THE BEST OF THE BIBLE

365 Must-Read Bible Passages

D0001861

Tyndale House Publishers, Inc.
WHEATON, ILLINOIS

Library of Congress Cataloging-in-Publication Data

Bible. English. New Living Translation Selections. 1996.
  The best of the Bible: 365 must-read Bible passages.
    p. cm.
  ISBN 0-8423-7053-6 (pbk. : alk. paper)
    1. Bible—Meditations. 2. Devotional calendars. I. Title.
BS195.L58 1996
220.5′208—dc20
                                               96-20668

Printed in the United States of America

00 01 99 98 97 96
9   8   7   6   5   4   3   2   1

Introduction

There are many plans to help you read through the Bible. The approach taken here is designed to help you get a flavor of the whole Bible by reading selections from it throughout the year. You will be reading the Bible's "best"—the most-loved stories and important passages.

In addition to the Bible text, each day's reading has a question designed to help you interact with the story and the characters. These questions ask how you react to situations, people, yourself, and God. A thought is offered each day as well. These thoughts offer ways to apply the lessons to your life.

Enjoy the time you spend in God's Word. May he grant you understanding and bless you throughout the year.

A Note to Readers

With 40 million copies in print, *The Living Bible* has been meeting a great need in people's hearts for more than thirty years. But even good things can be improved, so ninety evangelical scholars from various theological backgrounds and denominations were commissioned in 1989 to begin revising *The Living Bible*. The end result of this seven-year process is the *Holy Bible*, New Living Translation— a general-purpose translation that is accurate, easy to read, and excellent for study.

The goal of any Bible translation is to convey the meaning of the ancient Hebrew and Greek texts as accurately as possible to the modern reader. The New Living Translation is based on the most recent scholarship in the theory of translation. The challenge for the translators was to create a text that would make the same impact in the life of modern readers that the original text had for the original readers. In the New Living Translation, this is accomplished by translating entire thoughts (rather than just words) into natural, everyday English. The end result is a translation that is easy to read and understand and that accurately communicates the meaning of the original text.

We believe that this new translation, which combines the latest in scholarship with the best in translation style, will speak to your heart. We present the New Living Translation with the prayer that God will use it to speak his timeless truth to the church and to the world in a fresh, new way.

The Publishers
July 1996

How It All Started

GENESIS 1:1–2:3

In the beginning God created the heavens and the earth. ²The earth was empty, a formless mass cloaked in darkness. And the Spirit of God was hovering over its surface. ³Then God said, "Let there be light," and there was light. ⁴And God saw that it was good. Then he separated the light from the darkness. ⁵God called the light "day" and the darkness "night." Together these made up one day.

⁶And God said, "Let there be space between the waters, to separate water from water." ⁷And so it was. God made this space to separate the waters above from the waters below. ⁸And God called the space "sky." This happened on the second day.

⁹And God said, "Let the waters beneath the sky be gathered into one place so dry ground may appear." And so it was. ¹⁰God named the dry ground "land" and the water "seas." And God saw that it was good. ¹¹Then God said, "Let the land burst forth with every sort of grass and seed-bearing plant. And let there be trees that grow seed-bearing fruit. The seeds will then produce the kinds of plants and trees from which they came." And so it was. ¹²The land was filled with seed-bearing plants and trees, and their seeds produced plants and trees of like kind. And God saw that it was good. ¹³This all happened on the third day.

¹⁴And God said, "Let bright lights appear in the sky to separate the day from the night. They will be signs to mark off the seasons, the days, and the years. ¹⁵Let their light shine down upon the earth." And so it was. ¹⁶For God made two great lights, the sun and the moon, to shine down upon the earth. The greater one, the sun, presides during the day; the lesser one, the moon, presides through the night. He also made the stars. ¹⁷God set these lights in the heavens to light the earth, ¹⁸to govern the day and the night, and to separate the light from the darkness. And God saw that it was good. ¹⁹This all happened on the fourth day.

²⁰And God said, "Let the waters swarm with fish and other life. Let the skies be filled with birds of every kind." ²¹So God created great sea creatures

and every sort of fish and every kind of bird. And God saw that it was good. [22]Then God blessed them, saying, "Let the fish multiply and fill the oceans. Let the birds increase and fill the earth." [23]This all happened on the fifth day.

[24]And God said, "Let the earth bring forth every kind of animal—livestock, small animals, and wildlife." And so it was. [25]God made all sorts of wild animals, livestock, and small animals, each able to reproduce more of its own kind. And God saw that it was good.

[26]Then God said, "Let us make people in our image, to be like ourselves. They will be masters over all life—the fish in the sea, the birds in the sky, and all the livestock, wild animals, and small animals."

[27]So God created people in his own image;
God patterned them after himself;
male and female he created them.

[28]God blessed them and told them, "Multiply and fill the earth and subdue it. Be masters over the fish and birds and all the animals." [29]And God said, "Look! I have given you the seed-bearing plants throughout the earth and all the fruit trees for your food. [30]And I have given all the grasses and other green plants to the animals and birds for their food." And so it was. [31]Then God looked over all he had made, and he saw that it was excellent in every way. This all happened on the sixth day.

[2:1]So the creation of the heavens and the earth and everything in them was completed. [2]On the seventh day, having finished his task, God rested from all his work. [3]And God blessed the seventh day and declared it holy, because it was the day when he rested from his work of creation.

∿∿∿ **Why do human beings have value and worth?** How are we made like God? The phrase "Let us make people . . . like ourselves" does not mean that God created us exactly like himself, especially in a physical sense. Instead, we are reflections of God's glory. We share many of his characteristics. Our worth is not defined by possessions, achievements, physical attractiveness, or popularity. Self-worth is knowing that God created us in his likeness. Criticizing or downgrading ourselves is criticizing what God has made. Because we are like God, we can feel positive about ourselves and our abilities. Knowing that you are a person of infinite worth gives you the freedom to love God, know him personally, and make valuable contributions to those around you.

Adam and Eve

GENESIS 2:15–3:24

The LORD God placed the man in the Garden of Eden to tend and care for it. ¹⁶But the LORD God gave him this warning: "You may freely eat any fruit in the garden ¹⁷except fruit from the tree of the knowledge of good and evil. If you eat of its fruit, you will surely die." ¹⁸And the LORD God said, "It is not good for the man to be alone. I will make a companion who will help him." ¹⁹So the LORD God formed from the soil every kind of animal and bird. He brought them to Adam to see what he would call them, and Adam chose a name for each one. ²⁰He gave names to all the livestock, birds, and wild animals. But still there was no companion suitable for him. ²¹So the LORD God caused Adam to fall into a deep sleep. He took one of Adam's ribs and closed up the place from which he had taken it. ²²Then the LORD God made a woman from the rib and brought her to Adam.

²³"At last!" Adam exclaimed. "She is part of my own flesh and bone! She will be called 'woman,' because she was taken out of a man." ²⁴This explains why a man leaves his father and mother and is joined to his wife, and the two are united into one. ²⁵Now, although Adam and his wife were both naked, neither of them felt any shame.

³:¹Now the serpent was the shrewdest of all the creatures the LORD God had made. "Really?" he asked the woman. "Did God really say you must not eat any of the fruit in the garden?"

²"Of course we may eat it," the woman told him. ³"It's only the fruit from the tree at the center of the garden that we are not allowed to eat. God says we must not eat it or even touch it, or we will die."

⁴"You won't die!" the serpent hissed. ⁵"God knows that your eyes will be opened when you eat it. You will become just like God, knowing everything, both good and evil."

⁶The woman was convinced. The fruit looked so fresh and delicious, and it would make her so wise! So she ate some of the fruit. She also gave some to her husband, who was with her. Then he ate it, too. ⁷At that moment, their eyes were opened, and they suddenly felt shame at their nakedness. So they strung fig leaves together around their hips to cover themselves.

⁸Toward evening they heard the LORD God walking about in the garden, so they hid themselves among the trees. ⁹The LORD God called to Adam, "Where are you?"

¹⁰He replied, "I heard you, so I hid. I was afraid because I was naked."

¹¹"Who told you that you were naked?" the LORD God asked. "Have you eaten the fruit I commanded you not to eat?"

¹²"Yes," Adam admitted, "but it was the woman you gave me who brought me the fruit, and I ate it."

3

¹³Then the LORD God asked the woman, "How could you do such a thing?"

"The serpent tricked me," she replied. "That's why I ate it."

¹⁴So the LORD God said to the serpent, "Because you have done this, you will be punished. You are singled out from all the domestic and wild animals of the whole earth to be cursed. You will grovel in the dust as long as you live, crawling along on your belly. ¹⁵From now on, you and the woman will be enemies, and your offspring and her offspring will be enemies. He will crush your head, and you will strike his heel."

¹⁶Then he said to the woman, "You will bear children with intense pain and suffering. And though your desire will be for your husband, he will be your master."

¹⁷And to Adam he said, "Because you listened to your wife and ate the fruit I told you not to eat, I have placed a curse on the ground. All your life you will struggle to scratch a living from it. ¹⁸It will grow thorns and thistles for you, though you will eat of its grains. ¹⁹All your life you will sweat to produce food, until your dying day. Then you will return to the ground from which you came. For you were made from dust, and to the dust you will return."

²⁰Then Adam named his wife Eve, because she would be the mother of all people everywhere. ²¹And the LORD God made clothing from animal skins for Adam and his wife.

²²Then the LORD God said, "The people have become as we are, knowing everything, both good and evil. What if they eat the fruit of the tree of life? Then they will live forever!" ²³So the LORD God banished Adam and his wife from the Garden of Eden, and he sent Adam out to cultivate the ground from which he had been made. ²⁴After banishing them from the garden, the LORD God stationed mighty angelic beings to the east of Eden. And a flaming sword flashed back and forth, guarding the way to the tree of life.

〰〰 **In what ways are you like those first humans?** Adam and Eve got what they wanted: an intimate knowledge of both good and evil. But they got it by doing what was wrong, and the results were disastrous. Many people think that freedom means doing anything they want. God says true freedom comes from obedience and knowing what *not* to do and then doing what is right. The restrictions he gives us are for our good, helping us avoid evil. We have the freedom to walk in front of a speeding car, but we don't need to be hit to realize it would be foolish to do so. Don't listen to Satan's temptations. Don't think you have to experience evil to learn more about life.

Cain and Abel

GENESIS 4:1 16

Now Adam slept with his wife, Eve, and she became pregnant. When the time came, she gave birth to Cain, and she said, "With the LORD's help, I have brought forth a man!" ²Later she gave birth to a second son and named him Abel.

When they grew up, Abel became a shepherd, while Cain was a farmer. ³At harvest time Cain brought to the LORD a gift of his farm produce, ⁴while Abel brought several choice lambs from the best of his flock. The LORD accepted Abel's offering, ⁵but he did not accept Cain's. This made Cain very angry and dejected.

⁶"Why are you so angry?" the LORD asked him. "Why do you look so dejected? ⁷You will be accepted if you respond in the right way. But if you refuse to respond correctly, then watch out! Sin is waiting to attack and destroy you, and you must subdue it."

⁸Later Cain suggested to his brother, Abel, "Let's go out into the fields." And while they were together there, Cain attacked and killed his brother.

⁹Afterward the LORD asked Cain, "Where is your brother? Where is Abel?"

"I don't know!" Cain retorted. "Am I supposed to keep track of him wherever he goes?"

¹⁰But the LORD said, "What have you done? Listen—your brother's blood cries out to me from the ground! ¹¹You are hereby banished from the ground you have defiled with your brother's blood. ¹²No longer will it yield abundant crops for you, no matter how hard you work! From now on you will be a homeless fugitive on the earth, constantly wandering from place to place."

¹³Cain replied to the LORD, "My punishment is too great for me to bear! ¹⁴You have banished me from my land and from your presence; you have made me a wandering fugitive. All who see me will try to kill me!"

¹⁵The LORD replied, "They will not kill you, for I will give seven times your punishment to anyone who does." Then the LORD put a mark on Cain to warn anyone who might try to kill him. ¹⁶So Cain left the LORD's presence and settled in the land of Nod, east of Eden.

〜�dwー **How do you handle anger?** How do you react when someone suggests that you have done something wrong? Do you move to correct the mistake? Or do you deny that you need to correct it? After Cain's offering was rejected, God gave him the chance to right his wrong and try again. God even encouraged him to do this! But Cain refused, and the rest of his life is a startling example of what happens to those who refuse to admit their mistakes. The next time someone suggests you are wrong, take an honest look at yourself and choose God's way instead of Cain's.

JANUARY

Noah Gets to Build a Boat
GENESIS 6:9-22

This is the history of Noah and his family. Noah was a righteous man, the only blameless man living on earth at the time. He consistently followed God's will and enjoyed a close relationship with him. [10]Noah had three sons: Shem, Ham, and Japheth.

[11]Now the earth had become corrupt in God's sight, and it was filled with violence. [12]God observed all this corruption in the world, and he saw violence and depravity everywhere. [13]So God said to Noah, "I have decided to destroy all living creatures, for the earth is filled with violence because of them. Yes, I will wipe them all from the face of the earth!

[14]"Make a boat from resinous wood and seal it with tar, inside and out. Then construct decks and stalls throughout its interior. [15]Make it 450 feet long, 75 feet wide, and 45 feet high. [16]Construct an opening all the way around the boat, 18 inches below the roof. Then put three decks inside the boat—bottom, middle, and upper—and put a door in the side.

[17]"Look! I am about to cover the earth with a flood that will destroy every living thing. Everything on earth will die! [18]But I solemnly swear to keep you safe in the boat, with your wife and your sons and their wives. [19]Bring a pair of every kind of animal—a male and a female—into the boat with you to keep them alive during the flood. [20]Pairs of each kind of bird and each kind of animal, large and small alike, will come to you to be kept alive. [21]And remember, take enough food for your family and for all the animals." [22]So Noah did everything exactly as God had commanded him.

〰〰 **What is the most difficult act that God has asked you to do?**
Although Noah lived among evil people, he tried to do what pleased God by conducting his affairs according to God's will. For a lifetime he walked step by step in faith, a living example to his generation. Like Noah, we live in a world filled with evil. Are we being an influence on others, or are we being influenced? Either the three-foot space around us is becoming more like us, or we are becoming more like it.

JANUARY

All Aboard!
GENESIS 7:1-24

Finally, the day came when the LORD said to Noah, "Go into the boat with all your family, for among all the people of the earth, I consider you alone to be righteous. [2]Take along seven pairs of each animal that I have approved for eating and for sacrifice, and take one pair of each of the others. [3]Then select seven pairs of every kind of bird. There must be a male and a female in each pair to ensure that every kind of living creature will survive the flood. ⁴One week from today I will begin forty days and forty nights of rain. And I will wipe from the earth all the living things I have created."

⁵So Noah did exactly as the LORD had commanded him. ⁶He was 600 years old when the flood came, ⁷and he went aboard the boat to escape—he and his wife and his sons and their wives. ⁸With them were all the various kinds of animals—those approved for eating and sacrifice and those that were not—along with all the birds and other small animals. ⁹They came into the boat in pairs, male and female, just as God had commanded Noah. ¹⁰One week later, the flood came and covered the earth.

¹¹When Noah was 600 years old, on the seventeenth day of the second month, the underground waters burst forth on the earth, and the rain fell in mighty torrents from the sky. ¹²The rain continued to fall for forty days and forty nights. ¹³But Noah had gone into the boat that very day with his wife and his sons—Shem, Ham, and Japheth—and their wives. ¹⁴With them in the boat were pairs of every kind of breathing animal—domestic and wild, large and small—along with birds and flying insects of every kind. ¹⁵Two by two they came into the boat, ¹⁶male and female, just as God had commanded. Then the LORD shut them in.

¹⁷For forty days the floods prevailed, covering the ground and lifting the boat high above the earth. ¹⁸As the waters rose higher and higher above the ground, the boat floated safely on the surface. ¹⁹Finally, the water covered even the highest mountains on the earth, ²⁰standing more than twenty-two feet above the highest peaks. ²¹All the living things on earth died—birds, domestic animals, wild animals, all kinds of small animals, and all the people. ²²Everything died that breathed and lived on dry land. ²³Every living thing on the earth was wiped out—people, animals both large and small, and birds. They were all destroyed, and only Noah was left alive, along with those who were with him in the boat. ²⁴And the water covered the earth for 150 days.

〰️〰️ **If you were alive at this time and were invited to get on the boat, would you have accepted?** Many have wondered how this animal-kingdom roundup happened. Did Noah and his sons spend years collecting them? In reality, the creation, along with Noah, was doing just as God had commanded. There seemed to be no problem gathering the animals—God took care of the details of that job while Noah was doing his part by building the ark. Often we do just the opposite of Noah. We worry about details in our life over which we have no control while neglecting specific areas (such as attitudes, relationships, responsibilities) that *are* under our control. Like Noah, concentrate on what God has given you to do, and leave the rest to him.

A Long Wait

GENESIS 8:1-22

But God remembered Noah and all the animals in the boat. He sent a wind to blow across the waters, and the floods began to disappear. ²The underground water sources ceased their gushing, and the torrential rains stopped. ³So the flood gradually began to recede. After 150 days, ⁴exactly five months from the time the flood began, the boat came to rest on the mountains of Ararat. ⁵Two and a half months later, as the waters continued to go down, other mountain peaks began to appear.

⁶After another forty days, Noah opened the window he had made in the boat ⁷and released a raven that flew back and forth until the earth was dry. ⁸Then he sent out a dove to see if it could find dry ground. ⁹But the dove found no place to land because the water was still too high. So it returned to the boat, and Noah held out his hand and drew the dove back inside. ¹⁰Seven days later, Noah released the dove again. ¹¹This time, toward evening, the bird returned to him with a fresh olive leaf in its beak. Noah now knew that the water was almost gone. ¹²A week later, he released the dove again, and this time it did not come back.

¹³Finally, when Noah was 601 years old, ten and a half months after the flood began, Noah lifted back the cover to look. The water was drying up. ¹⁴Two more months went by, and at last the earth was dry! ¹⁵Then God said to Noah, ¹⁶"Leave the boat, all of you. ¹⁷Release all the animals and birds so they can breed and reproduce in great numbers." ¹⁸So Noah, his wife, and his sons and their wives left the boat. ¹⁹And all the various kinds of animals and birds came out, pair by pair.

²⁰Then Noah built an altar to the LORD and sacrificed on it the animals and birds that had been approved for that purpose. ²¹And the LORD was pleased with the sacrifice and said to himself, "I will never again curse the earth, destroying all living things, even though people's thoughts and actions are bent toward evil from childhood. ²²As long as the earth remains, there will be springtime and harvest, cold and heat, winter and summer, day and night."

∿∿ **How would you have spent your time on the boat?** Occasionally Noah would send a bird out to test the earth and see if it was dry. But Noah didn't get out of the ark until God told him to. He was waiting for God's timing. God knew that even though the water was gone, the earth was not dry enough for Noah and his family to venture out. What patience Noah showed, especially after spending an entire year inside his boat! We, like Noah, must trust God to give us patience during those difficult times when we must wait.

Rules and Rainbows

GENESIS 9:1-17

God blessed Noah and his sons and told them, "Multiply and fill the earth. ²All the wild animals, large and small, and all the birds and fish will be afraid of you. I have placed them in your power. ³I have given them to you for food, just as I have given you grain and vegetables. ⁴But you must never eat animals that still have their lifeblood in them. ⁵And murder is forbidden. Animals that kill people must die, and any person who murders must be killed. ⁶Yes, you must execute anyone who murders another person, for to kill a person is to kill a living being made in God's image. ⁷Now you must have many children and repopulate the earth. Yes, multiply and fill the earth!"

⁸Then God told Noah and his sons, ⁹"I am making a covenant with you and your descendants, ¹⁰and with the animals you brought with you—all these birds and livestock and wild animals. ¹¹I solemnly promise never to send another flood to kill all living creatures and destroy the earth." ¹²And God said, "I am giving you a sign as evidence of my eternal covenant with you and all living creatures. ¹³I have placed my rainbow in the clouds. It is the sign of my permanent promise to you and to all the earth. ¹⁴When I send clouds over the earth, the rainbow will be seen in the clouds, ¹⁵and I will remember my covenant with you and with everything that lives. Never again will there be a flood that will destroy all life. ¹⁶When I see the rainbow in the clouds, I will remember the eternal covenant between God and every living creature on earth." ¹⁷Then God said to Noah, "Yes, this is the sign of my covenant with all the creatures of the earth."

〜〴〳 **What could you do the next time you see a rainbow?** Noah stepped out of the ark onto an earth devoid of human life. But God gave him a reassuring promise. This covenant had three parts: (1) Never again will a flood do such destruction. (2) As long as the earth remains, the seasons will always come as expected. (3) A rainbow will be visible when it rains as a sign to all that God will keep his promises. The earth's order and seasons are still preserved, and rainbows still remind us of God's faithfulness to his Word.

The Tower of Babel

GENESIS 11:1-9

At one time the whole world spoke a single language and used the same words. ²As the people migrated eastward, they found a plain in the land of Babylonia and settled there. ³They began to talk about construction projects. "Come," they said, "let's make great piles of burnt brick and collect natural asphalt to use as mortar. ⁴Let's build a great city with a tower that reaches to the skies—a monument to our greatness! This will bring us together and keep us from scattering all over the world."

⁵But the LORD came down to see the city and the tower the people were building. ⁶"Look!" he said. "If they can accomplish this when they have just begun to take advantage of their common language and political unity, just think of what they will do later. Nothing will be impossible for them! ⁷Come, let's go down and give them different languages. Then they won't be able to understand each other."

⁸In that way, the LORD scattered them all over the earth; and that ended the building of the city. ⁹That is why the city was called Babel, because it was there that the LORD confused the people by giving them many languages, thus scattering them across the earth.

〰〰 **Whom do you trust more than God?** The tower of Babel was a great human achievement, a wonder of the world. But it was a monument to the people themselves rather than to God. We often build monuments to ourselves (expensive clothes, big house, fancy car, important job) to call attention to our achievements. These may not be wrong in themselves, but when we use them to give us identity and self-worth, they take God's place in our life. We are free to develop in many areas, but we are not free to think we have replaced God. What "monuments" are in your life?

9

JANUARY

God's Promises to Abraham

GENESIS 12:1-9; 17:1-8

Then the LORD told Abram, "Leave your country, your relatives, and your father's house, and go to the land that I will show you. ²I will cause you to become the father of a great nation. I will bless you and make you famous, and I will make you a blessing to others. ³I will bless those who bless you and curse those who curse you. All the families of the earth will be blessed through you."

⁴So Abram departed as the LORD had instructed him, and Lot went with him. Abram was seventy-five years old when he left Haran. ⁵He took his wife, Sarai, his nephew Lot, and all his wealth—his livestock and all the people who had joined his household at Haran—and finally arrived in Canaan. ⁶Traveling through Canaan, they came to a place near Shechem and set up camp beside the oak at Moreh. At that time, the area was inhabited by Canaanites.

⁷Then the LORD appeared to Abram and said, "I am going to give this land to your offspring." And Abram built an altar there to commemorate

the LORD's visit. ⁸After that, Abram traveled southward and set up camp in the hill country between Bethel on the west and Ai on the east. There he built an altar and worshiped the LORD. ⁹Then Abram traveled south by stages toward the Negev.

17:1 When Abram was ninety-nine years old, the LORD appeared to him and said, "I am God Almighty; serve me faithfully and live a blameless life. ²I will make a covenant with you, by which I will guarantee to make you into a mighty nation." ³At this, Abram fell face down in the dust. Then God said to him, ⁴"This is my covenant with you: I will make you the father of not just one nation, but a multitude of nations! ⁵What's more, I am changing your name. It will no longer be Abram; now you will be known as Abraham, for you will be the father of many nations. ⁶I will give you millions of descendants who will represent many nations. Kings will be among them!

⁷"I will continue this everlasting covenant between us, generation after generation. It will continue between me and your offspring forever. And I will always be your God and the God of your descendants after you. ⁸Yes, I will give all this land of Canaan to you and to your offspring forever. And I will be their God."

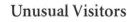 **How does God affect the way you make decisions?** God promised to bless Abram and make him great, but there was one condition: Abram had to do what God wanted him to do. This meant leaving his home and friends and traveling to a new land where God promised to build a great nation from Abram's family. Abram obeyed, leaving his home for God's promise of even greater blessings in the future. God may be trying to lead you to a place of greater service and usefulness for him. Don't let the comfort and security of your present position make you miss God's plan for you.

JANUARY

Unusual Visitors
GENESIS 18:1-15

The LORD appeared again to Abraham while he was camped near the oak grove belonging to Mamre. One day about noon, as Abraham was sitting at the entrance to his tent, ²he suddenly noticed three men standing nearby. He got up and ran to meet them, welcoming them by bowing low to the ground. ³"My lord," he said, "if it pleases you, stop here for a while. ⁴Rest in the shade of this tree while my servants get some water to wash your feet. ⁵Let me prepare some food to refresh you. Please stay awhile before continuing on your journey."

"All right," they said. "Do as you have said."

⁶So Abraham ran back to the tent and said to Sarah, "Quick! Get three measures of your best flour, and bake some bread." ⁷Then Abraham ran out

to the herd and chose a fat calf and told a servant to hurry and butcher it. ⁸When the food was ready, he took some cheese curds and milk and the roasted meat, and he served it to the men. As they ate, Abraham waited on them there beneath the trees.

⁹"Where is Sarah, your wife?" they asked him.

"In the tent," Abraham replied.

¹⁰Then one of them said, "About this time next year I will return, and your wife Sarah will have a son."

Now Sarah was listening to this conversation from the tent nearby. ¹¹And since Abraham and Sarah were both very old, and Sarah was long past the age of having children, ¹²she laughed silently to herself. "How could a worn-out woman like me have a baby?" she thought. "And when my master—my husband—is also so old?"

¹³Then the LORD said to Abraham, "Why did Sarah laugh? Why did she say, 'Can an old woman like me have a baby?' ¹⁴Is anything too hard for the LORD? About a year from now, just as I told you, I will return, and Sarah will have a son." ¹⁵Sarah was afraid, so she denied that she had laughed. But he said, "That is not true. You did laugh."

〜�**What is your basic attitude toward strangers?** Abraham was eager to show hospitality to these three visitors, as was Lot (19:2). In Abraham's day, a person's reputation was largely connected to his hospitality—the sharing of home and food. Even strangers were to be treated as highly honored guests. Meeting another's need for food or shelter was and still is one of the most immediate and practical ways to obey God. It is also a time-honored relationship builder. Hebrews 13:2 suggests that we, like Abraham, might actually entertain angels. This thought should be on our mind the next time we have the opportunity to meet a stranger's needs.

Destruction of Sodom and Gomorrah
GENESIS 19:1-29

That evening the two angels came to the entrance of the city of Sodom, and Lot was sitting there as they arrived. When he saw them, he stood up to meet them. Then he welcomed them and bowed low to the ground. ²"My lords," he said, "come to my home to wash your feet, and be my guests for the night. You may then get up in the morning as early as you like and be on your way again."

"Oh no," they said, "we'll just spend the night out here in the city square."

³But Lot insisted, so at last they went home with him. He set a great feast before them, complete with fresh bread made without yeast. After the meal, ⁴as they were preparing to retire for the night, all the men of Sodom, young

and old, came from all over the city and surrounded the house. ⁵They shouted to Lot, "Where are the men who came to spend the night with you? Bring them out so we can have sex with them."

⁶Lot stepped outside to talk to them, shutting the door behind him. ⁷"Please, my brothers," he begged, "don't do such a wicked thing. ⁸Look— I have two virgin daughters. Do with them as you wish, but leave these men alone, for they are under my protection."

⁹"Stand back!" they shouted. "Who do you think you are? We let you settle among us, and now you are trying to tell us what to do! We'll treat you far worse than those other men!" And they lunged at Lot and began breaking down the door. ¹⁰But the two angels reached out and pulled Lot in and bolted the door. ¹¹Then they blinded the men of Sodom so they couldn't find the doorway.

¹²"Do you have any other relatives here in the city?" the angels asked. "Get them out of this place—sons-in-law, sons, daughters, or anyone else. ¹³For we will destroy the city completely. The stench of the place has reached the LORD, and he has sent us to destroy it."

¹⁴So Lot rushed out to tell his daughters' fiancés, "Quick, get out of the city! The LORD is going to destroy it." But the young men thought he was only joking.

¹⁵At dawn the next morning the angels became insistent. "Hurry," they said to Lot. "Take your wife and your two daughters who are here. Get out of here right now, or you will be caught in the destruction of the city."

¹⁶When Lot still hesitated, the angels seized his hand and the hands of his wife and two daughters and rushed them to safety outside the city, for the LORD was merciful. ¹⁷"Run for your lives!" the angels warned. "Do not stop anywhere in the valley. And don't look back! Escape to the mountains, or you will die."

¹⁸"Oh no, my lords, please," Lot begged. ¹⁹"You have been so kind to me and saved my life, and you have granted me such mercy. But I cannot go to the mountains. Disaster would catch up to me there, and I would soon die. ²⁰See, there is a small village nearby. Please let me go there instead; don't you see how small it is? Then my life will be saved."

²¹"All right," the angel said, "I will grant your request. I will not destroy that little village. ²²But hurry! For I can do nothing until you are there." From that time on, that village was known as Zoar.

²³The sun was rising as Lot reached the village. ²⁴Then the LORD rained down fire and burning sulfur from the heavens on Sodom and Gomorrah. ²⁵He utterly destroyed them, along with the other cities and villages of the plain, eliminating all life—people, plants, and animals alike. ²⁶But Lot's wife looked back as she was following along behind him, and she became a pillar of salt.

²⁷The next morning Abraham was up early and hurried out to the place where he had stood in the LORD's presence. ²⁸He looked out across the plain to Sodom and Gomorrah and saw columns of smoke and fumes, as from a

furnace, rising from the cities there. [29]But God had listened to Abraham's request and kept Lot safe, removing him from the disaster that engulfed the cities on the plain.

~~~ **How does God feel about sin?** Lot's wife turned back to look at the smoldering city of Sodom. Clinging to the past, she was unwilling to turn completely from sin. Are you looking back longingly at sin while trying to move forward with God? You can't make progress with God as long as you are holding on to pieces of your old life. Jesus said it this way in Matthew 6:24: "No one can serve two masters."

12

Hagar and Ishmael
GENESIS 21:8-21

As time went by and Isaac grew and was weaned, Abraham gave a big party to celebrate the happy occasion. [9]But Sarah saw Ishmael—the son of Abraham and her Egyptian servant Hagar—making fun of Isaac. [10]So she turned to Abraham and demanded, "Get rid of that servant and her son. He is not going to share the family inheritance with my son, Isaac. I won't have it!" [11]This upset Abraham very much because Ishmael was his son. [12]But God told Abraham, "Do not be upset over the boy and your servant wife. Do just as Sarah says, for Isaac is the son through whom your descendants will be counted. [13]But I will make a nation of the descendants of Hagar's son because he also is your son."

[14]So Abraham got up early the next morning, prepared food for the journey, and strapped a container of water to Hagar's shoulders. He sent her away with their son, and she walked out into the wilderness of Beersheba, wandering aimlessly. [15]When the water was gone, she left the boy in the shade of a bush. [16]Then she went and sat down by herself about a hundred yards away. "I don't want to watch the boy die," she said, as she burst into tears.

[17]Then God heard the boy's cries, and the angel of God called to Hagar from the sky, "Hagar, what's wrong? Do not be afraid! God has heard the boy's cries from the place where you laid him. [18]Go to him and comfort him, for I will make a great nation from his descendants."

[19]Then God opened Hagar's eyes, and she saw a well. She immediately filled her water container and gave the boy a drink. [20]And God was with the boy as he grew up in the wilderness of Paran. He became an expert archer, [21]and his mother arranged a marriage for him with a young woman from Egypt.

~~~ **How does God deal with the messes in your life?** What happened to Ishmael, and who are his descendants? Ishmael became ruler of a large tribe or nation. The Ishmaelites were nomads living in the wilderness of

Sinai and Paran, south of Israel. One of Ishmael's daughters married Esau, Ishmael's nephew (28:9). While people sometimes make mistakes, God always keeps his promises and always cares for his children. God was with Ishmael as he grew up (v. 20), and he is with you, too.

Abraham's Painful Decision

GENESIS 22:1-19

Later on God tested Abraham's faith and obedience. "Abraham!" God called. "Yes," he replied. "Here I am."

[2] "Take your son, your only son—yes, Isaac, whom you love so much—and go to the land of Moriah. Sacrifice him there as a burnt offering on one of the mountains, which I will point out to you."

[3] The next morning Abraham got up early. He saddled his donkey and took two of his servants with him, along with his son Isaac. Then he chopped wood to build a fire for a burnt offering and set out for the place where God had told him to go. [4] On the third day of the journey, Abraham saw the place in the distance. [5] "Stay here with the donkey," Abraham told the young men. "The boy and I will travel a little farther. We will worship there, and then we will come right back."

[6] Abraham placed the wood for the burnt offering on Isaac's shoulders, while he himself carried the knife and the fire. As the two of them went on together, [7] Isaac said, "Father?"

"Yes, my son," Abraham replied.

"We have the wood and the fire," said the boy, "but where is the lamb for the sacrifice?"

[8] "God will provide a lamb, my son," Abraham answered. And they both went on together.

[9] When they arrived at the place where God had told Abraham to go, he built an altar and placed the wood on it. Then he tied Isaac up and laid him on the altar over the wood. [10] And Abraham took the knife and lifted it up to kill his son as a sacrifice to the LORD. [11] At that moment the angel of the LORD shouted to him from heaven, "Abraham! Abraham!"

"Yes," he answered. "I'm listening."

[12] "Lay down the knife," the angel said. "Do not hurt the boy in any way, for now I know that you truly fear God. You have not withheld even your beloved son from me."

[13] Then Abraham looked up and saw a ram caught by its horns in a bush. So he took the ram and sacrificed it as a burnt offering on the altar in place of his son. [14] Abraham named the place "The LORD Will Provide." This name has now become a proverb: "On the mountain of the LORD it will be provided."

15

¹⁵Then the angel of the LORD called again to Abraham from heaven, ¹⁶"This is what the LORD says: Because you have obeyed me and have not withheld even your beloved son, I swear by my own self that ¹⁷I will bless you richly. I will multiply your descendants into countless millions, like the stars of the sky and the sand on the seashore. They will conquer their enemies, ¹⁸and through your descendants, all the nations of the earth will be blessed—all because you have obeyed me." ¹⁹Then they returned to Abraham's young men and traveled home again to Beersheba, where Abraham lived for quite some time.

⌇⌇ **What do you have trouble giving up to God?** Why did God ask Abraham to perform human sacrifice? Heathen nations practiced human sacrifice, but God condemned this as a terrible sin (Lev. 20:1-5). God did not want Isaac to die, but he wanted Abraham to prove that he loved God more than he loved his promised and long-awaited son. God was testing Abraham. The purpose of testing is to strengthen our character and deepen our commitment to God and his perfect timing. Through this difficult experience, Abraham strengthened his commitment to obey God. He also learned about God's ability to provide.

14

JANUARY

A Man Named Eliezer
GENESIS 24:1-27

Abraham was now a very old man, and the LORD had blessed him in every way. ²One day Abraham said to the man in charge of his household, who was his oldest servant, ³"Swear by the LORD, the God of heaven and earth, that you will not let my son marry one of these local Canaanite women. ⁴Go instead to my homeland, to my relatives, and find a wife there for my son Isaac."

⁵The servant asked, "But suppose I can't find a young woman who will travel so far from home? May I then take Isaac there to live among your relatives?"

⁶"No!" Abraham warned. "Be careful never to take my son there. ⁷For the LORD, the God of heaven, who took me from my father's house and my native land, solemnly promised to give this land to my offspring. He will send his angel ahead of you, and he will see to it that you find a young woman there to be my son's wife. ⁸If she is unwilling to come back with you, then you are free from this oath. But under no circumstances are you to take my son there."

⁹So the servant took a solemn oath that he would follow Abraham's instructions. ¹⁰He loaded ten of Abraham's camels with gifts and set out, taking with him the best of everything his master owned. He traveled to Aram-naharaim and went to the village where Abraham's brother Nahor

had settled. ¹¹There the servant made the camels kneel down beside a well just outside the village. It was evening, and the women were coming out to draw water.

¹²"O LORD, God of my master," he prayed. "Give me success and show kindness to my master, Abraham. Help me to accomplish the purpose of my journey. ¹³See, here I am, standing beside this spring, and the young women of the village are coming out to draw water. ¹⁴This is my request. I will ask one of them for a drink. If she says, 'Yes, certainly, and I will water your camels, too!'—let her be the one you have appointed as Isaac's wife. By this I will know that you have shown kindness to my master."

¹⁵As he was still praying, a young woman named Rebekah arrived with a water jug on her shoulder. Her father was Bethuel, who was the son of Abraham's brother Nahor and his wife, Milcah. ¹⁶Now Rebekah was very beautiful, and she was a virgin; no man had ever slept with her. She went down to the spring, filled her jug, and came up again. ¹⁷Running over to her, the servant asked, "Please give me a drink."

¹⁸"Certainly, sir," she said, and she quickly lowered the jug for him to drink. ¹⁹When he had finished, she said, "I'll draw water for your camels, too, until they have had enough!" ²⁰So she quickly emptied the jug into the watering trough and ran down to the well again. She kept carrying water to the camels until they had finished drinking. ²¹The servant watched her in silence, wondering whether or not she was the one the LORD intended him to meet. ²²Then at last, when the camels had finished drinking, he gave her a gold ring for her nose and two large gold bracelets for her wrists.

²³"Whose daughter are you?" he asked. "Would your father have any room to put us up for the night?"

²⁴"My father is Bethuel," she replied. "My grandparents are Nahor and Milcah. ²⁵Yes, we have plenty of straw and food for the camels, and we have a room for guests."

²⁶The man fell down to the ground and worshiped the LORD. ²⁷"Praise be to the LORD, the God of my master, Abraham," he said. "The LORD has been so kind and faithful to Abraham, for he has led me straight to my master's relatives."

〰〰 **How do you approach difficult tasks?** Was it right for Abraham's servant to ask God for such a specific sign? The sign he requested was only slightly out of the ordinary. The hospitality of the day required women at the well to offer water to weary travelers but not to their animals. Eliezer was simply asking God to show him a woman with an attitude of service—someone who would go beyond the expected. An offer to water his camels would indicate that kind of attitude. Eliezer did not ask for a woman with looks or wealth. He knew the importance of having the right heart, and he asked God to help him with his task.

Isaac and Rebekah

GENESIS 24:28-67

The young woman [Rebekah] ran home to tell her family about all that had happened. ²⁹Now Rebekah had a brother named Laban. ³⁰When he saw the nose-ring and the bracelets on his sister's wrists, and when he heard her story, he rushed out to the spring, where the man was still standing beside his camels. Laban said to him, ³¹"Come and stay with us, you who are blessed by the LORD. Why do you stand here outside the village when we have a room all ready for you and a place prepared for the camels!"

³²So the man went home with Laban, and Laban unloaded the camels, gave him straw to bed them down, fed them, and provided water for the camel drivers to wash their feet. ³³Then supper was served. But Abraham's servant said, "I don't want to eat until I have told you why I have come."

"All right," Laban said, "tell us your mission."

³⁴"I am Abraham's servant," he explained. ³⁵"And the LORD has blessed my master richly; he has become a great man. The LORD has given him flocks of sheep and herds of cattle, a fortune in silver and gold, and many servants and camels and donkeys. ³⁶When Sarah, my master's wife, was very old, she gave birth to my master's son, and my master has given him everything he owns. ³⁷And my master made me swear that I would not let Isaac marry one of the local Canaanite women. ³⁸Instead, I was to come to his relatives here in this far-off land, to his father's home. I was told to bring back a young woman from here to marry his son.

³⁹" 'But suppose I can't find a young woman willing to come back with me?' I asked him. ⁴⁰'You will,' he told me, 'for the LORD, in whose presence I have walked, will send his angel with you and will make your mission successful. Yes, you must get a wife for my son from among my relatives, from my father's family. ⁴¹But if you go to my relatives and they refuse to let her come, you will be free from your oath.'

⁴²"So this afternoon when I came to the spring I prayed this prayer: 'O LORD, the God of my master, Abraham, if you are planning to make my mission a success, please guide me in a special way. ⁴³Here I am, standing beside this spring. I will say to some young woman who comes to draw water, "Please give me a drink of water!" ⁴⁴And she will reply, "Certainly! And I'll water your camels, too!" LORD, let her be the one you have selected to be the wife of my master's son.'

⁴⁵"Before I had finished praying these words, I saw Rebekah coming along with her water jug on her shoulder. She went down to the spring and drew water and filled the jug. So I said to her, 'Please give me a drink.' ⁴⁶She quickly lowered the jug from her shoulder so I could drink, and she said, 'Certainly, sir, and I will water your camels, too!' And she did. ⁴⁷When I

asked her whose daughter she was, she told me, 'My father is Bethuel, the son of Nahor and his wife, Milcah.' So I gave her the ring and the bracelets.

[48]"Then I bowed my head and worshiped the LORD. I praised the LORD, the God of my master, Abraham, because he had led me along the right path to find a wife from the family of my master's relatives. [49]So tell me— will you or won't you show true kindness to my master? When you tell me, then I'll know what my next step should be, whether to move this way or that."

[50]Then Laban and Bethuel replied, "The LORD has obviously brought you here, so what can we say? [51]Here is Rebekah; take her and go. Yes, let her be the wife of your master's son, as the LORD has directed."

[52]At this reply, Abraham's servant bowed to the ground and worshiped the LORD. [53]Then he brought out silver and gold jewelry and lovely clothing for Rebekah. He also gave valuable presents to her mother and brother. [54]Then they had supper, and the servant and the men with him stayed there overnight. But early the next morning, he said, "Send me back to my master."

[55]"But we want Rebekah to stay at least ten days," her brother and mother said. "Then she can go."

[56]But he said, "Don't hinder my return. The LORD has made my mission successful, and I want to report back to my master."

[57]"Well," they said, "we'll call Rebekah and ask her what she thinks." [58]So they called Rebekah. "Are you willing to go with this man?" they asked her. And she replied, "Yes, I will go."

[59]So they said good-bye to Rebekah and sent her away with Abraham's servant and his men. The woman who had been Rebekah's childhood nurse went along with her. [60]They blessed her with this blessing as she parted:

> "Our sister, may you become
> the mother of many millions!
> May your descendants overcome
> all their enemies."

[61]Then Rebekah and her servants mounted the camels and left with Abraham's servant.

[62]Meanwhile, Isaac, whose home was in the Negev, had returned from Beer-lahairoi. [63]One evening as he was taking a walk out in the fields, meditating, he looked up and saw the camels coming. [64]When Rebekah looked up and saw Isaac, she quickly dismounted. [65]"Who is that man walking through the fields to meet us?" she asked the servant.

And he replied, "It is my master." So Rebekah covered her face with her veil. [66]Then the servant told Isaac the whole story.

[67]And Isaac brought Rebekah into his mother's tent, and she became his wife. He loved her very much, and she was a special comfort to him after the death of his mother.

〰️〰️ **What unexpected good thing has God done for you recently?**
Rebekah had physical beauty, but she also had inner beauty. Appearance is important to us, and we spend time and money improving it. But how much effort do we put into developing our inner beauty? Patience, kindness, and joy are the beauty treatments that help us become truly lovely—on the inside.

16

Jacob and Esau
GENESIS 25:19-34

This is the history of the family of Isaac, the son of Abraham. ²⁰When Isaac was forty years old, he married Rebekah, the daughter of Bethuel the Aramean from Paddan-aram and the sister of Laban. ²¹Isaac pleaded with the LORD to give Rebekah a child because she was childless. So the LORD answered Isaac's prayer, and his wife became pregnant with twins. ²²But the two children struggled with each other in her womb. So she went to ask the LORD about it. "Why is this happening to me?" she asked.

²³And the LORD told her, "The sons in your womb will become two rival nations. One nation will be stronger than the other; the descendants of your older son will serve the descendants of your younger son."

²⁴And when the time came, the twins were born. ²⁵The first was very red at birth. He was covered with so much hair that one would think he was wearing a piece of clothing. So they called him Esau. ²⁶Then the other twin was born with his hand grasping Esau's heel. So they called him Jacob. Isaac was sixty years old when the twins were born.

²⁷As the boys grew up, Esau became a skillful hunter, a man of the open fields, while Jacob was the kind of person who liked to stay at home. ²⁸Isaac loved Esau in particular because of the wild game he brought home, but Rebekah favored Jacob.

²⁹One day when Jacob was cooking some stew, Esau arrived home exhausted and hungry from a hunt. ³⁰Esau said to Jacob, "I'm starved! Give me some of that red stew you've made." (This was how Esau got his other name, Edom—"Red.")

³¹Jacob replied, "All right, but trade me your birthright for it."

³²"Look, I'm dying of starvation!" said Esau. "What good is my birthright to me now?"

³³So Jacob insisted, "Well then, swear to me right now that it is mine." So Esau swore an oath, thereby selling all his rights as the firstborn to his younger brother. ³⁴Then Jacob gave Esau some bread and lentil stew. Esau ate and drank and went on about his business, indifferent to the fact that he had given up his birthright.

~\/\/~ **How do you treat your family members?** Esau traded the lasting benefits of his birthright for the immediate pleasure of food. He acted on impulse, satisfying his immediate desires without pausing to consider the long-range consequences of what he was about to do. We can fall into the same trap. When we see something we want, our first impulse is to get it. At first we feel intensely satisfied and sometimes even powerful because we have obtained what we set out to get. But immediate pleasure often causes us to lose sight of the future. We can avoid making Esau's mistake by comparing the short-term satisfaction with its long-range consequences before we act.

JANUARY **17**

Jacob Tricks His Father

GENESIS 27:1–40

When Isaac was old and almost blind, he called for Esau, his older son, and said, "My son?"

"Yes, Father?" Esau replied.

²"I am an old man now," Isaac said, "and I expect every day to be my last. ³Take your bow and a quiver full of arrows out into the open country, and hunt some wild game for me. ⁴Prepare it just the way I like it so it's savory and good, and bring it here for me to eat. Then I will pronounce the blessing that belongs to you, my firstborn son, before I die."

⁵But Rebekah overheard the conversation. So when Esau left to hunt for the wild game, ⁶she said to her son Jacob, "I overheard your father asking Esau ⁷to prepare him a delicious meal of wild game. He wants to bless Esau in the LORD's presence before he dies. ⁸Now, my son, do exactly as I tell you. ⁹Go out to the flocks and bring me two fine young goats. I'll prepare your father's favorite dish from them. ¹⁰Take the food to your father; then he can eat it and bless you instead of Esau before he dies."

¹¹"But Mother!" Jacob replied. "He won't be fooled that easily. Think how hairy Esau is and how smooth my skin is! ¹²What if my father touches me? He'll see that I'm trying to trick him, and then he'll curse me instead of blessing me."

¹³"Let the curse fall on me, dear son," said Rebekah. "Just do what I tell you. Go out and get the goats."

¹⁴So Jacob followed his mother's instructions, bringing her the two goats. She took them and cooked a delicious meat dish, just the way Isaac liked it. ¹⁵Then she took Esau's best clothes, which were there in the house, and dressed Jacob with them. ¹⁶She made him a pair of gloves from the hairy skin of the young goats, and she fastened a strip of the goat's skin around his neck. ¹⁷Then she gave him the meat dish, with its rich aroma, and some freshly baked bread. ¹⁸Jacob carried the platter of food to his father and said, "My father?"

"Yes, my son," he answered. "Who is it—Esau or Jacob?"

[19]Jacob replied, "It's Esau, your older son. I've done as you told me. Here is the wild game, cooked the way you like it. Sit up and eat it so you can give me your blessing."

[20]Isaac asked, "How were you able to find it so quickly, my son?"

"Because the LORD your God put it in my path!" Jacob replied.

[21]Then Isaac said to Jacob, "Come over here. I want to touch you to make sure you really are Esau." [22]So Jacob went over to his father, and Isaac touched him. "The voice is Jacob's, but the hands are Esau's," Isaac said to himself. [23]But he did not recognize Jacob because Jacob's hands felt hairy just like Esau's. So Isaac pronounced his blessing on Jacob. [24]"Are you really my son Esau?" he asked.

"Yes, of course," Jacob replied.

[25]Then Isaac said, "Now, my son, bring me the meat. I will eat it, and then I will give you my blessing." So Jacob took the food over to his father, and Isaac ate it. He also drank the wine that Jacob served him. Then Isaac said, [26]"Come here and kiss me, my son."

[27]So Jacob went over and kissed him. And when Isaac caught the smell of his clothes, he was finally convinced, and he blessed his son. He said, "The smell of my son is the good smell of the open fields that the LORD has blessed. [28]May God always give you plenty of dew for healthy crops and good harvests of grain and wine. [29]May many nations become your servants. May you be the master of your brothers. May all your mother's sons bow low before you. All who curse you are cursed, and all who bless you are blessed."

[30]As soon as Isaac had blessed Jacob, and almost before Jacob had left his father, Esau returned from his hunting trip. [31]Esau prepared his father's favorite meat dish and brought it to him. Then he said, "I'm back, Father, and I have the wild game. Sit up and eat it so you can give me your blessing."

[32]But Isaac asked him, "Who are you?"

"Why, it's me, of course!" he replied. "It's Esau, your older son."

[33]Isaac began to tremble uncontrollably and said, "Then who was it that just served me wild game? I have already eaten it, and I blessed him with an irrevocable blessing before you came."

[34]When Esau understood, he let out a loud and bitter cry. "O my father, bless me, too!" he begged.

[35]But Isaac said, "Your brother was here, and he tricked me. He has carried away your blessing."

[36]Esau said bitterly, "No wonder his name is Jacob, for he has deceived me twice, first taking my birthright and now stealing my blessing. Oh, haven't you saved even one blessing for me?"

[37]Isaac said to Esau, "I have made Jacob your master and have declared that all his brothers will be his servants. I have guaranteed him an abundance of grain and wine—what is there left to give?"

[38]Esau pleaded, "Not one blessing left for me? O my father, bless me, too!" Then Esau broke down and wept.

[39]His father, Isaac, said to him, "You will live off the land and what it yields, [40]and you will live by your sword. You will serve your brother for a time, but then you will shake loose from him and be free."

〜〰 **How honestly have you treated your parents?** How we react to a moral dilemma often exposes our real motives. Frequently we are more worried about getting caught than about doing what is right. Jacob did not seem concerned about the deceitfulness of his mother's plan; instead, he was afraid of getting in trouble while carrying it out. If you are worried about getting caught, you are probably in a position that is less than honest. Let your fear of getting caught be a warning to do right. Jacob paid a huge price for carrying out this dishonest plan.

JANUARY

Jacob Meets God
GENESIS 28:10-22

18

Meanwhile, Jacob left Beersheba and traveled toward Haran. [11]At sundown he arrived at a good place to set up camp and stopped there for the night. Jacob found a stone for a pillow and lay down to sleep. [12]As he slept, he dreamed of a stairway that reached from earth to heaven. And he saw the angels of God going up and down on it.

[13]At the top of the stairway stood the LORD, and he said, "I am the LORD, the God of your grandfather Abraham and the God of your father, Isaac. The ground you are lying on belongs to you. I will give it to you and your descendants. [14]Your descendants will be as numerous as the dust of the earth! They will cover the land from east to west and from north to south. All the families of the earth will be blessed through you and your descendants. [15]What's more, I will be with you, and I will protect you wherever you go. I will someday bring you safely back to this land. I will be with you constantly until I have finished giving you everything I have promised."

[16]Then Jacob woke up and said, "Surely the LORD is in this place, and I wasn't even aware of it." [17]He was afraid and said, "What an awesome place this is! It is none other than the house of God—the gateway to heaven!" [18]The next morning he got up very early. He took the stone he had used as a pillow and set it upright as a memorial pillar. Then he poured olive oil over it. [19]He named the place Bethel—"house of God"—though the name of the nearby village was Luz.

[20]Then Jacob made this vow: "If God will be with me and protect me on this journey and give me food and clothing, [21]and if he will bring me back safely to my father, then I will make the LORD my God. [22]This memorial

pillar will become a place for worshiping God, and I will give God a tenth of everything he gives me."

〜〰〜 **In what places in your life has God been the most real?** God's covenant promise to Abraham and Isaac was offered to Jacob as well. But it was not enough to be Abraham's grandson; Jacob had to establish his own personal relationship with God. God has no grandchildren; each of us must have a personal relationship with him. It is not enough to hear wonderful stories about Christians in your family. You need to become part of the story yourself (see Gal. 3:6-7).

19
JANUARY

Jacob's Marriages
GENESIS 29:14-30

After Jacob had been there about a month, [15]Laban said to him, "You shouldn't work for me without pay just because we are relatives. How much do you want?"

[16]Now Laban had two daughters: Leah, who was the oldest, and her younger sister, Rachel. [17]Leah had pretty eyes, but Rachel was beautiful in every way, with a lovely face and shapely figure. [18]Since Jacob was in love with Rachel, he told her father, "I'll work for you seven years if you'll give me Rachel, your younger daughter, as my wife."

[19]"Agreed!" Laban replied. "I'd rather give her to you than to someone outside the family."

[20]So Jacob spent the next seven years working to pay for Rachel. But his love for her was so strong that it seemed to him but a few days. [21]Finally, the time came for him to marry her. "I have fulfilled my contract," Jacob said to Laban. "Now give me my wife so we can be married."

[22]So Laban invited everyone in the neighborhood to celebrate with Jacob at a wedding feast. [23]That night, when it was dark, Laban took Leah to Jacob, and he slept with her. [24]And Laban gave Leah a servant, Zilpah, to be her maid.

[25]But when Jacob woke up in the morning—it was Leah! "What sort of trick is this?" Jacob raged at Laban. "I worked seven years for Rachel. What do you mean by this trickery?"

[26]"It's not our custom to marry off a younger daughter ahead of the first-born," Laban replied. [27]"Wait until the bridal week is over, and you can have Rachel, too—that is, if you promise to work another seven years for me."

[28]So Jacob agreed to work seven more years. A week after Jacob had married Leah, Laban gave him Rachel, too. [29]And Laban gave Rachel a servant, Bilhah, to be her maid. [30]So Jacob slept with Rachel, too, and he loved her more than Leah. He then stayed and worked the additional seven years.

〜⋌〜 **What are the qualities that make up the way you love others?**
People often wonder if waiting a long time for something they want is worth it.
Jacob waited seven years to marry Rachel. After being tricked, he agreed to
work seven more years for her! The most important goals and desires are
worth working and waiting for. Movies and television have created the illusion
that people have to wait only about an hour to solve their problems or get what
they want. Don't be trapped into thinking the same is true in real life. Patience
is hardest when we need it the most, but it is the key to achieving our goals.

JANUARY **20**

Jacob Returns Home
Genesis 32:1–33:16

As Jacob and his household started on their way again, angels of God came
to meet him. ²When Jacob saw them, he exclaimed, "This is God's camp!"
So he named the place Mahanaim.

³Jacob now sent messengers to his brother, Esau, in Edom, the land of
Seir. ⁴He told them, "Give this message to my master Esau: 'Humble greetings from your servant Jacob! I have been living with Uncle Laban until
recently, ⁵and now I own oxen, donkeys, sheep, goats, and many servants,
both men and women. I have sent these messengers to inform you of my
coming, hoping that you will be friendly to us.' "

⁶The messengers returned with the news that Esau was on his way to
meet Jacob—with an army of four hundred men! ⁷Jacob was terrified at the
news. He divided his household, along with the flocks and herds and camels, into two camps. ⁸He thought, "If Esau attacks one group, perhaps the
other can escape."

⁹Then Jacob prayed, "O God of my grandfather Abraham and my father,
Isaac—O LORD, you told me to return to my land and to my relatives, and
you promised to treat me kindly. ¹⁰I am not worthy of all the faithfulness
and unfailing love you have shown to me, your servant. When I left home,
I owned nothing except a walking stick, and now my household fills two
camps! ¹¹O LORD, please rescue me from my brother, Esau. I am afraid that
he is coming to kill me, along with my wives and children. ¹²But you promised to treat me kindly and to multiply my descendants until they become
as numerous as the sands along the seashore—too many to count."

¹³Jacob stayed where he was for the night and prepared a present for
Esau: ¹⁴two hundred female goats, twenty male goats, two hundred ewes,
twenty rams, ¹⁵thirty female camels with their young, forty cows, ten bulls,
twenty female donkeys, and ten male donkeys. ¹⁶He told his servants to lead
them on ahead, each group of animals by itself, separated by a distance in
between.

¹⁷He gave these instructions to the men leading the first group: "When

you meet Esau, he will ask, 'Where are you going? Whose servants are you? Whose animals are these?' ¹⁸You should reply, 'These belong to your servant Jacob. They are a present for his master Esau! He is coming right behind us.'" ¹⁹Jacob gave the same instructions to each of the herdsmen and told them, "You are all to say the same thing to Esau when you see him. ²⁰And be sure to say, 'Your servant Jacob is right behind us.'" Jacob's plan was to appease Esau with the presents before meeting him face to face. "Perhaps," Jacob hoped, "he will be friendly to us." ²¹So the presents were sent on ahead, and Jacob spent that night in the camp.

²²But during the night Jacob got up and sent his two wives, two concubines, and eleven sons across the Jabbok River. ²³After they were on the other side, he sent over all his possessions. ²⁴This left Jacob all alone in the camp, and a man came and wrestled with him until dawn. ²⁵When the man saw that he couldn't win the match, he struck Jacob's hip and knocked it out of joint at the socket. ²⁶Then the man said, "Let me go, for it is dawn."

But Jacob panted, "I will not let you go unless you bless me."

²⁷"What is your name?" the man asked.

He replied, "Jacob."

²⁸"Your name will no longer be Jacob," the man told him. "It is now Israel, because you have struggled with both God and men and have won."

²⁹"What is your name?" Jacob asked him.

"Why do you ask?" the man replied. Then he blessed Jacob there.

³⁰Jacob named the place Peniel—"face of God"—for he said, "I have seen God face to face, yet my life has been spared." ³¹The sun rose as he left Peniel, and he was limping because of his hip. ³²That is why even today the people of Israel don't eat meat from near the hip, in memory of what happened that night.

33:1 Then, in the distance, Jacob saw Esau coming with his four hundred men. ²Jacob now arranged his family into a column, with his two concubines and their children at the front, Leah and her children next, and Rachel and Joseph last. ³Then Jacob went on ahead. As he approached his brother, he bowed low seven times before him. ⁴Then Esau ran to meet him and embraced him affectionately and kissed him. Both of them were in tears.

⁵Then Esau looked at the women and children and asked, "Who are these people with you?"

"These are the children God has graciously given to me," Jacob replied. ⁶Then the concubines came forward with their children and bowed low before him. ⁷Next Leah came with her children, and they bowed down. Finally, Rachel and Joseph came and made their bows.

⁸"And what were all the flocks and herds I met as I came?" Esau asked. Jacob replied, "They are gifts, my lord, to ensure your goodwill."

⁹"Brother, I have plenty," Esau answered. "Keep what you have."

¹⁰"No, please accept them," Jacob said, "for what a relief it is to see your friendly smile. It is like seeing the smile of God! ¹¹Please take my gifts, for

God has been very generous to me. I have more than enough." Jacob continued to insist, so Esau finally accepted them.

[12]"Well, let's be going," Esau said. "I will stay with you and lead the way."

[13]But Jacob replied, "You can see, my lord, that some of the children are very young, and the flocks and herds have their young, too. If they are driven too hard, they may die. [14]So go on ahead of us. We will follow at our own pace and meet you at Seir."

[15]"Well," Esau said, "at least let me leave some of my men to guide and protect you."

"There is no reason for you to be so kind to me," Jacob insisted.

[16]So Esau started back to Seir that same day.

〰〰 **What happens inside you when you try to avoid a problem?** It is refreshing to see Esau's change of heart when the two brothers meet again. The bitterness over losing his birthright and blessing (25:29-34) seems gone. Instead, Esau is content with what he has. Jacob even exclaims how great it is to see his brother obviously pleased with him (33:10). Life can deal us some bad situations. We can feel cheated, as Esau did, but we don't have to remain bitter. We can remove bitterness from our lives by honestly expressing our feelings to God, forgiving those who have wronged us, and being content with what we have.

JANUARY

21

Jacob's Children
GENESIS 37:1-36

So Jacob settled again in the land of Canaan, where his father had lived. [2]This is the history of Jacob's family.

When Joseph was seventeen years old, he often tended his father's flocks with his half brothers, the sons of his father's wives Bilhah and Zilpah. But Joseph reported to his father some of the bad things his brothers were doing. [3]Now Jacob loved Joseph more than any of his other children because Joseph had been born to him in his old age. So one day he gave Joseph a special gift—a beautiful robe. [4]But his brothers hated Joseph because of their father's partiality. They couldn't say a kind word to him.

[5]One night Joseph had a dream and promptly reported the details to his brothers, causing them to hate him even more. [6]"Listen to this dream," he announced. [7]"We were out in the field tying up bundles of grain. My bundle stood up, and then your bundles all gathered around and bowed low before it!"

[8]"So you are going to be our king, are you?" his brothers taunted. And they hated him all the more for his dream and what he had said.

[9]Then Joseph had another dream and told his brothers about it. "Listen

to this dream," he said. "The sun, moon, and eleven stars bowed low before me!"

¹⁰This time he told his father as well as his brothers, and his father rebuked him. "What do you mean?" his father asked. "Will your mother, your brothers, and I actually come and bow before you?" ¹¹But while his brothers were jealous of Joseph, his father gave it some thought and wondered what it all meant.

¹²Soon after this, Joseph's brothers went to pasture their father's flocks at Shechem. ¹³When they had been gone for some time, Jacob said to Joseph, "Your brothers are over at Shechem with the flocks. I'm going to send you to them."

"I'm ready to go," Joseph replied.

¹⁴"Go and see how your brothers and the flocks are getting along," Jacob said. "Then come back and bring me word." So Jacob sent him on his way, and Joseph traveled to Shechem from his home in the valley of Hebron.

¹⁵When he arrived there, a man noticed him wandering around the countryside. "What are you looking for?" he asked.

¹⁶"For my brothers and their flocks," Joseph replied. "Have you seen them?"

¹⁷"Yes," the man told him, "but they are no longer here. I heard your brothers say they were going to Dothan." So Joseph followed his brothers to Dothan and found them there.

¹⁸When Joseph's brothers saw him coming, they recognized him in the distance and made plans to kill him. ¹⁹"Here comes that dreamer!" they exclaimed. ²⁰"Come on, let's kill him and throw him into a deep pit. We can tell our father that a wild animal has eaten him. Then we'll see what becomes of all his dreams!"

²¹But Reuben came to Joseph's rescue. "Let's not kill him," he said. ²²"Why should we shed his blood? Let's just throw him alive into this pit here. That way he will die without our having to touch him." Reuben was secretly planning to help Joseph escape, and then he would bring him back to his father.

²³So when Joseph arrived, they pulled off his beautiful robe ²⁴and threw him into the pit. This pit was normally used to store water, but it was empty at the time. ²⁵Then, just as they were sitting down to eat, they noticed a caravan of camels in the distance coming toward them. It was a group of Ishmaelite traders taking spices, balm, and myrrh from Gilead to Egypt.

²⁶Judah said to the others, "What can we gain by killing our brother? That would just give us a guilty conscience. ²⁷Let's sell Joseph to those Ishmaelite traders. Let's not be responsible for his death; after all, he is our brother!" And his brothers agreed. ²⁸So when the traders came by, his brothers pulled Joseph out of the pit and sold him for twenty pieces of silver, and the Ishmaelite traders took him along to Egypt.

²⁹Some time later, Reuben returned to get Joseph out of the pit. When he discovered that Joseph was missing, he tore his clothes in anguish and frus-

tration. ³⁰Then he went back to his brothers and lamented, "The boy is gone! What can I do now?"

³¹Then Joseph's brothers killed a goat and dipped the robe in its blood. ³²They took the beautiful robe to their father and asked him to identify it. "We found this in the field," they told him. "It's Joseph's robe, isn't it?"

³³Their father recognized it at once. "Yes," he said, "it is my son's robe. A wild animal has attacked and eaten him. Surely Joseph has been torn in pieces!" ³⁴Then Jacob tore his clothes and put on sackcloth. He mourned deeply for his son for many days. ³⁵His family all tried to comfort him, but it was no use. "I will die in mourning for my son," he would say, and then begin to weep.

³⁶Meanwhile, in Egypt, the traders sold Joseph to Potiphar, an officer of Pharaoh, the king of Egypt. Potiphar was captain of the palace guard.

~✻ **How are disagreements settled in your family?** Could jealousy ever make you feel like killing someone? Before saying, "Of course not," look at what happened in this story. Ten men were willing to kill their younger brother over a cloak and a few reported dreams. Their deep-seated jealousy had grown into ugly rage, blinding them completely to what was right. Jealousy can be hard to recognize because our reasons for it seem to make sense. But left unchecked, jealousy grows quickly and leads to serious sins. The longer you cultivate jealous feelings, the harder it is to uproot them. The time to deal with jealousy is when you notice yourself keeping score of what others own or have accomplished.

JANUARY 22

Joseph in Trouble
GENESIS 39:1-23

Now when Joseph arrived in Egypt with the Ishmaelite traders, he was purchased by Potiphar, a member of the personal staff of Pharaoh, the king of Egypt. Potiphar was the captain of the palace guard.

²The LORD was with Joseph and blessed him greatly as he served in the home of his Egyptian master. ³Potiphar noticed this and realized that the LORD was with Joseph, giving him success in everything he did. ⁴So Joseph naturally became quite a favorite with him. Potiphar soon put Joseph in charge of his entire household and entrusted him with all his business dealings. ⁵From the day Joseph was put in charge, the LORD began to bless Potiphar for Joseph's sake. All his household affairs began to run smoothly, and his crops and livestock flourished. ⁶So Potiphar gave Joseph complete administrative responsibility over everything he owned. With Joseph there, he didn't have a worry in the world, except to decide what he wanted to eat!

Now Joseph was a very handsome and well-built young man. ⁷And about this time, Potiphar's wife began to desire him and invited him to sleep with her. ⁸But Joseph refused. "Look," he told her, "my master trusts me with everything in his entire household. ⁹No one here has more authority than I do! He has held back nothing from me except you, because you are his wife. How could I ever do such a wicked thing? It would be a great sin against God."

¹⁰She kept putting pressure on him day after day, but he refused to sleep with her, and he kept out of her way as much as possible. ¹¹One day, however, no one else was around when he was doing his work inside the house. ¹²She came and grabbed him by his shirt, demanding, "Sleep with me!" Joseph tore himself away, but as he did, his shirt came off. She was left holding it as he ran from the house.

¹³When she saw that she had his shirt and that he had fled, ¹⁴she began screaming. Soon all the men around the place came running. "My husband has brought this Hebrew slave here to insult us!" she sobbed. "He tried to rape me, but I screamed. ¹⁵When he heard my loud cries, he ran and left his shirt behind with me."

¹⁶She kept the shirt with her, and when her husband came home that night, ¹⁷she told him her story. "That Hebrew slave you've had around here tried to make a fool of me," she said. ¹⁸"I was saved only by my screams. He ran out, leaving his shirt behind!"

¹⁹After hearing his wife's story, Potiphar was furious! ²⁰He took Joseph and threw him into the prison where the king's prisoners were held. ²¹But the LORD was with Joseph there, too, and he granted Joseph favor with the chief jailer. ²²Before long, the jailer put Joseph in charge of all the other prisoners and over everything that happened in the prison. ²³The chief jailer had no more worries after that, because Joseph took care of everything. The LORD was with him, making everything run smoothly and successfully.

~∿∿∕ **How do you feel about getting in trouble for doing right?** Potiphar's wife failed to seduce Joseph, who resisted this temptation by saying it would be a sin against God. Joseph didn't say, "I'd be hurting you," or "I'd be sinning against Potiphar," or "I'd be sinning against myself." Under pressure, such excuses are easily rationalized away. Remember that sexual sin is not just between two consenting adults. It is an act of disobedience to God.

23 JANUARY

Dreams in Prison
GENESIS 40:1-23

Some time later, Pharaoh's chief cup-bearer and chief baker offended him. ²Pharaoh became very angry with these officials, ³and he put them in the prison where Joseph was, in the palace of Potiphar, the captain of the guard.

⁴They remained in prison for quite some time, and Potiphar assigned Joseph to take care of them.

⁵One night the cup-bearer and the baker each had a dream, and each dream had its own meaning. ⁶The next morning Joseph noticed the dejected look on their faces. ⁷"Why do you look so worried today?" he asked.

⁸And they replied, "We both had dreams last night, but there is no one here to tell us what they mean."

"Interpreting dreams is God's business," Joseph replied. "Tell me what you saw."

⁹The cup-bearer told his dream first. "In my dream," he said, "I saw a vine in front of me. ¹⁰It had three branches that began to bud and blossom, and soon there were clusters of ripe grapes. ¹¹I was holding Pharaoh's wine cup in my hand, so I took the grapes and squeezed the juice into it. Then I placed the cup in Pharaoh's hand."

¹²"I know what the dream means," Joseph said. "The three branches mean three days. ¹³Within three days Pharaoh will take you out of prison and return you to your position as his chief cup-bearer. ¹⁴And please have some pity on me when you are back in his favor. Mention me to Pharaoh, and ask him to let me out of here. ¹⁵For I was kidnapped from my homeland, the land of the Hebrews, and now I'm here in jail, but I did nothing to deserve it."

¹⁶When the chief baker saw that the first dream had such a good meaning, he told his dream to Joseph, too. "In my dream," he said, "there were three baskets of pastries on my head. ¹⁷In the top basket were all kinds of bakery goods for Pharaoh, but the birds came and ate them."

¹⁸"I'll tell you what it means," Joseph told him. "The three baskets mean three days. ¹⁹Three days from now Pharaoh will cut off your head and impale your body on a pole. Then birds will come and peck away at your flesh."

²⁰Pharaoh's birthday came three days later, and he gave a banquet for all his officials and household staff. He sent for his chief cup-bearer and chief baker, and they were brought to him from the prison. ²¹He then restored the chief cup-bearer to his former position, ²²but he sentenced the chief baker to be impaled on a pole, just as Joseph had predicted. ²³Pharaoh's cup-bearer, however, promptly forgot all about Joseph, never giving him another thought.

〰〰 **When have you helped someone even though you had your own problems?** When the subject of dreams came up, Joseph focused everyone's attention on God. Rather than using the situation to make himself look good, he turned it into a powerful witness for the Lord. One secret of effective witnessing is to recognize opportunities to relate God to the other person's experience. When the opportunity arises, we must have the courage to speak, as Joseph did.

Dreams in the Palace

GENESIS 41:1-36

Two years later, Pharaoh dreamed that he was standing on the bank of the Nile River. ²In his dream, seven fat, healthy-looking cows suddenly came up out of the river and began grazing along its bank. ³Then seven other cows came up from the river, but these were very ugly and gaunt. These cows went over and stood beside the fat cows. ⁴Then the thin, ugly cows ate the fat ones! At this point in the dream, Pharaoh woke up.

⁵Soon he fell asleep again and had a second dream. This time he saw seven heads of grain on one stalk, with every kernel well formed and plump. ⁶Then suddenly, seven more heads appeared on the stalk, but these were shriveled and withered by the east wind. ⁷And these thin heads swallowed up the seven plump, well-formed heads! Then Pharaoh woke up again and realized it was a dream.

⁸The next morning, as he thought about it, Pharaoh became very concerned as to what the dreams might mean. So he called for all the magicians and wise men of Egypt and told them about his dreams, but not one of them could suggest what they meant. ⁹Then the king's cup-bearer spoke up. "Today I have been reminded of my failure," he said. ¹⁰"Some time ago, you were angry with the chief baker and me, and you imprisoned us in the palace of the captain of the guard. ¹¹One night the chief baker and I each had a dream, and each dream had a meaning. ¹²We told the dreams to a young Hebrew man who was a servant of the captain of the guard. He told us what each of our dreams meant, ¹³and everything happened just as he said it would. I was restored to my position as cup-bearer, and the chief baker was executed and impaled on a pole."

¹⁴Pharaoh sent for Joseph at once, and he was brought hastily from the dungeon. After a quick shave and change of clothes, he went in and stood in Pharaoh's presence. ¹⁵"I had a dream last night," Pharaoh told him, "and none of these men can tell me what it means. But I have heard that you can interpret dreams, and that is why I have called for you."

¹⁶"It is beyond my power to do this," Joseph replied. "But God will tell you what it means and will set you at ease."

¹⁷So Pharaoh told him the dream. "I was standing on the bank of the Nile River," he said. ¹⁸"Suddenly, seven fat, healthy-looking cows came up out of the river and began grazing along its bank. ¹⁹But then seven other cows came up from the river. They were very thin and gaunt—in fact, I've never seen such ugly animals in all the land of Egypt. ²⁰These thin, ugly cows ate up the seven fat ones that had come out of the river first, ²¹but afterward they were still as ugly and gaunt as before! Then I woke up.

²²"A little later I had another dream. This time there were seven heads of grain on one stalk, and all seven heads were plump and full. ²³Then out of

32

the same stalk came seven withered heads, shriveled by the east wind. ^{24}And the withered heads swallowed up the plump ones! I told these dreams to my magicians, but not one of them could tell me what they mean."

^{25}"Both dreams mean the same thing," Joseph told Pharaoh. "God was telling you what he is about to do. ^{26}The seven fat cows and the seven plump heads of grain both represent seven years of prosperity. ^{27}The seven thin, ugly cows and the seven withered heads of grain represent seven years of famine. ^{28}This will happen just as I have described it, for God has shown you what he is about to do. ^{29}The next seven years will be a period of great prosperity throughout the land of Egypt. ^{30}But afterward there will be seven years of famine so great that all the prosperity will be forgotten and wiped out. Famine will destroy the land. ^{31}This famine will be so terrible that even the memory of the good years will be erased. ^{32}As for having the dream twice, it means that the matter has been decreed by God and that he will make these events happen soon.

^{33}"My suggestion is that you find the wisest man in Egypt and put him in charge of a nationwide program. ^{34}Let Pharaoh appoint officials over the land, and let them collect one-fifth of all the crops during the seven good years. ^{35}Have them gather all the food and grain of these good years into the royal storehouses, and store it away so there will be food in the cities. ^{36}That way there will be enough to eat when the seven years of famine come. Otherwise disaster will surely strike the land, and all the people will die."

〰️〽️ **Whom has God used to give you guidance?** Our most important opportunities may come when we least expect them. Joseph was brought hastily from the dungeon and pushed before Pharaoh. Did he have time to prepare? Yes and no. He had no warning that he would be suddenly pulled from prison and questioned by the king. Yet Joseph was ready for almost anything because of his right relationship with God. It was not Joseph's knowledge of dreams that helped him interpret their meaning. It was his knowledge of God. Be ready for opportunities by getting to know God better. Then you will be ready to take on almost anything that comes your way.

JANUARY 25

Joseph in Charge
GENESIS 41:37-57

Joseph's suggestions were well received by Pharaoh and his advisers. ^{38}As they discussed who should be appointed for the job, Pharaoh said, "Who could do it better than Joseph? For he is a man who is obviously filled with the spirit of God." ^{39}Turning to Joseph, Pharaoh said, "Since God has revealed the meaning of the dreams to you, you are the wisest man in the land! ^{40}I hereby appoint you to direct this project. You will manage my household and organize all my people. Only I will have a rank higher than yours."

⁴¹And Pharaoh said to Joseph, "I hereby put you in charge of the entire land of Egypt." ⁴²Then Pharaoh placed his own signet ring on Joseph's finger as a symbol of his authority. He dressed him in beautiful clothing and placed the royal gold chain about his neck. ⁴³Pharaoh also gave Joseph the chariot of his second-in-command, and wherever he went the command was shouted, "Kneel down!" So Joseph was put in charge of all Egypt. ⁴⁴And Pharaoh said to Joseph, "I am the king, but no one will move a hand or a foot in the entire land of Egypt without your approval."

⁴⁵Pharaoh renamed him Zaphenath-paneah and gave him a wife—a young woman named Asenath, the daughter of Potiphera, priest of Heliopolis. So Joseph took charge of the entire land of Egypt. ⁴⁶He was thirty years old when he entered the service of Pharaoh, the king of Egypt. And when Joseph left Pharaoh's presence, he made a tour of inspection throughout the land.

⁴⁷And sure enough, for the next seven years there were bumper crops everywhere. ⁴⁸During those years, Joseph took a portion of all the crops grown in Egypt and stored them for the government in nearby cities. ⁴⁹After seven years, the granaries were filled to overflowing. There was so much grain, like sand on the seashore, that the people could not keep track of the amount.

⁵⁰During this time, before the arrival of the first of the famine years, two sons were born to Joseph and his wife, Asenath, the daughter of Potiphera, priest of Heliopolis. ⁵¹Joseph named his older son Manasseh, for he said, "God has made me forget all my troubles and the family of my father." ⁵²Joseph named his second son Ephraim, for he said, "God has made me fruitful in this land of my suffering."

⁵³At last the seven years of plenty came to an end. ⁵⁴Then the seven years of famine began, just as Joseph had predicted. There were crop failures in all the surrounding countries, too, but in Egypt there was plenty of grain in the storehouses. ⁵⁵Throughout the land of Egypt the people began to starve. They pleaded with Pharaoh for food, and he told them, "Go to Joseph and do whatever he tells you." ⁵⁶So with severe famine everywhere in the land, Joseph opened up the storehouses and sold grain to the Egyptians. ⁵⁷And people from surrounding lands also came to Egypt to buy grain from Joseph because the famine was severe throughout the world.

How well do you handle big responsibilities? Joseph rose quickly to the top, from prison walls to Pharaoh's palace. His training for this important position involved being first a slave and then a prisoner. In each situation he learned the importance of serving God and others. Whatever your situation, no matter how undesirable, consider it part of your training program for serving God.

Joseph Sees His Brothers Again

GENESIS 42:1-38

When Jacob heard that there was grain available in Egypt, he said to his sons, "Why are you standing around looking at one another? ²I have heard there is grain in Egypt. Go down and buy some for us before we all starve to death." ³So Joseph's ten older brothers went down to Egypt to buy grain. ⁴Jacob wouldn't let Joseph's younger brother, Benjamin, go with them, however, for fear some harm might come to him. ⁵So Jacob's sons arrived in Egypt along with others to buy food, for the famine had reached Canaan as well.

⁶Since Joseph was governor of all Egypt and in charge of the sale of the grain, it was to him that his brothers came. They bowed low before him, with their faces to the ground. ⁷Joseph recognized them instantly, but he pretended to be a stranger. "Where are you from?" he demanded roughly.

"From the land of Canaan," they replied. "We have come to buy grain."

⁸Joseph's brothers didn't recognize him, but Joseph recognized them. ⁹And he remembered the dreams he had had many years before. He said to them, "You are spies! You have come to see how vulnerable our land has become."

¹⁰"No, my lord!" they exclaimed. "We have come to buy food. ¹¹We are all brothers and honest men, sir! We are not spies!"

¹²"Yes, you are!" he insisted. "You have come to discover how vulnerable the famine has made us."

¹³"Sir," they said, "there are twelve of us brothers, and our father is in the land of Canaan. Our youngest brother is there with our father, and one of our brothers is no longer with us."

¹⁴But Joseph insisted, "As I said, you are spies! ¹⁵This is how I will test your story. I swear by the life of Pharaoh that you will not leave Egypt unless your youngest brother comes here. ¹⁶One of you go and get your brother! I'll keep the rest of you here, bound in prison. Then we'll find out whether or not your story is true. If it turns out that you don't have a younger brother, then I'll know you are spies."

¹⁷So he put them all in prison for three days. ¹⁸On the third day Joseph said to them, "I am a God-fearing man. If you do as I say, you will live. ¹⁹We'll see how honorable you really are. Only one of you will remain in the prison. The rest of you may go on home with grain for your families. ²⁰But bring your youngest brother back to me. In this way, I will know whether or not you are telling me the truth. If you are, I will spare you." To this they agreed.

²¹Speaking among themselves, they said, "This has all happened because of what we did to Joseph long ago. We saw his terror and anguish and heard his pleadings, but we wouldn't listen. That's why this trouble has come upon us."

²²"Didn't I tell you not to do it?" Reuben asked. "But you wouldn't listen. And now we are going to die because we murdered him."

²³Of course, they didn't know that Joseph understood them as he was standing there, for he had been speaking to them through an interpreter. ²⁴Now he left the room and found a place where he could weep. Returning, he talked some more with them. He then chose Simeon from among them and had him tied up right before their eyes.

²⁵Joseph then ordered his servants to fill the men's sacks with grain, but he also gave secret instructions to return each brother's payment at the top of his sack. He also gave them provisions for their journey. ²⁶So they loaded up their donkeys with the grain and started for home.

²⁷But when they stopped for the night and one of them opened his sack to get some grain to feed the donkeys, he found his money in the sack. ²⁸"Look!" he exclaimed to his brothers. "My money is here in my sack!" They were filled with terror and said to each other, "What has God done to us?" ²⁹So they came to their father, Jacob, in the land of Canaan and told him all that had happened.

³⁰"The man who is ruler over the land spoke very roughly to us," they told him. "He took us for spies. ³¹But we said, 'We are honest men, not spies. ³²We are twelve brothers, sons of one father; one brother has disappeared, and the youngest is with our father in the land of Canaan.' ³³Then the man, the ruler of the land, told us, 'This is the way I will find out if you are honest men. Leave one of your brothers here with me, and take grain for your families and go on home. ³⁴But bring your youngest brother back to me. Then I will know that you are honest men and not spies. If you prove to be what you say, then I will give you back your brother, and you may come as often as you like to buy grain.' "

³⁵As they emptied out the sacks, there at the top of each one was the bag of money paid for the grain. Terror gripped them, as it did their father. ³⁶Jacob exclaimed, "You have deprived me of my children! Joseph has disappeared, Simeon is gone, and now you want to take Benjamin, too. Everything is going against me!"

³⁷Then Reuben said to his father, "You may kill my two sons if I don't bring Benjamin back to you. I'll be responsible for him."

³⁸But Jacob replied, "My son will not go down with you, for his brother Joseph is dead, and he alone is left of his mother's children. If anything should happen to him, you would bring my gray head down to the grave in deep sorrow."

〰〰 **What would you do with a chance for revenge?** Joseph remembered his dreams about his brothers bowing down to him (37:6-9). Those dreams were coming true! As a young boy, Joseph was boastful about his dreams. As a man, he no longer flaunted his superior status. He did not feel the need to say "I told you so." It was not yet time to reveal his identity, so he kept quiet. Sometimes it is best for us to remain quiet, even when we would like to have the last word.

Back to Joseph

GENESIS 43:1-34

But there was no relief from the terrible famine throughout the land.
²When the grain they had brought from Egypt was almost gone, Jacob said
to his sons, "Go again and buy us a little food."

³But Judah said, "The man wasn't joking when he warned that we
couldn't see him again unless Benjamin came along. ⁴If you let him come
with us, we will go down and buy some food. ⁵But if you don't let Benjamin
go, we may as well stay at home. Remember that the man said, 'You won't
be allowed to come and see me unless your brother is with you.' "

⁶"Why did you ever tell him you had another brother?" Jacob moaned.
"Why did you have to treat me with such cruelty?"

⁷"But the man specifically asked us about our family," they replied. "He
wanted to know whether our father was still living, and he asked us if we
had another brother so we told him. How could we have known he would
say, 'Bring me your brother'?"

⁸Judah said to his father, "Send the boy with me, and we will be on our
way. Otherwise we will all die of starvation—and not only we, but you and
our little ones. ⁹I personally guarantee his safety. If I don't bring him back
to you, then let me bear the blame forever. ¹⁰For we could have gone and
returned twice by this time if you had let him come without delay."

¹¹So their father, Jacob, finally said to them, "If it can't be avoided, then at
least do this. Fill your bags with the best products of the land. Take them to
the man as gifts—balm, honey, spices, myrrh, pistachio nuts, and almonds.
¹²Take double the money that you found in your sacks, as it was probably
someone's mistake. ¹³Then take your brother and go back to the man.
¹⁴May God Almighty give you mercy as you go before the man, that he
might release Simeon and return Benjamin. And if I must bear the anguish
of their deaths, then so be it."

¹⁵So they took Benjamin and the gifts and double the money and hurried
to Egypt, where they presented themselves to Joseph. ¹⁶When Joseph saw
that Benjamin was with them, he said to the manager of his household,
"These men will eat with me this noon. Take them inside and prepare a big
feast." ¹⁷So the man did as he was told and took them to Joseph's palace.

¹⁸They were badly frightened when they saw where they were being
taken. "It's because of the money returned to us in our sacks," they said.
"He plans to pretend that we stole it. Then he will seize us as slaves and take
our donkeys."

¹⁹As the brothers arrived at the entrance to the palace, they went over to
the man in charge of Joseph's household. ²⁰They said to him, "Sir, after our
first trip to Egypt to buy food, ²¹as we were returning home, we stopped for
the night and opened our sacks. The money we had used to pay for the

grain was there in our sacks. Here it is; we have brought it back again. ²²We also have additional money to buy more grain. We have no idea how the money got into our sacks."

²³"Relax. Don't worry about it," the household manager told them. "Your God, the God of your ancestors, must have put it there. We collected your money all right." Then he released Simeon and brought him out to them.

²⁴The brothers were then led into the palace and given water to wash their feet and food for their donkeys. ²⁵They were told they would be eating there, so they prepared their gifts for Joseph's arrival at noon.

²⁶When Joseph came, they gave him their gifts and bowed low before him. ²⁷He asked them how they had been getting along, and then he said, "How is your father—the old man you spoke about? Is he still alive?"

²⁸"Yes," they replied. "He is alive and well." Then they bowed again before him.

²⁹Looking at his brother Benjamin, Joseph asked, "Is this your youngest brother, the one you told me about? May God be gracious to you, my son." ³⁰Then Joseph made a hasty exit because he was overcome with emotion for his brother and wanted to cry. Going into his private room, he wept there. ³¹ Then he washed his face and came out, keeping himself under control. "Bring on the food!" he ordered.

³²Joseph ate by himself, and his brothers were served at a separate table. The Egyptians sat at their own table because Egyptians despise Hebrews and refuse to eat with them. ³³Joseph told each of his brothers where to sit, and to their amazement, he seated them in the order of their ages, from oldest to youngest. ³⁴Their food was served to them from Joseph's own table. He gave the largest serving to Benjamin—five times as much as to any of the others. So they all feasted and drank freely with him.

〰️ **How well do you know how to forgive?** Judah accepted full responsibility for Benjamin's safety. He did not know what that might mean for him, but he was determined to carry it out. In the end it was Judah's stirring words that caused Joseph to break down and reveal himself to his brothers (44:18-34). Accepting and fulfilling responsibilities is difficult, but it builds character and confidence, earns others' respect, and motivates us to complete our work. When you have been given an assignment to complete or a responsibility to fulfill, commit yourself to seeing it through.

Crisis in the Palace

GENESIS 44:1-34

When his brothers were ready to leave, Joseph gave these instructions to the man in charge of his household: "Fill each of their sacks with as much grain as they can carry, and put each man's money back into his sack. ²Then put my personal silver cup at the top of the youngest brother's sack, along with his grain money." So the household manager did as he was told.

³The brothers were up at dawn and set out on their journey with their loaded donkeys. ⁴But when they were barely out of the city, Joseph said to his household manager, "Chase after them and stop them. Ask them, 'Why have you repaid an act of kindness with such evil? ⁵What do you mean by stealing my master's personal silver drinking cup, which he uses to predict the future? What a wicked thing you have done!' "

⁶So the man caught up with them and spoke to them in the way he had been instructed. ⁷"What are you talking about?" the brothers responded. "What kind of people do you think we are, that you accuse us of such a terrible thing? ⁸Didn't we bring back the money we found in our sacks? Why would we steal silver or gold from your master's house? ⁹If you find his cup with any one of us, let that one die. And all the rest of us will be your master's slaves forever."

¹⁰"Fair enough," the man replied, "except that only the one who stole it will be a slave. The rest of you may go free."

¹¹They quickly took their sacks from the backs of their donkeys and opened them. ¹²Joseph's servant began searching the oldest brother's sack, going on down the line to the youngest. The cup was found in Benjamin's sack! ¹³At this, they tore their clothing in despair, loaded the donkeys again, and returned to the city. ¹⁴Joseph was still at home when Judah and his brothers arrived, and they fell to the ground before him.

¹⁵"What were you trying to do?" Joseph demanded. "Didn't you know that a man such as I would know who stole it?"

¹⁶And Judah said, "Oh, my lord, what can we say to you? How can we plead? How can we prove our innocence? God is punishing us for our sins. My lord, we have all returned to be your slaves—we and our brother who had your cup in his sack."

¹⁷"No," Joseph said. "Only the man who stole the cup will be my slave. The rest of you may go home to your father."

¹⁸Then Judah stepped forward and said, "My lord, let me say just this one word to you. Be patient with me for a moment, for I know you could have me killed in an instant, as though you were Pharaoh himself. ¹⁹You asked us, my lord, if we had a father or a brother. ²⁰We said, 'Yes, we have a father, an old man, and a child of his old age, his youngest son. His brother is dead, and he alone is left of his mother's children, and his

father loves him very much.' ²¹And you said to us, 'Bring him here so I can see him.' ²²But we said to you, 'My lord, the boy cannot leave his father, for his father would die.' ²³But you told us, 'You may not see me again unless your youngest brother is with you.' ²⁴So we returned to our father and told him what you had said. ²⁵And when he said, 'Go back again and buy us a little food,' ²⁶we replied, 'We can't unless you let our youngest brother go with us. We won't be allowed to see the man in charge of the grain unless our youngest brother is with us.' ²⁷Then my father said to us, 'You know that my wife had two sons, ²⁸and that one of them went away and never returned—doubtless torn to pieces by some wild animal. I have never seen him since. ²⁹If you take away his brother from me, too, and any harm comes to him, you would bring my gray head down to the grave in deep sorrow.'

³⁰"And now, my lord, I cannot go back to my father without the boy. Our father's life is bound up in the boy's life. ³¹When he sees that the boy is not with us, our father will die. We will be responsible for bringing his gray head down to the grave in sorrow. ³²My lord, I made a pledge to my father that I would take care of the boy. I told him, 'If I don't bring him back to you, I will bear the blame forever.' ³³Please, my lord, let me stay here as a slave instead of the boy, and let the boy return with his brothers. ³⁴For how can I return to my father if the boy is not with me? I cannot bear to see what this would do to him."

〜�♪〜 **How do you react when someone points out a mistake you've made?** When Judah was younger, he showed no regard for his brother Joseph or his father, Jacob. First he convinced his brothers to sell Joseph as a slave (37:27); then he joined his brothers in lying to his father about Joseph's fate (37:32). But what a change had taken place in Judah! The man who had sold one favored little brother into slavery now offered to become a slave himself to save another favored little brother. He was so concerned for his father and younger brother that he was willing to die for them. When you are ready to give up hope on yourself or others, remember that God can change even the most selfish personality.

29 JANUARY

Finding a Lost Son
GENESIS 45:1-28

Joseph could stand it no longer. "Out, all of you!" he cried out to his attendants. He wanted to be alone with his brothers when he told them who he was. ²Then he broke down and wept aloud. His sobs could be heard throughout the palace, and the news was quickly carried to Pharaoh's palace.

³"I am Joseph!" he said to his brothers. "Is my father still alive?" But his brothers were speechless! They were stunned to realize that Joseph was

standing there in front of them. ⁴"Come over here," he said. So they came closer. And he said again, "I am Joseph, your brother whom you sold into Egypt. ⁵But don't be angry with yourselves that you did this to me, for God did it. He sent me here ahead of you to preserve your lives. ⁶These two years of famine will grow to seven, during which there will be neither plowing nor harvest. ⁷God has sent me here to keep you and your families alive so that you will become a great nation. ⁸Yes, it was God who sent me here, not you! And he has made me a counselor to Pharaoh—manager of his entire household and ruler over all Egypt.

⁹"Hurry, return to my father and tell him, 'This is what your son Joseph says: God has made me master over all the land of Egypt. Come down to me right away! ¹⁰You will live in the land of Goshen so you can be near me with all your children and grandchildren, your flocks and herds, and all that you have. ¹¹I will take care of you there, for there are still five years of famine ahead of us. Otherwise you and your household will come to utter poverty.' "

¹²Then Joseph said, "You can see for yourselves, and so can my brother Benjamin, that I really am Joseph! ¹³Tell my father how I am honored here in Egypt. Tell him about everything you have seen, and bring him to me quickly." ¹⁴Weeping with joy, he embraced Benjamin, and Benjamin also began to weep. ¹⁵Then Joseph kissed each of his brothers and wept over them, and then they began talking freely with him.

¹⁶The news soon reached Pharaoh: "Joseph's brothers have come!" Pharaoh was very happy to hear this and so were his officials.

¹⁷Pharaoh said to Joseph, "Tell your brothers to load their pack animals and return quickly to their homes in Canaan. ¹⁸Tell them to bring your father and all of their families, and to come here to Egypt to live. Tell them, 'Pharaoh will assign to you the very best territory in the land of Egypt. You will live off the fat of the land!' ¹⁹And tell your brothers to take wagons from Egypt to carry their wives and little ones and to bring your father here. ²⁰Don't worry about your belongings, for the best of all the land of Egypt is yours."

²¹So the sons of Jacob did as they were told. Joseph gave them wagons, as Pharaoh had commanded, and he supplied them with provisions for the journey. ²²And he gave each of them new clothes—but to Benjamin he gave five changes of clothes and three hundred pieces of silver! ²³He sent his father ten donkeys loaded with the good things of Egypt, and ten donkeys loaded with grain and all kinds of other food to be eaten on his journey. ²⁴So he sent his brothers off, and as they left, he called after them, "Don't quarrel along the way!" ²⁵And they left Egypt and returned to their father, Jacob, in the land of Canaan.

²⁶"Joseph is still alive!" they told him. "And he is ruler over all the land of Egypt!" Jacob was stunned at the news—he couldn't believe it. ²⁷But when they had given him Joseph's messages, and when he saw the wagons loaded with the food sent by Joseph, his spirit revived.

²⁸Then Jacob said, "It must be true! My son Joseph is alive! I will go and see him before I die."

〰️〰️ **When did you last let your family know you appreciate them?** Although Joseph's brothers had wanted to get rid of him, God used even their evil actions to fulfill his ultimate plan. He sent Joseph ahead to preserve their lives, save Egypt, and prepare the way for the beginning of the nation of Israel. God is in control. His plans are not dictated by human actions. When others intend evil toward you, remember that they are only God's tools. As Joseph said to his brothers, "As far as I am concerned, God turned into good what you meant for evil. He brought me to the high position I have today so I could save the lives of many people" (50:20).

JANUARY

Jacob's Final Words

GENESIS 49:1-33

Then Jacob called together all his sons and said, "Gather around me, and I will tell you what is going to happen to you in the days to come.

² "Come and listen, O sons of Jacob;
  listen to Israel, your father.

³ "Reuben, you are my oldest son,
  the child of my vigorous youth.
  You are first on the list in rank and honor.
⁴ But you are as unruly as the waves of the sea,
  and you will be first no longer.
  For you slept with one of my wives;
  you dishonored me in my own bed.

⁵ "Simeon and Levi are two of a kind—
  men of violence.
⁶ O my soul, stay away from them.
  May I never be a party to their wicked plans.
  For in their anger they murdered men,
  and they crippled oxen just for sport.
⁷ Cursed be their anger, for it is fierce;
  cursed be their wrath, for it is cruel.
  Therefore, I will scatter their descendants
  throughout the nation of Israel.

⁸ "Judah, your brothers will praise you.
  You will defeat your enemies.
  All your relatives will bow before you.
⁹ Judah is a young lion

that has finished eating its prey.
Like a lion he crouches and lies down;
    like a lioness—who will dare to rouse him?
¹⁰The scepter will not depart from Judah,
    nor the ruler's staff from his descendants,
until the coming of the one to whom it belongs,
    the one whom all nations will obey.
¹¹He ties his foal to a grapevine,
    the colt of his donkey to a choice vine.
He washes his clothes in wine
    because his harvest is so plentiful.
¹²His eyes are darker than wine,
    and his teeth are whiter than milk.

¹³"Zebulun will settle on the shores of the sea
    and will be a harbor for ships;
    his borders will extend to Sidon.

¹⁴"Issachar is a strong beast of burden,
    resting among the sheepfolds.
¹⁵When he sees how good the countryside is,
    how pleasant the land,
he will bend his shoulder to the task
    and submit to forced labor.

¹⁶"Dan will govern his people
    like any other tribe in Israel.
¹⁷He will be a snake beside the road,
    a poisonous viper along the path,
that bites the horse's heels
    so the rider is thrown off.
¹⁸I trust in you for salvation, O LORD!

¹⁹"Gad will be plundered by marauding bands,
    but he will turn and plunder them.

²⁰"Asher will produce rich foods,
    food fit for kings.

²¹"Naphtali is a deer let loose,
    producing magnificent fawns.

²²"Joseph is a fruitful tree,
    a fruitful tree beside a fountain.
    His branches reach over the wall.
²³He has been attacked by archers,
    who shot at him and harassed him.
²⁴But his bow remained strong,

and his arms were strengthened
by the Mighty One of Jacob,
the Shepherd, the Rock of Israel.
²⁵May the God of your ancestors help you;
may the Almighty bless you
with the blessings of the heavens above,
blessings of the earth beneath,
and blessings of the breasts and womb.
²⁶May the blessings of your ancestors
be greater than the blessings of the eternal mountains,
reaching to the utmost bounds of the everlasting hills.
These blessings will fall on the head of Joseph,
who is a prince among his brothers.

²⁷"Benjamin is a wolf that prowls.
He devours his enemies in the morning,
and in the evening he divides the plunder."

²⁸These are the twelve tribes of Israel, and these are the blessings with which Jacob blessed his twelve sons. Each received a blessing that was appropriate to him.

²⁹Then Jacob told them, "Soon I will die. Bury me with my father and grandfather in the cave in Ephron's field. ³⁰This is the cave in the field of Machpelah, near Mamre in Canaan, which Abraham bought from Ephron the Hittite for a permanent burial place. ³¹There Abraham and his wife Sarah are buried. There Isaac and his wife, Rebekah, are buried. And there I buried Leah. ³²It is the cave that my grandfather Abraham bought from the Hittites." ³³Then when Jacob had finished this charge to his sons, he lay back in the bed, breathed his last, and died.

〰️ **What's the strongest impression you've made on others?** In the middle of his prophecy to Dan, Jacob exclaimed, "I trust in you for salvation, O Lord!" He was emphasizing to Dan that he would be a strong leader only if his trust was in God, not in his natural strength or ability. Those who are strong, attractive, or talented often find it easier to trust in themselves than in God, who gave them their gifts. Remember to thank God for what you are and have so your trust does not become misplaced.

31

JANUARY

Moses Is Born
EXODUS 1:8–2:10

Then a new king came to the throne of Egypt who knew nothing about Joseph or what he had done. ⁹He told his people, "These Israelites are becoming a threat to us because there are so many of them. ¹⁰We must find a way to put an end to this. If we don't and if war breaks out, they will join our enemies and fight against us. Then they will escape from the country."

[11]So the Egyptians made the Israelites their slaves and put brutal slave drivers over them, hoping to wear them down under heavy burdens. They forced them to build the cities of Pithom and Rameses as supply centers for the king. [12]But the more the Egyptians oppressed them, the more quickly the Israelites multiplied! The Egyptians soon became alarmed [13]and decided to make their slavery more bitter still. [14]They were ruthless with the Israelites, forcing them to make bricks and mortar and to work long hours in the fields.

[15]Then Pharaoh, the king of Egypt, gave this order to the Hebrew midwives, Shiphrah and Puah: [16]"When you help the Hebrew women give birth, kill all the boys as soon as they are born. Allow only the baby girls to live." [17]But because the midwives feared God, they refused to obey the king and allowed the boys to live, too.

[18]Then the king called for the midwives. "Why have you done this?" he demanded. "Why have you allowed the boys to live?"

[19]"Sir," they told him, "the Hebrew women are very strong. They have their babies so quickly that we cannot get there in time! They are not slow in giving birth like Egyptian women."

[20]So God blessed the midwives, and the Israelites continued to multiply, growing more and more powerful. [21]And because the midwives feared God, he gave them families of their own.

[22]Then Pharaoh gave this order to all his people: "Throw all the newborn Israelite boys into the Nile River. But you may spare the baby girls."

[2:1]During this time, a man and woman from the tribe of Levi got married. [2]The woman became pregnant and gave birth to a son. She saw what a beautiful baby he was and kept him hidden for three months. [3]But when she could no longer hide him, she got a little basket made of papyrus reeds and waterproofed it with tar and pitch. She put the baby in the basket and laid it among the reeds along the edge of the Nile River. [4]The baby's sister then stood at a distance, watching to see what would happen to him.

[5]Soon after this, one of Pharaoh's daughters came down to bathe in the river, and her servant girls walked along the riverbank. When the princess saw the little basket among the reeds, she told one of her servant girls to get it for her. [6]As the princess opened it, she found the baby boy. His helpless cries touched her heart. "He must be one of the Hebrew children," she said.

[7]Then the baby's sister approached the princess. "Should I go and find one of the Hebrew women to nurse the baby for you?" she asked.

[8]"Yes, do!" the princess replied. So the girl rushed home and called the baby's mother.

[9]"Take this child home and nurse him for me," the princess told her. "I will pay you for your help." So the baby's mother took her baby home and nursed him.

[10]Later, when he was older, the child's mother brought him back to the

princess, who adopted him as her son. The princess named him Moses, for she said, "I drew him out of the water."

〜∧↙ **How have you appreciated the gift of birth?** Moses' mother knew how wrong it would be to destroy her child. But there was little she could do to change Pharaoh's new law. Her only alternative was to hide the child and later place him in a tiny reed basket on the river. God used her courageous act to place her son, the Hebrew of his choice, in the house of Pharaoh. Do you sometimes feel surrounded by evil and frustrated by how little you can do about it? When faced with evil, look for ways to act against it. Then trust God to use your effort, however small it seems, in his war against evil.

Moses on the Run
EXODUS 2:11-25

Many years later, when Moses had grown up, he went out to visit his people, the Israelites, and he saw how hard they were forced to work. During his visit, he saw an Egyptian beating one of the Hebrew slaves. ¹²After looking around to make sure no one was watching, Moses killed the Egyptian and buried him in the sand.

¹³The next day, as Moses was out visiting his people again, he saw two Hebrew men fighting. "What are you doing, hitting your neighbor like that?" Moses said to the one in the wrong.

¹⁴"Who do you think you are?" the man replied. "Who appointed you to be our prince and judge? Do you plan to kill me as you killed that Egyptian yesterday?"

Moses was badly frightened because he realized that everyone knew what he had done. ¹⁵And sure enough, when Pharaoh heard about it, he gave orders to have Moses arrested and killed. But Moses fled from Pharaoh and escaped to the land of Midian.

When Moses arrived in Midian, he sat down beside a well. ¹⁶Now it happened that the priest of Midian had seven daughters who came regularly to this well to draw water and fill the water troughs for their father's flocks. ¹⁷But other shepherds would often come and chase the girls and their flocks away. This time, however, Moses came to their aid, rescuing the girls from the shepherds. Then he helped them draw water for their flocks.

¹⁸When the girls returned to Reuel, their father, he asked, "How did you get the flocks watered so quickly today?"

¹⁹"An Egyptian rescued us from the shepherds," they told him. "And then he drew water for us and watered our flocks."

²⁰"Well, where is he then?" their father asked. "Did you just leave him there? Go and invite him home for a meal!"

²¹Moses was happy to accept the invitation, and he settled down to live with them. In time, Reuel gave Moses one of his daughters, Zipporah, to be

his wife. [22]Later they had a baby boy, and Moses named him Gershom, for he said, "I have been a stranger in a foreign land."

[23]Years passed, and the king of Egypt died. But the Israelites still groaned beneath their burden of slavery. They cried out for help, and their pleas for deliverance rose up to God. [24]God heard their cries and remembered his covenant promise to Abraham, Isaac, and Jacob. [25]He looked down on the Israelites and felt deep concern for their welfare.

~√√∠ When was the last time you found yourself running from God? Moses tried to make sure no one was watching before he killed the Egyptian. But as it turned out, someone did see him, and Moses had to flee the country. Sometimes we mistakenly think we can get away with doing wrong if no one sees or catches us. Sooner or later, however, doing wrong will catch up with us as it did with Moses. Even if we are not caught in this life, we will still have to face God's evaluation of our actions.

2 FEBRUARY

God's Burning Bush
EXODUS 3:1-22

One day Moses was tending the flock of his father-in-law, Jethro, the priest of Midian, and he went deep into the wilderness near Sinai, the mountain of God. [2]Suddenly, the angel of the LORD appeared to him as a blazing fire in a bush. Moses was amazed because the bush was engulfed in flames, but it didn't burn up. [3]"Amazing!" Moses said to himself. "Why isn't that bush burning up? I must go over to see this."

[4]When the LORD saw that he had caught Moses' attention, God called to him from the bush, "Moses! Moses!"

"Here I am!" Moses replied.

[5]"Do not come any closer," God told him. "Take off your sandals, for you are standing on holy ground." [6]Then he said, "I am the God of your ancestors— the God of Abraham, the God of Isaac, and the God of Jacob." When Moses heard this, he hid his face in his hands because he was afraid to look at God.

[7]Then the LORD told him, "You can be sure I have seen the misery of my people in Egypt. I have heard their cries for deliverance from their harsh slave drivers. Yes, I am aware of their suffering. [8]So I have come to rescue them from the Egyptians and lead them out of Egypt into their own good and spacious land. It is a land flowing with milk and honey—the land where the Canaanites, Hittites, Amorites, Perizzites, Hivites, and Jebusites live. [9]The cries of the people of Israel have reached me, and I have seen how the Egyptians have oppressed them with heavy tasks. [10]Now go, for I am sending you to Pharaoh. You will lead my people, the Israelites, out of Egypt."

[11]"But who am I to appear before Pharaoh?" Moses asked God. "How can you expect me to lead the Israelites out of Egypt?"

¹²Then God told him, "I will be with you. And this will serve as proof that I have sent you: When you have brought the Israelites out of Egypt, you will return here to worship God at this very mountain."

¹³But Moses protested, "If I go to the people of Israel and tell them, 'The God of your ancestors has sent me to you,' they won't believe me. They will ask, 'Which god are you talking about? What is his name?' Then what should I tell them?"

¹⁴God replied, "I AM THE ONE WHO ALWAYS IS. Just tell them, 'I AM has sent me to you.'" ¹⁵God also said, "Tell them, 'The LORD, the God of your ancestors—the God of Abraham, the God of Isaac, and the God of Jacob— has sent me to you.' This will be my name forever; it has always been my name, and it will be used throughout all generations.

¹⁶"Now go and call together all the leaders of Israel. Tell them, 'The LORD, the God of your ancestors—the God of Abraham, Isaac, and Jacob— appeared to me in a burning bush. He said, "You can be sure that I am watching over you and have seen what is happening to you in Egypt. ¹⁷I promise to rescue you from the oppression of the Egyptians. I will lead you to the land now occupied by the Canaanites, Hittites, Amorites, Perizzites, Hivites, and Jebusites—a land flowing with milk and honey."'

¹⁸"The leaders of the people of Israel will accept your message. Then all of you must go straight to the king of Egypt and tell him, 'The LORD, the God of the Hebrews, has met with us. Let us go on a three-day journey into the wilderness to offer sacrifices to the LORD our God.'

¹⁹"But I know that the king of Egypt will not let you go except under heavy pressure. ²⁰So I will reach out and strike at the heart of Egypt with all kinds of miracles. Then at last he will let you go. ²¹And I will see to it that the Egyptians treat you well. They will load you down with gifts so you will not leave empty-handed. ²²The Israelite women will ask for silver and gold jewelry and fine clothing from their Egyptian neighbors and their neighbors' guests. With this clothing, you will dress your sons and daughters. In this way, you will plunder the Egyptians!"

〰〰 **In what ways has God made himself known to you?** God spoke to Moses from an unexpected source: a burning bush. When Moses saw it, he went to investigate. God often uses unexpected sources when communicating to us, too. Be willing to investigate. Whether he uses people, thoughts, or experiences, be ready for God's surprises. He may have guidance for you that can come when you are ready to listen to a "burning bush."

3

Moses Isn't Sure
EXODUS 4:1-17

But Moses protested again, "Look, they won't believe me! They won't do what I tell them. They'll just say, 'The LORD never appeared to you.' "

²Then the LORD asked him, "What do you have there in your hand?"

"A shepherd's staff," Moses replied.

³"Throw it down on the ground," the LORD told him. So Moses threw it down, and it became a snake! Moses was terrified, so he turned and ran away.

⁴Then the LORD told him, "Take hold of its tail." So Moses reached out and grabbed it, and it became a shepherd's staff again.

⁵"Perform this sign, and they will believe you," the LORD told him. "Then they will realize that the LORD, the God of their ancestors—the God of Abraham, the God of Isaac, and the God of Jacob—really has appeared to you."

⁶Then the LORD said to Moses, "Put your hand inside your robe." Moses did so, and when he took it out again, his hand was white as snow with leprosy. ⁷"Now put your hand back into your robe again," the LORD said. Moses did, and when he took it out this time, it was as healthy as the rest of his body.

⁸"If they do not believe the first miraculous sign, they will believe the second," the LORD said. ⁹"And if they do not believe you even after these two signs, then take some water from the Nile River and pour it out on the dry ground. When you do, it will turn into blood."

¹⁰But Moses pleaded with the LORD, "O Lord, I'm just not a good speaker. I never have been, and I'm not now, even after you have spoken to me. I'm clumsy with words."

¹¹"Who makes mouths?" the LORD asked him. "Who makes people so they can speak or not speak, hear or not hear, see or not see? Is it not I, the LORD? ¹²Now go, and do as I have told you. I will help you speak well, and I will tell you what to say."

¹³But Moses again pleaded, "Lord, please! Send someone else."

¹⁴Then the LORD became angry with Moses. "All right," he said. "What about your brother, Aaron the Levite? He is a good speaker. And look! He is on his way to meet you now. And when he sees you, he will be very glad. ¹⁵You will talk to him, giving him the words to say. I will help both of you to speak clearly, and I will tell you what to do. ¹⁶Aaron will be your spokesman to the people, and you will be as God to him, telling him what to say. ¹⁷And be sure to take your shepherd's staff along so you can perform the miraculous signs I have shown you."

～∿∠ **How willing are you to do what you feel God wants you to do?**
Moses pleaded with God to let him out of his mission. After all, he was not a good speaker and would probably embarrass both himself and God. But God looked at Moses' problem quite differently. All Moses needed was some help, and who better than God could help him say and do the right things. God made his mouth and would give him the words to say. It is easy for us to focus on our weaknesses. But if God asks us to do something, he will help us get the job done. He will provide words, strength, courage, and ability where needed.

Resistance
EXODUS 5:1-23

After this presentation to Israel's leaders, Moses and Aaron went to see Pharaoh. They told him, "This is what the LORD, the God of Israel, says: 'Let my people go, for they must go out into the wilderness to hold a religious festival in my honor.' "

²"Is that so?" retorted Pharaoh. "And who is the LORD that I should listen to him and let Israel go? I don't know the LORD, and I will not let Israel go."

³But Aaron and Moses persisted. "The God of the Hebrews has met with us," they declared. "Let us take a three-day trip into the wilderness so we can offer sacrifices to the LORD our God. If we don't, we will surely die by disease or the sword."

⁴"Who do you think you are," Pharaoh shouted, "distracting the people from their tasks? Get back to work! ⁵Look, there are many people here in Egypt, and you are stopping them from doing their work."

⁶That same day Pharaoh sent this order to the slave drivers and foremen he had set over the people of Israel: ⁷"Do not supply the people with any more straw for making bricks. Let them get it themselves! ⁸But don't reduce their production quotas by a single brick. They obviously don't have enough to do. If they did, they wouldn't be talking about going into the wilderness to offer sacrifices to their God. ⁹Load them down with more work. Make them sweat! That will teach them to listen to these liars!"

¹⁰So the slave drivers and foremen informed the people: "Pharaoh has ordered us not to provide straw for you. ¹¹Go and get it yourselves. Find it wherever you can. But you must produce just as many bricks as before!" ¹²So the people scattered throughout the land in search of straw.

¹³The slave drivers were brutal. "Meet your daily quota of bricks, just as you did before!" they demanded. ¹⁴Then they whipped the Israelite foremen in charge of the work crews. "Why haven't you met your quotas either yesterday or today?" they demanded.

¹⁵So the Israelite foremen went to Pharaoh and pleaded with him. "Please don't treat us like this," they begged. ¹⁶"We are given no straw, but we are

still told to make as many bricks as before. We are beaten for something that isn't our fault! It is the fault of your slave drivers for making such unreasonable demands."

[17]But Pharaoh replied, "You're just lazy! You obviously don't have enough to do. If you did, you wouldn't be saying, 'Let us go, so we can offer sacrifices to the LORD.' [18]Now, get back to work! No straw will be given to you, but you must still deliver the regular quota of bricks."

[19]Since Pharaoh would not let up on his demands, the Israelite foremen could see that they were in serious trouble. [20]As they left Pharaoh's court, they met Moses and Aaron, who were waiting outside for them. [21]The foremen said to them, "May the LORD judge you for getting us into this terrible situation with Pharaoh and his officials. You have given them an excuse to kill us!"

[22]So Moses went back to the LORD and protested, "Why have you mistreated your own people like this, Lord? Why did you send me? [23]Since I gave Pharaoh your message, he has been even more brutal to your people. You have not even begun to rescue them!"

〰〰 **What have people said when you've tried to obey God?** Pharaoh would not listen to Moses and Aaron because he did not know or respect God. People who do not know God may not listen to his Word or his messengers. Like Moses and Aaron, we need to persist. When others reject you or your faith, don't be surprised or discouraged. Continue to tell them about God, trusting him to open minds and soften stubborn hearts.

5

Rejection
EXODUS 6:1-13

"Now you will see what I will do to Pharaoh," the LORD told Moses. "When he feels my powerful hand upon him, he will let the people go. In fact, he will be so anxious to get rid of them that he will force them to leave his land!"

[2]And God continued, "I am the LORD. [3]I appeared to Abraham, to Isaac, and to Jacob as God Almighty, though I did not reveal my name, the LORD, to them. [4]And I entered into a solemn covenant with them. Under its terms, I swore to give them the land of Canaan, where they were living. [5]You can be sure that I have heard the groans of the people of Israel, who are now slaves to the Egyptians. I have remembered my covenant with them.

[6]"Therefore, say to the Israelites: 'I am the LORD, and I will free you from your slavery in Egypt. I will redeem you with mighty power and great acts of judgment. [7]I will make you my own special people, and I will be your God. And you will know that I am the LORD your God who has rescued you from

your slavery in Egypt. [8]I will bring you into the land I swore to give to Abraham, Isaac, and Jacob. It will be your very own property. I am the LORD!' "

[9]So Moses told the people what the LORD had said, but they wouldn't listen anymore. They had become too discouraged by the increasing burden of their slavery.

[10]Then the LORD said to Moses, [11]"Go back to Pharaoh, and tell him to let the people of Israel leave Egypt."

[12]"But LORD!" Moses objected. "My own people won't listen to me anymore. How can I expect Pharaoh to listen? I'm no orator!"

[13]But the LORD ordered Moses and Aaron to return to Pharaoh, king of Egypt, and to demand that he let the people of Israel leave Egypt.

〰️〰️ **What would it cost you to do what God wants?** Small problems need only small answers. But when we face great problems, God has an opportunity to exercise his great power. As the Hebrews' troubles grew steadily worse, God planned to intervene with his mighty power and perform great miracles to deliver them. How big are your problems? Big problems put you in a perfect position to watch God give big answers.

FEBRUARY

A Stubborn Ruler

EXODUS 7:1-13

Then the LORD said to Moses, "Pay close attention to this. I will make you seem like God to Pharaoh. Your brother, Aaron, will be your prophet; he will speak for you. [2]Tell Aaron everything I say to you and have him announce it to Pharaoh. He will demand that the people of Israel be allowed to leave Egypt. [3]But I will cause Pharaoh to be stubborn so I can multiply my miraculous signs and wonders in the land of Egypt. [4]Even then Pharaoh will refuse to listen to you. So I will crush Egypt with a series of disasters, after which I will lead the forces of Israel out with great acts of judgment. [5]When I show the Egyptians my power and force them to let the Israelites go, they will realize that I am the LORD."

[6]So Moses and Aaron did just as the LORD had commanded them. [7]Moses was eighty years old, and Aaron was eighty-three at the time they made their demands to Pharaoh.

[8]Then the LORD said to Moses and Aaron, [9]"Pharaoh will demand that you show him a miracle to prove that God has sent you. When he makes this demand, say to Aaron, 'Throw down your shepherd's staff,' and it will become a snake."

[10]So Moses and Aaron went to see Pharaoh, and they performed the miracle just as the LORD had told them. Aaron threw down his staff before Pharaoh and his court, and it became a snake. [11]Then Pharaoh called in his wise men and magicians, and they did the same thing with their secret arts.

[12]Their staffs became snakes, too! But then Aaron's snake swallowed up their snakes. [13]Pharaoh's heart, however, remained hard and stubborn. He still refused to listen, just as the LORD had predicted.

~∿↯⁓ **How does stubbornness affect your relationship with God?**
After repeated warnings, Pharaoh still refused to obey God. He hardened his heart every time there was a break in the plagues. His stubborn disobedience brought suffering upon himself and his entire country. While persistence is good, stubbornness is usually self-centered. Stubbornness toward God is always disobedience. Avoid disobedience because the consequences may spill onto others.

7

Five out of Ten Plagues
EXODUS 7:14–9:7

Then the LORD said to Moses, "Pharaoh is very stubborn, and he continues to refuse to let the people go. [15]So go to Pharaoh in the morning as he goes down to the river. Stand on the riverbank and meet him there. Be sure to take along the shepherd's staff that turned into a snake. [16]Say to him, 'The LORD, the God of the Hebrews, has sent me to say, "Let my people go, so they can worship me in the wilderness." Until now, you have refused to listen to him. [17]Now the LORD says, "You are going to find out that I am the LORD." Look! I will hit the water of the Nile with this staff, and the river will turn to blood. [18]The fish in it will die, and the river will stink. The Egyptians will not be able to drink any water from the Nile.' "

[19]Then the LORD said to Moses: "Tell Aaron to point his staff toward the waters of Egypt—all its rivers, canals, marshes, and reservoirs. Everywhere in Egypt the water will turn into blood, even the water stored in wooden bowls and stone pots in the people's homes."

[20]So Moses and Aaron did just as the LORD had commanded them. As Pharaoh and all of his officials watched, Moses raised his staff and hit the water of the Nile. Suddenly, the whole river turned to blood! [21]The fish in the river died, and the water became so foul that the Egyptians couldn't drink it. There was blood everywhere throughout the land of Egypt. [22]But again the magicians of Egypt used their secret arts, and they, too, turned water into blood. So Pharaoh's heart remained hard and stubborn. He refused to listen to Moses and Aaron, just as the LORD had predicted. [23]Pharaoh returned to his palace and put the whole thing out of his mind. [24]Then the Egyptians dug wells along the riverbank to get drinking water, for they couldn't drink from the river. [25]An entire week passed from the time the LORD turned the water of the Nile to blood.

[8:1]Then the LORD said to Moses, "Go to Pharaoh once again and tell him, 'This is what the LORD says: Let my people go, so they can worship me. [2]If you refuse, then listen carefully to this: I will send vast hordes of frogs across your entire land from one border to the other. ³The Nile River will swarm with them. They will come up out of the river and into your houses, even into your bedrooms and onto your beds! Every home in Egypt will be filled with them. They will fill even your ovens and your kneading bowls. ⁴You and your people will be overwhelmed by frogs!' "

⁵Then the LORD said to Moses, "Tell Aaron to point his shepherd's staff toward all the rivers, canals, and marshes of Egypt so there will be frogs in every corner of the land." ⁶Aaron did so, and frogs covered the whole land of Egypt! ⁷But the magicians were able to do the same thing with their secret arts. They, too, caused frogs to come up on the land.

⁸Then Pharaoh summoned Moses and Aaron and begged, "Plead with the LORD to take the frogs away from me and my people. I will let the people go, so they can offer sacrifices to the LORD."

⁹"You set the time!" Moses replied. "Tell me when you want me to pray for you, your officials, and your people. I will pray that you and your houses will be rid of the frogs. Then only the frogs in the Nile River will remain alive."

¹⁰"Do it tomorrow," Pharaoh said.

"All right," Moses replied, "it will be as you have said. Then you will know that no one is as powerful as the LORD our God. ¹¹All the frogs will be destroyed, except those in the river."

¹²So Moses and Aaron left Pharaoh, and Moses pleaded with the LORD about the frogs he had sent. ¹³And the LORD did as Moses had promised. The frogs in the houses, the courtyards, and the fields all died. ¹⁴They were piled into great heaps, and a terrible stench filled the land. ¹⁵But when Pharaoh saw that the frogs were gone, he hardened his heart. He refused to listen to Moses and Aaron, just as the LORD had predicted.

¹⁶So the LORD said to Moses, "Tell Aaron to strike the dust with his staff. The dust will turn into swarms of gnats throughout the land of Egypt." ¹⁷So Moses and Aaron did just as the LORD had commanded them. Suddenly, gnats infested the entire land, covering the Egyptians and their animals. All the dust in the land of Egypt turned into gnats. ¹⁸Pharaoh's magicians tried to do the same thing with their secret arts, but this time they failed. And the gnats covered all the people and animals.

¹⁹"This is the finger of God!" the magicians exclaimed to Pharaoh. But Pharaoh's heart remained hard and stubborn. He wouldn't listen to them, just as the LORD had predicted.

²⁰Next the LORD told Moses, "Get up early in the morning and meet Pharaoh as he goes down to the river. Say to him, 'This is what the LORD says: Let my people go, so they can worship me. ²¹If you refuse, I will send swarms of flies throughout Egypt. Your homes will be filled with them, and the ground will be covered with them. ²²But it will be very different in the land of Goshen, where the Israelites live. No flies will be found there. Then you will know that I am the LORD and that I have power even in the heart of

your land. ²³I will make a clear distinction between your people and my people. This miraculous sign will happen tomorrow.' "

²⁴And the LORD did just as he had said. There were terrible swarms of flies in Pharaoh's palace and in every home in Egypt. The whole country was thrown into chaos by the flies.

²⁵Pharaoh hastily called for Moses and Aaron. "All right! Go ahead and offer sacrifices to your God," he said. "But do it here in this land. Don't go out into the wilderness."

²⁶But Moses replied, "That won't do! The Egyptians would detest the sacrifices that we offer to the LORD our God. If we offer them here where they can see us, they will be sure to stone us. ²⁷We must take a three-day trip into the wilderness to offer sacrifices to the LORD our God, just as he has commanded us."

²⁸"All right, go ahead," Pharaoh replied. "I will let you go to offer sacrifices to the LORD your God in the wilderness. But don't go too far away. Now hurry, and pray for me."

²⁹"As soon as I go," Moses said, "I will ask the LORD to cause the swarms of flies to disappear from you and all your people. But I am warning you, don't change your mind again and refuse to let the people go to sacrifice to the LORD."

³⁰So Moses left Pharaoh and asked the LORD to remove all the flies. ³¹And the LORD did as Moses asked and caused the swarms to disappear. Not a single fly remained in the land! ³²But Pharaoh hardened his heart again and refused to let the people go.

⁹:¹"Go back to Pharaoh," the LORD commanded Moses. "Tell him, 'This is what the LORD, the God of the Hebrews, says: Let my people go, so they can worship me. ²If you continue to oppress them and refuse to let them go, ³the LORD will send a deadly plague to destroy your horses, donkeys, camels, cattle, and sheep. ⁴But the LORD will again make a distinction between the property of the Israelites and that of the Egyptians. Not a single one of Israel's livestock will die!' "

⁵The LORD announced that he would send the plague the very next day, ⁶and he did it, just as he had said. The next morning all the livestock of the Egyptians began to die, but the Israelites didn't lose a single animal from their flocks and herds. ⁷Pharaoh sent officials to see whether it was true that none of the Israelites' animals were dead. But even after he found it to be true, his heart remained stubborn. He still refused to let the people go.

〰️〽️ **When do you try to bargain with God?** Pharaoh wanted a compromise. He would allow the Hebrews to sacrifice, but only if they would do it nearby. God's requirement, however, was firm: The Hebrews had to leave Egypt. Sometimes people urge believers to compromise and give only partial obedience to God's commands. But commitment and obedience to God cannot be negotiated. When it comes to obeying God, half measures won't do.

Four More Plagues

EXODUS 9:8–10:29

Then the LORD said to Moses and Aaron, "Take soot from a furnace, and have Moses toss it into the sky while Pharaoh watches. ⁹It will spread like fine dust over the whole land of Egypt, causing boils to break out on people and animals alike."

¹⁰So they gathered soot from a furnace and went to see Pharaoh. As Pharaoh watched, Moses tossed the soot into the air, and terrible boils broke out on the people and animals throughout Egypt. ¹¹Even the magicians were unable to stand before Moses, because the boils had broken out on them, too. ¹²But the LORD made Pharaoh even more stubborn, and he refused to listen, just as the LORD had predicted.

¹³Then the LORD said to Moses, "Get up early in the morning. Go to Pharaoh and tell him, 'The LORD, the God of the Hebrews, says: Let my people go, so they can worship me. ¹⁴If you don't, I will send a plague that will really speak to you and your officials and all the Egyptian people. I will prove to you that there is no other God like me in all the earth. ¹⁵I could have killed you all by now. I could have attacked you with a plague that would have wiped you from the face of the earth. ¹⁶But I have let you live for this reason—that you might see my power and that my fame might spread throughout the earth. ¹⁷But you are still lording it over my people, and you refuse to let them go. ¹⁸So tomorrow at this time I will send a hailstorm worse than any in all of Egypt's history. ¹⁹Quick! Order your livestock and servants to come in from the fields. Every person or animal left outside will die beneath the hail.' "

²⁰Some of Pharaoh's officials believed what the LORD said. They immediately brought their livestock and servants in from the fields. ²¹But those who had no respect for the word of the LORD left them out in the open.

²²Then the LORD said to Moses, "Lift your hand toward the sky, and cause the hail to fall throughout Egypt, on the people, the animals, and the crops."

²³So Moses lifted his staff toward the sky, and the LORD sent thunder and hail, and lightning struck the earth. The LORD sent a tremendous hailstorm against all the land of Egypt. ²⁴Never in all the history of Egypt had there been a storm like that, with such severe hail and continuous lightning. ²⁵It left all of Egypt in ruins. Everything left in the fields was destroyed—people, animals, and crops alike. Even all the trees were destroyed. ²⁶The only spot in all Egypt without hail that day was the land of Goshen, where the people of Israel lived.

²⁷Then Pharaoh urgently sent for Moses and Aaron. "I finally admit my fault," he confessed. "The LORD is right, and my people and I are wrong. ²⁸Please beg the LORD to end this terrifying thunder and hail. I will let you go at once."

²⁹"All right," Moses replied. "As soon as I leave the city, I will lift my hands and pray to the LORD. Then the thunder and hail will stop. This will prove to you that the earth belongs to the LORD. ³⁰But as for you and your officials, I know that you still do not fear the LORD God as you should." ³¹All the flax and barley were destroyed because the barley was ripe and the flax was in bloom. ³²But the wheat and the spelt were not destroyed because they had not yet sprouted from the ground.

³³So Moses left Pharaoh and went out of the city. As he lifted his hands to the LORD, all at once the thunder and hail stopped, and the downpour ceased. ³⁴When Pharaoh saw this, he and his officials sinned yet again by stubbornly refusing to do as they had promised. ³⁵Pharaoh refused to let the people leave, just as the LORD had predicted.

10:1 Then the LORD said to Moses, "Return to Pharaoh and again make your demands. I have made him and his officials stubborn so I can continue to display my power by performing miraculous signs among them. ²You will be able to tell wonderful stories to your children and grandchildren about the marvelous things I am doing among the Egyptians to prove that I am the LORD."

³So Moses and Aaron went to Pharaoh and said, "This is what the LORD, the God of the Hebrews, says: How long will you refuse to submit to me? Let my people go, so they can worship me. ⁴If you refuse, watch out! For tomorrow I will cover the whole country with locusts. ⁵There will be so many that you won't be able to see the ground. They will devour everything that escaped the hailstorm, including all the trees in the fields. ⁶They will overrun your palaces and the homes of your officials and all the houses of Egypt. Never in the history of Egypt has there been a plague like this one!" And with that, Moses turned and walked out.

⁷The court officials now came to Pharaoh and appealed to him. "How long will you let these disasters go on? Please let the Israelites go to serve the LORD their God! Don't you realize that Egypt lies in ruins?"

⁸So Moses and Aaron were brought back to Pharaoh. "All right, go and serve the LORD your God," he said. "But tell me, just whom do you want to take along?"

⁹"Young and old, all of us will go," Moses replied. "We will take our sons and daughters and our flocks and herds. We must all join together in a festival to the LORD."

¹⁰Pharaoh retorted, "The LORD will certainly need to be with you if you try to take your little ones along! I can see through your wicked intentions. ¹¹Never! Only the men may go and serve the LORD, for that is what you requested." And Pharaoh threw them out of the palace.

¹²Then the LORD said to Moses, "Raise your hand over the land of Egypt to bring on the locusts. Let them cover the land and eat all the crops still left after the hailstorm."

¹³So Moses raised his staff, and the LORD caused an east wind to blow all that day and through the night. When morning arrived, the east wind had

brought the locusts. [14]And the locusts swarmed over the land of Egypt from border to border. It was the worst locust plague in Egyptian history, and there has never again been one like it. [15]For the locusts covered the surface of the whole country, making the ground look black. They ate all the plants and all the fruit on the trees that had survived the hailstorm. Not one green thing remained, neither tree nor plant, throughout the land of Egypt.

[16]Pharaoh quickly sent for Moses and Aaron. "I confess my sin against the LORD your God and against you," he said to them. [17]"Forgive my sin only this once, and plead with the LORD your God to take away this terrible plague."

[18]So Moses left Pharaoh and pleaded with the LORD. [19]The LORD responded by sending a strong west wind that blew the locusts out into the Red Sea. Not a single locust remained in all the land of Egypt. [20]But the LORD made Pharaoh stubborn once again, and he did not let the people go.

[21]Then the LORD said to Moses, "Lift your hand toward heaven, and a deep and terrifying darkness will descend on the land of Egypt." [22]So Moses lifted his hand toward heaven, and there was deep darkness over the entire land for three days. [23]During all that time the people scarcely moved, for they could not see. But there was light as usual where the people of Israel lived.

[24]Then Pharaoh called for Moses. "Go and worship the LORD," he said. "But let your flocks and herds stay here. You can even take your children with you."

[25]"No," Moses said, "we must take our flocks and herds for sacrifices and burnt offerings to the LORD our God. [26]All our property must go with us; not a hoof can be left behind. We will have to choose our sacrifices for the LORD our God from among these animals. And we won't know which sacrifices he will require until we get there."

[27]So the LORD hardened Pharaoh's heart once more, and he would not let them go. [28]"Get out of here!" Pharaoh shouted at Moses. "Don't ever let me see you again! The day you do, you will die!"

[29]"Very well," Moses replied. "I will never see you again."

〰〰 **How does God get your attention?** God gave Pharaoh many opportunities to heed Moses' warnings. But finally God seemed to say, "All right, Pharaoh, have it your way," and Pharaoh's heart became permanently hardened. Did God intentionally harden Pharaoh's heart and overrule his free will? No, he simply confirmed that Pharaoh freely chose a life of resisting God. Similarly, after a lifetime of resisting God, you may find it impossible to turn to him. Don't wait until just the *right* time before turning to God. Do it now while you still have the chance. If you continually ignore God's voice, eventually you will be unable to hear it at all.

9

The Ultimate Plague

EXODUS 11:1-10; 12:29-36

Then the LORD said to Moses, "I will send just one more disaster on Pharaoh and the land of Egypt. After that, Pharaoh will let you go. In fact, he will be so anxious to get rid of you that he will practically force you to leave the country. ²Tell all the Israelite men and women to ask their Egyptian neighbors for articles of silver and gold."

³(Now the LORD had caused the Egyptians to look favorably on the people of Israel, and Moses was considered a very great man in the land of Egypt. He was respected by Pharaoh's officials and the Egyptian people alike.)

⁴So Moses announced to Pharaoh, "This is what the LORD says: About midnight I will pass through Egypt. ⁵All the firstborn sons will die in every family in Egypt, from the oldest son of Pharaoh, who sits on the throne, to the oldest son of his lowliest slave. Even the firstborn of the animals will die. ⁶Then a loud wail will be heard throughout the land of Egypt; there has never been such wailing before, and there never will be again. ⁷But among the Israelites it will be so peaceful that not even a dog will bark. Then you will know that the LORD makes a distinction between the Egyptians and the Israelites. ⁸All the officials of Egypt will come running to me, bowing low. 'Please leave!' they will beg. 'Hurry! And take all your followers with you.' Only then will I go!" Then, burning with anger, Moses left Pharaoh's presence.

⁹Now the LORD had told Moses, "Pharaoh will not listen to you. But this will give me the opportunity to do even more mighty miracles in the land of Egypt." ¹⁰Although Moses and Aaron did these miracles in Pharaoh's presence, the LORD hardened his heart so he wouldn't let the Israelites leave the country.

12:29 And at midnight the LORD killed all the firstborn sons in the land of Egypt, from the firstborn son of Pharaoh, who sat on the throne, to the firstborn son of the captive in the dungeon. Even the firstborn of their livestock were killed. ³⁰Pharaoh and his officials and all the people of Egypt woke up during the night, and loud wailing was heard throughout the land of Egypt. There was not a single house where someone had not died.

³¹Pharaoh sent for Moses and Aaron during the night. "Leave us!" he cried. "Go away, all of you! Go and serve the LORD as you have requested. ³²Take your flocks and herds, and be gone. Go, but give me a blessing as you leave." ³³All the Egyptians urged the people of Israel to get out of the land as quickly as possible, for they thought, "We will all die!"

³⁴The Israelites took with them their bread dough made without yeast. They wrapped their kneading bowls in their spare clothing and carried them on their shoulders. ³⁵And the people of Israel did as Moses had

instructed and asked the Egyptians for clothing and articles of silver and gold. [36]The LORD caused the Egyptians to look favorably on the Israelites, and they gave the Israelites whatever they asked for. So, like a victorious army, they plundered the Egyptians!

~~\/\/~~ **What does it mean to *fear* God in your life?** You may wonder how Pharaoh could be so foolish as to see God's miraculous power and still not listen to Moses. But Pharaoh had his mind made up long before the plagues began. He couldn't believe that someone was greater than he. This stubborn unbelief led to a heart so hard that even a major catastrophe couldn't soften him. Finally, it took the greatest of all calamities, the loss of his son, to force him to recognize God's authority. But even then he wanted God to leave, not to rule his country. We must not wait for great calamities to drive us to God but must open our hearts and minds to his direction now.

FEBRUARY

A Narrow Escape

EXODUS 13:17–14:31

When Pharaoh finally let the people go, God did not lead them on the road that runs through Philistine territory, even though that was the shortest way from Egypt to the Promised Land. God said, "If the people are faced with a battle, they might change their minds and return to Egypt." [18]So God led them along a route through the wilderness toward the Red Sea, and the Israelites left Egypt like a marching army.

[19]Moses took the bones of Joseph with him, for Joseph had made the sons of Israel swear that they would take his bones with them when God led them out of Egypt as he was sure God would.

[20]Leaving Succoth, they camped at Etham on the edge of the wilderness. [21]The LORD guided them by a pillar of cloud during the day and a pillar of fire at night. That way they could travel whether it was day or night. [22]And the LORD did not remove the pillar of cloud or pillar of fire from their sight.

[14:1] Then the LORD gave these instructions to Moses: [2]"Tell the people to march toward Pi-hahiroth between Migdol and the sea. Camp there along the shore, opposite Baal-zephon. [3]Then Pharaoh will think, 'Those Israelites are confused. They are trapped between the wilderness and the sea!' [4]And once again I will harden Pharaoh's heart, and he will chase after you. I have planned this so I will receive great glory at the expense of Pharaoh and his armies. After this, the Egyptians will know that I am the LORD!" So the Israelites camped there as they were told.

[5]When word reached the king of Egypt that the Israelites were not planning to return to Egypt after three days, Pharaoh and his officials changed their minds. "What have we done, letting all these slaves get away?" they asked. [6]So Pharaoh called out his troops and led the chase in his chariot.

⁷He took with him six hundred of Egypt's best chariots, along with the rest of the chariots of Egypt, each with a commander. ⁸The LORD continued to strengthen Pharaoh's resolve, and he chased after the people of Israel who had escaped so defiantly. ⁹All the forces in Pharaoh's army—all his horses, chariots, and charioteers—were used in the chase. The Egyptians caught up with the people of Israel as they were camped beside the shore near Pi-hahiroth, across from Baal-zephon.

¹⁰As Pharaoh and his army approached, the people of Israel could see them in the distance, marching toward them. The people began to panic, and they cried out to the LORD for help.

¹¹Then they turned against Moses and complained, "Why did you bring us out here to die in the wilderness? Weren't there enough graves for us in Egypt? Why did you make us leave? ¹²Didn't we tell you to leave us alone while we were still in Egypt? Our Egyptian slavery was far better than dying out here in the wilderness!"

¹³But Moses told the people, "Don't be afraid. Just stand where you are and watch the LORD rescue you. The Egyptians that you see today will never be seen again. ¹⁴The LORD himself will fight for you. You won't have to lift a finger in your defense!"

¹⁵Then the LORD said to Moses, "Why are you crying out to me? Tell the people to get moving! ¹⁶Use your shepherd's staff—hold it out over the water, and a path will open up before you through the sea. Then all the people of Israel will walk through on dry ground. ¹⁷Yet I will harden the hearts of the Egyptians, and they will follow the Israelites into the sea. Then I will receive great glory at the expense of Pharaoh and his armies, chariots, and charioteers. ¹⁸When I am finished with Pharaoh and his army, all Egypt will know that I am the LORD!"

¹⁹Then the angel of God, who had been leading the people of Israel, moved to a position behind them, and the pillar of cloud also moved around behind them. ²⁰The cloud settled between the Israelite and Egyptian camps. As night came, the pillar of cloud turned into a pillar of fire, lighting the Israelite camp. But the cloud became darkness to the Egyptians, and they couldn't find the Israelites.

²¹Then Moses raised his hand over the sea, and the LORD opened up a path through the water with a strong east wind. The wind blew all that night, turning the seabed into dry land. ²²So the people of Israel walked through the sea on dry ground, with walls of water on each side! ²³Then the Egyptians—all of Pharaoh's horses, chariots, and charioteers—followed them across the bottom of the sea. ²⁴But early in the morning, the LORD looked down on the Egyptian army from the pillar of fire and cloud, and he threw them into confusion. ²⁵Their chariot wheels began to come off, making their chariots impossible to drive. "Let's get out of here!" the Egyptians shouted. "The LORD is fighting for Israel against us!"

²⁶When all the Israelites were on the other side, the LORD said to Moses, "Raise your hand over the sea again. Then the waters will rush back over

the Egyptian chariots and charioteers." ²⁷So as the sun began to rise, Moses raised his hand over the sea. The water roared back into its usual place, and the LORD swept the terrified Egyptians into the surging currents. ²⁸The waters covered all the chariots and charioteers—the entire army of Pharaoh. Of all the Egyptians who had chased the Israelites into the sea, not a single one survived.

²⁹The people of Israel had walked through the middle of the sea on dry land, as the water stood up like a wall on both sides. ³⁰This was how the LORD rescued Israel from the Egyptians that day. And the Israelites could see the bodies of the Egyptians washed up on the shore. ³¹When the people of Israel saw the mighty power that the LORD had displayed against the Egyptians, they feared the LORD and put their faith in him and his servant Moses.

〰〰 **When have you experienced God's protection?** The people were hostile and despairing, but Moses encouraged them to watch the wonderful way God would rescue them. Moses had a positive attitude! When it looked as if they were trapped, Moses called upon God to intervene. We may not be chased by an army, but we may still feel trapped. Instead of giving in to despair, we should adopt Moses' attitude to "watch" and see what God will do.

FEBRUARY **11**

God Provides Water
EXODUS 15:22-27; 17:1-7

Then Moses led the people of Israel away from the Red Sea, and they moved out into the Shur Desert. They traveled in this desert for three days without water. ²³When they came to Marah, they finally found water. But the people couldn't drink it because it was bitter. (That is why the place was called Marah, which means "bitter.")

²⁴Then the people turned against Moses. "What are we going to drink?" they demanded.

²⁵So Moses cried out to the LORD for help, and the LORD showed him a branch. Moses took the branch and threw it into the water. This made the water good to drink.

It was there at Marah that the LORD laid before them the following conditions to test their faithfulness to him: ²⁶"If you will listen carefully to the voice of the LORD your God and do what is right in his sight, obeying his commands and laws, then I will not make you suffer the diseases I sent on the Egyptians; for I am the LORD who heals you."

²⁷After leaving Marah, they came to Elim, where there were twelve springs and seventy palm trees. They camped there beside the springs.

17:1 At the LORD's command, the people of Israel left the Sin Desert and moved from place to place. Eventually they came to Rephidim, but there was no water to be found there. ²So once more the people grumbled and complained to Moses. "Give us water to drink!" they demanded.

"Quiet!" Moses replied. "Why are you arguing with me? And why are you testing the LORD?"

³But tormented by thirst, they continued to complain, "Why did you ever take us out of Egypt? Why did you bring us here? We, our children, and our livestock will all die!"

⁴Then Moses pleaded with the LORD, "What should I do with these people? They are about to stone me!"

⁵The LORD said to Moses, "Take your shepherd's staff, the one you used when you struck the water of the Nile. Then call some of the leaders of Israel and walk on ahead of the people. ⁶I will meet you by the rock at Mount Sinai. Strike the rock, and water will come pouring out. Then the people will be able to drink." Moses did just as he was told; and as the leaders looked on, water gushed out.

⁷Moses named the place Massah—"the place of testing"—and Meribah— "the place of arguing"—because the people of Israel argued with Moses and tested the LORD by saying, "Is the LORD going to take care of us or not?"

〰〰 **What do you complain to God about?** Again the people complained about their problem instead of praying. Some problems can be solved by careful thought or by rearranging our priorities. Some can be solved by discussion and good counsel. But some problems can be solved only by prayer. We should make a determined effort to pray when we feel like complaining, because complaining only adds to our worries and stress. Prayer quiets our thoughts and emotions and prepares us to listen.

12

FEBRUARY

God's Unusual
Food Supply

EXODUS 16:1-36

Then [the Israelites] left Elim and journeyed into the Sin Desert, between Elim and Mount Sinai. They arrived there a month after leaving Egypt. ²There, too, the whole community of Israel spoke bitterly against Moses and Aaron.

³"Oh, that we were back in Egypt," they moaned. "It would have been better if the LORD had killed us there! At least there we had plenty to eat. But now you have brought us into this desert to starve us to death."

⁴Then the LORD said to Moses, "Look, I'm going to rain down food from heaven for you. The people can go out each day and pick up as much food as they need for that day. I will test them in this to see whether they will follow my instructions. ⁵Tell them to pick up twice as much as usual on the sixth day of each week."

⁶Then Moses and Aaron called a meeting of all the people of Israel and told them, "In the evening you will realize that it was the LORD who brought you out of the land of Egypt. ⁷In the morning you will see the glorious presence of the LORD. He has heard your complaints, which are against the LORD and not against us. ⁸The LORD will give you meat to eat in the evening and bread in the morning, for he has heard all your complaints against him. Yes, your complaints are against the LORD, not against us."

⁹Then Moses said to Aaron, "Say this to the entire community of Israel: 'Come into the LORD's presence, and hear his reply to your complaints.' "
¹⁰And as Aaron spoke to the people, they looked out toward the desert. Within the guiding cloud, they could see the awesome glory of the LORD.

¹¹And the LORD said to Moses, ¹²"I have heard the people's complaints. Now tell them, 'In the evening you will have meat to eat, and in the morning you will be filled with bread. Then you will know that I am the LORD your God.' "

¹³That evening vast numbers of quail arrived and covered the camp. The next morning the desert all around the camp was wet with dew. ¹⁴When the dew disappeared later in the morning, thin flakes, white like frost, covered the ground. ¹⁵The Israelites were puzzled when they saw it. "What is it?" they asked.

And Moses told them, "It is the food the LORD has given you. ¹⁶The LORD says that each household should gather as much as it needs. Pick up two quarts for each person."

¹⁷So the people of Israel went out and gathered this food— some getting more, and some getting less. ¹⁸By gathering two quarts for each person, everyone had just enough. Those who gathered a lot had nothing left over, and those who gathered only a little had enough. Each family had just what it needed.

¹⁹Then Moses told them, "Do not keep any of it overnight." ²⁰But, of course, some of them didn't listen and kept some of it until morning. By then it was full of maggots and had a terrible smell. And Moses was very angry with them.

²¹The people gathered the food morning by morning, each family according to its need. And as the sun became hot, the food they had not picked up melted and disappeared. ²²On the sixth day, there was twice as much as usual on the ground—four quarts for each person instead of two. The leaders of the people came and asked Moses why this had happened. ²³He replied, "The LORD has appointed tomorrow as a day of rest, a holy Sabbath to the LORD. On this day we will rest from our normal daily tasks. So bake or boil as much as you want today, and set aside what is left for tomorrow."

²⁴The next morning the leftover food was wholesome and good, without maggots or odor. ²⁵Moses said, "This is your food for today, for today is a Sabbath to the LORD. There will be no food on the ground today. ²⁶Gather the food for six days, but the seventh day is a Sabbath. There will be no food on the ground for you on that day."

²⁷Some of the people went out anyway to gather food, even though it was the Sabbath day. But there was none to be found. ²⁸"How long will these people refuse to obey my commands and instructions?" the LORD asked Moses. ²⁹"Do they not realize that I have given them the seventh day, the Sabbath, as a day of rest? That is why I give you twice as much food on the sixth day, so there will be enough for two days. On the Sabbath day you must stay in your places. Do not pick up food from the ground on that day." ³⁰So the people rested on the seventh day.

³¹In time, the food became known as manna. It was white like coriander seed, and it tasted like honey cakes.

³²Then Moses gave them this command from the LORD: "Take two quarts of manna and keep it forever as a treasured memorial of the LORD's provision. By doing this, later generations will be able to see the bread that the LORD provided in the wilderness when he brought you out of Egypt."

³³Moses said to Aaron, "Get a container and put two quarts of manna into it. Then store it in a sacred place as a reminder for all future generations." ³⁴Aaron did this, just as the LORD had commanded Moses. He eventually placed it for safekeeping in the Ark of the Covenant. ³⁵So the people of Israel ate manna for forty years until they arrived in the land of Canaan, where there were crops to eat.

³⁶(The container used to measure the manna was an omer, which held about two quarts.)

〜⌇⌇⌐ **For what specific gift did you last say thanks to God?** It happened again. As the Israelites encountered danger, shortages, and inconvenience, they complained bitterly and longed to be back in Egypt. But as always, God provided for their needs. Difficult circumstances often lead to stress, and complaining is a natural response. The Israelites didn't really want to be back in Egypt; they just wanted life to get a little easier. In the pressure of the moment, they could not focus on the cause of their stress (in this case, lack of trust in God); they could only think about the quickest way of escape. When pressure comes your way, resist the temptation to make a quick escape. Instead, focus on God's power and wisdom to help you deal with the cause of your stress.

13 FEBRUARY

Helpful Advice
EXODUS 18:1-27

Word soon reached Jethro, the priest of Midian and Moses' father-in-law, about all the wonderful things God had done for Moses and his people, the Israelites. He had heard about how the LORD had brought them safely out of Egypt.

²Some time before this, Moses had sent his wife, Zipporah, and his two sons to live with Jethro, his father-in-law. ³The name of Moses' first son was

Gershom, for Moses had said when the boy was born, "I have been a stranger in a foreign land." [4]The name of his second son was Eliezer, for Moses had said at his birth, "The God of my fathers was my helper; he delivered me from the sword of Pharaoh." [5]Jethro now came to visit Moses, and he brought Moses' wife and two sons with him. They arrived while Moses and the people were camped near the mountain of God. [6]Moses was told, "Jethro, your father-in-law, has come to visit you. Your wife and your two sons are with him."

[7]So Moses went out to meet his father-in-law. He bowed to him respectfully and greeted him warmly. They asked about each other's health and then went to Moses' tent to talk further. [8]Moses told his father-in-law about everything the LORD had done to rescue Israel from Pharaoh and the Egyptians. He also told him about the problems they had faced along the way and how the LORD had delivered his people from all their troubles. [9]Jethro was delighted when he heard about all that the LORD had done for Israel as he brought them out of Egypt.

[10]"Praise be to the LORD," Jethro said, "for he has saved you from the Egyptians and from Pharaoh. He has rescued Israel from the power of Egypt! [11]I know now that the LORD is greater than all other gods, because his people have escaped from the proud and cruel Egyptians."

[12]Then Jethro presented a burnt offering and gave sacrifices to God. As Jethro was doing this, Aaron and the leaders of Israel came out to meet him. They all joined him in a sacrificial meal in God's presence.

[13]The next day, Moses sat as usual to hear the people's complaints against each other. They were lined up in front of him from morning till evening. [14]When Moses' father-in-law saw all that Moses was doing for the people, he said, "Why are you trying to do all this alone? The people have been standing here all day to get your help."

[15]Moses replied, "Well, the people come to me to seek God's guidance. [16]When an argument arises, I am the one who settles the case. I inform the people of God's decisions and teach them his laws and instructions."

[17]"This is not good!" his father-in-law exclaimed. [18]"You're going to wear yourself out—and the people, too. This job is too heavy a burden for you to handle all by yourself. [19]Now let me give you a word of advice, and may God be with you. You should continue to be the people's representative before God, bringing him their questions to be decided. [20]You should tell them God's decisions, teach them God's laws and instructions, and show them how to conduct their lives. [21]But find some capable, honest men who fear God and hate bribes. Appoint them as judges over groups of one thousand, one hundred, fifty, and ten. [22]These men can serve the people, resolving all the ordinary cases. Anything that is too important or too complicated can be brought to you. But they can take care of the smaller matters themselves. They will help you carry the load, making the task easier for you. [23]If you follow this advice, and if God directs you to do so, then

you will be able to endure the pressures, and all these people will go home in peace."

²⁴Moses listened to his father-in-law's advice and followed his suggestions. ²⁵He chose capable men from all over Israel and made them judges over the people. They were put in charge of groups of one thousand, one hundred, fifty, and ten. ²⁶These men were constantly available to administer justice. They brought the hard cases to Moses, but they judged the smaller matters themselves.

²⁷Soon after this, Moses said good-bye to his father-in-law, who returned to his own land.

〰〰 **Who are the dependable advisers in your life?** Moses told his father-in-law all that God had done, convincing him that the Lord was greater than any other god. Our relatives are often the hardest people to tell about God. Yet we should look for opportunities to tell them what God is doing in our life because we can have an important influence on them.

14

FEBRUARY

An Appointment with God

EXODUS 19:1-25

The Israelites arrived in the wilderness of Sinai exactly two months after they left Egypt. ²After breaking camp at Rephidim, they came to the base of Mount Sinai and set up camp there.

³Then Moses climbed the mountain to appear before God. The LORD called out to him from the mountain and said, "Give these instructions to the descendants of Jacob, the people of Israel: ⁴'You have seen what I did to the Egyptians. You know how I brought you to myself and carried you on eagle's wings. ⁵Now if you will obey me and keep my covenant, you will be my own special treasure from among all the nations of the earth; for all the earth belongs to me. ⁶And you will be to me a kingdom of priests, my holy nation.' Give this message to the Israelites."

⁷Moses returned from the mountain and called together the leaders of the people and told them what the LORD had said. ⁸They all responded together, "We will certainly do everything the LORD asks of us." So Moses brought the people's answer back to the LORD.

⁹Then the LORD said to Moses, "I am going to come to you in a thick cloud so the people themselves can hear me as I speak to you. Then they will always have confidence in you."

Moses told the LORD what the people had said. ¹⁰Then the LORD told Moses, "Go down and prepare the people for my visit. Purify them today and tomorrow, and have them wash their clothing. ¹¹Be sure they are ready on the third day, for I will come down upon Mount Sinai as all the people watch. ¹²Set boundary lines that the people may not pass. Warn them, 'Be careful! Do not go up on the mountain or even touch its boundaries. Those who do will certainly die! [13]Any people or animals that cross the boundary must be stoned to death or shot with arrows. They must not be touched by human hands.' The people must stay away from the mountain until they hear one long blast from the ram's horn. Then they must gather at the foot of the mountain."

[14]So Moses went down to the people. He purified them for worship and had them wash their clothing. [15]He told them, "Get ready for an important event two days from now. And until then, abstain from having sexual intercourse."

[16]On the morning of the third day, there was a powerful thunder and lightning storm, and a dense cloud came down upon the mountain. There was a long, loud blast from a ram's horn, and all the people trembled. [17]Moses led them out from the camp to meet with God, and they stood at the foot of the mountain. [18]All Mount Sinai was covered with smoke because the LORD had descended on it in the form of fire. The smoke billowed into the sky like smoke from a furnace, and the whole mountain shook with a violent earthquake. [19]As the horn blast grew louder and louder, Moses spoke, and God thundered his reply for all to hear. [20]The LORD came down on the top of Mount Sinai and called Moses to the top of the mountain. So Moses climbed the mountain.

[21]Then the LORD told Moses, "Go back down and warn the people not to cross the boundaries. They must not come up here to see the LORD, for those who do will die. [22]Even the priests who regularly come near to the LORD must purify themselves, or I will destroy them."

[23]"But LORD, the people cannot come up on the mountain!" Moses protested. "You already told them not to. You told me to set boundaries around the mountain and to declare it off limits."

[24]But the LORD said, "Go down anyway and bring Aaron back with you. In the meantime, do not let the priests or the people cross the boundaries to come up here. If they do, I will punish them."

[25]So Moses went down to the people and told them what the LORD had said.

〰〰 **How would you prepare to meet with God?** In Genesis 15 and 17, God made a covenant with Abraham, promising to make his descendants into a great nation. Here that promise was being realized as God restated his agreement with the Israelite nation, the descendants of Abraham. God promised to bless and care for them. The people promised to obey him. The covenant was thus sealed. But the good intentions of the people quickly wore off. Have you made a commitment to God? How are you holding up your end of the bargain?

The Ten Commandments
EXODUS 20:1-22

Then God instructed the people as follows:

²"I am the LORD your God, who rescued you from slavery in Egypt.
³"Do not worship any other gods besides me.
⁴"Do not make idols of any kind, whether in the shape of birds or animals or fish. ⁵You must never worship or bow down to them, for I, the LORD your God, am a jealous God who will not share your affection with any other god! I do not leave unpunished the sins of those who hate me, but I punish the children for the sins of their parents to the third and fourth generations. ⁶But I lavish my love on those who love me and obey my commands, even for a thousand generations.
⁷"Do not misuse the name of the LORD your God. The LORD will not let you go unpunished if you misuse his name.
⁸"Remember to observe the Sabbath day by keeping it holy. ⁹Six days a week are set apart for your daily duties and regular work, ¹⁰but the seventh day is a day of rest dedicated to the LORD your God. On that day no one in your household may do any kind of work. This includes you, your sons and daughters, your male and female servants, your livestock, and any foreigners living among you. ¹¹For in six days the LORD made the heavens, the earth, the sea, and everything in them; then he rested on the seventh day. That is why the LORD blessed the Sabbath day and set it apart as holy.
¹²"Honor your father and mother. Then you will live a long, full life in the land the LORD your God will give you.
¹³"Do not murder.
¹⁴"Do not commit adultery.
¹⁵"Do not steal.
¹⁶"Do not testify falsely against your neighbor.
¹⁷"Do not covet your neighbor's house. Do not covet your neighbor's wife, male or female servant, ox or donkey, or anything else your neighbor owns."

¹⁸When the people heard the thunder and the loud blast of the horn, and when they saw the lightning and the smoke billowing from the mountain, they stood at a distance, trembling with fear.
¹⁹And they said to Moses, "You tell us what God says, and we will listen. But don't let God speak directly to us. If he does, we will die!"
²⁰"Don't be afraid," Moses said, "for God has come in this way to show you his awesome power. From now on, let your fear of him keep you from sinning!"

²¹As the people stood in the distance, Moses entered into the deep darkness where God was.

²²And the LORD said to Moses, "Say this to the people of Israel: You are witnesses that I have spoken to you from heaven."

〜∿〜 **How often do you think about God's standards?** The command to "honor your father and mother" is the first commandment with a promise attached. To live in peace for generations in the Promised Land, the Israelites would need to respect authority and build strong families. But what does it mean to "honor" your parents? Partly, it means speaking well of them and politely to them. It also means acting in a way that shows them courtesy and respect (but not to obey them if this means disobedience to God). It means following their teaching and example of putting God first. Parents have a special place in God's sight. Even those who find it difficult to get along with their parents are still commanded to honor them.

FEBRUARY **16**

The Gold Calf

EXODUS 32:1-29

When Moses failed to come back down the mountain right away, the people went to Aaron. "Look," they said, "make us some gods who can lead us. This man Moses, who brought us here from Egypt, has disappeared. We don't know what has happened to him."

²So Aaron said, "Tell your wives and sons and daughters to take off their gold earrings, and then bring them to me."

³All the people obeyed Aaron and brought him their gold earrings. ⁴Then Aaron took the gold, melted it down, and molded and tooled it into the shape of a calf. The people exclaimed, "O Israel, these are the gods who brought you out of Egypt!"

⁵When Aaron saw how excited the people were about it, he built an altar in front of the calf and announced, "Tomorrow there will be a festival to the LORD!"

⁶So the people got up early the next morning to sacrifice burnt offerings and peace offerings. After this, they celebrated with feasting and drinking, and indulged themselves in pagan revelry.

⁷Then the LORD told Moses, "Quick! Go down the mountain! The people you brought from Egypt have defiled themselves. ⁸They have already turned from the way I commanded them to live. They have made an idol shaped like a calf, and they have worshiped and sacrificed to it. They are saying, 'These are your gods, O Israel, who brought you out of Egypt.' "

⁹Then the LORD said, "I have seen how stubborn and rebellious these people are. ¹⁰Now leave me alone so my anger can blaze against them and

destroy them all. Then I will make you, Moses, into a great nation instead of them."

[11]But Moses pleaded with the LORD his God not to do it. "O LORD!" he exclaimed. "Why are you so angry with your own people whom you brought from the land of Egypt with such great power and mighty acts? [12]The Egyptians will say, 'God tricked them into coming to the mountains so he could kill them and wipe them from the face of the earth.' Turn away from your fierce anger. Change your mind about this terrible disaster you are planning against your people! [13]Remember your covenant with your servants—Abraham, Isaac, and Jacob. You swore by your own self, 'I will make your descendants as numerous as the stars of heaven. Yes, I will give them all of this land that I have promised to your descendants, and they will possess it forever.' "

[14]So the LORD withdrew his threat and didn't bring against his people the disaster he had threatened.

[15]Then Moses turned and went down the mountain. He held in his hands the two stone tablets inscribed with the terms of the covenant. They were inscribed on both sides, front and back. [16]These stone tablets were God's work; the words on them were written by God himself.

[17]When Joshua heard the noise of the people shouting below them, he exclaimed to Moses, "It sounds as if there is a war in the camp!"

[18]But Moses replied, "No, it's neither a cry of victory nor a cry of defeat. It is the sound of a celebration."

[19]When they came near the camp, Moses saw the calf and the dancing. In terrible anger, he threw the stone tablets to the ground, smashing them at the foot of the mountain. [20]He took the calf they had made and melted it in the fire. And when the metal had cooled, he ground it into powder and mixed it with water. Then he made the people drink it.

[21]After that, he turned to Aaron. "What did the people do to you?" he demanded. "How did they ever make you bring such terrible sin upon them?"

[22]"Don't get upset, sir," Aaron replied. "You yourself know these people and what a wicked bunch they are. [23]They said to me, 'Make us some gods to lead us, for something has happened to this man Moses, who led us out of Egypt.' [24]So I told them, 'Bring me your gold earrings.' When they brought them to me, I threw them into the fire—and out came this calf!"

[25]When Moses saw that Aaron had let the people get completely out of control—and much to the amusement of their enemies—[26]he stood at the entrance to the camp and shouted, "All of you who are on the LORD's side, come over here and join me." And all the Levites came.

[27]He told them, "This is what the LORD, the God of Israel, says: Strap on your swords! Go back and forth from one end of the camp to the other, killing even your brothers, friends, and neighbors." [28]The Levites obeyed Moses, and about three thousand people died that day.

[29]Then Moses told the Levites, "Today you have been ordained for the

service of the LORD, for you obeyed him even though it meant killing your own sons and brothers. Because of this, he will now give you a great blessing."

〜〜 **What distracts you from obeying God?** Idols again! Even though Israel had seen the invisible God in action, they still wanted the familiar gods they could see and shape into whatever image they desired. How much like them we are! Our great temptation is still to shape God to our liking, to make him convenient to obey or ignore. God responds in great anger when his mercy is trampled on. The gods we create blind us to the love the living God wants to shower on us. God cannot work in us when we elevate anyone or anything above him. What idols are in your life?

Instructions about God's Tent

EXODUS 40:1-38

The LORD now said to Moses, [2]"Set up the Tabernacle on the first day of the new year. [3]Place the Ark of the Covenant inside, and install the inner curtain to enclose the Ark within the Most Holy Place. [4]Then bring in the table, and arrange the utensils on it. And bring in the lampstand, and set up the lamps.

[5]"Place the incense altar just outside the inner curtain, opposite the Ark of the Covenant. Set up the curtain made for the entrance of the Tabernacle. [6]Place the altar of burnt offering in front of the Tabernacle entrance. [7]Set the large washbasin between the Tabernacle and the altar and fill it with water. [8]Then set up the courtyard around the outside of the tent, and hang the curtain for the courtyard entrance.

[9]"Take the anointing oil and sprinkle it on the Tabernacle and on all its furnishings to make them holy. [10]Sprinkle the anointing oil on the altar of burnt offering and its utensils, sanctifying them. Then the altar will become most holy. [11]Next anoint the large washbasin and its pedestal to make them holy.

[12]"Bring Aaron and his sons to the entrance of the Tabernacle, and wash them with water. [13]Clothe Aaron with the holy garments and anoint him, setting him apart to serve me as a priest. [14]Then bring his sons and dress them in their tunics. [15]Anoint them as you did their father, so they may serve me as priests. With this anointing, Aaron's descendants are set apart for the priesthood forever, from generation to generation."

[16]Moses proceeded to do everything as the LORD had commanded him. [17]So the Tabernacle was set up on the first day of the new year. [18]Moses put it together by setting its frames into their bases and attaching the crossbars and raising the posts. [19]Then he spread the coverings over the Tabernacle framework and put on the roof layers, just as the LORD had commanded him.

²⁰He placed inside the Ark the stone tablets inscribed with the terms of the covenant, and then he attached the Ark's carrying poles. He also set the Ark's cover—the place of atonement—on top of it. ²¹Then he brought the Ark of the Covenant into the Tabernacle and set up the inner curtain to shield it from view, just as the LORD had commanded.

²²Next he placed the table in the Tabernacle, along the north side of the Holy Place, just outside the inner curtain. ²³And he arranged the Bread of the Presence on the table that stands before the LORD, just as the LORD had commanded.

²⁴He set the lampstand in the Tabernacle across from the table on the south side of the Holy Place. ²⁵Then he set up the lamps in the LORD's presence, just as the LORD had commanded. ²⁶He also placed the incense altar in the Tabernacle, in the Holy Place in front of the inner curtain. ²⁷On it he burned the fragrant incense made from sweet spices, just as the LORD had commanded.

²⁸He attached the curtain at the entrance of the Tabernacle, ²⁹and he placed the altar of burnt offering near the Tabernacle entrance. On it he offered a burnt offering and a grain offering, just as the LORD had commanded.

³⁰Next he placed the large washbasin between the Tabernacle and the altar. He filled it with water so the priests could use it to wash themselves. ³¹Moses and Aaron and Aaron's sons washed their hands and feet in the basin. ³²Whenever they walked past the altar to enter the Tabernacle, they were to stop and wash, just as the LORD had commanded Moses.

³³Then he hung the curtains forming the courtyard around the Tabernacle and the altar. And he set up the curtain at the entrance of the courtyard. So at last Moses finished the work.

³⁴Then the cloud covered the Tabernacle, and the glorious presence of the LORD filled it. ³⁵Moses was no longer able to enter the Tabernacle because the cloud had settled down over it, and the Tabernacle was filled with the awesome glory of the LORD.

³⁶Now whenever the cloud lifted from the Tabernacle and moved, the people of Israel would set out on their journey, following it. ³⁷But if the cloud stayed, they would stay until it moved again. ³⁸The cloud of the LORD rested on the Tabernacle during the day, and at night there was fire in the cloud so all the people of Israel could see it. This continued throughout all their journeys.

〰〰〰 **When are you most aware of God's presence in your life?** God told Moses how to build the Tabernacle, and Moses delegated jobs in order to do it. God allows people to participate with him in carrying out his will. Your task is not just to sit and watch God work but to give your best effort when work needs to be done.

Moses under Fire

NUMBERS 12:1-16

While [the Israelites] were at Hazeroth, Miriam and Aaron criticized Moses because he had married a Cushite woman. ²They said, "Has the LORD spoken only through Moses? Hasn't he spoken through us, too?" But the LORD heard them.

³Now Moses was more humble than any other person on earth. ⁴So immediately the LORD called to Moses, Aaron, and Miriam and said, "Go out to the Tabernacle, all three of you!" And the three of them went out. ⁵Then the LORD descended in the pillar of cloud and stood at the entrance of the Tabernacle. "Aaron and Miriam!" he called, and they stepped forward. ⁶And the LORD said to them, "Now listen to me! Even with prophets, I the LORD communicate by visions and dreams. ⁷But that is not how I communicate with my servant Moses. He is entrusted with my entire house. ⁸I speak to him face to face, directly and not in riddles! He sees the LORD as he is. Should you not be afraid to criticize him?"

⁹The LORD was furious with them, and he departed. ¹⁰As the cloud moved from above the Tabernacle, Miriam suddenly became white as snow with leprosy. When Aaron saw what had happened, ¹¹he cried out to Moses, "Oh, my lord! Please don't punish us for this sin we have so foolishly committed. ¹²Don't let her be like a stillborn baby, already decayed at birth."

¹³So Moses cried out to the LORD, "Heal her, O God, I beg you!"

¹⁴And the LORD said to Moses, "If her father had spit in her face, wouldn't she have been defiled for seven days? Banish her from the camp for seven days, and after that she may return."

¹⁵So Miriam was excluded from the camp for seven days, and the people waited until she was brought back before they traveled again. ¹⁶Then they left Hazeroth and camped in the wilderness of Paran.

〰️ **What do you do when you find yourself feeling jealous of someone?** People often argue over minor disagreements, leaving the real issue untouched. Miriam and Aaron were really jealous of Moses' position and influence. Since they could not find fault with the way Moses was leading the people, they chose to criticize his wife. When you are in a disagreement, stop and ask yourself if you are arguing over the real issue or if you have introduced a smoke screen by attacking someone's character. If you are unjustly criticized, remember that your critics may be afraid to face the real problem. Don't take this type of criticism personally. Ask God to help you identify the real issue and deal with it.

Spying on the Promised Land
NUMBERS 13:1–14:4

The LORD now said to Moses, [2]"Send men to explore the land of Canaan, the land I am giving to Israel. Send one leader from each of the twelve ancestral tribes." [3]So Moses did as the LORD commanded him. He sent out twelve men, all tribal leaders of Israel, from their camp in the wilderness of Paran. [4]These were the tribes and the names of the leaders:

Tribe	Leader
Reuben	Shammua son of Zaccur
[5] Simeon	Shaphat son of Hori
[6] Judah	Caleb son of Jephunneh
[7] Issachar	Igal son of Joseph
[8] Ephraim	Hoshea son of Nun
[9] Benjamin	Palti son of Raphu
[10] Zebulun	Gaddiel son of Sodi
[11] Manasseh son of Joseph	Gaddi son of Susi
[12] Dan	Ammiel son of Gemalli
[13] Asher	Sethur son of Michael
[14] Naphtali	Nahbi son of Vophsi
[15] Gad	Geuel son of Maki

[16]These are the names of the men Moses sent to explore the land. By this time Moses had changed Hoshea's name to Joshua.

[17]Moses gave the men these instructions as he sent them out to explore the land: "Go northward through the Negev into the hill country. [18]See what the land is like and find out whether the people living there are strong or weak, few or many. [19]What kind of land do they live in? Is it good or bad? Do their towns have walls or are they unprotected? [20]How is the soil? Is it fertile or poor? Are there many trees? Enter the land boldly, and bring back samples of the crops you see." (It happened to be the season for harvesting the first ripe grapes.)

[21]So they went up and explored the land from the wilderness of Zin as far as Rehob, near Lebo-hamath. [22]Going northward, they passed first through the Negev and arrived at Hebron, where Ahiman, Sheshai, and Talmai—all descendants of Anak—lived. (The ancient town of Hebron was founded seven years before the Egyptian city of Zoan.) [23]When they came to what is now known as the valley of Eshcol, they cut down a cluster of grapes so large that it took two of them to carry it on a pole between them! They also took samples of the pomegranates and figs. [24]At that time the Israelites renamed the valley Eshcol—"cluster"—because of the cluster of grapes they had cut there.

[25]After exploring the land for forty days, the men returned [26]to Moses,

Aaron, and the people of Israel at Kadesh in the wilderness of Paran. They reported to the whole community what they had seen and showed them the fruit they had taken from the land. ²⁷This was their report to Moses: "We arrived in the land you sent us to see, and it is indeed a magnificent country—a land flowing with milk and honey. Here is some of its fruit as proof. ²⁸But the people living there are powerful, and their cities and towns are fortified and very large. We also saw the descendants of Anak who are living there! ²⁹The Amalekites live in the Negev, and the Hittites, Jebusites, and Amorites live in the hill country. The Canaanites live along the coast of the Mediterranean Sea and along the Jordan Valley."

³⁰But Caleb tried to encourage the people as they stood before Moses. "Let's go at once to take the land," he said. "We can certainly conquer it!"

³¹But the other men who had explored the land with him answered, "We can't go up against them! They are stronger than we are!" ³²So they spread discouraging reports about the land among the Israelites: "The land we explored will swallow up any who go to live there. All the people we saw were huge. ³³We even saw giants there, the descendants of Anak. We felt like grasshoppers next to them, and that's what we looked like to them!"

14:1 Then all the people began weeping aloud, and they cried all night. ²Their voices rose in a great chorus of complaint against Moses and Aaron. "We wish we had died in Egypt, or even here in the wilderness!" they wailed. ³"Why is the LORD taking us to this country only to have us die in battle? Our wives and little ones will be carried off as slaves! Let's get out of here and return to Egypt!" ⁴Then they plotted among themselves, "Let's choose a leader and go back to Egypt!"

〜〜〜 **How does God affect the word *impossible* in your mind?** The Israelites didn't trust God—they believed victory was impossible. In their self-doubt, their decision made sense. But they failed to realize that God doesn't always operate from a human perspective. A promise from God is a sure thing, no matter how unlikely it seems. Caleb stood for the truth he knew about God. God had said very plainly that he would help the people conquer the Promised Land. But the other spies forgot what they knew about God and made their decision on the basis of what they knew of themselves. Are you willing to stand against the pressure of popular opinion to do what God's Word says?

20

A Majority That Was Wrong
NUMBERS 14:5-45

Then Moses and Aaron fell face down on the ground before the people of Israel. [6]Two of the men who had explored the land, Joshua son of Nun and Caleb son of Jephunneh, tore their clothing. [7]They said to the community of Israel, "The land we explored is a wonderful land! [8]And if the LORD is pleased with us, he will bring us safely into that land and give it to us. It is a rich land flowing with milk and honey, and he will give it to us! [9]Do not rebel against the LORD, and don't be afraid of the people of the land. They are only helpless prey to us! They have no protection, but the LORD is with us! Don't be afraid of them!"

[10]But the whole community began to talk about stoning Joshua and Caleb. Then the glorious presence of the LORD appeared to all the Israelites from above the Tabernacle. [11]And the LORD said to Moses, "How long will these people reject me? Will they never believe me, even after all the miraculous signs I have done among them? [12]I will disown them and destroy them with a plague. Then I will make you into a nation far greater and mightier than they are!"

[13]"But what will the Egyptians think when they hear about it?" Moses pleaded with the LORD. "They know full well the power you displayed in rescuing these people from Egypt. [14]They will tell this to the inhabitants of this land, who are well aware that you are with this people. They know, LORD, that you have appeared in full view of your people in the pillar of cloud that hovers over them. They know that you go before them in the pillar of cloud by day and the pillar of fire by night. [15]Now if you slaughter all these people, the nations that have heard of your fame will say, [16]'The LORD was not able to bring them into the land he swore to give them, so he killed them in the wilderness.'

[17]"Please, Lord, prove that your power is as great as you have claimed it to be. For you said, [18]'The LORD is slow to anger and rich in unfailing love, forgiving every kind of sin and rebellion. Even so he does not leave sin unpunished, but he punishes the children for the sins of their parents to the third and fourth generations.' [19]Please pardon the sins of this people because of your magnificent, unfailing love, just as you have forgiven them ever since they left Egypt."

[20]Then the LORD said, "I will pardon them as you have requested. [21]But as surely as I live, and as surely as the earth is filled with the LORD's glory, [22]not one of these people will ever enter that land. They have seen my glorious presence and the miraculous signs I performed both in Egypt and in the wilderness, but again and again they tested me by refusing to listen. [23]They will never even see the land I swore to give their ancestors. None of those who have treated me with contempt will enter it. [24]But my servant Caleb is

different from the others. He has remained loyal to me, and I will bring him into the land he explored. His descendants will receive their full share of that land. ²⁵Now turn around and don't go on toward the land where the Amalekites and Canaanites live. Tomorrow you must set out for the wilderness in the direction of the Red Sea."

²⁶Then the LORD said to Moses and Aaron, ²⁷"How long will this wicked nation complain about me? I have heard everything the Israelites have been saying. ²⁸Now tell them this: 'As surely as I live, I will do to you the very things I heard you say. I, the LORD, have spoken! ²⁹You will all die here in this wilderness! Because you complained against me, none of you who are twenty years old or older and were counted in the census ³⁰will enter the land I swore to give you. The only exceptions will be Caleb son of Jephunneh and Joshua son of Nun.

³¹" 'You said your children would be taken captive. Well, I will bring them safely into the land, and they will enjoy what you have despised. ³²But as for you, your dead bodies will fall in this wilderness. ³³And your children will be like shepherds, wandering in the wilderness forty years. In this way, they will pay for your faithlessness, until the last of you lies dead in the wilderness.

³⁴" 'Because the men who explored the land were there for forty days, you must wander in the wilderness for forty years—a year for each day, suffering the consequences of your sins. You will discover what it is like to have me for an enemy.' ³⁵I, the LORD, have spoken! I will do these things to every member of the community who has conspired against me. They will all die here in this wilderness!"

³⁶Then the ten scouts who had incited the rebellion against the LORD by spreading discouraging reports about the land ³⁷were struck dead with a plague before the LORD. ³⁸Of the twelve who had explored the land, only Joshua and Caleb remained alive.

³⁹When Moses reported the LORD's words to the Israelites, there was much sorrow among the people. ⁴⁰So they got up early the next morning and set out for the hill country of Canaan. "Let's go," they said. "We realize that we have sinned, but now we are ready to enter the land the LORD has promised us."

⁴¹But Moses said, "Why are you now disobeying the LORD's orders to return to the wilderness? It won't work. ⁴²Do not go into the land now. You will only be crushed by your enemies because the LORD is not with you. ⁴³When you face the Amalekites and Canaanites in battle, you will be slaughtered. The LORD will abandon you because you have abandoned the LORD."

⁴⁴But the people pushed ahead toward the hill country of Canaan, despite the fact that neither Moses nor the Ark of the LORD's covenant left the camp. ⁴⁵Then the Amalekites and the Canaanites who lived in those hills came down and attacked them and chased them as far as Hormah.

~~∿~~ **How often are your decisions based on peer pressure?** When the Israelites realized their foolish mistake, they were suddenly ready to return to God. But God didn't confuse their admission of guilt with true repentance because he knew their hearts. Sure enough, they soon went their own way again. Sometimes good actions or intentions come too late. We must not only act rightly but also act at the right time. The kind of obedience God wants is complete and instant.

21 FEBRUARY

Another Hard Lesson
NUMBERS 21:4-9

Then the people of Israel set out from Mount Hor, taking the road to the Red Sea to go around the land of Edom. But the people grew impatient along the way, [5]and they began to murmur against God and Moses. "Why have you brought us out of Egypt to die here in the wilderness?" they complained. "There is nothing to eat here and nothing to drink. And we hate this wretched manna!"

[6]So the LORD sent poisonous snakes among them, and many of them were bitten and died. [7]Then the people came to Moses and cried out, "We have sinned by speaking against the LORD and against you. Pray that the LORD will take away the snakes." So Moses prayed for the people.

[8]Then the LORD told him, "Make a replica of a poisonous snake and attach it to the top of a pole. Those who are bitten will live if they simply look at it!" [9]So Moses made a snake out of bronze and attached it to the top of a pole. Whenever those who were bitten looked at the bronze snake, they recovered!

~~∿~~ **What can you do to avoid repeating mistakes?** When the bronze serpent was hung on the pole, the Israelites didn't know the fuller meaning Jesus Christ would bring to this event (see John 3:14-15). Jesus explained that just as the Israelites were rescued from death by looking at the serpent on the pole, all believers today can be rescued from eternal death by looking to Jesus on the cross. It was not the serpent that healed the people but their belief that God could heal them, which was demonstrated by their obedience to God's instructions. In the same way, we should continue to look to Christ (see Heb. 12:2).

22 FEBRUARY

Balaam and His Donkey
NUMBERS 22:1-38

Then the people of Israel traveled to the plains of Moab and camped east of the Jordan River, across from Jericho. [2]Balak son of Zippor, the Moabite king, knew what the Israelites had done to the Amorites. [3]And when they saw how many Israelites there were, he and his people were terrified. ⁴The king of Moab said to the leaders of Midian, "This mob will devour everything in sight, like an ox devours grass!"

So Balak, king of Moab, ⁵sent messengers to Balaam son of Beor, who was living in his native land of Pethor near the Euphrates River. He sent this message to request that Balaam come to help him:

"A vast horde of people has arrived from Egypt. They cover the face of the earth and are threatening me. ⁶Please come and curse them for me because they are so numerous. Then perhaps I will be able to conquer them and drive them from the land. I know that blessings fall on the people you bless. I also know that the people you curse are doomed."

⁷Balak's messengers, officials of both Moab and Midian, set out and took money with them to pay Balaam to curse Israel. They went to Balaam and urgently explained to him what Balak wanted. ⁸"Stay here overnight," Balaam said. "In the morning I will tell you whatever the LORD directs me to say." So the officials from Moab stayed there with Balaam.

⁹That night God came to Balaam and asked him, "Who are these men with you?"

¹⁰So Balaam said to God, "Balak son of Zippor, king of Moab, has sent me this message: ¹¹'A vast horde of people has come from Egypt and has spread out over the whole land. Come at once to curse them. Perhaps then I will be able to conquer them and drive them from the land.' "

¹²"Do not go with them," God told Balaam. "You are not to curse these people, for I have blessed them!"

¹³The next morning Balaam got up and told Balak's officials, "Go on home! The LORD will not let me go with you."

¹⁴So the Moabite officials returned to King Balak and reported, "Balaam refused to come with us." ¹⁵Then Balak tried again. This time he sent a larger number of even more distinguished officials than those he had sent the first time. ¹⁶They went to Balaam and gave him this message:

"This is what Balak son of Zippor says: Please don't let anything stop you from coming. ¹⁷I will pay you well and do anything you ask of me. Just come and curse these people for me!"

¹⁸But Balaam answered them, "Even if Balak were to give me a palace filled with silver and gold, I would be powerless to do anything against the will of the LORD my God. ¹⁹But stay here one more night to see if the LORD has anything else to say to me."

²⁰That night God came to Balaam and told him, "Since these men have come for you, get up and go with them. But be sure to do only what I tell you to do."

²¹So the next morning Balaam saddled his donkey and started off with

the Moabite officials. ²²But God was furious that Balaam was going, so he sent the angel of the LORD to stand in the road to block his way. As Balaam and two servants were riding along, ²³Balaam's donkey suddenly saw the angel of the LORD standing in the road with a drawn sword in his hand. The donkey bolted off the road into a field, but Balaam beat it and turned it back onto the road. ²⁴Then the angel of the LORD stood at a place where the road narrowed between two vineyard walls. ²⁵When the donkey saw the angel of the LORD standing there, it tried to squeeze by and crushed Balaam's foot against the wall. So Balaam beat the donkey again. ²⁶Then the angel of the LORD moved farther down the road and stood in a place so narrow that the donkey could not get by at all. ²⁷This time when the donkey saw the angel, it lay down under Balaam. In a fit of rage Balaam beat it again with his staff.

²⁸Then the LORD caused the donkey to speak. "What have I done to you that deserves your beating me these three times?" it asked Balaam.

²⁹"Because you have made me look like a fool!" Balaam shouted. "If I had a sword with me, I would kill you!"

³⁰"But I am the same donkey you always ride on," the donkey answered. "Have I ever done anything like this before?"

"No," he admitted.

³¹Then the LORD opened Balaam's eyes, and he saw the angel of the LORD standing in the roadway with a drawn sword in his hand. Balaam fell face down on the ground before him.

³²"Why did you beat your donkey those three times?" the angel of the LORD demanded. "I have come to block your way because you are stubbornly resisting me. ³³Three times the donkey saw me and shied away; otherwise, I would certainly have killed you by now and spared the donkey."

³⁴Then Balaam confessed to the angel of the LORD, "I have sinned. I did not realize you were standing in the road to block my way. I will go back home if you are against my going."

³⁵But the angel of the LORD told him, "Go with these men, but you may say only what I tell you to say." So Balaam went on with Balak's officials. ³⁶When King Balak heard that Balaam was on the way, he went out to meet him at a Moabite town on the Arnon River at the border of his land.

³⁷"Did I not send you an urgent invitation? Why didn't you come right away?" Balak asked Balaam. "Didn't you believe me when I said I would reward you richly?"

³⁸Balaam replied, "I have come, but I have no power to say just anything. I will speak only the messages that God gives me."

∿∧⁄⁄ **What happens when you do what you know you shouldn't do?**
God let Balaam go with Balak's messengers, but he was angry about Balaam's greedy attitude. Balaam claimed that he would not go against God just for money, but his resolve was beginning to slip. His greed for the wealth offered by the king blinded him so that he could not see how God was trying to stop

him. Though we may know what God wants us to do, we can become blinded by our greedy desire for money, possessions, or prestige. We can avoid Balaam's mistake by looking past the allure of fame or fortune to the long-range benefits of following God.

Moses Reviews God's Actions

DEUTERONOMY 29:1-29

These are the terms of the covenant the LORD commanded Moses to make with the Israelites while they were in the land of Moab, in addition to the covenant he had made with them at Mount Sinai.

²Moses summoned all the Israelites and said to them, "You have seen with your own eyes everything the LORD did in Egypt to Pharaoh and all his servants and his whole country—³all the great tests of strength, the miraculous signs, and the amazing wonders. ⁴But to this day the LORD has not given you minds that understand, nor eyes that see, nor ears that hear! ⁵For forty years I led you through the wilderness, yet your clothes and sandals did not wear out. ⁶You had no bread or wine or other strong drink, but he gave you food so you would know that he is the LORD your God. ⁷When we came here, King Sihon of Heshbon and King Og of Bashan came out to fight against us, but we defeated them. ⁸We took their land and gave it to the tribes of Reuben and Gad and to the half-tribe of Manasseh as their inheritance.

⁹"Therefore, obey the terms of this covenant so that you will prosper in everything you do. ¹⁰All of you—your tribal leaders, your judges, your officers, all the men of Israel—are standing today before the LORD your God. ¹¹With you are your little ones, your wives, and the foreigners living among you who chop your wood and carry your water. ¹²You are standing here today to enter into a covenant with the LORD your God. The LORD is making this covenant with you today, and he has sealed it with an oath. ¹³He wants to confirm you today as his people and to confirm that he is your God, just as he promised you, and as he swore to your ancestors Abraham, Isaac, and Jacob. ¹⁴But you are not the only ones with whom the LORD is making this covenant with its obligations. ¹⁵The LORD your God is making this covenant with you who stand in his presence today and also with all future generations of Israel.

¹⁶"Surely you remember how we lived in the land of Egypt and how we traveled through the lands of enemy nations as we left. ¹⁷You have seen their detestable idols made of wood, stone, silver, and gold. ¹⁸The LORD made this covenant with you so that no man, woman, family, or tribe among you would turn away from the LORD our God to worship these gods of other nations, and so that no root among you would bear bitter and poisonous fruit. ¹⁹Let none of those who hear the warnings of this curse consider

themselves immune, thinking, 'I am safe, even though I am walking in my own stubborn way.' This would lead to utter ruin! [20]The LORD will not pardon such people. His anger and jealousy will burn against them. All the curses written in this book will come down on them, and the LORD will erase their names from under heaven. [21]The LORD will separate them from all the tribes of Israel, to pour out on them all the covenant curses recorded in this Book of the Law.

[22]"Then the generations to come, both your own descendants and the foreigners who come from distant lands, will see the devastation of the land and the diseases the LORD will send against it. [23]They will find its soil turned into sulfur and salt, with nothing planted and nothing growing, not even a blade of grass. It will be just like Sodom and Gomorrah, Admah and Zeboiim, which the LORD destroyed in his anger. [24]The surrounding nations will ask, 'Why has the LORD done this to his land? Why was he so angry?'

[25]"And they will be told, 'This happened because the people of the land broke the covenant they made with the LORD, the God of their ancestors, when he brought them out of the land of Egypt. [26]They turned to serve and worship other gods that were foreign to them, gods that the LORD had not designated for them. [27]That is why the LORD's anger burned against this land, bringing down on it all the curses recorded in this book. [28]In great anger and fury the LORD uprooted his people from their land and exiled them to another land, where they still live today!'

[29]"There are secret things that belong to the LORD our God, but the revealed things belong to us and our descendants forever, so that we may obey these words of the law."

〜∿∠ **How do you keep track of what God has done for you?** Moses cautioned that the day the Hebrews chose to turn from God, a root would be planted that would produce bitter fruit. When we do wrong, we plant an evil seed that begins to grow out of control, eventually yielding a crop of sorrow and pain. But we can prevent those seeds of sin from taking root. If you have done something wrong, confess it to God and others immediately. If the seed never finds fertile soil, its bitter fruit will never ripen.

24 FEBRUARY

Moses Challenges the People
DEUTERONOMY 30:1-20

"Suppose all these things happen to you—the blessings and the curses I have listed—and you meditate on them as you are living among the nations to which the LORD your God has exiled you. [2]If at that time you return to the LORD your God, and you and your children begin wholeheartedly to obey all the commands I have given you today, [3]then the LORD your God will restore your fortunes. He will have mercy on you and gather you back from all the nations where he has scattered you. ⁴Though you are at the ends of the earth, the LORD your God will go and find you and bring you back again. ⁵He will return you to the land that belonged to your ancestors, and you will possess that land again. He will make you even more prosperous and numerous than your ancestors!

⁶"The LORD your God will cleanse your heart and the hearts of all your descendants so that you will love him with all your heart and soul, and so you may live! ⁷The LORD your God will inflict all these curses on your enemies and persecutors. ⁸Then you will again obey the LORD and keep all the commands I am giving you today. ⁹The LORD your God will make you successful in everything you do. He will give you many children and numerous livestock, and your fields will produce abundant harvests, for the LORD will delight in being good to you as he was to your ancestors. ¹⁰The LORD your God will delight in you if you obey his voice and keep the commands and laws written in this Book of the Law, and if you turn to the LORD your God with all your heart and soul.

¹¹"This command I am giving you today is not too difficult for you to understand or perform. ¹²It is not up in heaven, so distant that you must ask, 'Who will go to heaven and bring it down so we can hear and obey it?' ¹³It is not beyond the sea, so far away that you must ask, 'Who will cross the sea to bring it to us so we can hear and obey it?' ¹⁴The message is very close at hand; it is on your lips and in your heart so that you can obey it.

¹⁵"Now listen! Today I am giving you a choice between prosperity and disaster, between life and death. ¹⁶I have commanded you today to love the LORD your God and to keep his commands, laws, and regulations by walking in his ways. If you do this, you will live and become a great nation, and the LORD your God will bless you and the land you are about to enter and occupy. ¹⁷But if your heart turns away and you refuse to listen, and if you are drawn away to serve and worship other gods, ¹⁸then I warn you now that you will certainly be destroyed. You will not live a long, good life in the land you are crossing the Jordan to occupy.

¹⁹"Today I have given you the choice between life and death, between blessings and curses. I call on heaven and earth to witness the choice you make. Oh, that you would choose life, that you and your descendants might live! ²⁰Choose to love the LORD your God and to obey him and commit yourself to him, for he is your life. Then you will live long in the land the LORD swore to give your ancestors Abraham, Isaac, and Jacob."

〰️ **How do you show that you love God?** Moses challenged Israel to show their love for God by choosing to obey him and thereby continue to experience his blessings. God doesn't force his will on anyone. He lets us decide whether to follow him or reject him. This decision, however, is a life-or-death matter. God wants us to realize this, for he would like us all to choose life. Daily, in each new situation, we must decide again.

Moses Appoints
New Leaders
DEUTERONOMY 31:1-8

When Moses had finished saying these things to all the people of Israel, ²he said, "I am now 120 years old and am no longer able to lead you. The LORD has told me that I will not cross the Jordan River. ³But the LORD your God himself will cross over ahead of you. He will destroy the nations living there, and you will take possession of their land. Joshua is your new leader, and he will go with you, just as the LORD promised. ⁴The LORD will destroy the nations living in the land, just as he destroyed Sihon and Og, the kings of the Amorites. ⁵The LORD will hand over to you the people who live there, and you will deal with them as I have commanded you. ⁶Be strong and courageous! Do not be afraid of them! The LORD your God will go ahead of you. He will neither fail you nor forsake you."

⁷Then Moses called for Joshua, and as all Israel watched he said to him, "Be strong and courageous! For you will lead these people into the land that the LORD swore to give their ancestors. You are the one who will deliver it to them as their inheritance. ⁸Do not be afraid or discouraged, for the LORD is the one who goes before you. He will be with you; he will neither fail you nor forsake you."

〰️〰️ If you were Joshua, who would be "Moses" in your life?
Joshua had been Moses' assistant for many years and had learned much from him (Josh. 1:1). One of his key qualifications was his faith. Joshua had been appointed to take over the leadership of Israel and guide the people into the Promised Land (Moses could not enter the land due to his disobedience— Numbers 20:12). Indeed, this was a frightening task with 3 million people to care for, settle disputes for, and lead into battle. Finding courage would be Joshua's greatest test. He was strong and courageous because he knew God was with him and because he had faith that God would do all he had promised Israel.

The Death of Moses
DEUTERONOMY 34:1-12

Then Moses went to Mount Nebo from the plains of Moab and climbed Pisgah Peak, which is across from Jericho. And the LORD showed him the whole land, from Gilead as far as Dan; ²all the land of Naphtali; the land of Ephraim and Manasseh; all the land of Judah, extending to the Mediterranean Sea; ³the Negev; the Jordan Valley with Jericho—the city of palms—as far as Zoar. ⁴Then the LORD said to Moses, "This is the land I promised on oath to Abraham, Isaac, and Jacob, and I told them I would give it to their descendants. I have now allowed you to see it, but you will not enter the land."

⁵So Moses, the servant of the LORD, died there in the land of Moab, just as the LORD had said. ⁶He was buried in a valley near Beth-peor in Moab, but to this day no one knows the exact place. ⁷Moses was 120 years old when he died, yet his eyesight was clear, and he was as strong as ever. ⁸The people of Israel mourned thirty days for Moses on the plains of Moab, until the customary period of mourning was over.

⁹Now Joshua son of Nun was full of the spirit of wisdom, for Moses had laid his hands on him. So the people of Israel obeyed him and did everything just as the LORD had commanded Moses.

¹⁰There has never been another prophet like Moses, whom the LORD knew face to face. ¹¹The LORD sent Moses to perform all the miraculous signs and wonders in the land of Egypt against Pharaoh, all his servants, and his entire land. ¹²And it was through Moses that the LORD demonstrated his mighty power and terrifying acts in the sight of all Israel.

~\/\~ **How would you most like to be remembered?** Moses, the man who did not want to be sent to Egypt because he was "clumsy with words" (Exod. 4:10), delivered the three addresses to Israel that make up the book of Deuteronomy. God gave him the power to develop from a stuttering shepherd into a national leader and powerful orator. His courage, humility, and wisdom molded the Hebrew slaves into a nation. But Moses was one person who did not let success go to his head. In the end God was still Moses' best friend. His love, respect, and awe for God had grown daily throughout his life. Moses knew that it was not any greatness in himself that made him successful; it was the greatness of the all-powerful God in whom he trusted. Allow God to lead and guide you, to be your friend, and, like Moses, you will live a life of honor, integrity, courage, humility, and wisdom.

FEBRUARY

God Takes Over
JOSHUA 1:1-18

After the death of Moses the LORD's servant, the LORD spoke to Joshua son of Nun, Moses' assistant. He said, ²"Now that my servant Moses is dead, you must lead my people across the Jordan River into the land I am giving them. ³I promise you what I promised Moses: 'Everywhere you go, you will be on land I have given you—⁴from the Negev Desert in the south to the Lebanon mountains in the north, from the Euphrates River on the east to the Mediterranean Sea on the west, and all the land of the Hittites.' ⁵No one will be able to stand their ground against you as long as you live. For I will be with you as I was with Moses. I will not fail you or abandon you.

⁶"Be strong and courageous, for you will lead my people to possess all the land I swore to give their ancestors. ⁷Be strong and very courageous. Obey all the laws Moses gave you. Do not turn away from them, and you will be successful in everything you do. ⁸Study this Book of the Law continually. Meditate on it day and night so you may be sure to obey all that is written in it. Only then will you succeed. ⁹I command you—be strong and courageous! Do not be afraid or discouraged. For the LORD your God is with you wherever you go."

¹⁰Joshua then commanded the leaders of Israel, ¹¹"Go through the camp and tell the people to get their provisions ready. In three days you will cross the Jordan River and take possession of the land the LORD your God has given you."

¹²Then Joshua called together the tribes of Reuben, Gad, and the half-tribe of Manasseh. He told them, ¹³"Remember what Moses, the servant of the LORD, commanded you: 'The LORD your God is giving you rest and has given you this land.' ¹⁴Your wives, children, and cattle may remain here on the east side of the Jordan River, but your warriors, fully armed, must lead the other tribes across the Jordan to help them conquer their territory. Stay with them ¹⁵until the LORD gives rest to them as he has given rest to you, and until they, too, possess the land the LORD your God is giving them. Only then may you settle here on the east side of the Jordan River in the land that Moses, the servant of the LORD, gave you."

¹⁶They answered Joshua, "We will do whatever you command us, and we will go wherever you send us. ¹⁷We will obey you just as we obeyed Moses. And may the LORD your God be with you as he was with Moses. ¹⁸Anyone who rebels against your word and does not obey your every command will be put to death. So be strong and courageous!"

〰〰 **Which of these qualities would you most need to be like Joshua?** Many people think success is based on power, influential personal contacts, and a relentless drive to get ahead. But the strategy for success that God taught Joshua goes against such criteria. He told Joshua that to succeed he must (1) be strong and brave because the task ahead would not be easy, (2) obey God's Law, and (3) daily read and study God's Word. To be successful, follow God's words to Joshua. You may not succeed by the world's standards, but you will be a success in God's eyes, and his opinion lasts forever.

28 FEBRUARY

Spies Visit Jericho
JOSHUA 2:1-24

Then Joshua secretly sent out two spies from the Israelite camp at Acacia. He instructed them, "Spy out the land on the other side of the Jordan River, especially around Jericho." So the two men set out and came to the house of a prostitute named Rahab and stayed there that night.

²But someone told the king of Jericho, "Some Israelites have come here tonight to spy out the land." ³So the king of Jericho sent orders to Rahab: "Bring out the men who have come into your house. They are spies sent here to discover the best way to attack us."

⁴Rahab, who had hidden the two men, replied, "The men were here earlier, but I didn't know where they were from. ⁵They left the city at dusk, as the city gates were about to close, and I don't know where they went. If you hurry, you can probably catch up with them." ⁶(But she had taken them up to the roof and hidden them beneath piles of flax.) ⁷So the king's men went looking for the spies along the road leading to the shallow crossing places of the Jordan River. And as soon as the king's men had left, the city gate was shut.

⁸Before the spies went to sleep that night, Rahab went up on the roof to talk with them. ⁹"I know the LORD has given you this land," she told them. "We are all afraid of you. Everyone is living in terror. ¹⁰For we have heard how the LORD made a dry path for you through the Red Sea when you left Egypt. And we know what you did to Sihon and Og, the two Amorite kings east of the Jordan River, whose people you completely destroyed. ¹¹No wonder our hearts have melted in fear! No one has the courage to fight after hearing such things. For the LORD your God is the supreme God of the heavens above and the earth below. ¹²Now swear to me by the LORD that you will be kind to me and my family since I have helped you. Give me some guarantee that ¹³when Jericho is conquered, you will let me live, along with my father and mother, my brothers and sisters, and all their families."

¹⁴"We offer our own lives as a guarantee for your safety," the men agreed. "If you don't betray us, we will keep our promise when the LORD gives us the land."

¹⁵Then, since Rahab's house was built into the city wall, she let them down by a rope through the window. ¹⁶"Escape to the hill country," she told them. "Hide there for three days until the men who are searching for you have returned; then go on your way."

¹⁷Before they left, the men told her, "We can guarantee your safety ¹⁸only if you leave this scarlet rope hanging from the window. And all your family members—your father, mother, brothers, and all your relatives—must be here inside the house. ¹⁹If they go out into the street, they will be killed, and we cannot be held to our oath. But we swear that no one inside this house will be killed—not a hand will be laid on any of them. ²⁰If you betray us, however, we are not bound by this oath in any way."

²¹"I accept your terms," she replied. And she sent them on their way, leaving the scarlet rope hanging from the window.

²²The spies went up into the hill country and stayed there three days. The men who were chasing them had searched everywhere along the road, but they finally returned to the city without success. ²³Then the two spies came

down from the hill country, crossed the Jordan River, and reported to Joshua all that had happened to them. [24]"The LORD will certainly give us the whole land," they said, "for all the people in the land are terrified of us."

~\/~ **What persons has God used in your life unexpectedly?** Why would the spies stop at the house of Rahab the prostitute? (1) It was a good place to gather information and have no questions asked in return. (2) Rahab's house was in an ideal location for a quick escape because it was built into the city wall. (3) God directed the spies to Rahab's house because he knew her heart was open to him and that she would be instrumental in the Israelite victory over Jericho. God often uses people with simple faith to accomplish his great purposes, no matter what kind of past they have had or how insignificant they seem to be. Rahab didn't allow her past to keep her from the new role God had for her.

The Invasion of Canaan

JOSHUA 3:1-17

Early the next morning Joshua and all the Israelites left Acacia and arrived at the banks of the Jordan River, where they camped before crossing. ²Three days later, the Israelite leaders went through the camp ³giving these instructions to the people: "When you see the Levitical priests carrying the Ark of the Covenant of the LORD your God, follow them. ⁴Since you have never traveled this way before, they will guide you. Stay about a half mile behind them, keeping a clear distance between you and the Ark. Make sure you don't come any closer."

⁵Then Joshua told the people, "Purify yourselves, for tomorrow the LORD will do great wonders among you."

⁶In the morning Joshua said to the priests, "Lift up the Ark of the Covenant and lead the people across the river." And so they started out.

⁷The LORD told Joshua, "Today I will begin to make you great in the eyes of all the Israelites. Now they will know that I am with you, just as I was with Moses. ⁸Give these instructions to the priests who are carrying the Ark of the Covenant: 'When you reach the banks of the Jordan River, take a few steps into the river and stop.' "

⁹So Joshua told the Israelites, "Come and listen to what the LORD your God says. ¹⁰Today you will know that the living God is among you. He will surely drive out the Canaanites, Hittites, Hivites, Perizzites, Girgashites, Amorites, and Jebusites. ¹¹Think of it! The Ark of the Covenant, which belongs to the Lord of the whole earth, will lead you across the Jordan River! ¹²Now choose twelve men, one from each tribe. ¹³The priests will be carrying the Ark of the LORD, the Lord of all the earth. When their feet touch the water, the flow of water will be cut off upstream, and the river will pile up there in one heap."

¹⁴When the people set out to cross the Jordan, the priests who were carrying the Ark of the Covenant went ahead of them. ¹⁵Now it was the harvest season, and the Jordan was overflowing its banks. But as soon as the feet of the priests who were carrying the Ark touched the water at the river's edge, ¹⁶the water began piling up at a town upstream called Adam, which is near

Zarethan. And the water below that point flowed on to the Dead Sea until the riverbed was dry. Then all the people crossed over near the city of Jericho. ¹⁷Meanwhile, the priests who were carrying the Ark of the LORD's covenant stood on dry ground in the middle of the riverbed as the people passed by them. They waited there until everyone had crossed the Jordan on dry ground.

∿∿ **How would you illustrate God's guidance in your life?** Just before crossing over into the Promised Land, Joshua gathered the people to hear the words of the Lord. Their excitement was high. No doubt they wanted to rush on, but Joshua made them stop and listen. We live in a fast-paced age where we feel we have to rush just to keep up. It is easy to get caught up in our daily tasks, becoming too busy for what God says is most important—listening to his words. Take time to focus on what God wants from you during all your activities. Knowing what God has said before you rush into your day may help you avoid foolish mistakes.

MARCH

The Battle of Jericho
JOSHUA 5:13–6:27

As Joshua approached the city of Jericho, he looked up and saw a man facing him with sword in hand. Joshua went up to him and asked, "Are you friend or foe?"

¹⁴"Neither one," he replied. "I am commander of the LORD's army."

At this, Joshua fell with his face to the ground in reverence. "I am at your command," Joshua said. "What do you want your servant to do?"

¹⁵The commander of the LORD's army replied, "Take off your sandals, for this is holy ground." And Joshua did as he was told.

6:1 Now the gates of Jericho were tightly shut because the people were afraid of the Israelites. No one was allowed to go in or out. ²But the LORD said to Joshua, "I have given you Jericho, its king, and all its mighty warriors. ³Your entire army is to march around the city once a day for six days. ⁴Seven priests will walk ahead of the Ark, each carrying a ram's horn. On the seventh day you are to march around the city seven times, with the priests blowing the horns. ⁵When you hear the priests give one long blast on the horns, have all the people give a mighty shout. Then the walls of the city will collapse, and the people can charge straight into the city."

⁶So Joshua called together the priests and said, "Take up the Ark of the Covenant, and assign seven priests to walk in front of it, each carrying a ram's horn." ⁷Then he gave orders to the people: "March around the city, and the armed men will lead the way in front of the Ark of the LORD."

⁸After Joshua spoke to the people, the seven priests with the rams' horns started marching in the presence of the LORD, blowing the horns as they marched. And the priests carrying the Ark of the LORD's covenant followed

behind them. [9]Armed guards marched both in front of the priests and behind the Ark, with the priests continually blowing the horns. [10]"Do not shout; do not even talk," Joshua commanded. "Not a single word from any of you until I tell you to shout. Then shout!" [11]So the Ark of the LORD was carried around the city once that day, and then everyone returned to spend the night in the camp.

[12]Joshua got up early the next morning, and the priests again carried the Ark of the LORD. [13]The seven priests with the rams' horns marched in front of the Ark of the LORD, blowing their horns. Armed guards marched both in front of the priests with the horns and behind the Ark of the LORD. All this time the priests were sounding their horns. [14]On the second day they marched around the city once and returned to the camp. They followed this pattern for six days.

[15]On the seventh day the Israelites got up at dawn and marched around the city as they had done before. But this time they went around the city seven times. [16]The seventh time around, as the priests sounded the long blast on their horns, Joshua commanded the people, "Shout! For the LORD has given you the city! [17]The city and everything in it must be completely destroyed as an offering to the LORD. Only Rahab the prostitute and the others in her house will be spared, for she protected our spies. [18]Do not take any of the things set apart for destruction, or you yourselves will be completely destroyed, and you will bring trouble on all Israel. [19]Everything made from silver, gold, bronze, or iron is sacred to the LORD and must be brought into his treasury."

[20]When the people heard the sound of the horns, they shouted as loud as they could. Suddenly, the walls of Jericho collapsed, and the Israelites charged straight into the city from every side and captured it. [21]They completely destroyed everything in it—men and women, young and old, cattle, sheep, donkeys—everything.

[22]Then Joshua said to the two spies, "Keep your promise. Go to the prostitute's house and bring her out, along with all her family."

[23]The young men went in and brought out Rahab, her father, mother, brothers, and all the other relatives who were with her. They moved her whole family to a safe place near the camp of Israel.

[24]Then the Israelites burned the city and everything in it. Only the things made from silver, gold, bronze, or iron were kept for the treasury of the LORD's house. [25]So Joshua spared Rahab the prostitute and her relatives who were with her in the house, because she had hidden the spies Joshua sent to Jericho. And she lives among the Israelites to this day.

[26]At that time Joshua invoked this curse:

> "May the curse of the LORD fall on anyone
> who tries to rebuild the city of Jericho.
> At the cost of his firstborn son,
> he will lay its foundation.
> At the cost of his youngest son,
> he will set up its gates."

²⁷So the LORD was with Joshua, and his name became famous throughout the land.

〜〜〜 **How serious are you about allowing God to use you?** It must have seemed strange to the Israelites that instead of going to battle, they were going to march around the city for a week! But this was God's plan, and the Israelites had a guaranteed victory if they would follow it. As strange as the plan sounded, it worked. God may require you to do things that don't make sense at first. Even as you follow him, you may wonder how things can possibly work out. Like the Israelites, take one day at a time and follow step by step. You may not see the logic of God's plan until after you have obeyed.

MARCH

3

Ultimate Consequences

JOSHUA 7:1-26

But Israel was unfaithful concerning the things set apart for the LORD. A man named Achan had stolen some of these things, so the LORD was very angry with the Israelites. Achan was the son of Carmi, of the family of Zimri, of the clan of Zerah, and of the tribe of Judah.

²Joshua sent some of his men from Jericho to spy out the city of Ai, east of Bethel, near Beth-aven. ³When they returned, they told Joshua, "It's a small town, and it won't take more than two or three thousand of us to destroy it. There's no need for all of us to go there."

⁴So approximately three thousand warriors were sent, but they were soundly defeated. The men of Ai ⁵chased the Israelites from the city gate as far as the quarries, and they killed about thirty-six who were retreating down the slope. The Israelites were paralyzed with fear at this turn of events, and their courage melted away.

⁶Joshua and the leaders of Israel tore their clothing in dismay, threw dust on their heads, and bowed down facing the Ark of the LORD until evening. ⁷Then Joshua cried out, "Sovereign LORD, why did you bring us across the Jordan River if you are going to let the Amorites kill us? If only we had been content to stay on the other side! ⁸Lord, what am I to say, now that Israel has fled from its enemies? ⁹For when the Canaanites and all the other people living in the land hear about it, they will surround us and wipe us off the face of the earth. And then what will happen to the honor of your great name?"

¹⁰But the LORD said to Joshua, "Get up! Why are you lying on your face like this? ¹¹Israel has sinned and broken my covenant! They have stolen the things that I commanded to be set apart for me. And they have not only stolen them; they have also lied about it and hidden the things among their belongings. ¹²That is why the Israelites are running from their enemies in defeat. For now Israel has been set apart for destruction. I will not remain

with you any longer unless you destroy the things among you that were set apart for destruction.

¹³"Get up! Command the people to purify themselves in preparation for tomorrow. For this is what the LORD, the God of Israel, says: Hidden among you, O Israel, are things set apart for the LORD. You will never defeat your enemies until you remove these things. ¹⁴In the morning you must present yourselves by tribes, and the LORD will point out the tribe to which the guilty man belongs. That tribe must come forward with its clans, and the LORD will point out the guilty clan. That clan will then come forward, and the LORD will point out the guilty family. Finally, each member of the guilty family must come one by one. ¹⁵The one who has stolen what was set apart for destruction will himself be burned with fire, along with everything he has, for he has broken the covenant of the LORD and has done a horrible thing in Israel."

¹⁶Early the next morning, Joshua brought the tribes of Israel before the LORD, and the tribe of Judah was singled out. ¹⁷Then the clans of Judah came forward, and the clan of Zerah was singled out. Then the families of Zerah came before the LORD, and the family of Zimri was singled out. ¹⁸Every member of Zimri's family was brought forward person by person, and Achan was singled out.

¹⁹Then Joshua said to Achan, "My son, give glory to the LORD, the God of Israel, by telling the truth. Make your confession and tell me what you have done. Don't hide it from me."

²⁰Achan replied, "I have sinned against the LORD, the God of Israel. ²¹For I saw a beautiful robe imported from Babylon, two hundred silver coins, and a bar of gold weighing more than a pound. I wanted them so much that I took them. They are hidden in the ground beneath my tent, with the silver buried deeper than the rest."

²²So Joshua sent some men to make a search. They ran to the tent and found the stolen goods hidden there, just as Achan had said, with the silver buried beneath the rest. ²³They took the things from the tent and brought them to Joshua and all the Israelites. Then they laid them on the ground in the presence of the LORD.

²⁴Then Joshua and all the Israelites took Achan, the silver, the robe, the bar of gold, his sons, daughters, cattle, donkeys, sheep, tent, and everything he had, and they brought them to the valley of Achor. ²⁵Then Joshua said to Achan, "Why have you brought trouble on us? The LORD will now bring trouble on you." And all the Israelites stoned Achan and his family and burned their bodies. ²⁶They piled a great heap of stones over Achan, which remains to this day. That is why the place has been called the Valley of Trouble ever since. So the LORD was no longer angry.

〜✓〜 **What strongly negative or positive consequences have you experienced?** When Joshua first went against Ai, he did not consult God but relied on the strength of his army to defeat the small city. Only after Israel was defeated did they turn to God and ask, "What happened?" Too often we rely on our own skills and strength, especially when the task before us seems easy. We go to God only when the obstacles seem too great. However, only God knows what lies ahead. Consulting him, even when we are on a winning streak, may save us from grave mistakes or misjudgments. God may want us to learn lessons, remove pride, or consult others before he will work through us.

MARCH

The Longest Day

JOSHUA 10:1-15

Now Adoni-zedek, king of Jerusalem, heard that Joshua had captured and completely destroyed Ai and killed its king, just as he had destroyed the city of Jericho and killed its king. He also learned that the Gibeonites had made peace with Israel and were now their allies. ²He and his people became very afraid when they heard all this because Gibeon was a large city—as large as the royal cities and larger than Ai. And the Gibeonite men were mighty warriors. ³So King Adoni-zedek of Jerusalem sent messengers to several other kings: Hoham of Hebron, Piram of Jarmuth, Japhia of Lachish, and Debir of Eglon. ⁴"Come and help me destroy Gibeon," he urged them, "for they have made peace with Joshua and the people of Israel." ⁵So these five Amorite kings combined their armies for a united attack. They moved all their troops into place and attacked Gibeon.

⁶The men of Gibeon quickly sent messengers to Joshua at Gilgal, "Don't abandon your servants now!" they pleaded. "Come quickly and save us! For all the Amorite kings who live in the hill country have come out against us with their armies."

⁷So Joshua and the entire Israelite army left Gilgal and set out to rescue Gibeon. ⁸"Do not be afraid of them," the LORD said to Joshua, "for I will give you victory over them. Not a single one of them will be able to stand up to you."

⁹Joshua traveled all night from Gilgal and took the Amorite armies by surprise. ¹⁰The LORD threw them into a panic, and the Israelites slaughtered them in great numbers at Gibeon. Then the Israelites chased the enemy along the road to Beth-horon and attacked them at Azekah and Makkedah, killing them along the way. ¹¹As the Amorites retreated down the road from Beth-horon, the LORD destroyed them with a terrible hailstorm that continued until they reached Azekah. The hail killed more of the enemy than the Israelites killed with the sword.

¹²On the day the LORD gave the Israelites victory over the Amorites, Joshua prayed to the LORD in front of all the people of Israel. He said,

"Let the sun stand still over Gibeon,
    and the moon over the valley of Aijalon."

¹³So the sun and moon stood still until the Israelites had defeated their enemies.

Is this event not recorded in *The Book of Jashar?* The sun stopped in the middle of the sky, and it did not set as on a normal day. ¹⁴The LORD fought for Israel that day. Never before or since has there been a day like that one, when the LORD answered such a request from a human being.

¹⁵Then Joshua and the Israelite army returned to their camp at Gilgal.

〰〽 **How do you know God is powerful?** How did the sun stand still? Of course, in relation to the earth the sun always stands still, but the wording should not cause us to doubt the miracle. After all, we are not confused when someone tells us the sun rises or sets. The point is that the day was prolonged, not that God used a particular method to prolong it. Regardless of God's chosen method, the Bible is clear that the day was prolonged by a miracle, and God's intervention turned the tide of battle for his people. Do not be afraid to ask God for what might seem impossible. If it is in his will, he has the power to do it.

MARCH

Joshua Warns the Leaders

JOSHUA 23:1-16

5

The years passed, and the LORD had given the people of Israel rest from all their enemies. Joshua, who was now very old, ²called together all the elders, leaders, judges, and officers of Israel. He said to them, "I am an old man now. ³You have seen everything the LORD your God has done for you during my lifetime. The LORD your God has fought for you against your enemies. ⁴I have allotted to you as an inheritance all the land of the nations yet unconquered, as well as the land of those we have already conquered—from the Jordan River to the Mediterranean Sea in the west. ⁵This land will be yours, for the LORD your God will drive out all the people living there now. You will live there instead of them, just as the LORD your God promised you.

⁶"So be strong! Be very careful to follow all the instructions written in the Book of the Law of Moses. Do not deviate from them in any way. ⁷Make sure you do not associate with the other people still remaining in the land. Do not even mention the names of their gods, much less swear by them or worship them. ⁸But be faithful to the LORD your God as you have done until now.

⁹"For the LORD has driven out great and powerful nations for you, and no one has yet been able to defeat you. ¹⁰Each one of you will put to flight a thousand of the enemy, for the LORD your God fights for you, just as he has promised. ¹¹So be very careful to love the LORD your God.

¹²"But if you turn away from him and intermarry with the survivors of these nations remaining among you, ¹³then know for certain that the LORD your God will no longer drive them out from your land. Instead, they will be a snare and a trap to you, a pain in your side and a thorn in your eyes,

and you will be wiped out from this good land the LORD your God has given you.

¹⁴"Soon I will die, going the way of all the earth. Deep in your hearts you know that every promise of the LORD your God has come true. Not a single one has failed! ¹⁵But as surely as the LORD your God has given you the good things he promised, he will also bring disaster on you if you disobey him. He will completely wipe you out from this good land he has given you. ¹⁶If you break the covenant of the LORD your God by worshiping and serving other gods, his anger will burn against you, and you will quickly be wiped out from the good land he has given you."

〰〰 **Which of Joshua's warnings do you most need to obey?** Joshua knew the nation's weak spots. Before dying, he called the people together and gave commands to help them where they were most likely to slip: (1) Follow all that is written in the book of the laws of Moses without turning aside. (2) Don't associate with the heathen nations or worship their gods. (3) Don't intermarry with the heathen nations. These temptations were right in their backyard. Our associations and relationships can be temptations to us as well. It's wise to identify our weak spots *before* we break down. Then we can develop strategies to overcome these temptations instead of being overcome by them.

6

MARCH

Joshua's Last Words
JOSHUA 24:1-31

Then Joshua summoned all the people of Israel to Shechem, along with their elders, leaders, judges, and officers. So they came and presented themselves to God.

²Joshua said to the people, "This is what the LORD, the God of Israel, says: Your ancestors, including Terah, the father of Abraham and Nahor, lived beyond the Euphrates River, and they worshiped other gods. ³But I took your ancestor Abraham from the land beyond the Euphrates and led him into the land of Canaan. I gave him many descendants through his son Isaac. ⁴To Isaac I gave Jacob and Esau. To Esau I gave the hill country of Seir, while Jacob and his children went down into Egypt.

⁵"Then I sent Moses and Aaron, and I brought terrible plagues on Egypt; and afterward I brought you out as a free people. ⁶But when your ancestors arrived at the Red Sea, the Egyptians chased after you with chariots and horses. ⁷When you cried out to the LORD, I put darkness between you and the Egyptians. I brought the sea crashing down on the Egyptians, drowning them. With your very own eyes you saw what I did. Then you lived in the wilderness for many years.

⁸"Finally, I brought you into the land of the Amorites on the east side of the Jordan. They fought against you, but I gave you victory over them, and

you took possession of their land. ⁹Then Balak son of Zippor, king of Moab, started a war against Israel. He asked Balaam son of Beor to curse you, ¹⁰but I would not listen to him. Instead, I made Balaam bless you, and so I rescued you from Balak.

¹¹"When you crossed the Jordan River and came to Jericho, the men of Jericho fought against you. There were also many others who fought you, including the Amorites, the Perizzites, the Canaanites, the Hittites, the Girgashites, the Hivites, and the Jebusites. But I gave you victory over them. ¹²And I sent hornets ahead of you to drive out the two kings of the Amorites. It was not your swords or bows that brought you victory. ¹³I gave you land you had not worked for, and I gave you cities you did not build—the cities in which you are now living. I gave you vineyards and olive groves for food, though you did not plant them.

¹⁴"So honor the LORD and serve him wholeheartedly. Put away forever the idols your ancestors worshiped when they lived beyond the Euphrates River and in Egypt. Serve the LORD alone. ¹⁵But if you are unwilling to serve the LORD, then choose today whom you will serve. Would you prefer the gods your ancestors served beyond the Euphrates? Or will it be the gods of the Amorites in whose land you now live? But as for me and my family, we will serve the LORD."

¹⁶The people replied, "We would never forsake the LORD and worship other gods. ¹⁷For the LORD our God is the one who rescued us and our ancestors from slavery in the land of Egypt. He performed mighty miracles before our very eyes. As we traveled through the wilderness among our enemies, he preserved us. ¹⁸It was the LORD who drove out the Amorites and the other nations living here in the land. So we, too, will serve the LORD, for he alone is our God."

¹⁹Then Joshua said to the people, "You are not able to serve the LORD, for he is a holy and jealous God. He will not forgive your rebellion and sins. ²⁰If you forsake the LORD and serve other gods, he will turn against you and destroy you, even though he has been so good to you."

²¹But the people answered Joshua, saying, "No, we are determined to serve the LORD!"

²²"You are accountable for this decision," Joshua said. "You have chosen to serve the LORD."

"Yes," they replied, "we are accountable."

²³"All right then," Joshua said, "destroy the idols among you, and turn your hearts to the LORD, the God of Israel."

²⁴The people said to Joshua, "We will serve the LORD our God. We will obey him alone."

²⁵So Joshua made a covenant with the people that day at Shechem, committing them to a permanent and binding contract between themselves and the LORD. ²⁶Joshua recorded these things in the Book of the Law of God. As a reminder of their agreement, he took a huge stone and rolled it beneath the oak tree beside the Tabernacle of the LORD.

²⁷Joshua said to all the people, "This stone has heard everything the LORD said to us. It will be a witness to testify against you if you go back on your word to God."
²⁸Then Joshua sent the people away, each to his own inheritance.
²⁹Soon after this, Joshua son of Nun, the servant of the LORD, died at the age of 110. ³⁰They buried him in the land he had inherited, at Timnath-serah in the hill country of Ephraim, north of Mount Gaash.
³¹Israel served the LORD throughout the lifetime of Joshua and of the leaders who outlived him—those who had personally experienced all that the LORD had done for Israel.

〜〴〲 **How can you get hope from history?** The people had to decide whether they would obey the Lord, who had proven his trustworthiness, or obey the local gods, which were only man-made idols. It's easy to slip into a quiet rebellion—going about life in your own way. But the time comes when you have to choose who or what will control you. The choice is yours. Will it be God, your own limited personality, or another imperfect substitute? Once you have chosen to be controlled by God's Spirit, reaffirm your choice every day.

7
MARCH

Judge Deborah
JUDGES 4:4-24

Deborah, the wife of Lappidoth, was a prophet who had become a judge in Israel. ⁵She would hold court under the Palm of Deborah, which stood between Ramah and Bethel in the hill country of Ephraim, and the Israelites came to her to settle their disputes. ⁶One day she sent for Barak son of Abinoam, who lived in Kedesh in the land of Naphtali. She said to him, "This is what the LORD, the God of Israel, commands you: Assemble ten thousand warriors from the tribes of Naphtali and Zebulun at Mount Tabor. ⁷I will lure Sisera, commander of Jabin's army, along with his chariots and warriors, to the Kishon River. There I will give you victory over him."

⁸Barak told her, "I will go, but only if you go with me!"

⁹"Very well," she replied, "I will go with you. But since you have made this choice, you will receive no honor. For the LORD's victory over Sisera will be at the hands of a woman." So Deborah went with Barak to Kedesh. ¹⁰At Kedesh, Barak called together the tribes of Zebulun and Naphtali, and ten thousand warriors marched up with him. Deborah also marched with them.

¹¹Now Heber the Kenite, a descendant of Moses' brother-in-law Hobab, had moved away from the other members of his tribe and pitched his tent by the Oak of Zaanannim, near Kedesh.

¹²When Sisera was told that Barak son of Abinoam had gone up to Mount Tabor, ¹³he called for all nine hundred of his iron chariots and all of his warriors, and they marched from Harosheth-haggoyim to the Kishon River.

¹⁴Then Deborah said to Barak, "Get ready! Today the Lord will give you victory over Sisera, for the Lord is marching ahead of you." So Barak led his ten thousand warriors down the slopes of Mount Tabor into battle. ¹⁵When Barak attacked, the Lord threw Sisera and all his charioteers and warriors into a panic. Then Sisera leaped down from his chariot and escaped on foot. ¹⁶Barak chased the enemy and their chariots all the way to Harosheth-haggoyim, killing all of Sisera's warriors. Not a single one was left alive.

¹⁷Meanwhile, Sisera ran to the tent of Jael, the wife of Heber the Kenite, because Heber's family was on friendly terms with King Jabin of Hazor. ¹⁸Jael went out to meet Sisera and said to him, "Come into my tent, sir. Come in. Don't be afraid." So he went into her tent, and she covered him with a blanket.

¹⁹"Please give me some water," he said. "I'm thirsty." So she gave him some milk to drink and covered him again.

²⁰"Stand at the door of the tent," he told her. "If anybody comes and asks you if there is anyone here, say no."

²¹But when Sisera fell asleep from exhaustion, Jael quietly crept up to him with a hammer and tent peg. Then she drove the tent peg through his temple and into the ground, and so he died.

²²When Barak came looking for Sisera, Jael went out to meet him. She said, "Come, and I will show you the man you are looking for." So he followed her into the tent and found Sisera lying there dead, with the tent peg through his temple.

²³So on that day Israel saw God subdue Jabin, the Canaanite king. ²⁴And from that time on Israel became stronger and stronger against King Jabin, until they finally destroyed him.

〰〰 **How do people know that you care about them?** How did Deborah command such respect? She was responsible for leading the people into battle, but more than that, she influenced them to live for God after the battle was over. Her personality drew people together and commanded the respect of even Barak, a military general. She was also a prophetess, whose main role was to encourage the people to obey God. If you are a leader among your friends, don't forget about the spiritual condition of those being led. A true leader is concerned about persons, not just success.

MARCH

Gideon Becomes a Judge

JUDGES 6:1-40

Again the Israelites did what was evil in the Lord's sight. So the Lord handed them over to the Midianites for seven years. ²The Midianites were so cruel that the Israelites fled to the mountains, where they made hiding places for themselves in caves and dens. ³Whenever the Israelites planted their crops, marauders from Midian, Amalek, and the people of the east would attack Israel, [4]camping in the land and destroying crops as far away as Gaza. They left the Israelites with nothing to eat, taking all the sheep, oxen, and donkeys. [5]These enemy hordes, coming with their cattle and tents as thick as locusts, arrived on droves of camels too numerous to count. And they stayed until the land was stripped bare. [6]So Israel was reduced to starvation by the Midianites. Then the Israelites cried out to the LORD for help.

[7]When they cried out to the LORD because of Midian, [8]the LORD sent a prophet to the Israelites. He said, "This is what the LORD, the God of Israel, says: I brought you up out of slavery in Egypt [9]and rescued you from the Egyptians and from all who oppressed you. I drove out your enemies and gave you their land. [10]I told you, 'I am the LORD your God. You must not worship the gods of the Amorites, in whose land you now live.' But you have not listened to me."

[11]Then the angel of the LORD came and sat beneath the oak tree at Ophrah, which belonged to Joash of the clan of Abiezer. Gideon son of Joash had been threshing wheat at the bottom of a winepress to hide the grain from the Midianites. [12]The angel of the LORD appeared to him and said, "Mighty hero, the LORD is with you!"

[13]"Sir," Gideon replied, "if the LORD is with us, why has all this happened to us? And where are all the miracles our ancestors told us about? Didn't they say, 'The LORD brought us up out of Egypt'? But now the LORD has abandoned us and handed us over to the Midianites."

[14]Then the LORD turned to him and said, "Go with the strength you have and rescue Israel from the Midianites. I am sending you!"

[15]"But Lord," Gideon replied, "how can I rescue Israel? My clan is the weakest in the whole tribe of Manasseh, and I am the least in my entire family!"

[16]The LORD said to him, "I will be with you. And you will destroy the Midianites as if you were fighting against one man."

[17]Gideon replied, "If you are truly going to help me, show me a sign to prove that it is really the LORD speaking to me. [18]Don't go away until I come back and bring my offering to you."

The LORD answered, "I will stay here until you return."

[19]Gideon hurried home. He cooked a young goat, and with half a bushel of flour he baked some bread without yeast. Then, carrying the meat in a basket and the broth in a pot, he brought them out and presented them to the angel, who was under the oak tree.

[20]The angel of God said to him, "Place the meat and the unleavened bread on this rock, and pour the broth over it." And Gideon did as he was told. [21]Then the angel of the LORD touched the meat and bread with the staff in his hand, and fire flamed up from the rock and consumed all he had brought. And the angel of the LORD disappeared.

[22]When Gideon realized that it was the angel of the LORD, he cried out, "Sovereign LORD, I have seen the angel of the LORD face to face!"

[23]"It is all right," the LORD replied. "Do not be afraid. You will not die."

²⁴And Gideon built an altar to the LORD there and named it "The LORD Is Peace." The altar remains in Ophrah in the land of the clan of Abiezer to this day.

²⁵That night the LORD said to Gideon, "Take the second best bull from your father's herd, the one that is seven years old. Pull down your father's altar to Baal, and cut down the Asherah pole standing beside it. ²⁶Then build an altar to the LORD your God here on this hill, laying the stones carefully. Sacrifice the bull as a burnt offering on the altar, using as fuel the wood of the Asherah pole you cut down." ²⁷So Gideon took ten of his servants and did as the LORD had commanded. But he did it at night because he was afraid of the other members of his father's household and the people of the town. He knew what would happen if they found out who had done it.

²⁸Early the next morning, as the people of the town began to stir, someone discovered that the altar of Baal had been knocked down and that the Asherah pole beside it was gone. In their place a new altar had been built, and it had the remains of a sacrifice on it. ²⁹The people said to each other, "Who did this?" And after asking around and making a careful search, they learned that it was Gideon, the son of Joash.

³⁰"Bring out your son," they shouted to Joash. "He must die for destroying the altar of Baal and for cutting down the Asherah pole."

³¹But Joash shouted to the mob, "Why are you defending Baal? Will you argue his case? Whoever pleads his case will be put to death by morning! If Baal truly is a god, let him defend himself and destroy the one who knocked down his altar!" ³²From then on Gideon was called Jerubbaal, which means "Let Baal defend himself," because he knocked down Baal's altar.

³³Soon afterward the armies of Midian, Amalek, and the people of the east formed an alliance against Israel and crossed the Jordan, camping in the valley of Jezreel. ³⁴Then the Spirit of the LORD took possession of Gideon. He blew a ram's horn as a call to arms, and the men of the clan of Abiezer came to him. ³⁵He also sent messengers throughout Manasseh, Asher, Zebulun, and Naphtali, summoning their warriors, and all of them responded.

³⁶Then Gideon said to God, "If you are truly going to use me to rescue Israel as you promised, ³⁷prove it to me in this way. I will put some wool on the threshing floor tonight. If the fleece is wet with dew in the morning but the ground is dry, then I will know that you are going to help me rescue Israel as you promised." ³⁸And it happened just that way. When Gideon got up the next morning, he squeezed the fleece and wrung out a whole bowlful of water.

³⁹Then Gideon said to God, "Please don't be angry with me, but let me make one more request. This time let the fleece remain dry while the ground around it is wet with dew." ⁴⁰So that night God did as Gideon asked. The fleece was dry in the morning, but the ground was covered with dew.

〰〰 **What examples of obedience can be found in your life?** Gideon questioned God about the problems he and his nation faced and about God's apparent lack of help. What he didn't acknowledge was the fact that the people had brought calamity upon themselves when they decided to disobey and neglect God. How easy it is to overlook personal accountability and blame our problems on God and others. Unfortunately, this does not solve our problems. When problems come, the first place to look is within. Our first action should be confession to God of sins that may have created our problems.

9 MARCH

Gideon and the Midianites

JUDGES 7:1-25

So Jerubbaal (that is, Gideon) and his army got up early and went as far as the spring of Harod. The armies of Midian were camped north of them in the valley near the hill of Moreh. ²The LORD said to Gideon, "You have too many warriors with you. If I let all of you fight the Midianites, the Israelites will boast to me that they saved themselves by their own strength. ³Therefore, tell the people, 'Whoever is timid or afraid may leave and go home.'" Twenty-two thousand of them went home, leaving only ten thousand who were willing to fight.

⁴But the LORD told Gideon, "There are still too many! Bring them down to the spring, and I will sort out who will go with you and who will not." ⁵When Gideon took his warriors down to the water, the LORD told him, "Divide the men into two groups. In one group put all those who cup water in their hands and lap it up with their tongues like dogs. In the other group put all those who kneel down and drink with their mouths in the stream." ⁶Only three hundred of the men drank from their hands. All the others got down on their knees and drank with their mouths in the stream. ⁷The LORD told Gideon, "With these three hundred men I will rescue you and give you victory over the Midianites. Send all the others home." ⁸So Gideon collected the provisions and rams' horns of the other warriors and sent them home. But he kept the three hundred men with him.

Now the Midianite camp was in the valley just below Gideon. ⁹During the night, the LORD said, "Get up! Go down into the Midianite camp, for I have given you victory over them! ¹⁰But if you are afraid to attack, go down to the camp with your servant Purah. ¹¹Listen to what the Midianites are saying, and you will be greatly encouraged. Then you will be eager to attack."

So Gideon took Purah and went down to the outposts of the enemy camp. ¹²The armies of Midian, Amalek, and the people of the east had settled in the valley like a swarm of locusts. Their camels were like grains of sand on the seashore—too many to count! ¹³Gideon crept up just as a man was telling his friend about a dream. The man said, "I had this dream, and in my dream a loaf of barley bread came tumbling down into the Midianite camp. It hit a tent, turned it over, and knocked it flat!"

¹⁴His friend said, "Your dream can mean only one thing—God has given Gideon son of Joash, the Israelite, victory over all the armies united with Midian!"

¹⁵When Gideon heard the dream and its interpretation, he thanked God. Then he returned to the Israelite camp and shouted, "Get up! For the LORD has given you victory over the Midianites!" ¹⁶He divided the three hundred men into three groups and gave each man a ram's horn and a clay jar with a torch in it. ¹⁷Then he said to them, "Keep your eyes on me. When I come to the edge of the camp, do just as I do. ¹⁸As soon as my group blows the rams' horns, those of you on the other sides of the camp blow your horns and shout, 'For the LORD and for Gideon!' "

¹⁹It was just after midnight, after the changing of the guard, when Gideon and the one hundred men with him reached the outer edge of the Midianite camp. Suddenly, they blew the horns and broke their clay jars. ²⁰Then all three groups blew their horns and broke their jars. They held the blazing torches in their left hands and the horns in their right hands and shouted, "A sword for the LORD and for Gideon!" ²¹Each man stood at his position around the camp and watched as all the Midianites rushed around in a panic, shouting as they ran. ²²When the three hundred Israelites blew their horns, the LORD caused the warriors in the camp to fight against each other with their swords. Those who were not killed fled to places as far away as Beth-shittah near Zererah and to the border of Abel-meholah near Tabbath.

²³Then Gideon sent for the warriors of Naphtali, Asher, and Manasseh, who joined in the chase after the fleeing army of Midian. ²⁴Gideon also sent messengers throughout the hill country of Ephraim, saying, "Come down to attack the Midianites. Cut them off at the shallows of the Jordan River at Beth-barah." And the men of Ephraim did as they were told. ²⁵They captured Oreb and Zeeb, the two Midianite generals, killing Oreb at the rock of Oreb, and Zeeb at the winepress of Zeeb. And they continued to chase the Midianites. Afterward the Israelites brought the heads of Oreb and Zeeb to Gideon, who was by the Jordan.

〜〜 **In what area of your life do you need to trust God more?** Facing overwhelming odds, Gideon was afraid. God understood his fear, but he didn't excuse Gideon from his task. Instead he allowed Gideon to slip into the enemy camp and overhear a conversation that would give him courage. Are you facing a battle? God can give you the strength you need for any situation. And don't be startled by the way he helps you. Like Gideon, you must listen to God and be ready to take the first step. Only after you begin to obey God will you find the courage to move ahead.

10

The Birth of Samson
JUDGES 13:1-25

Again the Israelites did what was evil in the LORD's sight, so the LORD handed them over to the Philistines, who kept them in subjection for forty years. ²In those days, a man named Manoah from the tribe of Dan lived in the town of Zorah. His wife was unable to become pregnant, and they had no children. ³The angel of the LORD appeared to Manoah's wife and said, "Even though you have been unable to have children, you will soon become pregnant and give birth to a son. ⁴You must not drink wine or any other alcoholic drink or eat any forbidden food. ⁵You will become pregnant and give birth to a son, and his hair must never be cut. For he will be dedicated to God as a Nazirite from birth. He will rescue Israel from the Philistines."

⁶The woman ran and told her husband, "A man of God appeared to me! He was like one of God's angels, terrifying to look at. I didn't ask where he was from, and he didn't tell me his name. ⁷But he told me, 'You will become pregnant and give birth to a son. You must not drink wine or any other alcoholic drink or eat any forbidden food. For your son will be dedicated to God as a Nazirite from the moment of his birth until the day of his death.' "

⁸Then Manoah prayed to the LORD. He said, "Lord, please let the man of God come back to us again and give us more instructions about this son who is to be born."

⁹God answered his prayer, and the angel of God appeared once again to his wife as she was sitting in the field. But her husband, Manoah, was not with her. ¹⁰So she quickly ran and told her husband, "The man who appeared to me the other day is here again!"

¹¹Manoah ran back with his wife and asked, "Are you the man who talked to my wife the other day?"

"Yes," he replied, "I am."

¹²So Manoah asked him, "When your words come true, what kind of rules should govern the boy's life and work?"

¹³The angel of the LORD replied, "Be sure your wife follows the instructions I gave her. ¹⁴She must not eat grapes or raisins, drink wine or any other alcoholic drink, or eat any forbidden food."

¹⁵Then Manoah said to the angel of the LORD, "Please stay here until we can prepare a young goat for you to eat."

¹⁶"I will stay," the angel of the LORD replied, "but I will not eat anything. However, you may prepare a burnt offering as a sacrifice to the LORD." (Manoah didn't realize it was the angel of the LORD.)

¹⁷Then Manoah asked the angel of the LORD, "What is your name? For when all this comes true, we want to honor you."

¹⁸"Why do you ask my name?" the angel of the LORD replied. "You wouldn't understand if I told you."

¹⁹Then Manoah took a young goat and a grain offering and offered it on a rock as a sacrifice to the LORD. And as Manoah and his wife watched, the LORD did an amazing thing. ²⁰As the flames from the altar shot up toward the sky, the angel of the LORD ascended in the fire. When Manoah and his wife saw this, they fell with their faces to the ground.

²¹The angel did not appear again to Manoah and his wife. Manoah finally realized it was the angel of the LORD, ²²and he said to his wife, "We will die, for we have seen God!"

²³But his wife said, "If the LORD were going to kill us, he wouldn't have accepted our burnt offering and grain offering. He wouldn't have appeared to us and told us this wonderful thing and done these miracles."

²⁴When her son was born, they named him Samson. And the LORD blessed him as he grew up. ²⁵And in Mahaneh-dan, which is located between the towns of Zorah and Eshtaol, the Spirit of the LORD began to take hold of him.

〰⋏⋎⟋ **In which part of your life do you need more discipline?** Samson's tribe, Dan, continued to wander in their inherited land (18:1), which was yet unconquered (Josh. 19:47-48). Samson's visits to the tribal army camp stirred his heart, and God's Spirit began preparing him for his role as judge and leader against the Philistines. Perhaps there are things that "excite" you. These may indicate areas where God wants to use you. God uses a variety of means to develop and prepare us: hereditary traits, environmental influences, and personal experiences. As with Samson, this preparation often begins long before adulthood. Be sensitive to the Holy Spirit's leading and the tasks God has prepared for you. Your past may be more useful to you than you imagine.

MARCH

11

Samson's Riddle
JUDGES 14:1-20

One day when Samson was in Timnah, he noticed a certain Philistine woman. ²When he returned home, he told his father and mother, "I want to marry a young Philistine woman I saw in Timnah."

³His father and mother objected strenuously, "Isn't there one woman in our tribe or among all the Israelites you could marry? Why must you go to the pagan Philistines to find a wife?"

But Samson told his father, "Get her for me. She is the one I want." ⁴His father and mother didn't realize the LORD was at work in this, creating an opportunity to disrupt the Philistines, who ruled over Israel at that time.

⁵As Samson and his parents were going down to Timnah, a young lion attacked Samson near the vineyards of Timnah. ⁶At that moment the Spirit of the LORD powerfully took control of him, and he ripped the lion's jaws apart with his bare hands. He did it as easily as if it were a young goat. But

he didn't tell his father or mother about it. ⁷When Samson arrived in Timnah, he talked with the woman and was very pleased with her.

⁸Later, when he returned to Timnah for the wedding, he turned off the path to look at the carcass of the lion. And he found that a swarm of bees had made some honey in the carcass. ⁹He scooped some of the honey into his hands and ate it along the way. He also gave some to his father and mother, and they ate it. But he didn't tell them he had taken the honey from the carcass of the lion.

¹⁰As his father was making final arrangements for the marriage, Samson threw a party at Timnah, as was the custom of the day. ¹¹Thirty young men from the town were invited to be his companions. ¹²Samson said to them, "Let me tell you a riddle. If you solve my riddle during these seven days of the celebration, I will give you thirty plain linen robes and thirty fancy robes. ¹³But if you can't solve it, then you must give me thirty linen robes and thirty fancy robes."

"All right," they agreed, "let's hear your riddle."

¹⁴So he said:

"From the one who eats came something to eat;
   out of the strong came something sweet."

Three days later they were still trying to figure it out. ¹⁵On the fourth day they said to Samson's wife, "Get the answer to the riddle from your husband, or we will burn down your father's house with you in it. Did you invite us to this party just to make us poor?"

¹⁶So Samson's wife came to him in tears and said, "You don't love me; you hate me! You have given my people a riddle, but you haven't told me the answer."

"I haven't even given the answer to my father or mother," he replied. "Why should I tell you?" ¹⁷So she cried whenever she was with him and kept it up for the rest of the celebration. At last, on the seventh day, he told her the answer because of her persistent nagging. Then she gave the answer to the young men.

¹⁸So before sunset of the seventh day, the men of the town came to Samson with their answer:

"What is sweeter than honey?
   What is stronger than a lion?"

Samson replied, "If you hadn't plowed with my heifer, you wouldn't have found the answer to my riddle!" ¹⁹Then the Spirit of the LORD powerfully took control of him. He went down to the town of Ashkelon, killed thirty men, took their belongings, and gave their clothing to the men who had answered his riddle. But Samson was furious about what had happened, and he went back home to live with his father and mother. ²⁰So his wife was given in marriage to the man who had been Samson's best man at the wedding.

〜〰〜 **How carefully do you consider the wisdom of your parents?**
Samson's parents objected to his marrying the Philistine woman for several reasons: (1) It was against God's law (Exod. 34:15-17; Deut. 7:1-4). A stark example of what happened when the Israelites married their heathen neighbors can be found in Judges 3:5-8. (2) The Philistines were Israel's greatest enemies. Marriage to a hated Philistine would be a disgrace to Samson's family. But Samson's father gave in to Samson's demand and allowed the marriage, even though he had the right to refuse his son. Perhaps his father knew Samson wouldn't listen anyway. Your parents know you better than anyone. Be careful to listen to their advice as you make decisions for your life.

MARCH

Samson and the Jawbone

12

JUDGES 15:1-20

Later on, during the wheat harvest, Samson took a young goat as a present to his wife. He intended to sleep with her, but her father wouldn't let him in. ²"I really thought you hated her," her father explained, "so I gave her in marriage to your best man. But look, her sister is more beautiful than she is. Marry her instead."

³Samson said, "This time I cannot be blamed for everything I am going to do to you Philistines." ⁴Then he went out and caught three hundred foxes. He tied their tails together in pairs, and he fastened a torch to each pair of tails. ⁵Then he lit the torches and let the foxes run through the fields of the Philistines. He burned all their grain to the ground, including the grain still in piles and all that had been bundled. He also destroyed their grapevines and olive trees.

⁶"Who did this?" the Philistines demanded.

"Samson," was the reply, "because his father-in-law from Timnah gave Samson's wife to be married to his best man." So the Philistines went and got the woman and her father and burned them to death.

⁷"Because you did this," Samson vowed, "I will take my revenge on you, and I won't stop until I'm satisfied!" ⁸So he attacked the Philistines with great fury and killed many of them. Then he went to live in a cave in the rock of Etam.

⁹The Philistines retaliated by setting up camp in Judah and raiding the town of Lehi. ¹⁰The men of Judah asked the Philistines, "Why have you attacked us?"

The Philistines replied, "We've come to capture Samson. We have come to pay him back for what he did to us."

¹¹So three thousand men of Judah went down to get Samson at the cave

in the rock of Etam. They said to Samson, "Don't you realize the Philistines rule over us? What are you doing to us?"

But Samson replied, "I only paid them back for what they did to me."

¹²But the men of Judah told him, "We have come to tie you up and hand you over to the Philistines."

"All right," Samson said. "But promise that you won't kill me yourselves."

¹³"We will tie you up and hand you over to the Philistines," they replied. "We won't kill you." So they tied him up with two new ropes and led him away from the rock.

¹⁴As Samson arrived at Lehi, the Philistines came shouting in triumph. But the Spirit of the LORD powerfully took control of Samson, and he snapped the ropes on his arms as if they were burnt strands of flax, and they fell from his wrists. ¹⁵Then he picked up a donkey's jawbone that was lying on the ground and killed a thousand Philistines with it. ¹⁶And Samson said,

"With the jawbone of a donkey,
    I've made heaps on heaps!
With the jawbone of a donkey,
    I've killed a thousand men!"

¹⁷When he finished speaking, he threw away the jawbone; and the place was named Jawbone Hill.

¹⁸Now Samson was very thirsty, and he cried out to the LORD, "You have accomplished this great victory by the strength of your servant. Must I now die of thirst and fall into the hands of these pagan people?" ¹⁹So God caused water to gush out of a hollow in the ground at Lehi, and Samson was revived as he drank. Then he named that place "The Spring of the One Who Cried Out," and it is still in Lehi to this day.

²⁰Samson was Israel's judge for twenty years, while the Philistines ruled the land.

〰️〰️ **What proof do you have that mistakes usually don't correct themselves?** Samson's reply in verse 11 tells the story of this chapter: "I only paid them back for what they did to me." Revenge is an uncontrollable monster. Each act of retaliation brings another. It is a boomerang that cannot be thrown without cost to the thrower. The revenge cycle can be halted only by forgiveness. Are you trying to get revenge for a wrong someone has done to you? Break the cycle now by first refusing to take revenge, then by forgiving the one who wronged you. Don't let revenge get control of you.

Samson and Delilah
JUDGES 16.1-21

One day Samson went to the Philistine city of Gaza and spent the night with a prostitute. ²Word soon spread that Samson was there, so the men of Gaza gathered together and waited all night at the city gates. They kept quiet during the night, saying to themselves, "When the light of morning comes, we will kill him."

³But Samson stayed in bed only until midnight. Then he got up, took hold of the city gates with its two posts, and lifted them, bar and all, right out of the ground. He put them on his shoulders and carried them all the way to the top of the hill across from Hebron.

⁴Later Samson fell in love with a woman named Delilah, who lived in the valley of Sorek. ⁵The leaders of the Philistines went to her and said, "Find out from Samson what makes him so strong and how he can be over- powered and tied up securely. Then each of us will give you eleven hundred pieces of silver."

⁶So Delilah said to Samson, "Please tell me what makes you so strong and what it would take to tie you up securely."

⁷Samson replied, "If I am tied up with seven new bowstrings that have not yet been dried, I will be as weak as anyone else."

⁸So the Philistine leaders brought Delilah seven new bowstrings, and she tied Samson up with them. ⁹She had hidden some men in one of the rooms of her house, and she cried out, "Samson! The Philistines have come to cap- ture you!" But Samson snapped the bowstrings as if they were string that had been burned in a fire. So the secret of his strength was not discovered.

¹⁰Afterward Delilah said to him, "You made fun of me and told me a lie! Now please tell me how you can be tied up securely."

¹¹Samson replied, "If I am tied up with brand-new ropes that have never been used, I will be as weak as anyone else."

¹²So Delilah took new ropes and tied him up with them. The men were hiding in the room as before, and again Delilah cried out, "Samson! The Philistines have come to capture you!" But Samson snapped the ropes from his arms as if they were thread.

¹³Then Delilah said, "You have been making fun of me and telling me lies! Won't you please tell me how you can be tied up securely?"

Samson replied, "If you weave the seven braids of my hair into the fabric on your loom and tighten it with the loom shuttle, I will be as weak as any- one else."

So while he slept, Delilah wove the seven braids of his hair into the fabric ¹⁴and tightened it with the loom shuttle. Again she cried out, "Samson! The Philistines have come to capture you!" But Samson woke up, pulled back the loom shuttle, and yanked his hair away from the loom and the fabric.

¹⁵Then Delilah pouted, "How can you say you love me when you don't confide in me? You've made fun of me three times now, and you still haven't told me what makes you so strong!" ¹⁶So day after day she nagged him until he couldn't stand it any longer.

¹⁷Finally, Samson told her his secret. "My hair has never been cut," he confessed, "for I was dedicated to God as a Nazirite from birth. If my head were shaved, my strength would leave me, and I would become as weak as anyone else."

¹⁸Delilah realized he had finally told her the truth, so she sent for the Philistine leaders. "Come back one more time," she said, "for he has told me everything." So the Philistine leaders returned and brought the money with them. ¹⁹Delilah lulled Samson to sleep with his head in her lap, and she called in a man to shave off his hair, making his capture certain. And his strength left him. ²⁰Then she cried out, "Samson! The Philistines have come to capture you!"

When he woke up, he thought, "I will do as before and shake myself free." But he didn't realize the LORD had left him.

²¹So the Philistines captured him and gouged out his eyes. They took him to Gaza, where he was bound with bronze chains and made to grind grain in the prison.

〰〰 In what situations do you find yourself flirting with disaster?
Samson was deceived because he wanted to believe Delilah's lies. Although he could strangle a lion, he could not smother his burning lust and see Delilah for who she really was. How can you keep your desire for love and sexual pleasure from deceiving you? (1) You must decide what kind of a person you will love *before* passion takes over. Determine whether a person's character and faith in God are as desirable as his or her physical appearance. (2) Since most of the time you spend with your spouse will *not* involve sex, your companion's personality, temperament, and commitment to solve problems must be as gratifying as his or her kisses. (3) Be patient. Wait for time to reveal what is beneath the pleasant appearance and attentive touch.

14 MARCH

Samson's Death
JUDGES 16:22-31

But before long his hair began to grow back.

²³The Philistine leaders held a great festival, offering sacrifices and praising their god, Dagon. They said, "Our god has given us victory over our enemy Samson!"

²⁴When the people saw him, they praised their god, saying, "Our god has delivered our enemy to us! The one who killed so many of us is now in our power!"

²⁵Half drunk by now, the people demanded, "Bring out Samson so he can perform for us!" So he was brought from the prison and made to stand at the center of the temple, between the two pillars supporting the roof. ²⁶Samson said to the servant who was leading him by the hand, "Place my hands against the two pillars. I want to rest against them." ²⁷The temple was completely filled with people. All the Philistine leaders were there, and there were about three thousand on the roof who were watching Samson and making fun of him.

²⁸Then Samson prayed to the LORD, "Sovereign LORD, remember me again. O God, please strengthen me one more time so that I may pay back the Philistines for the loss of my eyes." ²⁹Then Samson put his hands on the center pillars of the temple and pushed against them with all his might. ³⁰"Let me die with the Philistines," he prayed. And the temple crashed down on the Philistine leaders and all the people. So he killed more people when he died than he had during his entire lifetime.

³¹Later his brothers and other relatives went down to get his body. They took him back home and buried him between Zorah and Eshtaol, where his father, Manoah, was buried. Samson had been Israel's judge for twenty years.

〰〰 **How well do you understand God's patience?** In spite of Samson's past, God still answered his prayer and destroyed the heathen temple and worshipers. God still loved him. He was willing to hear Samson's prayer of confession and repentance and use him this final time. Sin in our life keeps us from feeling like praying. But perfect moral behavior is not a condition for prayer. Don't let guilt feelings over sin keep you apart from God. No matter how long you have been away from God, he is ready to hear from you and restore you to a right relationship. Every situation can be salvaged if you are willing to turn again to him. If God could still work in Samson's situation, he can certainly make something worthwhile out of yours.

MARCH 15

Ruth and Naomi: A Friendship
RUTH 1:1-22

In the days when the judges ruled in Israel, a man from Bethlehem in Judah left the country because of a severe famine. He took his wife and two sons and went to live in the country of Moab. ²The man's name was Elimelech, and his wife was Naomi. Their two sons were Mahlon and Kilion. They were Ephrathites from Bethlehem in the land of Judah. During their stay in Moab, ³Elimelech died and Naomi was left with her two sons. ⁴The two sons married Moabite women. One married a woman named Orpah, and the other a woman named Ruth. But about ten years later, ⁵both Mahlon and Kilion died. This left Naomi alone, without her husband or sons.

⁶Then Naomi heard in Moab that the LORD had blessed his people in Judah by giving them good crops again. So Naomi and her daughters-in-law got ready to leave Moab to return to her homeland. ⁷With her two daughters-in-law she set out from the place where she had been living, and they took the road that would lead them back to Judah.

⁸But on the way, Naomi said to her two daughters-in-law, "Go back to your mothers' homes instead of coming with me. And may the LORD reward you for your kindness to your husbands and to me. ⁹May the LORD bless you with the security of another marriage." Then she kissed them good-bye, and they all broke down and wept.

¹⁰"No," they said. "We want to go with you to your people."

¹¹But Naomi replied, "Why should you go on with me? Can I still give birth to other sons who could grow up to be your husbands? ¹²No, my daughters, return to your parents' homes, for I am too old to marry again. And even if it were possible, and I were to get married tonight and bear sons, then what? ¹³Would you wait for them to grow up and refuse to marry someone else? No, of course not, my daughters! Things are far more bitter for me than for you, because the LORD himself has caused me to suffer."

¹⁴And again they wept together, and Orpah kissed her mother-in-law good-bye. But Ruth insisted on staying with Naomi. ¹⁵"See," Naomi said to her, "your sister-in-law has gone back to her people and to her gods. You should do the same."

¹⁶But Ruth replied, "Don't ask me to leave you and turn back. I will go wherever you go and live wherever you live. Your people will be my people, and your God will be my God. ¹⁷I will die where you die and will be buried there. May the LORD punish me severely if I allow anything but death to separate us!" ¹⁸So when Naomi saw that Ruth had made up her mind to go with her, she stopped urging her.

¹⁹So the two of them continued on their journey. When they came to Bethlehem, the entire town was stirred by their arrival. "Is it really Naomi?" the women asked.

²⁰"Don't call me Naomi," she told them. "Instead, call me Mara, for the Almighty has made life very bitter for me. ²¹I went away full, but the LORD has brought me home empty. Why should you call me Naomi when the LORD has caused me to suffer and the Almighty has sent such tragedy?"

²²So Naomi returned from Moab, accompanied by her daughter-in-law Ruth, the young Moabite woman. They arrived in Bethlehem at the beginning of the barley harvest.

〰️〰️ **How do difficulties affect your friendships?** Naomi had experienced severe hardships. She had left Israel married and secure; she returned widowed and poor. Naomi changed her name to express her bitterness and pain. Naomi was not rejecting God by openly expressing her feelings. However, she seems to have lost sight of the tremendous resources she had in her relationship with Ruth and with God. When you face bitter times, God welcomes your honest prayers, but be careful not to overlook the love, strength, and resources that he provides in relationships. And don't allow bitterness and disappointment to blind you to positive opportunities.

Ruth Meets Boaz

RUTH 2:1-23

Now there was a wealthy and influential man in Bethlehem named Boaz, who was a relative of Naomi's husband, Elimelech.

²One day Ruth said to Naomi, "Let me go out into the fields to gather left-over grain behind anyone who will let me do it."

And Naomi said, "All right, my daughter, go ahead." ³So Ruth went out to gather grain behind the harvesters. And as it happened, she found herself working in a field that belonged to Boaz, the relative of her father-in-law, Elimelech.

⁴While she was there, Boaz arrived from Bethlehem and greeted the harvesters. "The LORD be with you!" he said.

"The LORD bless you!" the harvesters replied.

⁵Then Boaz asked his foreman, "Who is that girl over there?"

⁶And the foreman replied, "She is the young woman from Moab who came back with Naomi. ⁷She asked me this morning if she could gather grain behind the harvesters. She has been hard at work ever since, except for a few minutes' rest over there in the shelter."

⁸Boaz went over and said to Ruth, "Listen, my daughter. Stay right here with us when you gather grain; don't go to any other fields. Stay right behind the women working in my field. ⁹See which part of the field they are harvesting, and then follow them. I have warned the young men not to bother you. And when you are thirsty, help yourself to the water they have drawn from the well."

¹⁰Ruth fell at his feet and thanked him warmly. "Why are you being so kind to me?" she asked. "I am only a foreigner."

¹¹"Yes, I know," Boaz replied. "But I also know about the love and kindness you have shown your mother-in-law since the death of your husband. I have heard how you left your father and mother and your own land to live here among complete strangers. ¹²May the LORD, the God of Israel, under whose wings you have come to take refuge, reward you fully."

¹³"I hope I continue to please you, sir," she replied. "You have comforted me by speaking so kindly to me, even though I am not as worthy as your workers."

¹⁴At lunchtime Boaz called to her, "Come over here and help yourself to some of our food. You can dip your bread in the wine if you like." So she sat with his harvesters, and Boaz gave her food—more than she could eat.

¹⁵When Ruth went back to work again, Boaz ordered his young men, "Let her gather grain right among the sheaves without stopping her. ¹⁶And pull out some heads of barley from the bundles and drop them on purpose for her. Let her pick them up, and don't give her a hard time!"

¹⁷So Ruth gathered barley there all day, and when she beat out the grain that evening, it came to about half a bushel. ¹⁸She carried it back into town and showed it to her mother-in-law. Ruth also gave her the food that was left over from her lunch.

¹⁹"So much!" Naomi exclaimed. "Where did you gather all this grain today? Where did you work? May the LORD bless the one who helped you!"

So Ruth told her mother-in-law about the man in whose field she had worked. And she said, "The man I worked with today is named Boaz."

²⁰"May the LORD bless him!" Naomi told her daughter-in-law. "He is showing his kindness to us as well as to your dead husband. That man is one of our closest relatives, one of our family redeemers."

²¹Then Ruth said, "What's more, Boaz even told me to come back and stay with his harvesters until the entire harvest is completed."

²²"This is wonderful!" Naomi exclaimed. "Do as he said. Stay with his workers right through the whole harvest. You will be safe there, unlike in other fields."

²³So Ruth worked alongside the women in Boaz's fields and gathered grain with them until the end of the barley harvest. Then she worked with them through the wheat harvest, too. But all the while she lived with her mother-in-law.

〰〰 **When have you found your reputation to be an advantage?**
Foreigners were not always warmly welcomed in Israel, but Boaz gladly welcomed Ruth because she had gained a reputation for showing kindness and generosity to others. Boaz was so impressed with Ruth that he let her follow directly behind his reapers in order to pick up the choicest grain that was dropped. Ruth's past actions were a report card by which others judged her. Her good reputation was her most valuable asset. It came as a result of her hard work, her strong moral character, and her sensitivity, kindness, and loyalty to Naomi. A good reputation is built upon godly character and kindness toward others. What kind of reputation are you building?

17 MARCH

Ruth Finds a Husband
RUTH 3:1-18

One day Naomi said to Ruth, "My daughter, it's time that I found a permanent home for you, so that you will be provided for. ²Boaz is a close relative of ours, and he's been very kind by letting you gather grain with his workers. Tonight he will be winnowing barley at the threshing floor. ³Now do as

I tell you—take a bath and put on perfume and dress in your nicest clothes. Then go to the threshing floor, but don't let Boaz see you until he has finished his meal. [4]Be sure to notice where he lies down; then go and uncover his feet and lie down there. He will tell you what to do."

[5]"I will do everything you say," Ruth replied. [6]So she went down to the threshing floor that night and followed the instructions of her mother-in-law.

[7]After Boaz had finished his meal and was in good spirits, he lay down beside the heap of grain and went to sleep. Then Ruth came quietly, uncovered his feet, and lay down. [8]Around midnight, Boaz suddenly woke up and turned over. He was surprised to find a woman lying at his feet! [9]"Who are you?" he demanded.

"I am your servant Ruth," she replied. "Spread the corner of your covering over me, for you are my family redeemer."

[10]"The LORD bless you, my daughter!" Boaz exclaimed. "You are showing more family loyalty now than ever by not running after a younger man, whether rich or poor. [11]Now don't worry about a thing, my daughter. I will do what is necessary, for everyone in town knows you are an honorable woman. [12]But there is one problem. While it is true that I am one of your family redeemers, there is another man who is more closely related to you than I am. [13]Stay here tonight, and in the morning I will talk to him. If he is willing to redeem you, then let him marry you. But if he is not willing, then as surely as the LORD lives, I will marry you! Now lie down here until morning."

[14]So Ruth lay at Boaz's feet until the morning, but she got up before it was light enough for people to recognize each other. For Boaz said, "No one must know that a woman was here at the threshing floor." [15]Boaz also said to her, "Bring your cloak and spread it out." He measured out six scoops of barley into the cloak and helped her put it on her back. Then Boaz returned to the town.

[16]When Ruth went back to her mother-in-law, Naomi asked, "What happened, my daughter?"

Ruth told Naomi everything Boaz had done for her, [17]and she added, "He gave me these six scoops of barley and said, 'Don't go back to your mother-in-law empty-handed.' "

[18]Then Naomi said to her, "Just be patient, my daughter, until we hear what happens. The man won't rest until he has followed through on this. He will settle it today."

~∿⌖~ **What unexpected methods has God used in your life?** As a foreigner, Ruth may have thought that Naomi's advice was odd. But Ruth followed her advice because she knew Naomi was kind, trustworthy, and had integrity. Each of us knows a parent, older friend, or relative who is always looking out for our best interests. The experience and knowledge of such a person can be invaluable. Imagine what Ruth's life would have been like had she ignored her mother-in-law. Take care to listen to the advice of trusted people. It may change your life.

18

A Happy Ending
RUTH 4:1-22

So Boaz went to the town gate and took a seat there. When the family redeemer he had mentioned came by, Boaz called out to him, "Come over here, friend. I want to talk to you." So they sat down together. ²Then Boaz called ten leaders from the town and asked them to sit as witnesses. ³And Boaz said to the family redeemer, "You know Naomi, who came back from Moab. She is selling the land that belonged to our relative Elimelech. ⁴I felt that I should speak to you about it so that you can redeem it if you wish. If you want the land, then buy it here in the presence of these witnesses. But if you don't want it, let me know right away, because I am next in line to redeem it after you."

The man replied, "All right, I'll redeem it."

⁵Then Boaz told him, "Of course, your purchase of the land from Naomi also requires that you marry Ruth, the Moabite widow. That way, she can have children who will carry on her husband's name and keep the land in the family."

⁶"Then I can't redeem it," the family redeemer replied, "because this might endanger my own estate. You redeem the land; I cannot do it."

⁷In those days it was the custom in Israel for anyone transferring a right of purchase to remove his sandal and hand it to the other party. This publicly validated the transaction. ⁸So the other family redeemer drew off his sandal as he said to Boaz, "You buy the land."

⁹Then Boaz said to the leaders and to the crowd standing around, "You are witnesses that today I have bought from Naomi all the property of Elimelech, Kilion, and Mahlon. ¹⁰And with the land I have acquired Ruth, the Moabite widow of Mahlon, to be my wife. This way she can have a son to carry on the family name of her dead husband and to inherit the family property here in his hometown. You are all witnesses today."

¹¹Then the leaders and all the people standing there replied, "We are witnesses! May the LORD make the woman who is now coming into your home like Rachel and Leah, from whom all the nation of Israel descended! May you be great in Ephrathah and famous in Bethlehem. ¹²And may the LORD give you descendants by this young woman who will be like those of our ancestor Perez, the son of Tamar and Judah."

¹³So Boaz married Ruth and took her home to live with him. When he slept with her, the LORD enabled her to become pregnant, and she gave birth to a son. ¹⁴And the women of the town said to Naomi, "Praise the LORD who has given you a family redeemer today! May he be famous in Israel. ¹⁵May this child restore your youth and care for you in your old age. For he is the son of your daughter-in-law who loves you so much and who has been better to you than seven sons!"

¹⁶Naomi took care of the baby and cared for him as if he were her own. ¹⁷The neighbor women said, "Now at last Naomi has a son again!" And they named him Obed. He became the father of Jesse and the grandfather of David.

¹⁸This is their family line beginning with their ancestor Perez:

> Perez was the father of Hezron.
> ¹⁹ Hezron was the father of Ram.
> Ram was the father of Amminadab.
> ²⁰ Amminadab was the father of Nahshon.
> Nahshon was the father of Salmon.
> ²¹ Salmon was the father of Boaz.
> Boaz was the father of Obed.
> ²² Obed was the father of Jesse.
> Jesse was the father of David.

〰〰 What future reasons could there be for obeying God today?
God brought great blessings out of Naomi's tragedy, even greater blessings than "seven sons" (indicating the great blessing of an abundance of heirs). Throughout her tough times, Naomi continued to trust God. And God, in his time, blessed her greatly. Even in our sorrow and calamity, God can bring great blessings. Be like Naomi, and don't turn your back on God when tragedy strikes. Don't ask, "How can God allow this to happen to me?" Instead, trust him. He will be with you even in the hard times.

MARCH **19**

A Serious Prayer
1 SAMUEL 1:1-28

There was a man named Elkanah who lived in Ramah in the hill country of Ephraim. He was the son of Jeroham and grandson of Elihu, from the family of Tohu and the clan of Zuph. ²Elkanah had two wives, Hannah and Peninnah. Peninnah had children, while Hannah did not.

³Each year Elkanah and his family would travel to Shiloh to worship and sacrifice to the LORD Almighty at the Tabernacle. The priests of the LORD at that time were the two sons of Eli—Hophni and Phinehas. ⁴On the day Elkanah presented his sacrifice, he would give portions of the sacrifice to Peninnah and each of her children. ⁵But he gave Hannah a special portion because he loved her very much, even though the LORD had given her no children. ⁶But Peninnah made fun of Hannah because the LORD had closed her womb. ⁷Year after year it was the same—Peninnah would taunt Hannah as they went to the Tabernacle. Hannah would finally be reduced to tears and would not even eat.

⁸"What's the matter, Hannah?" Elkanah would ask. "Why aren't you

eating? Why be so sad just because you have no children? You have me—isn't that better than having ten sons?"

⁹Once when they were at Shiloh, Hannah went over to the Tabernacle after supper to pray to the LORD. Eli the priest was sitting at his customary place beside the entrance. ¹⁰Hannah was in deep anguish, crying bitterly as she prayed to the LORD. ¹¹And she made this vow: "O LORD Almighty, if you will look down upon my sorrow and answer my prayer and give me a son, then I will give him back to you. He will be yours for his entire lifetime, and as a sign that he has been dedicated to the LORD, his hair will never be cut."

¹²As she was praying to the LORD, Eli watched her. ¹³Seeing her lips moving but hearing no sound, he thought she had been drinking. ¹⁴"Must you come here drunk?" he demanded. "Throw away your wine!"

¹⁵"Oh no, sir!" she replied, "I'm not drunk! But I am very sad, and I was pouring out my heart to the LORD. ¹⁶Please don't think I am a wicked woman! For I have been praying out of great anguish and sorrow."

¹⁷"In that case," Eli said, "cheer up! May the God of Israel grant the request you have asked of him."

¹⁸"Oh, thank you, sir!" she exclaimed. Then she went back and began to eat again, and she was no longer sad.

¹⁹The entire family got up early the next morning and went to worship the LORD once more. Then they returned home to Ramah. When Elkanah slept with Hannah, the LORD remembered her request, ²⁰and in due time she gave birth to a son. She named him Samuel, for she said, "I asked the LORD for him."

²¹The next year Elkanah, Peninnah, and their children went on their annual trip to offer a sacrifice to the LORD. ²²But Hannah did not go. She told her husband, "Wait until the baby is weaned. Then I will take him to the Tabernacle and leave him there with the LORD permanently."

²³"Whatever you think is best," Elkanah agreed. "Stay here for now, and may the LORD help you keep your promise." So she stayed home and nursed the baby.

²⁴When the child was weaned, Hannah took him to the Tabernacle in Shiloh. They brought along a three-year-old bull for the sacrifice and half a bushel of flour and some wine. ²⁵After sacrificing the bull, they took the child to Eli. ²⁶"Sir, do you remember me?" Hannah asked. "I am the woman who stood here several years ago praying to the LORD. ²⁷I asked the LORD to give me this child, and he has given me my request. ²⁸Now I am giving him to the LORD, and he will belong to the LORD his whole life." And they worshiped the LORD there.

〰️✓ **What promises have you made to God lately that you have kept?** Be careful what you promise in prayer because God may take you up on it. Hannah so desperately wanted a child that she was willing to strike a bargain with God. God took her up on her promise, and, to Hannah's credit, she did her part, even though it was painful. Although we are not in a position to barter with

God, he may choose to answer a prayer that has an attached promise. When you pray, ask yourself, Will I follow through on any promises I make to God if he grants my request? It is dishonest and dangerous to ignore a promise, especially to God. God keeps his promises, and he expects you to keep yours.

God Calls Samuel

1 SAMUEL 3:1–4:1

Meanwhile, the boy Samuel was serving the LORD by assisting Eli. Now in those days messages from the LORD were very rare, and visions were quite uncommon. ²One night Eli, who was almost blind by now, had just gone to bed. ³The lamp of God had not yet gone out, and Samuel was sleeping in the Tabernacle near the Ark of God. ⁴Suddenly, the LORD called out, "Samuel! Samuel!"

"Yes?" Samuel replied. "What is it?" ⁵He jumped up and ran to Eli. "Here I am. What do you need?"

"I didn't call you," Eli replied. "Go on back to bed." So he did.

⁶Then the LORD called out again, "Samuel!"

Again Samuel jumped up and ran to Eli. "Here I am," he said. "What do you need?"

"I didn't call you, my son," Eli said. "Go on back to bed."

⁷Samuel did not yet know the LORD because he had never had a message from the LORD before. ⁸So now the LORD called a third time, and once more Samuel jumped up and ran to Eli. "Here I am," he said. "What do you need?"

Then Eli realized it was the LORD who was calling the boy. ⁹So he said to Samuel, "Go and lie down again, and if someone calls again, say, 'Yes, LORD, your servant is listening.' " So Samuel went back to bed.

¹⁰And the LORD came and called as before, "Samuel! Samuel!"

And Samuel replied, "Yes, your servant is listening."

¹¹Then the LORD said to Samuel, "I am about to do a shocking thing in Israel. ¹²I am going to carry out all my threats against Eli and his family. ¹³I have warned him continually that judgment is coming for his family, because his sons are blaspheming God and he hasn't disciplined them. ¹⁴So I have vowed that the sins of Eli and his sons will never be forgiven by sacrifices or offerings."

¹⁵Samuel stayed in bed until morning, then got up and opened the doors of the Tabernacle as usual. He was afraid to tell Eli what the LORD had said to him. ¹⁶But Eli called out to him, "Samuel, my son."

"Here I am," Samuel replied.

¹⁷"What did the LORD say to you? Tell me everything. And may God punish you if you hide anything from me!" ¹⁸So Samuel told Eli everything; he

didn't hold anything back. "It is the LORD's will," Eli replied. "Let him do what he thinks best."

¹⁹As Samuel grew up, the LORD was with him, and everything Samuel said was wise and helpful. ²⁰All the people of Israel from one end of the land to the other knew that Samuel was confirmed as a prophet of the LORD. ²¹The LORD continued to appear at Shiloh and gave messages to Samuel there at the Tabernacle. ⁴:¹And Samuel's words went out to all the people of Israel.

〰〽〟 **When you read God's Word, what do you expect him to say to you?** Although this was a time when God still gave direct and audible messages to his people, such messages became rare in the days of Eli. Why? Look at the attitude of Eli's sons. They either refused to listen to God or allowed greed to get in the way of any communication with him. Listening and responding is vital in a relationship with God. Although God may not use the sound of a human voice, he speaks just as clearly today through his Word. To receive his messages, we must be ready to listen and to act upon what he tells us. Like Samuel, be ready to say, "Yes, I'm listening" when God speaks to you.

MARCH

Samuel's Disappointing Sons

1 SAMUEL 8:1-5

As Samuel grew old, he appointed his sons to be judges over Israel. ²Joel and Abijah, his oldest sons, held court in Beersheba. ³But they were not like their father, for they were greedy for money. They accepted bribes and perverted justice.

⁴Finally, the leaders of Israel met at Ramah to discuss the matter with Samuel. ⁵"Look," they told him, "you are now old, and your sons are not like you. Give us a king like all the other nations have."

〰〽〟 **What positive lessons have you learned from others' mistakes?** Israel wanted a king for several reasons: (1) Samuel's sons were not fit to lead Israel. (2) It was hoped that a king would unite the tribes into one nation and one army. (3) The people wanted to be like the neighboring nations. This is exactly what God didn't want. Having a king would make it easy to forget that God was their real leader. We cannot ask God to lead our personal life if we continue to live by the world's standards and values, for God requires obedience. Faith in God must touch all the practical areas of our life. Is God the leader of your life?

The People Want a King

1 SAMUEL 8:6-22

Samuel was very upset with their request and went to the LORD for advice. [7]"Do as they say," the LORD replied, "for it is me they are rejecting, not you. They don't want me to be their king any longer. [8]Ever since I brought them from Egypt they have continually forsaken me and followed other gods. And now they are giving you the same treatment. [9]Do as they ask, but solemnly warn them about how a king will treat them."

[10]So Samuel passed on the LORD's warning to the people. [11]"This is how a king will treat you," Samuel said. "The king will draft your sons into his army and make them run before his chariots. [12]Some will be commanders of his troops, while others will be slave laborers. Some will be forced to plow in his fields and harvest his crops, while others will make his weapons and chariot equipment. [13]The king will take your daughters from you and force them to cook and bake and make perfumes for him. [14]He will take away the best of your fields and vineyards and olive groves and give them to his own servants. [15]He will take a tenth of your harvest and distribute it among his officers and attendants. [16]He will want your male and female slaves and demand the finest of your cattle and donkeys for his own use. [17]He will demand a tenth of your flocks, and you will be his slaves. [18]When that day comes, you will beg for relief from this king you are demanding, but the LORD will not help you."

[19]But the people refused to listen to Samuel's warning. "Even so, we still want a king," they said. [20]"We want to be like the nations around us. Our king will govern us and lead us into battle."

[21]So Samuel told the LORD what the people had said, [22]and the LORD replied, "Do as they say, and give them a king." Then Samuel agreed and sent the people home.

〰〰 **What has God taught you about being responsible for your own choices?** Samuel carefully explained all the negative consequences of having a king, but the Israelites refused to listen. When you have an important decision to make, weigh the positives and negatives carefully, considering everyone who might be affected by your choice. When you want something badly enough, it is difficult to see the potential negative consequences. But don't discount the negatives. Unless you have a plan to handle each one, they will cause you great difficulty later.

23

MARCH

Saul and the Lost Donkeys

1 SAMUEL 9:1-21

Kish was a rich, influential man from the tribe of Benjamin. He was the son of Abiel and grandson of Zeror, from the family of Becorath and the clan of Aphiah. ²His son Saul was the most handsome man in Israel—head and shoulders taller than anyone else in the land.

³One day Kish's donkeys strayed away, and he told Saul, "Take a servant with you, and go look for them." ⁴So Saul took one of his servants and traveled all through the hill country of Ephraim, the land of Shalishah, the Shaalim area, and the entire land of Benjamin, but they couldn't find the donkeys anywhere. ⁵Finally, they entered the region of Zuph, and Saul said to his servant, "Let's go home. By now my father will be more worried about us than about the donkeys!"

⁶But the servant said, "I've just thought of something! There is a man of God who lives here in this town. He is held in high honor by all the people because everything he says comes true. Let's go find him. Perhaps he can tell us which way to go."

⁷"But we don't have anything to offer him," Saul replied. "Even our food is gone, and we don't have a thing to give him."

⁸"Well," the servant said, "I have one small silver piece. We can at least offer it to him and see what happens!" ⁹(In those days if people wanted a message from God, they would say, "Let's go and ask the seer," for prophets used to be called seers.)

¹⁰"All right," Saul agreed, "let's try it!" So they started into the town where the man of God was.

¹¹As they were climbing a hill toward the town, they met some young women coming out to draw water. So Saul and his servant asked, "Is the seer here today?"

¹²"Yes," they replied. "Stay right on this road. He is at the town gates. He has just arrived to take part in a public sacrifice up on the hill. ¹³Hurry and catch him before he goes up the hill to eat. The guests won't start until he arrives to bless the food."

¹⁴So they entered the town, and as they passed through the gates, Samuel was coming out toward them to climb the hill. ¹⁵Now the LORD had told Samuel the previous day, ¹⁶"About this time tomorrow I will send you a man from the land of Benjamin. Anoint him to be the leader of my people, Israel. He will rescue them from the Philistines, for I have looked down on my people in mercy and have heard their cry."

¹⁷When Samuel noticed Saul, the LORD said, "That's the man I told you about! He will rule my people."

¹⁸Just then Saul approached Samuel at the gateway and asked, "Can you please tell me where the seer's house is?"

¹⁹"I am the seer!" Samuel replied. "Go on up the hill ahead of me to the place of sacrifice, and we'll eat there together. In the morning I will tell you what you want to know and send you on your way. ²⁰And don't worry about those donkeys that were lost three days ago, for they have been found. And I am here to tell you that you and your family are the focus of all Israel's hopes."

²¹Saul replied, "But I'm only from Benjamin, the smallest tribe in Israel, and my family is the least important of all the families of that tribe! Why are you talking like this to me?"

~\/~ **What is God's part in your daily decisions?** Often we think that events just happen to us, but as we learn from this story about Saul, God may use common occurrences to lead us where he wants. It is important to evaluate all situations as potential "divine appointments" designed to shape our life. Think of all the good and bad circumstances that have affected you lately. Can you see God's purpose in them? Perhaps he is building a certain quality in you or leading you to serve him in a new area.

MARCH **24**

Saul Becomes King

1 SAMUEL 10:1-27

Then Samuel took a flask of olive oil and poured it over Saul's head. He kissed Saul on the cheek and said, "I am doing this because the LORD has appointed you to be the leader of his people Israel. ²When you leave me today, you will see two men beside Rachel's tomb at Zelzah, on the border of Benjamin. They will tell you that the donkeys have been found and that your father is worried about you and is asking, 'Have you seen my son?'

³"When you get to the oak of Tabor, you will see three men coming toward you who are on their way to worship God at Bethel. One will be bringing three young goats, another will have three loaves of bread, and the third will be carrying a skin of wine. ⁴They will greet you and offer you two of the loaves, which you are to accept.

⁵"When you arrive at Gibeah of God, where the garrison of the Philistines is located, you will meet a band of prophets coming down from the altar on the hill. They will be playing a harp, a tambourine, a flute, and a lyre, and they will be prophesying. ⁶At that time the Spirit of the LORD will come upon you with power, and you will prophesy with them. You will be changed into a different person. ⁷After these signs take place, do whatever you think is best, for God will be with you. ⁸Then go down to Gilgal ahead of me and wait for me there seven days. I will join you there to sacrifice burnt offerings and peace offerings. When I arrive, I will give you further instructions."

⁹As Saul turned and started to leave, God changed his heart, and all Sam-

uel's signs were fulfilled that day. [10]When Saul and his servant arrived at Gibeah, they saw the prophets coming toward them. Then the Spirit of God came upon Saul, and he, too, began to prophesy. [11]When his friends heard about it, they exclaimed, "What? Is Saul a prophet? How did the son of Kish become a prophet?" [12]But one of the neighbors responded, "It doesn't matter who his father is; anyone can become a prophet." So that is the origin of the saying "Is Saul a prophet?"

[13]When Saul had finished prophesying, he climbed the hill to the altar. [14]"Where in the world have you been?" Saul's uncle asked him.

"We went to look for the donkeys," Saul replied, "but we couldn't find them. So we went to the prophet Samuel to ask him where they were."

[15]"Oh? And what did he say?" his uncle asked.

[16]"He said the donkeys had been found," Saul replied. But Saul didn't tell his uncle that Samuel had anointed him to be king.

[17]Later Samuel called all the people of Israel to meet before the LORD at Mizpah. [18]And he gave them this message from the LORD, the God of Israel: "I brought you from Egypt and rescued you from the Egyptians and from all of the nations that were oppressing you. [19]But though I have done so much for you, you have rejected me and said, 'We want a king instead!' Now, therefore, present yourselves before the LORD by tribes and clans."

[20]So Samuel called the tribal leaders together before the LORD, and the tribe of Benjamin was chosen. [21]Then he brought each family of the tribe of Benjamin before the LORD, and the family of the Matrites was chosen. And finally Saul son of Kish was chosen from among them. But when they looked for him, he had disappeared! [22]So they asked the LORD, "Where is he?"

And the LORD replied, "He is hiding among the baggage." [23]So they found him and brought him out, and he stood head and shoulders above anyone else.

[24]Then Samuel said to all the people, "This is the man the LORD has chosen as your king. No one in all Israel is his equal!"

And all the people shouted, "Long live the king!"

[25]Then Samuel told the people what the rights and duties of a king were. He wrote them down on a scroll and placed it before the LORD. Then Samuel sent the people home again.

[26]When Saul returned to his home at Gibeah, a band of men whose hearts God had touched became his constant companions. [27]But there were some wicked men who complained, "How can this man save us?" And they despised him and refused to bring him gifts. But Saul ignored them.

How do you evaluate people? Saul, who not long before was a farmer searching for donkeys, was now king. Although he was tall, handsome, and wealthy, it is surprising that he was God's choice to be king since he was not a deeply religious man. But God does not choose people according to our expectations. He may not even choose the one best qualified for the task but rather the one who will fulfill his larger purpose. Sometimes this means allowing a poor leader to be selected to teach people a valuable lesson. God may want to use you for a great work, or he may choose someone else who seems less fit. In either case, try to look for God's greater purpose.

A Son to Make a
Father Proud

1 SAMUEL 14:1-23

One day Jonathan said to the young man who carried his armor, "Come on, let's go over to where the Philistines have their outpost." But Jonathan did not tell his father what he was doing. ²Meanwhile, Saul and his six hundred men were camped on the outskirts of Gibeah, around the pomegranate tree at Migron. ³(Among Saul's men was Ahijah the priest, who was wearing the linen ephod. Ahijah was the son of Ahitub, Ichabod's brother. Ahitub was the son of Phinehas and the grandson of Eli, the priest of the LORD who had served at Shiloh.)

No one realized that Jonathan had left the Israelite camp. ⁴To reach the Philistine outpost, Jonathan had to go down between two rocky cliffs that were called Bozez and Seneh. ⁵The cliff on the north was in front of Micmash, and the one on the south was in front of Geba. ⁶"Let's go across to see those pagans," Jonathan said to his armor bearer. "Perhaps the LORD will help us, for nothing can hinder the LORD. He can win a battle whether he has many warriors or only a few!"

⁷"Do what you think is best," the youth replied. "I'm with you completely, whatever you decide."

⁸"All right then," Jonathan told him. "We will cross over and let them see us. ⁹If they say to us, 'Stay where you are or we'll kill you,' then we will stop and not go up to them. ¹⁰But if they say, 'Come on up and fight,' then we will go up. That will be the LORD's sign that he will help us defeat them."

¹¹When the Philistines saw them coming, they shouted, "Look! The Hebrews are crawling out of their holes!" ¹²Then they shouted to Jonathan, "Come on up here, and we'll teach you a lesson!"

"Come on, climb right behind me," Jonathan said to his armor bearer, "for the LORD will help us defeat them!" ¹³So they climbed up using both hands and feet, and the Philistines fell back as Jonathan and his armor bearer killed them right and left. ¹⁴They killed about twenty men in all, and their bodies were scattered over about half an acre. ¹⁵Suddenly, panic broke out in the Philistine army, both in the camp and in the field, including even the outposts and raiding parties. And just then an earthquake struck, and everyone was terrified.

¹⁶Saul's lookouts in Gibeah saw a strange sight—the vast army of Philistines began to melt away in every direction. ¹⁷"Find out who isn't here,"

Saul ordered. And when they checked, they found that Jonathan and his armor bearer were gone. [18]Then Saul shouted to Ahijah, "Bring the ephod here!" For at that time Ahijah was wearing the ephod in front of the Israelites. [19]But while Saul was talking to the priest, the shouting and confusion in the Philistine camp grew louder and louder. So Saul said to Ahijah, "Never mind; let's get going!"

[20]Then Saul and his six hundred men rushed out to the battle and found the Philistines killing each other. There was terrible confusion everywhere. [21]Even the Hebrews who had gone over to the Philistine army revolted and joined in with Saul, Jonathan, and the rest of the Israelites. [22]Likewise, the men who were hiding in the hills joined the chase when they saw the Philistines running away. [23]So the LORD saved Israel that day, and the battle continued to rage even out beyond Beth-aven.

What would it mean to have a friend like Jonathan? Jonathan and his bodyguard weren't much of a force to attack the huge Philistine army. But while everyone else was afraid, they trusted God, knowing that the size of the enemy army had no relationship to God's ability to help them. God honored the faith and brave action of these two men with a tremendous victory. Have you ever felt surrounded by the "enemy" or faced overwhelming odds? God is never intimidated by the size of the enemy or the complexity of a problem. With him, there are always enough resources to resist the pressures and win your battles. If God has called you to action, then bravely commit what few resources you have to God and rely upon him to give you the victory.

MARCH

Samuel Appoints David

1 SAMUEL 16:1-13

Finally, the LORD said to Samuel, "You have mourned long enough for Saul. I have rejected him as king of Israel. Now fill your horn with olive oil and go to Bethlehem. Find a man named Jesse who lives there, for I have selected one of his sons to be my new king."

[2]But Samuel asked, "How can I do that? If Saul hears about it, he will kill me."

"Take a heifer with you," the LORD replied, "and say that you have come to make a sacrifice to the LORD. [3]Invite Jesse to the sacrifice, and I will show you which of his sons to anoint for me."

[4]So Samuel did as the LORD instructed him. When he arrived at Bethlehem, the leaders of the town became afraid. "What's wrong?" they asked. "Do you come in peace?"

[5]"Yes," Samuel replied. "I have come to sacrifice to the LORD. Purify yourselves and come with me to the sacrifice." Then Samuel performed the purification rite for Jesse and his sons and invited them, too.

⁶When they arrived, Samuel took one look at Eliab and thought, "Surely this is the LORD's anointed!" ⁷But the LORD said to Samuel, "Don't judge by his appearance or height, for I have rejected him. The LORD doesn't make decisions the way you do! People judge by outward appearance, but the LORD looks at a person's thoughts and intentions."

⁸Then Jesse told his son Abinadab to step forward and walk in front of Samuel. But Samuel said, "This is not the one the LORD has chosen." ⁹Next Jesse summoned Shammah, but Samuel said, "Neither is this the one the LORD has chosen." ¹⁰In the same way all seven of Jesse's sons were presented to Samuel. But Samuel said to Jesse, "The LORD has not chosen any of these." ¹¹Then Samuel asked, "Are these all the sons you have?"

"There is still the youngest," Jesse replied. "But he's out in the fields watching the sheep."

"Send for him at once," Samuel said. "We will not sit down to eat until he arrives."

¹²So Jesse sent for him. He was ruddy and handsome, with pleasant eyes. And the LORD said, "This is the one; anoint him."

¹³So as David stood there among his brothers, Samuel took the olive oil he had brought and poured it on David's head. And the Spirit of the LORD came mightily upon him from that day on. Then Samuel returned to Ramah.

〰〰 **What do you appreciate in people other than perhaps their looks?** Saul was tall and handsome; he was an impressive-looking man. Samuel may have been trying to find someone who looked like Saul to be Israel's next king, but God warned him against judging by appearance alone. Appearance doesn't reveal what people are really like or their true value. Fortunately, God judges by character, not appearance. And because only God can see on the inside, only he can accurately judge people. We spend hours each week maintaining our outward appearance, while we should be spending time developing our inner character. While everyone can see your face, only you and God know what your heart really looks like. Which is the more attractive part of you?

David and Goliath's Challenge

MARCH **27**

1 SAMUEL 17:1-31

The Philistines now mustered their army for battle and camped between Socoh in Judah and Azekah at Ephes-dammim. ²Saul countered by gathering his troops near the valley of Elah. ³So the Philistines and Israelites faced each other on opposite hills, with the valley between them.

⁴Then Goliath, a Philistine champion from Gath, came out of the Philistine ranks to face the forces of Israel. He was a giant of a man, measuring

over nine feet tall! [5]He wore a bronze helmet and a coat of mail that weighed 125 pounds. [6]He also wore bronze leggings, and he slung a bronze javelin over his back. [7]The shaft of his spear was as heavy and thick as a weaver's beam, tipped with an iron spearhead that weighed fifteen pounds. An armor bearer walked ahead of him carrying a huge shield.

[8]Goliath stood and shouted across to the Israelites, "Do you need a whole army to settle this? Choose someone to fight for you, and I will represent the Philistines. We will settle this dispute in single combat! [9]If your man is able to kill me, then we will be your slaves. But if I kill him, you will be our slaves! [10]I defy the armies of Israel! Send me a man who will fight with me!" [11]When Saul and the Israelites heard this, they were terrified and deeply shaken.

[12]Now David was the son of a man named Jesse, an Ephrathite from Bethlehem in the land of Judah. Jesse was an old man at that time, and he had eight sons in all. [13]Jesse's three oldest sons—Eliab, Abinadab, and Shammah—had already joined Saul's army to fight the Philistines. [14]David was the youngest of Jesse's sons. Since David's three oldest brothers were in the army, they stayed with Saul's forces all the time. [15]But David went back and forth between working for Saul and helping his father with the sheep in Bethlehem.

[16]For forty days, twice a day, morning and evening, the Philistine giant strutted in front of the Israelite army.

[17]One day Jesse said to David, "Take this half-bushel of roasted grain and these ten loaves of bread to your brothers. [18]And give these ten cuts of cheese to their captain. See how your brothers are getting along, and bring me back a letter from them."

[19]David's brothers were with Saul and the Israelite army at the valley of Elah, fighting against the Philistines. [20]So David left the sheep with another shepherd and set out early the next morning with the gifts. He arrived at the outskirts of the camp just as the Israelite army was leaving for the battlefield with shouts and battle cries. [21]Soon the Israelite and Philistine forces stood facing each other, army against army. [22]David left his things with the keeper of supplies and hurried out to the ranks to greet his brothers. [23]As he was talking with them, he saw Goliath, the champion from Gath, come out from the Philistine ranks, shouting his challenge to the army of Israel.

[24]As soon as the Israelite army saw him, they began to run away in fright. [25]"Have you seen the giant?" the men were asking. "He comes out each day to challenge Israel. And have you heard about the huge reward the king has offered to anyone who kills him? The king will give him one of his daughters for a wife, and his whole family will be exempted from paying taxes!"

[26]David talked to some others standing there to verify the report. "What will a man get for killing this Philistine and putting an end to his abuse of Israel?" he asked them. "Who is this pagan Philistine anyway, that he is allowed to defy the armies of the living God?" [27]And David received the

same reply as before: "What you have been hearing is true. That is the reward for killing the giant."

²⁸But when David's oldest brother, Eliab, heard David talking to the men, he was angry. "What are you doing around here anyway?" he demanded. "What about those few sheep you're supposed to be taking care of? I know about your pride and dishonesty. You just want to see the battle!"

²⁹"What have I done now?" David replied. "I was only asking a question!" ³⁰He walked over to some others and asked them the same thing and received the same answer. ³¹Then David's question was reported to King Saul, and the king sent for him.

〜∿⌇ **How does your confidence in God affect your decision to accept challenges?** What a difference perspective can make. Saul saw only a giant and a young boy. David, however, saw a mortal man defying almighty God. He knew he would not be alone when he faced Goliath; God would fight for him. He looked at his situation from God's point of view. Viewing impossible situations from God's point of view helps us to put giant problems in perspective.

MARCH 28

David Kills Goliath
1 SAMUEL 17:32-58

"Don't worry about a thing," David told Saul. "I'll go fight this Philistine!"

³³"Don't be ridiculous!" Saul replied. "There is no way you can go against this Philistine. You are only a boy, and he has been in the army since he was a boy!"

³⁴But David persisted. "I have been taking care of my father's sheep," he said. "When a lion or a bear comes to steal a lamb from the flock, ³⁵I go after it with a club and take the lamb from its mouth. If the animal turns on me, I catch it by the jaw and club it to death. ³⁶I have done this to both lions and bears, and I'll do it to this pagan Philistine, too, for he has defied the armies of the living God! ³⁷The LORD who saved me from the claws of the lion and the bear will save me from this Philistine!"

Saul finally consented. "All right, go ahead," he said. "And may the LORD be with you!"

³⁸Then Saul gave David his own armor—a bronze helmet and a coat of mail. ³⁹David put it on, strapped the sword over it, and took a step or two to see what it was like, for he had never worn such things before. "I can't go in these," he protested. "I'm not used to them." So he took them off again. ⁴⁰He picked up five smooth stones from a stream and put them in his shepherd's bag. Then, armed only with his shepherd's staff and sling, he started across to fight Goliath.

⁴¹Goliath walked out toward David with his shield bearer ahead of him, ⁴²sneering in contempt at this ruddy-faced boy. ⁴³"Am I a dog," he roared at

David, "that you come at me with a stick?" And he cursed David by the names of his gods. ⁴⁴"Come over here, and I'll give your flesh to the birds and wild animals!" Goliath yelled.

⁴⁵David shouted in reply, "You come to me with sword, spear, and javelin, but I come to you in the name of the LORD Almighty—the God of the armies of Israel, whom you have defied. ⁴⁶Today the LORD will conquer you, and I will kill you and cut off your head. And then I will give the dead bodies of your men to the birds and wild animals, and the whole world will know that there is a God in Israel! ⁴⁷And everyone will know that the LORD does not need weapons to rescue his people. It is his battle, not ours. The LORD will give you to us!"

⁴⁸As Goliath moved closer to attack, David quickly ran out to meet him. ⁴⁹Reaching into his shepherd's bag and taking out a stone, he hurled it from his sling and hit the Philistine in the forehead. The stone sank in, and Goliath stumbled and fell face downward to the ground. ⁵⁰So David triumphed over the Philistine giant with only a stone and sling. And since he had no sword, ⁵¹he ran over and pulled Goliath's sword from its sheath. David used it to kill the giant and cut off his head.

When the Philistines saw that their champion was dead, they turned and ran. ⁵²Then the Israelites gave a great shout of triumph and rushed after the Philistines, chasing them as far as Gath and the gates of Ekron. The bodies of the dead and wounded Philistines were strewn all along the road from Shaaraim, as far as Gath and Ekron. ⁵³Then the Israelite army returned and plundered the deserted Philistine camp. ⁵⁴(David took Goliath's head to Jerusalem, but he stored the Philistine's armor in his own tent.)

⁵⁵As Saul watched David go out to fight Goliath, he asked Abner, the general of his army, "Abner, whose son is he?"

"I really don't know," Abner said.

⁵⁶"Well, find out!" the king told him.

⁵⁷After David had killed Goliath, Abner brought him to Saul with the Philistine's head still in his hand. ⁵⁸"Tell me about your father, my boy," Saul said.

And David replied, "His name is Jesse, and we live in Bethlehem."

~√∠ **What "giants" need to be defeated in your life?** Criticism couldn't stop David. While the rest of the army stood around, he knew the importance of taking action. With God to fight for him, there was no reason to wait. People may try to discourage you with negative comments or mockery, but continue to do what you know is right. By doing what is right, you will be pleasing God, whose opinion matters most.

Trouble between Saul and David

1 SAMUEL 18:1-30

After David had finished talking with Saul, he met Jonathan, the king's son. There was an immediate bond of love between them, and they became the best of friends. ²From that day on Saul kept David with him at the palace and wouldn't let him return home. ³And Jonathan made a special vow to be David's friend, ⁴and he sealed the pact by giving him his robe, tunic, sword, bow, and belt.

⁵Whatever Saul asked David to do, David did it successfully. So Saul made him a commander in his army, an appointment that was applauded by the fighting men and officers alike. ⁶But something happened when the victorious Israelite army was returning home after David had killed Goliath. Women came out from all the towns along the way to celebrate and to cheer for King Saul, and they sang and danced for joy with tambourines and cymbals. ⁷This was their song:

> "Saul has killed his thousands,
> and David his ten thousands!"

⁸This made Saul very angry. "What's this?" he said. "They credit David with ten thousands and me with only thousands. Next they'll be making him their king!" ⁹So from that time on Saul kept a jealous eye on David.

¹⁰The very next day, in fact, a tormenting spirit from God overwhelmed Saul, and he began to rave like a madman. David began to play the harp, as he did whenever this happened. But Saul, who had a spear in his hand, ¹¹suddenly hurled it at David, intending to pin him to the wall. But David jumped aside and escaped. This happened another time, too, ¹²for Saul was afraid of him, and he was jealous because the LORD had left him and was now with David. ¹³Finally, Saul banned him from his presence and appointed him commander over only a thousand men, but David faithfully led his troops into battle.

¹⁴David continued to succeed in everything he did, for the LORD was with him. ¹⁵When Saul recognized this, he became even more afraid of him. ¹⁶But all Israel and Judah loved David because he was so successful at leading his troops into battle.

¹⁷One day Saul said to David, "I am ready to give you my older daughter, Merab, as your wife. But first you must prove yourself to be a real warrior by fighting the LORD's battles." For Saul thought to himself, "I'll send him out against the Philistines and let them kill him rather than doing it myself."

¹⁸"Who am I, and what is my family in Israel that I should be the king's son-in-law?" David exclaimed. "My father's family is nothing!" ¹⁹So when the time came for the wedding, Saul gave Merab in marriage to Adriel, a man from Meholah.

²⁰In the meantime, Saul's daughter Michal had fallen in love with David, and Saul was delighted when he heard about it. ²¹"Here's another chance to see him killed by the Philistines!" Saul said to himself. But to David he said, "I have a way for you to become my son-in-law after all!"

²²Then Saul told his men to say confidentially to David, "The king really likes you, and so do we. Why don't you accept the king's offer and become his son-in-law?"

²³When Saul's men said these things to David, he replied, "How can a poor man from a humble family afford the bride price for the daughter of a king?"

²⁴When Saul's men reported this back to the king, ²⁵he told them, "Tell David that all I want for the bride price is one hundred Philistine foreskins! Vengeance on my enemies is all I really want." But what Saul had in mind was that David would be killed in the fight.

²⁶David was delighted to accept the offer. So before the time limit expired, ²⁷he and his men went out and killed two hundred Philistines and presented all their foreskins to the king. So Saul gave Michal to David to be his wife.

²⁸When the king realized how much the LORD was with David and how much Michal loved him, ²⁹he became even more afraid of him, and he remained David's enemy for the rest of his life. ³⁰Whenever the Philistine army attacked, David was more successful against them than all the rest of Saul's officers. So David's name became very famous throughout the land.

〰️〰️ **How do you treat your friends who succeed?** When David and Jonathan met, they became close friends at once. Their friendship is one of the deepest and closest recorded in the Bible because they (1) based their friendship on commitment to God, not just each other; (2) let nothing come between them, not even career or family problems; (3) drew closer together when their friendship was tested; and (4) were able to remain friends to the end. Jonathan, the prince of Israel, later realized that David, and not he, would be king (1 Sam. 23:17). But that did not weaken his love for David. Jonathan would much rather lose the throne of Israel than his closest friend. Think about your friendships. On what are they based? How do you show your friends how much you care about them?

30

David and Jonathan
1 SAMUEL 20:1-42

David now fled from Naioth in Ramah and found Jonathan. "What have I done?" he exclaimed. "What is my crime? How have I offended your father that he is so determined to kill me?"

²"That's not true!" Jonathan protested. "I'm sure he's not planning any such thing, for he always tells me everything he's going to do, even the little

things. I know he wouldn't hide something like this from me. It just isn't so!"

³Then David took an oath before Jonathan and said, "Your father knows perfectly well about our friendship, so he has said to himself, 'I won't tell Jonathan—why should I hurt him?' But I swear to you that I am only a step away from death! I swear it by the LORD and by your own soul!"

⁴"Tell me what I can do!" Jonathan exclaimed.

⁵David replied, "Tomorrow we celebrate the new moon festival. I've always eaten with your father on this occasion, but tomorrow I'll hide in the field and stay there until the evening of the third day. ⁶If your father asks where I am, tell him I asked permission to go home to Bethlehem for an annual family sacrifice. ⁷If he says, 'Fine!' then you will know all is well. But if he is angry and loses his temper, then you will know he was planning to kill me. ⁸Show me this kindness as my sworn friend—for we made a covenant together before the LORD—or kill me yourself if I have sinned against your father. But please don't betray me to him!"

⁹"Never!" Jonathan exclaimed. "You know that if I had the slightest notion my father was planning to kill you, I would tell you at once."

¹⁰Then David asked, "How will I know whether or not your father is angry?"

¹¹"Come out to the field with me," Jonathan replied. And they went out there together. ¹²Then Jonathan told David, "I promise by the LORD, the God of Israel, that by this time tomorrow, or the next day at the latest, I will talk to my father and let you know at once how he feels about you. If he speaks favorably about you, I will let you know. ¹³But if he is angry and wants you killed, may the LORD kill me if I don't warn you so you can escape and live. May the LORD be with you as he used to be with my father. ¹⁴And may you treat me with the faithful love of the LORD as long as I live. But if I die, ¹⁵treat my family with this faithful love, even when the LORD destroys all your enemies."

¹⁶So Jonathan made a covenant with David, saying, "May the LORD destroy all your enemies!" ¹⁷And Jonathan made David reaffirm his vow of friendship again, for Jonathan loved David as much as he loved himself.

¹⁸Then Jonathan said, "Tomorrow we celebrate the new moon festival. You will be missed when your place at the table is empty. ¹⁹The day after tomorrow, toward evening, go to the place where you hid before, and wait there by the stone pile. ²⁰I will come out and shoot three arrows to the side of the stone pile as though I were shooting at a target. ²¹Then I will send a boy to bring the arrows back. If you hear me tell him, 'They're on this side,' then you will know, as surely as the LORD lives, that all is well, and there is no trouble. ²²But if I tell him, 'Go farther—the arrows are still ahead of you,' then it will mean that you must leave immediately, for the LORD is sending you away. ²³And may the LORD make us keep our promises to each other, for he has witnessed them."

²⁴So David hid himself in the field, and when the new moon festival

began, the king sat down to eat. ²⁵He sat at his usual place against the wall, with Jonathan sitting opposite him and Abner beside him. But David's place was empty. ²⁶Saul didn't say anything about it that day, for he said to himself, "Something must have made David ceremonially unclean. Yes, that must be why he's not here." ²⁷But when David's place was empty again the next day, Saul asked Jonathan, "Why hasn't the son of Jesse been here for dinner either yesterday or today?"

²⁸Jonathan replied, "David earnestly asked me if he could go to Bethlehem. ²⁹He wanted to take part in a family sacrifice. His brother demanded that he be there, so I told him he could go. That's why he isn't here."

³⁰Saul boiled with rage at Jonathan. "You stupid son of a whore!" he swore at him. "Do you think I don't know that you want David to be king in your place, shaming yourself and your mother? ³¹As long as that son of Jesse is alive, you'll never be king. Now go and get him so I can kill him!"

³²"But what has he done?" Jonathan demanded. "Why should he be put to death?" ³³Then Saul hurled his spear at Jonathan, intending to kill him. So at last Jonathan realized that his father was really determined to kill David. ³⁴Jonathan left the table in fierce anger and refused to eat all that day, for he was crushed by his father's shameful behavior toward David.

³⁵The next morning, as agreed, Jonathan went out into the field and took a young boy with him to gather his arrows. ³⁶"Start running," he told the boy, "so you can find the arrows as I shoot them." So the boy ran, and Jonathan shot an arrow beyond him. ³⁷When the boy had almost reached the arrow, Jonathan shouted, "The arrow is still ahead of you. ³⁸Hurry, hurry, don't wait." So the boy quickly gathered up the arrows and ran back to his master. ³⁹He, of course, didn't understand what Jonathan meant; only Jonathan and David knew. ⁴⁰Then Jonathan gave his bow and arrows to the boy and told him to take them back to the city.

⁴¹As soon as the boy was gone, David came out from where he had been hiding near the stone pile. Then David bowed to Jonathan with his face to the ground. Both of them were in tears as they embraced each other and said good-bye, especially David. ⁴²At last Jonathan said to David, "Go in peace, for we have made a pact in the LORD's name. We have entrusted each other and each other's children into the LORD's hands forever." Then David left, and Jonathan returned to the city.

〰〽〰 **How much can your friends trust you?** Jonathan asked David to keep a promise to treat his children kindly in the future. Years later David took great pains to fulfill this promise: He invited Jonathan's son, Mephibosheth, into his palace to live (2 Sam. 9). When you make promises to your friends, do you keep them? Would you keep a promise you made many years earlier?

David Spares Saul's Life

1 SAMUEL 24:1-22

After Saul returned from fighting the Philistines, he was told that David had gone into the wilderness of En-gedi. [2]So Saul chose three thousand special troops from throughout Israel and went to search for David and his men near the rocks of the wild goats. [3]At the place where the road passes some sheepfolds, Saul went into a cave to relieve himself. But as it happened, David and his men were hiding in that very cave!

[4]"Now's your opportunity!" David's men whispered to him. "Today is the day the LORD was talking about when he said, 'I will certainly put Saul into your power, to do with as you wish.' " Then David crept forward and cut off a piece of Saul's robe.

[5]But then David's conscience began bothering him because he had cut Saul's robe. [6]"The LORD knows I shouldn't have done it," he said to his men. "It is a serious thing to attack the LORD's anointed one, for the LORD himself has chosen him." [7]So David sharply rebuked his men and did not let them kill Saul.

After Saul had left the cave and gone on his way, [8]David came out and shouted after him, "My lord the king!" And when Saul looked around, David bowed low before him.

[9]Then he shouted to Saul, "Why do you listen to the people who say I am trying to harm you? [10]This very day you can see with your own eyes it isn't true. For the LORD placed you at my mercy back there in the cave, and some of my men told me to kill you, but I spared you. For I said, 'I will never harm him—he is the LORD's anointed one.' [11]Look, my father, at what I have in my hand. It is a piece of your robe! I cut it off, but I didn't kill you. This proves that I am not trying to harm you and that I have not sinned against you, even though you have been hunting for me to kill me. [12]The LORD will decide between us. Perhaps the LORD will punish you for what you are trying to do to me, but I will never harm you. [13]As that old proverb says, 'From evil people come evil deeds.' So you can be sure I will never harm you. [14]Who is the king of Israel trying to catch anyway? Should he spend his time chasing one who is as worthless as a dead dog or a flea? [15]May the LORD judge which of us is right and punish the guilty one. He is my advocate, and he will rescue me from your power!"

[16]Saul called back, "Is that really you, my son David?" Then he began to cry. [17]And he said to David, "You are a better man than I am, for you have repaid me good for evil. [18]Yes, you have been wonderfully kind to me today, for when the LORD put me in a place where you could have killed me, you didn't do it. [19]Who else would let his enemy get away when he had him in his power? May the LORD reward you well for the kindness you have shown me today. [20]And now I realize that you are surely going to be king, and

137

Israel will flourish under your rule. ²¹Now, swear to me by the LORD that when that happens you will not kill my family and destroy my line of descendants!"

²²So David promised, and Saul went home. But David and his men went back to their stronghold.

〰️ **Do you treat others the way you want to be treated?** The means we use to accomplish a goal are just as important as the goal we are trying to accomplish. David's goal was to become king, so his men urged him to kill Saul when he had the chance. David's refusal was not an example of cowardice but of courage—the courage to stand against the group and do what he knew was right. Don't compromise your moral standards by giving in to group pressure or taking the easy way out. Be willing to do right, not what *seems* right. Being in tune with God will help you to know the difference.

David and Abigail
1 SAMUEL 25:1-42

Now Samuel died, and all Israel gathered for his funeral. They buried him near his home at Ramah.

Then David moved down to the wilderness of Maon. ²There was a wealthy man from Maon who owned property near the village of Carmel. He had three thousand sheep and a thousand goats, and it was sheep-shearing time. ³This man's name was Nabal, and his wife, Abigail, was a sensible and beautiful woman. But Nabal, a descendant of Caleb, was mean and dishonest in all his dealings.

⁴When David heard that Nabal was shearing his sheep, ⁵he sent ten of his young men to Carmel. He told them to deliver this message: ⁶"Peace and prosperity to you, your family, and everything you own! ⁷I am told that you are shearing your sheep and goats. While your shepherds stayed among us near Carmel, we never harmed them, and nothing was ever stolen from them. ⁸Ask your own servants, and they will tell you this is true. So would you please be kind to us, since we have come at a time of celebration? Please give us any provisions you might have on hand." ⁹David's young men gave this message to Nabal and waited for his reply.

¹⁰"Who is this fellow David?" Nabal sneered. "Who does this son of Jesse think he is? There are lots of servants these days who run away from their masters. ¹¹Should I take my bread and water and the meat I've slaughtered for my shearers and give it to a band of outlaws who come from who knows where?" ¹²So David's messengers returned and told him what Nabal had said.

¹³"Get your swords!" was David's reply as he strapped on his own. Four hundred men started off with David, and two hundred remained behind to guard their equipment.

¹⁴Meanwhile, one of Nabal's servants went to Abigail and told her, "David sent men from the wilderness to talk to our master, and he insulted them. ¹⁵But David's men were very good to us, and we never suffered any harm from them. Nothing was stolen from us the whole time they were with us. ¹⁶In fact, day and night they were like a wall of protection to us and the

139

sheep. [17]You'd better think fast, for there is going to be trouble for our master and his whole family. He's so ill-tempered that no one can even talk to him!"

[18]Abigail lost no time. She quickly gathered two hundred loaves of bread, two skins of wine, five dressed sheep, nearly a bushel of roasted grain, one hundred raisin cakes, and two hundred fig cakes. She packed them on donkeys and said to her servants, [19]"Go on ahead. I will follow you shortly." But she didn't tell her husband what she was doing.

[20]As she was riding her donkey into a mountain ravine, she saw David and his men coming toward her. [21]David had just been saying, "A lot of good it did to help this fellow. We protected his flocks in the wilderness, and nothing he owned was lost or stolen. But he has repaid me evil for good. [22]May God deal with me severely if even one man of his household is still alive tomorrow morning!"

[23]When Abigail saw David, she quickly got off her donkey and bowed low before him. [24]She fell at his feet and said, "I accept all blame in this matter, my lord. Please listen to what I have to say. [25]I know Nabal is a wicked and ill-tempered man; please don't pay any attention to him. He is a fool, just as his name suggests. But I never even saw the messengers you sent.

[26]"Now, my lord, as surely as the LORD lives and you yourself live, since the LORD has kept you from murdering and taking vengeance into your own hands, let all your enemies be as cursed as Nabal is. [27]And here is a present I have brought to you and your young men. [28]Please forgive me if I have offended in any way. The LORD will surely reward you with a lasting dynasty, for you are fighting the LORD's battles. And you have not done wrong throughout your entire life.

[29]"Even when you are chased by those who seek your life, you are safe in the care of the LORD your God, secure in his treasure pouch! But the lives of your enemies will disappear like stones shot from a sling! [30]When the LORD has done all he promised and has made you leader of Israel, [31]don't let this be a blemish on your record. Then you won't have to carry on your conscience the staggering burden of needless bloodshed and vengeance. And when the LORD has done these great things for you, please remember me!"

[32]David replied to Abigail, "Praise the LORD, the God of Israel, who has sent you to meet me today! [33]Thank God for your good sense! Bless you for keeping me from murdering the man and carrying out vengeance with my own hands. [34]For I swear by the LORD, the God of Israel, who has kept me from hurting you, that if you had not hurried out to meet me, not one of Nabal's men would be alive tomorrow morning." [35]Then David accepted her gifts and told her, "Return home in peace. We will not kill your husband."

[36]When Abigail arrived home, she found that Nabal had thrown a big party and was celebrating like a king. He was very drunk, so she didn't tell him anything about her meeting with David until the next morning. [37]The next morning when he was sober, she told him what had happened. As a result he had a stroke, and he lay on his bed paralyzed. [38]About ten days later, the LORD struck him and he died.

³⁹When David heard that Nabal was dead, he said, "Praise the LORD, who has paid back Nabal and kept me from doing it myself. Nabal has received the punishment for his sin." Then David wasted no time in sending messengers to Abigail to ask her to become his wife.

⁴⁰When the messengers arrived at Carmel, they told Abigail, "David has sent us to ask if you will marry him."

⁴¹She bowed low to the ground and responded, "Yes, I am even willing to become a slave to David's servants!" ⁴²Quickly getting ready, she took along five of her servant girls as attendants, mounted her donkey, and went with David's messengers. And so she became his wife.

How does God keep you from making big mistakes? David was in no mood to listen when he set out for Nabal's ranch. Nevertheless, he stopped to hear what Abigail had to say. If he had ignored her, he would have been guilty of taking vengeance into his own hands. No matter how right we think we are, we must always be careful to stop and listen to what others have to say. The extra time and effort can save us much pain and trouble in the long run.

APRIL

Saul and the Occult

1 SAMUEL 28:1-25

About that time the Philistines mustered their armies for another war with Israel. King Achish told David, "You and your men will be expected to join me in battle."

²"Very well!" David agreed. "Now you will see for yourself what we can do." Then Achish told David, "I will make you my personal bodyguard for life."

³Meanwhile, Samuel had died, and all Israel had mourned for him. He was buried in Ramah, his hometown. And Saul had banned all mediums and psychics from the land of Israel.

⁴The Philistines set up their camp at Shunem, and Saul and the armies of Israel camped at Gilboa. ⁵When Saul saw the vast Philistine army, he became frantic with fear. ⁶He asked the LORD what he should do, but the LORD refused to answer him, either by dreams or by sacred lots or by the prophets. ⁷Saul then said to his advisers, "Find a woman who is a medium, so I can go and ask her what to do."

His advisers replied, "There is a medium at Endor."

⁸So Saul disguised himself by wearing ordinary clothing instead of his royal robes. Then he went to the woman's home at night, accompanied by two of his men.

"I have to talk to a man who has died," he said. "Will you call up his spirit for me?"

⁹"Are you trying to get me killed?" the woman demanded. "You know

141

that Saul has expelled all the mediums and psychics from the land. Why are you setting a trap for me?"

¹⁰But Saul took an oath in the name of the LORD and promised, "As surely as the LORD lives, nothing bad will happen to you for doing this."

¹¹Finally, the woman said, "Well, whose spirit do you want me to call up?"

"Call up Samuel," Saul replied.

¹²When the woman saw Samuel, she screamed, "You've deceived me! You are Saul!"

¹³"Don't be afraid!" the king told her. "What do you see?"

"I see a god coming up out of the earth," she said.

¹⁴"What does he look like?" Saul asked.

"He is an old man wrapped in a robe," she replied. Saul realized that it was Samuel, and he fell to the ground before him.

¹⁵"Why have you disturbed me by calling me back?" Samuel asked.

"Because I am in deep trouble," Saul replied. "The Philistines are at war with us, and God has left me and won't reply by prophets or dreams. So I have called for you to tell me what to do."

¹⁶But Samuel replied, "Why ask me if the LORD has left you and has become your enemy? ¹⁷The LORD has done just as he said he would. He has taken the kingdom from you and given it to your rival, David. ¹⁸The LORD has done this because you did not obey his instructions concerning the Amalekites. ¹⁹What's more, the LORD will hand you and the army of Israel over to the Philistines tomorrow, and you and your sons will be here with me. The LORD will bring the entire army of Israel down in defeat."

²⁰Saul fell full length on the ground, paralyzed with fright because of Samuel's words. He was also faint with hunger, for he had eaten nothing all day and all night. ²¹When the woman saw how distraught he was, she said, "Sir, I obeyed your command at the risk of my life. ²²Now do what I say, and let me give you something to eat so you can regain your strength for the trip back."

²³But Saul refused. The men who were with him also urged him to eat, so he finally yielded and got up from the ground and sat on the couch. ²⁴The woman had been fattening a calf, so she hurried out and killed it. She kneaded dough and baked unleavened bread. ²⁵She brought the meal to Saul and his men, and they ate it. Then they went out into the night.

〰〰 **What kinds of things could be considered "occult practices"? How would God feel about your involvement in such things?** God had strictly forbidden the Israelites to have anything to do with divination, sorcery, witchcraft, mediums, spiritists, or anyone who consults the spirits of the dead (Deut. 18:9-14). In fact, sorcerers were to be put to death (Exod. 22:18). Practitioners of the occult have Satan and demons as the source of their information; God does not reveal his will to them. Instead he speaks through his own channels: the Bible; his Son; Jesus Christ, and the Holy Spirit. In this instance, God brought Samuel back to give Saul a prediction regarding his fate, a message

Saul already knew. This in no way justifies efforts to contact the dead or communicate with persons or spirits from the past. God is against all such practices (Gal. 5:19-21).

David Becomes King
over All Israel

APRIL

3

2 SAMUEL 5:1-12

Then all the tribes of Israel went to David at Hebron and told him, "We are all members of your family. ²For a long time, even while Saul was our king, you were the one who really led Israel. And the LORD has told you, 'You will be the shepherd of my people Israel. You will be their leader.' " ³So there at Hebron, David made a covenant with the leaders of Israel before the LORD. And they anointed him king of Israel.

⁴David was thirty years old when he began to reign, and he reigned forty years in all. ⁵He had reigned over Judah from Hebron for seven years and six months, and from Jerusalem he reigned over all Israel and Judah for thirty-three years.

⁶David then led his troops to Jerusalem to fight against the Jebusites. "You'll never get in here," the Jebusites taunted. "Even the blind and lame could keep you out!" For the Jebusites thought they were safe. ⁷But David captured the fortress of Zion, now called the City of David.

⁸When the insulting message from the defenders of the city reached David, he told his own troops, "Go up through the water tunnel into the city and destroy those 'lame' and 'blind' Jebusites. How I hate them." That is the origin of the saying, "The blind and the lame may not enter the house." ⁹So David made the fortress his home, and he called it the City of David. He built additional fortifications around the city, starting at the Millo and working inward. ¹⁰And David became more and more powerful, because the LORD God Almighty was with him.

¹¹Then King Hiram of Tyre sent messengers to David, along with carpenters and stonemasons to build him a palace. Hiram also sent many cedar logs for lumber. ¹²And David realized that the LORD had made him king over Israel and had made his kingdom great for the sake of his people Israel.

⤳ **How could you become a person who is pleasing to God, as David was?** David now realized why the Lord had made him the king. Although the heathen kingdoms based their greatness on conquest, power, armies, and wealth, David knew that his greatness came only from God. To be great means keeping a close relationship with God personally and nationally. To do this, David had to keep his ambition under control. Although he was famous, successful, and well liked, he gave God first place in his life and

143

served the people according to God's purposes. Do you seek greatness from God or from people? In the drive for success, remember to keep your ambition under God's control.

4 APRIL

The King's Kindness
2 SAMUEL 9:1-13

One day David began wondering if anyone in Saul's family was still alive, for he had promised Jonathan that he would show kindness to them. ²He summoned a man named Ziba, who had been one of Saul's servants. "Are you Ziba?" the king asked.

"Yes sir, I am," Ziba replied.

³The king then asked him, "Is anyone still alive from Saul's family? If so, I want to show God's kindness to them in any way I can."

Ziba replied, "Yes, one of Jonathan's sons is still alive, but he is crippled."

⁴"Where is he?" the king asked.

"In Lo-debar," Ziba told him, "at the home of Makir son of Ammiel." ⁵So David sent for him and brought him from Makir's home. ⁶His name was Mephibosheth; he was Jonathan's son and Saul's grandson. When he came to David, he bowed low in great fear and said, "I am your servant."

⁷But David said, "Don't be afraid! I've asked you to come so that I can be kind to you because of my vow to your father, Jonathan. I will give you all the land that once belonged to your grandfather Saul, and you may live here with me at the palace!"

⁸Mephibosheth fell to the ground before the king. "Should the king show such kindness to a dead dog like me?" he exclaimed.

⁹Then the king summoned Saul's servant Ziba and said, "I have given your master's grandson everything that belonged to Saul and his family. ¹⁰You and your sons and servants are to farm the land for him to produce food for his family. But Mephibosheth will live here at the palace with me."

Ziba, who had fifteen sons and twenty servants, replied, ¹¹"Yes, my lord; I will do all that you have commanded." And from that time on, Mephibosheth ate regularly with David, as though he were one of his own sons. ¹²Mephibosheth had a young son named Mica. And from then on, all the members of Ziba's household were Mephibosheth's servants. ¹³And Mephibosheth, who was crippled in both feet, moved to Jerusalem to live at the palace.

〰〰 **What promises need to be kept in your life?** David had made a promise to his best friend, Jonathan, to take care of Jonathan's son, Mephibosheth (1 Sam. 20:14-17). David's treatment of Mephibosheth shows his integrity as a leader who accepted his obligation to show love and mercy. His generous provision for Jonathan's son goes beyond any political benefit he might have received. Do you keep your promises? Can you be generous with those less deserving? Each time you show compassion, your character is strengthened.

APRIL

David and Bathsheba

2 SAMUEL 11:1-27

The following spring, the time of year when kings go to war, David sent Joab and the Israelite army to destroy the Ammonites. In the process they laid siege to the city of Rabbah. But David stayed behind in Jerusalem.

²Late one afternoon David got out of bed after taking a nap and went for a stroll on the roof of the palace. As he looked out over the city, he noticed a woman of unusual beauty taking a bath. ³He sent someone to find out who she was, and he was told, "She is Bathsheba, the daughter of Eliam and the wife of Uriah the Hittite." ⁴Then David sent for her; and when she came to the palace, he slept with her. (She had just completed the purification rites after having her menstrual period.) Then she returned home. ⁵When Bathsheba discovered that she was pregnant, she sent a message to inform David.

⁶So David sent word to Joab: "Send me Uriah the Hittite." ⁷When Uriah arrived, David asked him how Joab and the army were getting along and how the war was progressing. ⁸Then he told Uriah, "Go on home and relax." David even sent a gift to Uriah after he had left the palace. ⁹But Uriah wouldn't go home. He stayed that night at the palace entrance with some of the king's other servants.

¹⁰When David heard what Uriah had done, he summoned him and asked, "What's the matter with you? Why didn't you go home last night after being away for so long?"

¹¹Uriah replied, "The Ark and the armies of Israel and Judah are living in tents, and Joab and his officers are camping in the open fields. How could I go home to wine and dine and sleep with my wife? I swear that I will never be guilty of acting like that."

¹²"Well, stay here tonight," David told him, "and tomorrow you may return to the army." So Uriah stayed in Jerusalem that day and the next. ¹³ Then David invited him to dinner and got him drunk. But even then he couldn't get Uriah to go home to his wife. Again he slept at the palace entrance.

¹⁴So the next morning David wrote a letter to Joab and gave it to Uriah to deliver. ¹⁵The letter instructed Joab, "Station Uriah on the front lines where the battle is fiercest. Then pull back so that he will be killed." ¹⁶So Joab assigned Uriah to a spot close to the city wall where he knew the enemy's strongest men were fighting. ¹⁷And Uriah was killed along with several other Israelite soldiers.

145

¹⁸Then Joab sent a battle report to David. ¹⁹He told his messenger, "Report all the news of the battle to the king. ²⁰But he might get angry and ask, 'Why did the troops go so close to the city? Didn't they know there would be shooting from the walls? ²¹Wasn't Gideon's son Abimelech killed at Thebez by a woman who threw a millstone down on him?' Then tell him, 'Uriah the Hittite was killed, too.' "

²²So the messenger went to Jerusalem and gave a complete report to David. ²³"The enemy came out against us," he said. "And as we chased them back to the city gates, ²⁴the archers on the wall shot arrows at us. Some of our men were killed, including Uriah the Hittite."

²⁵"Well, tell Joab not to be discouraged," David said. "The sword kills one as well as another! Fight harder next time, and conquer the city!"

²⁶When Bathsheba heard that her husband was dead, she mourned for him. ²⁷When the period of mourning was over, David sent for her and brought her to the palace, and she became one of his wives. Then she gave birth to a son. But the LORD was very displeased with what David had done.

〰〰 **How often are you tempted to correct one sin by committing another?** In the episode with Bathsheba, David allowed himself to fall deeper and deeper into sin. (1) David abandoned his purpose by staying home from war (v. 1). (2) He focused on his own desires (v. 3). (3) When temptation came, he looked into it instead of turning away from it (v. 3). (4) He sinned deliberately (v. 4). (5) He tried to cover up his sin by deceiving others (vv. 6-15). (6) He committed murder to continue the cover-up (vv. 15, 17). Eventually David's sin was exposed (12:9) and punished (12:10-14). (7) The consequences of David's sin were far-reaching, affecting many others (11:18; 12:11, 14-15). David could have chosen to stop and turn from evil at any stage along the way. But once sin gets started, it is difficult to stop (James 1:14-15). The deeper the mess, the less we want to admit having caused it. It's much easier to stop sliding down a hill when you are near the top than when you are halfway down. The best solution is to stop sin before it starts.

APRIL

David and Nathan
2 SAMUEL 12:1-25

So the LORD sent Nathan the prophet to tell David this story: "There were two men in a certain town. One was rich, and one was poor. ²The rich man owned many sheep and cattle. ³The poor man owned nothing but a little lamb he had worked hard to buy. He raised that little lamb, and it grew up with his children. It ate from the man's own plate and drank from his cup. He cuddled it in his arms like a baby daughter. ⁴One day a guest arrived at the home of the rich man. But instead of killing a lamb from his own flocks for food, he took the poor man's lamb and killed it and served it to his guest."

⁵David was furious. "As surely as the LORD lives," he vowed, "any man who would do such a thing deserves to die! ⁶He must repay four lambs to the poor man for the one he stole and for having no pity."

⁷Then Nathan said to David, "You are that man! The LORD, the God of Israel, says, 'I anointed you king of Israel and saved you from the power of Saul. ⁸I gave you his house and his wives and the kingdoms of Israel and Judah. And if that had not been enough, I would have given you much, much more. ⁹Why, then, have you despised the word of the LORD and done this horrible deed? For you have murdered Uriah and stolen his wife. ¹⁰From this time on, the sword will be a constant threat to your family, because you have despised me by taking Uriah's wife to be your own.

¹¹" 'Because of what you have done, I, the LORD, will cause your own household to rebel against you. I will give your wives to another man, and he will go to bed with them in public view. ¹²You did it secretly, but I will do this to you openly in the sight of all Israel.' "

¹³Then David confessed to Nathan, "I have sinned against the LORD."

Nathan replied, "Yes, but the LORD has forgiven you, and you won't die for this sin. ¹⁴But you have given the enemies of the LORD great opportunity to despise and blaspheme him, so your child will die."

¹⁵After Nathan returned to his home, the LORD made Bathsheba's baby deathly ill. ¹⁶David begged God to spare the child. He went without food and lay all night on the bare ground. ¹⁷The leaders of the nation pleaded with him to get up and eat with them, but he refused. ¹⁸Then on the seventh day the baby died. David's advisers were afraid to tell him. "He was so broken up about the baby being sick," they said. "What will he do to himself when we tell him the child is dead?"

¹⁹But when David saw them whispering, he realized what had happened. "Is the baby dead?" he asked.

"Yes," they replied. ²⁰Then David got up from the ground, washed himself, put on lotions, and changed his clothes. Then he went to the Tabernacle and worshiped the LORD. After that, he returned to the palace and ate. ²¹His advisers were amazed. "We don't understand you," they told him. "While the baby was still living, you wept and refused to eat. But now that the baby is dead, you have stopped your mourning and are eating again."

²²David replied, "I fasted and wept while the child was alive, for I said, 'Perhaps the LORD will be gracious to me and let the child live.' ²³But why should I fast when he is dead? Can I bring him back again? I will go to him one day, but he cannot return to me."

²⁴Then David comforted Bathsheba, his wife, and slept with her. She became pregnant and gave birth to a son, and they named him Solomon. The LORD loved the child ²⁵and sent word through Nathan the prophet that his name should be Jedidiah—"beloved of the LORD"—because the LORD loved him.

~~\/\/~~ **Which of your friends love you enough to correct you?** David repented of his sin, but God's judgment was that his child would die. The consequences of David's sin were irreversible. Sometimes an apology isn't enough. When God forgives us and restores our relationship to him, he doesn't eliminate all the consequences of our wrongdoing. We may be tempted to say, "If this is wrong, I can always apologize to God," but we must remember that we may set into motion events with consequences that cannot be reversed.

APRIL

Family Consequences of Sin
2 SAMUEL 13:1-19

David's son Absalom had a beautiful sister named Tamar. And Amnon, her half brother, fell desperately in love with her. ²Amnon became so obsessed with Tamar that he became ill. She was a virgin, and it seemed impossible that he could ever fulfill his love for her.

³Now Amnon had a very crafty friend—his cousin Jonadab. He was the son of David's brother Shimea. ⁴One day Jonadab said to Amnon, "What's the trouble? Why should the son of a king look so dejected morning after morning?"

So Amnon told him, "I am in love with Tamar, Absalom's sister."

⁵"Well," Jonadab said, "I'll tell you what to do. Go back to bed and pretend you are sick. When your father comes to see you, ask him to let Tamar come and prepare some food for you. Tell him you'll feel better if she feeds you."

⁶So Amnon pretended to be sick. And when the king came to see him, Amnon asked him, "Please let Tamar come to take care of me and cook something for me to eat." ⁷So David agreed and sent Tamar to Amnon's house to prepare some food for him.

⁸When Tamar arrived at Amnon's house, she went to the room where he was lying down so he could watch her mix some dough. Then she baked some special bread for him. ⁹But when she set the serving tray before him, he refused to eat. "Everyone get out of here," Amnon told his servants. So they all left. ¹⁰Then he said to Tamar, "Now bring the food into my bedroom and feed it to me here." So Tamar took it to him. ¹¹But as she was feeding him, he grabbed her and demanded, "Come to bed with me, my darling sister."

¹²"No, my brother!" she cried. "Don't be foolish! Don't do this to me! You know what a serious crime it is to do such a thing in Israel. ¹³Where could I go in my shame? And you would be called one of the greatest fools in Israel. Please, just speak to the king about it, and he will let you marry me."

¹⁴But Amnon wouldn't listen to her, and since he was stronger than she was, he raped her. ¹⁵Then suddenly Amnon's love turned to hate, and he hated her even more than he had loved her. "Get out of here!" he snarled at her.

¹⁶"No, no!" Tamar cried. "To reject me now is a greater wrong than what you have already done to me."

But Amnon wouldn't listen to her. ¹⁷He shouted for his servant and demanded, "Throw this woman out, and lock the door behind her!"

¹⁸So the servant put her out. She was wearing a long, beautiful robe, as was the custom in those days for the king's virgin daughters. ¹⁹But now Tamar tore her robe and put ashes on her head. And then, with her face in her hands, she went away crying.

〰️〰️ **What actions do you take to avoid temptation?** Love and lust are very different. After Amnon raped his half sister, his "love" turned to hate. Although he had claimed to be in love, he was actually overcome by lust. Love is patient; lust requires immediate sexual satisfaction. Love is kind; lust is harsh. Love does not demand its own way; lust does. And he yielded to the temptation to do evil. You can avoid this mistake: (1) Ask God in earnest prayer to help you stay away from people, places, and situations that offer temptation. (2) Memorize and meditate on portions of Scripture that combat your specific weaknesses. At the root of most temptation is a real need or desire that God can fill. (3) Find another believer with whom you can openly share your temptations, and call this person for help when temptation strikes.

APRIL

Family Revenge

2 SAMUEL 13:20-39

Her brother Absalom saw her and asked, "Is it true that Amnon has been with you? Well, don't be so upset. Since he's your brother anyway, don't worry about it." So Tamar lived as a desolate woman in Absalom's house. ²¹When King David heard what had happened, he was very angry. ²²And though Absalom never spoke to Amnon about it, he hated Amnon deeply because of what he had done to his sister.

²³Two years later, when Absalom's sheep were being sheared at Baal-hazor near Ephraim, Absalom invited all the king's sons to come to a feast. ²⁴He went to the king and said, "My sheep-shearers are now at work. Would the king and his servants please come to celebrate the occasion with me?"

²⁵The king replied, "No, my son. If we all came, we would be too much of a burden on you." Absalom pressed him, but the king wouldn't come, though he sent his thanks.

²⁶"Well, then," Absalom said, "if you can't come, how about sending my brother Amnon instead?"

"Why Amnon?" the king asked. ²⁷But Absalom kept on pressing the king until he finally agreed to let all his sons attend, including Amnon.

²⁸Absalom told his men, "Wait until Amnon gets drunk; then at my signal, kill him! Don't be afraid. I'm the one who has given the command.

Take courage and do it!" ²⁹So at Absalom's signal they murdered Amnon. Then the other sons of the king jumped on their mules and fled.

³⁰As they were on the way back to Jerusalem, this report reached David: "Absalom has killed all your sons; not one is left alive!" ³¹The king jumped up, tore his robe, and fell prostrate on the ground. His advisers also tore their clothes in horror and sorrow.

³²But just then Jonadab, the son of David's brother Shimea, arrived and said, "No, not all your sons have been killed! It was only Amnon! Absalom has been plotting this ever since Amnon raped his sister Tamar. ³³No, your sons aren't all dead! It was only Amnon." ³⁴Meanwhile Absalom escaped.

Then the watchman on the Jerusalem wall saw a great crowd coming toward the city from the west. He ran to tell the king, "I see a crowd of people coming from the Horonaim road along the side of the hill."

³⁵"Look!" Jonadab told the king. "There they are now! Your sons are coming, just as I said." ³⁶They soon arrived, weeping and sobbing, and the king and his officials wept bitterly with them. ³⁷And David mourned many days for his son Amnon.

Absalom fled to his grandfather, Talmai son of Ammihud, the king of Geshur. ³⁸He stayed there in Geshur for three years. ³⁹And David, now reconciled to Amnon's death, longed to be reunited with his son Absalom.

〜〰〜 **Are you more likely to have committed David's sin or Absalom's?** Absalom tried to comfort Tamar and persuade her not to turn the incident into a public scandal. Secretly, he planned to take revenge against Amnon himself. This he did two years later. Absalom told Tamar the rape was only a family matter. But God's standards for moral conduct are not suspended when we deal with family matters. Family problems must be dealt with openly and honestly. If you're facing a problem with a family member, ask God for wisdom as you deal with it. He will help you discover constructive ways to work through the matter.

9 APRIL

Family Betrayal
2 SAMUEL 15:1-37

After this, Absalom bought a chariot and horses, and he hired fifty footmen to run ahead of him. ²He got up early every morning and went out to the gate of the city. When people brought a case to the king for judgment, Absalom would ask where they were from, and they would tell him their tribe. ³Then Absalom would say, "You've really got a strong case here! It's too bad the king doesn't have anyone to hear it. ⁴I wish I were the judge. Then people could bring their problems to me, and I would give them justice!" ⁵And when people tried to bow before him, Absalom wouldn't let them. Instead, he took them by the hand and embraced them. ⁶So in this way, Absalom stole the hearts of all the people of Israel.

[7]After four years, Absalom said to the king, "Let me go to Hebron to offer a sacrifice to the LORD in fulfillment of a vow I made to him. [8]For while I was at Geshur, I promised to sacrifice to him in Hebron if he would bring me back to Jerusalem."

[9]"All right," the king told him. "Go and fulfill your vow."

So Absalom went to Hebron. [10]But while he was there, he sent secret messengers to every part of Israel to stir up a rebellion against the king. "As soon as you hear the trumpets," his message read, "you will know that Absalom has been crowned king in Hebron." [11]He took two hundred men from Jerusalem with him as guests, but they knew nothing of his intentions. [12]While he was offering the sacrifices, he sent for Ahithophel, one of David's counselors who lived in Giloh. Soon many others also joined Absalom, and the conspiracy gained momentum.

[13]A messenger soon arrived in Jerusalem to tell King David, "All Israel has joined Absalom in a conspiracy against you!"

[14]"Then we must flee at once, or it will be too late!" David urged his men. "Hurry! If we get out of the city before he arrives, both we and the city of Jerusalem will be spared from disaster."

[15]"We are with you," his advisers replied. "Do what you think is best." [16]So the king and his household set out at once. He left no one behind except ten of his concubines to keep the palace in order. [17]The king and his people set out on foot, and they paused at the edge of the city [18]to let David's troops move past to lead the way. There were six hundred Gittites who had come with David from Gath, along with the king's bodyguard.

[19]Then the king turned to Ittai, the captain of the Gittites, and asked, "Why are you coming with us? Go on back with your men to King Absalom, for you are a guest in Israel, a foreigner in exile. [20]You arrived only yesterday, and now should I force you to wander with us? I don't even know where we will go. Go on back and take your troops with you, and may the LORD show you his unfailing love and faithfulness."

[21]But Ittai said to the king, "I vow by the LORD and by your own life that I will go wherever you go, no matter what happens—whether it means life or death."

[22]David replied, "All right, come with us." So Ittai and his six hundred men and their families went along.

[23]There was deep sadness throughout the land as the king and his followers passed by. They crossed the Kidron Valley and then went out toward the wilderness.

[24]Abiathar and Zadok and the Levites took the Ark of the Covenant of God and set it down beside the road. Then they offered sacrifices there until everyone had passed by. [25]David instructed Zadok to take the Ark of God back into the city. "If the LORD sees fit," David said, "he will bring me back to see the Ark and the Tabernacle again. [26]But if he is through with me, then let him do what seems best to him."

[27]Then the king told Zadok the priest, "Look, here is my plan. You and

Abiathar should return quietly to the city with your son Ahimaaz and Abiathar's son Jonathan. [28]I will stop at the shallows of the Jordan River and wait there for a message from you. Let me know what happens in Jerusalem before I disappear into the wilderness." [29]So Zadok and Abiathar took the Ark of God back to the city and stayed there.

[30]David walked up the road that led to the Mount of Olives, weeping as he went. His head was covered and his feet were bare as a sign of mourning. And the people who were with him covered their heads and wept as they climbed the mountain. [31]When someone told David that his adviser Ahithophel was now backing Absalom, David prayed, "O LORD, let Ahithophel give Absalom foolish advice!"

[32]As they reached the spot at the top of the Mount of Olives where people worshiped God, David found Hushai the Arkite waiting for him. Hushai had torn his clothing and put dirt on his head as a sign of mourning. [33]But David told him, "If you go with me, you will only be a burden. [34]Return to Jerusalem and tell Absalom, 'I will now be your adviser, just as I was your father's adviser in the past.' Then you can frustrate and counter Ahithophel's advice. [35]Zadok and Abiathar, the priests, are there. Tell them the plans that are being made to capture me, [36]and they will send their sons Ahimaaz and Jonathan to find me and tell me what is going on." [37]So David's friend Hushai returned to Jerusalem, getting there just as Absalom arrived.

〰〰 **Who helps you keep your motives clear?** Had David not escaped from Jerusalem, the ensuing fight might have destroyed both him and the innocent inhabitants of the city. Some fights that we think necessary may be costly and destructive to those around us. In such cases, it may be wise to back down and save the fight for another day—even if doing so hurts our pride. It takes courage to stand and fight, but it also takes courage to back down when you must for the sake of others.

10
APRIL

The Death of Absalom
2 SAMUEL 18:1-18

David now appointed generals and captains to lead his troops. [2]One-third were placed under Joab, one-third under Joab's brother Abishai son of Zeruiah, and one-third under Ittai the Gittite. The king told his troops, "I am going out with you."

[3]But his men objected strongly. "You must not go," they urged. "If we have to turn and run—and even if half of us die—it will make no difference to Absalom's troops; they will be looking only for you. You are worth ten thousand of us, and it is better that you stay here in the city and send us help if we need it."

[4]"If you think that's the best plan, I'll do it," the king finally agreed. So he

stood at the gate of the city as all the divisions of troops passed by. ⁵And the king gave this command to Joab, Abishai, and Ittai: "For my sake, deal gently with young Absalom." And all the troops heard the king give this order to his commanders.

⁶So the battle began in the forest of Ephraim, ʲand the Israelite troops were beaten back by David's men. There was a great slaughter, and twenty thousand men laid down their lives that day. ⁸The battle raged all across the countryside, and more men died because of the forest than were killed by the sword.

⁹During the battle, Absalom came unexpectedly upon some of David's men. He tried to escape on his mule, but as he rode beneath the thick branches of a great oak, his head got caught. His mule kept going and left him dangling in the air. ¹⁰One of David's men saw what had happened and told Joab, "I saw Absalom dangling in a tree."

¹¹"What?" Joab demanded. "You saw him there and didn't kill him? I would have rewarded you with ten pieces of silver and a hero's belt!"

¹²"I wouldn't do it for a thousand pieces of silver," the man replied. "We all heard the king say to you and Abishai and Ittai, 'For my sake, please don't harm young Absalom.' ¹³And if I had betrayed the king by killing his son—and the king would certainly find out who did it—you yourself would be the first to abandon me."

¹⁴"Enough of this nonsense," Joab said. Then he took three daggers and plunged them into Absalom's heart as he dangled from the oak still alive. ¹⁵Ten of Joab's young armor bearers then surrounded Absalom and killed him. ¹⁶Then Joab blew the trumpet, and his men returned from chasing the army of Israel. ¹⁷They threw Absalom's body into a deep pit in the forest and piled a great heap of stones over it. And the army of Israel fled to their homes.

¹⁸During his lifetime, Absalom had built a monument to himself in the King's Valley, for he had said, "I have no son to carry on my name." He named the monument after himself, and it is known as Absalom's Monument to this day.

〜�〜 **In what situations are you most likely to lose control?** The man who reported Absalom's predicament to Joab caught Joab in hypocrisy. He knew that if the king found out that his son had been killed, Joab would have turned on him instead of giving him a reward. Joab could not answer but only dismissed him. Those who do evil often do not take the time to consider what they are about to do. They don't care whether or not it is right or lawful. Don't rush into action without thinking. Consider whether what you are about to do is right or wrong.

11

Conflict over the Throne
1 KINGS 1:5-27

About that time David's son Adonijah, whose mother was Haggith, decided to make himself king in place of his aged father. So he provided himself with chariots and horses and recruited fifty men to run in front of him. ⁶Now his father, King David, had never disciplined him at any time, even by asking, "What are you doing?" Adonijah was a very handsome man and had been born next after Absalom. ⁷Adonijah took Joab son of Zeruiah and Abiathar the priest into his confidence, and they agreed to help him become king. ⁸But among those who remained loyal to David and refused to support Adonijah were Zadok the priest, Benaiah son of Jehoiada, Nathan the prophet, Shimei, Rei, and David's personal bodyguard.

⁹Adonijah went to the stone of Zoheleth near the spring of En-rogel, where he sacrificed sheep, oxen, and fattened calves. He invited all his brothers—the other sons of King David—and all the royal officials of Judah. ¹⁰But he did not invite Nathan the prophet, or Benaiah, or the king's bodyguard, or his brother Solomon.

¹¹Then Nathan the prophet went to Bathsheba, Solomon's mother, and asked her, "Did you realize that Haggith's son, Adonijah, has made himself king and that our lord David doesn't even know about it? ¹²If you want to save your own life and the life of your son Solomon, follow my counsel. ¹³Go at once to King David and say to him, 'My lord, didn't you promise me that my son Solomon would be the next king and would sit upon your throne? Then why has Adonijah become king?' ¹⁴And while you are still talking with him, I will come and confirm everything you have said."

¹⁵So Bathsheba went into the king's bedroom. He was very old now, and Abishag was taking care of him. ¹⁶Bathsheba bowed low before him.

"What can I do for you?" he asked her.

¹⁷She replied, "My lord, you vowed to me by the LORD your God that my son Solomon would be the next king and would sit on your throne. ¹⁸But instead, Adonijah has become the new king, and you do not even know about it. ¹⁹He has sacrificed many oxen, fattened calves, and sheep, and he has invited all your sons and Abiathar the priest and Joab, the commander of the army. But he did not invite your servant Solomon. ²⁰And now, my lord the king, all Israel is waiting for your decision as to who will become king after you. ²¹If you do not act, my son Solomon and I will be treated as criminals as soon as you are dead."

²²While she was still speaking with the king, Nathan the prophet arrived. ²³The king's advisers told him, "Nathan the prophet is here to see you."

Nathan went in and bowed low before the king. ²⁴He asked, "My lord, have you decided that Adonijah will be the next king and that he will sit on your throne? ²⁵Today he has sacrificed many oxen, fattened calves, and sheep, and he has invited your sons to attend the celebration. He also invited Joab, the commander of the army, and Abiathar the priest. They are feasting and drinking with him and shouting, 'Long live King Adonijah!' ²⁶But I myself, your servant, was not invited; neither were Zadok the priest, Benaiah son of Jehoiada, nor Solomon. ²⁷Has my lord really done this without letting any of his servants know who should be the next king?"

∿∿⌐ **What happens when you don't make wise decisions?** Because David had never interfered by opposing or even questioning his son, Adonijah did not know how to work within limits. The result was that he always wanted his own way, regardless of how it affected others. Adonijah did whatever he wanted and paid no respect to God's wishes. An undisciplined child may look cute to his or her parents, but an undisciplined adult destroys himself and others. Your parents set limits so that you will develop the self-restraint you will need later in order to control yourself. They discipline you now so that you will grow into a self-disciplined adult. As difficult as it sometimes is, be grateful that your parents love you enough to discipline you.

David Gives Solomon the Crown

APRIL **12**

1 KINGS 1:28-53

"Call Bathsheba," David said. So she came back in and stood before the king. ²⁹And the king vowed, "As surely as the LORD lives, who has rescued me from every danger, ³⁰today I decree that your son Solomon will be the next king and will sit on my throne, just as I swore to you before the LORD, the God of Israel."

³¹Then Bathsheba bowed low before him again and exclaimed, "May my lord King David live forever!"

³²Then King David ordered, "Call Zadok the priest, Nathan the prophet, and Benaiah son of Jehoiada." When they came into the king's presence, ³³the king said to them, "Take Solomon and my officers down to Gihon Spring. Solomon is to ride on my personal mule. ³⁴There Zadok the priest and Nathan the prophet are to anoint him king over Israel. Then blow the trumpets and shout, 'Long live King Solomon!' ³⁵When you bring him back here, he will sit on my throne. He will succeed me as king, for I have appointed him to be ruler over Israel and Judah."

³⁶"Amen!" Benaiah son of Jehoiada replied. "May the LORD, the God of my lord the king, decree it to be so. ³⁷And may the LORD be with Solomon as he has been with you, and may he make Solomon's reign even greater than yours!"

³⁸So Zadok the priest, Nathan the prophet, Benaiah son of Jehoiada, and the king's bodyguard took Solomon down to Gihon Spring, and Solomon

rode on King David's personal mule. ³⁹There Zadok the priest took a flask of olive oil from the sacred tent and poured it on Solomon's head. Then the trumpets were blown, and all the people shouted, "Long live King Solomon!" ⁴⁰And all the people returned with Solomon to Jerusalem, playing flutes and shouting for joy. The celebration was so joyous and noisy that the earth shook with the sound.

⁴¹Adonijah and his guests heard the celebrating and shouting just as they were finishing their banquet. When Joab heard the sound of trumpets, he asked, "What's going on? Why is the city in such an uproar?"

⁴²And while he was still speaking, Jonathan son of Abiathar the priest arrived. "Come in," Adonijah said to him, "for you are a good man. You must have good news."

⁴³"Not at all!" Jonathan replied. "Our lord King David has just declared Solomon king! ⁴⁴The king sent him down to Gihon Spring with Zadok the priest, Nathan the prophet, and Benaiah son of Jehoiada, protected by the king's bodyguard. They had him ride on the king's own mule, ⁴⁵and Zadok and Nathan have anointed him as the new king. They have just returned, and the whole city is celebrating and rejoicing. That's what all the noise is about. ⁴⁶Moreover, Solomon is now sitting on the royal throne as king. ⁴⁷All the royal officials went to King David and congratulated him, saying, 'May your God make Solomon's fame even greater than your own, and may Solomon's kingdom be even greater than yours!' Then the king bowed his head in worship as he lay in his bed, ⁴⁸and he spoke these words: 'Blessed be the LORD, the God of Israel, who today has chosen someone to sit on my throne while I am still alive to see it.' "

⁴⁹Then all of Adonijah's guests jumped up in panic from the banquet table and quickly went their separate ways. ⁵⁰Adonijah himself was afraid of Solomon, so he rushed to the sacred tent and caught hold of the horns of the altar. ⁵¹Word soon reached Solomon that Adonijah had seized the horns of the altar and that he was pleading, "Let Solomon swear today that he will not kill me!"

⁵²Solomon replied, "If he proves himself to be loyal, he will not be harmed. But if he does not, he will die." ⁵³So King Solomon summoned Adonijah, and they brought him down from the altar. He came and bowed low before the king, and Solomon dismissed him, saying, "Go on home."

〜〜〜 **When things in your world get confusing, how do you know God is still in control?** Sometimes it takes getting caught before someone is willing to give up his scheme. When Adonijah learned that his plans had been exposed, he ran in panic to the sacred altar, the highest symbol of God's mercy and forgiveness. He went there, however, *after* his plans for treason were exposed. If Adonijah had first considered what God wanted, he might have avoided trouble. Don't wait until you have made a mess of things to run to God. Seek God's guidance *before* you act.

Solomon's Wisdom

1 KINGS 3:1-15

Solomon made an alliance with Pharaoh, the king of Egypt, and married one of his daughters. He brought her to live in the City of David until he could finish building his palace and the Temple of the LORD and the wall around the city. [2]At that time the people of Israel sacrificed their offerings at local altars, for a temple honoring the name of the LORD had not yet been built.

[3]Solomon loved the LORD and followed all the instructions of his father, David, except that Solomon, too, offered sacrifices and burned incense at the local altars. [4]The most important of these altars was at Gibeon, so the king went there and sacrificed one thousand burnt offerings. [5]That night the LORD appeared to Solomon in a dream, and God said, "What do you want? Ask, and I will give it to you!"

[6]Solomon replied, "You were wonderfully kind to my father, David, because he was honest and true and faithful to you. And you have continued this great kindness to him today by giving him a son to succeed him. [7]O LORD my God, now you have made me king instead of my father, David, but I am like a little child who doesn't know his way around. [8]And here I am among your own chosen people, a nation so great they are too numerous to count! [9]Give me an understanding mind so that I can govern your people well and know the difference between right and wrong. For who by himself is able to govern this great nation of yours?"

[10]The Lord was pleased with Solomon's reply and was glad that he had asked for wisdom. [11]So God replied, "Because you have asked for wisdom in governing my people and have not asked for a long life or riches for yourself or the death of your enemies—[12]I will give you what you asked for! I will give you a wise and understanding mind such as no one else has ever had or ever will have! [13]And I will also give you what you did not ask for— riches and honor! No other king in all the world will be compared to you for the rest of your life! [14]And if you follow me and obey my commands as your father, David, did, I will give you a long life."

[15]Then Solomon woke up and realized it had been a dream. He returned to Jerusalem and stood before the Ark of the Lord's covenant, where he sacrificed burnt offerings and peace offerings. Then he invited all his officials to a great banquet.

〜〰〜 **Which of Solomon's choices would you have made?** When given a chance to have anything in the world, Solomon asked for wisdom in order to lead well and make right decisions. We can ask God for this same wisdom (James 1:5). Notice that Solomon asked for wisdom to carry out his job. He did not ask God to do the job for him. We should not ask God to do *for* us what he

wants to do *through* us. Instead, we should ask God to give us the wisdom to
know what to do and the courage to follow through on it.

14 APRIL

Solomon Solves a Problem
1 KINGS 3:16-28

Some time later, two prostitutes came to the king to have an argument settled. ¹⁷"Please, my lord," one of them began, "this woman and I live in the
same house. I gave birth to a baby while she was with me in the house.
¹⁸Three days later, she also had a baby. We were alone; there were only two
of us in the house. ¹⁹But her baby died during the night when she rolled
over on it. ²⁰Then she got up in the night and took my son from beside me
while I was asleep. She laid her dead child in my arms and took mine to
sleep beside her. ²¹And in the morning when I tried to nurse my son, he was
dead! But when I looked more closely in the morning light, I saw that it
wasn't my son at all."

²²Then the other woman interrupted, "It certainly was your son, and the
living child is mine."

"No," the first woman said, "the dead one is yours, and the living one is
mine." And so they argued back and forth before the king.

²³Then the king said, "Let's get the facts straight. Both of you claim the
living child is yours, and each says that the dead child belongs to the other.
²⁴All right, bring me a sword." So a sword was brought to the king. ²⁵Then
he said, "Cut the living child in two and give half to each of these women!"

²⁶Then the woman who really was the mother of the living child, and
who loved him very much, cried out, "Oh no, my lord! Give her the child—
please do not kill him!"

But the other woman said, "All right, he will be neither yours nor mine;
divide him between us!"

²⁷Then the king said, "Do not kill him, but give the baby to the woman
who wants him to live, for she is his mother!"

²⁸Word of the king's decision spread quickly throughout all Israel, and
the people were awed as they realized the great wisdom God had given him
to render decisions with justice.

〜〰〜 **In what situation in your life do you presently need God's wisdom?** Solomon's settlement of this dispute was a classic example of his wisdom. This wise ruling was verification that God had answered Solomon's prayer
and given him an understanding heart. We have God's wisdom available to us
as we pray and request it. But, like Solomon, we must put it into action. Apply-
ing wisdom to life demonstrates our understanding.

Solomon Builds
the Temple

1 KINGS 6:1-38

APRIL

15

It was in midspring, during the fourth year of Solomon's reign, that he began the construction of the Temple of the LORD. This was 480 years after the people of Israel were delivered from their slavery in the land of Egypt. ²The Temple that King Solomon built for the LORD was 90 feet long, 30 feet wide, and 45 feet high. ³The foyer at the front of the Temple was 30 feet wide, running across the entire width of the Temple. It projected outward 15 feet from the front of the Temple. ⁴Solomon also made narrow, recessed windows throughout the Temple.

⁵A complex of rooms was built against the outer walls of the Temple, all the way around the sides and rear of the building. ⁶The complex was three stories high, the bottom floor being 7½ feet wide, the second floor 9 feet wide, and the top floor 10½ feet wide. The rooms were connected to the walls of the Temple by beams resting on ledges built out from the wall. So the beams were not inserted into the walls themselves.

⁷The stones used in the construction of the Temple were prefinished at the quarry, so the entire structure was built without the sound of hammer, ax, or any other iron tool at the building site.

⁸The entrance to the bottom floor was on the south side of the Temple. There were winding stairs going up to the second floor, and another flight of stairs between the second and third floors. ⁹After completing the Temple structure, Solomon put in a ceiling made of beams and planks of cedar. ¹⁰As already stated, there was a complex of rooms on three sides of the building, attached to the Temple walls by cedar timbers. Each story of the complex was 7½ feet high.

¹¹Then the LORD gave this message to Solomon: ¹²"Concerning this Temple you are building, if you keep all my laws and regulations and obey all my commands, I will fulfill through you the promise I made to your father, David. ¹³I will live among the people of Israel and never forsake my people."

¹⁴So Solomon finished building the Temple. ¹⁵The entire inside, from floor to ceiling, was paneled with wood. He paneled the walls and ceilings with cedar, and he used cypress for the floors. ¹⁶He partitioned off an inner sanctuary—the Most Holy Place—at the far end of the Temple. It was 30 feet deep and was paneled with cedar from floor to ceiling. ¹⁷The main room of the Temple, outside the Most Holy Place, was 60 feet long. ¹⁸Cedar paneling completely covered the stone walls throughout the Temple, and the paneling was decorated with carvings of gourds and open flowers.

¹⁹Solomon prepared the inner sanctuary in the rear of the Temple, where the Ark of the LORD's covenant would be placed. ²⁰This inner sanctuary was 30 feet long, 30 feet wide, and 30 feet high. Solomon overlaid its walls and ceiling with pure gold. He also overlaid the altar made of cedar. ²¹Then he

159

overlaid the rest of the Temple's interior with pure gold, and he made gold chains to protect the entrance to the Most Holy Place. [22]So he finished overlaying the entire Temple with gold, including the altar that belonged to the Most Holy Place.

[23]Within the inner sanctuary Solomon placed two cherubim made of olive wood, each 15 feet tall. [24]The wingspan of each of the cherubim was 15 feet, each wing being 7$\frac{1}{2}$ feet long. [25]The two cherubim were identical in shape and size; [26]each was 15 feet tall. [27]Solomon placed them side by side in the inner sanctuary of the Temple. Their outspread wings reached from wall to wall, while their inner wings touched at the center of the room. [28]He overlaid the two cherubim with gold.

[29]All the walls of the inner sanctuary and the main room were decorated with carvings of cherubim, palm trees, and open flowers. [30]The floor in both rooms was overlaid with gold.

[31]For the entrance to the inner sanctuary, Solomon made double doors of olive wood with five-sided doorposts. [32]These doors were decorated with carvings of cherubim, palm trees, and open flowers, and the doors were overlaid with gold.

[33]Then he made four-sided doorposts of olive wood for the entrance to the Temple. [34]There were two folding doors of cypress wood, and each door was hinged to fold back upon itself. [35]These doors were decorated with carvings of cherubim, palm trees, and open flowers, and the doors were overlaid with gold.

[36]The walls of the inner courtyard were built so that there was one layer of cedar beams after every three layers of hewn stone.

[37]The foundation of the LORD's Temple was laid in midspring of the fourth year of Solomon's reign. [38]The entire building was completed in every detail by midautumn of the eleventh year of his reign. So it took seven years to build the Temple.

〜�〜 **What can you learn from Solomon about making and carrying out plans?** Verse 13 summarizes the temple's main purpose. God promised that his eternal presence would never leave the temple as long as one condition was met—the Israelites had to obey God's law. Knowing how many laws they had to follow, we may think this condition was difficult. But the Israelites' situation was much like ours today: They were not cut off from God for failing to keep some small subpoint of a law. Forgiveness was amply provided for all their sins, no matter how large or small. As you read the history of the kings, you will see that lawbreaking was the result, not the cause, of estrangement from God. The kings abandoned God in their hearts first and *then* failed to keep his laws. When we close our heart to God, his power and presence soon leave us.

Solomon and the Queen of Sheba

1 KINGS 10:1-13

When the queen of Sheba heard of Solomon's reputation, which brought honor to the name of the LORD, she came to test him with hard questions. ²She arrived in Jerusalem with a large group of attendants and a great caravan of camels loaded with spices, huge quantities of gold, and precious jewels. When she met with Solomon, they talked about everything she had on her mind. ³Solomon answered all her questions; nothing was too hard for the king to explain to her. ⁴When the queen of Sheba realized how wise Solomon was, and when she saw the palace he had built, ⁵she was breathless. She was also amazed at the food on his tables, the organization of his officials and their splendid clothing, the cup-bearers and their robes, and the burnt offerings Solomon made at the Temple of the LORD.

⁶She exclaimed to the king, "Everything I heard in my country about your achievements and wisdom is true! ⁷I didn't believe it until I arrived here and saw it with my own eyes. Truly I had not heard the half of it! Your wisdom and prosperity are far greater than what I was told. ⁸How happy these people must be! What a privilege for your officials to stand here day after day, listening to your wisdom! ⁹The LORD your God is great indeed! He delights in you and has placed you on the throne of Israel. Because the LORD loves Israel with an eternal love, he has made you king so you can rule with justice and righteousness."

¹⁰Then she gave the king a gift of nine thousand pounds of gold, and great quantities of spices and precious jewels. Never again were so many spices brought in as those the queen of Sheba gave to Solomon.

¹¹(When Hiram's ships brought gold from Ophir, they also brought rich cargoes of almug wood and precious jewels. ¹²The king used the almug wood to make railings for the Temple of the LORD and the royal palace, and to construct harps and lyres for the musicians. Never before or since has there been such a supply of beautiful almug wood.)

¹³King Solomon gave the queen of Sheba whatever she asked for, besides all the other customary gifts he had so generously given. Then she and all her attendants left and returned to their own land.

~✠~ **When are you tempted to try to impress people?** Because of Solomon's wisdom, the people were happy and the palace servants content. Wisdom's quality is shown by how well it works. In James 3:17 we learn that wisdom is peaceable. Are you seeking the kind of wisdom that establishes peace in your relationships?

17

APRIL

Solomon's Unwise Son
1 KINGS 12:1-24

Rehoboam went to Shechem, where all Israel had gathered to make him king. ²When Jeroboam son of Nebat heard of Solomon's death, he returned from Egypt, for he had fled to Egypt to escape from King Solomon. ³The leaders of Israel sent for Jeroboam, and the whole assembly of Israel went to speak with Rehoboam. ⁴"Your father was a hard master," they said. "Lighten the harsh labor demands and heavy taxes that your father imposed on us. Then we will be your loyal subjects."

⁵Rehoboam replied, "Give me three days to think this over. Then come back for my answer." So the people went away.

⁶Then King Rehoboam went to discuss the matter with the older men who had counseled his father, Solomon. "What is your advice?" he asked. "How should I answer these people?"

⁷The older counselors replied, "If you are willing to serve the people today and give them a favorable answer, they will always be your loyal subjects."

⁸But Rehoboam rejected the advice of the elders and instead asked the opinion of the young men who had grown up with him and who were now his advisers. ⁹"What is your advice?" he asked them. "How should I answer these people who want me to lighten the burdens imposed by my father?"

¹⁰The young men replied, "This is what you should tell those complainers: 'My little finger is thicker than my father's waist—if you think he was hard on you, just wait and see what I'll be like! ¹¹Yes, my father was harsh on you, but I'll be even harsher! My father used whips on you, but I'll use scorpions!' "

¹²Three days later, Jeroboam and all the people returned to hear Rehoboam's decision, just as the king had requested. ¹³But Rehoboam spoke harshly to them, for he rejected the advice of the older counselors ¹⁴and followed the counsel of his younger advisers. He told the people, "My father was harsh on you, but I'll be even harsher! My father used whips on you, but I'll use scorpions!" ¹⁵So the king paid no attention to the people's demands. This turn of events was the will of the LORD, for it fulfilled the LORD's message to Jeroboam son of Nebat through the prophet Ahijah from Shiloh.

¹⁶When all Israel realized that the king had rejected their request, they shouted, "Down with David and his dynasty! We have no share in Jesse's son! Let's go home, Israel! Look out for your own house, O David!" So the people of Israel returned home. ¹⁷But Rehoboam continued to rule over the Israelites who lived in the towns of Judah.

¹⁸King Rehoboam sent Adoniram, who was in charge of the labor force, to restore order, but all Israel stoned him to death. When this news reached King Rehoboam, he quickly jumped into his chariot and fled to Jerusalem.

¹⁹The northern tribes of Israel have refused to be ruled by a descendant of David to this day. ²⁰When the people of Israel learned of Jeroboam's return from Egypt, they called an assembly and made him king over all Israel. So only the tribe of Judah remained loyal to the family of David.

²¹When Rehoboam arrived at Jerusalem, he mobilized the armies of Judah and Benjamin—180,000 select troops—to fight against the army of Israel and to restore the kingdom to himself. ²²But God said to Shemaiah, the man of God, ²³"Say to Rehoboam son of Solomon, king of Judah, and to all the people of Judah and Benjamin, ²⁴'This is what the LORD says: Do not fight against your relatives, the Israelites. Go back home, for what has happened is my doing!'" So they obeyed the message of the LORD and went home, as the LORD had commanded.

⌁⌁⌁ **Who are the people you know will give you good advice?** Rehoboam asked for advice, but he didn't carefully evaluate that advice. If he had, he would have realized that the advice offered by the older men was wiser than that of his peers. To evaluate advice, ask yourself if it is realistic, workable, and consistent with the Bible. Determine whether following the advice will be fair, make improvements, and result in a wise solution. Seek counsel from those more experienced and wise. Advice is helpful only if we evaluate it with God's standards in mind.

APRIL

God Takes Care of Elijah
1 KINGS 17:1-24

18

Now Elijah, who was from Tishbe in Gilead, told King Ahab, "As surely as the LORD, the God of Israel, lives—the God whom I worship and serve—there will be no dew or rain during the next few years unless I give the word!"

²Then the LORD said to Elijah, ³"Go to the east and hide by Kerith Brook at a place east of where it enters the Jordan River. ⁴Drink from the brook and eat what the ravens bring you, for I have commanded them to bring you food."

⁵So Elijah did as the LORD had told him and camped beside Kerith Brook. ⁶The ravens brought him bread and meat each morning and evening, and he drank from the brook. ⁷But after a while the brook dried up, for there was no rainfall anywhere in the land.

⁸Then the LORD said to Elijah, ⁹"Go and live in the village of Zarephath, near the city of Sidon. There is a widow there who will feed you. I have given her my instructions."

¹⁰So he went to Zarephath. As he arrived at the gates of the village, he saw a widow gathering sticks, and he asked her, "Would you please bring me a

cup of water?" ¹¹As she was going to get it, he called to her, "Bring me a bite of bread, too."

¹²But she said, "I swear by the LORD your God that I don't have a single piece of bread in the house. And I have only a handful of flour left in the jar and a little cooking oil in the bottom of the jug. I was just gathering a few sticks to cook this last meal, and then my son and I will die."

¹³But Elijah said to her, "Don't be afraid! Go ahead and cook that 'last meal,' but bake me a little loaf of bread first. Afterward there will still be enough food for you and your son. ¹⁴For this is what the LORD, the God of Israel, says: There will always be plenty of flour and oil left in your containers until the time when the LORD sends rain and the crops grow again!"

¹⁵So she did as Elijah said, and she and Elijah and her son continued to eat from her supply of flour and oil for many days. ¹⁶For no matter how much they used, there was always enough left in the containers, just as the LORD had promised through Elijah.

¹⁷Some time later, the woman's son became sick. He grew worse and worse, and finally he died. ¹⁸She then said to Elijah, "O man of God, what have you done to me? Have you come here to punish my sins by killing my son?"

¹⁹But Elijah replied, "Give me your son." And he took the boy's body from her, carried him up to the upper room, where he lived, and laid the body on his bed. ²⁰Then Elijah cried out to the LORD, "O LORD my God, why have you brought tragedy on this widow who has opened her home to me, causing her son to die?"

²¹And he stretched himself out over the child three times and cried out to the LORD, "O LORD my God, please let this child's life return to him." ²²The LORD heard Elijah's prayer, and the life of the child returned, and he came back to life! ²³Then Elijah brought him down from the upper room and gave him to his mother. "Look, your son is alive!" he said.

²⁴Then the woman told Elijah, "Now I know for sure that you are a man of God, and that the LORD truly speaks through you."

〰〰 **How do obeying and trusting God go together in your life?** In a nation that was required by law to care for its prophets, it is ironic that God turned to ravens (unclean birds) and a widow (a foreigner from Jezebel's home territory) to care for Elijah. God has help where we least expect it. He provides for us in ways that go beyond our narrow definitions or expectations. No matter how bitter our trials or how seemingly hopeless our situation, we should look for God's hand of care. We may find his providence in some strange places!

Elijah versus the Priests of Baal

1 KINGS 18:16-46

So Obadiah went to tell Ahab that Elijah had come, and Ahab went out to meet him. [17]"So it's you, is it—Israel's troublemaker?" Ahab asked when he saw him.

[18]"I have made no trouble for Israel," Elijah replied. "You and your family are the troublemakers, for you have refused to obey the commands of the LORD and have worshiped the images of Baal instead. [19]Now bring all the people of Israel to Mount Carmel, with all 450 prophets of Baal and the 400 prophets of Asherah, who are supported by Jezebel."

[20]So Ahab summoned all the people and the prophets to Mount Carmel. [21]Then Elijah stood in front of them and said, "How long are you going to waver between two opinions? If the LORD is God, follow him! But if Baal is God, then follow him!" But the people were completely silent.

[22]Then Elijah said to them, "I am the only prophet of the LORD who is left, but Baal has 450 prophets. [23]Now bring two bulls. The prophets of Baal may choose whichever one they wish and cut it into pieces and lay it on the wood of their altar, but without setting fire to it. I will prepare the other bull and lay it on the wood on the altar, but not set fire to it. [24]Then call on the name of your god, and I will call on the name of the LORD. The god who answers by setting fire to the wood is the true God!" And all the people agreed.

[25]Then Elijah said to the prophets of Baal, "You go first, for there are many of you. Choose one of the bulls and prepare it and call on the name of your god. But do not set fire to the wood."

[26]So they prepared one of the bulls and placed it on the altar. Then they called on the name of Baal all morning, shouting, "O Baal, answer us!" But there was no reply of any kind. Then they danced wildly around the altar they had made.

[27]About noontime Elijah began mocking them. "You'll have to shout louder," he scoffed, "for surely he is a god! Perhaps he is deep in thought, or he is relieving himself. Or maybe he is away on a trip, or he is asleep and needs to be wakened!"

[28]So they shouted louder, and following their normal custom, they cut themselves with knives and swords until the blood gushed out. [29]They raved all afternoon until the time of the evening sacrifice, but still there was no reply, no voice, no answer.

[30]Then Elijah called to the people, "Come over here!" They all crowded around him as he repaired the altar of the LORD that had been torn down. [31]He took twelve stones, one to represent each of the tribes of Israel, [32]and he used the stones to rebuild the LORD's altar. Then he dug a trench around the altar large enough to hold about three gallons. [33]He piled wood on the altar, cut the bull into pieces, and laid the pieces on the wood. Then he said,

"Fill four large jars with water, and pour the water over the offering and the wood." After they had done this, ³⁴he said, "Do the same thing again!" And when they were finished, he said, "Now do it a third time!" So they did as he said, ³⁵and the water ran around the altar and even overflowed the trench.

³⁶At the customary time for offering the evening sacrifice, Elijah the prophet walked up to the altar and prayed, "O LORD, God of Abraham, Isaac, and Jacob, prove today that you are God in Israel and that I am your servant. Prove that I have done all this at your command. ³⁷O LORD, answer me! Answer me so these people will know that you, O LORD, are God and that you have brought them back to yourself."

³⁸Immediately the fire of the LORD flashed down from heaven and burned up the young bull, the wood, the stones, and the dust. It even licked up all the water in the ditch! ³⁹And when the people saw it, they fell on their faces and cried out, "The LORD is God! The LORD is God!"

⁴⁰Then Elijah commanded, "Seize all the prophets of Baal. Don't let a single one escape!" So the people seized them all, and Elijah took them down to the Kishon Valley and killed them there.

⁴¹Then Elijah said to Ahab, "Go and enjoy a good meal! For I hear a mighty rainstorm coming!"

⁴²So Ahab prepared a feast. But Elijah climbed to the top of Mount Carmel and fell to the ground and prayed. ⁴³Then he said to his servant, "Go and look out toward the sea."

The servant went and looked, but he returned to Elijah and said, "I didn't see anything." Seven times Elijah told him to go and look, and seven times he went. ⁴⁴Finally the seventh time, his servant told him, "I saw a little cloud about the size of a hand rising from the sea."

Then Elijah shouted, "Hurry to Ahab and tell him, 'Climb into your chariot and go back home. If you don't hurry, the rain will stop you!' "

⁴⁵And sure enough, the sky was soon black with clouds. A heavy wind brought a terrific rainstorm, and Ahab left quickly for Jezreel. ⁴⁶Now the LORD gave special strength to Elijah. He tucked his cloak into his belt and ran ahead of Ahab's chariot all the way to the entrance of Jezreel.

How would you describe your attitude toward God's power today? Just as God flashed down fire from heaven for Elijah, he will help us accomplish what he commands us to do. The proof may not be as dramatic in our life as in Elijah's, but God will make resources available to us in creative ways to accomplish his purposes. He will give you the wisdom to deal with your peers, the courage to take a stand for truth, or the means to provide help for someone in need. Like Elijah, we can have faith that God will provide whatever we need to do what he commands.

Spiritual Burnout
1 KINGS 19:1-21

When Ahab got home, he told Jezebel what Elijah had done and that he had slaughtered the prophets of Baal. ²So Jezebel sent this message to Elijah: "May the gods also kill me if by this time tomorrow I have failed to take your life like those whom you killed."

³Elijah was afraid and fled for his life. He went to Beersheba, a town in Judah, and he left his servant there. ⁴Then he went on alone into the desert, traveling all day. He sat down under a solitary broom tree and prayed that he might die. "I have had enough, LORD," he said. "Take my life, for I am no better than my ancestors."

⁵Then he lay down and slept under the broom tree. But as he was sleeping, an angel touched him and told him, "Get up and eat!" ⁶He looked around and saw some bread baked on hot stones and a jar of water! So he ate and drank and lay down again.

⁷Then the angel of the LORD came again and touched him and said, "Get up and eat some more, for there is a long journey ahead of you."

⁸So he got up and ate and drank, and the food gave him enough strength to travel forty days and forty nights to Mount Sinai, the mountain of God. ⁹There he came to a cave, where he spent the night.

But the LORD said to him, "What are you doing here, Elijah?"

¹⁰Elijah replied, "I have zealously served the LORD God Almighty. But the people of Israel have broken their covenant with you, torn down your altars, and killed every one of your prophets. I alone am left, and now they are trying to kill me, too."

¹¹"Go out and stand before me on the mountain," the LORD told him. And as Elijah stood there, the LORD passed by, and a mighty windstorm hit the mountain. It was such a terrible blast that the rocks were torn loose, but the LORD was not in the wind. After the wind there was an earthquake, but the LORD was not in the earthquake. ¹²And after the earthquake there was a fire, but the LORD was not in the fire. And after the fire there was the sound of a gentle whisper. ¹³When Elijah heard it, he wrapped his face in his cloak and went out and stood at the entrance of the cave.

And a voice said, "What are you doing here, Elijah?"

¹⁴He replied again, "I have zealously served the LORD God Almighty. But the people of Israel have broken their covenant with you, torn down your altars, and killed every one of your prophets. I alone am left, and now they are trying to kill me, too."

¹⁵Then the LORD told him, "Go back the way you came, and travel to the wilderness of Damascus. When you arrive there, anoint Hazael to be king of Aram. ¹⁶Then anoint Jehu son of Nimshi to be king of Israel, and anoint Elisha son of Shaphat from Abel-meholah to replace you as my prophet.

¹⁷Anyone who escapes from Hazael will be killed by Jehu, and those who escape Jehu will be killed by Elisha! ¹⁸Yet I will preserve seven thousand others in Israel who have never bowed to Baal or kissed him!"

¹⁹So Elijah went and found Elisha son of Shaphat plowing a field with a team of oxen. There were eleven teams of oxen ahead of him, and he was plowing with the twelfth team. Elijah went over to him and threw his cloak across his shoulders and walked away again. ²⁰Elisha left the oxen standing there, ran after Elijah, and said to him, "First let me go and kiss my father and mother good-bye, and then I will go with you!"

Elijah replied, "Go on back! But consider what I have done to you."

²¹Elisha then returned to his oxen, killed them, and used the wood from the plow to build a fire to roast their flesh. He passed around the meat to the other plowmen, and they all ate. Then he went with Elijah as his assistant.

〜〜〜 **When was the last time you felt sorry for yourself?** Elijah knew that the gentle whisper was God's voice. He realized that God doesn't reveal himself only in powerful, miraculous ways. To look for God only in something big (camps, churches, conferences, visible leaders) may be to miss him because he is often found gently whispering in the quietness of a humbled heart. Are you listening for God? Step back from the noise and activity of your busy life and listen humbly and quietly for his guidance. It may come when you least expect it.

21 APRIL

The Stolen Vineyard

1 KINGS 21:1-29

King Ahab had a palace in Jezreel, and near the palace was a vineyard owned by a man named Naboth. ²One day Ahab said to Naboth, "Since your vineyard is so convenient to the palace, I would like to buy it to use as a vegetable garden. I will give you a better vineyard in exchange, or if you prefer, I will pay you for it."

³But Naboth replied, "The LORD forbid that I should give you the inheritance that was passed down by my ancestors." ⁴So Ahab went home angry and sullen because of Naboth's answer. The king went to bed with his face to the wall and refused to eat!

⁵"What in the world is the matter?" his wife, Jezebel, asked him. "What has made you so upset that you are not eating?"

⁶"I asked Naboth to sell me his vineyard or to trade it, and he refused!" Ahab told her.

⁷"Are you the king of Israel or not?" Jezebel asked. "Get up and eat and don't worry about it. I'll get you Naboth's vineyard!"

⁸So she wrote letters in Ahab's name, sealed them with his seal, and sent them to the elders and other leaders of the city where Naboth lived. ⁹In her letters she commanded: "Call the citizens together for fasting and prayer

and give Naboth a place of honor. [10]Find two scoundrels who will accuse him of cursing God and the king. Then take him out and stone him to death."

[11]So the elders and other leaders followed the instructions Jezebel had written in the letters. [12]They called for a fast and put Naboth at a prominent place before the people. [13]Then two scoundrels accused him before all the people of cursing God and the king. So he was dragged outside the city and stoned to death. [14]The city officials then sent word to Jezebel, "Naboth has been stoned to death."

[15]When Jezebel heard the news, she said to Ahab, "You know the vineyard Naboth wouldn't sell you? Well, you can have it now! He's dead!" [16]So Ahab immediately went down to the vineyard to claim it.

[17]But the LORD said to Elijah, who was from Tishbe, [18]"Go down to meet King Ahab, who rules in Samaria. He will be at Naboth's vineyard in Jezreel, taking possession of it. [19]Give him this message: 'This is what the LORD says: Isn't killing Naboth bad enough? Must you rob him, too? Because you have done this, dogs will lick your blood outside the city just as they licked the blood of Naboth!' "

[20]"So my enemy has found me!" Ahab exclaimed to Elijah.

"Yes," Elijah answered, "I have come because you have sold yourself to what is evil in the LORD's sight. [21]The LORD is going to bring disaster to you and sweep you away. He will not let a single one of your male descendants, slave or free alike, survive in Israel! [22]He is going to destroy your family as he did the family of Jeroboam son of Nebat and the family of Baasha son of Ahijah, for you have made him very angry and have led all of Israel into sin. [23]The LORD has also told me that the dogs of Jezreel will eat the body of your wife, Jezebel, at the city wall. [24]The members of your family who die in the city will be eaten by dogs, and those who die in the field will be eaten by vultures."

[25]No one else so completely sold himself to what was evil in the LORD's sight as did Ahab, for his wife, Jezebel, influenced him. [26]He was especially guilty because he worshiped idols just as the Amorites had done—the people whom the LORD had driven from the land ahead of the Israelites.

[27]When Ahab heard this message, he tore his clothing, dressed in sackcloth, and fasted. He even slept in sackcloth and went about in deep mourning.

[28]Then another message from the LORD came to Elijah, who was from Tishbe: [29]"Do you see how Ahab has humbled himself before me? Because he has done this, I will not do what I promised during his lifetime. It will happen to his sons; I will destroy all his descendants."

~~√∿∟ **How important is justice in your life?** Ahab refused to admit his sin against God. Instead he accused Elijah of being his enemy. When we are blinded by envy and hatred, it is almost impossible to see our own sin. Ahab was more wicked than any other king of Israel, but when he repented in deep humility, God took notice and reduced his punishment. The same Lord who was merciful to Ahab wants to be merciful to you. No matter what you have done, it is never too late to humble yourself, turn to God, and ask for forgiveness.

22 APRIL

The Death of King Ahab
1 KINGS 22:29-40

So the king of Israel and King Jehoshaphat of Judah led their armies against Ramoth-gilead. ³⁰Now King Ahab said to Jehoshaphat, "As we go into battle, I will disguise myself so no one will recognize me, but you wear your royal robes." So Ahab disguised himself, and they went into battle.

³¹Now the king of Aram had issued these orders to his thirty-two charioteers: "Attack only the king of Israel!" ³²So when the Aramean charioteers saw Jehoshaphat in his royal robes, they went after him. "There is the king of Israel!" they shouted. But when Jehoshaphat cried out, ³³the charioteers realized he was not the king of Israel, and they stopped chasing him.

³⁴An Aramean soldier, however, randomly shot an arrow at the Israelite troops, and the arrow hit the king of Israel between the joints of his armor. "Get me out of here!" Ahab groaned to the driver of his chariot. "I have been badly wounded!" ³⁵The battle raged all that day, and Ahab was propped up in his chariot facing the Arameans. The blood from his wound ran down to the floor of his chariot, and as evening arrived he died. ³⁶Just as the sun was setting, the cry ran through his troops: "It's all over—return home!" ³⁷So the king died, and his body was taken to Samaria and buried there. ³⁸Then his chariot was washed beside the pool of Samaria, where the prostitutes bathed, and dogs came and licked the king's blood, just as the LORD had promised.

³⁹The rest of the events in Ahab's reign and the story of the ivory palace and the cities he built are recorded in *The Book of the History of the Kings of Israel.* ⁴⁰When Ahab died, he was buried among his ancestors. Then his son Ahaziah became the next king.

When are you tempted to think that you can hide from God?
Ahab could not escape God's judgment. Ben-hadad sent thirty-two of his best chariot captains with the sole purpose of killing Ahab. Thinking he could escape, Ahab tried a disguise, but a random shot struck him while the chariots chased the wrong king, Jehoshaphat. It was foolish for Ahab to think he could escape with a disguise. Sometimes people today try to escape reality by disguising themselves—acting differently, changing schools, moving to a new town. When life seems rotten, trying to escape will make no difference, for you will only take your problems along with you. Turn to God to help you deal with the true source of your problems. He wants to help you through the "rotten" times and give you life in its fullest.

Elijah's Chariot

2 KINGS 2:1-12

When the LORD was about to take Elijah up to heaven in a whirlwind, Elijah and Elisha were traveling from Gilgal. ²And Elijah said to Elisha, "Stay here, for the LORD has told me to go to Bethel."

But Elisha replied, "As surely as the LORD lives and you yourself live, I will never leave you!" So they went on together to Bethel.

³The group of prophets from Bethel came to Elisha and asked him, "Did you know that the LORD is going to take your master away from you today?"

"Quiet!" Elisha answered. "Of course I know it."

⁴Then Elijah said to Elisha, "Stay here, for the LORD has told me to go to Jericho."

But Elisha replied again, "As surely as the LORD lives and you yourself live, I will never leave you." So they went on together to Jericho.

⁵Then the group of prophets from Jericho came to Elisha and asked him, "Did you know that the LORD is going to take your master away from you today?"

"Quiet!" he answered again. "Of course I know it."

⁶Then Elijah said to Elisha, "Stay here, for the LORD has told me to go to the Jordan River."

But again Elisha replied, "As surely as the LORD lives and you yourself live, I will never leave you." So they went on together.

⁷Fifty men from the group of prophets also went and watched from a distance as Elijah and Elisha stopped beside the Jordan River. ⁸Then Elijah folded his cloak together and struck the water with it. The river divided, and the two of them went across on dry ground!

⁹When they came to the other side, Elijah said to Elisha, "What can I do for you before I am taken away?"

And Elisha replied, "Please let me become your rightful successor."

¹⁰"You have asked a difficult thing," Elijah replied. "If you see me when I am taken from you, then you will get your request. But if not, then you won't."

¹¹As they were walking along and talking, suddenly a chariot of fire appeared, drawn by horses of fire. It drove between them, separating them, and Elijah was carried by a whirlwind into heaven. ¹²Elisha saw it and cried out, "My father! My father! The chariots and charioteers of Israel!" And as they disappeared from sight, Elisha tore his robe in two.

〰️〰️ **When you make a commitment, how far will you go to carry it out?** Elisha asked for twice as much power as Elijah had. This was a bold request, but God granted it. Why? Because Elisha's motives were pure. His main goal was not to be better or more powerful than Elijah but to accomplish more for God. If our motives are pure, we don't have to be afraid to ask great things from God. When we ask God for great power or ability, we need to examine our motives and get rid of any selfishness we find.

24 APRIL

Elisha's Miracles
2 KINGS 2:13-25

Then Elisha picked up Elijah's cloak and returned to the bank of the Jordan River. [14]He struck the water with the cloak and cried out, "Where is the LORD, the God of Elijah?" Then the river divided, and Elisha went across.

[15]When the group of prophets from Jericho saw what happened, they exclaimed, "Elisha has become Elijah's successor!" And they went to meet him and bowed down before him. [16]"Sir," they said, "just say the word and fifty of our strongest men will search the wilderness for your master. Perhaps the Spirit of the LORD has left him on some mountain or in some valley."

"No," Elisha said, "don't send them." [17]But they kept urging him until he was embarrassed, and he finally said, "All right, send them." So fifty men searched for three days but did not find Elijah. [18]Elisha was still at Jericho when they returned. "Didn't I tell you not to go?" he asked.

[19]Now the leaders of the town of Jericho visited Elisha. "We have a problem, my lord," they told him. "This town is located in beautiful natural surroundings, as you can see. But the water is bad, and the land is unproductive."

[20]Elisha said, "Bring me a new bowl with salt in it." So they brought it to him. [21]Then he went out to the spring that supplied the town with water and threw the salt into it. And he said, "This is what the LORD says: I have made this water wholesome. It will no longer cause death or infertility." [22]And sure enough! The water has remained wholesome ever since, just as Elisha said.

[23]Elisha left Jericho and went up to Bethel. As he was walking along the road, a group of boys from the town began mocking and making fun of him. "Go away, you baldhead!" they chanted. "Go away, you baldhead!" [24]Elisha turned around and looked at them, and he cursed them in the name of the LORD. Then two bears came out of the woods and mauled forty-two of them. [25]From there Elisha went to Mount Carmel and finally returned to Samaria.

〰️ **How would someone else know that you have a deep respect for God?** Some young men made fun of God's messenger and paid for it with their lives. Making fun of religious leaders has been a popular sport through the ages. To take a stand for God is to be different from the world and vulnerable to verbal abuse. When we are cynical and sarcastic toward religious leaders, we are in danger of mocking not just the person but also the spiritual message. We need to pray for leaders, not laugh at them. True leaders, those who follow God, need to be heard with respect and encouraged in their ministry.

The Healing of Naaman

2 KINGS 5:1-27

The king of Aram had high admiration for Naaman, the commander of his army, because through him the LORD had given Aram great victories. But though Naaman was a mighty warrior, he suffered from leprosy. ²Now groups of Aramean raiders had invaded the land of Israel, and among their captives was a young girl who had been given to Naaman's wife as a maid. ³One day the girl said to her mistress, "I wish my master would go to see the prophet in Samaria. He would heal him of his leprosy."

⁴So Naaman told the king what the young girl from Israel had said. ⁵"Go and visit the prophet," the king told him. "I will send a letter of introduction for you to carry to the king of Israel." So Naaman started out, taking as gifts 750 pounds of silver, 150 pounds of gold, and ten sets of clothing. ⁶The letter to the king of Israel said: "With this letter I present my servant Naaman. I want you to heal him of his leprosy."

⁷When the king of Israel read it, he tore his clothes in dismay and said, "This man sends me a leper to heal! Am I God, that I can kill and give life? He is only trying to find an excuse to invade us again."

⁸But when Elisha, the man of God, heard about the king's reaction, he sent this message to him: "Why are you so upset? Send Naaman to me, and he will learn that there is a true prophet here in Israel."

⁹So Naaman went with his horses and chariots and waited at the door of Elisha's house. ¹⁰But Elisha sent a messenger out to him with this message: "Go and wash yourself seven times in the Jordan River. Then your skin will be restored, and you will be healed of leprosy."

¹¹But Naaman became angry and stalked away. "I thought he would surely come out to meet me!" he said. "I expected him to wave his hand over the leprosy and call on the name of the LORD his God and heal me! ¹²Aren't the Abana River and Pharpar River of Damascus better than all the rivers of Israel put together? Why shouldn't I wash in them and be healed?" So Naaman turned and went away in a rage.

¹³But his officers tried to reason with him and said, "Sir, if the prophet had told you to do some great thing, wouldn't you have done it? So you should certainly obey him when he says simply to go and wash and be cured!" ¹⁴So Naaman went down to the Jordan River and dipped himself seven times, as the man of God had instructed him. And his flesh became as healthy as a young child's, and he was healed!

¹⁵Then Naaman and his entire party went back to find the man of God. They stood before him, and Naaman said, "I know at last that there is no God in all the world except in Israel. Now please accept my gifts."

¹⁶But Elisha replied, "As surely as the LORD lives, whom I serve, I will not accept any gifts." And though Naaman urged him to take the gifts, Elisha refused.

¹⁷Then Naaman said, "All right, but please allow me to load two of my mules with earth from this place, and I will take it back home with me. From now on I will never again offer any burnt offerings or sacrifices to any other god except the LORD. ¹⁸However, may the LORD pardon me in this one thing. When my master the king goes into the temple of the god Rimmon to worship there and leans on my arm, may the LORD pardon me when I bow, too."

¹⁹"Go in peace," Elisha said. So Naaman started home again.

²⁰But Gehazi, Elisha's servant, said to himself, "My master should not have let this Aramean get away without accepting his gifts. As surely as the LORD lives, I will chase after him and get something from him." ²¹So Gehazi set off after him.

When Naaman saw him running after him, he climbed down from his chariot and went to meet him. "Is everything all right?" Naaman asked.

²²"Yes," Gehazi said, "but my master has sent me to tell you that two young prophets from the hill country of Ephraim have just arrived. He would like 75 pounds of silver and two sets of clothing to give to them."

²³"By all means, take 150 pounds of silver," Naaman insisted. He gave him two sets of clothing, tied up the money in two bags, and sent two of his servants to carry the gifts for Gehazi. ²⁴But when they arrived at the hill, Gehazi took the gifts from the servants and sent the men back. Then he hid the gifts inside the house.

²⁵When he went in to his master, Elisha asked him, "Where have you been, Gehazi?"

"I haven't been anywhere," he replied.

²⁶But Elisha asked him, "Don't you realize that I was there in spirit when Naaman stepped down from his chariot to meet you? Is this the time to receive money and clothing and olive groves and vineyards and sheep and oxen and servants? ²⁷Because you have done this, you and your children and your children's children will suffer from Naaman's leprosy forever." When Gehazi left the room, he was leprous; his skin was as white as snow.

⌇⌇⌇ **What "small" things have you refused to do for God?** Naaman, a great hero, was used to getting respect, and he was outraged when Elisha treated him like an ordinary person. To wash in a great river would be one thing, but the Jordan was small and dirty. To wash in the Jordan, Naaman thought, was beneath a man of his position. But Naaman had to humble himself and obey Elisha's commands in order to be healed. Obedience to God begins with humility. We must believe that his way is better than our own. We may not always understand his ways of working, but by humbly obeying, we will receive his blessings. We must remember that (1) God's ways are best; (2) God wants our obedience more than anything else; and (3) God can use anything to accomplish his purposes.

The King Who Was Seven Years Old

2 KINGS 11:1-21

When Athaliah, the mother of King Ahaziah of Judah, learned that her son was dead, she set out to destroy the rest of the royal family. ²But Ahaziah's sister Jehosheba, the daughter of King Jehoram, took Ahaziah's infant son, Joash, and stole him away from among the rest of the king's children, who were about to be killed. Jehosheba put Joash and his nurse in a bedroom to hide him from Athaliah, so the child was not murdered. ³Joash and his nurse remained hidden in the Temple of the LORD for six years while Athaliah ruled over the land.

⁴In the seventh year of Athaliah's reign, Jehoiada the priest summoned the commanders, the Carite mercenaries, and the guards to come to the Temple of the LORD. He made a pact with them and made them swear an oath of loyalty there in the LORD's Temple; then he showed them the king's son. ⁵Jehoiada told them, "This is what you must do. A third of you who are on duty on the Sabbath are to guard the royal palace itself. ⁶Another third of you are to stand guard at the Sur Gate. And the final third must stand guard behind the palace guard. These three groups will all guard the palace. ⁷The other two units who are off duty on the Sabbath must stand guard for the king at the LORD's Temple. ⁸Form a bodyguard for the king and keep your weapons in hand. Any unauthorized person who approaches you must be killed. Stay right beside the king at all times."

⁹So the commanders did everything just as Jehoiada the priest ordered. The commanders took charge of the men reporting for duty that Sabbath, as well as those who were going off duty. They brought them all to Jehoiada the priest, ¹⁰and he supplied them with the spears and shields that had once belonged to King David and were stored in the Temple of the LORD. ¹¹The guards stationed themselves around the king, with their weapons ready. They formed a line from the south side of the Temple around to the north side and all around the altar.

¹²Then Jehoiada brought out Joash, the king's son, and placed the crown on his head. He presented Joash with a copy of God's covenant and proclaimed him king. They anointed him, and all the people clapped their hands and shouted, "Long live the king!"

¹³When Athaliah heard all the noise made by the guards and the people, she hurried to the LORD's Temple to see what was happening. ¹⁴And she saw

the newly crowned king standing in his place of authority by the pillar, as was the custom at times of coronation. The officers and trumpeters were surrounding him, and people from all over the land were rejoicing and blowing trumpets. When Athaliah saw all this, she tore her clothes in despair and shouted, "Treason! Treason!"

¹⁵Then Jehoiada the priest ordered the commanders who were in charge of the troops, "Take her out of the Temple, and kill anyone who tries to rescue her. Do not kill her here in the Temple of the LORD." ¹⁶So they seized her and led her out to the gate where horses enter the palace grounds, and she was killed there.

¹⁷Then Jehoiada made a covenant between the LORD and the king and the people that they would be the LORD's people. He also made a covenant between the king and the people. ¹⁸And all the people of the land went over to the temple of Baal and tore it down. They demolished the altars and smashed the idols to pieces, and they killed Mattan the priest of Baal in front of the altars.

Jehoiada the priest stationed guards at the Temple of the LORD. ¹⁹Then the commanders, the Carite mercenaries, the guards, and all the people of the land escorted the king from the Temple of the LORD. They went through the gate of the guards and into the palace, and the king took his seat on the royal throne. ²⁰So all the people of the land rejoiced, and the city was peaceful because Athaliah had been killed at the king's palace.

²¹Joash was seven years old when he became king.

〜〰〜 **Who were your best examples in childhood?** The covenant recorded in verse 17 was in fact a recommitment to a very old covenant—the one set up in the book of Deuteronomy for the righteous rule of the nation. It was meant to function as a constitution for the people. This covenant, however, had been virtually ignored for over 100 years. The new king was only seven years old. But Jehoiada, the priest, wisely prepared for the king's future rule by recommitting the nation and the king to the Lord. What a godly example for the young king. Think of the people who have been good examples in your life. What effect did they have on you? How can you thank them?

27
APRIL

Discovery of the Lost Book
2 KINGS 22:1–23:3

Josiah was eight years old when he became king, and he reigned in Jerusalem thirty-one years. His mother was Jedidah, the daughter of Adaiah from Bozkath. ²He did what was pleasing in the LORD's sight and followed the example of his ancestor David. He did not turn aside from doing what was right.

³In the eighteenth year of his reign, King Josiah sent Shaphan son of Azaliah and grandson of Meshullam, the court secretary, to the Temple of

the LORD. He told him, ⁴"Go up to Hilkiah the high priest and have him count the money the gatekeepers have collected from the people at the LORD's Temple. ⁵Entrust this money to the men assigned to supervise the Temple's restoration. Then they can use it to pay workers to repair the Temple of the LORD. ⁶They will need to hire carpenters, builders, and masons. Also have them buy the timber and the cut stone needed to repair the Temple. ⁷But there will be no need for the construction supervisors to keep account of the money they receive, for they are honest people."

⁸Hilkiah the high priest said to Shaphan the court secretary, "I have found the Book of the Law in the LORD's Temple!" Then Hilkiah gave the scroll to Shaphan, and he read it.

⁹Shaphan returned to the king and reported, "Your officials have given the money collected at the Temple of the LORD to the workers and supervisors at the Temple." ¹⁰Shaphan also said to the king, "Hilkiah the priest has given me a scroll." So Shaphan read it to the king.

¹¹When the king heard what was written in the Book of the Law, he tore his clothes in despair. ¹²Then he gave these orders to Hilkiah the priest, Ahikam son of Shaphan, Acbor son of Micaiah, Shaphan the court secretary, and Asaiah the king's personal adviser: ¹³"Go to the Temple and speak to the LORD for me and for the people and for all Judah. Ask him about the words written in this scroll that has been found. The LORD's anger is burning against us because our ancestors have not obeyed the words in this scroll. We have not been doing what this scroll says we must do."

¹⁴So Hilkiah the priest, Ahikam, Acbor, Shaphan, and Asaiah went to the newer Mishneh section of Jerusalem to consult with the prophet Huldah. She was the wife of Shallum son of Tikvah and grandson of Harhas, the keeper of the Temple wardrobe. ¹⁵She said to them, "The LORD, the God of Israel, has spoken! Go and tell the man who sent you, ¹⁶'This is what the LORD says: I will destroy this city and its people, just as I stated in the scroll you read. ¹⁷For my people have abandoned me and worshiped pagan gods, and I am very angry with them for everything they have done. My anger is burning against this place, and it will not be quenched.'

¹⁸"But go to the king of Judah who sent you to seek the LORD and tell him: 'This is what the LORD, the God of Israel, says concerning the message you have just heard: ¹⁹You were sorry and humbled yourself before the LORD when you heard what I said against this city and its people, that this land would be cursed and become desolate. You tore your clothing in despair and wept before me in repentance. So I have indeed heard you, says the LORD. ²⁰I will not send the promised disaster against this city until after you have died and been buried in peace. You will not see the disaster I am going to bring on this place.' " So they took her message back to the king.

²³:¹ Then the king summoned all the leaders of Judah and Jerusalem. ²And the king went up to the Temple of the LORD with all the people of Judah and Jerusalem, and the priests, and the prophets—all the people from the least to the greatest. There the king read to them the entire Book

of the Covenant that had been found in the LORD's Temple. ³The king took his place of authority beside the pillar and renewed the covenant in the LORD's presence. He pledged to obey the LORD by keeping all his commands, regulations, and laws with all his heart and soul. In this way, he confirmed all the terms of the covenant that were written in the scroll, and all the people pledged themselves to the covenant.

〰〰 **What happens in your life when the Bible is a "lost book"?**
When Josiah heard the law, he tore his clothes in grief. He immediately instituted reforms. With just one reading of God's law, he changed the course of the nation. Today many people own Bibles, but few are affected by the truths found in God's Word. The Word of God should cause us, like Josiah, to take action immediately to reform our life and bring it into harmony with God's will.

28 APRIL

Rebuilding the Temple
EZRA 3:1-13

Now in early autumn, when the Israelites had settled in their towns, all the people assembled together as one person in Jerusalem. ²Then Jeshua son of Jehozadak with his fellow priests and Zerubbabel son of Shealtiel with his family began to rebuild the altar of the God of Israel so they could sacrifice burnt offerings on it, as instructed in the law of Moses, the man of God. ³Even though the people were afraid of the local residents, they rebuilt the altar at its old site. Then they immediately began to sacrifice burnt offerings on the altar to the LORD. They did this each morning and evening.

⁴They celebrated the Festival of Shelters as prescribed in the law of Moses, sacrificing the burnt offerings specified for each day of the festival. ⁵They also offered the regular burnt offerings and the offerings required for the new moon celebrations and the other annual festivals to the LORD. Freewill offerings were also sacrificed to the LORD by the people. ⁶Fifteen days before the Festival of Shelters began, the priests had begun to sacrifice burnt offerings to the LORD. This was also before they had started to lay the foundation of the LORD's Temple.

⁷Then they hired masons and carpenters and bought cedar logs from the people of Tyre and Sidon, paying them with food, wine, and olive oil. The logs were brought down from the Lebanon mountains and floated along the coast of the Mediterranean Sea to Joppa, for King Cyrus had given permission for this.

⁸The construction of the Temple of God began in midspring, during the second year after they arrived in Jerusalem. The work force was made up of everyone who had returned from exile, including Zerubbabel son of Shealtiel, Jeshua son of Jehozadak and his fellow priests, and all the Levites. The Levites who were twenty years old or older were put in charge of rebuilding

the LORD's Temple. ⁹The workers at the Temple of God were supervised by Jeshua with his sons and relatives, and Kadmiel and his sons, all descendants of Hodaviah. They were helped in this task by the Levites of the family of Henadad.

¹⁰When the builders completed the foundation of the LORD's Temple, the priests put on their robes and took their places to blow their trumpets. And the Levites, descendants of Asaph, clashed their cymbals to praise the LORD, just as King David had prescribed. ¹¹With praise and thanks, they sang this song to the LORD:

"He is so good!
His faithful love for Israel endures forever!"

Then all the people gave a great shout, praising the LORD because the foundation of the LORD's Temple had been laid.

¹²Many of the older priests, Levites, and other leaders remembered the first Temple, and they wept aloud when they saw the new Temple's foundation. The others, however, were shouting for joy. ¹³The joyful shouting and weeping mingled together in a loud commotion that could be heard far in the distance.

〜〰〜 **How do you feel when you're working on a large, important project?** Fifty years after its destruction, the Temple was being rebuilt (536 B.C.). Some of the older people remembered Solomon's Temple and wept because the new Temple would not be as glorious as the first one. But the beauty of the building is not nearly so important to God as the attitudes of the builders and worshipers. God cares more about what we *are* than what we accomplish. Our world is always changing, and magnificent accomplishments decay and disappear. Do not be concerned if it seems as if your work for God is not so great as what others have done. Your relationship with him is more important.

Nehemiah Returns to Jerusalem

APRIL **29**

NEHEMIAH 2:1-20

Early the following spring, during the twentieth year of King Artaxerxes' reign, I was serving the king his wine. I had never appeared sad in his presence before this time. ²So the king asked me, "Why are you so sad? You aren't sick, are you? You look like a man with deep troubles."

Then I was badly frightened, ³but I replied, "Long live the king! Why shouldn't I be sad? For the city where my ancestors are buried is in ruins, and the gates have been burned down."

⁴The king asked, "Well, how can I help you?"

With a prayer to the God of heaven, ⁵I replied, "If it please Your Majesty and if you are pleased with me, your servant, send me to Judah to rebuild the city where my ancestors are buried."

⁶The king, with the queen sitting beside him, asked, "How long will you be gone? When will you return?" So the king agreed, and I set a date for my departure.

⁷I also said to the king, "If it please Your Majesty, give me letters to the governors of the province west of the Euphrates River, instructing them to let me travel safely through their territories on my way to Judah. ⁸And please send a letter to Asaph, the manager of the king's forest, instructing him to give me timber. I will need it to make beams for the gates of the Temple fortress, for the city walls, and for a house for myself." And the king granted these requests, because the gracious hand of God was on me.

⁹When I came to the governors of the province west of the Euphrates River, I delivered the king's letters to them. The king, I should add, had sent along army officers and horsemen to protect me. ¹⁰But when Sanballat the Horonite and Tobiah the Ammonite official heard of my arrival, they were very angry that someone had come who was interested in helping Israel.

¹¹Three days after my arrival at Jerusalem, ¹²I slipped out during the night, taking only a few others with me. I had not told anyone about the plans God had put in my heart for Jerusalem. We took no pack animals with us, except the donkey that I myself was riding. ¹³I went out through the Valley Gate, past the Jackal's Well, and over to the Dung Gate to inspect the broken walls and burned gates. ¹⁴Then I went to the Fountain Gate and to the King's Pool, but my donkey couldn't get through the rubble. ¹⁵So I went up the Kidron Valley instead, inspecting the wall before I turned back and entered again at the Valley Gate.

¹⁶The city officials did not know I had been out there or what I was doing, for I had not yet said anything to anyone about my plans. I had not yet spoken to the religious and political leaders, the officials, or anyone else in the administration. ¹⁷But now I said to them, "You know full well the tragedy of our city. It lies in ruins, and its gates are burned. Let us rebuild the wall of Jerusalem and rid ourselves of this disgrace!" ¹⁸Then I told them about how the gracious hand of God had been on me, and about my conversation with the king.

They replied at once, "Good! Let's rebuild the wall!" So they began the good work.

¹⁹But when Sanballat, Tobiah, and Geshem the Arab heard of our plan, they scoffed contemptuously. "What are you doing, rebelling against the king like this?" they asked.

²⁰But I replied, "The God of heaven will help us succeed. We his servants will start rebuilding this wall. But you have no stake or claim in Jerusalem."

〰〰 **What relationships in your past need to be rebuilt?** After his prayer, Nehemiah asked the king for permission to go to Judah. As soon as he got a positive answer, he began asking for additional help. Sometimes when we have needs, we hesitate to ask the right people for help because we are afraid to approach them. Not Nehemiah! He went directly to the person who could help him the most. Don't be reluctant to ask those to help who are most qualified. They may be more interested and approachable than you think. God's answers to prayer may come as a result of our asking others.

Nehemiah's Concern for the Poor

NEHEMIAH 5:1-19

About this time some of the men and their wives raised a cry of protest against their fellow Jews. [2]They were saying, "We have such large families. We need more money just so we can buy the food we need to survive." [3]Others said, "We have mortgaged our fields, vineyards, and homes to get food during the famine." [4]And others said, "We have already borrowed to the limit on our fields and vineyards to pay our taxes. [5]We belong to the same family, and our children are just like theirs. Yet we must sell our children into slavery just to get enough money to live. We have already sold some of our daughters, and we are helpless to do anything about it, for our fields and vineyards are already mortgaged to others."

[6]When I heard their complaints, I was very angry. [7]After thinking about the situation, I spoke out against these nobles and officials. I told them, "You are oppressing your own relatives by charging them interest when they borrow money!" Then I called a public meeting to deal with the problem.

[8]At the meeting I said to them, "The rest of us are doing all we can to redeem our Jewish relatives who have had to sell themselves to pagan foreigners, but you are selling them back into slavery again. How often must we redeem them?" And they had nothing to say in their defense.

[9]Then I pressed further, "What you are doing is not right! Should you not walk in the fear of our God in order to avoid being mocked by enemy nations? [10]I myself, as well as my brothers and my workers, have been lending the people money and grain, but now let us stop this business of loans. [11]You must restore their fields, vineyards, olive groves, and homes to them this very day. Repay the interest you charged on their money, grain, wine, and olive oil."

[12]Then they replied, "We will give back everything and demand nothing more from the people. We will do as you say." Then I called the priests and made the nobles and officials formally vow to do what they had promised.

[13]I shook out the fold of my robe and said, "If you fail to keep your promise, may God shake you from your homes and from your property!"

The whole assembly responded, "Amen," and they praised the LORD. And the people did as they had promised.

¹⁴I would like to mention that for the entire twelve years that I was governor of Judah—from the twentieth until the thirty-second year of the reign of King Artaxerxes—neither I nor my officials drew on our official food allowance. ¹⁵This was quite a contrast to the former governors who had laid heavy burdens on the people, demanding a daily ration of food and wine, besides a pound of silver. Even their assistants took advantage of the people. But because of my fear of God, I did not act that way. ¹⁶I devoted myself to working on the wall and refused to acquire any land. And I required all my officials to spend time working on the wall. ¹⁷I asked for nothing, even though I regularly fed 150 Jewish officials at my table, besides all the visitors from other lands! ¹⁸The provisions required at my expense for each day were one ox, six fat sheep, and a large number of domestic fowl. And every ten days we needed a large supply of all kinds of wine. Yet I refused to claim the governor's food allowance because the people were already having a difficult time.

¹⁹Remember, O my God, all that I have done for these people, and bless me for it.

~√∠ **How do you express your concern for the poor?** God's concern for the poor is revealed in almost every book of the Bible. Here, Nehemiah insisted that fairness to the poor and oppressed was central to following God. The books of Moses clearly spelled out the Israelites' responsibility to care for the poor (Exod. 22:22-27; Lev. 25:35-37; Deut. 14:28-29; 15:7-11). The way we help those in need ought to mirror God's love and concern.

Reading God's Word

NEHEMIAH 8:1-18

All the people assembled together as one person at the square just inside the Water Gate. They asked Ezra the scribe to bring out the Book of the Law of Moses, which the LORD had given for Israel to obey. ²So on October 8 Ezra the priest brought the scroll of the law before the assembly, which included the men and women and all the children old enough to understand. ³He faced the square just inside the Water Gate from early morning until noon and read aloud to everyone who could understand. All the people paid close attention to the Book of the Law. ⁴Ezra the scribe stood on a high wooden platform that had been made for the occasion. To his right stood Mattithiah, Shema, Anaiah, Uriah, Hilkiah, and Maaseiah. To his left stood Pedaiah, Mishael, Malkijah, Hashum, Hashbaddanah, Zechariah, and Meshullam. ⁵Ezra stood on the platform in full view of all the people. When they saw him open the book, they all rose to their feet.

⁶Then Ezra praised the LORD, the great God, and all the people chanted, "Amen! Amen!" as they lifted their hands toward heaven. Then they bowed down and worshiped the LORD with their faces to the ground.

⁷Now the Levites—Jeshua, Bani, Sherebiah, Jamin, Akkub, Shabbethai, Hodiah, Maaseiah, Kelita, Azariah, Jozabad, Hanan, and Pelaiah—instructed the people who were standing there. ⁸They read from the Book of the Law of God and clearly explained the meaning of what was being read, helping the people understand each passage. ⁹Then Nehemiah the governor, Ezra the priest and scribe, and the Levites who were interpreting for the people said to them, "Don't weep on such a day as this! For today is a sacred day before the LORD your God." All the people had been weeping as they listened to the words of the law.

¹⁰And Nehemiah continued, "Go and celebrate with a feast of choice foods and sweet drinks, and share gifts of food with people who have nothing prepared. This is a sacred day before our Lord. Don't be dejected and sad, for the joy of the LORD is your strength!"

¹¹And the Levites, too, quieted the people, telling them, "Hush! Don't weep! For this is a sacred day." ¹²So the people went away to eat and drink at a festive meal, to share gifts of food, and to celebrate with great joy because they had heard God's words and understood them.

¹³On October 9 the family leaders and the priests and Levites met with Ezra to go over the law in greater detail. ¹⁴As they studied the law, they discovered that the LORD had commanded through Moses that the Israelites should live in shelters during the festival to be held that month. ¹⁵He had said that a proclamation should be made throughout their towns and especially in Jerusalem, telling the people to go to the hills to get branches from olive, wild olive, myrtle, palm, and fig trees. They were to use these branches to make shelters in which they would live during the festival, as it was prescribed in the law.

¹⁶So the people went out and cut branches and used them to build shelters on the roofs of their houses, in their courtyards, in the courtyards of God's Temple, or in the squares just inside the Water Gate and the Ephraim Gate. ¹⁷So everyone who had returned from captivity lived in these shelters for the seven days of the festival, and everyone was filled with great joy! The Israelites had not celebrated this way since the days of Joshua son of Nun. ¹⁸Ezra read from the Book of the Law of God on each of the seven days of the festival. Then on October 15 they held a solemn assembly, as the law of Moses required.

〰〰 **What are your expectations when you open God's Word?** The people paid close attention to Ezra as he read God's Word, and their lives were changed. Because we hear the Bible so often, we can become dulled to its words and immune to its teachings. Instead, we should *listen* carefully to every verse and ask the Holy Spirit to help us answer the question, How does this apply to *my* life?

MAY

The Fall of a Queen
ESTHER 1:1-22

This happened in the days of King Xerxes, who reigned over 127 provinces stretching from India to Ethiopia. ²At that time he ruled his empire from his throne at the fortress of Susa. ³In the third year of his reign, he gave a banquet for all his princes and officials. He invited all the military officers of Media and Persia, as well as the noblemen and provincial officials. ⁴The celebration lasted six months—a tremendous display of the opulent wealth and glory of his empire.

⁵When it was all over, the king gave a special banquet for all the palace servants and officials—from the greatest to the least. It lasted for seven days and was held at Susa in the courtyard of the palace garden. ⁶The courtyard was decorated with beautifully woven white and blue linen hangings,

fastened by purple ribbons to silver rings embedded in marble pillars. Gold and silver couches stood on a mosaic pavement of porphyry, marble, mother-of-pearl, and other costly stones. [7]Drinks were served in gold goblets of many designs, and there was an abundance of royal wine, just as the king had commanded. [8]The only restriction on the drinking was that no one should be compelled to take more than he wanted. But those who wished could have as much as they pleased, for the king had instructed his staff to let everyone decide this matter for himself.

[9]Queen Vashti gave a banquet for the women of the palace at the same time.

[10]On the seventh day of the feast, when King Xerxes was half drunk with wine, he told Mehuman, Biztha, Harbona, Bigtha, Abagtha, Zethar, and Carcas, the seven eunuchs who attended him, [11]to bring Queen Vashti to him with the royal crown on her head. He wanted all the men to gaze on her beauty, for she was a very beautiful woman. [12]But when they conveyed the king's order to Queen Vashti, she refused to come. This made the king furious, and he burned with anger.

[13]He immediately consulted with his advisers, who knew all the Persian laws and customs, for he always asked their advice. [14]The names of these men were Carshena, Shethar, Admatha, Tarshish, Meres, Marsena, and Memucan—seven high officials of Persia and Media. They were his closest associates and held the highest positions in the empire. [15]"What must be done to Queen Vashti?" the king demanded. "What penalty does the law provide for a queen who refuses to obey the king's orders, properly sent through his eunuchs?"

[16]Memucan answered the king and his princes, "Queen Vashti has wronged not only the king but also every official and citizen throughout your empire. [17]Women everywhere will begin to despise their husbands when they learn that Queen Vashti has refused to appear before the king. [18]Before this day is out, the wife of every one of us, your officials throughout the empire, will hear what the queen did and will start talking to their husbands the same way. There will be no end to the contempt and anger throughout your realm. [19]So if it please the king, we suggest that you issue a written decree, a law of the Persians and Medes that cannot be revoked. It should order that Queen Vashti be forever banished from your presence and that you choose another queen more worthy than she. [20]When this decree is published throughout your vast empire, husbands everywhere, whatever their rank, will receive proper respect from their wives!"

[21]The king and his princes thought this made good sense, so he followed Memucan's counsel. [22]He sent letters to all parts of the empire, to each province in its own script and language, proclaiming that every man should be the ruler of his home.

How often do you take the important people in your life for granted? Xerxes made a rash, half-drunk decision, based purely on feelings. His self-restraint and practical wisdom were weakened by too much wine, and

he later regretted his decision (2:1). Poor decisions are made when clear thinking is not involved. Make your decisions through careful thinking, not on the
spur of the moment.

3

A Strange Way to
Become Queen
ESTHER 2:1-23

But after Xerxes' anger had cooled, he began thinking about Vashti and what
she had done and the decree he had made. ²So his attendants suggested, "Let
us search the empire to find beautiful young virgins for the king. ³Let the
king appoint agents in each province to bring these beautiful young women
into the royal harem at Susa. Hegai, the eunuch in charge, will see that they
are all given beauty treatments. ⁴After that, the young woman who pleases
you most will be made queen instead of Vashti." This advice was very appealing to the king, so he put the plan into effect immediately.

⁵Now at the fortress of Susa there was a certain Jew named Mordecai son
of Jair. He was from the tribe of Benjamin and was a descendant of Kish
and Shimei. ⁶His family had been exiled from Jerusalem to Babylon by King
Nebuchadnezzar, along with King Jehoiachin of Judah and many others. ⁷
This man had a beautiful and lovely young cousin, Hadassah, who was also
called Esther. When her father and mother had died, Mordecai adopted her
into his family and raised her as his own daughter. ⁸As a result of the king's
decree, Esther, along with many other young women, was brought to the
king's harem at the fortress of Susa and placed in Hegai's care. ⁹Hegai was
very impressed with Esther and treated her kindly. He quickly ordered a
special menu for her and provided her with beauty treatments. He also
assigned her seven maids specially chosen from the king's palace, and he
moved her and her maids into the best place in the harem.

¹⁰Esther had not told anyone of her nationality and family background,
for Mordecai had told her not to. ¹¹Every day Mordecai would take a walk
near the courtyard of the harem to ask about Esther and to find out what
was happening to her.

¹²Before each young woman was taken to the king's bed, she was given
the prescribed twelve months of beauty treatments—six months with oil
of myrrh, followed by six months with special perfumes and ointments.
¹³When the time came for her to go in to the king, she was given her choice
of whatever clothing or jewelry she wanted to enhance her beauty. ¹⁴That
evening she was taken to the king's private rooms, and the next morning
she was brought to the second harem, where the king's wives lived. There
she would be under the care of Shaashgaz, another of the king's eunuchs.
She would live there for the rest of her life, never going to the king again
unless he had especially enjoyed her and requested her by name.

¹⁵When it was Esther's turn to go to the king, she accepted the advice of Hegai, the eunuch in charge of the harem. She asked for nothing except what he suggested, and she was admired by everyone who saw her. ¹⁶When Esther was taken to King Xerxes at the royal palace in early winter of the seventh year of his reign, ¹⁷the king loved her more than any of the other young women. He was so delighted with her that he set the royal crown on her head and declared her queen instead of Vashti. ¹⁸To celebrate the occasion, he gave a banquet in Esther's honor for all his princes and servants, giving generous gifts to everyone and declaring a public festival for the provinces.

¹⁹Even after all the young women had been transferred to the second harem and Mordecai had become a palace official, ²⁰Esther continued to keep her nationality and family background a secret. She was still following Mordecai's orders, just as she did when she was living in his home.

²¹One day as Mordecai was on duty at the palace, two of the king's eunuchs, Bigthana and Teresh—who were guards at the door of the king's private quarters—became angry at King Xerxes and plotted to assassinate him. ²²But Mordecai heard about the plot and passed the information on to Queen Esther. She then told the king about it and gave Mordecai credit for the report. ²³When an investigation was made and Mordecai's story was found to be true, the two men were hanged on a gallows. This was all duly recorded in *The Book of the History of King Xerxes' Reign.*

∿∿ **When have difficult or confusing events in your life actually been a preparation for something you would later experience?** God placed Esther on the throne even before the Jews faced the possibility of complete destruction (3:5ff.) so that when trouble came, someone would be in a position to help. No human effort could thwart God's plan to send the Messiah to earth as a Jew. If your family has to move and you have to change to a new school and church, you may not be able to see God's purpose in your situation. But remember that God is in control. He may be placing you in a special place for a special purpose. Ask him to help you discover it.

MAY

The Jews in Danger

ESTHER 3:1-15

Some time later, King Xerxes promoted Haman son of Hammedatha the Agagite to prime minister, making him the most powerful official in the empire next to the king himself. ²All the king's officials would bow down before Haman to show him respect whenever he passed by, for so the king had commanded. But Mordecai refused to bow down or show him respect.

³Then the palace officials at the king's gate asked Mordecai, "Why are you disobeying the king's command?" ⁴They spoke to him day after day, but still

he refused to comply with the order. So they spoke to Haman about this to see if he would tolerate Mordecai's conduct, since Mordecai had told them he was a Jew.

⁵When Haman saw that Mordecai would not bow down or show him respect, he was filled with rage. ⁶So he decided it was not enough to lay hands on Mordecai alone. Since he had learned that Mordecai was a Jew, he decided to destroy all the Jews throughout the entire empire of Xerxes.

⁷So in the month of April, during the twelfth year of King Xerxes' reign, lots were cast (the lots were called *purim*) to determine the best day and month to take action. And the day selected was March 7, nearly a year later.

⁸Then Haman approached King Xerxes and said, "There is a certain race of people scattered through all the provinces of your empire. Their laws are different from those of any other nation, and they refuse to obey even the laws of the king. So it is not in the king's interest to let them live. ⁹If it please Your Majesty, issue a decree that they be destroyed, and I will give 375 tons of silver to the government administrators so they can put it into the royal treasury."

¹⁰The king agreed, confirming his decision by removing his signet ring from his finger and giving it to Haman son of Hammedatha the Agagite— the enemy of the Jews. ¹¹"Keep the money," the king told Haman, "but go ahead and do as you like with these people."

¹²On April 17 Haman called in the king's secretaries and dictated letters to the princes, the governors of the respective provinces, and the local officials of each province in their own scripts and languages. These letters were signed in the name of King Xerxes, sealed with his ring, ¹³and sent by messengers into all the provinces of the empire. The letters decreed that all Jews—young and old, including women and children—must be killed, slaughtered, and annihilated on a single day. This was scheduled to happen nearly a year later on March 7. The property of the Jews would be given to those who killed them. ¹⁴A copy of this decree was to be issued in every province and made known to all the people, so that they would be ready to do their duty on the appointed day. ¹⁵At the king's command, the decree went out by the swiftest messengers, and it was proclaimed in the fortress of Susa. Then the king and Haman sat down to drink, but the city of Susa fell into confusion.

〰〰 **In what situations are you tempted to compromise your faith?** Mordecai's faith was based on conviction. He did not first take a poll to determine the safest or most popular course of action; he had the courage to stand alone. Doing what is right is not always popular. Those who do right will be in the minority, but to obey God is more important than to obey people (Acts 5:29).

The Queen Decides
to Help

ESTHER 4:1-17

When Mordecai learned what had been done, he tore his clothes, put on sackcloth and ashes, and went out into the city, crying with a loud and bitter wail. ²He stood outside the gate of the palace, for no one was allowed to enter while wearing clothes of mourning. ³And as news of the king's decree reached all the provinces, there was great mourning among the Jews. They fasted, wept, and wailed, and many people lay in sackcloth and ashes.

⁴When Queen Esther's maids and eunuchs came and told her about Mordecai, she was deeply distressed. She sent clothing to him to replace the sackcloth, but he refused it. ⁵Then Esther sent for Hathach, one of the king's eunuchs who had been appointed as her attendant. She ordered him to go to Mordecai and find out what was troubling him and why he was in mourning. ⁶So Hathach went out to Mordecai in the square in front of the palace gate.

⁷Mordecai told him the whole story and told him how much money Haman had promised to pay into the royal treasury for the destruction of the Jews. ⁸Mordecai gave Hathach a copy of the decree issued in Susa that called for the death of all Jews, and he asked Hathach to show it to Esther. He also asked Hathach to explain it to her and to urge her to go to the king to beg for mercy and plead for her people. ⁹So Hathach returned to Esther with Mordecai's message.

¹⁰Then Esther told Hathach to go back and relay this message to Mordecai: ¹¹"The whole world knows that anyone who appears before the king in his inner court without being invited is doomed to die unless the king holds out his gold scepter. And the king has not called for me to come to him in more than a month." ¹²So Hathach gave Esther's message to Mordecai.

¹³Mordecai sent back this reply to Esther: "Don't think for a moment that you will escape there in the palace when all other Jews are killed. ¹⁴If you keep quiet at a time like this, deliverance for the Jews will arise from some other place, but you and your relatives will die. What's more, who can say but that you have been elevated to the palace for just such a time as this?"

¹⁵Then Esther sent this reply to Mordecai: ¹⁶"Go and gather together all the Jews of Susa and fast for me. Do not eat or drink for three days, night or day. My maids and I will do the same. And then, though it is against the law, I will go in to see the king. If I must die, I am willing to die." ¹⁷So Mordecai went away and did as Esther told him.

〰️✒️ In what ways has your faith cost you? Esther risked her life by coming before the king. Her courageous act is a model for us to follow In approaching a difficult or dangerous task. We should: (1) Calculate the cost. Esther realized her life was at stake. (2) Set priorities. She believed that the safety of the Jewish race was more important than her life. (3) Prepare. She gathered support and fasted. (4) Determine your course of action and move ahead boldly. She didn't think too long about it, allowing the interlude to lessen her commitment to what she had to do. Do you have to complete a difficult school assignment, confront a friend on a delicate subject, or make a difficult decision? Take action with confidence by following Esther's inspiring example.

MAY

Esther Risks Her Life

ESTHER 5:1-14

Three days later, Esther put on her royal robes and entered the inner court of the palace, just across from the king's hall. The king was sitting on his royal throne, facing the entrance. ²When he saw Queen Esther standing there in the inner court, he welcomed her, holding out the gold scepter to her. So Esther approached and touched its tip.

³Then the king asked her, "What do you want, Queen Esther? What is your request? I will give it to you, even if it is half the kingdom!"

⁴And Esther replied, "If it please Your Majesty, let the king and Haman come today to a banquet I have prepared for the king."

⁵The king turned to his attendants and said, "Tell Haman to come quickly to a banquet, as Esther has requested." So the king and Haman went to Esther's banquet.

⁶And while they were drinking wine, the king said to Esther, "Now tell me what you really want. What is your request? I will give it to you, even if it is half the kingdom!"

⁷Esther replied, "This is my request and deepest wish. ⁸If Your Majesty is pleased with me and wants to grant my request, please come with Haman tomorrow to the banquet I will prepare for you. Then tomorrow I will explain what this is all about."

⁹What a happy man Haman was as he left the banquet! But when he saw Mordecai sitting at the gate, not standing up or trembling nervously before him, he was furious. ¹⁰However, he restrained himself and went on home. Then he gathered together his friends and Zeresh, his wife, ¹¹and boasted to them about his great wealth and his many children. He bragged about the honors the king had given him and how he had been promoted over all the other officials and leaders.

¹²Then Haman added, "And that's not all! Queen Esther invited only me and the king himself to the banquet she prepared for us. And she has invited me to dine with her and the king again tomorrow!" ¹³Then he added, "But all this is meaningless as long as I see Mordecai the Jew just sitting there at the palace gate."

¹⁴So Haman's wife, Zeresh, and all his friends suggested, "Set up a gallows

that stands seventy-five feet tall, and in the morning ask the king to hang Mordecai on it. When this is done, you can go on your merry way to the banquet with the king." This pleased Haman immensely, and he ordered the gallows set up.

〜〜 **When was the last time you did something scary to obey God?** God was in control, yet Mordecai and Esther had to act. We cannot understand how both can be true at the same time, and yet they are. God chooses to work through those *willing* to act for him. We should pray as if all depended on God and act as if all depended on us. We should avoid two extremes: doing nothing or feeling that we must do everything.

MAY 7

God Protects His People
ESTHER 6:1–7:10

That night the king had trouble sleeping, so he ordered an attendant to bring the historical records of his kingdom so they could be read to him. [2]In those records he discovered an account of how Mordecai had exposed the plot of Bigthana and Teresh, two of the eunuchs who guarded the door to the king's private quarters. They had plotted to assassinate the king. [3]"What reward or recognition did we ever give Mordecai for this?" the king asked.

His attendants replied, "Nothing has been done."

[4]"Who is that in the outer court?" the king inquired. Now, as it happened, Haman had just arrived in the outer court of the palace to ask the king to hang Mordecai from the gallows he had prepared.

[5]So the attendants replied to the king, "Haman is out there."

"Bring him in," the king ordered. [6]So Haman came in, and the king said, "What should I do to honor a man who truly pleases me?"

Haman thought to himself, "Whom would the king wish to honor more than me?" [7]So he replied, "If the king wishes to honor someone, [8]he should bring out one of the king's own royal robes, as well as the king's own horse with a royal emblem on its head. [9]Instruct one of the king's most noble princes to dress the man in the king's robe and to lead him through the city square on the king's own horse. Have the prince shout as they go, 'This is what happens to those the king wishes to honor!' "

[10]"Excellent!" the king said to Haman. "Hurry and get the robe and my horse, and do just as you have said for Mordecai the Jew, who sits at the gate of the palace. Do not fail to carry out everything you have suggested."

[11]So Haman took the robe and put it on Mordecai, placed him on the king's own horse, and led him through the city square, shouting, "This is what happens to those the king wishes to honor!" [12]Afterward Mordecai returned to the palace gate, but Haman hurried home dejected and completely humiliated.

¹³When Haman told his wife, Zeresh, and all his friends what had happened, they said, "Since Mordecai—this man who has humiliated you—is a Jew, you will never succeed in your plans against him. It will be fatal to continue to oppose him." ¹⁴While they were still talking, the king's eunuchs arrived to take Haman to the banquet Esther had prepared.

7:1 So the king and Haman went to Queen Esther's banquet. ²And while they were drinking wine that day, the king again asked her, "Tell me what you want, Queen Esther. What is your request? I will give it to you, even if it is half the kingdom!"

³And so Queen Esther replied, "If Your Majesty is pleased with me and wants to grant my request, my petition is that my life and the lives of my people will be spared. ⁴For my people and I have been sold to those who would kill, slaughter, and annihilate us. If we had only been sold as slaves, I could remain quiet, for that would have been a matter too trivial to warrant disturbing the king."

⁵"Who would do such a thing?" King Xerxes demanded. "Who would dare touch you?"

⁶Esther replied, "This wicked Haman is our enemy." Haman grew pale with fright before the king and queen. ⁷Then the king jumped to his feet in a rage and went out into the palace garden.

But Haman stayed behind to plead for his life with Queen Esther, for he knew that he was doomed. ⁸In despair he fell on the couch where Queen Esther was reclining, just as the king returned from the palace garden. "Will he even assault the queen right here in the palace, before my very eyes?" the king roared. And as soon as the king spoke, his attendants covered Haman's face, signaling his doom.

⁹Then Harbona, one of the king's eunuchs, said, "Haman has set up a gallows that stands seventy-five feet tall in his own courtyard. He intended to use it to hang Mordecai, the man who saved the king from assassination."

"Then hang Haman on it!" the king ordered. ¹⁰So they hanged Haman on the gallows he had set up for Mordecai, and the king's anger was pacified.

When is it helpful to remember that God is still in control of the world? Unable to sleep, the king decided to review the history of his reign, and his servants read to him about Mordecai's good deed. This seems coincidental, but God is *always* at work. God has been working quietly and patiently throughout your life as well. The events that have come together for good are not mere coincidence; they are the result of God's sovereign control over the course of people's lives (Rom. 8:28).

The Testing of Job

JOB 1:1-22

There was a man named Job who lived in the land of Uz. He was blameless, a man of complete integrity. He feared God and stayed away from evil. ²He had seven sons and three daughters. ³He owned seven thousand sheep, three thousand camels, five hundred teams of oxen, and five hundred female donkeys, and he employed many servants. He was, in fact, the richest person in that entire area.

⁴Every year when Job's sons had birthdays, they invited their brothers and sisters to join them for a celebration. On these occasions they would get together to eat and drink. ⁵When these celebrations ended—and sometimes they lasted several days—Job would purify his children. He would get up early in the morning and offer a burnt offering for each of them. For Job said to himself, "Perhaps my children have sinned and have cursed God in their hearts." This was Job's regular practice.

⁶One day the angels came to present themselves before the LORD, and Satan the Accuser came with them. ⁷"Where have you come from?" the LORD asked Satan.

And Satan answered the LORD, "I have been going back and forth across the earth, watching everything that's going on."

⁸Then the LORD asked Satan, "Have you noticed my servant Job? He is the finest man in all the earth—a man of complete integrity. He fears God and will have nothing to do with evil."

⁹Satan replied to the LORD, "Yes, Job fears God, but not without good reason! ¹⁰You have always protected him and his home and his property from harm. You have made him prosperous in everything he does. Look how rich he is! ¹¹But take away everything he has, and he will surely curse you to your face!"

¹²"All right, you may test him," the LORD said to Satan. "Do whatever you want with everything he possesses, but don't harm him physically." So Satan left the LORD's presence.

¹³One day when Job's sons and daughters were dining at the oldest brother's house, ¹⁴a messenger arrived at Job's home with this news: "Your oxen were plowing, with the donkeys feeding beside them, ¹⁵when the Sabeans raided us. They stole all the animals and killed all the farmhands. I am the only one who escaped to tell you."

¹⁶While he was still speaking, another messenger arrived with this news: "The fire of God has fallen from heaven and burned up your sheep and all the shepherds. I am the only one who escaped to tell you."

¹⁷While he was still speaking, a third messenger arrived with this news: "Three bands of Chaldean raiders have stolen your camels and killed your servants. I am the only one who escaped to tell you."

¹⁸While he was still speaking, another messenger arrived with this news: "Your sons and daughters were feasting in their oldest brother's home. ¹⁹Suddenly, a powerful wind swept in from the desert and hit the house on all sides. The house collapsed, and all your children are dead. I am the only one who escaped to tell you."

²⁰Job stood up and tore his robe in grief. Then he shaved his head and fell to the ground before God. ²¹He said,

> "I came naked from my mother's womb,
>   and I will be stripped of everything when I die.
> The LORD gave me everything I had,
>   and the LORD has taken it away.
> Praise the name of the LORD!"

²²In all of this, Job did not sin by blaming God.

〰〰 **In what situations do you most quickly question God's care?**
As we see calamity and suffering in the book of Job, we must remember that we live in a fallen world, where good behavior is not always rewarded and bad behavior is not always punished. Sin has twisted justice and made our world unpredictable and ugly. The book of Job shows a good man suffering for no apparent reason. Sadly, our world is like that. But Job's story does not end in despair. Through Job's life we can see that faith in God is justified even when our situations look hopeless. Faith based on rewards or prosperity is hollow. To be unshakable, faith must be built on the confidence that God's ultimate purpose will come to pass. Be sure that your faith is based on the unchangeable God who loves you.

9 MAY

Job and His Friends
JOB 2:1-13

One day the angels came again to present themselves before the LORD, and Satan the Accuser came with them. ²"Where have you come from?" the LORD asked Satan.

And Satan answered the LORD, "I have been going back and forth across the earth, watching everything that's going on."

³Then the LORD asked Satan, "Have you noticed my servant Job? He is the finest man in all the earth—a man of complete integrity. He fears God and will have nothing to do with evil. And he has maintained his integrity, even though you persuaded me to harm him without cause."

⁴Satan replied to the LORD, "Skin for skin—he blesses you only because you bless him. A man will give up everything he has to save his life. ⁵But take away his health, and he will surely curse you to your face!"

⁶"All right, do with him as you please," the LORD said to Satan. "But spare

his life." [7]So Satan left the LORD's presence, and he struck Job with a terrible case of boils from head to foot. [8]Then Job scraped his skin with a piece of broken pottery as he sat among the ashes. [9]His wife said to him, "Are you still trying to maintain your integrity? Curse God and die."

[10]But Job replied, "You talk like a godless woman. Should we accept only good things from the hand of God and never anything bad?" So in all this, Job said nothing wrong.

[11]Three of Job's friends were Eliphaz the Temanite, Bildad the Shuhite, and Zophar the Naamathite. When they heard of the tragedy he had suffered, they got together and traveled from their homes to comfort and console him. [12]When they saw Job from a distance, they scarcely recognized him. Wailing loudly, they tore their robes and threw dust into the air over their heads to demonstrate their grief. [13]Then they sat on the ground with him for seven days and nights. And no one said a word, for they saw that his suffering was too great for words.

〰️ **How do you normally respond to someone else's pain? How should you respond?** Why did the friends arrive and then just sit quietly? According to Jewish tradition, people who come to comfort someone in mourning are not to speak until the mourner speaks. Often the best response to another person's suffering is silence. Job's friends realized that his pain was too deep to be healed with mere words, so they said nothing. (If only they had continued to just sit quietly!) Often, we feel we must say something spiritual and insightful to a hurting friend. Perhaps what he or she needs most is just our presence, showing that we care. Pat answers and trite quotations say much less than caring silence and loving companionship.

MAY **10**

God Speaks to Job
JOB 38:1-41

Then the LORD answered Job from the whirlwind:

[2]"Who is this that questions my wisdom with such ignorant words? [3]Brace yourself, because I have some questions for you, and you must answer them.

[4]"Where were you when I laid the foundations of the earth? Tell me, if you know so much. [5]Do you know how its dimensions were determined and who did the surveying? [6]What supports its foundations, and who laid its cornerstone [7]as the morning stars sang together and all the angels shouted for joy?

[8]"Who defined the boundaries of the sea as it burst from the womb, [9]and as I clothed it with clouds and thick darkness? [10]For I locked it behind

barred gates, limiting its shores. [11]I said, 'Thus far and no farther will you come. Here your proud waves must stop!'

[12]"Have you ever commanded the morning to appear and caused the dawn to rise in the east? [13]Have you ever told the daylight to spread to the ends of the earth, to bring an end to the night's wickedness? [14]For the features of the earth take shape as the light approaches, and the dawn is robed in red. [15]The light disturbs the haunts of the wicked, and it stops the arm that is raised in violence.

[16]"Have you explored the springs from which the seas come? Have you walked about and explored their depths? [17]Do you know where the gates of death are located? Have you seen the gates of utter gloom? [18]Do you realize the extent of the earth? Tell me about it if you know!

[19]"Where does the light come from, and where does the darkness go? [20]Can you take it to its home? Do you know how to get there? [21]But of course you know all this! For you were born before it was all created, and you are so very experienced!

[22]"Have you visited the treasuries of the snow? Have you seen where the hail is made and stored? [23]I have reserved it for the time of trouble, for the day of battle and war. [24]Where is the path to the origin of light? Where is the home of the east wind?

[25]"Who created a channel for the torrents of rain? Who laid out the path for the lightning? [26]Who makes the rain fall on barren land, in a desert where no one lives? [27]Who sends the rain that satisfies the parched ground and makes the tender grass spring up?

[28]"Does the rain have a father? Where does dew come from? [29]Who is the mother of the ice? Who gives birth to the frost from the heavens? [30]For the water turns to ice as hard as rock, and the surface of the water freezes.

[31]"Can you hold back the movements of the stars? Are you able to restrain the Pleiades or Orion? [32]Can you ensure the proper sequence of the seasons or guide the constellation of the Bear with her cubs across the heavens? [33]Do you know the laws of the universe and how God rules the earth?

[34]"Can you shout to the clouds and make it rain? [35]Can you make lightning appear and cause it to strike as you direct it? [36]Who gives intuition and instinct? [37]Who is wise enough to count all the clouds? Who can tilt the water jars of heaven, [38]turning the dry dust to clumps of mud?

[39]"Can you stalk prey for a lioness and satisfy the young lions' appetites [40]as they lie in their dens or crouch in the thicket? [41]Who provides food for the ravens when their young cry out to God as they wander about in hunger?"

〰〰〰 **What things around you remind you of God's greatness?** God stated that he has all the forces of nature at his command and that he can unleash or restrain them at will. No one completely understands such common occurrences as rain or snow, and no one can command them—only God who created them has that power. God's point was that if Job could not explain such common events in nature, how could he possibly explain or question God? And if nature is beyond our grasp, God's moral purposes may not be what we imagine either. Your job is not to question God but to worship and serve him because of who he is and what he has done for you.

The Rest of Job's Story

JOB 42:1-17

Then Job replied to the LORD:
²"I know that you can do anything, and no one can stop you. ³You ask, 'Who is this that questions my wisdom with such ignorance?' It is I. And I was talking about things I did not understand, things far too wonderful for me.

⁴"You said, 'Listen and I will speak! I have some questions for you, and you must answer them.'

⁵"I had heard about you before, but now I have seen you with my own eyes. ⁶I take back everything I said, and I sit in dust and ashes to show my repentance."

⁷After the LORD had finished speaking to Job, he said to Eliphaz the Temanite: "I am angry with you and with your two friends, for you have not been right in what you said about me, as my servant Job was. ⁸Now take seven young bulls and seven rams and go to my servant Job and offer a burnt offering for yourselves. My servant Job will pray for you, and I will accept his prayer on your behalf. I will not treat you as you deserve, for you have not been right in what you said about me, as my servant Job was."

⁹So Eliphaz the Temanite, Bildad the Shuhite, and Zophar the Naamathite did as the LORD commanded them, and the LORD accepted Job's prayer.

¹⁰When Job prayed for his friends, the LORD restored his fortunes. In fact, the LORD gave him twice as much as before! ¹¹Then all his brothers, sisters, and former friends came and feasted with him in his home. And they consoled him and comforted him because of all the trials the LORD had brought against him. And each of them brought him a gift of money and a gold ring.

¹²So the LORD blessed Job in the second half of his life even more than in the beginning. For now he had fourteen thousand sheep, six thousand camels, one thousand teams of oxen, and one thousand female donkeys. ¹³He also gave Job seven more sons and three more daughters. ¹⁴He named his first daughter Jemimah, the second Keziah, and the third Keren-happuch. ¹⁵In all the land there were no other women as lovely as the daughters of Job. And their father put them into his will along with their brothers.

¹⁶Job lived 140 years after that, living to see four generations of his children and grandchildren. ¹⁷Then he died, an old man who had lived a long, good life.

〰️〰️ **What difference does it make to know and remember that God always has the last word?** Job's friends had persistently asked him to admit his sin and ask for forgiveness, and eventually Job did indeed repent. Ironically, Job's repentance was not the kind called for by his friends. He did not ask for forgiveness for secret sins but forgiveness for questioning God's sovereignty and justice. Job repented of his attitude and acknowledged God's great power and perfect justice. We sin when we angrily ask, "If God is in control, how could he let this happen?" Since we are locked into time, unable to see beyond today, we cannot know the reasons for everything that happens. Thus, we must often choose between anger and trust. Will you trust God with your unanswered questions?

12

MAY

Two Kinds of Lives

PSALM 1:1-6

Oh, the joys of those
    who do not follow the advice of the wicked,
    or stand around with sinners,
    or join in with scoffers.
2 But they delight in doing everything the LORD wants;
    day and night they think about his law.
3 They are like trees planted along the riverbank,
    bearing fruit each season without fail.
Their leaves never wither,
    and in all they do, they prosper.

4 But this is not true of the wicked.
    They are like worthless chaff, scattered by the wind.
5 They will be condemned at the time of judgment.
    Sinners will have no place among the godly.

6 For the LORD watches over the path of the godly,
    but the path of the wicked leads to destruction.

〰️〰️ **What kind of person do you really want to be?** God doesn't judge people on the basis of race, sex, or national origin. He judges them on the basis of their faith in him and their response to his revealed will. Those who diligently try to obey God are blessed. They are like healthy, fruit-bearing trees with strong roots, and God promises to watch over them. God's wisdom guides their lives. In contrast, those who don't trust and obey God have meaningless lives that blow away like dust. There are only two paths of life before you—God's way of obedience or the way of rebellion and destruction. Be sure to choose God's path because the path you choose determines how you will spend eternity.

The Value of Humans

PSALM 8:1-9

O LORD, our Lord, the majesty of your name fills the earth!
Your glory is higher than the heavens.

2 You have taught children and nursing infants
to give you praise.
They silence your enemies
who were seeking revenge.

3 When I look at the night sky and see the work of your fingers—
the moon and the stars you have set in place—
4 what are mortals that you should think of us,
mere humans that you should care for us?
5 For you made us only a little lower than God,
and you crowned us with glory and honor.
6 You put us in charge of everything you made,
giving us authority over all things—
7 the sheep and the cattle
and all the wild animals,
8 the birds in the sky, the fish in the sea,
and everything that swims the ocean currents.

9 O LORD, our Lord, the majesty of your name fills the earth!

How do you know you have worth? When we look at the marvels of creation, we wonder how God could be concerned for people who constantly disappoint him. Yet God created us only a little lower than the angels. The next time you question your worth as a person or feel down about yourself, remember that God considers you to be highly valuable. We have great worth because we bear the stamp of the Creator. Because God has already declared how valuable you are to him, you can be set free from feelings of worthlessness.

A Sheep's Song

PSALM 23:1-6

The LORD is my shepherd;
I have everything I need.
2 He lets me rest in green meadows;
he leads me beside peaceful streams.

³ He renews my strength.
He guides me along right paths,
     bringing honor to his name.

⁴ Even when I walk
     through the dark valley of death,
I will not be afraid,
     for you are close beside me.
Your rod and your staff
     protect and comfort me.

⁵ You prepare a feast for me
     in the presence of my enemies.
You welcome me as a guest,
     anointing my head with oil.
My cup overflows with blessings.
⁶ Surely your goodness and unfailing love will pursue me
     all the days of my life,
and I will live in the house of the LORD
     forever.

〰️✒️ **What is the most comforting phrase to you in this psalm?**
When we allow God our Shepherd to guide us, we have contentment. When we
choose to sin, however, we are choosing to go our own way, and we cannot
blame God for the environment in which we find ourselves. Our Shepherd knows
the "green meadows" and "peaceful streams" that will restore us. We will
reach these places only by following him obediently. Rebelling against the Shepherd's leading is actually rebelling against our own best interests for the future.
We must remember this the next time we are tempted to go our own way rather
than the Shepherd's way.

15 MAY

A Confession
PSALM 51:1-19

Have mercy on me, O God,
     because of your unfailing love.
Because of your great compassion,
     blot out the stain of my sins.
² Wash me clean from my guilt.
     Purify me from my sin.

³ For I recognize my shameful deeds—
     they haunt me day and night.
⁴ Against you, and you alone, have I sinned;
     I have done what is evil in your sight.

You will be proved right in what you say,
    and your judgment against me is just.

5 For I was born a sinner—
    yes, from the moment my mother conceived me.
6 But you desire honesty from the heart,
    so you can teach me to be wise in my inmost being.

7 Purify me from my sins, and I will be clean;
    wash me, and I will be whiter than snow.
8 Oh, give me back my joy again;
    you have broken me—
    now let me rejoice.
9 Don't keep looking at my sins.
    Remove the stain of my guilt.
10 Create in me a clean heart, O God.
    Renew a right spirit within me.
11 Do not banish me from your presence,
    and don't take your Holy Spirit from me.
12 Restore to me again the joy of your salvation,
    and make me willing to obey you.
13 Then I will teach your ways to sinners,
    and they will return to you.
14 Forgive me for shedding blood, O God who saves;
    then I will joyfully sing of your forgiveness.
15 Unseal my lips, O Lord,
    that I may praise you.

16 You would not be pleased with sacrifices,
    or I would bring them.
    If I brought you a burnt offering,
    you would not accept it.
17 The sacrifice you want is a broken spirit.
    A broken and repentant heart, O God,
    you will not despise.

18 Look with favor on Zion and help her;
    rebuild the walls of Jerusalem.
19 Then you will be pleased with worthy sacrifices
    and with our whole burnt offerings;
    and bulls will again be sacrificed on your altar.

What examples of repentance have been part of your life?

Because we are born as sinners (v. 5), our natural inclination is to please ourselves rather than God. David followed that inclination when he took another
man's wife. We also follow it when we sin in any way, acting according to our
own selfish desires. Like David, we must ask God to cleanse us from within

(v. 7), clearing our heart and mind for new thoughts and desires. Right conduct can come only from a clean heart and mind. Ask God to create in you a clean heart and mind.

16

What God Is Like
PSALM 103:1-22

Praise the LORD, I tell myself;
    with my whole heart, I will praise his holy name.
2 Praise the LORD, I tell myself,
    and never forget the good things he does for me.
3 He forgives all my sins
    and heals all my diseases.
4 He ransoms me from death
    and surrounds me with love and tender mercies.
5 He fills my life with good things.
    My youth is renewed like the eagle's!
6 The LORD gives righteousness
    and justice to all who are treated unfairly.
7 He revealed his character to Moses
    and his deeds to the people of Israel.
8 The LORD is merciful and gracious;
    he is slow to get angry and full of unfailing love.
9 He will not constantly accuse us,
    nor remain angry forever.
10 He has not punished us for all our sins,
    nor does he deal with us as we deserve.
11 For his unfailing love toward those who fear him
    is as great as the height of the heavens above the earth.
12 He has removed our rebellious acts
    as far away from us as the east is from the west.
13 The LORD is like a father to his children,
    tender and compassionate to those who fear him.
14 For he understands how weak we are;
    he knows we are only dust.
15 Our days on earth are like grass;
    like wildflowers, we bloom and die.
16 The wind blows, and we are gone—
    as though we had never been here.
17 But the love of the LORD remains forever
    with those who fear him.
His salvation extends to the children's children
18   of those who are faithful to his covenant,

of those who obey his commandments!

¹⁹ The LORD has made the heavens his throne;
   from there he rules over everything.
²⁰ Praise the LORD, you angels of his,
   you mighty creatures who carry out his plans,
   listening for each of his commands.
²¹ Yes, praise the LORD, you armies of angels
   who serve him and do his will!
²² Praise the LORD, everything he has created,
   everywhere in his kingdom.
   As for me—I, too, will praise the LORD.

⌇⌁⌇ **Which characteristic of God in this psalm helps you understand him better?** David's praise focused on God's glorious acts. It is easy to complain about life, but David's list gives us plenty for which to praise God—his love, forgiveness, salvation, kindness, mercy, justice, patience, tenderness—we receive all of these without deserving any of them. No matter how difficult your life's journey, you can always count your blessings—past, present, and future. When you feel like you have nothing for which to praise God, read David's list.

MAY **17**

How Well God Knows Us

PSALM 139:1-24

   O LORD, you have examined my heart
   and know everything about me.
² You know when I sit down or stand up.
   You know my every thought when far away.
³ You chart the path ahead of me
   and tell me where to stop and rest.
   Every moment you know where I am.
⁴ You know what I am going to say
   even before I say it, LORD.
⁵ You both precede and follow me.
   You place your hand of blessing on my head.
⁶ Such knowledge is too wonderful for me,
   too great for me to know!

⁷ I can never escape from your spirit!
   I can never get away from your presence!
⁸ If I go up to heaven, you are there;
   if I go down to the place of the dead, you are there.
⁹ If I ride the wings of the morning,

if I dwell by the farthest oceans,
¹⁰ even there your hand will guide me,
and your strength will support me.
¹¹ I could ask the darkness to hide me
and the light around me to become night—
¹²   but even in darkness I cannot hide from you.
To you the night shines as bright as day.
Darkness and light are both alike to you.

¹³ You made all the delicate, inner parts of my body
and knit me together in my mother's womb.
¹⁴ Thank you for making me so wonderfully complex!
Your workmanship is marvelous—and how well I know it.
¹⁵ You watched me as I was being formed in utter seclusion,
as I was woven together in the dark of the womb.
¹⁶ You saw me before I was born.
Every day of my life was recorded in your book.
Every moment was laid out
before a single day had passed.

¹⁷ How precious are your thoughts about me, O God!
They are innumerable!
¹⁸ I can't even count them;
they outnumber the grains of sand!
And when I wake up in the morning,
you are still with me!

¹⁹ O God, if only you would destroy the wicked!
Get out of my life, you murderers!
²⁰ They blaspheme you;
your enemies take your name in vain.
²¹ O LORD, shouldn't I hate those who hate you?
Shouldn't I despise those who resist you?
²² Yes, I hate them with complete hatred,
for your enemies are my enemies.

²³ Search me, O God, and know my heart;
test me and know my thoughts.
²⁴ Point out anything in me that offends you,
and lead me along the path of everlasting life.

What do you feel when you read this psalm? God's character goes into the creation of every person. When you feel worthless or even begin to hate yourself, remember that God's Spirit is ready and willing to work within you to make your character all God meant it to be. God thinks of you constantly (vv. 17-18). We should have as much respect for ourselves as our Maker has for us.

God for All People
and Time

PSALM 145:1-21

I will praise you, my God and King,
and bless your name forever and ever.
2 I will bless you every day,
and I will praise you forever.
3 Great is the LORD! He is most worthy of praise!
His greatness is beyond discovery!

4 Let each generation tell its children
of your mighty acts.
5 I will meditate on your majestic, glorious splendor
and your wonderful miracles.
6 Your awe-inspiring deeds will be on every tongue;
I will proclaim your greatness.
7 Everyone will share the story of your wonderful goodness;
they will sing with joy of your righteousness.

8 The LORD is kind and merciful,
slow to get angry, full of unfailing love.
9 The LORD is good to everyone.
He showers compassion on all his creation.
10 All of your works will thank you, LORD,
and your faithful followers will bless you.
11 They will talk together about the glory of your kingdom;
they will celebrate examples of your power.
12 They will tell about your mighty deeds
and about the majesty and glory of your reign.
13 For your kingdom is an everlasting kingdom.
You rule generation after generation.

The LORD is faithful in all he says;
he is gracious in all he does.
14 The LORD helps the fallen
and lifts up those bent beneath their loads.
15 All eyes look to you for help;
you give them their food as they need it.
16 When you open your hand,
you satisfy the hunger and thirst of every living thing.

17 The LORD is righteous in everything he does;
he is filled with kindness.
18 The LORD is close to all who call on him,
yes, to all who call on him sincerely.

^{19}He fulfills the desires of those who fear him;
   he hears their cries for help and rescues them.
^{20}The LORD protects all those who love him,
   but he destroys the wicked.

^{21}I will praise the LORD,
   and everyone on earth will bless his holy name
   forever and forever.

〰〰 **Which of God's qualities do you most need today?** Sometimes our burdens seem more than we can bear, and we wonder how we can go on. David stands at this bleak intersection of life's road and points toward the Lord, the great burden-bearer. God is able to lift us up because: (1) His greatness is unsearchable (v. 3). (2) He does mighty acts across many generations (v. 4). (3) He is full of glorious splendor and majesty (v. 5). (4) He does wonderful and awesome acts (vv. 5-6). (5) He is righteous (v. 7). (6) He is gracious, compassionate, patient, and merciful (vv. 8-9). (7) He rules over an everlasting kingdom (v. 13). (8) He is our source of all our daily needs (vv. 15-16). (9) He is righteous and gracious in all his dealings (v. 17). (10) He remains near to those who call on him (v. 18). (11) He hears our cries and saves us (vv. 19-20). If you are bending under a burden and feel that you are about to fall, turn to God for help. He is ready to lift you up and bear your burden.

19 MAY

Wise Words about Life
PROVERBS 4:1-27

My children, listen to me. Listen to your father's instruction. Pay attention and grow wise, ^{2}for I am giving you good guidance. Don't turn away from my teaching. ^{3}For I, too, was once my father's son, tenderly loved by my mother as an only child.

^{4}My father told me, "Take my words to heart. Follow my instructions and you will live. ^{5}Learn to be wise, and develop good judgment. Don't forget or turn away from my words. ^{6}Don't turn your back on wisdom, for she will protect you. Love her, and she will guard you. ^{7}Getting wisdom is the most important thing you can do! And whatever else you do, get good judgment. ^{8}If you prize wisdom, she will exalt you. Embrace her and she will honor you. ^{9}She will place a lovely wreath on your head; she will present you with a beautiful crown."

^{10}My child, listen to me and do as I say, and you will have a long, good life. ^{11}I will teach you wisdom's ways and lead you in straight paths. ^{12}If you live a life guided by wisdom, you won't limp or stumble as you run. ^{13}Carry out my instructions; don't forsake them. Guard them, for they will lead you to a fulfilled life.

¹⁴Do not do as the wicked do or follow the path of evildoers. ¹⁵Avoid their haunts. Turn away and go somewhere else, ¹⁶for evil people cannot sleep until they have done their evil deed for the day. They cannot rest unless they have caused someone to stumble. ¹⁷They eat wickedness and drink violence!

¹⁸The way of the righteous is like the first gleam of dawn, which shines ever brighter until the full light of day. ¹⁹But the way of the wicked is like complete darkness. Those who follow it have no idea what they are stumbling over.

²⁰Pay attention, my child, to what I say. Listen carefully. ²¹Don't lose sight of my words. Let them penetrate deep within your heart, ²²for they bring life and radiant health to anyone who discovers their meaning.

²³Above all else, guard your heart, for it affects everything you do.

²⁴Avoid all perverse talk; stay far from corrupt speech.

²⁵Look straight ahead, and fix your eyes on what lies before you. ²⁶Mark out a straight path for your feet; then stick to the path and stay safe. ²⁷Don't get sidetracked; keep your feet from following evil.

〜〽〰 **What priority does finding wisdom have in your life?** If you want wisdom, you must decide to go after it. It takes resolve—a determination not to abandon the search once you begin no matter how difficult the road may become. This is not a once-in-a-lifetime step but a daily process of choosing between two paths—the wicked (vv. 14-17, 19) and the Just (v. 18). Nothing else is more important or more valuable. Choose your path wisely today.

MAY

Wise Words about Sex

PROVERBS 5:1-23

My son, pay attention to my wisdom; listen carefully to my wise counsel. ²Then you will learn to be discreet and will store up knowledge.

³The lips of an immoral woman are as sweet as honey, and her mouth is smoother than oil. ⁴But the result is as bitter as poison, sharp as a double-edged sword. ⁵Her feet go down to death; her steps lead straight to the grave. ⁶For she does not care about the path to life. She staggers down a crooked trail and doesn't even realize where it leads.

⁷So now, my sons, listen to me. Never stray from what I am about to say: ⁸Run from her! Don't go near the door of her house! ⁹If you do, you will lose your honor and hand over to merciless people everything you have achieved in life. ¹⁰Strangers will obtain your wealth, and someone else will enjoy the fruit of your labor. ¹¹Afterward you will groan in anguish when disease consumes your body, ¹²and you will say, "How I hated discipline! If only I had not demanded my own way! ¹³Oh, why didn't I listen to my

teachers? Why didn't I pay attention to those who gave me instruction? [14]I have come to the brink of utter ruin, and now I must face public disgrace." [15]Drink water from your own well—share your love only with your wife. [16]Why spill the water of your springs in public, having sex with just anyone? [17]You should reserve it for yourselves. Don't share it with strangers.

[18]Let your wife be a fountain of blessing for you. Rejoice in the wife of your youth. [19]She is a loving doe, a graceful deer. Let her breasts satisfy you always. May you always be captivated by her love. [20]Why be captivated, my son, with an immoral woman, or embrace the breasts of an adulterous woman?

[21]For the LORD sees clearly what a man does, examining every path he takes. [22]An evil man is held captive by his own sins; they are ropes that catch and hold him. [23]He will die for lack of self-control; he will be lost because of his incredible folly.

How does the above passage match what you hear around you every day? God does not intend marriage to be boring and dull. Sex is a gift that God gives to married people for their mutual enjoyment. Real happiness comes when we decide to find pleasure in the relationship God has given or will give us and to commit ourselves to making it pleasurable for the one God gives us to love. That may not be what you read in the newspaper or what your friends think, but if you commit yourself to purity, you won't shortchange your future.

21 MAY

A Summary of Life

ECCLESIASTES 12:1-14

Don't let the excitement of youth cause you to forget your Creator. Honor him in your youth before you grow old and no longer enjoy living. [2]It will be too late then to remember him, when the light of the sun and moon and stars is dim to your old eyes, and there is no silver lining left among the clouds. [3]Your limbs will tremble with age, and your strong legs will grow weak. Your teeth will be too few to do their work, and you will be blind, too. [4]And when your teeth are gone, keep your lips tightly closed when you eat! Even the chirping of birds will wake you up. But you yourself will be deaf and tuneless, with a quavering voice. [5]You will be afraid of heights and of falling, white-haired and withered, dragging along without any sexual desire. You will be standing at death's door. And as you near your everlasting home, the mourners will walk along the streets.

[6]Yes, remember your Creator now while you are young, before the silver cord of life snaps and the golden bowl is broken. Don't wait until the water jar is smashed at the spring and the pulley is broken at the well. [7]For then the dust will return to the earth, and the spirit will return to God who gave it.

[8]"All is meaningless," says the Teacher, "utterly meaningless."

⁹Because the Teacher was wise, he taught the people everything he knew. He collected proverbs and classified them. ¹⁰Indeed, the Teacher taught the plain truth, and he did so in an interesting way.

¹¹A wise teacher's words spur students to action and emphasize important truths. The collected sayings of the wise are like guidance from a shepherd.

¹²But, my child, be warned: There is no end of opinions ready to be expressed. Studying them can go on forever and become very exhausting!

¹³Here is my final conclusion: Fear God and obey his commands, for this is the duty of every person. ¹⁴God will judge us for everything we do, including every secret thing, whether good or bad.

⌇⋀⋌ In what way can you remember your Creator today? A life without God produces a bitter, lonely, and hopeless old person. A life centered around God is fulfilling; it makes the "evil years"—when disabilities, sicknesses, and handicaps could cause barriers to enjoying life—satisfying because of the hope of eternal life. Being young is exciting, but the excitement of youth can become a barrier to closeness with God. However, those things that most young people live for (sports, sex, popularity) become increasingly unimportant with old age. Make your strength available to God when it is still yours—during your youthful years. Don't waste it on evil or meaningless activities that become bad habits and make you callous. Seek God now.

MAY 22

God Chooses Isaiah
ISAIAH 6:1-13

In the year King Uzziah died, I saw the Lord. He was sitting on a lofty throne, and the train of his robe filled the Temple. ²Hovering around him were mighty seraphim, each with six wings. With two wings they covered their faces, with two they covered their feet, and with the remaining two they flew. ³In a great chorus they sang, "Holy, holy, holy is the LORD Almighty! The whole earth is filled with his glory!" ⁴The glorious singing shook the Temple to its foundations, and the entire sanctuary was filled with smoke.

⁵Then I said, "My destruction is sealed, for I am a sinful man and a member of a sinful race. Yet I have seen the King, the LORD Almighty!"

⁶Then one of the seraphim flew over to the altar, and he picked up a burning coal with a pair of tongs. ⁷He touched my lips with it and said, "See, this coal has touched your lips. Now your guilt is removed, and your sins are forgiven."

⁸Then I heard the Lord asking, "Whom should I send as a messenger to my people? Who will go for us?"

And I said, "Lord, I'll go! Send me."

⁹And he said, "Yes, go. But tell my people this: 'You will hear my words, but you will not understand. You will see what I do, but you will not perceive its meaning.' ¹⁰Harden the hearts of these people. Close their ears, and shut their eyes. That way, they will not see with their eyes, hear with their ears, understand with their hearts, and turn to me for healing."

¹¹Then I said, "Lord, how long must I do this?"

And he replied, "Until their cities are destroyed, with no one left in them. Until their houses are deserted and the whole country is an utter wasteland. ¹²Do not stop until the LORD has sent everyone away to distant lands and the entire land of Israel lies deserted. ¹³Even if only a tenth—a remnant—survive, it will be invaded again and burned. Israel will remain a stump, like a tree that is cut down, but the stump will be a holy seed that will grow again."

〜〜〜 **When did you last realize your continuing need for God's forgiveness?** Isaiah's lofty view of God in verses 1-4 gives us a sense of God's greatness, mystery, and power. His recognition of his sinfulness before God encourages us to confess our sin. His picture of forgiveness reminds us that we, too, are forgiven. When we recognize how great our God is, how sinful we are, and the extent of his forgiveness, we are energized to do his work. How does your concept of the greatness of God measure up to Isaiah's?

23 MAY

The Suffering Servant
ISAIAH 53:1-12

Who has believed our message? To whom will the LORD reveal his saving power? ²My servant grew up in the LORD's presence like a tender green shoot, sprouting from a root in dry and sterile ground. There was nothing beautiful or majestic about his appearance, nothing to attract us to him. ³He was despised and rejected—a man of sorrows, acquainted with bitterest grief. We turned our backs on him and looked the other way when he went by. He was despised, and we did not care.

⁴Yet it was our weaknesses he carried; it was our sorrows that weighed him down. And we thought his troubles were a punishment from God for his own sins! ⁵But he was wounded and crushed for our sins. He was beaten that we might have peace. He was whipped, and we were healed! ⁶All of us have strayed away like sheep. We have left God's paths to follow our own. Yet the LORD laid on him the guilt and sins of us all.

⁷He was oppressed and treated harshly, yet he never said a word. He was led as a lamb to the slaughter. And as a sheep is silent before the shearers, he did not open his mouth. ⁸From prison and trial they led him away to his death. But who among the people realized that he was dying for their sins— that he was suffering their punishment? ⁹He had done no wrong, and he

never deceived anyone. But he was buried like a criminal; he was put in a rich man's grave. ¹⁰But it was the LORD's good plan to crush him and fill him with grief. Yet when his life is made an offering for sin, he will have a multitude of children, many heirs. He will enjoy a long life, and the LORD's plan will prosper in his hands. ¹¹When he sees all that is accomplished by his anguish, he will be satisfied. And because of what he has experienced, my righteous servant will make it possible for many to be counted righteous, for he will bear all their sins. ¹²I will give him the honors of one who is mighty and great, because he exposed himself to death. He was counted among those who were sinners. He bore the sins of many and interceded for sinners.

~\/~ **How would you describe what Jesus did for you?** Isaiah speaks of the people of Israel straying from God and compares them to wandering sheep. Yet God would send the Messiah to bring them back into the fold. We have the hindsight to see and know the identity of the promised Messiah who has come and died for our sins. But if we can see all that Jesus did and still reject him, our sin is much greater than that of the ancient Israelites who could not see what we have seen. Have you given your life to Jesus Christ, the Good Shepherd (John 10:11-16), or are you still like a wandering sheep?

MAY 24

God Calls a Prophet
JEREMIAH 1:1-9

These are the words of Jeremiah son of Hilkiah, one of the priests from Anathoth, a town in the land of Benjamin. ²The LORD first gave messages to Jeremiah during the thirteenth year of King Josiah's reign in Judah. ³He continued to give messages throughout the reign of Josiah's son, King Jehoiakim, until the eleventh year of King Zedekiah's reign in Judah. In August of that year, the people of Jerusalem were taken away as captives.

⁴The LORD gave me a message. He said, ⁵"I knew you before I formed you in your mother's womb. Before you were born I set you apart and appointed you as my spokesman to the world."

⁶"O Sovereign LORD," I said, "I can't speak for you! I'm too young!"

⁷"Don't say that," the LORD replied, "for you must go wherever I send you and say whatever I tell you. ⁸And don't be afraid of the people, for I will be with you and take care of you. I, the LORD, have spoken!"

⁹Then the LORD touched my mouth and said, "See, I have put my words in your mouth!"

~\/~ **What is your reaction to the possibility of God using your life?** Often people struggle with new challenges because they lack self-confidence, feeling that they have inadequate ability, training, or experience. Jeremiah thought he was "too young" and inexperienced to be God's spokesman to the world. But God promised to be with him. We should not allow feelings of inadequacy to keep us from obeying God's call. He will *always* be with us. When you find yourself avoiding something you know you should do, be careful not to use your lack of self-confidence as an excuse. If God gives you a job to do, he will provide all you need to do it.

25 MAY

The Book Burning
JEREMIAH 36:1-32

During the fourth year that Jehoiakim son of Josiah was king in Judah, the LORD gave this message to Jeremiah: ²"Get a scroll, and write down all my messages against Israel, Judah, and the other nations. Begin with the first message back in the days of Josiah, and write down every message you have given, right up to the present time. ³Perhaps the people of Judah will repent if they see in writing all the terrible things I have planned for them. Then I will be able to forgive their sins and wrongdoings."

⁴So Jeremiah sent for Baruch son of Neriah, and as Jeremiah dictated, Baruch wrote down all the prophecies that the LORD had given him. ⁵Then Jeremiah said to Baruch, "I am a prisoner here and unable to go to the Temple. ⁶So you go to the Temple on the next day of fasting, and read the messages from the LORD that are on this scroll. On that day people will be there from all over Judah. ⁷Perhaps even yet they will turn from their evil ways and ask the LORD's forgiveness before it is too late. For the LORD's terrible anger has been pronounced against them."

⁸Baruch did as Jeremiah told him and read these messages from the LORD to the people at the Temple. ⁹This happened on the day of sacred fasting held in late autumn, during the fifth year of the reign of Jehoiakim son of Josiah. People from all over Judah came to attend the services at the Temple on that day. ¹⁰Baruch read Jeremiah's words to all the people from the Temple room of Gemariah son of Shaphan. This room was just off the upper courtyard of the Temple, near the New Gate entrance.

¹¹When Micaiah son of Gemariah and grandson of Shaphan heard the messages from the LORD, ¹²he went down to the secretary's room in the palace where the administrative officials were meeting. Elishama the secretary was there, along with Delaiah son of Shemaiah, Elnathan son of Acbor, Gemariah son of Shaphan, Zedekiah son of Hananiah, and all the others with official responsibilities. ¹³When Micaiah told them about the messages Baruch was reading to the people, ¹⁴the officials sent Jehudi son of Nethaniah, grandson of Shelemiah, and great-grandson of Cushi, to ask Baruch to come and read the messages to them, too. So Baruch took the scroll and

went to them. [15]"Sit down and read the scroll to us," the officials said, and Baruch did as they requested.

[16]By the time Baruch had finished reading, they were badly frightened. "We must tell the king what we have heard," they said. [17]"But first, tell us how you got these messages. Did they come directly from Jeremiah?"

[18]So Baruch explained, "Jeremiah dictated them to me word by word, and I wrote down his words with ink on this scroll."

[19]"You and Jeremiah should both hide," the officials told Baruch. "Don't tell anyone where you are!" [20]Then the officials left the scroll for safekeeping in the room of Elishama the secretary and went to tell the king.

[21]The king sent Jehudi to get the scroll. Jehudi brought it from Elishama's room and read it to the king as all his officials stood by. [22]It was late autumn, and the king was in a winterized part of the palace, sitting in front of a fire to keep warm. [23]Whenever Jehudi finished reading three or four columns, the king took his knife and cut off that section of the scroll. He then threw it into the fire, section by section, until the whole scroll was burned up. [24]Neither the king nor his officials showed any signs of fear or repentance at what they heard. [25]Even when Elnathan, Delaiah, and Gemariah begged the king not to burn the scroll, he wouldn't listen.

[26]Then the king commanded his son Jerahmeel, Seraiah son of Azriel, and Shelemiah son of Abdeel to arrest Baruch and Jeremiah. But the LORD had hidden them.

[27]After the king had burned Jeremiah's scroll, the LORD gave Jeremiah another message. He said, [28]"Get another scroll, and write everything again just as you did on the scroll King Jehoiakim burned. [29]Then say to the king, 'This is what the LORD says: You burned the scroll because it said the king of Babylon would destroy this land and everything in it. [30]Now this is what the LORD says about King Jehoiakim of Judah: He will have no heirs to sit on the throne of David. His dead body will be thrown out to lie unburied— exposed to hot days and frosty nights. [31]I will punish him and his family and his officials because of their sins. I will pour out on them and on all the people of Judah and Jerusalem all the disasters I have promised, for they would not listen to my warnings.'"

[32]Then Jeremiah took another scroll and dictated again to his secretary Baruch. He wrote everything that had been on the scroll King Jehoiakim had burned in the fire. Only this time, he added much more!

〰️〰️ **How much risk is involved in your relationship with God?** God told Jeremiah to write his words on a scroll. Because he was not allowed to go to the Temple, Jeremiah asked his scribe, Baruch, to whom he had dictated the scroll, to read it to the people gathered there. Baruch then read it to the officials, and finally Jehudi read it to the king himself. Although the king burned the scroll, he could not destroy God's Word. Today many people try to put God's Word aside or say that it contains errors and therefore cannot be trusted. People may reject God's Word, but they cannot destroy it. God's Word will stand forever (Ps. 119:89). As you read this book, realize that the words are God's timeless message to all the world and to you personally.

26 MAY

Jeremiah in the Well

JEREMIAH 38:1-13

Now Shephatiah son of Mattan, Gedaliah son of Pashhur, Jehucal son of Shelemiah, and Pashhur son of Malkijah heard what Jeremiah had been telling the people. He was saying, ²"This is what the LORD says: Everyone who stays in Jerusalem will die from war, famine, or disease, but those who surrender to the Babylonians will live. ³The LORD also says: The city of Jerusalem will surely be handed over to the army of the king of Babylon, who will capture it."

⁴So these officials went to the king and said, "Sir, this man must die! That kind of talk will undermine the morale of the few fighting men we have left, as well as that of all the people, too. This man is a traitor!"

⁵So King Zedekiah agreed. "All right," he said. "Do as you like. I will do nothing to stop you."

⁶So the officials took Jeremiah from his cell and lowered him by ropes into an empty cistern in the prison yard. It belonged to Malkijah, a member of the royal family. There was no water in the cistern, but there was a thick layer of mud at the bottom, and Jeremiah sank down into it.

⁷But Ebed-melech the Ethiopian, an important palace official, heard that Jeremiah was in the cistern. At that time the king was holding court at the Benjamin Gate, ⁸so Ebed-melech rushed from the palace to speak with him. ⁹"My lord the king," he said, "these men have done a very evil thing in putting Jeremiah the prophet into the cistern. He will soon die of hunger, for almost all the bread in the city is gone."

¹⁰So the king told Ebed-melech, "Take along thirty of my men, and pull Jeremiah out of the cistern before he dies."

¹¹So Ebed-melech took the men with him and went to a room in the palace beneath the treasury, where he found some old rags and discarded clothing. He carried these to the cistern and lowered them to Jeremiah on a rope. ¹²Ebed-melech called down to Jeremiah, "Put these rags under your armpits to protect you from the ropes." Then when Jeremiah was ready, ¹³they pulled him out. So Jeremiah was returned to the courtyard of the guard—the palace prison—where he remained.

〰️ **What part of your life compares in any way with Jeremiah's time in the well?** Ebed-melech feared God more than people. He alone among the palace officials stood up against the murder plot. His obedience could have cost him his life. Because he obeyed, however, he was spared when Jerusalem fell (39:15-18). You can either go along with the crowd or speak up for God. When someone is treated unkindly or unjustly, for example, reach out to that person with God's love. You may be the only one who does. And when you're being treated unkindly yourself, be sure to thank God when he sends an "Ebed-melech" your way.

A Valley of Dry Bones

EZEKIEL 37:1-14

The LORD took hold of me, and I was carried away by the Spirit of the LORD to a valley filled with bones. [2]He led me around among the old, dry bones that covered the valley floor. They were scattered everywhere across the ground. [3]Then he asked me, "Son of man, can these bones become living people again?"

"O Sovereign LORD," I replied, "you alone know the answer to that."

[4]Then he said to me, "Speak to these bones and say, 'Dry bones, listen to the word of the LORD! [5]This is what the Sovereign LORD says: Look! I am going to breathe into you and make you live again! [6]I will put flesh and muscles on you and cover you with skin. I will put breath into you, and you will come to life. Then you will know that I am the LORD.' "

[7]So I spoke these words, just as he told me. Suddenly as I spoke, there was a rattling noise all across the valley. The bones of each body came together and attached themselves as they had been before. [8]Then as I watched, muscles and flesh formed over the bones. Then skin formed to cover their bodies, but they still had no breath in them.

[9]Then he said to me, "Speak to the winds and say: 'This is what the Sovereign LORD says: Come, O breath, from the four winds! Breathe into these dead bodies so that they may live again.' "

[10]So I spoke as he commanded me, and the wind entered the bodies, and they began to breathe. They all came to life and stood up on their feet—a great army of them.

[11]Then he said to me, "Son of man, these bones represent the people of Israel. They are saying, 'We have become old, dry bones—all hope is gone.' [12]Now give them this message from the Sovereign LORD: O my people, I will open your graves of exile and cause you to rise again. Then I will bring you back to the land of Israel. [13]When this happens, O my people, you will know that I am the LORD. [14]I will put my Spirit in you, and you will live and return home to your own land. Then you will know that I am the LORD. You will see that I have done everything just as I promised. I, the LORD, have spoken!"

〰️〰️ **What can you do to help you understand God's plan for the world?** The dry bones represented the people's spiritually dead condition. Your church may seem like a heap of dried-up bones to you, spiritually dead with no hope of vitality. But just as God promised to restore his nation, he can

215

restore any church, no matter how dry or dead it may be. Rather than give up, pray for renewal, for God can restore it to life. The hope and prayer of every church should be that God will put his Spirit into it (v. 14). In fact, God is at work calling his people back to himself, bringing new life into dead churches.

28 MAY

Coping with Pressure to Conform

DANIEL 1:1-21

During the third year of King Jehoiakim's reign in Judah, King Nebuchadnezzar of Babylon came to Jerusalem and besieged it with his armies. ²The Lord gave him victory over King Jehoiakim of Judah. When Nebuchadnezzar returned to Babylon, he took with him some of the sacred objects from the Temple of God and placed them in the treasure-house of his god in the land of Babylonia.

³Then the king ordered Ashpenaz, who was in charge of the palace officials, to bring to the palace some of the young men of Judah's royal family and other noble families, who had been brought to Babylon as captives. ⁴"Select only strong, healthy, and good-looking young men," he said. "Make sure they are well versed in every branch of learning, are gifted with knowledge and good sense, and have the poise needed to serve in the royal palace. Teach these young men the language and literature of the Babylonians." ⁵The king assigned them a daily ration of the best food and wine from his own kitchens. They were to be trained for a three-year period, and then some of them would be made his advisers in the royal court.

⁶Daniel, Hananiah, Mishael, and Azariah were four of the young men chosen, all from the tribe of Judah. ⁷The chief official renamed them with these Babylonian names:

Daniel was called Belteshazzar.
Hananiah was called Shadrach.
Mishael was called Meshach.
Azariah was called Abednego.

⁸But Daniel made up his mind not to defile himself by eating the food and wine given to them by the king. He asked the chief official for permission to eat other things instead. ⁹Now God had given the chief official great respect for Daniel. ¹⁰But he was alarmed by Daniel's suggestion. "My lord the king has ordered that you eat this food and wine," he said. "If you become pale and thin compared to the other youths your age, I am afraid the king will have me beheaded for neglecting my duties." ¹¹Daniel talked it over with the attendant who had been appointed by the chief official to look after Daniel, Hananiah, Mishael, and Azariah. ¹²"Test us for ten days on a diet of vegetables and water," Daniel said. ¹³"At the end

of the ten days, see how we look compared to the other young men who are eating the king's rich food. Then you can decide whether or not to let us continue eating our diet." [14]So the attendant agreed to Daniel's suggestion and tested them for ten days.

[15]At the end of the ten days, Daniel and his three friends looked healthier and better nourished than the young men who had been eating the food assigned by the king. [16]So after that, the attendant fed them only vegetables instead of the rich foods and wines. [17]God gave these four young men an unusual aptitude for learning the literature and science of the time. And God gave Daniel special ability in understanding the meanings of visions and dreams.

[18]When the three-year training period ordered by the king was completed, the chief official brought all the young men to King Nebuchadnezzar. [19]The king talked with each of them, and none of them impressed him as much as Daniel, Hananiah, Mishael, and Azariah. So they were appointed to his regular staff of advisers. [20]In all matters requiring wisdom and balanced judgment, the king found the advice of these young men to be ten times better than that of all the magicians and enchanters in his entire kingdom.

[21]Daniel remained there until the first year of King Cyrus's reign.

How might Daniel react to the pressure situations in your life?
It is easier to resist temptation if you have thought through your convictions well before the temptation arises. Daniel and his friends made their decision to be faithful to the laws of their religion before they were faced with the king's delicacies, so they did not hesitate to stick with their convictions. Sometimes we get into trouble because we have not previously decided where to draw the line. Before such situations arise, decide on your commitments. Then when temptation comes, you will be ready and able to resist.

MAY 29

A King's Dream
DANIEL 2:1-24

One night during the second year of his reign, Nebuchadnezzar had a dream that disturbed him so much that he couldn't sleep. [2]He called in his magicians, enchanters, sorcerers, and astrologers, and he demanded that they tell him what he had dreamed. As they stood before the king, [3]he said, "I have had a dream that troubles me. Tell me what I dreamed, for I must know what it means."

[4]Then the astrologers answered the king in Aramaic, "Long live the king! Tell us the dream, and we will tell you what it means."

[5]But the king said to the astrologers, "I am serious about this. If you don't tell me what my dream was and what it means, you will be torn limb from limb, and your houses will be demolished into heaps of rubble! [6]But if you

tell me what I dreamed and what the dream means, I will give you many wonderful gifts and honors. Just tell me the dream and what it means!" ⁷They said again, "Please, Your Majesty. Tell us the dream, and we will tell you what it means."

⁸The king replied, "I can see through your trick! You are trying to stall for time because you know I am serious about what I said. ⁹If you don't tell me the dream, you will be condemned. You have conspired to tell me lies in hopes that something will change. But tell me the dream, and then I will know that you can tell me what it means."

¹⁰The astrologers replied to the king, "There isn't a man alive who can tell Your Majesty his dream! And no king, however great and powerful, has ever asked such a thing of any magician, enchanter, or astrologer! ¹¹This is an impossible thing the king requires. No one except the gods can tell you your dream, and they do not live among people."

¹²The king was furious when he heard this, and he sent out orders to execute all the wise men of Babylon. ¹³And because of the king's decree, men were sent to find and kill Daniel and his friends. ¹⁴When Arioch, the commander of the king's guard, came to kill them, Daniel handled the situation with wisdom and discretion. ¹⁵He asked Arioch, "Why has the king issued such a harsh decree?" So Arioch told him all that had happened. ¹⁶Daniel went at once to see the king and requested more time so he could tell the king what the dream meant.

¹⁷Then Daniel went home and told his friends Hananiah, Mishael, and Azariah what had happened. ¹⁸He urged them to ask the God of heaven to show them his mercy by telling them the secret, so they would not be executed along with the other wise men of Babylon. ¹⁹That night the secret was revealed to Daniel in a vision. Then Daniel praised the God of heaven, ²⁰saying,

"Praise the name of God forever and ever,
    for he alone has all wisdom and power.
²¹ He determines the course of world events;
    he removes kings and sets others on the throne.
He gives wisdom to the wise
    and knowledge to the scholars.
²² He reveals deep and mysterious things
    and knows what lies hidden in darkness,
    though he himself is surrounded by light.
²³ I thank and praise you, God of my ancestors,
    for you have given me wisdom and strength.
You have told me what we asked of you
    and revealed to us what the king demanded."

²⁴Then Daniel went in to see Arioch, who had been ordered to execute the wise men of Babylon. Daniel said to him, "Don't kill the wise men. Take me to the king, and I will tell him the meaning of his dream."

~◝◞◟◝ **What do you do in seemingly hopeless situations?** Daniel was at a crisis point. Imagine going to see the powerful, temperamental king who had just angrily ordered your death! Daniel did not shrink back in fear, however, but he confidently believed that God would tell him all that the king wanted to know. When the king gave Daniel time to find the answer, Daniel found his three friends and they prayed. When you find yourself in a tight spot, share your needs with trusted friends who also believe in God's power. Prayer is more effective than panic. Panic confirms your hopelessness; prayer confirms your hope in God. Daniel's trust in God saved himself, his three friends, and all the wise men.

MAY

The Meaning of the Dream

DANIEL 2:25-49

Then Arioch quickly took Daniel to the king and said, "I have found one of the captives from Judah who will tell Your Majesty the meaning of your dream!"

²⁶The king said to Daniel (also known as Belteshazzar), "Is this true? Can you tell me what my dream was and what it means?"

²⁷Daniel replied, "There are no wise men, enchanters, magicians, or fortune-tellers who can tell the king such things. ²⁸But there is a God in heaven who reveals secrets, and he has shown King Nebuchadnezzar what will happen in the future. Now I will tell you your dream and the visions you saw as you lay on your bed.

²⁹"While Your Majesty was sleeping, you dreamed about coming events. The revealer of mysteries has shown you what is going to happen. ³⁰And it is not because I am wiser than any living person that I know the secret of your dream, but because God wanted you to understand what you were thinking about.

³¹"Your Majesty, in your vision you saw in front of you a huge and powerful statue of a man, shining brilliantly, frightening and awesome. ³²The head of the statue was made of fine gold, its chest and arms were of silver, its belly and thighs were of bronze, ³³its legs were of iron, and its feet were a combination of iron and clay. ³⁴But as you watched, a rock was cut from a mountain by supernatural means. It struck the feet of iron and clay, smashing them to bits. ³⁵The whole statue collapsed into a heap of iron, clay, bronze, silver, and gold. The pieces were crushed as small as chaff on a threshing floor, and the wind blew them all away without a trace. But the rock that knocked the statue down became a great mountain that covered the whole earth.

³⁶"That was the dream; now I will tell Your Majesty what it means. ³⁷Your Majesty, you are a king over many kings. The God of heaven has given you

219

sovereignty, power, strength, and honor. [38]He has made you the ruler over all the inhabited world and has put even the animals and birds under your control. You are the head of gold.

[39]"But after your kingdom comes to an end, another great kingdom, inferior to yours, will rise to take your place. After that kingdom has fallen, yet a third great kingdom, represented by the bronze belly and thighs, will rise to rule the world. [40]Following that kingdom, there will be a fourth great kingdom, as strong as iron. That kingdom will smash and crush all previous empires, just as iron smashes and crushes everything it strikes. [41]The feet and toes you saw that were a combination of iron and clay show that this kingdom will be divided. [42]Some parts of it will be as strong as iron, and others as weak as clay. [43]This mixture of iron and clay also shows that these kingdoms will try to strengthen themselves by forming alliances with each other through intermarriage. But this will not succeed, just as iron and clay do not mix.

[44]"During the reigns of those kings, the God of heaven will set up a kingdom that will never be destroyed; no one will ever conquer it. It will shatter all these kingdoms into nothingness, but it will stand forever. [45]That is the meaning of the rock cut from the mountain by supernatural means, crushing to dust the statue of iron, bronze, clay, silver, and gold.

"The great God has shown Your Majesty what will happen in the future. The dream is true, and its meaning is certain."

[46]Then King Nebuchadnezzar bowed to the ground before Daniel and worshiped him, and he commanded his people to offer sacrifices and burn sweet incense before him. [47]The king said to Daniel, "Truly, your God is the God of gods, the Lord over kings, a revealer of mysteries, for you have been able to reveal this secret."

[48]Then the king appointed Daniel to a high position and gave him many valuable gifts. He made Daniel ruler over the whole province of Babylon, as well as chief over all his wise men. [49]At Daniel's request, the king appointed Shadrach, Meshach, and Abednego to be in charge of all the affairs of the province of Babylon, while Daniel remained in the king's court.

〜�〜 **Who gets the credit when things go right in your life?** Nebuchadnezzar honored Daniel and Daniel's God. If Daniel had taken the credit himself, the king would have honored only Daniel. Because Daniel gave God the credit, the king honored both of them. Part of our mission in this world is to show nonbelievers what God is like. We can do that by giving God credit for the great things he does in our life. Our acts of love and compassion may make an impression on people, and if we give God credit for our actions, they will want to know more about him. Give thanks to God for what he is doing in and through you.

Three Friends in a Furnace

DANIEL 3:1-30

King Nebuchadnezzar made a gold statue ninety feet tall and nine feet wide and set it up on the plain of Dura in the province of Babylon. ²Then he sent messages to the princes, prefects, governors, advisers, counselors, judges, magistrates, and all the provincial officials to come to the dedication of the statue he had set up. ³When all these officials had arrived and were standing before the image King Nebuchadnezzar had set up, ⁴a herald shouted out, "People of all races and nations and languages, listen to the king's command! ⁵When you hear the sound of the horn, flute, zither, lyre, harp, pipes, and other instruments, bow to the ground to worship King Nebuchadnezzar's gold statue. ⁶Anyone who refuses to obey will immediately be thrown into a blazing furnace."

⁷So at the sound of the musical instruments, all the people, whatever their race or nation or language, bowed to the ground and worshiped the statue that King Nebuchadnezzar had set up.

⁸But some of the astrologers went to the king and informed on the Jews. ⁹They said to King Nebuchadnezzar, "Long live the king! ¹⁰You issued a decree requiring all the people to bow down and worship the gold statue when they hear the sound of the musical instruments. ¹¹That decree also states that those who refuse to obey must be thrown into a blazing furnace. ¹²But there are some Jews—Shadrach, Meshach, and Abednego—whom you have put in charge of the province of Babylon. They have defied Your Majesty by refusing to serve your gods or to worship the gold statue you have set up."

¹³Then Nebuchadnezzar flew into a rage and ordered Shadrach, Meshach, and Abednego to be brought before him. When they were brought in, ¹⁴Nebuchadnezzar said to them, "Is it true, Shadrach, Meshach, and Abednego, that you refuse to serve my gods or to worship the gold statue I have set up? ¹⁵I will give you one more chance. If you bow down and worship the statue I have made when you hear the sound of the musical instruments, all will be well. But if you refuse, you will be thrown immediately into the blazing furnace. What god will be able to rescue you from my power then?"

¹⁶Shadrach, Meshach, and Abednego replied, "O Nebuchadnezzar, we do not need to defend ourselves before you. ¹⁷If we are thrown into the blazing furnace, the God whom we serve is able to save us. He will rescue us from your power, Your Majesty. ¹⁸But even if he doesn't, Your Majesty can be sure that we will never serve your gods or worship the gold statue you have set up."

¹⁹Nebuchadnezzar was so furious with Shadrach, Meshach, and Abednego that his face became distorted with rage. He commanded that the furnace be heated seven times hotter than usual. ²⁰Then he ordered some of

the strongest men of his army to bind Shadrach, Meshach, and Abednego and throw them into the blazing furnace. [21]So they tied them up and threw them into the furnace, fully clothed. [22]And because the king, in his anger, had demanded such a hot fire in the furnace, the flames leaped out and killed the soldiers as they threw the three men in! [23]So Shadrach, Meshach, and Abednego, securely tied, fell down into the roaring flames.

[24]But suddenly, as he was watching, Nebuchadnezzar jumped up in amazement and exclaimed to his advisers, "Didn't we tie up three men and throw them into the furnace?"

"Yes," they said, "we did indeed, Your Majesty."

[25]"Look!" Nebuchadnezzar shouted. "I see four men, unbound, walking around in the fire. They aren't even hurt by the flames! And the fourth looks like a divine being!"

[26]Then Nebuchadnezzar came as close as he could to the door of the flaming furnace and shouted: "Shadrach, Meshach, and Abednego, servants of the Most High God, come out! Come here!" So Shadrach, Meshach, and Abednego stepped out of the fire. [27]Then the princes, prefects, governors, and advisers crowded around them and saw that the fire had not touched them. Not a hair on their heads was singed, and their clothing was not scorched. They didn't even smell of smoke!

[28]Then Nebuchadnezzar said, "Praise to the God of Shadrach, Meshach, and Abednego! He sent his angel to rescue his servants who trusted in him. They defied the king's command and were willing to die rather than serve or worship any god except their own God. [29]Therefore, I make this decree: If any people, whatever their race or nation or language, speak a word against the God of Shadrach, Meshach, and Abednego, they will be torn limb from limb, and their houses will be crushed into heaps of rubble. There is no other god who can rescue like this!" [30]Then the king promoted Shadrach, Meshach, and Abednego to even higher positions in the province of Babylon.

~\/\/~ **What examples can you give of God's protection in your life?** Why didn't the three men just bow to the image and tell God that they didn't mean it? They had determined never to worship another god, and they courageously took their stand. As a result, they were condemned and led away to be executed. They did not know whether they would be delivered from the fire; all they knew was that they would not bow to an idol. Are you ready to take a stand for God no matter what? When you stand for God, you will stand out. It may be painful, and it may not always have a happy ending. Be prepared to say, "If he delivers me, or if he doesn't, I will serve only God."

The Writing on the Wall

DANIEL 5:1-31

A number of years later, King Belshazzar gave a great feast for a thousand of his nobles and drank wine with them. [2]While Belshazzar was drinking, he gave orders to bring in the gold and silver cups that his predecessor, Nebuchadnezzar, had taken from the Temple in Jerusalem, so that he and his nobles, his wives, and his concubines might drink from them. [3]So they brought these gold cups taken from the Temple of God in Jerusalem, and the king and his nobles, his wives, and his concubines drank from them. [4]They drank toasts from them to honor their idols made of gold, silver, bronze, iron, wood, and stone.

[5]At that very moment they saw the fingers of a human hand writing on the plaster wall of the king's palace, near the lampstand. The king himself saw the hand as it wrote, [6]and his face turned pale with fear. Such terror gripped him that his knees knocked together and his legs gave way beneath him.

[7]The king shouted for the enchanters, astrologers, and fortune-tellers to be brought before him. He said to these wise men of Babylon, "Whoever can read this writing and tell me what it means will be dressed in purple robes of royal honor and will wear a gold chain around his neck. He will become the third highest ruler in the kingdom!" [8]But when all the king's wise men came in, none of them could read the writing or tell him what it meant. [9]So the king grew even more alarmed, and his face turned ashen white. His nobles, too, were shaken.

[10]But when the queen mother heard what was happening, she hurried to the banquet hall. She said to Belshazzar, "Long live the king! Don't be so pale and afraid about this. [11]There is a man in your kingdom who has within him the spirit of the holy gods. During Nebuchadnezzar's reign, this man was found to have insight, understanding, and wisdom as though he himself were a god. Your predecessor, King Nebuchadnezzar, made him chief over all the magicians, enchanters, astrologers, and fortune-tellers of Babylon. [12]This man Daniel, whom the king named Belteshazzar, has a sharp mind and is filled with divine knowledge and understanding. He can

interpret dreams, explain riddles, and solve difficult problems. Call for Daniel, and he will tell you what the writing means."

¹³So Daniel was brought in before the king. The king asked him, "Are you Daniel, who was exiled from Judah by my predecessor, King Nebuchadnezzar? ¹⁴I have heard that you have the spirit of the gods within you and that you are filled with insight, understanding, and wisdom. ¹⁵My wise men and enchanters have tried to read this writing on the wall, but they cannot. ¹⁶I am told that you can give interpretations and solve difficult problems. If you can read these words and tell me their meaning, you will be clothed in purple robes of royal honor, and you will wear a gold chain around your neck. You will become the third highest ruler in the kingdom."

¹⁷Daniel answered the king, "Keep your gifts or give them to someone else, but I will tell you what the writing means. ¹⁸Your Majesty, the Most High God gave sovereignty, majesty, glory, and honor to your predecessor, Nebuchadnezzar. ¹⁹He made him so great that people of all races and nations and languages trembled before him in fear. He killed those he wanted to kill and spared those he wanted to spare. He honored those he wanted to honor and disgraced those he wanted to disgrace. ²⁰But when his heart and mind were hardened with pride, he was brought down from his royal throne and stripped of his glory. ²¹He was driven from human society. He was given the mind of an animal, and he lived among the wild donkeys. He ate grass like a cow, and he was drenched with the dew of heaven, until he learned that the Most High God rules the kingdoms of the world and appoints anyone he desires to rule over them.

²²"You are his successor, O Belshazzar, and you knew all this, yet you have not humbled yourself. ²³For you have defied the Lord of heaven and have had these cups from his Temple brought before you. You and your nobles and your wives and concubines have been drinking wine from them while praising gods of silver, gold, bronze, iron, wood, and stone—gods that neither see nor hear nor know anything at all. But you have not honored the God who gives you the breath of life and controls your destiny! ²⁴So God has sent this hand to write a message.

²⁵"This is the message that was written: MENE, MENE, TEKEL, PARSIN. ²⁶This is what these words mean:

> *Mene* means 'numbered'—God has numbered the days of your reign and has brought it to an end.
> ²⁷ *Tekel* means 'weighed'—you have been weighed on the balances and have failed the test.
> ²⁸ *Parsin* means 'divided'—your kingdom has been divided and given to the Medes and Persians."

²⁹Then at Belshazzar's command, Daniel was dressed in purple robes, a gold chain was hung around his neck, and he was proclaimed the third highest ruler in the kingdom.

30That very night Belshazzar, the Babylonian king, was killed. 31And Darius the Mede took over the kingdom at the age of sixty-two.

〰️ **What reasons would God have for passing Judgment on the society in which you live?** The writing on the wall was a message for all those who defy God. Although Belshazzar had power and wealth, his kingdom was totally corrupt, and he could not withstand the judgment of God. God's time of judgment comes for all people. If you have forgotten God and slipped into a sinful way of life, turn away from your sin now before he denies you more opportunities to repent. Ask God to forgive you, and begin to live by his standards of justice.

JUNE

Daniel and the Lions

DANIEL 6:1-28

Darius the Mede decided to divide the kingdom into 120 provinces, and he appointed a prince to rule over each province. 2The king also chose Daniel and two others as administrators to supervise the princes and to watch out for the king's interests. 3Daniel soon proved himself more capable than all the other administrators and princes. Because of his great ability, the king made plans to place him over the entire empire. 4Then the other administrators and princes began searching for some fault in the way Daniel was handling his affairs, but they couldn't find anything to criticize. He was faithful and honest and always responsible. 5So they concluded, "Our only chance of finding grounds for accusing Daniel will be in connection with the requirements of his religion."

6So the administrators and princes went to the king and said, "Long live King Darius! 7We administrators, prefects, princes, advisers, and other officials have unanimously agreed that Your Majesty should make a law that will be strictly enforced. Give orders that for the next thirty days anyone who prays to anyone, divine or human—except to Your Majesty—will be thrown to the lions. 8And let Your Majesty issue and sign this law so it cannot be changed, a law of the Medes and Persians, which cannot be revoked." 9So King Darius signed the law.

10But when Daniel learned that the law had been signed, he went home and knelt down as usual in his upstairs room, with its windows open toward Jerusalem. He prayed three times a day, just as he had always done, giving thanks to his God. 11The officials went together to Daniel's house and found him praying and asking for God's help. 12So they went back to the king and reminded him about his law. "Did you not sign a law that for the next thirty days anyone who prays to anyone, divine or human—except to Your Majesty—will be thrown to the lions?"

"Yes," the king replied, "that decision stands; it is a law of the Medes and Persians, which cannot be revoked."

¹³Then they told the king, "That man Daniel, one of the captives from Judah, is paying no attention to you or your law. He still prays to his God three times a day."

¹⁴Hearing this, the king was very angry with himself for signing the law, and he tried to find a way to save Daniel. He spent the rest of the day looking for a way to get Daniel out of this predicament. ¹⁵In the evening the men went together to the king and said, "Your Majesty knows that according to the law of the Medes and the Persians, no law that the king signs can be changed."

¹⁶So at last the king gave orders for Daniel to be arrested and thrown into the den of lions. The king said to him, "May your God, whom you worship continually, rescue you." ¹⁷A stone was brought and placed over the mouth of the den. The king sealed the stone with his own royal seal and the seals of his nobles, so that no one could rescue Daniel from the lions. ¹⁸Then the king returned to his palace and spent the night fasting. He refused his usual entertainment and couldn't sleep at all that night.

¹⁹Very early the next morning, the king hurried out to the lions' den. ²⁰When he got there, he called out in anguish, "Daniel, servant of the living God! Was your God, whom you worship continually, able to rescue you from the lions?"

²¹Daniel answered, "Long live the king! ²²My God sent his angel to shut the lions' mouths so that they would not hurt me, for I have been found innocent in his sight. And I have not wronged you, Your Majesty."

²³The king was overjoyed and ordered that Daniel be lifted from the den. Not a scratch was found on him because he had trusted in his God. ²⁴Then the king gave orders to arrest the men who had maliciously accused Daniel. He had them thrown into the lions' den, along with their wives and children. The lions leaped on them and tore them apart before they even hit the floor of the den.

²⁵Then King Darius sent this message to the people of every race and nation and language throughout the world:

"Peace and prosperity to you!

²⁶"I decree that everyone throughout my kingdom should tremble with fear before the God of Daniel.

For he is the living God,
  and he will endure forever.
His kingdom will never be destroyed,
  and his rule will never end.
²⁷ He rescues and saves his people;
  he performs miraculous signs and wonders
  in the heavens and on earth.
He has rescued Daniel
  from the power of the lions."

²⁸So Daniel prospered during the reign of Darius and the reign of Cyrus the Persian.

⤳ **When is your regular prayer time?** Although Daniel knew about the law against praying, he still prayed three times a day, "just as he had always done." Daniel had a disciplined prayer life. Our prayers are not usually interrupted by threats but simply by the pressure of our schedules. Don't let threats or pressures cut into your prayer time. Pray regularly, no matter what.

JUNE

Bending God's Directions

JONAH 1:1–2:10

The LORD gave this message to Jonah son of Amittai: ²"Get up and go to the great city of Nineveh! Announce my judgment against it because I have seen how wicked its people are."

³But Jonah got up and went in the opposite direction in order to get away from the LORD. He went down to the seacoast, to the port of Joppa, where he found a ship leaving for Tarshish. He bought a ticket and went on board, hoping that by going away to the west he could escape from the LORD.

⁴But as the ship was sailing along, suddenly the LORD flung a powerful wind over the sea, causing a violent storm that threatened to send them to the bottom. ⁵Fearing for their lives, the desperate sailors shouted to their gods for help and threw the cargo overboard to lighten the ship. And all this time Jonah was sound asleep down in the hold. ⁶So the captain went down after him. "How can you sleep at a time like this?" he shouted. "Get up and pray to your god! Maybe he will have mercy on us and spare our lives."

⁷Then the crew cast lots to see which of them had offended the gods and caused the terrible storm. When they did this, Jonah lost the toss. ⁸"What have you done to bring this awful storm down on us?" they demanded. "Who are you? What is your line of work? What country are you from? What is your nationality?"

⁹And Jonah answered, "I am a Hebrew, and I worship the LORD, the God of heaven, who made the sea and the land." ¹⁰Then he told them that he was running away from the LORD.

The sailors were terrified when they heard this. "Oh, why did you do it?" they groaned. ¹¹And since the storm was getting worse all the time, they asked him, "What should we do to you to stop this storm?"

¹²"Throw me into the sea," Jonah said, "and it will become calm again. For I know that this terrible storm is all my fault."

¹³Instead, the sailors tried even harder to row the boat ashore. But the stormy sea was too violent for them, and they couldn't make it. ¹⁴Then they cried out to the LORD, Jonah's God. "O LORD," they pleaded, "don't make us die for this man's sin. And don't hold us responsible for his death, because it

isn't our fault. O LORD, you have sent this storm upon him for your own good reasons."

¹⁵Then the sailors picked Jonah up and threw him into the raging sea, and the storm stopped at once! ¹⁶The sailors were awestruck by the LORD's great power, and they offered him a sacrifice and vowed to serve him.

¹⁷Now the LORD had arranged for a great fish to swallow Jonah. And Jonah was inside the fish for three days and three nights.

²:¹Then Jonah prayed to the LORD his God from inside the fish. ²He said, "I cried out to the LORD in my great trouble, and he answered me. I called to you from the world of the dead, and LORD, you heard me! ³You threw me into the ocean depths, and I sank down to the heart of the sea. I was buried beneath your wild and stormy waves. ⁴Then I said, 'O LORD, you have driven me from your presence. How will I ever again see your holy Temple?'

⁵"I sank beneath the waves, and death was very near. The waters closed in around me, and seaweed wrapped itself around my head. ⁶I sank down to the very roots of the mountains. I was locked out of life and imprisoned in the land of the dead. But you, O LORD my God, have snatched me from the yawning jaws of death!

⁷"When I had lost all hope, I turned my thoughts once more to the LORD. And my earnest prayer went out to you in your holy Temple. ⁸Those who worship false gods turn their backs on all God's mercies. ⁹But I will offer sacrifices to you with songs of praise, and I will fulfill all my vows. For my salvation comes from the LORD alone."

¹⁰Then the LORD ordered the fish to spit up Jonah on the beach, and it did.

~~~ **When did you last try to avoid doing what you knew God wanted you to do?** Jonah was afraid. He knew that God had a specific job for him, but he didn't want to do it. When God gives us directions through his Word, sometimes we run in fear, claiming that God is asking too much. Fear made Jonah run. But running got him into worse trouble. In the end, Jonah knew that it was best to do what God had asked in the first place. But by then he had paid a costly price for running. It is far better to obey from the start.

4 JUNE

Wrong Motives
JONAH 3:1–4:11

Then the LORD spoke to Jonah a second time: ²"Get up and go to the great city of Nineveh, and deliver the message of judgment I have given you."

³This time Jonah obeyed the LORD's command and went to Nineveh, a city so large that it took three days to see it all. ⁴On the day Jonah entered the city, he shouted to the crowds: "Forty days from now Nineveh will be destroyed!" ⁵The people of Nineveh believed God's message, and from the

greatest to the least, they decided to go without food and wear sackcloth to show their sorrow.

⁶When the king of Nineveh heard what Jonah was saying, he stepped down from his throne and took off his royal robes. He dressed himself in sackcloth and sat on a heap of ashes. ⁷Then the king and his nobles sent this decree throughout the city: "No one, not even the animals, may eat or drink anything at all. ⁸Everyone is required to wear sackcloth and pray earnestly to God. Everyone must turn from their evil ways and stop all their violence. ⁹Who can tell? Perhaps even yet God will have pity on us and hold back his fierce anger from destroying us."

¹⁰When God saw that they had put a stop to their evil ways, he had mercy on them and didn't carry out the destruction he had threatened.

4:1 This change of plans upset Jonah, and he became very angry. ²So he complained to the LORD about it: "Didn't I say before I left home that you would do this, LORD? That is why I ran away to Tarshish! I knew that you were a gracious and compassionate God, slow to get angry and filled with unfailing love. I knew how easily you could cancel your plans for destroying these people. ³Just kill me now, LORD! I'd rather be dead than alive because nothing I predicted is going to happen."

⁴The LORD replied, "Is it right for you to be angry about this?"

⁵Then Jonah went out to the east side of the city and made a shelter to sit under as he waited to see if anything would happen to the city. ⁶And the LORD God arranged for a leafy plant to grow there, and soon it spread its broad leaves over Jonah's head, shading him from the sun. This eased some of his discomfort, and Jonah was very grateful for the plant.

⁷But God also prepared a worm! The next morning at dawn the worm ate through the stem of the plant, so that it soon died and withered away. ⁸And as the sun grew hot, God sent a scorching east wind to blow on Jonah. The sun beat down on his head until he grew faint and wished to die. "Death is certainly better than this!" he exclaimed.

⁹Then God said to Jonah, "Is it right for you to be angry because the plant died?"

"Yes," Jonah retorted, "even angry enough to die!"

¹⁰Then the LORD said, "You feel sorry about the plant, though you did nothing to put it there. And a plant is only, at best, short lived. ¹¹But Nineveh has more than 120,000 people living in spiritual darkness, not to mention all the animals. Shouldn't I feel sorry for such a great city?"

〰〰 **About what things do you complain to God?** Jonah revealed the reason for his reluctance to go to Nineveh (4:2). He didn't want the Ninevites forgiven; he wanted them destroyed. Jonah did not understand that the God of Israel is also the God of the whole world. Are you surprised when some unexpected person turns to God? Is it possible that your view is as narrow as Jonah's? We must not forget that, in reality, *we* do not deserve to be forgiven by God.

5

Beginnings
LUKE 1:1-4; JOHN 1:1-18

You will be reading various parts of the four Gospels in order to have a fairly chronological biography of Jesus' life.

Most honorable Theophilus:
Many people have written accounts about the events that took place among us. [2]They used as their source material the reports circulating among us from the early disciples and other eyewitnesses of what God has done in fulfillment of his promises. [3]Having carefully investigated all of these accounts from the beginning, I have decided to write a careful summary for you, [4]to reassure you of the truth of all you were taught.

John 1:1 In the beginning the Word already existed. He was with God, and he was God. [2]He was in the beginning with God. [3]He created everything there is. Nothing exists that he didn't make. [4]Life itself was in him, and this life gives light to everyone. [5]The light shines through the darkness, and the darkness can never extinguish it.

[6]God sent John the Baptist [7]to tell everyone about the light so that everyone might believe because of his testimony. [8]John himself was not the light; he was only a witness to the light. [9]The one who is the true light, who gives light to everyone, was going to come into the world.

[10]But although the world was made through him, the world didn't recognize him when he came. [11]Even in his own land and among his own people, he was not accepted. [12]But to all who believed him and accepted him, he gave the right to become children of God. [13]They are reborn! This is not a physical birth resulting from human passion or plan—this rebirth comes from God.

[14]So the Word became human and lived here on earth among us. He was full of unfailing love and faithfulness. And we have seen his glory, the glory of the only Son of the Father.

[15]John pointed him out to the people. He shouted to the crowds, "This is the one I was talking about when I said, 'Someone is coming who is far greater than I am, for he existed long before I did.'"

[16]We have all benefited from the rich blessings he brought to us—one gracious blessing after another. [17]For the law was given through Moses; God's unfailing love and faithfulness came through Jesus Christ. [18]No one has ever seen God. But his only Son, who is himself God, is near to the Father's heart; he has told us about him.

〰〰〰 **Have you personally received Jesus as your Savior and become a child of God?** There was a lot of interest in Jesus, and many people had written firsthand accounts about him. Luke may have used these accounts and all other available resources as material for an accurate and complete account of Jesus' life, teachings, and ministry. Because truth was important to Luke, he relied heavily on eyewitness accounts. Christianity doesn't say, "Close your eyes and believe," but rather, "Check it out for yourself." The Bible encourages you to investigate its claims thoroughly because your conclusion about Jesus is a life-and-death matter.

The Angel and Zechariah

LUKE 1:5-25

It all begins with a Jewish priest, Zechariah, who lived when Herod was king of Judea. Zechariah was a member of the priestly order of Abijah. His wife, Elizabeth, was also from the priestly line of Aaron. ⁶Zechariah and Elizabeth were righteous in God's eyes, careful to obey all of the Lord's commandments and regulations. ⁷They had no children because Elizabeth was barren, and now they were both very old.

⁸One day Zechariah was serving God in the Temple, for his order was on duty that week. ⁹As was the custom of the priests, he was chosen by lot to enter the sanctuary and burn incense in the Lord's presence. ¹⁰While the incense was being burned, a great crowd stood outside, praying.

¹¹Zechariah was in the sanctuary when an angel of the Lord appeared, standing to the right of the incense altar. ¹²Zechariah was overwhelmed with fear. ¹³But the angel said, "Don't be afraid, Zechariah! For God has heard your prayer, and your wife, Elizabeth, will bear you a son! And you are to name him John. ¹⁴You will have great joy and gladness, and many will rejoice with you at his birth, ¹⁵for he will be great in the eyes of the Lord. He must never touch wine or hard liquor, and he will be filled with the Holy Spirit, even before his birth. ¹⁶And he will persuade many Israelites to turn to the Lord their God. ¹⁷He will be a man with the spirit and power of Elijah, the prophet of old. He will precede the coming of the Lord, preparing the people for his arrival. He will turn the hearts of the fathers to their children, and he will change disobedient minds to accept godly wisdom."

¹⁸Zechariah said to the angel, "How can I know this will happen? I'm an old man now, and my wife is also well along in years."

¹⁹Then the angel said, "I am Gabriel! I stand in the very presence of God. It was he who sent me to bring you this good news! ²⁰And now, since you didn't believe what I said, you won't be able to speak until the child is born. For my words will certainly come true at the proper time."

²¹Meanwhile, the people were waiting for Zechariah to come out, wondering why he was taking so long. ²²When he finally did come out, he couldn't speak to them. Then they realized from his gestures that he must have seen a vision in the Temple sanctuary.

²³He stayed at the Temple until his term of service was over, and then he

returned home. [24]Soon afterward his wife, Elizabeth, became pregnant and went into seclusion for five months. [25]"How kind the Lord is!" she exclaimed. "He has taken away my disgrace of having no children!"

〰〰 **How would you react to an angel's visit?** When told he would have a son, Zechariah doubted the angel's word. From his human perspective, his doubts were understandable—but with God, anything is possible. Although Zechariah and Elizabeth were past the age of childbearing, God gave them a child. It is easy to doubt or misunderstand what God wants to do in our life. Even God's people sometimes make the mistake of trusting their reason or experience instead of God. When tempted to think that one of God's promises is impossible, try to look at the situation from God's perspective. He is not bound by human limitations.

7

Mary and Elizabeth
LUKE 1:26-56

In the sixth month of Elizabeth's pregnancy, God sent the angel Gabriel to Nazareth, a village in Galilee, [27]to a virgin named Mary. She was engaged to be married to a man named Joseph, a descendant of King David. [28]Gabriel appeared to her and said, "Greetings, favored woman! The Lord is with you!"

[29]Confused and disturbed, Mary tried to think what the angel could mean. [30]"Don't be frightened, Mary," the angel told her, "for God has decided to bless you! [31]You will become pregnant and have a son, and you are to name him Jesus. [32]He will be very great and will be called the Son of the Most High. And the Lord God will give him the throne of his ancestor David. [33]And he will reign over Israel forever; his Kingdom will never end!"

[34]Mary asked the angel, "But how can I have a baby? I am a virgin."

[35]The angel replied, "The Holy Spirit will come upon you, and the power of the Most High will overshadow you. So the baby born to you will be holy, and he will be called the Son of God. [36]What's more, your relative Elizabeth has become pregnant in her old age! People used to say she was barren, but she's already in her sixth month. [37]For nothing is impossible with God."

[38]Mary responded, "I am the Lord's servant, and I am willing to accept whatever he wants. May everything you have said come true." And then the angel left.

[39]A few days later Mary hurried to the hill country of Judea, to the town [40]where Zechariah lived. She entered the house and greeted Elizabeth. [41]At the sound of Mary's greeting, Elizabeth's child leaped within her, and Elizabeth was filled with the Holy Spirit.

[42]Elizabeth gave a glad cry and exclaimed to Mary, "You are blessed by God above all other women, and your child is blessed. [43]What an honor this is, that the mother of my Lord should visit me! [44]When you came in and

greeted me, my baby jumped for joy the instant I heard your voice! ⁴⁵You are blessed, because you believed that the Lord would do what he said."

⁴⁶Mary responded,
"Oh, how I praise the Lord.
⁴⁷ How I rejoice in God my Savior!
⁴⁸For he took notice of his lowly servant girl,
and now generation after generation
will call me blessed.
⁴⁹For he, the Mighty One, is holy,
and he has done great things for me.
⁵⁰His mercy goes on from generation to generation,
to all who fear him.
⁵¹His mighty arm does tremendous things!
How he scatters the proud and haughty ones!
⁵²He has taken princes from their thrones
and exalted the lowly.
⁵³He has satisfied the hungry with good things
and sent the rich away with empty hands.
⁵⁴And how he has helped his servant Israel!
He has not forgotten his promise to be merciful.
⁵⁵For he promised our ancestors—Abraham and his children—
to be merciful to them forever."

⁵⁶Mary stayed with Elizabeth about three months and then went back to her own home.

What gives you joy in your life? A young unmarried girl who became pregnant risked disaster. Unless the father of the child agreed to marry her, she would probably remain unmarried for life. If her own father rejected her, she could be forced into begging or prostitution in order to earn her living. And Mary, with her story about being made pregnant by the Holy Spirit, risked being considered crazy as well. Still Mary said, despite the possible risks, "May everything you have said come true." When Mary said that, she didn't know about the tremendous opportunity she would have. She only knew that God was asking her to serve him, and she willingly obeyed. Don't wait to see the bottom line before offering your life to God. Offer yourself willingly to God.

JUNE

John the Baptist Is Born
LUKE 1:57-80

Now it was time for Elizabeth's baby to be born, and it was a boy. ⁵⁸The word spread quickly to her neighbors and relatives that the Lord had been very kind to her, and everyone rejoiced with her.

⁵⁹When the baby was eight days old, all the relatives and friends came for the circumcision ceremony. They wanted to name him Zechariah, after his father. ⁶⁰But Elizabeth said, "No! His name is John!"

⁶¹"What?" they exclaimed. "There is no one in all your family by that name." ⁶²So they asked the baby's father, communicating to him by making gestures. ⁶³He motioned for a writing tablet, and to everyone's surprise he wrote, "His name is John!" ⁶⁴Instantly Zechariah could speak again, and he began praising God.

⁶⁵Wonder fell upon the whole neighborhood, and the news of what had happened spread throughout the Judean hills. ⁶⁶Everyone who heard about it reflected on these events and asked, "I wonder what this child will turn out to be? For the hand of the Lord is surely upon him in a special way."

⁶⁷Then his father, Zechariah, was filled with the Holy Spirit and gave this prophecy:

⁶⁸"Praise the Lord, the God of Israel,
    because he has visited his people and redeemed them.
⁶⁹He has sent us a mighty Savior
    from the royal line of his servant David,
⁷⁰just as he promised
    through his holy prophets long ago.
⁷¹Now we will be saved from our enemies
    and from all who hate us.
⁷²He has been merciful to our ancestors
    by remembering his sacred covenant with them,
⁷³   the covenant he gave to our ancestor Abraham.
⁷⁴We have been rescued from our enemies,
    so we can serve God without fear,
⁷⁵   in holiness and righteousness forever.

⁷⁶"And you, my little son,
    will be called the prophet of the Most High,
    because you will prepare the way for the Lord.
⁷⁷You will tell his people how to find salvation
    through forgiveness of their sins.
⁷⁸Because of God's tender mercy,
    the light from heaven is about to break upon us,
⁷⁹to give light to those who sit in darkness and in the shadow
        of death,
    and to guide us to the path of peace."

⁸⁰John grew up and became strong in spirit. Then he lived out in the wilderness until he began his public ministry to Israel.

〰️〰️ **When did you last say thank you to your parents for what they've done for you over the years?** Zechariah had just recalled hundreds of years of God's sovereign work in history, beginning with Abraham and going on into eternity. Then, in tender contrast, he personalized the story. His son had been chosen for a key role in the drama of the ages. Although God has unlimited power, he chooses to work through frail humans who begin as helpless babies. Don't minimize what God can do through those who are faithful to him—even you.

A Family Tree
MATTHEW 1:1-25

This is a record of the ancestors of Jesus the Messiah, a descendant of King David and of Abraham:

> ² Abraham was the father of Isaac.
> Isaac was the father of Jacob.
> Jacob was the father of Judah and his brothers.
> ³ Judah was the father of Perez and Zerah (their mother was Tamar).
> Perez was the father of Hezron.
> Hezron was the father of Ram.
> ⁴ Ram was the father of Amminadab.
> Amminadab was the father of Nahshon.
> Nahshon was the father of Salmon.
> ⁵ Salmon was the father of Boaz (his mother was Rahab).
> Boaz was the father of Obed (his mother was Ruth).
> Obed was the father of Jesse.
> ⁶ Jesse was the father of King David.
> David was the father of Solomon (his mother was Bathsheba, the widow of Uriah).
> ⁷ Solomon was the father of Rehoboam.
> Rehoboam was the father of Abijah.
> Abijah was the father of Asaph.
> ⁸ Asaph was the father of Jehoshaphat.
> Jehoshaphat was the father of Jehoram.
> Jehoram was the father of Uzziah.
> ⁹ Uzziah was the father of Jotham.
> Jotham was the father of Ahaz.
> Ahaz was the father of Hezekiah.
> ¹⁰ Hezekiah was the father of Manasseh.
> Manasseh was the father of Amos.
> Amos was the father of Josiah.
> ¹¹ Josiah was the father of Jehoiachin and his brothers (born at the time of the exile to Babylon).
> ¹² After the Babylonian exile:

Jehoiachin was the father of Shealtiel.
Shealtiel was the father of Zerubbabel.
¹³Zerubbabel was the father of Abiud.
Abiud was the father of Eliakim.
Eliakim was the father of Azor.
¹⁴Azor was the father of Zadok.
Zadok was the father of Akim.
Akim was the father of Eliud.
¹⁵Eliud was the father of Eleazar.
Eleazar was the father of Matthan.
Matthan was the father of Jacob.
¹⁶Jacob was the father of Joseph, the husband of Mary.
Mary was the mother of Jesus, who is called the Messiah.

¹⁷All those listed above include fourteen generations from Abraham to King David, and fourteen from David's time to the Babylonian exile, and fourteen from the Babylonian exile to the Messiah.

¹⁸Now this is how Jesus the Messiah was born. His mother, Mary, was engaged to be married to Joseph. But while she was still a virgin, she became pregnant by the Holy Spirit. ¹⁹Joseph, her fiancé, being a just man, decided to break the engagement quietly, so as not to disgrace her publicly.

²⁰As he considered this, he fell asleep, and an angel of the Lord appeared to him in a dream. "Joseph, son of David," the angel said, "do not be afraid to go ahead with your marriage to Mary. For the child within her has been conceived by the Holy Spirit. ²¹And she will have a son, and you are to name him Jesus, for he will save his people from their sins." ²²All of this happened to fulfill the Lord's message through his prophet:

²³"Look! The virgin will conceive a child!
    She will give birth to a son,
    and he will be called Immanuel
    (meaning, God is with us)."

²⁴When Joseph woke up, he did what the angel of the Lord commanded. He brought Mary home to be his wife, ²⁵but she remained a virgin until her son was born. And Joseph named him Jesus.

〰〰 **Which of these people have you read about in the Old Testament? What do you remember about them?** In the first seventeen verses of Matthew we meet forty-six people spanning two thousand years. All were ancestors of Jesus, but they varied considerably in personality, spirituality, and experience. Some were heroes of faith—like Abraham, Isaac, Ruth, and David. Some had shady reputations—like Rahab and Tamar. Many were very ordinary—like Hezron, Aram, Nahshon, and Achim. Others were evil—like Manasseh and Abijah. God's work in history is not limited by human failures or sins; he works through ordinary people. Just as God used all kinds of people to bring his Son into the world, he uses all kinds today to accomplish his will. You, too, are part of the story of God's work in the world.

10

Jesus Is Born!

LUKE 2:1-20

At that time the Roman emperor, Augustus, decreed that a census should be taken throughout the Roman Empire. [2](This was the first census taken when Quirinius was governor of Syria.) [3]All returned to their own towns to register for this census. [4]And because Joseph was a descendant of King David, he had to go to Bethlehem in Judea, David's ancient home. He traveled there from the village of Nazareth in Galilee. [5]He took with him Mary, his fiancée, who was obviously pregnant by this time.

[6]And while they were there, the time came for her baby to be born. [7]She gave birth to her first child, a son. She wrapped him snugly in strips of cloth and laid him in a manger, because there was no room for them in the village inn.

[8]That night some shepherds were in the fields outside the village, guarding their flocks of sheep. [9]Suddenly, an angel of the Lord appeared among them, and the radiance of the Lord's glory surrounded them. They were terribly frightened, [10]but the angel reassured them. "Don't be afraid!" he said. "I bring you good news of great joy for everyone! [11]The Savior—yes, the Messiah, the Lord—has been born tonight in Bethlehem, the city of David! [12]And this is how you will recognize him: You will find a baby lying in a manger, wrapped snugly in strips of cloth!"

[13]Suddenly, the angel was joined by a vast host of others—the armies of heaven—praising God:

[14]"Glory to God in the highest heaven,
    and peace on earth to all whom God favors."

[15]When the angels had returned to heaven, the shepherds said to each other, "Come on, let's go to Bethlehem! Let's see this wonderful thing that has happened, which the Lord has told us about."

[16]They ran to the village and found Mary and Joseph. And there was the baby, lying in the manger. [17]Then the shepherds told everyone what had happened and what the angel had said to them about this child. [18]All who heard the shepherds' story were astonished, [19]but Mary quietly treasured these things in her heart and thought about them often. [20]The shepherds went back to their fields and flocks, glorifying and praising God for what the angels had told them, and because they had seen the child, just as the angel had said.

~⟋⟍⟋ **What does Christmas mean to you?** The greatest event in history had just happened! The Messiah was born! For ages the Jews had waited for this, and when it finally happened, the announcement came to humble shepherds. The good news about Jesus is that he comes to all, including the plain and the ordinary. He comes to anyone with a heart humble enough to accept him. Whoever you are, whatever you do, you can have Jesus in your life. Don't think you need extraordinary qualifications—he accepts you as you are.

11 JUNE

Jesus' First Trip to Church
LUKE 2:21-40

Eight days later, when the baby was circumcised, he was named Jesus, the name given him by the angel even before he was conceived.

²²Then it was time for the purification offering, as required by the law of Moses after the birth of a child; so his parents took him to Jerusalem to present him to the Lord. ²³The law of the Lord says, "If a woman's first child is a boy, he must be dedicated to the Lord." ²⁴So they offered a sacrifice according to what was required in the law of the Lord—"either a pair of turtledoves or two young pigeons."

²⁵Now there was a man named Simeon who lived in Jerusalem. He was a righteous man and very devout. He was filled with the Holy Spirit, and he eagerly expected the Messiah to come and rescue Israel. ²⁶The Holy Spirit had revealed to him that he would not die until he had seen the Lord's Messiah. ²⁷That day the Spirit led him to the Temple. So when Mary and Joseph came to present the baby Jesus to the Lord as the law required, ²⁸Simeon was there. He took the child in his arms and praised God, saying,

> ²⁹"Lord, now I can die in peace!
>   As you promised me,
> ³⁰I have seen the Savior
> ³¹   you have given to all people.
> ³²He is a light to reveal God to the nations,
>   and he is the glory of your people Israel!"

³³Joseph and Mary were amazed at what was being said about Jesus. ³⁴Then Simeon blessed them, and he said to Mary, "This child will be rejected by many in Israel, and it will be their undoing. But he will be the greatest joy to many others. ³⁵Thus, the deepest thoughts of many hearts will be revealed. And a sword will pierce your very soul."

³⁶Anna, a prophet, was also there in the Temple. She was the daughter of Phanuel, of the tribe of Asher, and was very old. She was a widow, for her husband had died when they had been married only seven years. ³⁷She was now eighty-four years old. She never left the Temple but stayed there day

and night, worshiping God with fasting and prayer. [38]She came along just as Simeon was talking with Mary and Joseph, and she began praising God. She talked about Jesus to everyone who had been waiting for the promised King to come and deliver Jerusalem.

[39]When Jesus' parents had fulfilled all the requirements of the law of the Lord, they returned home to Nazareth in Galilee. [40]There the child grew up healthy and strong. He was filled with wisdom beyond his years, and God placed his special favor upon him.

 How would you react to holding Jesus when he was a baby?
Although Simeon and Anna were very old, they still hoped to see the Messiah. Led by the Holy Spirit, they were among the first to bear witness to Jesus. In the Jewish culture, elders were respected, so Simeon's and Anna's prophecies carried extra weight. Our society, however, values youthfulness over wisdom, and contributions by the elderly are often ignored. As Christians, we should reverse those values wherever we can. Encourage older people to share their wisdom and experience. Listen carefully when they speak. Offer them your friendship, and help them find ways to continue to serve God.

JUNE **12**

Foreign Visitors
MATTHEW 2:1-12

Jesus was born in the town of Bethlehem in Judea, during the reign of King Herod. About that time some wise men from eastern lands arrived in Jerusalem, asking, [2]"Where is the newborn king of the Jews? We have seen his star as it arose, and we have come to worship him."

[3]Herod was deeply disturbed by their question, as was all of Jerusalem. [4]He called a meeting of the leading priests and teachers of religious law. "Where did the prophets say the Messiah would be born?" he asked them.

[5]"In Bethlehem," they said, "for this is what the prophet wrote:

[6] 'O Bethlehem of Judah,
you are not just a lowly village in Judah,
for a ruler will come from you
who will be the shepherd for my people Israel.' "

[7]Then Herod sent a private message to the wise men, asking them to come see him. At this meeting he learned the exact time when they first saw the star. [8]Then he told them, "Go to Bethlehem and search carefully for the child. And when you find him, come back and tell me so that I can go and worship him, too!"

[9]After this interview the wise men went their way. Once again the star appeared to them, guiding them to Bethlehem. It went ahead of them and stopped over the place where the child was. [10]When they saw the star, they

were filled with joy! [11]They entered the house where the child and his mother, Mary, were, and they fell down before him and worshiped him. Then they opened their treasure chests and gave him gifts of gold, frankincense, and myrrh. [12]But when it was time to leave, they went home another way, because God had warned them in a dream not to return to Herod.

〜⋎〜 **What gifts have you ever given Christ?** The astrologers traveled thousands of miles to see the King of the Jews. When they finally found him, they responded with joy, worship, and gifts. How different from the approach people often take today. We expect God to come looking for us, to explain himself, prove who he is, and give *us* gifts. But those who are wise still seek and worship Jesus today, not for what they can get, but for who he is.

13 JUNE

Escape and Return
MATTHEW 2:13-23

After the wise men were gone, an angel of the Lord appeared to Joseph in a dream. "Get up and flee to Egypt with the child and his mother," the angel said. "Stay there until I tell you to return, because Herod is going to try to kill the child." [14]That night Joseph left for Egypt with the child and Mary, his mother, [15]and they stayed there until Herod's death. This fulfilled what the Lord had spoken through the prophet: "I called my Son out of Egypt."

[16]Herod was furious when he learned that the wise men had outwitted him. He sent soldiers to kill all the boys in and around Bethlehem who were two years old and under, because the wise men had told him the star first appeared to them about two years earlier. [17]Herod's brutal action fulfilled the prophecy of Jeremiah:

[18]"A cry of anguish is heard in Ramah—
weeping and mourning unrestrained.
Rachel weeps for her children,
refusing to be comforted—for they are dead."

[19]When Herod died, an angel of the Lord appeared in a dream to Joseph in Egypt and told him, [20]"Get up and take the child and his mother back to the land of Israel, because those who were trying to kill the child are dead." [21]So Joseph returned immediately to Israel with Jesus and his mother. [22]But when he learned that the new ruler was Herod's son Archelaus, he was afraid. Then, in another dream, he was warned to go to Galilee. [23]So they went and lived in a town called Nazareth. This fulfilled what was spoken by the prophets concerning the Messiah: "He will be called a Nazarene."

〜⋎〜 **How has knowing God brought excitement into your life?** Herod was afraid that this newborn King would one day take his throne. He completely misunderstood the reason for Christ's coming. Jesus didn't want Herod's throne—he wanted to be king of Herod's life. Jesus wanted to give Herod eternal life, not take away his present life. Today people are often afraid that Christ wants to take things away, when in reality he wants to give them real freedom, peace, and joy. Jesus wants to be King of your life. Have you let him sit on the throne?

JUNE 14

Jesus in the Temple Again
LUKE 2:41-52

Every year Jesus' parents went to Jerusalem for the Passover festival. [42]When Jesus was twelve years old, they attended the festival as usual. [43]After the celebration was over, they started home to Nazareth, but Jesus stayed behind in Jerusalem. His parents didn't miss him at first, [44]because they assumed he was with friends among the other travelers. But when he didn't show up that evening, they started to look for him among their relatives and friends. [45]When they couldn't find him, they went back to Jerusalem to search for him there. [46]Three days later they finally discovered him. He was in the Temple, sitting among the religious teachers, discussing deep questions with them. [47]And all who heard him were amazed at his understanding and his answers.

[48]His parents didn't know what to think. "Son!" his mother said to him. "Why have you done this to us? Your father and I have been frantic, searching for you everywhere."

[49]"But why did you need to search?" he asked. "You should have known that I would be in my Father's house." [50]But they didn't understand what he meant.

[51]Then he returned to Nazareth with them and was obedient to them; and his mother stored all these things in her heart. [52]So Jesus grew both in height and in wisdom, and he was loved by God and by all who knew him.

〜✍️ **What four words would summarize your teenage years?** The second chapter of Luke shows us that although Jesus was unique, he had a normal childhood and adolescence. In terms of development, he went through the same progression we do. He grew physically and mentally, he related to other people, and he was loved by God. A full human life is not unbalanced. It was important to Jesus—and it should be important to all believers—to develop fully and harmoniously in these key areas: physical, mental, social, and spiritual. Make sure you're letting God help you grow in each of these areas.

15

Baptism and Temptation

MARK 1:1-13

Here begins the Good News about Jesus the Messiah, the Son of God. [2]In the book of the prophet Isaiah, God said,

> "Look, I am sending my messenger before you,
>   and he will prepare your way.
> [3] He is a voice shouting in the wilderness:
> 'Prepare a pathway for the Lord's coming!
>   Make a straight road for him!' "

[4]This messenger was John the Baptist. He lived in the wilderness and was preaching that people should be baptized to show that they had turned from their sins and turned to God to be forgiven. [5]People from Jerusalem and from all over Judea traveled out into the wilderness to see and hear John. And when they confessed their sins, he baptized them in the Jordan River. [6]His clothes were woven from camel hair, and he wore a leather belt; his food was locusts and wild honey. [7]He announced: "Someone is coming soon who is far greater than I am—so much greater that I am not even worthy to be his slave. [8]I baptize you with water, but he will baptize you with the Holy Spirit!"

[9]One day Jesus came from Nazareth in Galilee, and he was baptized by John in the Jordan River. [10]And when Jesus came up out of the water, he saw the heavens split open and the Holy Spirit descending like a dove on him. [11]And a voice came from heaven saying, "You are my beloved Son, and I am fully pleased with you."

[12]Immediately the Holy Spirit compelled Jesus to go into the wilderness. [13]He was there for forty days, being tempted by Satan. He was out among the wild animals, and angels took care of him.

〰〰〰 **What are your most difficult temptations? Compare them to Jesus' temptations.** To identify fully with human beings, Jesus had to endure Satan's temptations. Although Jesus is God, he is also man, and as a human being he was not exempt from Satan's attacks. Because Jesus faced temptations and overcame them, he can assist us in two important ways: (1) as an example of how to face temptation without sinning and (2) as our helper who knows just what we need because he went through the same experience. When you face temptation, trust Jesus to help you overcome it.

John the Baptist and Jesus
JOHN 1:19-34

This was the testimony of John when the Jewish leaders sent priests and Temple assistants from Jerusalem to ask John whether he claimed to be the Messiah. [20]He flatly denied it. "I am not the Messiah," he said.

[21]"Well then, who are you?" they asked. "Are you Elijah?"

"No," he replied.

"Are you the Prophet?"

"No."

[22]"Then who are you? Tell us, so we can give an answer to those who sent us. What do you have to say about yourself?"

[23]John replied in the words of Isaiah:

"I am a voice shouting in the wilderness,
'Prepare a straight pathway for the Lord's coming!' "

[24]Then those who were sent by the Pharisees [25]asked him, "If you aren't the Messiah or Elijah or the Prophet, what right do you have to baptize?"

[26]John told them, "I baptize with water, but right here in the crowd is someone you do not know, [27]who will soon begin his ministry. I am not even worthy to be his slave." [28]This incident took place at Bethany, a village east of the Jordan River, where John was baptizing.

[29]The next day John saw Jesus coming toward him and said, "Look! There is the Lamb of God who takes away the sin of the world! [30]He is the one I was talking about when I said, 'Soon a man is coming who is far greater than I am, for he existed long before I did.' [31]I didn't know he was the one, but I have been baptizing with water in order to point him out to Israel."

[32]Then John said, "I saw the Holy Spirit descending like a dove from heaven and resting upon him. [33]I didn't know he was the one, but when God sent me to baptize with water, he told me, 'When you see the Holy Spirit descending and resting upon someone, he is the one you are looking for. He is the one who baptizes with the Holy Spirit.' [34]I saw this happen to Jesus, so I testify that he is the Son of God."

~~~ **To whom did you last talk about Christ?** Although John the Baptist was a well-known preacher and attracted large crowds, he was content to let Jesus take the higher place. This is true humility, the basis for greatness in preaching, teaching, or any other work we do for Christ. When you are content to do what God wants you to do and let Jesus Christ be honored for it, God will do great things through you.

17

Jesus' First Disciples
JOHN 1:35-51

The following day, John was again standing with two of his disciples. ³⁶As Jesus walked by, John looked at him and then declared, "Look! There is the Lamb of God!" ³⁷Then John's two disciples turned and followed Jesus.

³⁸Jesus looked around and saw them following. "What do you want?" he asked them.

They replied, "Rabbi" (which means Teacher), "where are you staying?"

³⁹"Come and see," he said. It was about four o'clock in the afternoon when they went with him to the place, and they stayed there the rest of the day.

⁴⁰Andrew, Simon Peter's brother, was one of these men who had heard what John said and then followed Jesus. ⁴¹The first thing Andrew did was to find his brother, Simon, and tell him, "We have found the Messiah" (which means the Christ).

⁴²Then Andrew brought Simon to meet Jesus. Looking intently at Simon, Jesus said, "You are Simon, the son of John—but you will be called Cephas" (which means Peter).

⁴³The next day Jesus decided to go to Galilee. He found Philip and said to him, "Come, be my disciple." ⁴⁴Philip was from Bethsaida, Andrew and Peter's hometown.

⁴⁵Philip went off to look for Nathanael and told him, "We have found the very person Moses and the prophets wrote about! His name is Jesus, the son of Joseph from Nazareth."

⁴⁶"Nazareth!" exclaimed Nathanael. "Can anything good come from there?"

"Just come and see for yourself," Philip said.

⁴⁷As they approached, Jesus said, "Here comes an honest man—a true son of Israel."

⁴⁸"How do you know about me?" Nathanael asked.

And Jesus replied, "I could see you under the fig tree before Philip found you."

⁴⁹Nathanael replied, "Teacher, you are the Son of God—the King of Israel!"

⁵⁰Jesus asked him, "Do you believe all this just because I told you I had seen you under the fig tree? You will see greater things than this." ⁵¹Then he said, "The truth is, you will all see heaven open and the angels of God going up and down upon the Son of Man."

How would someone know that you're a disciple of Jesus?

These new disciples used several names for Jesus: Lamb of God (v. 36), Messiah (v. 41), Son of God (v. 49), and King of Israel (v. 49). As they got to know Jesus, their appreciation for him grew. The more time we spend getting to know Christ, the more we will understand and appreciate who he is. We may be drawn to him for his teaching, but we will come to know him as the Son of God. Although these disciples made this verbal shift in a few days, they would not fully understand Jesus until three years later (Acts 2). What they so easily professed had to be worked out in experience. We may find that words of faith come easily, but deep appreciation for Christ comes with living by faith.

JUNE

Jesus and Surprises

18

JOHN 2:1-25

The next day Jesus' mother was a guest at a wedding celebration in the village of Cana in Galilee. ²Jesus and his disciples were also invited to the celebration. ³The wine supply ran out during the festivities, so Jesus' mother spoke to him about the problem. "They have no more wine," she told him.

⁴"How does that concern you and me?" Jesus asked. "My time has not yet come."

⁵But his mother told the servants, "Do whatever he tells you."

⁶Six stone waterpots were standing there; they were used for Jewish ceremonial purposes and held twenty to thirty gallons each. ⁷Jesus told the servants, "Fill the jars with water." When the jars had been filled to the brim, ⁸he said, "Dip some out and take it to the master of ceremonies." So they followed his instructions.

⁹When the master of ceremonies tasted the water that was now wine, not knowing where it had come from (though, of course, the servants knew), he called the bridegroom over. ¹⁰"Usually a host serves the best wine first," he said. "Then, when everyone is full and doesn't care, he brings out the less expensive wines. But you have kept the best until now!"

¹¹This miraculous sign at Cana in Galilee was Jesus' first display of his glory. And his disciples believed in him.

¹²After the wedding he went to Capernaum for a few days with his mother, his brothers, and his disciples.

¹³It was time for the annual Passover celebration, and Jesus went to Jerusalem. ¹⁴In the Temple area he saw merchants selling cattle, sheep, and doves for sacrifices; and he saw money changers behind their counters. ¹⁵Jesus made a whip from some ropes and chased them all out of the Temple. He drove out the sheep and oxen, scattered the money changers' coins over the floor, and turned over their tables. ¹⁶Then, going over to the people who sold doves, he told them, "Get these things out of here. Don't turn my Father's house into a marketplace!"

¹⁷Then his disciples remembered this prophecy from the Scriptures: "Passion for God's house burns within me."

¹⁸"What right do you have to do these things?" the Jewish leaders demanded. "If you have this authority from God, show us a miraculous sign to prove it."

¹⁹"All right," Jesus replied. "Destroy this temple, and in three days I will raise it up."

²⁰"What!" they exclaimed. "It took forty-six years to build this Temple, and you can do it in three days?" ²¹But by "this temple," Jesus meant his body. ²²After he was raised from the dead, the disciples remembered that he had said this. And they believed both Jesus and the Scriptures.

²³Because of the miraculous signs he did in Jerusalem at the Passover celebration, many people were convinced that he was indeed the Messiah. ²⁴But Jesus didn't trust them, because he knew what people were really like. ²⁵No one needed to tell him about human nature.

〜ᔕ〜 **How has Christ been unpredictable in your life?** Jesus was on a mission to save the world, the greatest mission in the history of mankind. Yet he took time to attend a wedding and take part in its festivities. Jesus valued these wedding festivities because they involved people, and Jesus came to be with people. Our mission can often be accomplished in joyous times of celebration with others. Bring balance to your life by bringing Jesus into times of pleasure and play as well as times of school and work.

19 JUNE

Jesus and Nicodemus
JOHN 3:1-21

After dark one evening, a Jewish religious leader named Nicodemus, a Pharisee, ²came to speak with Jesus. "Teacher," he said, "we all know that God has sent you to teach us. Your miraculous signs are proof enough that God is with you."

³Jesus replied, "I assure you, unless you are born again, you can never see the Kingdom of God."

⁴"What do you mean?" exclaimed Nicodemus. "How can an old man go back into his mother's womb and be born again?"

⁵Jesus replied, "The truth is, no one can enter the Kingdom of God without being born of water and the Spirit. ⁶Humans can reproduce only human life, but the Holy Spirit gives new life from heaven. ⁷So don't be surprised at my statement that you must be born again. ⁸Just as you can hear the wind but can't tell where it comes from or where it is going, so you can't explain how people are born of the Spirit."

⁹"What do you mean?" Nicodemus asked.

¹⁰Jesus replied, "You are a respected Jewish teacher, and yet you don't understand these things? ¹¹I assure you, I am telling you what we know and have seen, and yet you won't believe us. ¹²But if you don't even believe me

when I tell you about things that happen here on earth, how can you possibly believe if I tell you what is going on in heaven? [13]For only I, the Son of Man, have come to earth and will return to heaven again. [14]And as Moses lifted up the bronze snake on a pole in the wilderness, so I, the Son of Man, must be lifted up on a pole, [15]so that everyone who believes in me will have eternal life.

[16]"For God so loved the world that he gave his only Son, so that everyone who believes in him will not perish but have eternal life. [17]God did not send his Son into the world to condemn it, but to save it.

[18]"There is no judgment awaiting those who trust him. But those who do not trust him have already been judged for not believing in the only Son of God. [19]Their judgment is based on this fact: The light from heaven came into the world, but they loved the darkness more than the light, for their actions were evil. [20]They hate the light because they want to sin in the darkness. They stay away from the light for fear their sins will be exposed and they will be punished. [21]But those who do what is right come to the light gladly, so everyone can see that they are doing what God wants."

~∿∿⌇ **When did you first meet Jesus? How?** The entire gospel comes to a focus in verse 16. True love is not self-centered; it reaches out and draws others in. God sets the pattern of true love here, the basis for all love relationships: If you love someone dearly, you will be willing to pay dearly for that person's love. God paid with the life of his Son, the highest price he could pay. Jesus accepted our punishment, paid the price for our sins, and then offered us the new life that he bought for us. When we share the gospel with others, our love must be like his—we must willingly giving up our own comfort and security so that others might join us in receiving God's love.

JUNE **20**

John Gets into Trouble
JOHN 3:22-36; LUKE 3:19-20

Afterward Jesus and his disciples left Jerusalem, but they stayed in Judea for a while and baptized there.

[23]At this time John the Baptist was baptizing at Aenon, near Salim, because there was plenty of water there and people kept coming to him for baptism. [24]This was before John was put into prison. [25]At that time a certain Jew began an argument with John's disciples over ceremonial cleansing. [26]John's disciples came to him and said, "Teacher, the man you met on the other side of the Jordan River, the one you said was the Messiah, is also baptizing people. And everybody is going over there instead of coming here to us."

[27]John replied, "God in heaven appoints each person's work. [28]You yourselves know how plainly I told you that I am not the Messiah. I am here to prepare the way for him—that is all. [29]The bride will go where the bride-

groom is. A bridegroom's friend rejoices with him. I am the bridegroom's friend, and I am filled with joy at his success. ³⁰He must become greater and greater, and I must become less and less.

³¹"He has come from above and is greater than anyone else. I am of the earth, and my understanding is limited to the things of earth, but he has come from heaven. ³²He tells what he has seen and heard, but how few believe what he tells them! ³³Those who believe him discover that God is true. ³⁴For he is sent by God. He speaks God's words, for God's Spirit is upon him without measure or limit. ³⁵The Father loves his Son, and he has given him authority over everything. ³⁶And all who believe in God's Son have eternal life. Those who don't obey the Son will never experience eternal life, but the wrath of God remains upon them."

Luke 3:19 John also publicly criticized Herod Antipas, ruler of Galilee, for marrying Herodias, his brother's wife, and for many other wrongs he had done. ²⁰So Herod put John in prison, adding this sin to his many others.

〜ﮧﺢ **When has knowing Christ ever gotten you into trouble?** John, the author of this Gospel, has been demonstrating that Jesus is the true Son of God. Jesus sets before us the greatest choice in life. We are responsible to decide today whom we will obey (Josh. 24:15), and God wants us to choose him and life (Deut. 30:15-20). The wrath of God is God's final judgment and rejection of the sinner. To put off the choice is to choose not to follow Christ. Indecision is a fatal decision.

JUNE

Jesus Changes a Town
JOHN 4:1-42

Jesus learned that the Pharisees had heard, "Jesus is baptizing and making more disciples than John" ²(though Jesus himself didn't baptize them—his disciples did). ³So he left Judea to return to Galilee.

⁴He had to go through Samaria on the way. ⁵Eventually he came to the Samaritan village of Sychar, near the parcel of ground that Jacob gave to his son Joseph. ⁶Jacob's well was there; and Jesus, tired from the long walk, sat wearily beside the well about noontime. ⁷Soon a Samaritan woman came to draw water, and Jesus said to her, "Please give me a drink." ⁸He was alone at the time because his disciples had gone into the village to buy some food.

⁹The woman was surprised, for Jews refuse to have anything to do with Samaritans. She said to Jesus, "You are a Jew, and I am a Samaritan woman. Why are you asking me for a drink?"

¹⁰Jesus replied, "If you only knew the gift God has for you and who I am, you would ask me, and I would give you living water."

¹¹"But sir, you don't have a rope or a bucket," she said, "and this is a very deep well. Where would you get this living water? ¹²And besides, are you

greater than our ancestor Jacob who gave us this well? How can you offer better water than he and his sons and his cattle enjoyed?"

¹³Jesus replied, "People soon become thirsty again after drinking this water. ¹⁴But the water I give them takes away thirst altogether. It becomes a perpetual spring within them, giving them eternal life."

¹⁵"Please, sir," the woman said, "give me some of that water! Then I'll never be thirsty again, and I won't have to come here to haul water."

¹⁶"Go and get your husband," Jesus told her.

¹⁷"I don't have a husband," the woman replied.

Jesus said, "You're right! You don't have a husband—¹⁸for you have had five husbands, and you aren't even married to the man you're living with now."

¹⁹"Sir," the woman said, "you must be a prophet. ²⁰So tell me, why is it that you Jews insist that Jerusalem is the only place of worship, while we Samaritans claim it is here at Mount Gerizim, where our ancestors worshiped?"

²¹Jesus replied, "Believe me, the time is coming when it will no longer matter whether you worship the Father here or in Jerusalem. ²²You Samaritans know so little about the one you worship, while we Jews know all about him, for salvation comes through the Jews. ²³But the time is coming and is already here when true worshipers will worship the Father in spirit and in truth. The Father is looking for anyone who will worship him that way. ²⁴For God is Spirit, so those who worship him must worship in spirit and in truth."

²⁵The woman said, "I know the Messiah will come—the one who is called Christ. When he comes, he will explain everything to us."

²⁶Then Jesus told her, "I am the Messiah!"

²⁷Just then his disciples arrived. They were astonished to find him talking to a woman, but none of them asked him why he was doing it or what they had been discussing. ²⁸The woman left her water jar beside the well and went back to the village and told everyone, ²⁹"Come and meet a man who told me everything I ever did! Can this be the Messiah?" ³⁰So the people came streaming from the village to see him.

³¹Meanwhile, the disciples were urging Jesus to eat. ³²"No," he said, "I have food you don't know about."

³³"Who brought it to him?" the disciples asked each other.

³⁴Then Jesus explained: "My nourishment comes from doing the will of God, who sent me, and from finishing his work. ³⁵Do you think the work of harvesting will not begin until the summer ends four months from now? Look around you! Vast fields are ripening all around us and are ready now for the harvest. ³⁶The harvesters are paid good wages, and the fruit they harvest is people brought to eternal life. What joy awaits both the planter and the harvester alike! ³⁷You know the saying, 'One person plants and someone else harvests.' And it's true. ³⁸I sent you to harvest where you didn't plant; others had already done the work, and you will gather the harvest."

³⁹Many Samaritans from the village believed in Jesus because the woman had said, "He told me everything I ever did!" ⁴⁰When they came out to see

him, they begged him to stay at their village. So he stayed for two days, ⁴¹long enough for many of them to hear his message and believe. ⁴²Then they said to the woman, "Now we believe because we have heard him ourselves, not just because of what you told us. He is indeed the Savior of the world."

~~~ **In what ways has Jesus affected your town?** The Samaritan woman immediately shared her experience with others. Despite her reputation, many took her invitation and came out to meet Jesus. Perhaps there are sins in your past of which you're ashamed. But Christ is changing you. As people see these changes, they become curious. Use these opportunities to introduce them to Christ.

22

Jesus' Preaching and Healing
JOHN 4:43-54

At the end of the two days' stay, Jesus went on into Galilee. ⁴⁴He had previously said, "A prophet is honored everywhere except in his own country." ⁴⁵The Galileans welcomed him, for they had been in Jerusalem at the Passover celebration and had seen all his miraculous signs.

⁴⁶In the course of his journey through Galilee, he arrived at the town of Cana, where he had turned the water into wine. There was a government official in the city of Capernaum whose son was very sick. ⁴⁷When he heard that Jesus had come from Judea and was traveling in Galilee, he went over to Cana. He found Jesus and begged him to come to Capernaum with him to heal his son, who was about to die.

⁴⁸Jesus asked, "Must I do miraculous signs and wonders before you people will believe in me?"

⁴⁹The official pleaded, "Lord, please come now before my little boy dies."

⁵⁰Then Jesus told him, "Go back home. Your son will live!" And the man believed Jesus' word and started home.

⁵¹While he was on his way, some of his servants met him with the news that his son was alive and well. ⁵²He asked them when the boy had begun to feel better, and they replied, "Yesterday afternoon at one o'clock his fever suddenly disappeared!" ⁵³Then the father realized it was the same time that Jesus had told him, "Your son will live." And the officer and his entire household believed in Jesus. ⁵⁴This was Jesus' second miraculous sign in Galilee after coming from Judea.

~~~ **Why do you believe in Christ?** This government official not only believed that Jesus could heal; he also obeyed Jesus by returning home, thus demonstrating his faith. It isn't enough for us to say we believe that Jesus can take care of our problems. We need to act as if he can. When you pray about a need or problem, live as though you believe Jesus can do what he says.

Jesus Rejected

Luke 4:14-30

Then Jesus returned to Galilee, filled with the Holy Spirit's power. Soon he became well known throughout the surrounding country. ¹⁵He taught in their synagogues and was praised by everyone.

¹⁶When he came to the village of Nazareth, his boyhood home, he went as usual to the synagogue on the Sabbath and stood up to read the Scriptures. ¹⁷The scroll containing the messages of Isaiah the prophet was handed to him, and he unrolled the scroll to the place where it says:

> ¹⁸"The Spirit of the Lord is upon me,
> for he has appointed me to preach Good News to the poor.
> He has sent me to proclaim
> that captives will be released,
> that the blind will see,
> that the downtrodden will be freed from their oppressors,
> ¹⁹ and that the time of the Lord's favor has come."

²⁰He rolled up the scroll, handed it back to the attendant, and sat down. Everyone in the synagogue stared at him intently. ²¹Then he said, "This Scripture has come true today before your very eyes!"

²²All who were there spoke well of him and were amazed by the gracious words that fell from his lips. "How can this be?" they asked. "Isn't this Joseph's son?"

²³Then he said, "Probably you will quote me that proverb, 'Physician, heal yourself'—meaning, 'Why don't you do miracles here in your hometown like those you did in Capernaum?' ²⁴But the truth is, no prophet is accepted in his own hometown.

²⁵"Certainly there were many widows in Israel who needed help in Elijah's time, when there was no rain for three and a half years and hunger stalked the land. ²⁶Yet Elijah was not sent to any of them. He was sent instead to a widow of Zarephath—a foreigner in the land of Sidon. ²⁷Or think of the prophet Elisha, who healed Naaman, a Syrian, rather than the many lepers in Israel who needed help."

²⁸When they heard this, the people in the synagogue were furious. ²⁹Jumping up, they mobbed him and took him to the edge of the hill on which the city was built. They intended to push him over the cliff, ³⁰but he slipped away through the crowd and left them.

∿⌇ How would Jesus be received in your church next Sunday?

Jesus went to the synagogue "as usual." Even though he was the perfect Son of God and his local synagogue left much to be desired, he attended services every week. Jesus' example makes most excuses for not attending church sound weak and self-serving. Make regular worship a part of your life.

24 JUNE

Jesus Calls People to Follow
MARK 1:16-39

One day as Jesus was walking along the shores of the Sea of Galilee, he saw Simon and his brother, Andrew, fishing with a net, for they were commercial fishermen. [17]Jesus called out to them, "Come, be my disciples, and I will show you how to fish for people!" [18]And they left their nets at once and went with him.

[19]A little farther up the shore Jesus saw Zebedee's sons, James and John, in a boat mending their nets. [20]He called them, too, and immediately they left their father, Zebedee, in the boat with the hired men and went with him.

[21]Jesus and his companions went to the town of Capernaum, and every Sabbath day he went into the synagogue and taught the people. [22]They were amazed at his teaching, for he taught as one who had real authority—quite unlike the teachers of religious law.

[23]A man possessed by an evil spirit was in the synagogue, [24]and he began shouting, "Why are you bothering us, Jesus of Nazareth? Have you come to destroy us? I know who you are—the Holy One sent from God!"

[25]Jesus cut him short. "Be silent! Come out of the man." [26]At that, the evil spirit screamed and threw the man into a convulsion, but then he left him.

[27]Amazement gripped the audience, and they began to discuss what had happened. "What sort of new teaching is this?" they asked excitedly. "It has such authority! Even evil spirits obey his orders!" [28]The news of what he had done spread quickly through that entire area of Galilee.

[29]After Jesus and his disciples left the synagogue, they went over to Simon and Andrew's home, and James and John were with them. [30]Simon's mother-in-law was sick in bed with a high fever. They told Jesus about her right away. [31]He went to her bedside, and as he took her by the hand and helped her to sit up, the fever suddenly left, and she got up and prepared a meal for them.

[32]That evening at sunset, many sick and demon-possessed people were brought to Jesus. [33]And a huge crowd of people from all over Capernaum gathered outside the door to watch. [34]So Jesus healed great numbers of sick people who had many different kinds of diseases, and he ordered many demons to come out of their victims. But because they knew who he was, he refused to allow the demons to speak.

[35]The next morning Jesus awoke long before daybreak and went out alone into the wilderness to pray. [36]Later Simon and the others went out to find him. [37]They said, "Everyone is asking for you."

³⁸But he replied, "We must go on to other towns as well, and I will preach to them, too, because that is why I came." ³⁹So he traveled throughout the region of Galilee, preaching in the synagogues and expelling demons from many people.

〰〰 **What specific things have you left behind to follow Christ?** We often assume that Jesus' disciples were great men of faith from the first time they met Jesus. But they had to grow in their faith just as all believers do. Although it took time for Jesus' call and his message to get through, the disciples *followed*. In the same way, we may question and falter, but we must never stop following Jesus.

JUNE

Miracles and Questions

LUKE 5:1-39

One day as Jesus was preaching on the shore of the Sea of Galilee, great crowds pressed in on him to listen to the word of God. ²He noticed two empty boats at the water's edge, for the fishermen had left them and were washing their nets. ³Stepping into one of the boats, Jesus asked Simon, its owner, to push it out into the water. So he sat in the boat and taught the crowds from there.

⁴When he had finished speaking, he said to Simon, "Now go out where it is deeper and let down your nets, and you will catch many fish."

⁵"Master," Simon replied, "we worked hard all last night and didn't catch a thing. But if you say so, we'll try again." ⁶And this time their nets were so full they began to tear! ⁷A shout for help brought their partners in the other boat, and soon both boats were filled with fish and on the verge of sinking.

⁸When Simon Peter realized what had happened, he fell to his knees before Jesus and said, "Oh, Lord, please leave me—I'm too much of a sinner to be around you." ⁹For he was awestruck by the size of their catch, as were the others with him. ¹⁰His partners, James and John, the sons of Zebedee, were also amazed.

Jesus replied to Simon, "Don't be afraid! From now on you'll be fishing for people!" ¹¹And as soon as they landed, they left everything and followed Jesus.

¹²In one of the villages, Jesus met a man with an advanced case of leprosy. When the man saw Jesus, he fell to the ground, face down in the dust, begging to be healed. "Lord," he said, "if you want to, you can make me well again."

¹³Jesus reached out and touched the man. "I want to," he said. "Be healed!" And instantly the leprosy disappeared. ¹⁴Then Jesus instructed him not to tell anyone what had happened. He said, "Go right to the priest and let him examine you. Take along the offering required in the law of Moses for those who have been healed of leprosy, so everyone will have proof of your heal-

ing." [15]Yet despite Jesus' instructions, the report of his power spread even faster, and vast crowds came to hear him preach and to be healed of their diseases. [16]But Jesus often withdrew to the wilderness for prayer.

[17]One day while Jesus was teaching, some Pharisees and teachers of religious law were sitting nearby. (It seemed that these men showed up from every village in all Galilee and Judea, as well as from Jerusalem.) And the Lord's healing power was strongly with Jesus. [18]Some men came carrying a paralyzed man on a sleeping mat. They tried to push through the crowd to Jesus, [19]but they couldn't reach him. So they went up to the roof, took off some tiles, and lowered the sick man down into the crowd, still on his mat, right in front of Jesus. [20]Seeing their faith, Jesus said to the man, "Son, your sins are forgiven."

[21]"Who does this man think he is?" the Pharisees and teachers of religious law said to each other. "This is blasphemy! Who but God can forgive sins?"

[22]Jesus knew what they were thinking, so he asked them, "Why do you think this is blasphemy? [23]Is it easier to say, 'Your sins are forgiven' or 'Get up and walk'? [24]I will prove that I, the Son of Man, have the authority on earth to forgive sins." Then Jesus turned to the paralyzed man and said, "Stand up, take your mat, and go on home, because you are healed!"

[25]And immediately, as everyone watched, the man jumped to his feet, picked up his mat, and went home praising God. [26]Everyone was gripped with great wonder and awe. And they praised God, saying over and over again, "We have seen amazing things today."

[27]Later, as Jesus left the town, he saw a tax collector named Levi sitting at his tax-collection booth. "Come, be my disciple!" Jesus said to him. [28]So Levi got up, left everything, and followed him.

[29]Soon Levi held a banquet in his home with Jesus as the guest of honor. Many of Levi's fellow tax collectors and other guests were there. [30]But the Pharisees and their teachers of religious law complained bitterly to Jesus' disciples, "Why do you eat and drink with such scum?"

[31]Jesus answered them, "Healthy people don't need a doctor—sick people do. [32]I have come to call sinners to turn from their sins, not to spend my time with those who think they are already good enough."

[33]The religious leaders complained that Jesus' disciples were feasting instead of fasting. "John the Baptist's disciples always fast and pray," they declared, "and so do the disciples of the Pharisees. Why are yours always feasting?"

[34]Jesus asked, "Do wedding guests fast while celebrating with the groom? [35]Someday he will be taken away from them, and then they will fast."

[36]Then Jesus gave them this illustration: "No one tears a piece of cloth from a new garment and uses it to patch an old garment. For then the new garment would be torn, and the patch wouldn't even match the old garment. [37]And no one puts new wine into old wineskins. The new wine would burst the old skins, spilling the wine and ruining the skins. [38]New wine

must be put into new wineskins. ³⁹But no one who drinks the old wine seems to want the fresh and the new. 'The old is better,' they say."

〰〰 **How do Jesus' miracles affect you today?** It wasn't the sick man's faith that impressed Jesus but the faith of his friends. Jesus responded to their faith and healed the man. For better or worse, our faith affects others. We cannot make another person a Christian, but we can do much through our words, actions, and love to give him or her a chance to respond. Look for opportunities to bring your friends to the living Christ.

Jesus Demonstrates He Is God's Son

JOHN 5:1-47

Afterward Jesus returned to Jerusalem for one of the Jewish holy days. ²Inside the city, near the Sheep Gate, was the pool of Bethesda, with five covered porches. ³Crowds of sick people—blind, lame, or paralyzed—lay on the porches. ⁵One of the men lying there had been sick for thirty-eight years. ⁶When Jesus saw him and knew how long he had been ill, he asked him, "Would you like to get well?"

⁷"I can't, sir," the sick man said, "for I have no one to help me into the pool when the water is stirred up. While I am trying to get there, someone else always gets in ahead of me."

⁸Jesus told him, "Stand up, pick up your sleeping mat, and walk!"

⁹Instantly, the man was healed! He rolled up the mat and began walking! But this miracle happened on the Sabbath day. ¹⁰So the Jewish leaders objected. They said to the man who was cured, "You can't work on the Sabbath! It's illegal to carry that sleeping mat!"

¹¹He replied, "The man who healed me said to me, 'Pick up your sleeping mat and walk.'"

¹²"Who said such a thing as that?" they demanded.

¹³The man didn't know, for Jesus had disappeared into the crowd. ¹⁴But afterward Jesus found him in the Temple and told him, "Now you are well; so stop sinning, or something even worse may happen to you." ¹⁵Then the man went to find the Jewish leaders and told them it was Jesus who had healed him.

¹⁶So the Jewish leaders began harassing Jesus for breaking the Sabbath rules. ¹⁷But Jesus replied, "My Father never stops working, so why should I?" ¹⁸So the Jewish leaders tried all the more to kill him. In addition to disobeying the Sabbath rules, he had spoken of God as his Father, thereby making himself equal with God.

¹⁹Jesus replied, "I assure you, the Son can do nothing by himself. He does only what he sees the Father doing. Whatever the Father does, the Son also

does. [20]For the Father loves the Son and tells him everything he is doing, and the Son will do far greater things than healing this man. You will be astonished at what he does. [21]He will even raise from the dead anyone he wants to, just as the Father does. [22]And the Father leaves all judgment to his Son, [23]so that everyone will honor the Son, just as they honor the Father. But if you refuse to honor the Son, then you are certainly not honoring the Father who sent him.

[24]"I assure you, those who listen to my message and believe in God who sent me have eternal life. They will never be condemned for their sins, but they have already passed from death into life.

[25]"And I assure you that the time is coming, in fact it is here, when the dead will hear my voice—the voice of the Son of God. And those who listen will live. [26]The Father has life in himself, and he has granted his Son to have life in himself. [27]And he has given him authority to judge all mankind because he is the Son of Man. [28]Don't be so surprised! Indeed, the time is coming when all the dead in their graves will hear the voice of God's Son, [29]and they will rise again. Those who have done good will rise to eternal life, and those who have continued in evil will rise to judgment. [30]But I do nothing without consulting the Father. I judge as I am told. And my judgment is absolutely just, because it is according to the will of God who sent me; it is not merely my own.

[31]"If I were to testify on my own behalf, my testimony would not be valid. [32]But someone else is also testifying about me, and I can assure you that everything he says about me is true. [33]In fact, you sent messengers to listen to John the Baptist, and he preached the truth. [34]But the best testimony about me is not from a man, though I have reminded you about John's testimony so you might be saved. [35]John shone brightly for a while, and you benefited and rejoiced. [36]But I have a greater witness than John—my teachings and my miracles. They have been assigned to me by the Father, and they testify that the Father has sent me. [37]And the Father himself has also testified about me. You have never heard his voice or seen him face to face, [38]and you do not have his message in your hearts, because you do not believe me—the one he sent to you.

[39]"You search the Scriptures because you believe they give you eternal life. But the Scriptures point to me! [40]Yet you refuse to come to me so that I can give you this eternal life.

[41]"Your approval or disapproval means nothing to me, [42]because I know you don't have God's love within you. [43]For I have come to you representing my Father, and you refuse to welcome me, even though you readily accept others who represent only themselves. [44]No wonder you can't believe! For you gladly honor each other, but you don't care about the honor that comes from God alone.

[45]"Yet it is not I who will accuse you of this before the Father. Moses will accuse you! Yes, Moses, on whom you set your hopes. [46]But if you had

believed Moses, you would have believed me because he wrote about me. [47]And since you don't believe what he wrote, how will you believe what I say?"

∿∿ **What do you find most attractive about Jesus?** Whose approval do you seek? The religious leaders enjoyed great prestige in Israel, but their stamp of approval meant nothing to Jesus. He was concerned about God's approval. This is a good principle for us. If even the highest officials in the world approve of our actions and God does not, we should be concerned. But if God approves, even though others don't, we should be content.

Jesus and Disciples

MARK 2:23–3:19

One Sabbath day as Jesus was walking through some grainfields, his disciples began breaking off heads of wheat. [24]But the Pharisees said to Jesus, "They shouldn't be doing that! It's against the law to work by harvesting grain on the Sabbath."

[25]But Jesus replied, "Haven't you ever read in the Scriptures what King David did when he and his companions were hungry? [26]He went into the house of God (during the days when Abiathar was high priest), ate the special bread reserved for the priests alone, and then gave some to his companions. That was breaking the law, too." [27]Then he said to them, "The Sabbath was made to benefit people, and not people to benefit the Sabbath. [28]And I, the Son of Man, am master even of the Sabbath!"

[3:1]Jesus went into the synagogue again and noticed a man with a deformed hand. [2]Since it was the Sabbath, Jesus' enemies watched him closely. Would he heal the man's hand on the Sabbath? If he did, they planned to condemn him. [3]Jesus said to the man, "Come and stand in front of everyone." [4]Then he turned to his critics and asked, "Is it legal to do good deeds on the Sabbath, or is it a day for doing harm? Is this a day to save life or to destroy it?" But they wouldn't answer him. [5]He looked around at them angrily, because he was deeply disturbed by their hard hearts. Then he said to the man, "Reach out your hand." The man reached out his hand, and it became normal again! [6]At once the Pharisees went away and met with the supporters of Herod to discuss plans for killing Jesus.

[7]Jesus and his disciples went out to the lake, followed by a huge crowd from all over Galilee, Judea, [8]Jerusalem, Idumea, from east of the Jordan River, and even from as far away as Tyre and Sidon. The news about his miracles had spread far and wide, and vast numbers of people came to see him for themselves.

[9]Jesus instructed his disciples to bring around a boat and to have it ready in case he was crowded off the beach. [10]There had been many healings that day. As a result, many sick people were crowding around him, trying to

touch him. [11]And whenever those possessed by evil spirits caught sight of him, they would fall down in front of him shrieking, "You are the Son of God!" [12]But Jesus strictly warned them not to say who he was.

[13]Afterward Jesus went up on a mountain and called the ones he wanted to go with him. And they came to him. [14]Then he selected twelve of them to be his regular companions, calling them apostles. He sent them out to preach, [15]and he gave them authority to cast out demons. [16]These are the names of the twelve he chose:

> Simon (he renamed him Peter),
> [17]James and John (the sons of Zebedee, but Jesus nicknamed them "Sons of Thunder"),
> [18]Andrew,
> Philip,
> Bartholomew,
> Matthew,
> Thomas,
> James (son of Alphaeus),
> Thaddaeus,
> Simon (the Zealot),
> [19]Judas Iscariot (who later betrayed him).

〜✕〜 **How would Jesus treat your personal traditions?** Jesus used the example of David to point out how ridiculous the Pharisees' accusations were (this incident occurred in 1 Samuel 21:1-6). God created the Sabbath for our benefit, not his own. God derives no benefit from having us rest on the Sabbath, but we are restored both physically and spiritually when we take time to rest and to focus on God. For the Pharisees, Sabbath laws had become more important than Sabbath rest. Both David and Jesus understood that the intent of God's law is to promote love for God and others. When we apply a law to other people, we should make sure that we understand its purpose and intent so we don't make harmful or inappropriate judgments.

28 JUNE

Jesus Gives the Beatitudes
MATTHEW 5:1-16

One day as the crowds were gathering, Jesus went up the mountainside with his disciples and sat down to teach them.

> [3] "God blesses those who realize their need for him,
>   for the Kingdom of Heaven is given to them.
> [4] God blesses those who mourn,
>   for they will be comforted.

⁵ God blesses those who are gentle and lowly,
   for the whole earth will belong to them.
⁶ God blesses those who are hungry and thirsty for justice,
   for they will receive it in full.
⁷ God blesses those who are merciful,
   for they will be shown mercy.
⁸ God blesses those whose hearts are pure,
   for they will see God.
⁹ God blesses those who work for peace,
   for they will be called the children of God.
¹⁰God blesses those who are persecuted because they live for God,
   for the Kingdom of Heaven is theirs.

¹¹"God blesses you when you are mocked and persecuted and lied about because you are my followers. ¹²Be happy about it! Be very glad! For a great reward awaits you in heaven. And remember, the ancient prophets were persecuted, too.

¹³"You are the salt of the earth. But what good is salt if it has lost its flavor? Can you make it useful again? It will be thrown out and trampled underfoot as worthless. ¹⁴You are the light of the world—like a city on a mountain, glowing in the night for all to see. ¹⁵Don't hide your light under a basket! Instead, put it on a stand and let it shine for all. ¹⁶In the same way, let your good deeds shine out for all to see, so that everyone will praise your heavenly Father."

〜〰〜 **Which of the Beatitudes can you claim?** Jesus began his sermon with words that seem to contradict each other. But God's way of living usually contradicts the world's. If you want to live for God, you must be ready to say and do what seems strange to the world. You must be willing to give when others take, to love when others hate, to help when others abuse. In doing this, you will one day receive everything, while the others will end up with nothing.

Jesus on Law, Anger, and Lust

JUNE

MATTHEW 5:17-30

"Don't misunderstand why I have come. I did not come to abolish the law of Moses or the writings of the prophets. No, I came to fulfill them. ¹⁸I assure you, until heaven and earth disappear, even the smallest detail of God's law will remain until its purpose is achieved. ¹⁹So if you break the smallest commandment and teach others to do the same, you will be the least in the Kingdom of Heaven. But anyone who obeys God's laws and teaches them will be great in the Kingdom of Heaven. ²⁰"But I warn you—unless you obey God better than the teachers of religious law and the Pharisees do, you can't enter the Kingdom of Heaven at all!

[21]"You have heard that the law of Moses says, 'Do not murder. If you commit murder, you are subject to judgment.' [22]But I say, if you are angry with someone, you are subject to judgment! If you say to your friend, 'You idiot,' you are in danger of being brought before the court. And if you curse someone, you are in danger of the fires of hell.

[23]"So if you are standing before the altar in the Temple, offering a sacrifice to God, and you suddenly remember that someone has something against you, [24]leave your sacrifice there beside the altar. Go and be reconciled to that person. Then come and offer your sacrifice to God. [25]Come to terms quickly with your enemy before it is too late and you are dragged into court, handed over to an officer, and thrown in jail. [26]I assure you that you won't be free again until you have paid the last penny.

[27]"You have heard that the law of Moses says, 'Do not commit adultery.' [28]But I say, anyone who even looks at a woman with lust in his eye has already committed adultery with her in his heart. [29]So if your eye—even if it is your good eye—causes you to lust, gouge it out and throw it away. It is better for you to lose one part of your body than for your whole body to be thrown into hell. [30]And if your hand—even if it is your stronger hand—causes you to sin, cut it off and throw it away. It is better for you to lose one part of your body than for your whole body to be thrown into hell."

⌁〜⋀⁄⌐ **How do Jesus' views compare with yours?** Some believe that if lustful thoughts are sin, they might as well do the lustful actions, too. This is harmful in several ways: (1) It causes you to excuse your sin rather than eliminate it. (2) It destroys marriages. (3) It is deliberate rebellion against God's Word. (4) It always hurts someone else in addition to yourself. While desire is not as dangerous as action, it is just as damaging to righteousness. Left unchecked, wrong desires will result in wrong actions and turn you away from God.

30 JUNE

Jesus on Relationships
MATTHEW 5:31-48

"You have heard that the law of Moses says, 'A man can divorce his wife by merely giving her a letter of divorce.' [32]But I say that a man who divorces his wife, unless she has been unfaithful, causes her to commit adultery. And anyone who marries a divorced woman commits adultery.

[33]"Again, you have heard that the law of Moses says, 'Do not break your vows; you must carry out the vows you have made to the Lord.' [34]But I say, don't make any vows! If you say, 'By heaven!' it is a sacred vow because heaven is God's throne. [35]And if you say, 'By the earth!' it is a sacred vow because the earth is his footstool. And don't swear, 'By Jerusalem!' for Jeru-

salem is the city of the great King. [36]Don't even swear, 'By my head!' for you can't turn one hair white or black. [37]Just say a simple, 'Yes, I will,' or 'No, I won't.' Your word is enough. To strengthen your promise with a vow shows that something is wrong.

[38]"You have heard that the law of Moses says, 'If an eye is injured, injure the eye of the person who did it. If a tooth gets knocked out, knock out the tooth of the person who did it.' [39]But I say, don't resist an evil person! If you are slapped on the right cheek, turn the other, too. [40]If you are ordered to court and your shirt is taken from you, give your coat, too. [41]If a soldier demands that you carry his gear for a mile, carry it two miles. [42]Give to those who ask, and don't turn away from those who want to borrow.

[43]"You have heard that the law of Moses says, 'Love your neighbor' and hate your enemy. [44]But I say, love your enemies! Pray for those who persecute you! [45]In that way, you will be acting as true children of your Father in heaven. For he gives his sunlight to both the evil and the good, and he sends rain on the just and on the unjust, too. [46]If you love only those who love you, what good is that? Even corrupt tax collectors do that much. [47]If you are kind only to your friends, how are you different from anyone else? Even pagans do that. [48]But you are to be perfect, even as your Father in heaven is perfect."

〜�bo〜 **What part of your life could be most radically changed by these words?** How can we be perfect? (1) *In character.* In this life we cannot be flawless, but we can aspire to be as much like Christ as possible. (2) *In holiness.* We are to separate ourselves from the world's sinful values and be devoted to God's desires rather than our own. (3) *In maturity.* We can't achieve Christlike character and holy living all at once, but we must grow toward maturity and wholeness. Just as we expect different behavior from a baby, a child, a teenager, and an adult, so God expects different behavior from us, depending on our stage of spiritual development. (4) *In love.* We can seek to love others as completely as God loves us. We can be perfect if our behavior is appropriate for our maturity level—perfect, yet with much room to grow. Our tendency to sin must never deter us from striving to be more like Christ. Christ calls all of his disciples to excel, to rise above mediocrity, and to mature in every area, becoming like him. Those who strive to become perfect will one day be perfect, even as Christ is perfect (1 John 3:2-3).

Jesus on Doing
Good Things

JULY

MATTHEW 6:1-18

"Take care! Don't do your good deeds publicly, to be admired, because then you will lose the reward from your Father in heaven. ²When you give a gift to someone in need, don't shout about it as the hypocrites do—blowing trumpets in the synagogues and streets to call attention to their acts of charity! I assure you, they have received all the reward they will ever get. ³But when you give to someone, don't tell your left hand what your right hand is doing. ⁴Give your gifts in secret, and your Father, who knows all secrets, will reward you.

⁵"And now about prayer. When you pray, don't be like the hypocrites who love to pray publicly on street corners and in the synagogues where everyone can see them. I assure you, that is all the reward they will ever get. ⁶But when you pray, go away by yourself, shut the door behind you, and pray to your Father secretly. Then your Father, who knows all secrets, will reward you.

⁷"When you pray, don't babble on and on as people of other religions do. They think their prayers are answered only by repeating their words again and again. ⁸Don't be like them, because your Father knows exactly what you need even before you ask him! ⁹Pray like this:

Our Father in heaven,
    may your name be honored.
¹⁰May your kingdom come soon.
May your will be done here on earth,
    just as it is in heaven.
¹¹Give us our food for today,
¹²and forgive us our sins,
    just as we have forgiven those who have sinned against us.
¹³And don't let us yield to temptation,
    but deliver us from the evil one.

¹⁴"If you forgive those who sin against you, your heavenly Father will forgive you. ¹⁵But if you refuse to forgive others, your Father will not forgive your sins.

ᵒ"And when you fast, don't make it obvious, as the hypocrites do, who ᴄry to look pale and disheveled so people will admire them for their fasting. I assure you, that is the only reward they will ever get. ¹⁷But when you fast, comb your hair and wash your face. ¹⁸Then no one will suspect you are fasting, except your Father, who knows what you do in secret. And your Father, who knows all secrets, will reward you."

 How does your public life compare to your private life? It's easier to do what's right when we gain recognition and praise. To be sure our motives are not selfish, we should do our good works quietly or in secret, with no thought of reward. Jesus says we should check our motives in three areas: generosity (v. 3), prayer (v. 6), and fasting (v. 16). Those acts should not be self-centered but God-centered, done not to make us look good but to make God look good. The reward God promises is not material, and it is never given to those who seek it. Doing something only for ourselves is not a loving sacrifice. With your next good deed, ask, Would I still do this if no one would ever know I did it?

2

JULY

Jesus on Money and Worry
MATTHEW 6:19-34

"Don't store up treasures here on earth, where they can be eaten by moths and get rusty, and where thieves break in and steal. ²⁰Store your treasures in heaven, where they will never become moth-eaten or rusty and where they will be safe from thieves. ²¹Wherever your treasure is, there your heart and thoughts will also be.

²²"Your eye is a lamp for your body. A pure eye lets sunshine into your soul. ²³But an evil eye shuts out the light and plunges you into darkness. If the light you think you have is really darkness, how deep that darkness will be!

²⁴"No one can serve two masters. For you will hate one and love the other, or be devoted to one and despise the other. You cannot serve both God and money.

²⁵"So I tell you, don't worry about everyday life—whether you have enough food, drink, and clothes. Doesn't life consist of more than food and clothing? ²⁶Look at the birds. They don't need to plant or harvest or put food in barns because your heavenly Father feeds them. And you are far more valuable to him than they are. ²⁷Can all your worries add a single moment to your life? Of course not.

²⁸"And why worry about your clothes? Look at the lilies and how they grow. They don't work or make their clothing, ²⁹yet Solomon in all his glory was not dressed as beautifully as they are. ³⁰And if God cares so wonderfully

for flowers that are here today and gone tomorrow, won't he more surely care for you? You have so little faith!

[31]"So don't worry about having enough food or drink or clothing. [32]Why be like the pagans who are so deeply concerned about these things? Your heavenly Father already knows all your needs, [33]and he will give you all you need from day to day if you live for him and make the Kingdom of God your primary concern.

[34]"So don't worry about tomorrow, for tomorrow will bring its own worries. Today's trouble is enough for today."

~✺⌇ **In what ways are money and worry related in your life?** To live for God and make his kingdom your primary concern means to turn to God first for help, to fill your thoughts with his desires, to take his character for your pattern, and to serve and obey him in everything. What is really important to you? People, objects, goals, and other desires all compete for priority. Any of these can quickly bump God out of first place if you don't actively choose to give him first place in *every* area of your life.

Jesus on Criticizing and Praying

JULY 3

MATTHEW 7:1-12

"Stop judging others, and you will not be judged. [2]For others will treat you as you treat them. Whatever measure you use in judging others, it will be used to measure how you are judged. [3]And why worry about a speck in your friend's eye when you have a log in your own? [4]How can you think of saying, 'Friend, let me help you get rid of that speck in your eye,' when you can't see past the log in your own eye? [5]Hypocrite! First get rid of the log from your own eye; then perhaps you will see well enough to deal with the speck in your friend's eye.

[6]"Don't give what is holy to unholy people. Don't give pearls to swine! They will trample the pearls, then turn and attack you.

[7]"Keep on asking, and you will be given what you ask for. Keep on looking, and you will find. Keep on knocking, and the door will be opened. [8]For everyone who asks, receives. Everyone who seeks, finds. And the door is opened to everyone who knocks. [9]You parents—if your children ask for a loaf of bread, do you give them a stone instead? [10]Or if they ask for a fish, do you give them a snake? Of course not! [11]If you sinful people know how to give good gifts to your children, how much more will your heavenly Father give good gifts to those who ask him.

[12]"Do for others what you would like them to do for you. This is a summary of all that is taught in the law and the prophets."

Which do you do more of, criticizing or praying? Why? Jesus tells us to examine our own motives and conduct instead of judging others. The traits that bother us in others are often those we dislike in ourselves. Our own bad habits and behavior patterns are the very ones that we most want to change in others. Do you find it easy to magnify others' faults while excusing your own? If you are ready to criticize someone, check to see if you deserve the same criticism. Judge yourself first, and then lovingly forgive and help your neighbor.

JULY 4

How Jesus Looks at Us
MATTHEW 7:13-29

"You can enter God's Kingdom only through the narrow gate. The highway to hell is broad, and its gate is wide for the many who choose the easy way. [14]But the gateway to life is small, and the road is narrow, and only a few ever find it.

[15]"Beware of false prophets who come disguised as harmless sheep, but are really wolves that will tear you apart. [16]You can detect them by the way they act, just as you can identify a tree by its fruit. You don't pick grapes from thornbushes, or figs from thistles. [17]A healthy tree produces good fruit, and an unhealthy tree produces bad fruit. [18]A good tree can't produce bad fruit, and a bad tree can't produce good fruit. [19]So every tree that does not produce good fruit is chopped down and thrown into the fire. [20]Yes, the way to identify a tree or a person is by the kind of fruit that is produced.

[21]"Not all people who sound religious are really godly. They refer to me as 'Lord,' but they still won't enter the Kingdom of Heaven. The decisive issue is whether they obey my Father in heaven. [22]On judgment day many will tell me, 'Lord, Lord, we prophesied in your name and cast out demons in your name and performed many miracles in your name.' [23]But I will reply, 'I never knew you. Go away; the things you did were unauthorized.'

[24]"Anyone who listens to my teaching and obeys me is wise, like a person who builds a house on solid rock. [25]Though the rain comes in torrents and the floodwaters rise and the winds beat against that house, it won't collapse, because it is built on rock. [26]But anyone who hears my teaching and ignores it is foolish, like a person who builds a house on sand. [27]When the rains and floods come and the winds beat against that house, it will fall with a mighty crash."

[28]After Jesus finished speaking, the crowds were amazed at his teaching, [29]for he taught as one who had real authority—quite unlike the teachers of religious law.

What is your foundation in life? Some sports fans can "talk" a great game, but that tells you nothing about their athletic skills. And not everyone who talks about heaven belongs to God's kingdom. Jesus is more concerned about our *walk* than our *talk*. He wants us to *do* right, not just *say* the right words. Your house (which represents your life, v. 25) will withstand the storms of life only if you do what is right instead of just talking about it. What you do cannot be separated from what you believe.

Jesus and Foreigners
LUKE 7:1-17

When Jesus had finished saying all this, he went back to Capernaum. ²Now the highly valued slave of a Roman officer was sick and near death. ³When the officer heard about Jesus, he sent some respected Jewish leaders to ask him to come and heal his slave. ⁴So they earnestly begged Jesus to come with them and help the man. "If anyone deserves your help, it is he," they said, ⁵"for he loves the Jews and even built a synagogue for us."

⁶So Jesus went with them. But just before they arrived at the house, the officer sent some friends to say, "Lord, don't trouble yourself by coming to my home, for I am not worthy of such an honor. ⁷I am not even worthy to come and meet you. Just say the word from where you are, and my servant will be healed. ⁸I know because I am under the authority of my superior officers, and I have authority over my soldiers. I only need to say, 'Go,' and they go, or 'Come,' and they come. And if I say to my slaves, 'Do this or that,' they do it."

⁹When Jesus heard this, he was amazed. Turning to the crowd, he said, "I tell you, I haven't seen faith like this in all the land of Israel!" ¹⁰And when the captain's friends returned to his house, they found the slave completely healed.

¹¹Soon afterward Jesus went with his disciples to the village of Nain, with a great crowd following him. ¹²A funeral procession was coming out as he approached the village gate. The boy who had died was the only son of a widow, and many mourners from the village were with her. ¹³When the Lord saw her, his heart overflowed with compassion. "Don't cry!" he said. ¹⁴ Then he walked over to the coffin and touched it, and the bearers stopped. "Young man," he said, "get up." ¹⁵Then the dead boy sat up and began to talk to those around him! And Jesus gave him back to his mother.

¹⁶Great fear swept the crowd, and they praised God, saying, "A mighty prophet has risen among us," and "We have seen the hand of God at work today." ¹⁷The report of what Jesus had done that day spread all over Judea and even out across its borders.

〰️ **What is your attitude toward foreigners? How can you show them God's love?** The Roman officer didn't come to Jesus, and he didn't expect Jesus to come to him. Just as this officer did not need to be present to have his orders carried out, so Jesus didn't need to be present to heal. The

267

officer's faith was especially amazing because he was a Gentile who had not been brought up to know a loving God. Jesus praised this man's faith. What would he say about yours?

Jesus Describes John

MATTHEW 11:1-30

When Jesus had finished giving these instructions to his twelve disciples, he went off teaching and preaching in towns throughout the country. [2]John the Baptist, who was now in prison, heard about all the things the Messiah was doing. So he sent his disciples to ask Jesus, [3]"Are you really the Messiah we've been waiting for, or should we keep looking for someone else?"

[4]Jesus told them, "Go back to John and tell him about what you have heard and seen— [5]the blind see, the lame walk, the lepers are cured, the deaf hear, the dead are raised to life, and the Good News is being preached to the poor. [6]And tell him: 'God blesses those who are not offended by me.' "

[7]When John's disciples had gone, Jesus began talking about him to the crowds. "Who is this man in the wilderness that you went out to see? Did you find him weak as a reed, moved by every breath of wind? [8]Or were you expecting to see a man dressed in expensive clothes? Those who dress like that live in palaces, not out in the wilderness. [9]Were you looking for a prophet? Yes, and he is more than a prophet. [10]John is the man to whom the Scriptures refer when they say,

'Look, I am sending my messenger before you,
and he will prepare your way before you.'

[11]"I assure you, of all who have ever lived, none is greater than John the Baptist. Yet even the most insignificant person in the Kingdom of Heaven is greater than he is! [12]And from the time John the Baptist began preaching and baptizing until now, the Kingdom of Heaven has been forcefully advancing, and violent people attack it. [13]For before John came, all the teachings of the Scriptures looked forward to this present time. [14]And if you are willing to accept what I say, he is Elijah, the one the prophets said would come. [15]Anyone who is willing to hear should listen and understand!

[16]"How shall I describe this generation? These people are like a group of children playing a game in the public square. They complain to their friends, [17]'We played wedding songs, and you weren't happy, so we played funeral songs, but you weren't sad.' [18]For John the Baptist didn't drink wine and he often fasted, and you say, 'He's demon possessed.' [19]And I, the Son of Man, feast and drink, and you say, 'He's a glutton and a drunkard, and a friend of the worst sort of sinners!' But wisdom is shown to be right by what results from it."

²⁰Then Jesus began to denounce the cities where he had done most of his miracles, because they hadn't turned from their sins and turned to God. ²¹"What horrors await you, Korazin and Bethsaida! For if the miracles I did in you had been done in wicked Tyre and Sidon, their people would have sat in deep repentance long ago, clothed in sackcloth and throwing ashes on their heads to show their remorse. ²²I assure you, Tyre and Sidon will be better off on the judgment day than you! ²³And you people of Capernaum, will you be exalted to heaven? No, you will be brought down to the place of the dead. For if the miracles I did for you had been done in Sodom, it would still be here today. ²⁴I assure you, Sodom will be better off on the judgment day than you."

²⁵Then Jesus prayed this prayer: "O Father, Lord of heaven and earth, thank you for hiding the truth from those who think themselves so wise and clever, and for revealing it to the childlike. ²⁶Yes, Father, it pleased you to do it this way!

²⁷"My Father has given me authority over everything. No one really knows the Son except the Father, and no one really knows the Father except the Son and those to whom the Son chooses to reveal him."

²⁸Then Jesus said, "Come to me, all of you who are weary and carry heavy burdens, and I will give you rest. ²⁹Take my yoke upon you. Let me teach you, because I am humble and gentle, and you will find rest for your souls. ³⁰For my yoke fits perfectly, and the burden I give you is light."

〰〰〰 **How would you want Jesus to summarize your life?** As John sat in prison, he began to have some doubts about whether Jesus really was the Messiah. Jesus answered John's doubts by pointing to the miracles in which the blind, lame, and deaf were healed, the lepers were cured, the dead were raised, and the gospel was preached to the poor. With so much evidence, Jesus' identity was obvious. If you sometimes doubt your salvation, the forgiveness of your sins, or God's work in your life, look at the evidence in Scripture and the changes in your life. When you doubt, don't turn away from Christ; turn *to* him.

JULY

7

Jesus and Women
LUKE 7:36–8:3

One of the Pharisees asked Jesus to come to his home for a meal, so Jesus accepted the invitation and sat down to eat. ³⁷A certain immoral woman heard he was there and brought a beautiful jar filled with expensive perfume. ³⁸Then she knelt behind him at his feet, weeping. Her tears fell on his feet, and she wiped them off with her hair. Then she kept kissing his feet and putting perfume on them.

³⁹When the Pharisee who was the host saw what was happening and who the woman was, he said to himself, "This proves that Jesus is no prophet. If

God had really sent him, he would know what kind of woman is touching him. She's a sinner!"

⁴⁰Then Jesus spoke up and answered his thoughts. "Simon," he said to the Pharisee, "I have something to say to you."

"All right, Teacher," Simon replied, "go ahead."

⁴¹Then Jesus told him this story: "A man loaned money to two people— five hundred pieces of silver to one and fifty pieces to the other. ⁴²But neither of them could repay him, so he kindly forgave them both, canceling their debts. Who do you suppose loved him more after that?"

⁴³Simon answered, "I suppose the one for whom he canceled the larger debt."

"That's right," Jesus said. ⁴⁴Then he turned to the woman and said to Simon, "Look at this woman kneeling here. When I entered your home, you didn't offer me water to wash the dust from my feet, but she has washed them with her tears and wiped them with her hair. ⁴⁵You didn't give me a kiss of greeting, but she has kissed my feet again and again from the time I first came in. ⁴⁶You neglected the courtesy of olive oil to anoint my head, but she has anointed my feet with rare perfume. ⁴⁷I tell you, her sins—and they are many—have been forgiven, so she has shown me much love. But a person who is forgiven little shows only little love." ⁴⁸Then Jesus said to the woman, "Your sins are forgiven."

⁴⁹The men at the table said among themselves, "Who does this man think he is, going around forgiving sins?"

⁵⁰And Jesus said to the woman, "Your faith has saved you; go in peace."

8:¹ Not long afterward Jesus began a tour of the nearby cities and villages to announce the Good News concerning the Kingdom of God. He took his twelve disciples with him, ²along with some women he had healed and from whom he had cast out evil spirits. Among them were Mary Magdalene, from whom he had cast out seven demons; ³Joanna, the wife of Chuza, Herod's business manager; Susanna; and many others who were contributing from their own resources to support Jesus and his disciples.

〰️〽️ **How would you have fit into the group that followed Jesus?**
Overflowing love is the natural response to forgiveness and the appropriate consequence of faith. But only those who realize the depth of their sin can appreciate the complete forgiveness God offers them. Jesus has rescued all of his followers, whether they were once extremely wicked or conventionally good, from eternal death. Do you appreciate the wideness of God's mercy? Are you grateful for his forgiveness?

Troubles for Jesus

MATTHEW 12:22-50

Then a demon-possessed man, who was both blind and unable to talk, was brought to Jesus. He healed the man so that he could both speak and see. ²³ The crowd was amazed. "Could it be that Jesus is the Son of David, the Messiah?" they wondered out loud.

²⁴But when the Pharisees heard about the miracle, they said, "No wonder he can cast out demons. He gets his power from Satan, the prince of demons."

²⁵Jesus knew their thoughts and replied, "Any kingdom at war with itself is doomed. A city or home divided against itself is doomed. ²⁶And if Satan is casting out Satan, he is fighting against himself. His own kingdom will not survive. ²⁷And if I am empowered by the prince of demons, what about your own followers? They cast out demons, too, so they will judge you for what you have said. ²⁸But if I am casting out demons by the Spirit of God, then the Kingdom of God has arrived among you. ²⁹Let me illustrate this. You can't enter a strong man's house and rob him without first tying him up. Only then can his house be robbed! ³⁰Anyone who isn't helping me opposes me, and anyone who isn't working with me is actually working against me.

³¹"Every sin or blasphemy can be forgiven—except blasphemy against the Holy Spirit, which can never be forgiven. ³²Anyone who blasphemes against me, the Son of Man, can be forgiven, but blasphemy against the Holy Spirit will never be forgiven, either in this world or in the world to come.

³³"A tree is identified by its fruit. Make a tree good, and its fruit will be good. Make a tree bad, and its fruit will be bad. ³⁴You brood of snakes! How could evil men like you speak what is good and right? For whatever is in your heart determines what you say. ³⁵A good person produces good words from a good heart, and an evil person produces evil words from an evil heart. ³⁶And I tell you this, that you must give an account on judgment day of every idle word you speak. ³⁷The words you say now reflect your fate then; either you will be justified by them or you will be condemned."

³⁸One day some teachers of religious law and Pharisees came to Jesus and said, "Teacher, we want you to show us a miraculous sign to prove that you are from God."

³⁹But Jesus replied, "Only an evil, faithless generation would ask for a miraculous sign; but the only sign I will give them is the sign of the prophet Jonah. ⁴⁰For as Jonah was in the belly of the great fish for three days and three nights, so I, the Son of Man, will be in the heart of the earth for three days and three nights. ⁴¹The people of Nineveh will rise up against this generation on judgment day and condemn it, because they repented at the preaching of Jonah. And now someone greater than Jonah is here—and you

refuse to repent. [42]The queen of Sheba will also rise up against this generation on judgment day and condemn it, because she came from a distant land to hear the wisdom of Solomon. And now someone greater than Solomon is here—and you refuse to listen to him.

[43]"When an evil spirit leaves a person, it goes into the desert, seeking rest but finding none. [44]Then it says, 'I will return to the person I came from.' So it returns and finds its former home empty, swept, and clean. [45]Then the spirit finds seven other spirits more evil than itself, and they all enter the person and live there. And so that person is worse off than before. That will be the experience of this evil generation."

[46]As Jesus was speaking to the crowd, his mother and brothers were outside, wanting to talk with him. [47]Someone told Jesus, "Your mother and your brothers are outside, and they want to speak to you."

[48]Jesus asked, "Who is my mother? Who are my brothers?" [49]Then he pointed to his disciples and said, "These are my mother and brothers. [50]Anyone who does the will of my Father in heaven is my brother and sister and mother!"

⌇⋏⋎⌇ When are you tempted to have Jesus prove himself to you?

Many people have thought, *If I could just see a real miracle, then I could really believe in God.* But Jesus' response to the Pharisees applies to us. Jesus knew that they had already seen enough miraculous proof to convince them that he was the Messiah—if they would just open their hearts. But the Pharisees had already decided not to believe in Jesus, and more miracles would not change that. We have plenty of evidence—Jesus' death, resurrection, ascension, and centuries of his work in the lives of believers around the world. Instead of looking for additional evidence or miracles, accept what God has already given and move forward. He may use your life as evidence to reach another person.

9
JULY

Jesus Seeks, Seeds, and Weeds
MARK 4:1-29

Once again Jesus began teaching by the lakeshore. There was such a large crowd along the shore that he got into a boat and sat down and spoke from there. [2]He began to teach the people by telling many stories such as this one:

[3]"Listen! A farmer went out to plant some seed. [4]As he scattered it across his field, some seed fell on a footpath, and the birds came and ate it. [5]Other seed fell on shallow soil with underlying rock. The plant sprang up quickly, [6]but it soon wilted beneath the hot sun and died because the roots had no nourishment in the shallow soil. [7]Other seed fell among thorns that shot up and choked out the tender blades so that it produced no grain. [8]Still other seed fell on fertile soil and produced a crop that was thirty, sixty, and even a

hundred times as much as had been planted." Then he said, [9]"Anyone who is willing to hear should listen and understand!"

[10]Later, when Jesus was alone with the twelve disciples and with the others who were gathered around, they asked him, "What do your stories mean?"

[11]He replied, "You are permitted to understand the secret about the Kingdom of God. But I am using these stories to conceal everything about it from outsiders, [12]so that the Scriptures might be fulfilled:

'They see what I do,
   but they don't perceive its meaning.
They hear my words,
   but they don't understand.
So they will not turn from their sins
   and be forgiven.'

[13]"But if you can't understand this story, how will you understand all the others I am going to tell? [14]The farmer I talked about is the one who brings God's message to others. [15]The seed that fell on the hard path represents those who hear the message, but then Satan comes at once and takes it away from them. [16]The rocky soil represents those who hear the message and receive it with joy. [17]But like young plants in such soil, their roots don't go very deep. At first they get along fine, but they wilt as soon as they have problems or are persecuted because they believe the word. [18]The thorny ground represents those who hear and accept the Good News, [19]but all too quickly the message is crowded out by the cares of this life, the lure of wealth, and the desire for nice things, so no crop is produced. [20]But the good soil represents those who hear and accept God's message and produce a huge harvest—thirty, sixty, or even a hundred times as much as had been planted."

[21]Then Jesus asked them, "Would anyone light a lamp and then put it under a basket or under a bed to shut out the light? Of course not! A lamp is placed on a stand, where its light will shine.

[22]"Everything that is now hidden or secret will eventually be brought to light. [23]Anyone who is willing to hear should listen and understand! [24]And be sure to pay attention to what you hear. The more you do this, the more you will understand—and even more, besides. [25]To those who are open to my teaching, more understanding will be given. But to those who are not listening, even what they have will be taken away from them."

[26]Jesus also said, "Here is another illustration of what the Kingdom of God is like: A farmer planted seeds in a field, [27]and then he went on with his other activities. As the days went by, the seeds sprouted and grew without the farmer's help, [28]because the earth produces crops on its own. First a leaf blade pushes through, then the heads of wheat are formed, and finally the

grain ripens. [29]And as soon as the grain is ready, the farmer comes and harvests it with a sickle."

〜〜〜 **What kind of soil is your life right now?** The four soils represent four different ways people respond to God's Word. Usually we think that Jesus was talking about four different kinds of people. But he may also have been talking about (1) different times or phases in a person's life or (2) how a person receives God's message in some areas of his life and resists it in others. For example, you may be open to God about your future but closed concerning how you spend your money. You may respond like good soil to God's demand for worship but like rocky soil to his demand to give to those in need. Ask God to help you strive to be like good soil in every area of your life at all times.

10

JULY

More of Jesus' Parables
MATTHEW 13:24-43

Here is another story Jesus told: "The Kingdom of Heaven is like a farmer who planted good seed in his field. [25]But that night as everyone slept, his enemy came and planted weeds among the wheat. [26]When the crop began to grow and produce grain, the weeds also grew. [27]The farmer's servants came and told him, 'Sir, the field where you planted that good seed is full of weeds!'

[28]" 'An enemy has done it!' the farmer exclaimed.

" 'Shall we pull out the weeds?' they asked.

[29]"He replied, 'No, you'll hurt the wheat if you do. [30]Let both grow together until the harvest. Then I will tell the harvesters to sort out the weeds and burn them and to put the wheat in the barn.' "

[31]Here is another illustration Jesus used: "The Kingdom of Heaven is like a mustard seed planted in a field. [32]It is the smallest of all seeds, but it becomes the largest of garden plants and grows into a tree where birds can come and find shelter in its branches."

[33]Jesus also used this illustration: "The Kingdom of Heaven is like yeast used by a woman making bread. Even though she used a large amount of flour, the yeast permeated every part of the dough."

[34]Jesus always used stories and illustrations like these when speaking to the crowds. In fact, he never spoke to them without using such parables. [35]This fulfilled the prophecy that said,

"I will speak to you in parables.
I will explain mysteries hidden since the creation of the world."

[36]Then, leaving the crowds outside, Jesus went into the house. His disciples said, "Please explain the story of the weeds in the field."

[37]"All right," he said. "I, the Son of Man, am the farmer who plants the

good seed. ³⁸The field is the world, and the good seed represents the people of the Kingdom. The weeds are the people who belong to the evil one. ³⁹The enemy who planted the weeds among the wheat is the Devil. The harvest is the end of the world, and the harvesters are the angels.

⁴⁰"Just as the weeds are separated out and burned, so it will be at the end of the world. ⁴¹I, the Son of Man, will send my angels, and they will remove from my Kingdom everything that causes sin and all who do evil, ⁴²and they will throw them into the furnace and burn them. There will be weeping and gnashing of teeth. ⁴³Then the godly will shine like the sun in their Father's Kingdom. Anyone who is willing to hear should listen and understand!"

〰〰 **How concerned are you about the eternal fate of the people you know?** The young thistles (weeds) and the young blades of wheat look the same and can't be distinguished until they are grown and ready for harvest. Thistles (unbelievers) and wheat (believers) must live side by side in this world. God allows unbelievers to remain for a while, just as a farmer allows weeds to remain in his field so the surrounding wheat isn't uprooted with them. At the harvest, however, the weeds will be uprooted and thrown away. God's harvest (judgment) of all people is coming. Be certain you are ready by making sure that your faith is sincere.

Even More Parables

MATTHEW 13:44-52

"The Kingdom of Heaven is like a treasure that a man discovered hidden in a field. In his excitement, he hid it again and sold everything he owned to get enough money to buy the field—and to get the treasure, too!

⁴⁵"Again, the Kingdom of Heaven is like a pearl merchant on the lookout for choice pearls. ⁴⁶When he discovered a pearl of great value, he sold everything he owned and bought it!

⁴⁷"Again, the Kingdom of Heaven is like a fishing net that is thrown into the water and gathers fish of every kind. ⁴⁸When the net is full, they drag it up onto the shore, sit down, sort the good fish into crates, and throw the bad ones away. ⁴⁹That is the way it will be at the end of the world. The angels will come and separate the wicked people from the godly, ⁵⁰throwing the wicked into the fire. There will be weeping and gnashing of teeth. ⁵¹Do you understand?"

"Yes," they said, "we do."

⁵²Then he added, "Every teacher of religious law who has become a disciple in the Kingdom of Heaven is like a person who brings out of the storehouse the new teachings as well as the old."

〰〰 **How and where did you find the hidden treasure?** The Kingdom of Heaven is more valuable than anything else we can have, and a person must be willing to give up everything to obtain it. The man who discovered the treasure in the field stumbled upon it by accident but knew its value when he found it. The merchant was earnestly searching for the pearl of great value, and when he found it, he sold everything he had to purchase it. If you have accepted Christ as your Savior, you, too, have found the treasure. Nothing is more valuable, and nothing is more important to share with others.

12 JULY

Jesus in Control
LUKE 8:22-56

One day Jesus said to his disciples, "Let's cross over to the other side of the lake." So they got into a boat and started out. ²³On the way across, Jesus lay down for a nap, and while he was sleeping the wind began to rise. A fierce storm developed that threatened to swamp them, and they were in real danger.

²⁴The disciples woke him up, shouting, "Master, Master, we're going to drown!"

So Jesus rebuked the wind and the raging waves. The storm stopped and all was calm! ²⁵Then he asked them, "Where is your faith?"

And they were filled with awe and amazement. They said to one another, "Who is this man, that even the winds and waves obey him?"

²⁶So they arrived in the land of the Gerasenes, across the lake from Galilee. ²⁷As Jesus was climbing out of the boat, a man who was possessed by demons came out to meet him. Homeless and naked, he had lived in a cemetery for a long time. ²⁸As soon as he saw Jesus, he shrieked and fell to the ground before him, screaming, "Why are you bothering me, Jesus, Son of the Most High God? Please, I beg you, don't torture me!" ²⁹For Jesus had already commanded the evil spirit to come out of him. This spirit had often taken control of the man. Even when he was shackled with chains, he simply broke them and rushed out into the wilderness, completely under the demon's power.

³⁰"What is your name?" Jesus asked.

"Legion," he replied—for the man was filled with many demons. ³¹The demons kept begging Jesus not to send them into the Bottomless Pit. ³²A large herd of pigs was feeding on the hillside nearby, and the demons pleaded with him to let them enter into the pigs. Jesus gave them permission. ³³So the demons came out of the man and entered the pigs, and the whole herd plunged down the steep hillside into the lake, where they drowned.

³⁴When the herdsmen saw it, they fled to the nearby city and the surrounding countryside, spreading the news as they ran. ³⁵A crowd soon gathered

around Jesus, for they wanted to see for themselves what had happened. And they saw the man who had been possessed by demons sitting quietly at Jesus' feet, clothed and sane. And the whole crowd was afraid. ³⁶Then those who had seen what happened told the others how the demon-possessed man had been healed. ³⁷And all the people in that region begged Jesus to go away and leave them alone, for a great wave of fear swept over them.

So Jesus returned to the boat and left, crossing back to the other side of the lake. ³⁸The man who had been demon possessed begged to go, too, but Jesus said, ³⁹"No, go back to your family and tell them all the wonderful things God has done for you." So he went all through the city telling about the great thing Jesus had done for him.

⁴⁰On the other side of the lake the crowds received Jesus with open arms because they had been waiting for him. ⁴¹And now a man named Jairus, a leader of the local synagogue, came and fell down at Jesus' feet, begging him to come home with him. ⁴²His only child was dying, a little girl twelve years old.

As Jesus went with him, he was surrounded by the crowds. ⁴³And there was a woman in the crowd who had had a hemorrhage for twelve years. She had spent everything she had on doctors and still could find no cure. ⁴⁴She came up behind Jesus and touched the fringe of his robe. Immediately, the bleeding stopped.

⁴⁵"Who touched me?" Jesus asked.

Everyone denied it, and Peter said, "Master, this whole crowd is pressing up against you."

⁴⁶But Jesus told him, "No, someone deliberately touched me, for I felt healing power go out from me." ⁴⁷When the woman realized that Jesus knew, she began to tremble and fell to her knees before him. The whole crowd heard her explain why she had touched him and that she had been immediately healed. ⁴⁸"Daughter," he said to her, "your faith has made you well. Go in peace."

⁴⁹While he was still speaking to her, a messenger arrived from Jairus's home with the message, "Your little girl is dead. There's no use troubling the Teacher now."

⁵⁰But when Jesus heard what had happened, he said to Jairus, "Don't be afraid. Just trust me, and she will be all right."

⁵¹When they arrived at the house, Jesus wouldn't let anyone go in with him except Peter, James, John, and the little girl's father and mother. ⁵²The house was filled with people weeping and wailing, but he said, "Stop the weeping! She isn't dead; she is only asleep."

⁵³But the crowd laughed at him because they all knew she had died. ⁵⁴Then Jesus took her by the hand and said in a loud voice, "Get up, my child!" ⁵⁵And at that moment her life returned, and she immediately stood up! Then Jesus told them to give her something to eat. ⁵⁶Her parents were overwhelmed, but Jesus insisted that they not tell anyone what had happened.

~√↙ **Which of these miracles gives you greatest comfort?** When caught in the storms of life, it is easy to think that God has lost control and that we are at the mercy of the winds of fate. In reality, God is sovereign. He controls the history of the world and our personal destinies. Just as Jesus calmed the waves, he can calm whatever storms you may face.

13 JULY

The Concerns of Jesus

MATTHEW 9:27-38

After Jesus left the girl's home, two blind men followed along behind him, shouting, "Son of David, have mercy on us!"

28They went right into the house where he was staying, and Jesus asked them, "Do you believe I can make you see?"

"Yes, Lord," they told him, "we do."

29Then he touched their eyes and said, "Because of your faith, it will happen." 30And suddenly they could see! Jesus sternly warned them, "Don't tell anyone about this." 31But instead, they spread his fame all over the region.

32When they left, some people brought to him a man who couldn't speak because he was possessed by a demon. 33So Jesus cast out the demon, and instantly the man could talk. The crowds marveled. "Nothing like this has ever happened in Israel!" they exclaimed.

34But the Pharisees said, "He can cast out demons because he is empowered by the prince of demons."

35Jesus traveled through all the cities and villages of that area, teaching in the synagogues and announcing the Good News about the Kingdom. And wherever he went, he healed people of every sort of disease and illness. 36He felt great pity for the crowds that came, because their problems were so great and they didn't know where to go for help. They were like sheep without a shepherd. 37He said to his disciples, "The harvest is so great, but the workers are so few. 38So pray to the Lord who is in charge of the harvest; ask him to send out more workers for his fields."

~√↙ **How do you picture Jesus caring for you?** Jesus didn't respond immediately to the blind men's pleas. He waited to see how earnest they were. Not everyone who says he or she wants help really wants it badly enough to do something about it. Jesus may have waited and questioned these men to make their desire and faith stronger. If it seems as if God is too slow in giving an answer to your prayers, maybe he is testing you as he did the blind men. Do you believe God can help you? Do you *really* want his help?

Some Don't Listen—
Some Need to Hear
MARK 6:1-13

Jesus left that part of the country and returned with his disciples to Nazareth, his hometown. ²The next Sabbath he began teaching in the synagogue, and many who heard him were astonished. They asked, "Where did he get all his wisdom and the power to perform such miracles? ³He's just the carpenter, the son of Mary and brother of James, Joseph, Judas, and Simon. And his sisters live right here among us." They were deeply offended and refused to believe in him.

⁴Then Jesus told them, "A prophet is honored everywhere except in his own hometown and among his relatives and his own family." ⁵And because of their unbelief, he couldn't do any mighty miracles among them except to place his hands on a few sick people and heal them. ⁶And he was amazed at their unbelief.

Then Jesus went out from village to village teaching. ⁷And he called his twelve disciples together and sent them out two by two, with authority to cast out evil spirits. ⁸He told them to take nothing with them except a walking stick—no food, no traveler's bag, no money. ⁹He told them to wear sandals but not to take even an extra coat. ¹⁰"When you enter each village, be a guest in only one home," he said. ¹¹"And if a village won't welcome you or listen to you, shake off its dust from your feet as you leave. It is a sign that you have abandoned that village to its fate."

¹²So the disciples went out, telling all they met to turn from their sins. ¹³And they cast out many demons and healed many sick people, anointing them with olive oil.

✎ **Do you have a clear idea of what God wants you to do?** Jesus was teaching effectively and wisely, but the people of his hometown saw him as only a carpenter. "He's no better than us—he's just a common laborer," they said. They were offended that others could be impressed by him and follow him. They rejected his authority because he was one of their peers. They thought they knew him, but their preconceived notions about who he was made it impossible for them to accept his message. Don't let prejudice blind you to truth. As you learn more about Jesus, try to see him for who he really is.

15

"Look, I am sending you out as sheep among wolves. Be as wary as snakes and harmless as doves. [17]But beware! For you will be handed over to the courts and beaten in the synagogues. [18]And you must stand trial before governors and kings because you are my followers. This will be your opportunity to tell them about me—yes, to witness to the world. [19]When you are arrested, don't worry about what to say in your defense, because you will be given the right words at the right time. [20]For it won't be you doing the talking—it will be the Spirit of your Father speaking through you.

[21]"Brother will betray brother to death, fathers will betray their own children, and children will rise against their parents and cause them to be killed. [22]And everyone will hate you because of your allegiance to me. But those who endure to the end will be saved. [23]When you are persecuted in one town, flee to the next. I assure you that I, the Son of Man, will return before you have reached all the towns of Israel.

[24]"A student is not greater than the teacher. A servant is not greater than the master. [25]The student shares the teacher's fate. The servant shares the master's fate. And since I, the master of the household, have been called the prince of demons, how much more will it happen to you, the members of the household! [26]But don't be afraid of those who threaten you. For the time is coming when everything will be revealed; all that is secret will be made public. [27]What I tell you now in the darkness, shout abroad when daybreak comes. What I whisper in your ears, shout from the housetops for all to hear!

[28]"Don't be afraid of those who want to kill you. They can only kill your body; they cannot touch your soul. Fear only God, who can destroy both soul and body in hell. [29]Not even a sparrow, worth only half a penny, can fall to the ground without your Father knowing it. [30]And the very hairs on your head are all numbered. [31]So don't be afraid; you are more valuable to him than a whole flock of sparrows.

[32]"If anyone acknowledges me publicly here on earth, I will openly acknowledge that person before my Father in heaven. [33]But if anyone denies me here on earth, I will deny that person before my Father in heaven.

[34]"Don't imagine that I came to bring peace to the earth! No, I came to bring a sword. [35]I have come to set a man against his father, and a daughter against her mother, and a daughter-in-law against her mother-in-law. [36]Your enemies will be right in your own household! [37]If you love your father or mother more than you love me, you are not worthy of being mine; or if you love your son or daughter more than me, you are not worthy of being mine. [38]If you refuse to take up your cross and follow me, you are not

worthy of being mine. [39]If you cling to your life, you will lose it; but if you give it up for me, you will find it. [40]"Anyone who welcomes you is welcoming me, and anyone who welcomes me is welcoming the Father who sent me. [41]If you welcome a prophet as one who speaks for God, you will receive the same reward a prophet gets. And if you welcome good and godly people because of their godliness, you will be given a reward like theirs. [42]And if you give even a cup of cold water to one of the least of my followers, you will surely be rewarded."

In what ways do Jesus' words speak to the fears you have?
Jesus said that God cares for the sparrows' every need. We are far more valuable to God than these little birds, so valuable that God sent his only Son to die for us (John 3:16). You are of great worth to God. You are never lost in his inventory. Because God places such value on you, you need never be afraid in the face of personal threats or difficult trials. But don't think that because you are valuable to God he will take away all your troubles. The real test of value is how well something holds up under the wear, tear, and abuse of everyday life. Those who stand up for Christ in spite of their troubles truly have lasting value and will receive great rewards.

Herod Kills
John the Baptist
JULY

16

MARK 6:14-29

Herod Antipas, the king, soon heard about Jesus, because people everywhere were talking about him. Some were saying, "This must be John the Baptist come back to life again. That is why he can do such miracles." [15]Others thought Jesus was the ancient prophet Elijah. Still others thought he was a prophet like the other great prophets of the past. [16]When Herod heard about Jesus, he said, "John, the man I beheaded, has come back from the dead." [17]For Herod had sent soldiers to arrest and imprison John as a favor to Herodias. She had been his brother Philip's wife, but Herod had married her. [18]John kept telling Herod, "It is illegal for you to marry your brother's wife." [19]Herodias was enraged and wanted John killed in revenge, but without Herod's approval she was powerless. [20]And Herod respected John, knowing that he was a good and holy man, so he kept him under his protection. Herod was disturbed whenever he talked with John, but even so, he liked to listen to him.

[21]Herodias's chance finally came. It was Herod's birthday, and he gave a party for his palace aides, army officers, and the leading citizens of Galilee. [22]Then his daughter, also named Herodias, came in and performed a dance that greatly pleased them all. "Ask me for anything you like," the king said

to the girl, "and I will give it to you." [23]Then he promised, "I will give you whatever you ask, up to half of my kingdom!"

[24]She went out and asked her mother, "What should I ask for?" Her mother told her, "Ask for John the Baptist's head!"

[25]So the girl hurried back to the king and told him, "I want the head of John the Baptist, right now, on a tray!"

[26]Then the king was very sorry, but he was embarrassed to break his oath in front of his guests. [27]So he sent an executioner to the prison to cut off John's head and bring it to him. The soldier beheaded John in the prison, [28]brought his head on a tray, and gave it to the girl, who took it to her mother. [29]When John's disciples heard what had happened, they came for his body and buried it in a tomb.

~∿⁄∠ **In what ways do you most want to be like John the Baptist?** As a ruler under Roman authority, Herod had no kingdom to give. The offer of half his kingdom was Herod's way to say that he would give Herodias's daughter almost anything she wanted. When Herodias asked for John's head, Herod would have been greatly embarrassed in front of his guests if he had denied her request. Words are powerful. Because they can lead to great sin, we should use them with great care.

17 JULY

Jesus: Cook, Water Walker, Healer
MATTHEW 14:13-36

As soon as Jesus heard the news, he went off by himself in a boat to a remote area to be alone. But the crowds heard where he was headed and followed by land from many villages. [14]A vast crowd was there as he stepped from the boat, and he had compassion on them and healed their sick.

[15]That evening the disciples came to him and said, "This is a desolate place, and it is getting late. Send the crowds away so they can go to the villages and buy food for themselves."

[16]But Jesus replied, "That isn't necessary—you feed them."

[17]"Impossible!" they exclaimed. "We have only five loaves of bread and two fish!"

[18]"Bring them here," he said. [19]Then he told the people to sit down on the grass. And he took the five loaves and two fish, looked up toward heaven, and asked God's blessing on the food. Breaking the loaves into pieces, he gave some of the bread and fish to each disciple, and the disciples gave them to the people. [20]They all ate as much as they wanted, and they picked up twelve baskets of leftovers. [21]About five thousand men had eaten from those five loaves, in addition to all the women and children!

[22]Immediately after this, Jesus made his disciples get back into the boat

and cross to the other side of the lake while he sent the people home. [23]Afterward he went up into the hills by himself to pray. Night fell while he was there alone. [24]Meanwhile, the disciples were in trouble far away from land, for a strong wind had risen, and they were fighting heavy waves.

[25]About three o'clock in the morning Jesus came to them, walking on the water. [26]When the disciples saw him, they screamed in terror, thinking he was a ghost. [27]But Jesus spoke to them at once. "It's all right," he said. "I am here! Don't be afraid."

[28]Then Peter called to him, "Lord, if it's really you, tell me to come to you by walking on water."

[29]"All right, come," Jesus said.

So Peter went over the side of the boat and walked on the water toward Jesus. [30]But when he looked around at the high waves, he was terrified and began to sink. "Save me, Lord!" he shouted.

[31]Instantly Jesus reached out his hand and grabbed him. "You don't have much faith," Jesus said. "Why did you doubt me?" [32]And when they climbed back into the boat, the wind stopped.

[33]Then the disciples worshiped him. "You really are the Son of God!" they exclaimed.

[34]After they had crossed the lake, they landed at Gennesaret. [35]The news of their arrival spread quickly throughout the whole surrounding area, and soon people were bringing all their sick to be healed. [36]The sick begged him to let them touch even the fringe of his robe, and all who touched it were healed.

~\/~ **Would you have been more likely to step out with Peter or to stay in the boat? Why?** Peter was not testing Jesus, something we are told not to do. Instead he was the only one in the boat to react in faith. His impulsive request led him to experience a rather unusual demonstration of God's power. Peter started to sink because he took his eyes off Jesus and focused on the high waves around him. Then his faith wavered when he realized what he was doing. We may not walk on water, but we do walk through tough situations. If we focus on the waves of difficult circumstances around us without looking to Christ for help, we too may despair and sink. To maintain your faith in the midst of difficult situations, keep your eyes on Christ rather than on your inadequacies.

Jesus Is the Bread from Heaven

JULY **18**

JOHN 6:22-40

The next morning, back across the lake, crowds began gathering on the shore, waiting to see Jesus. For they knew that he and his disciples had come over together and that the disciples had gone off in their boat, leaving him behind. ²³Several boats from Tiberias landed near the place where the Lord had blessed the bread and the people had eaten. ²⁴When the crowd saw that Jesus wasn't there, nor his disciples, they got into the boats and went across to Capernaum to look for him. ²⁵When they arrived and found him, they asked, "Teacher, how did you get here?"

²⁶Jesus replied, "The truth is, you want to be with me because I fed you, not because you saw the miraculous sign. ²⁷But you shouldn't be so concerned about perishable things like food. Spend your energy seeking the eternal life that I, the Son of Man, can give you. For God the Father has sent me for that very purpose."

²⁸They replied, "What does God want us to do?"

²⁹Jesus told them, "This is what God wants you to do: Believe in the one he has sent."

³⁰They replied, "You must show us a miraculous sign if you want us to believe in you. What will you do for us? ³¹After all, our ancestors ate manna while they journeyed through the wilderness! As the Scriptures say, 'Moses gave them bread from heaven to eat.' "

³²Jesus said, "I assure you, Moses didn't give them bread from heaven. My Father did. And now he offers you the true bread from heaven. ³³The true bread of God is the one who comes down from heaven and gives life to the world."

³⁴"Sir," they said, "give us that bread every day of our lives."

³⁵Jesus replied, "I am the bread of life. No one who comes to me will ever be hungry again. Those who believe in me will never thirst. ³⁶But you haven't believed in me even though you have seen me. ³⁷However, those the Father has given me will come to me, and I will never reject them. ³⁸For I have come down from heaven to do the will of God who sent me, not to do what I want. ³⁹And this is the will of God, that I should not lose even one of all those he has given me, but that I should raise them to eternal life at the last day. ⁴⁰For it is my Father's will that all who see his Son and believe in him should have eternal life—that I should raise them at the last day."

〜〜〜 **How is Jesus "bread" to you?** People eat bread to satisfy physical hunger and to sustain physical life. We can satisfy spiritual hunger and sustain spiritual life only by a right relationship with Jesus Christ. No wonder he called himself the bread of life. But bread must be eaten to sustain life, and Christ must be invited into our daily walk to sustain spiritual life.

Jesus Criticized and Deserted

JOHN 6:41-71

Then the people began to murmur in disagreement because he had said, "I am the bread from heaven." ⁴²They said, "This is Jesus, the son of Joseph. We know his father and mother. How can he say, 'I came down from heaven'?"

⁴³But Jesus replied, "Don't complain about what I said. ⁴⁴For people can't come to me unless the Father who sent me draws them to me, and at the last day I will raise them from the dead. ⁴⁵As it is written in the Scriptures, 'They will all be taught by God.' Everyone who hears and learns from the Father comes to me. ⁴⁶(Not that anyone has ever seen the Father; only I, who was sent from God, have seen him.)

⁴⁷"I assure you, anyone who believes in me already has eternal life. ⁴⁸Yes, I am the bread of life! ⁴⁹Your ancestors ate manna in the wilderness, but they all died. ⁵⁰However, the bread from heaven gives eternal life to everyone who eats it. ⁵¹I am the living bread that came down out of heaven. Anyone who eats this bread will live forever; this bread is my flesh, offered so the world may live."

⁵²Then the people began arguing with each other about what he meant. "How can this man give us his flesh to eat?" they asked.

⁵³So Jesus said again, "I assure you, unless you eat the flesh of the Son of Man and drink his blood, you cannot have eternal life within you. ⁵⁴But those who eat my flesh and drink my blood have eternal life, and I will raise them at the last day. ⁵⁵For my flesh is the true food, and my blood is the true drink. ⁵⁶All who eat my flesh and drink my blood remain in me, and I in them. ⁵⁷I live by the power of the living Father who sent me; in the same way, those who partake of me will live because of me. ⁵⁸I am the true bread from heaven. Anyone who eats this bread will live forever and not die as your ancestors did, even though they ate the manna."

⁵⁹He said these things while he was teaching in the synagogue in Capernaum.

⁶⁰Even his disciples said, "This is very hard to understand. How can anyone accept it?"

⁶¹Jesus knew within himself that his disciples were complaining, so he said to them, "Does this offend you? ⁶²Then what will you think if you see me, the Son of Man, return to heaven again? ⁶³It is the Spirit who gives eternal life. Human effort accomplishes nothing. And the very words I have spoken to you are spirit and life. ⁶⁴But some of you don't believe me." (For Jesus knew from the beginning who didn't believe, and he knew who would betray him.) ⁶⁵Then he said, "That is what I meant when I said that people can't come to me unless the Father brings them to me."

⁶⁶At this point many of his disciples turned away and deserted him. ⁶⁷Then Jesus turned to the Twelve and asked, "Are you going to leave, too?"

⁶⁸Simon Peter replied, "Lord, to whom would we go? You alone have the words that give eternal life. ⁶⁹We believe them, and we know you are the Holy One of God."

⁷⁰Then Jesus said, "I chose the twelve of you, but one is a devil." ⁷¹He was speaking of Judas, son of Simon Iscariot, one of the Twelve, who would betray him.

〰〰 **How do you react when you hear critical or derogatory comments about Jesus?** After many of Jesus' followers had deserted him, he asked the twelve disciples if they were also going to leave. Peter responded, "To whom would we go?" In his straightforward way, Peter answered for all of us—there is no other way. Jesus alone gives life. People look everywhere for eternal life and miss Christ, the only source. Stay with him, especially when you are confused or feel alone.

20
JULY

Jesus Teaches and Creates Purity
MARK 7:1-37

One day some Pharisees and teachers of religious law arrived from Jerusalem to confront Jesus. ²They noticed that some of Jesus' disciples failed to follow the usual Jewish ritual of hand washing before eating. ³(The Jews, especially the Pharisees, do not eat until they have poured water over their cupped hands, as required by their ancient traditions. ⁴Similarly, they eat nothing bought from the market unless they have immersed their hands in water. This is but one of many traditions they have clung to—such as their ceremony of washing cups, pitchers, and kettles.) ⁵So the Pharisees and teachers of religious law asked him, "Why don't your disciples follow our age-old customs? For they eat without first performing the hand-washing ceremony."

⁶Jesus replied, "You hypocrites! Isaiah was prophesying about you when he said,

⁷ 'These people honor me with their lips,
>   but their hearts are far away.
> Their worship is a farce,
>   for they replace God's commands with their own man-made
>   teachings.'

⁸For you ignore God's specific laws and substitute your own traditions."

⁹Then he said, "You reject God's laws in order to hold on to your own traditions. ¹⁰For instance, Moses gave you this law from God: 'Honor your father and mother,' and 'Anyone who speaks evil of father or mother must be put to death.' ¹¹But you say it is all right for people to say to their parents,

286

'Sorry, I can't help you. For I have vowed to give to God what I could have given to you.' [12]You let them disregard their needy parents. [13]As such, you break the law of God in order to protect your own tradition. And this is only one example. There are many, many others."

[14]Then Jesus called to the crowd to come and hear. "All of you listen," he said, "and try to understand. [15]You are not defiled by what you eat; you are defiled by what you say and do!

[17]Then Jesus went into a house to get away from the crowds, and his disciples asked him what he meant by the statement he had made. [18]"Don't you understand either?" he asked. "Can't you see that what you eat won't defile you? [19]Food doesn't come in contact with your heart, but only passes through the stomach and then comes out again." (By saying this, he showed that every kind of food is acceptable.)

[20]And then he added, "It is the thought-life that defiles you. [21]For from within, out of a person's heart, come evil thoughts, sexual immorality, theft, murder, [22]adultery, greed, wickedness, deceit, eagerness for lustful pleasure, envy, slander, pride, and foolishness. [23]All these vile things come from within; they are what defile you and make you unacceptable to God."

[24]Then Jesus left Galilee and went north to the region of Tyre. He tried to keep it secret that he was there, but he couldn't. As usual, the news of his arrival spread fast. [25]Right away a woman came to him whose little girl was possessed by an evil spirit. She had heard about Jesus, and now she came and fell at his feet. [26]She begged him to release her child from the demon's control.

Since she was a Gentile, born in Syrian Phoenicia, [27]Jesus told her, "First I should help my own family, the Jews. It isn't right to take food from the children and throw it to the dogs."

[28]She replied, "That's true, Lord, but even the dogs under the table are given some crumbs from the children's plates."

[29]"Good answer!" he said. "And because you have answered so well, I have healed your daughter." [30]And when she arrived home, her little girl was lying quietly in bed, and the demon was gone.

[31]Jesus left Tyre and went to Sidon, then back to the Sea of Galilee and the region of the Ten Towns. [32]A deaf man with a speech impediment was brought to him, and the people begged Jesus to lay his hands on the man to heal him. [33]Jesus led him to a private place away from the crowd. He put his fingers into the man's ears. Then, spitting onto his own fingers, he touched the man's tongue with the spittle. [34]And looking up to heaven, he sighed and commanded, "Be opened!" [35]Instantly the man could hear perfectly and speak plainly!

[36]Jesus told the crowd not to tell anyone, but the more he told them not to, the more they spread the news, [37]for they were completely amazed. Again and again they said, "Everything he does is wonderful. He even heals those who are deaf and mute."

〜〜〜 **What would God have to do to improve the purity of your life?**
An evil action begins with a single thought. Our thoughts can pollute us, leading us into sin. Allowing our thoughts to dwell on lust, envy, hate, or revenge will lead to evil actions. Don't be made unfit for God. Instead, "fix your thoughts on what is true and honorable and right. Think about things that are pure and lovely and admirable. Think about things that are excellent and worthy of praise" (Phil. 4:8).

21 JULY

Jesus Feeds and Warns
MATTHEW 15:32–16:12

Then Jesus called his disciples to him and said, "I feel sorry for these people. They have been here with me for three days, and they have nothing left to eat. I don't want to send them away hungry, or they will faint along the road."
³³The disciples replied, "And where would we get enough food out here in the wilderness for all of them to eat?"
³⁴Jesus asked, "How many loaves of bread do you have?"
They replied, "Seven, and a few small fish." ³⁵So Jesus told all the people to sit down on the ground. ³⁶Then he took the seven loaves and the fish, thanked God for them, broke them into pieces, and gave them to the disciples, who distributed the food to the crowd.
³⁷They all ate until they were full, and when the scraps were picked up, there were seven large baskets of food left over! ³⁸There were four thousand men who were fed that day, in addition to all the women and children. ³⁹Then Jesus sent the people home, and he got into a boat and crossed over to the region of Magadan.
¹⁶:¹One day the Pharisees and Sadducees came to test Jesus' claims by asking him to show them a miraculous sign from heaven.
²He replied, "You know the saying, 'Red sky at night means fair weather tomorrow, ³red sky in the morning means foul weather all day.' You are good at reading the weather signs in the sky, but you can't read the obvious signs of the times! ⁴Only an evil, faithless generation would ask for a miraculous sign, but the only sign I will give them is the sign of the prophet Jonah." Then Jesus left them and went away.
⁵Later, after they crossed to the other side of the lake, the disciples discovered they had forgotten to bring any food. ⁶"Watch out!" Jesus warned them. "Beware of the yeast of the Pharisees and Sadducees."
⁷They decided he was saying this because they hadn't brought any bread. ⁸Jesus knew what they were thinking, so he said, "You have so little faith! Why are you worried about having no food? ⁹Won't you ever understand? Don't you remember the five thousand I fed with five loaves, and the baskets of food that were left over? ¹⁰Don't you remember the four thousand I fed with seven loaves, with baskets of food left over? ¹¹How could you even

think I was talking about food? So again I say, 'Beware of the yeast of the Pharisees and Sadducees.' "

¹²Then at last they understood that he wasn't speaking about yeast or bread but about the false teaching of the Pharisees and Sadducees.

~∿⌐ **How do you evaluate what you hear?** Yeast is put into bread to make it rise, and it takes only a little to affect a whole batch of dough. Jesus used yeast as an example of how a small amount of evil can affect a large group of people. The wrong teachings of the Pharisees and Sadducees were leading many people astray. Beware of the tendency to say, "How can this little wrong possibly affect anyone?"

JULY **22**

Peter Identifies Jesus
MARK 8:22–9:1

When they arrived at Bethsaida, some people brought a blind man to Jesus, and they begged him to touch and heal the man. ²³Jesus took the blind man by the hand and led him out of the village. Then, spitting on the man's eyes, he laid his hands on him and asked, "Can you see anything now?"

²⁴The man looked around. "Yes," he said, "I see people, but I can't see them very clearly. They look like trees walking around."

²⁵Then Jesus placed his hands over the man's eyes again. As the man stared intently, his sight was completely restored, and he could see every-thing clearly. ²⁶Jesus sent him home, saying, "Don't go back into the village on your way home."

²⁷Jesus and his disciples left Galilee and went up to the villages of Caesa-rea Philippi. As they were walking along, he asked them, "Who do people say I am?"

²⁸"Well," they replied, "some say John the Baptist, some say Elijah, and others say you are one of the other prophets."

²⁹Then Jesus asked, "Who do you say I am?"

Peter replied, "You are the Messiah." ³⁰But Jesus warned them not to tell anyone about him.

³¹Then Jesus began to tell them that he, the Son of Man, would suffer many terrible things and be rejected by the leaders, the leading priests, and the teachers of religious law. He would be killed, and three days later he would rise again. ³²As he talked about this openly with his disciples, Peter took him aside and told him he shouldn't say things like that.

³³Jesus turned and looked at his disciples and then said to Peter very sternly, "Get away from me, Satan! You are seeing things merely from a human point of view, not from God's."

³⁴Then he called his disciples and the crowds to come over and listen. "If any of you wants to be my follower," he told them, "you must put aside

your selfish ambition, shoulder your cross, and follow me. [35]If you try to keep your life for yourself, you will lose it. But if you give up your life for my sake and for the sake of the Good News, you will find true life. [36]And how do you benefit if you gain the whole world but lose your own soul in the process? [37]Is anything worth more than your soul? [38]If a person is ashamed of me and my message in these adulterous and sinful days, I, the Son of Man, will be ashamed of that person when I return in the glory of my Father with the holy angels."

[9:1]Jesus went on to say, "I assure you that some of you standing here right now will not die before you see the Kingdom of God arrive in great power!"

〜〰️〜 **In what specific ways have you come to understand Jesus better in the last few weeks?** Jesus asked the disciples who others thought he was; then he focused on them: "Who do *you* say I am?" It is not enough to know what others say about Jesus. You must know, understand, and accept for yourself that he is the Messiah. You must move from curiosity to commitment, from admiration to adoration.

23 JULY

Jesus Is Transfigured
LUKE 9:28-45

About eight days later Jesus took Peter, James, and John to a mountain to pray. [29]And as he was praying, the appearance of his face changed, and his clothing became dazzling white. [30]Then two men, Moses and Elijah, appeared and began talking with Jesus. [31]They were glorious to see. And they were speaking of how he was about to fulfill God's plan by dying in Jerusalem.

[32]Peter and the others were very drowsy and had fallen asleep. Now they woke up and saw Jesus' glory and the two men standing with him. [33]As Moses and Elijah were starting to leave, Peter, not even knowing what he was saying, blurted out, "Master, this is wonderful! We will make three shrines—one for you, one for Moses, and one for Elijah." [34]But even as he was saying this, a cloud came over them; and terror gripped them as it covered them.

[35]Then a voice from the cloud said, "This is my Son, my Chosen One. Listen to him." [36]When the voice died away, Jesus was there alone. They didn't tell anyone what they had seen until long after this happened.

[37]The next day, after they had come down the mountain, a huge crowd met Jesus. [38]A man in the crowd called out to him, "Teacher, look at my boy, who is my only son. [39]An evil spirit keeps seizing him, making him scream. It throws him into convulsions so that he foams at the mouth. It is always hitting and injuring him. It hardly ever leaves him alone. [40]I begged your disciples to cast the spirit out, but they couldn't do it."

⁴¹"You stubborn, faithless people," Jesus said, "how long must I be with you and put up with you? Bring him here." ⁴²As the boy came forward, the demon knocked him to the ground and threw him into a violent convulsion. But Jesus rebuked the evil spirit and healed the boy. Then he gave him back to his father. ⁴³Awe gripped the people as they saw this display of God's power.

While everyone was marveling over all the wonderful things he was doing, Jesus said to his disciples, ⁴⁴"Listen to me and remember what I say. The Son of Man is going to be betrayed." ⁴⁵But they didn't know what he meant. Its significance was hidden from them, so they could not understand it, and they were afraid to ask him about it.

Would you rather leave the world and be with Christ or be with Christ in the world? Peter, James, and John experienced a wonderful moment on the mountain, and they didn't want to leave. Sometimes we, too, have such an exciting experience we want to stay where we are—away from the reality and problems of our daily life. Knowing that struggles await us in the valley encourages us to retreat from reality. Yet staying on the mountaintop does not allow us to minister to others. Instead of becoming spiritual giants, we would soon become giants of self-centeredness. We need times of retreat and renewal but only so we can return to minister to the world. Our faith must make sense off the mountain as well as on it.

JULY

Who's the Greatest?

MATTHEW 17:24–18:6

On their arrival in Capernaum, the tax collectors for the Temple tax came to Peter and asked him, "Doesn't your teacher pay the Temple tax?"

²⁵"Of course he does," Peter replied. Then he went into the house to talk to Jesus about it.

But before he had a chance to speak, Jesus asked him, "What do you think, Peter? Do kings tax their own people or the foreigners they have conquered?"

²⁶"They tax the foreigners," Peter replied.

"Well, then," Jesus said, "the citizens are free! ²⁷However, we don't want to offend them, so go down to the lake and throw in a line. Open the mouth of the first fish you catch, and you will find a coin. Take the coin and pay the tax for both of us."

^{18:1}About that time the disciples came to Jesus and asked, "Which of us is greatest in the Kingdom of Heaven?"

²Jesus called a small child over to him and put the child among them. ³Then he said, "I assure you, unless you turn from your sins and become as little children, you will never get into the Kingdom of Heaven. ⁴Therefore,

1-800-995-8777 chuck colson

anyone who becomes as humble as this little child is the greatest in the Kingdom of Heaven. 5And anyone who welcomes a little child like this on my behalf is welcoming me. 6But if anyone causes one of these little ones who trusts in me to lose faith, it would be better for that person to be thrown into the sea with a large millstone tied around the neck."

~~~ **When do you worry about status?** The disciples had become so preoccupied with the organization of Jesus' earthly kingdom that they had lost sight of its divine purpose. Instead of seeking a place of service, they sought positions of advantage. Jesus used a child to help his self-centered disciples get the point. We are not to be *childish* (like the disciples, arguing over petty issues) but rather *childlike*, with humble and sincere hearts. Are you being childlike or childish?

JULY

Who's on Our Side?

MARK 9:38-50

John said to Jesus, "Teacher, we saw a man using your name to cast out demons, but we told him to stop because he isn't one of our group." 39"Don't stop him!" Jesus said. "No one who performs miracles in my name will soon be able to speak evil of me. 40Anyone who is not against us is for us. 41If anyone gives you even a cup of water because you belong to the Messiah, I assure you, that person will be rewarded.

42"But if anyone causes one of these little ones who trusts in me to lose faith, it would be better for that person to be thrown into the sea with a large millstone tied around the neck. 43If your hand causes you to sin, cut it off. It is better to enter heaven with only one hand than to go into the unquenchable fires of hell with two hands. 45If your foot causes you to sin, cut it off. It is better to enter heaven with only one foot than to be thrown into hell with two feet. 47And if your eye causes you to sin, gouge it out. It is better to enter the Kingdom of God half blind than to have two eyes and be thrown into hell, 48'where the worm never dies and the fire never goes out.'

49"For everyone will be purified with fire. 50Salt is good for seasoning. But if it loses its flavor, how do you make it salty again? You must have the qualities of salt among yourselves and live in peace with each other."

~~~ **How do you respond to the beliefs of others?** Jesus used startling language to stress the importance of cutting sin out of our life. Painful self-discipline is sometimes required of his true followers. Giving up a relationship, attitude, or habit that is against God's will may seem just as painful as cutting off a hand. Our high goal, however, is worth any sacrifice; Christ is worth any possible loss. Nothing should stand in the way of faith and

obedience. We must be ruthless in removing sin from our life now in order to avoid being stuck with it for eternity. Make your choices from an eternal perspective.

Jesus Teaches
MATTHEW 18:10-22

"Beware that you don't despise a single one of these little ones. For I tell you that in heaven their angels are always in the presence of my heavenly Father. ¹²"If a shepherd has one hundred sheep, and one wanders away and is lost, what will he do? Won't he leave the ninety-nine others and go out into the hills to search for the lost one? ¹³And if he finds it, he will surely rejoice over it more than over the ninety-nine that didn't wander away! ¹⁴In the same way, it is not my heavenly Father's will that even one of these little ones should perish.

¹⁵"If another believer sins against you, go privately and point out the fault. If the other person listens and confesses it, you have won that person back. ¹⁶But if you are unsuccessful, take one or two others with you and go back again, so that everything you say may be confirmed by two or three witnesses. ¹⁷If that person still refuses to listen, take your case to the church. If the church decides you are right, but the other person won't accept it, treat that person as a pagan or a corrupt tax collector. ¹⁸I tell you this: Whatever you prohibit on earth is prohibited in heaven, and whatever you allow on earth is allowed in heaven.

¹⁹"I also tell you this: If two of you agree down here on earth concerning anything you ask, my Father in heaven will do it for you. ²⁰For where two or three gather together because they are mine, I am there among them."

²¹Then Peter came to him and asked, "Lord, how often should I forgive someone who sins against me? Seven times?"

²²"No!" Jesus replied, "seventy times seven!"

How do you react to the failures of others? The rabbis taught that people should forgive those who offend them—but only three times. Peter, trying to be especially generous, asked Jesus if seven (the "perfect" number) was enough times to forgive someone. But Jesus answered, "Seventy times seven," meaning that we shouldn't even keep track of how many times we forgive someone. We should always forgive those who are truly repentant, no matter how many times they ask.

27

Jesus Out in the Open

JOHN 7:1-31

After this, Jesus stayed in Galilee, going from village to village. He wanted to stay out of Judea where the Jewish leaders were plotting his death. ²But soon it was time for the Festival of Shelters, ³and Jesus' brothers urged him to go to Judea for the celebration. "Go where your followers can see your miracles!" they scoffed. ⁴"You can't become a public figure if you hide like this! If you can do such wonderful things, prove it to the world!" ⁵For even his brothers didn't believe in him.

⁶Jesus replied, "Now is not the right time for me to go. But you can go anytime, and it will make no difference. ⁷The world can't hate you, but it does hate me because I accuse it of sin and evil. ⁸You go on. I am not yet ready to go to this festival, because my time has not yet come." ⁹So Jesus remained in Galilee.

¹⁰But after his brothers had left for the festival, Jesus also went, though secretly, staying out of public view. ¹¹The Jewish leaders tried to find him at the festival and kept asking if anyone had seen him. ¹²There was a lot of discussion about him among the crowds. Some said, "He's a wonderful man," while others said, "He's nothing but a fraud, deceiving the people." ¹³But no one had the courage to speak favorably about him in public, for they were afraid of getting in trouble with the Jewish leaders.

¹⁴Then, midway through the festival, Jesus went up to the Temple and began to teach. ¹⁵The Jewish leaders were surprised when they heard him. "How does he know so much when he hasn't studied everything we've studied?" they asked.

¹⁶So Jesus told them, "I'm not teaching my own ideas, but those of God who sent me. ¹⁷Anyone who wants to do the will of God will know whether my teaching is from God or is merely my own. ¹⁸Those who present their own ideas are looking for praise for themselves, but those who seek to honor the one who sent them are good and genuine. ¹⁹None of you obeys the law of Moses! In fact, you are trying to kill me."

²⁰The crowd replied, "You're demon possessed! Who's trying to kill you?"

²¹Jesus replied, "I worked on the Sabbath by healing a man, and you were offended. ²²But you work on the Sabbath, too, when you obey Moses' law of circumcision. (Actually, this tradition of circumcision is older than the law of Moses; it goes back to Abraham.) ²³For if the correct time for circumcising your son falls on the Sabbath, you go ahead and do it, so as not to break the law of Moses. So why should I be condemned for making a man completely well on the Sabbath? ²⁴Think this through and you will see that I am right."

²⁵Some of the people who lived there in Jerusalem said among themselves, "Isn't this the man they are trying to kill? ²⁶But here he is, speaking in public, and they say nothing to him. Can it be that our leaders know that he

really is the Messiah? ²⁷But how could he be? For we know where this man comes from. When the Messiah comes, he will simply appear; no one will know where he comes from."

²⁸While Jesus was teaching in the Temple, he called out, "Yes, you know me, and you know where I come from. But I represent one you don't know, and he is true. ²⁹I know him because I have come from him, and he sent me to you." ³⁰Then the leaders tried to arrest him; but no one laid a hand on him, because his time had not yet come.

³¹Many among the crowds at the Temple believed in him. "After all," they said, "would you expect the Messiah to do more miraculous signs than this man has done?"

∿∿ Which of Jesus' teachings are difficult for you to accept?

Jesus' brothers had a difficult time believing in him. Some of these brothers would eventually become leaders in the church (James, for example), but for several years they were embarrassed by Jesus. After Jesus died and rose again, they finally believed. We today have every reason to believe because we have the full record of Jesus' miracles, death, and resurrection. We also have the evidence of what the gospel has done in people's lives through the centuries. Don't miss this opportunity to believe in God's Son.

JULY 28

A Warrant for Jesus' Arrest

JOHN 7:32-53

When the Pharisees heard that the crowds were murmuring such things, they and the leading priests sent Temple guards to arrest Jesus. ³³But Jesus told them, "I will be here a little longer. Then I will return to the one who sent me. ³⁴You will search for me but not find me. And you won't be able to come where I am."

³⁵The Jewish leaders were puzzled by this statement. "Where is he planning to go?" they asked. "Maybe he is thinking of leaving the country and going to the Jews in other lands, or maybe even to the Gentiles! ³⁶What does he mean when he says, 'You will search for me but not find me,' and 'You won't be able to come where I am'?"

³⁷On the last day, the climax of the festival, Jesus stood and shouted to the crowds, "If you are thirsty, come to me! ³⁸If you believe in me, come and drink! For the Scriptures declare that rivers of living water will flow out from within." ³⁹(When he said "living water," he was speaking of the Spirit, who would be given to everyone believing in him. But the Spirit had not yet been given, because Jesus had not yet entered into his glory.)

⁴⁰When the crowds heard him say this, some of them declared, "This man surely is the Prophet." ⁴¹Others said, "He is the Messiah." Still others said, "But he can't be! Will the Messiah come from Galilee? ⁴²For the

Scriptures clearly state that the Messiah will be born of the royal line of David, in Bethlehem, the village where King David was born." [43]So the crowd was divided in their opinion about him. [44]And some wanted him arrested, but no one touched him.

[45]The Temple guards who had been sent to arrest him returned to the leading priests and Pharisees. "Why didn't you bring him in?" they demanded.

[46]"We have never heard anyone talk like this!" the guards responded.

[47]"Have you been led astray, too?" the Pharisees mocked. [48]"Is there a single one of us rulers or Pharisees who believes in him? [49]These ignorant crowds do, but what do they know about it? A curse on them anyway!"

[50]Nicodemus, the leader who had met with Jesus earlier, then spoke up. [51]"Is it legal to convict a man before he is given a hearing?" he asked.

[52]They replied, "Are you from Galilee, too? Search the Scriptures and see for yourself—no prophet ever comes from Galilee!"

[53]Then the meeting broke up and everybody went home.

〰〰 **What does it mean to have "rivers of living water" flowing from within you?** The crowd was asking questions about Jesus. Some believed, others were hostile, and others disqualified Jesus as the Messiah because he was from Nazareth, not Bethlehem (Mic. 5:2). But he *was* born in Bethlehem (Luke 2:1-7), although he grew up in Nazareth. If they had looked more carefully, they would not have jumped to the wrong conclusions. When you search for God's truth, make sure you look carefully and thoughtfully at the Bible with an open heart and mind. Don't jump to conclusions before knowing more of what the Bible says.

 JULY

Jesus: Forgiveness and Light
JOHN 8:1-20

Jesus returned to the Mount of Olives, [2]but early the next morning he was back again at the Temple. A crowd soon gathered, and he sat down and taught them. [3]As he was speaking, the teachers of religious law and Pharisees brought a woman they had caught in the act of adultery. They put her in front of the crowd.

[4]"Teacher," they said to Jesus, "this woman was caught in the very act of adultery. [5]The law of Moses says to stone her. What do you say?"

[6]They were trying to trap him into saying something they could use against him, but Jesus stooped down and wrote in the dust with his finger. [7]They kept demanding an answer, so he stood up again and said, "All right, stone her. But let those who have never sinned throw the first stones!" [8]Then he stooped down again and wrote in the dust.

⁹When the accusers heard this, they slipped away one by one, beginning with the oldest, until only Jesus was left in the middle of the crowd with the woman. ¹⁰Then Jesus stood up again and said to her, "Where are your accusers? Didn't even one of them condemn you?"

¹¹"No, Lord," she said.

And Jesus said, "Neither do I. Go and sin no more."

¹²Jesus said to the people, "I am the light of the world. If you follow me, you won't be stumbling through the darkness, because you will have the light that leads to life."

¹³The Pharisees replied, "You are making false claims about yourself!"

¹⁴Jesus told them, "These claims are valid even though I make them about myself. For I know where I came from and where I am going, but you don't know this about me. ¹⁵You judge me with all your human limitations, but I am not judging anyone. ¹⁶And if I did, my judgment would be correct in every respect because I am not alone—I have with me the Father who sent me. ¹⁷Your own law says that if two people agree about something, their witness is accepted as fact. ¹⁸I am one witness, and my Father who sent me is the other."

¹⁹"Where is your father?" they asked.

Jesus answered, "Since you don't know who I am, you don't know who my Father is. If you knew me, then you would know my Father, too." ²⁰Jesus made these statements while he was teaching in the section of the Temple known as the Treasury. But he was not arrested, because his time had not yet come.

〰〰 **Who is the last person you had to forgive?** This passage makes a significant statement about judging others. Because Jesus upheld the legal penalty for adultery, stoning, he could not be accused of being against the law. But by saying that only a sinless person could throw the first stone, he highlighted the importance of compassion and forgiveness. When others are caught in sin, are you quick to pass judgment? To do so is to act as though you have never sinned. It is God's role to judge, not yours. Your role is to show forgiveness and compassion.

JULY

Jesus: Giver of Freedom

JOHN 8:21-59

Later Jesus said to them again, "I am going away. You will search for me and die in your sin. You cannot come where I am going."

²²The Jewish leaders asked, "Is he planning to commit suicide? What does he mean, 'You cannot come where I am going'?"

²³Then he said to them, "You are from below; I am from above. You are

of this world; I am not. ²⁴That is why I said that you will die in your sins; for unless you believe that I am who I say I am, you will die in your sins."

²⁵"Tell us who you are," they demanded.

Jesus replied, "I am the one I have always claimed to be. ²⁶I have much to say about you and much to condemn, but I won't. For I say only what I have heard from the one who sent me, and he is true." ²⁷But they still didn't understand that he was talking to them about his Father.

²⁸So Jesus said, "When you have lifted up the Son of Man on the cross, then you will realize that I am he and that I do nothing on my own, but I speak what the Father taught me. ²⁹And the one who sent me is with me—he has not deserted me. For I always do those things that are pleasing to him." ³⁰Then many who heard him say these things believed in him.

³¹Jesus said to the people who believed in him, "You are truly my disciples if you keep obeying my teachings. ³²And you will know the truth, and the truth will set you free."

³³"But we are descendants of Abraham," they said. "We have never been slaves to anyone on earth. What do you mean, 'set free'?"

³⁴Jesus replied, "I assure you that everyone who sins is a slave of sin. ³⁵A slave is not a permanent member of the family, but a son is part of the family forever. ³⁶So if the Son sets you free, you will indeed be free. ³⁷Yes, I realize that you are descendants of Abraham. And yet some of you are trying to kill me because my message does not find a place in your hearts. ³⁸I am telling you what I saw when I was with my Father. But you are following the advice of your father."

³⁹"Our father is Abraham," they declared.

"No," Jesus replied, "for if you were children of Abraham, you would follow his good example. ⁴⁰I told you the truth I heard from God, but you are trying to kill me. Abraham wouldn't do a thing like that. ⁴¹No, you are obeying your real father when you act that way."

They replied, "We were not born out of wedlock! Our true Father is God himself."

⁴²Jesus told them, "If God were your Father, you would love me, because I have come to you from God. I am not here on my own, but he sent me. ⁴³Why can't you understand what I am saying? It is because you are unable to do so! ⁴⁴For you are the children of your father the Devil, and you love to do the evil things he does. He was a murderer from the beginning and has always hated the truth. There is no truth in him. When he lies, it is consistent with his character; for he is a liar and the father of lies. ⁴⁵So when I tell the truth, you just naturally don't believe me! ⁴⁶Which of you can truthfully accuse me of sin? And since I am telling you the truth, why don't you believe me? ⁴⁷Anyone whose Father is God listens gladly to the words of God. Since you don't, it proves you aren't God's children."

⁴⁸The people retorted, "You Samaritan devil! Didn't we say all along that you were possessed by a demon?"

⁴⁹"No," Jesus said, "I have no demon in me. For I honor my Father—and

you dishonor me. [50]And though I have no wish to glorify myself, God wants to glorify me. Let him be the judge. [51]I assure you, anyone who obeys my teaching will never die!"

[52]The people said, "Now we know you are possessed by a demon. Even Abraham and the prophets died, but you say that those who obey your teaching will never die! [53]Are you greater than our father Abraham, who died? Are you greater than the prophets, who died? Who do you think you are?"

[54]Jesus answered, "If I am merely boasting about myself, it doesn't count. But it is my Father who says these glorious things about me. You say, 'He is our God,' [55]but you do not even know him. I know him. If I said otherwise, I would be as great a liar as you! But it is true—I know him and obey him. [56]Your ancestor Abraham rejoiced as he looked forward to my coming. He saw it and was glad."

[57]The people said, "You aren't even fifty years old. How can you say you have seen Abraham?"

[58]Jesus answered, "The truth is, I existed before Abraham was even born!" [59]At that point they picked up stones to kill him. But Jesus hid himself from them and left the Temple.

〰〰 **How has Christ made you free?** Jesus himself is the truth that makes us free. He is the source of truth, the perfect standard of what is right. He frees us from the consequences of sin, from self-deception, and from deception by Satan. He shows us clearly the way to everlasting life with God. Thus, Jesus does not give us freedom to do what we want but freedom to follow God. As you seek to serve God, Jesus' perfect truth frees you to be all that God meant you to be.

Jesus Sends Seventy Messengers

JULY

31

LUKE 10:1-24

The Lord now chose seventy-two other disciples and sent them on ahead in pairs to all the towns and villages he planned to visit. [2]These were his instructions to them: "The harvest is so great, but the workers are so few. Pray to the Lord who is in charge of the harvest, and ask him to send out more workers for his fields. [3]Go now, and remember that I am sending you out as lambs among wolves. [4]Don't take along any money, or a traveler's bag, or even an extra pair of sandals. And don't stop to greet anyone on the road.

[5]"Whenever you enter a home, give it your blessing. [6]If those who live there are worthy, the blessing will stand; if they are not, the blessing will return to you. [7]When you enter a town, don't move around from home to

home. Stay in one place, eating and drinking what they provide you. Don't hesitate to accept hospitality, because those who work deserve their pay.

8"If a town welcomes you, eat whatever is set before you 9and heal the sick. As you heal them, say, 'The Kingdom of God is near you now.' 10But if a town refuses to welcome you, go out into its streets and say, 11'We wipe the dust of your town from our feet as a public announcement of your doom. And don't forget the Kingdom of God is near!' 12The truth is, even wicked Sodom will be better off than such a town on the judgment day.

13"What horrors await you, Korazin and Bethsaida! For if the miracles I did in you had been done in wicked Tyre and Sidon, their people would have sat in deep repentance long ago, clothed in sackcloth and throwing ashes on their heads to show their remorse. 14Yes, Tyre and Sidon will be better off on the judgment day than you. 15And you people of Capernaum, will you be exalted to heaven? No, you will be brought down to the place of the dead."

16Then he said to the disciples, "Anyone who accepts your message is also accepting me. And anyone who rejects you is rejecting me. And anyone who rejects me is rejecting God who sent me."

17When the seventy-two disciples returned, they joyfully reported to him, "Lord, even the demons obey us when we use your name!"

18"Yes," he told them, "I saw Satan falling from heaven as a flash of lightning! 19And I have given you authority over all the power of the enemy, and you can walk among snakes and scorpions and crush them. Nothing will injure you. 20But don't rejoice just because evil spirits obey you; rejoice because your names are registered as citizens of heaven."

21Then Jesus was filled with the joy of the Holy Spirit and said, "O Father, Lord of heaven and earth, thank you for hiding the truth from those who think themselves so wise and clever, and for revealing it to the childlike. Yes, Father, it pleased you to do it this way.

22"My Father has given me authority over everything. No one really knows the Son except the Father, and no one really knows the Father except the Son and those to whom the Son chooses to reveal him."

23Then when they were alone, he turned to the disciples and said, "How privileged you are to see what you have seen. 24I tell you, many prophets and kings have longed to see and hear what you have seen and heard, but they could not."

〜〜 **What would have been most exciting about this trip for you?**
Jesus thanked God that spiritual truth was for everyone, not just the elite. Many of life's rewards seem to go to the intelligent, the rich, the good looking, or the powerful. But the Kingdom of God is equally available to all, regardless of position or ability. We come to Jesus, not through strength or brains, but through childlike trust. Jesus is not against those engaged in scholarly pursuits; he is against spiritual pride (being wise in your own eyes). We can thank God that we all have equal access to him through our Lord Jesus Christ. Trust in God, not in your personal qualifications, for your citizenship in the Kingdom.

Jesus Tells a Story and Visits Friends

LUKE 10:25-42

One day an expert in religious law stood up to test Jesus by asking him this question: "Teacher, what must I do to receive eternal life?"

26Jesus replied, "What does the law of Moses say? How do you read it?"

27The man answered, " 'You must love the Lord your God with all your heart, all your soul, all your strength, and all your mind.' And, 'Love your neighbor as yourself.' "

28"Right!" Jesus told him. "Do this and you will live!"

29The man wanted to justify his actions, so he asked Jesus, "And who is my neighbor?"

30Jesus replied with an illustration: "A Jewish man was traveling on a trip from Jerusalem to Jericho, and he was attacked by bandits. They stripped him of his clothes and money, beat him up, and left him half dead beside the road.

31"By chance a Jewish priest came along; but when he saw the man lying there, he crossed to the other side of the road and passed him by. 32A Temple assistant walked over and looked at him lying there, but he also passed by on the other side.

33"Then a despised Samaritan came along, and when he saw the man, he felt deep pity. 34Kneeling beside him, the Samaritan soothed his wounds with medicine and bandaged them. Then he put the man on his own donkey and took him to an inn, where he took care of him. 35The next day he handed the innkeeper two pieces of silver and told him to take care of the man. 'If his bill runs higher than that,' he said, 'I'll pay the difference the next time I am here.'

36"Now which of these three would you say was a neighbor to the man who was attacked by bandits?" Jesus asked.

37The man replied, "The one who showed him mercy."

Then Jesus said, "Yes, now go and do the same."

38As Jesus and the disciples continued on their way to Jerusalem, they came to a village where a woman named Martha welcomed them into her home. ³⁹Her sister, Mary, sat at the Lord's feet, listening to what he taught. ⁴⁰But Martha was worrying over the big dinner she was preparing. She came to Jesus and said, "Lord, doesn't it seem unfair to you that my sister just sits here while I do all the work? Tell her to come and help me."

⁴¹But the Lord said to her, "My dear Martha, you are so upset over all these details! ⁴²There is really only one thing worth being concerned about. Mary has discovered it—and I won't take it away from her."

 Who has been a good Samaritan to you? From the parable we learn three principles about loving our neighbors: (1) Lack of love is often easy to justify. (2) Our neighbor is anyone of any race or creed or social background who is in need. (3) Love means acting to meet a need. Wherever you live, there are needy people close by. There are no good reasons for refusing to help.

2

AUGUST

Jesus Teaches about Prayer
LUKE 11:1-13

Once when Jesus had been out praying, one of his disciples came to him as he finished and said, "Lord, teach us to pray, just as John taught his disciples." ²He said, "This is how you should pray:

"Father, may your name be honored for its holiness.
    May your Kingdom come soon.
³ Give us our food day by day.
⁴ And forgive us our sins—
    just as we forgive those who have sinned against us.
And don't let us yield to temptation."

⁵Then, teaching them more about prayer, he used this illustration: "Suppose you went to a friend's house at midnight, wanting to borrow three loaves of bread. You would say to him, ⁶'A friend of mine has just arrived for a visit, and I have nothing for him to eat.' ⁷He would call out from his bedroom, 'Don't bother me. The door is locked for the night, and we are all in bed. I can't help you this time.' ⁸But I tell you this—though he won't do it as a friend, if you keep knocking long enough, he will get up and give you what you want so his reputation won't be damaged.

⁹"And so I tell you, keep on asking, and you will be given what you ask for. Keep on looking, and you will find. Keep on knocking, and the door will be opened. ¹⁰For everyone who asks, receives. Everyone who seeks, finds. And the door is opened to everyone who knocks.

¹¹"You fathers—if your children ask for a fish, do you give them a snake instead? ¹²Or if they ask for an egg, do you give them a scorpion? Of course not! ¹³If you sinful people know how to give good gifts to your children,

how much more will your heavenly Father give the Holy Spirit to those who ask him."

~~~ **How could your prayer habits be improved?** When Jesus taught his disciples to pray, he made forgiveness the cornerstone of their relationship with God. God has forgiven our sins, so we must forgive those who have wronged us. To remain unforgiving shows we have not understood that we ourselves, along with all other human beings, need to be forgiven. Think of some people who have wronged you. Have you truly forgiven them, or do you still carry a grudge against them? How will God deal with you if he treats you as you treat others?

AUGUST

Accusations and Unbelief

LUKE 11:14-32

One day Jesus cast a demon out of a man who couldn't speak, and the man's voice returned to him. The crowd was amazed, [15]but some said, "No wonder he can cast out demons. He gets his power from Satan, the prince of demons!" [16]Trying to test Jesus, others asked for a miraculous sign from heaven to see if he was from God.

[17]He knew their thoughts, so he said, "Any kingdom at war with itself is doomed. A divided home is also doomed. [18]You say I am empowered by the prince of demons. But if Satan is fighting against himself by empowering me to cast out his demons, how can his kingdom survive? [19]And if I am empowered by the prince of demons, what about your own followers? They cast out demons, too, so they will judge you for what you have said. [20]But if I am casting out demons by the power of God, then the Kingdom of God has arrived among you. [21]For when Satan, who is completely armed, guards his palace, it is safe—[22]until someone who is stronger attacks and overpowers him, strips him of his weapons, and carries off his belongings.

[23]"Anyone who isn't helping me opposes me, and anyone who isn't working with me is actually working against me.

[24]"When an evil spirit leaves a person, it goes into the desert, searching for rest. But when it finds none, it says, 'I will return to the person I came from.' [25]So it returns and finds that its former home is all swept and clean. [26]Then the spirit finds seven other spirits more evil than itself, and they all enter the person and live there. And so that person is worse off than before."

[27]As he was speaking, a woman in the crowd called out, "God bless your mother—the womb from which you came, and the breasts that nursed you!"

[28]He replied, "But even more blessed are all who hear the word of God and put it into practice."

[29]As the crowd pressed in on Jesus, he said, "These are evil times, and this evil generation keeps asking me to show them a miraculous sign. But the

only sign I will give them is the sign of the prophet Jonah. [30]What happened to him was a sign to the people of Nineveh that God had sent him. What happens to me will be a sign that God has sent me, the Son of Man, to these people. [31]"The queen of Sheba will rise up against this generation on judgment day and condemn it, because she came from a distant land to hear the wisdom of Solomon. And now someone greater than Solomon is here—and you refuse to listen to him. [32]The people of Nineveh, too, will rise up against this generation on judgment day and condemn it, because they repented at the preaching of Jonah. And now someone greater than Jonah is here—and you refuse to repent."

〰〰 **What are your strongest reasons for being a faithful follower of Christ?** Jesus says, "Anyone who isn't helping me opposes me," while earlier he stated, "Anyone who is not against you is for you." People may be neutral toward Christians, but they cannot be neutral in their relationship to Jesus. You can't be neutral in the battle between Jesus and Satan. You can't be aloof or noncommittal because there are only two sides. Since God has already won the battle, why be on the losing side? If you aren't actively for Christ, you are against him.

4

AUGUST

Real Spirituality versus Unreal Spirituality

LUKE 11:33-54

"No one lights a lamp and then hides it or puts it under a basket. Instead, it is put on a lampstand to give light to all who enter the room. [34]Your eye is a lamp for your body. A pure eye lets sunshine into your soul. But an evil eye shuts out the light and plunges you into darkness. [35]Make sure that the light you think you have is not really darkness. [36]If you are filled with light, with no dark corners, then your whole life will be radiant, as though a floodlight is shining on you."

[37]As Jesus was speaking, one of the Pharisees invited him home for a meal. So he went in and took his place at the table. [38]His host was amazed to see that he sat down to eat without first performing the ceremonial washing required by Jewish custom. [39]Then the Lord said to him, "You Pharisees are so careful to clean the outside of the cup and the dish, but inside you are still filthy—full of greed and wickedness! [40]Fools! Didn't God make the inside as well as the outside? [41]So give to the needy what you greedily possess, and you will be clean all over.

[42]"But how terrible it will be for you Pharisees! For you are careful to tithe even the tiniest part of your income, but you completely forget about

justice and the love of God. You should tithe, yes, but you should not leave undone the more important things.

⁴³"How terrible it will be for you Pharisees! For how you love the seats of honor in the synagogues and the respectful greetings from everyone as you walk through the markets! ⁴⁴Yes, how terrible it will be for you. For you are like hidden graves in a field. People walk over them without knowing the corruption they are stepping on."

⁴⁵"Teacher," said an expert in religious law, "you have insulted us, too, in what you just said."

⁴⁶"Yes," said Jesus, "how terrible it will be for you experts in religious law! For you crush people beneath impossible religious demands, and you never lift a finger to help ease the burden. ⁴⁷How terrible it will be for you! For you build tombs for the very prophets your ancestors killed long ago. ⁴⁸Murderers! You agree with your ancestors that what they did was right. You would have done the same yourselves. ⁴⁹This is what God in his wisdom said about you: 'I will send prophets and apostles to them, and they will kill some and persecute the others.'

⁵⁰"And you of this generation will be held responsible for the murder of all God's prophets from the creation of the world—⁵¹from the murder of Abel to the murder of Zechariah, who was killed between the altar and the sanctuary. Yes, it will surely be charged against you.

⁵²"How terrible it will be for you experts in religious law! For you hide the key to knowledge from the people. You don't enter the Kingdom yourselves, and you prevent others from entering."

⁵³As Jesus finished speaking, the Pharisees and teachers of religious law were furious. From that time on they grilled him with many hostile questions, ⁵⁴trying to trap him into saying something they could use against him.

〰️〰️ **Who has noticed light in your life recently?** Jesus criticized the Pharisees harshly because they (1) washed their hands but not their hearts, (2) remembered to tithe but forgot justice, (3) loved people's praise, (4) made impossible religious demands, and (5) would not accept the truth about Jesus and prevented others from believing as well. They went wrong by focusing on outward appearances and ignoring the inner condition of their hearts. We do the same when our service is motivated by a desire to be seen rather than by a pure heart and love for others. Others may be fooled, but God isn't. Don't be a Christian on the outside only. Bring your inner life under God's control; then your outer life will naturally reflect him.

5

Religious and Rich Fools

LUKE 12:1-21

Meanwhile, the crowds grew until thousands were milling about and crushing each other. Jesus turned first to his disciples and warned them, "Beware of the yeast of the Pharisees—beware of their hypocrisy. ²The time is coming when everything will be revealed; all that is secret will be made public. ³Whatever you have said in the dark will be heard in the light, and what you have whispered behind closed doors will be shouted from the housetops for all to hear!

⁴"Dear friends, don't be afraid of those who want to kill you. They can only kill the body; they cannot do any more to you. ⁵But I'll tell you whom to fear. Fear God, who has the power to kill people and then throw them into hell.

⁶"What is the price of five sparrows? A couple of pennies? Yet God does not forget a single one of them. ⁷And the very hairs on your head are all numbered. So don't be afraid; you are more valuable to him than a whole flock of sparrows.

⁸"And I assure you of this: If anyone acknowledges me publicly here on earth, I, the Son of Man, will openly acknowledge that person in the presence of God's angels. ⁹But if anyone denies me here on earth, I will deny that person before God's angels. ¹⁰Yet those who speak against the Son of Man may be forgiven, but anyone who speaks blasphemies against the Holy Spirit will never be forgiven.

¹¹"And when you are brought to trial in the synagogues and before rulers and authorities, don't worry about what to say in your defense, ¹²for the Holy Spirit will teach you what needs to be said even as you are standing there."

¹³Then someone called from the crowd, "Teacher, please tell my brother to divide our father's estate with me."

¹⁴Jesus replied, "Friend, who made me a judge over you to decide such things as that?" ¹⁵Then he said, "Beware! Don't be greedy for what you don't have. Real life is not measured by how much we own."

¹⁶And he gave an illustration: "A rich man had a fertile farm that produced fine crops. ¹⁷In fact, his barns were full to overflowing. ¹⁸So he said, 'I know! I'll tear down my barns and build bigger ones. Then I'll have room enough to store everything. ¹⁹And I'll sit back and say to myself, My friend, you have enough stored away for years to come. Now take it easy! Eat, drink, and be merry!'

²⁰"But God said to him, 'You fool! You will die this very night. Then who will get it all?'

²¹"Yes, a person is a fool to store up earthly wealth but not have a rich relationship with God."

⚡ **In what situations do you get too caught up in the goals of this world?** Jesus says that the good life has nothing to do with being wealthy. This is the exact opposite of what society usually says. Advertisers spend millions of dollars to entice us to think that if we buy more and more of their products, we will be happier, more in tune, or more comfortable. How do you respond to the constant pressure to buy? Learn to tune out expensive enticements and concentrate on the truly good life—living in a relationship with God and doing his work.

AUGUST

Jesus Warns about Worry

Luke 12:22-48

Then turning to his disciples, Jesus said, "So I tell you, don't worry about everyday life—whether you have enough food to eat or clothes to wear. ²³For life consists of far more than food and clothing. ²⁴Look at the ravens. They don't need to plant or harvest or put food in barns because God feeds them. And you are far more valuable to him than any birds! ²⁵Can all your worries add a single moment to your life? Of course not! ²⁶And if worry can't do little things like that, what's the use of worrying over bigger things?

²⁷"Look at the lilies and how they grow. They don't work or make their clothing, yet Solomon in all his glory was not dressed as beautifully as they are. ²⁸And if God cares so wonderfully for flowers that are here today and gone tomorrow, won't he more surely care for you? You have so little faith! ²⁹And don't worry about food—what to eat and drink. Don't worry whether God will provide it for you. ³⁰These things dominate the thoughts of most people, but your Father already knows your needs. ³¹He will give you all you need from day to day if you make the Kingdom of God your primary concern.

³²"So don't be afraid, little flock. For it gives your Father great happiness to give you the Kingdom.

³³"Sell what you have and give to those in need. This will store up treasure for you in heaven! And the purses of heaven have no holes in them. Your treasure will be safe—no thief can steal it and no moth can destroy it. ³⁴Wherever your treasure is, there your heart and thoughts will also be.

³⁵"Be dressed for service and well prepared, ³⁶as though you were waiting for your master to return from the wedding feast. Then you will be ready to open the door and let him in the moment he arrives and knocks. ³⁷There will be special favor for those who are ready and waiting for his return. I tell you, he himself will seat them, put on an apron, and serve them as they sit and eat! ³⁸He may come in the middle of the night or just before dawn. But whenever he comes, there will be special favor for his servants who are ready!

³⁹"Know this: A homeowner who knew exactly when a burglar was

coming would not permit the house to be broken into. ⁴⁰You must be ready all the time, for the Son of Man will come when least expected."

⁴¹Peter asked, "Lord, is this illustration just for us or for everyone?"

⁴²And the Lord replied, "I'm talking to any faithful, sensible servant to whom the master gives the responsibility of managing his household and feeding his family. ⁴³If the master returns and finds that the servant has done a good job, there will be a reward. ⁴⁴I assure you, the master will put that servant in charge of all he owns. ⁴⁵But if the servant thinks, 'My master won't be back for a while,' and begins oppressing the other servants, partying, and getting drunk—⁴⁶well, the master will return unannounced and unexpected. He will tear the servant apart and banish him with the unfaithful. ⁴⁷The servant will be severely punished, for though he knew his duty, he refused to do it.

⁴⁸"But people who are not aware that they are doing wrong will be punished only lightly. Much is required from those to whom much is given, and much more is required from those to whom much more is given."

〜〴〰 **Do you feel worried or hopeful when you think about the future? Why?** Seeking the Kingdom of God means making Jesus the Lord and King of your life. He must control every area—your work, play, plans, relationships. Is the Kingdom only one of your many concerns, or is it central to all you do? Are you holding back any areas of your life from God's control? As Lord and Creator, he wants to help provide what you need as well as guide how you use what he provides.

7

AUGUST

Jesus Warns about Troubles
LUKE 12:49-59

"I have come to bring fire to the earth, and I wish that my task were already completed! ⁵⁰There is a terrible baptism ahead of me, and I am under a heavy burden until it is accomplished. ⁵¹Do you think I have come to bring peace to the earth? No, I have come to bring strife and division! ⁵²From now on families will be split apart, three in favor of me, and two against—or the other way around. ⁵³There will be a division between father and son, mother and daughter, mother-in-law and daughter-in-law."

⁵⁴Then Jesus turned to the crowd and said, "When you see clouds beginning to form in the west, you say, 'Here comes a shower.' And you are right. ⁵⁵When the south wind blows, you say, 'Today will be a scorcher.' And it is. ⁵⁶You hypocrites! You know how to interpret the appearance of the earth and the sky, but you can't interpret these present times.

⁵⁷"Why can't you decide for yourselves what is right? ⁵⁸If you are on the way to court and you meet your accuser, try to settle the matter before it

reaches the judge, or you may be sentenced and handed over to an officer and thrown in jail. ⁵⁹And if that happens, you won't be free again until you have paid the last penny."

~~~ **What examples have you seen of the problems Jesus mentions?** In these strange and unsettling words, Jesus revealed that his coming often results in conflict. He demands a response, and close groups can be torn apart when some choose to follow him and others refuse to do so. There is no middle ground with Jesus. Loyalties must be declared and commitments made, sometimes to the severing of other relationships. Life is easiest when a family unitedly believes in Christ, of course; but this often does not happen. Are you willing to risk your family's approval in order to gain eternal life?

Jesus and the Kingdom of God

About this time Jesus was informed that Pilate had murdered some people from Galilee as they were sacrificing at the Temple in Jerusalem. ²"Do you think those Galileans were worse sinners than other people from Galilee?" he asked. "Is that why they suffered? ³Not at all! And you will also perish unless you turn from your evil ways and turn to God. ⁴And what about the eighteen men who died when the Tower of Siloam fell on them? Were they the worst sinners in Jerusalem? ⁵No, and I tell you again that unless you repent, you will also perish."

⁶Then Jesus used this illustration: "A man planted a fig tree in his garden and came again and again to see if there was any fruit on it, but he was always disappointed. ⁷Finally, he said to his gardener, 'I've waited three years, and there hasn't been a single fig! Cut it down. It's taking up space we can use for something else.'

⁸"The gardener answered, 'Give it one more chance. Leave it another year, and I'll give it special attention and plenty of fertilizer. ⁹If we get figs next year, fine. If not, you can cut it down.' "

¹⁰One Sabbath day as Jesus was teaching in a synagogue, ¹¹he saw a woman who had been crippled by an evil spirit. She had been bent double for eighteen years and was unable to stand up straight. ¹²When Jesus saw her, he called her over and said, "Woman, you are healed of your sickness!" ¹³Then he touched her, and instantly she could stand straight. How she praised and thanked God!

¹⁴But the leader in charge of the synagogue was indignant that Jesus had healed her on the Sabbath day. "There are six days of the week for working," he said to the crowd. "Come on those days to be healed, not on the Sabbath."

¹⁵But the Lord replied, "You hypocrite! You work on the Sabbath day!

Don't you untie your ox or your donkey from their stalls on the Sabbath and lead them out for water? ¹⁶Wasn't it necessary for me, even on the Sabbath day, to free this dear woman from the bondage in which Satan has held her for eighteen years?" ¹⁷This shamed his enemies. And all the people rejoiced at the wonderful things he did.

¹⁸Then Jesus said, "What is the Kingdom of God like? How can I illustrate it? ¹⁹It is like a tiny mustard seed planted in a garden; it grows and becomes a tree, and the birds come and find shelter among its branches."

²⁰He also asked, "What else is the Kingdom of God like? ²¹It is like yeast used by a woman making bread. Even though she used a large amount of flour, the yeast permeated every part of the dough."

~~~ **When in your life would Jesus have to call for your repentance?**
In the Old Testament a fruitful tree was often used as a symbol of godly living (see Ps. 1:3). Jesus pointed out what would happen to the other kind of tree—the kind that took valuable time and space and still produced nothing for the patient gardener. This was one way Jesus warned his listeners that God would not tolerate forever their lack of productivity. Have you been enjoying God's special treatment without giving anything in return? If so, respond to the Gardener's patient care, and begin to bear the fruit God has created you to produce.

9

AUGUST

Jesus and a Blind Man
JOHN 9:1-41

As Jesus was walking along, he saw a man who had been blind from birth. ²"Teacher," his disciples asked him, "why was this man born blind? Was it a result of his own sins or those of his parents?"

³"It was not because of his sins or his parents' sins," Jesus answered. "He was born blind so the power of God could be seen in him. ⁴All of us must quickly carry out the tasks assigned us by the one who sent me, because there is little time left before the night falls and all work comes to an end. ⁵But while I am still here in the world, I am the light of the world."

⁶Then he spit on the ground, made mud with the saliva, and smoothed the mud over the blind man's eyes. ⁷He told him, "Go and wash in the pool of Siloam" (Siloam means Sent). So the man went and washed, and came back seeing!

⁸His neighbors and others who knew him as a blind beggar asked each other, "Is this the same man—that beggar?" ⁹Some said he was, and others said, "No, but he surely looks like him!"

And the beggar kept saying, "I am the same man!"

¹⁰They asked, "Who healed you? What happened?"

¹¹He told them, "The man they call Jesus made mud and smoothed it

over my eyes and told me, 'Go to the pool of Siloam and wash off the mud.' I went and washed, and now I can see!"

¹²"Where is he now?" they asked.

"I don't know," he replied.

¹³Then they took the man to the Pharisees. ¹⁴Now as it happened, Jesus had healed the man on a Sabbath. ¹⁵The Pharisees asked the man all about it. So he told them, "He smoothed the mud over my eyes, and when it was washed away, I could see!"

¹⁶Some of the Pharisees said, "This man Jesus is not from God, for he is working on the Sabbath." Others said, "But how could an ordinary sinner do such miraculous signs?" So there was a deep division of opinion among them.

¹⁷Then the Pharisees once again questioned the man who had been blind and demanded, "This man who opened your eyes—who do you say he is?"

The man replied, "I think he must be a prophet."

¹⁸The Jewish leaders wouldn't believe he had been blind, so they called in his parents. ¹⁹They asked them, "Is this your son? Was he born blind? If so, how can he see?"

²⁰His parents replied, "We know this is our son and that he was born blind, ²¹but we don't know how he can see or who healed him. He is old enough to speak for himself. Ask him." ²²They said this because they were afraid of the Jewish leaders, who had announced that anyone saying Jesus was the Messiah would be expelled from the synagogue. ²³That's why they said, "He is old enough to speak for himself. Ask him."

²⁴So for the second time they called in the man who had been blind and told him, "Give glory to God by telling the truth, because we know Jesus is a sinner."

²⁵"I don't know whether he is a sinner," the man replied. "But I know this: I was blind, and now I can see!"

²⁶"But what did he do?" they asked. "How did he heal you?"

²⁷"Look!" the man exclaimed. "I told you once. Didn't you listen? Why do you want to hear it again? Do you want to become his disciples, too?"

²⁸Then they cursed him and said, "You are his disciple, but we are disciples of Moses. ²⁹We know God spoke to Moses, but as for this man, we don't know anything about him."

³⁰"Why, that's very strange!" the man replied. "He healed my eyes, and yet you don't know anything about him! ³¹Well, God doesn't listen to sinners, but he is ready to hear those who worship him and do his will. ³²Never since the world began has anyone been able to open the eyes of someone born blind. ³³If this man were not from God, he couldn't do it."

³⁴"You were born in sin!" they answered. "Are you trying to teach us?" And they threw him out of the synagogue.

³⁵When Jesus heard what had happened, he found the man and said, "Do you believe in the Son of Man?"

³⁶The man answered, "Who is he, sir, because I would like to."

³⁷"You have seen him," Jesus said, "and he is speaking to you!"

³⁸"Yes, Lord," the man said, "I believe!" And he worshiped Jesus.

³⁹Then Jesus told him, "I have come to judge the world. I have come to give sight to the blind and to show those who think they see that they are blind."

⁴⁰The Pharisees who were standing there heard him and asked, "Are you saying we are blind?"

⁴¹"If you were blind, you wouldn't be guilty," Jesus replied. "But you remain guilty because you claim you can see."

〰𝓛 **What different stages of "seeing" have been part of your life?**
The longer this man experienced his new life through Christ, the more confident he became in the one who had healed him. He gained not only physical sight but also spiritual sight as he recognized Jesus first as a prophet, then as his Lord. When you turn to Christ, you begin to see him differently. The longer you walk with him, the better you will understand who he is. If you want to know more about Jesus, keep walking with him.

10 AUGUST

Jesus Is the Good Shepherd
JOHN 10:1-18

"I assure you, anyone who sneaks over the wall of a sheepfold, rather than going through the gate, must surely be a thief and a robber! ²For a shepherd enters through the gate. ³The gatekeeper opens the gate for him, and the sheep hear his voice and come to him. He calls his own sheep by name and leads them out. ⁴After he has gathered his own flock, he walks ahead of them, and they follow him because they recognize his voice. ⁵They won't follow a stranger; they will run from him because they don't recognize his voice."

⁶Those who heard Jesus use this illustration didn't understand what he meant, ⁷so he explained it to them. "I assure you, I am the gate for the sheep," he said. ⁸"All others who came before me were thieves and robbers. But the true sheep did not listen to them. ⁹Yes, I am the gate. Those who come in through me will be saved. Wherever they go, they will find green pastures. ¹⁰The thief's purpose is to steal and kill and destroy. My purpose is to give life in all its fullness.

¹¹"I am the good shepherd. The good shepherd lays down his life for the sheep. ¹²A hired hand will run when he sees a wolf coming. He will leave the sheep because they aren't his and he isn't their shepherd. And so the wolf attacks them and scatters the flock. ¹³The hired hand runs away because he is merely hired and has no real concern for the sheep.

¹⁴"I am the good shepherd; I know my own sheep, and they know me, ¹⁵just as my Father knows me and I know the Father. And I lay down my life for the sheep. ¹⁶I have other sheep, too, that are not in this sheepfold. I must

bring them also, and they will listen to my voice; and there will be one flock with one shepherd.

[17]"The Father loves me because I lay down my life that I may have it back again. [18]No one can take my life from me. I lay down my life voluntarily. For I have the right to lay it down when I want to and also the power to take it again. For my Father has given me this command."

〰〰 **How have you experienced God's guidance in your life?** In the sheepfold the shepherd functioned as a door, letting the sheep in and protecting them. Jesus is the door to God's salvation for us. He is our protector and offers us safety and security. Some people resent that Jesus is the door, the only way to God. But Jesus is God's Son. Why should we seek any other way or want to customize a different approach to God?

Jesus: The King Who Grieves

AUGUST 11

LUKE 13:22-35

Jesus went through the towns and villages, teaching as he went, always pressing on toward Jerusalem. [23]Someone asked him, "Lord, will only a few be saved?"

He replied, [24]"The door to heaven is narrow. Work hard to get in, because many will try to enter, [25]but when the head of the house has locked the door, it will be too late. Then you will stand outside knocking and pleading, 'Lord, open the door for us!' But he will reply, 'I do not know you.' [26]You will say, 'But we ate and drank with you, and you taught in our streets.' [27]And he will reply, 'I tell you, I don't know you. Go away, all you who do evil.'

[28]"And there will be great weeping and gnashing of teeth, for you will see Abraham, Isaac, Jacob, and all the prophets within the Kingdom of God, but you will be thrown out. [29]Then people will come from all over the world to take their places in the Kingdom of God. [30]And note this: Some who are despised now will be greatly honored then; and some who are greatly honored now will be despised then."

[31]A few minutes later some Pharisees said to him, "Get out of here if you want to live, because Herod Antipas wants to kill you!"

[32]Jesus replied, "Go tell that fox that I will keep on casting out demons and doing miracles of healing today and tomorrow; and the third day I will accomplish my purpose. [33]Yes, today, tomorrow, and the next day I must proceed on my way. For it wouldn't do for a prophet of God to be killed except in Jerusalem!

[34]"O Jerusalem, Jerusalem, the city that kills the prophets and stones God's messengers! How often I have wanted to gather your children

together as a hen protects her chicks beneath her wings, but you wouldn't let me. ³⁵And now look, your house is left to you empty. And you will never see me again until you say, 'Bless the one who comes in the name of the Lord!' "

〰〰 **How do you feel about those around you who don't know Christ?** There will be many surprises in God's Kingdom. Some who are despised now will be greatly honored then; some influential people here will be left outside the gates. Many "great" people on this earth (in God's eyes) are virtually ignored by the rest of the world. What matters to God is not a person's earthly popularity, status, wealth, heritage, or power but his or her commitment to Christ. How do your values match what the Bible tells you to value? Put God first, and you will join people from all over the world who will take their places at the feast in the Kingdom of Heaven.

12 AUGUST

Jesus on Seeking Honor
LUKE 14:1-14

One Sabbath day Jesus was in the home of a leader of the Pharisees. The people were watching him closely, ²because there was a man there whose arms and legs were swollen. ³Jesus asked the Pharisees and experts in religious law, "Well, is it permitted in the law to heal people on the Sabbath day, or not?" ⁴When they refused to answer, Jesus touched the sick man and healed him and sent him away. ⁵Then he turned to them and asked, "Which of you doesn't work on the Sabbath? If your son or your cow falls into a pit, don't you proceed at once to get him out?" ⁶Again they had no answer.

⁷When Jesus noticed that all who had come to the dinner were trying to sit near the head of the table, he gave them this advice: ⁸"If you are invited to a wedding feast, don't always head for the best seat. What if someone more respected than you has also been invited? ⁹The host will say, 'Let this person sit here instead.' Then you will be embarrassed and will have to take whatever seat is left at the foot of the table!

¹⁰"Do this instead—sit at the foot of the table. Then when your host sees you, he will come and say, 'Friend, we have a better place than this for you!' Then you will be honored in front of all the other guests. ¹¹For the proud will be humbled, but the humble will be honored."

¹²Then he turned to his host. "When you put on a luncheon or a dinner," he said, "don't invite your friends, brothers, relatives, and rich neighbors. For they will repay you by inviting you back. ¹³Instead, invite the poor, the crippled, the lame, and the blind. ¹⁴Then at the resurrection of the godly, God will reward you for inviting those who could not repay you."

~~✍~~ **When would others say that you look out for yourself too much?** Jesus advised people not to rush for the best seats at a feast. People today are just as eager to raise their social status, whether by being with the right people, dressing in the right clothes, or driving the right car. Dressing nicely or striving to be successful in school or in sports is not wrong in itself—it is wrong only when you want these things just to impress others. Whom do you try to impress? Rather than aiming for prestige, look for a place where you can serve.

Jesus on Being His Disciple
LUKE 14:15-35

Hearing this, a man sitting at the table with Jesus exclaimed, "What a privilege it would be to have a share in the Kingdom of God!"

[16]Jesus replied with this illustration: "A man prepared a great feast and sent out many invitations. [17]When all was ready, he sent his servant around to notify the guests that it was time for them to come. [18]But they all began making excuses. One said he had just bought a field and wanted to inspect it, so he asked to be excused. [19]Another said he had just bought five pair of oxen and wanted to try them out. [20]Another had just been married, so he said he couldn't come.

[21]"The servant returned and told his master what they had said. His master was angry and said, 'Go quickly into the streets and alleys of the city and invite the poor, the crippled, the lame, and the blind.' [22]After the servant had done this, he reported, 'There is still room for more.' [23]So his master said, 'Go out into the country lanes and behind the hedges and urge anyone you find to come, so that the house will be full. [24]For none of those I invited first will get even the smallest taste of what I had prepared for them.' "

[25]Great crowds were following Jesus. He turned around and said to them, [26]"If you want to be my follower you must love me more than your own father and mother, wife and children, brothers and sisters—yes, more than your own life. Otherwise, you cannot be my disciple. [27]And you cannot be my disciple if you do not carry your own cross and follow me.

[28]"But don't begin until you count the cost. For who would begin construction of a building without first getting estimates and then checking to see if there is enough money to pay the bills? [29]Otherwise, you might complete only the foundation before running out of funds. And then how everyone would laugh at you! [30]They would say, 'There's the person who started that building and ran out of money before it was finished!'

[31]"Or what king would ever dream of going to war without first sitting down with his counselors and discussing whether his army of ten thousand is strong enough to defeat the twenty thousand soldiers who are marching against him? [32]If he is not able, then while the enemy is still far away, he will

send a delegation to discuss terms of peace. [33]So no one can become my disciple without giving up everything for me.

[34]"Salt is good for seasoning. But if it loses its flavor, how do you make it salty again? [35]Flavorless salt is good neither for the soil nor for fertilizer. It is thrown away. Anyone who is willing to hear should listen and understand!"

〜〜〜 **What is it going to cost you to be a follower of Jesus? Are you willing to pay the price?** When a builder doesn't count the cost or estimates it inaccurately, his building may be left half completed. Will your Christian life be only half built and then abandoned because you did not count the cost of commitment to Jesus? What are those costs? Christians may face loss of social status or wealth. They may have to give up control over their money, their time, or their career. They may be hated, separated from their family, and even put to death. Following Christ does not mean a trouble-free life. We must carefully count the cost of becoming Christ's disciples so that we will know what we are getting into and won't be tempted later to turn back.

14 AUGUST

Two Parables of Losing and Finding
LUKE 15:1-10

Tax collectors and other notorious sinners often came to listen to Jesus teach. [2]This made the Pharisees and teachers of religious law complain that he was associating with such despicable people—even eating with them!

[3]So Jesus used this illustration: [4]"If you had one hundred sheep, and one of them strayed away and was lost in the wilderness, wouldn't you leave the ninety-nine others to go and search for the lost one until you found it? [5]And then you would joyfully carry it home on your shoulders. [6]When you arrived, you would call together your friends and neighbors to rejoice with you because your lost sheep was found. [7]In the same way, heaven will be happier over one lost sinner who returns to God than over ninety-nine others who are righteous and haven't strayed away!

[8]"Or suppose a woman has ten valuable silver coins and loses one. Won't she light a lamp and look in every corner of the house and sweep every nook and cranny until she finds it? [9]And when she finds it, she will call in her friends and neighbors to rejoice with her because she has found her lost coin. [10]In the same way, there is joy in the presence of God's angels when even one sinner repents."

〜〜〜 **How do these stories help you understand God's love for you?** It may seem foolish for the shepherd to leave ninety-nine sheep to go and search for just one. But the shepherd knew that the ninety-nine would be safe in the sheepfold, whereas the lost sheep was in danger. Because each sheep was of high value, the shepherd knew that it was worthwhile to search diligently for the lost one. God's love for each individual is so great that he seeks each one out and rejoices when he or she is "found." Jesus associated with sinners because he wanted to bring the lost sheep—people considered beyond hope—the gospel of God's Kingdom. Before you were a believer, God sought you; and his love is still seeking those who are yet lost.

A Son Who Was Found

LUKE 15:11-32

To illustrate the point further, Jesus told them this story: "A man had two sons. [12]The younger son told his father, 'I want my share of your estate now, instead of waiting until you die.' So his father agreed to divide his wealth between his sons.

[13]"A few days later this younger son packed all his belongings and took a trip to a distant land, and there he wasted all his money on wild living. [14]About the time his money ran out, a great famine swept over the land, and he began to starve. [15]He persuaded a local farmer to hire him to feed his pigs. [16]The boy became so hungry that even the pods he was feeding the pigs looked good to him. But no one gave him anything.

[17]"When he finally came to his senses, he said to himself, 'At home even the hired men have food enough to spare, and here I am, dying of hunger! [18]I will go home to my father and say, "Father, I have sinned against both heaven and you, [19]and I am no longer worthy of being called your son. Please take me on as a hired man."'

[20]"So he returned home to his father. And while he was still a long distance away, his father saw him coming. Filled with love and compassion, he ran to his son, embraced him, and kissed him. [21]His son said to him, 'Father, I have sinned against both heaven and you, and I am no longer worthy of being called your son.'

[22]"But his father said to the servants, 'Quick! Bring the finest robe in the house and put it on him. Get a ring for his finger, and sandals for his feet. [23]And kill the calf we have been fattening in the pen. We must celebrate with a feast, [24]for this son of mine was dead and has now returned to life. He was lost, but now he is found.' So the party began.

[25]"Meanwhile, the older son was in the fields working. When he returned home, he heard music and dancing in the house, [26]and he asked one of the servants what was going on. [27]'Your brother is back,' he was told, 'and your father has killed the calf we were fattening and has prepared a great feast. We are celebrating because of his safe return.'

[28]"The older brother was angry and wouldn't go in. His father came out and begged him, [29]but he replied, 'All these years I've worked hard for you and never once refused to do a single thing you told me to. And in all that

time you never gave me even one young goat for a feast with my friends. [30]Yet when this son of yours comes back after squandering your money on prostitutes, you celebrate by killing the finest calf we have.'

[31]"His father said to him, 'Look, dear son, you and I are very close, and everything I have is yours. [32]We had to celebrate this happy day. For your brother was dead and has come back to life! He was lost, but now he is found!' "

⌇⋀⋎⌇ **In what ways is this story like your life?** Some people need to hit bottom in order to come to their senses. The younger son's attitude was based on a desire to be free to live as he pleased. That is not so different from the desires of most people in our world today. It may take great sorrow and tragedy to cause them to look up to the only one who can help them. Are you trying to live life your way, selfishly pushing aside anything that gets in your way? Don't take leave of your senses. Stop and look before you hit bottom, and save yourself and your family much grief.

16 AUGUST

The Parable of the Shrewd Accountant

LUKE 16:1-18

Jesus told this story to his disciples: "A rich man hired a manager to handle his affairs, but soon a rumor went around that the manager was thoroughly dishonest. [2]So his employer called him in and said, 'What's this I hear about your stealing from me? Get your report in order, because you are going to be dismissed.'

[3]"The manager thought to himself, 'Now what? I'm through here, and I don't have the strength to go out and dig ditches, and I'm too proud to beg. [4]I know just the thing! And then I'll have plenty of friends to take care of me when I leave!'

[5]"So he invited each person who owed money to his employer to come and discuss the situation. He asked the first one, 'How much do you owe him?' [6]The man replied, 'I owe him eight hundred gallons of olive oil.' So the manager told him, 'Tear up that bill and write another one for four hundred gallons.'

[7]" 'And how much do you owe my employer?' he asked the next man. 'A thousand bushels of wheat,' was the reply. 'Here,' the manager said, 'take your bill and replace it with one for only eight hundred bushels.'

[8]"The rich man had to admire the dishonest rascal for being so shrewd. And it is true that the citizens of this world are more shrewd than the godly are. [9]I tell you, use your worldly resources to benefit others and make friends. In this way, your generosity stores up a reward for you in heaven.

[10]"Unless you are faithful in small matters, you won't be faithful in large

ones. If you cheat even a little, you won't be honest with greater responsibilities. ¹¹And if you are untrustworthy about worldly wealth, who will trust you with the true riches of heaven? ¹²And if you are not faithful with other people's money, why should you be trusted with money of your own?

¹³"No one can serve two masters. For you will hate one and love the other, or be devoted to one and despise the other. You cannot serve both God and money."

¹⁴The Pharisees, who dearly loved their money, naturally scoffed at all this. ¹⁵Then he said to them, "You like to look good in public, but God knows your evil hearts. What this world honors is an abomination in the sight of God.

¹⁶"Until John the Baptist began to preach, the laws of Moses and the messages of the prophets were your guides. But now the Good News of the Kingdom of God is preached, and eager multitudes are forcing their way in. ¹⁷But that doesn't mean that the law has lost its force in even the smallest point. It is stronger and more permanent than heaven and earth.

¹⁸"Anyone who divorces his wife and marries someone else commits adultery, and anyone who marries a divorced woman commits adultery."

〰️ **What does it mean to be an honest person?** Our integrity is often tested in regard to money matters. God calls us to be honest even in small details we could easily rationalize away. Heaven's riches are far more valuable than earthly wealth. But if we are not trustworthy with our money here (no matter how much or little we have), we will be unfit to handle the vast riches of God's Kingdom. Don't let your integrity slip in small matters, and it will not be compromised in crucial decisions.

The Rich Man and the Beggar

AUGUST

17

LUKE 16:19-31

Jesus said, "There was a certain rich man who was splendidly clothed and who lived each day in luxury. ²⁰At his door lay a diseased beggar named Lazarus. ²¹As Lazarus lay there longing for scraps from the rich man's table, the dogs would come and lick his open sores. ²²Finally, the beggar died and was carried by the angels to be with Abraham. The rich man also died and was buried, ²³and his soul went to the place of the dead. There, in torment, he saw Lazarus in the far distance with Abraham.

²⁴"The rich man shouted, 'Father Abraham, have some pity! Send Lazarus over here to dip the tip of his finger in water and cool my tongue, because I am in anguish in these flames.'

²⁵"But Abraham said to him, 'Son, remember that during your lifetime you had everything you wanted, and Lazarus had nothing. So now he is

here being comforted, and you are in anguish. ²⁶And besides, there is a great chasm separating us. Anyone who wanted to cross over to you from here is stopped at its edge, and no one there can cross over to us.'

²⁷"Then the rich man said, 'Please, Father Abraham, send him to my father's home. ²⁸For I have five brothers, and I want him to warn them about this place of torment so they won't have to come here when they die.'

²⁹"But Abraham said, 'Moses and the prophets have warned them. Your brothers can read their writings anytime they want to.'

³⁰"The rich man replied, 'No, Father Abraham! But if someone is sent to them from the dead, then they will turn from their sins.'

³¹"But Abraham said, 'If they won't listen to Moses and the prophets, they won't listen even if someone rises from the dead.' "

〜⋎〜 **Where are the poor people in your community? Whom do you know who is poor? How can you help the poor?** The Pharisees considered wealth to be a proof of a person's righteousness. Jesus startled them with this story in which a diseased beggar is rewarded and a rich man is punished. The rich man did not go to hell because of his wealth but because he was selfish, refusing to feed Lazarus, take him in, or care for him. The rich man was hard-hearted in spite of his great blessings. The amount of money we have is not as important as the way we use it. What is your attitude toward your money and possessions? Do you hoard them selfishly, or do you use them to help others?

AUGUST

Lazarus Dies

JOHN 11:1-36

A man named Lazarus was sick. He lived in Bethany with his sisters, Mary and Martha. ²This is the Mary who poured the expensive perfume on the Lord's feet and wiped them with her hair. Her brother, Lazarus, was sick. ³So the two sisters sent a message to Jesus telling him, "Lord, the one you love is very sick."

⁴But when Jesus heard about it he said, "Lazarus's sickness will not end in death. No, it is for the glory of God. I, the Son of God, will receive glory from this." ⁵Although Jesus loved Martha, Mary, and Lazarus, ⁶he stayed where he was for the next two days and did not go to them. ⁷Finally after two days, he said to his disciples, "Let's go to Judea again."

⁸But his disciples objected. "Teacher," they said, "only a few days ago the Jewish leaders in Judea were trying to kill you. Are you going there again?"

⁹Jesus replied, "There are twelve hours of daylight every day. As long as it is light, people can walk safely. They can see because they have the light of this world. ¹⁰Only at night is there danger of stumbling because there is no light." ¹¹Then he said, "Our friend Lazarus has fallen asleep, but now I will go and wake him up."

¹²The disciples said, "Lord, if he is sleeping, that means he is getting better!" ¹³They thought Jesus meant Lazarus was having a good night's rest, but Jesus meant Lazarus had died.

¹⁴Then he told them plainly, "Lazarus is dead. ¹⁵And for your sake, I am glad I wasn't there, because this will give you another opportunity to believe in me. Come, let's go see him."

¹⁶Thomas, nicknamed the Twin, said to his fellow disciples, "Let's go, too—and die with Jesus."

¹⁷When Jesus arrived at Bethany, he was told that Lazarus had already been in his grave for four days. ¹⁸Bethany was only a few miles down the road from Jerusalem, ¹⁹and many of the people had come to pay their respects and console Martha and Mary on their loss. ²⁰When Martha got word that Jesus was coming, she went to meet him. But Mary stayed at home. ²¹Martha said to Jesus, "Lord, if you had been here, my brother would not have died. ²²But even now I know that God will give you whatever you ask."

²³Jesus told her, "Your brother will rise again."

²⁴"Yes," Martha said, "when everyone else rises, on resurrection day."

²⁵Jesus told her, "I am the resurrection and the life. Those who believe in me, even though they die like everyone else, will live again. ²⁶They are given eternal life for believing in me and will never perish. Do you believe this, Martha?"

²⁷"Yes, Lord," she told him. "I have always believed you are the Messiah, the Son of God, the one who has come into the world from God." ²⁸Then she left him and returned to Mary. She called Mary aside from the mourners and told her, "The Teacher is here and wants to see you." ²⁹So Mary immediately went to him.

³⁰Now Jesus had stayed outside the village, at the place where Martha met him. ³¹When the people who were at the house trying to console Mary saw her leave so hastily, they assumed she was going to Lazarus's grave to weep. So they followed her there. ³²When Mary arrived and saw Jesus, she fell down at his feet and said, "Lord, if you had been here, my brother would not have died."

³³When Jesus saw her weeping and saw the other people wailing with her, he was moved with indignation and was deeply troubled. ³⁴"Where have you put him?" he asked them.

They told him, "Lord, come and see." ³⁵Then Jesus wept. ³⁶The people who were standing nearby said, "See how much he loved him."

ᔗᐱᓬ **In what situations have you been disappointed with God?**
Jesus loved this family and often stayed with them. He knew their pain but did not respond immediately. His delay had a specific purpose. God's timing, especially his delays, may make us think that he is not answering or is not answering in the way we want. But he will meet all our needs according to his perfect schedule and purpose. Patiently await his timing.

Jesus Raises Lazarus
JOHN 11:37-57

But some said, "This man healed a blind man. Why couldn't he keep Lazarus from dying?"

[38]And again Jesus was deeply troubled. Then they came to the grave. It was a cave with a stone rolled across its entrance. [39]"Roll the stone aside," Jesus told them.

But Martha, the dead man's sister, said, "Lord, by now the smell will be terrible because he has been dead for four days."

[40]Jesus responded, "Didn't I tell you that you will see God's glory if you believe?" [41]So they rolled the stone aside. Then Jesus looked up to heaven and said, "Father, thank you for hearing me. [42]You always hear me, but I said it out loud for the sake of all these people standing here, so they will believe you sent me." [43]Then Jesus shouted, "Lazarus, come out!" [44]And Lazarus came out, bound in graveclothes, his face wrapped in a headcloth. Jesus told them, "Unwrap him and let him go!"

[45]Many of the people who were with Mary believed in Jesus when they saw this happen. [46]But some went to the Pharisees and told them what Jesus had done. [47]Then the leading priests and Pharisees called the high council together to discuss the situation. "What are we going to do?" they asked each other. "This man certainly performs many miraculous signs. [48]If we leave him alone, the whole nation will follow him, and then the Roman army will come and destroy both our Temple and our nation."

[49]And one of them, Caiaphas, who was high priest that year, said, "How can you be so stupid? [50]Why should the whole nation be destroyed? Let this one man die for the people."

[51]This prophecy that Jesus should die for the entire nation came from Caiaphas in his position as high priest. He didn't think of it himself; he was inspired to say it. [52]It was a prediction that Jesus' death would be not for Israel only, but for the gathering together of all the children of God scattered around the world.

[53]So from that time on the Jewish leaders began to plot Jesus' death. [54]As a result, Jesus stopped his public ministry among the people and left Jerusalem. He went to a place near the wilderness, to the village of Ephraim, and stayed there with his disciples.

[55]It was now almost time for the celebration of Passover, and many people from the country arrived in Jerusalem several days early so they could go through the cleansing ceremony before the Passover began. [56]They wanted to see Jesus, and as they talked in the Temple, they asked each other, "What do you think? Will he come for the Passover?" [57]Meanwhile, the leading priests and Pharisees had publicly announced that anyone seeing Jesus must report him immediately so they could arrest him.

~\/\/~ **How would you have felt watching Lazarus walk out of the tomb?** John stresses that we have a God who cares. This portrait contrasts with the Greek concept of God that was popular in that day—a God with no emotions and no involvement with humans. Here we see many of Jesus' emotions—compassion, indignation, sorrow, even frustration. He often expressed deep emotion, so we need never be afraid to reveal our true feelings to him. He understands them, for he experienced them. Be honest, and don't try to hide anything from your Savior. He cares.

AUGUST

Jesus and Ten Lepers
LUKE 17:1-19

20

One day Jesus said to his disciples, "There will always be temptations to sin, but how terrible it will be for the person who does the tempting. ²It would be better to be thrown into the sea with a large millstone tied around the neck than to face the punishment in store for harming one of these little ones. ³I am warning you! If another believer sins, rebuke him; then if he repents, forgive him. ⁴Even if he wrongs you seven times a day and each time turns again and asks forgiveness, forgive him."

⁵One day the apostles said to the Lord, "We need more faith; tell us how to get it."

⁶"Even if you had faith as small as a mustard seed," the Lord answered, "you could say to this mulberry tree, 'May God uproot you and throw you into the sea,' and it would obey you!

⁷"When a servant comes in from plowing or taking care of sheep, he doesn't just sit down and eat. ⁸He must first prepare his master's meal and serve him his supper before eating his own. ⁹And the servant is not even thanked, because he is merely doing what he is supposed to do. ¹⁰In the same way, when you obey me you should say, 'We are not worthy of praise. We are servants who have simply done our duty.' "

¹¹As Jesus continued on toward Jerusalem, he reached the border between Galilee and Samaria. ¹²As he entered a village there, ten lepers stood at a distance, ¹³crying out, "Jesus, Master, have mercy on us!"

¹⁴He looked at them and said, "Go show yourselves to the priests." And as they went, their leprosy disappeared.

¹⁵One of them, when he saw that he was healed, came back to Jesus, shouting, "Praise God, I'm healed!" ¹⁶He fell face down on the ground at Jesus' feet, thanking him for what he had done. This man was a Samaritan.

¹⁷Jesus asked, "Didn't I heal ten men? Where are the other nine? ¹⁸Does only this foreigner return to give glory to God?" ¹⁹And Jesus said to the man, "Stand up and go. Your faith has made you well."

~~~ **For what are you thankful to God?** Jesus healed all ten lepers, but only one returned to thank him. It is possible to receive God's great gifts with an ungrateful spirit—nine of the ten men did so. Only the thankful man, however, learned that his faith had played a role in his healing; and only grateful Christians grow in understanding God's grace. God does not demand that we thank him, but he is pleased when we do so. And he uses our responsiveness to teach us more about himself.

AUGUST

Jesus and the Kingdom of God
LUKE 17:20-37

One day the Pharisees asked Jesus, "When will the Kingdom of God come?"

Jesus replied, "The Kingdom of God isn't ushered in with visible signs. [21]You won't be able to say, 'Here it is!' or 'It's over there!' For the Kingdom of God is among you."

[22]Later he talked again about this with his disciples. "The time is coming when you will long to share in the days of the Son of Man, but you won't be able to," he said. [23]"Reports will reach you that the Son of Man has returned and that he is in this place or that. Don't believe such reports or go out to look for him. [24]For when the Son of Man returns, you will know it beyond all doubt. It will be as evident as the lightning that flashes across the sky. [25]But first the Son of Man must suffer terribly and be rejected by this generation.

[26]"When the Son of Man returns, the world will be like the people were in Noah's day. [27]In those days before the flood, the people enjoyed banquets and parties and weddings right up to the time Noah entered his boat and the flood came to destroy them all.

[28]"And the world will be as it was in the days of Lot. People went about their daily business—eating and drinking, buying and selling, farming and building—[29]until the morning Lot left Sodom. Then fire and burning sulfur rained down from heaven and destroyed them all. [30]Yes, it will be 'business as usual' right up to the hour when the Son of Man returns. [31]On that day a person outside the house must not go into the house to pack. A person in the field must not return to town. [32]Remember what happened to Lot's wife! [33]Whoever clings to this life will lose it, and whoever loses this life will save it. [34]That night two people will be asleep in one bed; one will be taken away, and the other will be left. [35]Two women will be grinding flour together at the mill; one will be taken, the other left."

[37]"Lord, where will this happen?" the disciples asked.

Jesus replied, "Just as the gathering of vultures shows there is a carcass nearby, so these signs indicate that the end is near."

~~~~ **What difference would it make in your life if Jesus returned today?** Life will be going on as usual on the day Christ returns. There will be no warning. Most people will be going about their everyday tasks, indifferent to the things of God. They will be as surprised by Christ's return as the people in Noah's day were by the Flood (Gen. 6–8) or the people in Lot's day by the destruction of Sodom (Gen. 19). We don't know the time of Christ's return, but we do know that he is coming. He may come today, tomorrow, or centuries in the future. Whenever he comes, we must be morally and spiritually ready. Live as if Jesus were returning today.

AUGUST

Jesus Teaches about Prayer

LUKE 18:1-14

22

One day Jesus told his disciples a story to illustrate their need for constant prayer and to show them that they must never give up. [2]"There was a judge in a certain city," he said, "who was a godless man with great contempt for everyone. [3]A widow of that city came to him repeatedly, appealing for justice against someone who had harmed her. [4]The judge ignored her for a while, but eventually she wore him out. 'I fear neither God nor man,' he said to himself, [5]'but this woman is driving me crazy. I'm going to see that she gets justice, because she is wearing me out with her constant requests!' "

[6]Then the Lord said, "Learn a lesson from this evil judge. [7]Even he rendered a just decision in the end, so don't you think God will surely give justice to his chosen people who plead with him day and night? Will he keep putting them off? [8]I tell you, he will grant justice to them quickly! But when I, the Son of Man, return, how many will I find who have faith?"

[9]Then Jesus told this story to some who had great self-confidence and scorned everyone else: [10]"Two men went to the Temple to pray. One was a Pharisee, and the other was a dishonest tax collector. [11]The proud Pharisee stood by himself and prayed this prayer: 'I thank you, God, that I am not a sinner like everyone else, especially like that tax collector over there! For I never cheat, I don't sin, I don't commit adultery, [12]I fast twice a week, and I give you a tenth of my income.'

[13]"But the tax collector stood at a distance and dared not even lift his eyes to heaven as he prayed. Instead, he beat his chest in sorrow, saying, 'O God, be merciful to me, for I am a sinner.' [14]I tell you, this sinner, not the Pharisee, returned home justified before God. For the proud will be humbled, but the humble will be honored."

~~~~ **What is the tone of your prayers?** To repeat our prayers until the answer comes does not mean endless repetition or painfully long prayer sessions. Constant prayer means keeping our requests constantly before God as we live for him day by day, always believing he will answer. When we thus live by

faith, we are not to give up. God may delay answering, but his delays always have good reasons. We must not confuse them with neglect. As we persist in prayer we grow in character, faith, and hope.

23

Jesus on Family Matters
MARK 10:1-16

Then Jesus left Capernaum and went southward to the region of Judea and into the area east of the Jordan River. As always there were the crowds, and as usual he taught them.

²Some Pharisees came and tried to trap him with this question: "Should a man be allowed to divorce his wife?"

³"What did Moses say about divorce?" Jesus asked them.

⁴"Well, he permitted it," they replied. "He said a man merely has to write his wife an official letter of divorce and send her away."

⁵But Jesus responded, "He wrote those instructions only as a concession to your hard-hearted wickedness. ⁶But God's plan was seen from the beginning of creation, for 'He made them male and female.' ⁷'This explains why a man leaves his father and mother and is joined to his wife, ⁸and the two are united into one.' Since they are no longer two but one, ⁹let no one separate them, for God has joined them together."

¹⁰Later, when he was alone with his disciples in the house, they brought up the subject again. ¹¹He told them, "Whoever divorces his wife and marries someone else commits adultery against her. ¹²And if a woman divorces her husband and remarries, she commits adultery."

¹³One day some parents brought their children to Jesus so he could touch them and bless them, but the disciples told them not to bother him. ¹⁴But when Jesus saw what was happening, he was very displeased with his disciples. He said to them, "Let the children come to me. Don't stop them! For the Kingdom of God belongs to such as these. ¹⁵I assure you, anyone who doesn't have their kind of faith will never get into the Kingdom of God." ¹⁶Then he took the children into his arms and placed his hands on their heads and blessed them.

How far will you go to keep your word? Adults are not as trusting as little children. To feel secure, all children need is a loving look and gentle touch from someone who cares. Complete intellectual understanding is not one of their requirements. They believe us if they trust us. Jesus said that people should believe in him with this kind of childlike faith. We should not have to understand all the mysteries of the universe; it should be enough to know that God loves us and provides forgiveness for our sin. This doesn't mean that we should be childish or immature, but we should trust God with a child's simplicity and receptivity.

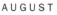

Jesus and the Rich Man

MARK 10:17-31

As he was starting out on a trip, a man came running up to Jesus, knelt down, and asked, "Good Teacher, what should I do to get eternal life?" [18]"Why do you call me good?" Jesus asked. "Only God is truly good. [19]But as for your question, you know the commandments: 'Do not murder. Do not commit adultery. Do not steal. Do not testify falsely. Do not cheat. Honor your father and mother.' "

[20]"Teacher," the man replied, "I've obeyed all these commandments since I was a child."

[21]Jesus felt genuine love for this man as he looked at him. "You lack only one thing," he told him. "Go and sell all you have and give the money to the poor, and you will have treasure in heaven. Then come, follow me." [22]At this, the man's face fell, and he went sadly away because he had many possessions.

[23]Jesus looked around and said to his disciples, "How hard it is for rich people to get into the Kingdom of God!" [24]This amazed them. But Jesus said again, "Dear children, it is very hard to get into the Kingdom of God. [25]It is easier for a camel to go through the eye of a needle than for a rich person to enter the Kingdom of God!"

[26]The disciples were astounded. "Then who in the world can be saved?" they asked.

[27]Jesus looked at them intently and said, "Humanly speaking, it is impossible. But not with God. Everything is possible with God."

[28]Then Peter began to mention all that he and the other disciples had left behind. "We've given up everything to follow you," he said.

[29]And Jesus replied, "I assure you that everyone who has given up house or brothers or sisters or mother or father or children or property, for my sake and for the Good News, [30]will receive now in return, a hundred times over, houses, brothers, sisters, mothers, children, and property—with persecutions. And in the world to come they will have eternal life. [31]But many who seem to be important now will be the least important then, and those who are considered least here will be the greatest then."

What is the most difficult thing Jesus could ask you to give up? This young man wanted to be sure he would get eternal life, so he asked what he could *do*. He said he'd never once broken any of the laws Jesus mentioned, but Jesus lovingly broke through his pride with a challenge that brought out his true motives: "Sell all you have and give the money to the poor." Here was the barrier that could keep this young man out of the Kingdom: his love of money. Money represented his pride of accomplishment and self-effort. Ironically, the young man's attitude made him unable to keep the first commandment, to let

327

nothing be more important than God (Exod. 20:3). He could not meet the one requirement Jesus gave—to turn his whole heart and life over to God. The man came to Jesus wondering what he could do; he left knowing what he was unable to do. What barriers are keeping you from turning your life over to Christ?

25 AUGUST

A Parable about Equal Pay
MATTHEW 20:1-19

"For the Kingdom of Heaven is like the owner of an estate who went out early one morning to hire workers for his vineyard. ²He agreed to pay the normal daily wage and sent them out to work.

³"At nine o'clock in the morning he was passing through the marketplace and saw some people standing around doing nothing. ⁴So he hired them, telling them he would pay them whatever was right at the end of the day. ⁵At noon and again around three o'clock he did the same thing. ⁶At five o'clock that evening he was in town again and saw some more people standing around. He asked them, 'Why haven't you been working today?'

⁷"They replied, 'Because no one hired us.'

"The owner of the estate told them, 'Then go on out and join the others in my vineyard.'

⁸"That evening he told the foreman to call the workers in and pay them, beginning with the last workers first. ⁹When those hired at five o'clock were paid, each received a full day's wage. ¹⁰When those hired earlier came to get their pay, they assumed they would receive more. But they, too, were paid a day's wage. ¹¹When they received their pay, they protested, ¹²'Those people worked only one hour, and yet you've paid them just as much as you paid us who worked all day in the scorching heat.'

¹³"He answered one of them, 'Friend, I haven't been unfair! Didn't you agree to work all day for the usual wage? ¹⁴Take it and go. I wanted to pay this last worker the same as you. ¹⁵Is it against the law for me to do what I want with my money? Should you be angry because I am kind?'

¹⁶"And so it is, that many who are first now will be last then; and those who are last now will be first then."

¹⁷As Jesus was on the way to Jerusalem, he took the twelve disciples aside privately and told them what was going to happen to him. ¹⁸"When we get to Jerusalem," he said, "the Son of Man will be betrayed to the leading priests and the teachers of religious law. They will sentence him to die. ¹⁹Then they will hand him over to the Romans to be mocked, whipped, and crucified. But on the third day he will be raised from the dead."

〰️ **How often are you jealous of what God has given to someone else?** This parable is a strong teaching about *grace,* God's generosity. We shouldn't begrudge those who turn to God in the last moments of life because, in reality, *no one* deserves eternal life. Many people we don't expect to see in the Kingdom may be there. The person who accepts Christ at the end of life will be there as well as the person who has believed and served God for many years. Do you resent God's gracious acceptance of the despised, the outcast, and the sinners who have turned to him for forgiveness? Are you ever jealous of what God has given to another person? Focus on God's gracious benefits to you, and be thankful for what you have.

AUGUST

26

Jesus on Serving Others

MARK 10:35-52

Then James and John, the sons of Zebedee, came over and spoke to him. "Teacher," they said, "we want you to do us a favor."

[36]"What is it?" he asked.

[37]"In your glorious Kingdom, we want to sit in places of honor next to you," they said, "one at your right and the other at your left."

[38]But Jesus answered, "You don't know what you are asking! Are you able to drink from the bitter cup of sorrow I am about to drink? Are you able to be baptized with the baptism of suffering I must be baptized with?"

[39]"Oh yes," they said, "we are able!"

And Jesus said, "You will indeed drink from my cup and be baptized with my baptism, [40]but I have no right to say who will sit on the thrones next to mine. God has prepared those places for the ones he has chosen."

[41]When the ten other disciples discovered what James and John had asked, they were indignant. [42]So Jesus called them together and said, "You know that in this world kings are tyrants, and officials lord it over the people beneath them. [43]But among you it should be quite different. Whoever wants to be a leader among you must be your servant, [44]and whoever wants to be first must be the slave of all. [45]For even I, the Son of Man, came here not to be served but to serve others, and to give my life as a ransom for many."

[46]And so they reached Jericho. Later, as Jesus and his disciples left town, a great crowd was following. A blind beggar named Bartimaeus (son of Timaeus) was sitting beside the road as Jesus was going by. [47]When Bartimaeus heard that Jesus from Nazareth was nearby, he began to shout out, "Jesus, Son of David, have mercy on me!"

[48]"Be quiet!" some of the people yelled at him.

But he only shouted louder, "Son of David, have mercy on me!"

[49]When Jesus heard him, he stopped and said, "Tell him to come here."

So they called the blind man. "Cheer up," they said. "Come on, he's calling you!" [50]Bartimaeus threw aside his coat, jumped up, and came to Jesus.

[51]"What do you want me to do for you?" Jesus asked.

"Teacher," the blind man said, "I want to see!"
⁵²And Jesus said to him, "Go your way. Your faith has healed you." And instantly the blind man could see! Then he followed Jesus down the road.

〰️⌇ **In what ways are you learning to be a servant?** James and John said they were willing to face any trial for Christ. Both did suffer: James died as a martyr (Acts 12:2), and John was forced to live in exile (Rev. 1:9). It is easy to say we will endure anything for Christ, and yet most of us complain over the most minor problems. If we say we are willing to suffer on a large scale for Christ, we must also be willing to suffer the irritations that may come with serving others.

27 AUGUST

Jesus and Zacchaeus
LUKE 19:1-27

Jesus entered Jericho and made his way through the town. ²There was a man there named Zacchaeus. He was one of the most influential Jews in the Roman tax-collecting business, and he had become very rich. ³He tried to get a look at Jesus, but he was too short to see over the crowds. ⁴So he ran ahead and climbed a sycamore tree beside the road, so he could watch from there.

⁵When Jesus came by, he looked up at Zacchaeus and called him by name. "Zacchaeus!" he said. "Quick, come down! For I must be a guest in your home today."

⁶Zacchaeus quickly climbed down and took Jesus to his house in great excitement and joy. ⁷But the crowds were displeased. "He has gone to be the guest of a notorious sinner," they grumbled.

⁸Meanwhile, Zacchaeus stood there and said to the Lord, "I will give half my wealth to the poor, Lord, and if I have overcharged people on their taxes, I will give them back four times as much!"

⁹Jesus responded, "Salvation has come to this home today, for this man has shown himself to be a son of Abraham. ¹⁰And I, the Son of Man, have come to seek and save those like him who are lost."

¹¹The crowd was listening to everything Jesus said. And because he was nearing Jerusalem, he told a story to correct the impression that the Kingdom of God would begin right away. ¹²He said, "A nobleman was called away to a distant empire to be crowned king and then return. ¹³Before he left, he called together ten servants and gave them ten pounds of silver to invest for him while he was gone. ¹⁴But his people hated him and sent a delegation after him to say they did not want him to be their king.

¹⁵"When he returned, the king called in the servants to whom he had given the money. He wanted to find out what they had done with the money and what their profits were. ¹⁶The first servant reported a tremen-

dous gain—ten times as much as the original amount! ¹⁷'Well done!' the king exclaimed. 'You are a trustworthy servant. You have been faithful with the little I entrusted to you, so you will be governor of ten cities as your reward.'

¹⁸"The next servant also reported a good gain—five times the original amount. ¹⁹'Well done!' the king said. 'You can be governor over five cities.'

²⁰"But the third servant brought back only the original amount of money and said, 'I hid it and kept it safe. ²¹I was afraid because you are a hard man to deal with, taking what isn't yours and harvesting crops you didn't plant.'

²²" 'You wicked servant!' the king roared. 'Hard, am I? If you knew so much about me and how tough I am, ²³why didn't you deposit the money in the bank so I could at least get some interest on it?' ²⁴Then turning to the others standing nearby, the king ordered, 'Take the money from this servant, and give it to the one who earned the most.'

²⁵" 'But, master,' they said, 'that servant has enough already!'

²⁶" 'Yes,' the king replied, 'but to those who use well what they are given, even more will be given. But from those who are unfaithful, even what little they have will be taken away. ²⁷And now about these enemies of mine who didn't want me to be their king—bring them in and execute them right here in my presence.' "

〰〰 **What personal physical characteristic has most affected how you feel about yourself?** Judging from the crowd's reaction to him, Zacchaeus must have been a very crooked tax collector. But after he met Jesus, he realized that his life needed straightening out. By giving to the poor and making restitution—with generous interest—to those he had cheated, Zacchaeus demonstrated inward change by outward action. It is not enough to follow Jesus in your head or heart alone. You must show your faith by changed behavior. Has your faith resulted in action? What changes do you need to make?

AUGUST

A Woman Anoints Jesus

JOHN 12:1-11

Six days before the Passover ceremonies began, Jesus arrived in Bethany, the home of Lazarus—the man he had raised from the dead. ²A dinner was prepared in Jesus' honor. Martha served, and Lazarus sat at the table with him. ³Then Mary took a twelve-ounce jar of expensive perfume made from essence of nard, and she anointed Jesus' feet with it and wiped his feet with her hair. And the house was filled with fragrance.

⁴But Judas Iscariot, one of his disciples—the one who would betray him—said, ⁵"That perfume was worth a small fortune. It should have been sold and the money given to the poor." ⁶Not that he cared for the poor—he

was a thief who was in charge of the disciples' funds, and he often took some for his own use.

[7]Jesus replied, "Leave her alone. She did it in preparation for my burial. [8]You will always have the poor among you, but I will not be here with you much longer."

[9]When all the people heard of Jesus' arrival, they flocked to see him and also to see Lazarus, the man Jesus had raised from the dead. [10]Then the leading priests decided to kill Lazarus, too, [11]for it was because of him that many of the people had deserted them and believed in Jesus.

〰️ **What have you ever "wasted" as an expression of love for Christ?** This act and Jesus' response to it do not teach us to ignore the poor so we can spend money extravagantly for Christ. This was a unique act for a specific occasion—an anointing that anticipated Jesus' burial and a public declaration of faith in him as Messiah. Jesus' words should have taught Judas a valuable lesson about the worth of money. Unfortunately, Judas did not take heed; soon he would sell his Master's life for thirty pieces of silver.

 AUGUST

Jesus Rides into Jerusalem
MATTHEW 21:1-17

As Jesus and the disciples approached Jerusalem, they came to the town of Bethphage on the Mount of Olives. Jesus sent two of them on ahead. [2]"Go into the village over there," he said, "and you will see a donkey tied there, with its colt beside it. Untie them and bring them here. [3]If anyone asks what you are doing, just say, 'The Lord needs them,' and he will immediately send them." [4]This was done to fulfill the prophecy,

[5] "Tell the people of Israel,
    'Look, your King is coming to you.
    He is humble, riding on a donkey—
    even on a donkey's colt.' "

[6]The two disciples did as Jesus said. [7]They brought the animals to him and threw their garments over the colt, and he sat on it.

[8]Most of the crowd spread their coats on the road ahead of Jesus, and others cut branches from the trees and spread them on the road. [9]He was in the center of the procession, and the crowds all around him were shouting,

"Praise God for the Son of David!
Bless the one who comes in the name of the Lord!
Praise God in highest heaven!"

[10]The entire city of Jerusalem was stirred as he entered. "Who is this?" they asked.

[11]And the crowds replied, "It's Jesus, the prophet from Nazareth in Galilee."
[12]Jesus entered the Temple and began to drive out the merchants and their customers. He knocked over the tables of the money changers and the stalls of those selling doves. [13]He said, "The Scriptures declare, 'My Temple will be called a place of prayer,' but you have turned it into a den of thieves!"
[14]The blind and the lame came to him, and he healed them there in the Temple. [15]The leading priests and the teachers of religious law saw these wonderful miracles and heard even the little children in the Temple shouting, "Praise God for the Son of David." But they were indignant [16]and asked Jesus, "Do you hear what these children are saying?"
"Yes," Jesus replied. "Haven't you ever read the Scriptures? For they say, 'You have taught children and infants to give you praise.' " [17]Then he returned to Bethany, where he stayed overnight.

〰〰 **If you had been part of the crowd that day, what would have been your most lasting memory?** This passage is one of the few places where the Gospels record that Jesus' glory is recognized on earth. Jesus boldly declared himself King, and the crowd gladly joined him. But these same people would bow to political pressure and desert him in just a few days. Today we celebrate this event on Palm Sunday. That day should remind us to guard against superficial acclaim for Christ. Think about this next time you celebrate Palm Sunday.

Jesus Explains Why He Must Die

AUGUST **30**

JOHN 12:20-36

Some Greeks who had come to Jerusalem to attend the Passover [21]paid a visit to Philip, who was from Bethsaida in Galilee. They said, "Sir, we want to meet Jesus." [22]Philip told Andrew about it, and they went together to ask Jesus.

[23]Jesus replied, "The time has come for the Son of Man to enter into his glory. [24]The truth is, a kernel of wheat must be planted in the soil. Unless it dies it will be alone—a single seed. But its death will produce many new kernels—a plentiful harvest of new lives. [25]Those who love their life in this world will lose it. Those who despise their life in this world will keep it for eternal life. [26]All those who want to be my disciples must come and follow me, because my servants must be where I am. And if they follow me, the Father will honor them. [27]Now my soul is deeply troubled. Should I pray, 'Father, save me from what lies ahead'? But that is the very reason why I came! [28]Father, bring glory to your name."

Then a voice spoke from heaven, saying, "I have already brought it glory, and I will do it again." ²⁹When the crowd heard the voice, some thought it was thunder, while others declared an angel had spoken to him. ³⁰Then Jesus told them, "The voice was for your benefit, not mine. ³¹The time of judgment for the world has come, when the prince of this world will be cast out. ³²And when I am lifted up on the cross, I will draw everyone to myself." ³³He said this to indicate how he was going to die.

³⁴"Die?" asked the crowd. "We understood from Scripture that the Messiah would live forever. Why are you saying the Son of Man will die? Who is this Son of Man you are talking about?"

³⁵Jesus replied, "My light will shine out for you just a little while longer. Walk in it while you can, so you will not stumble when the darkness falls. If you walk in the darkness, you cannot see where you are going. ³⁶Believe in the light while there is still time; then you will become children of the light." After saying these things, Jesus went away and was hidden from them.

How would you explain to someone why Jesus had to die on the cross? The crowd could not believe what Jesus was saying about the Messiah. They were waving palm branches for a victorious Messiah who would set up a political, earthly kingdom that would never end. From their reading of certain Scriptures, they thought the Messiah would never die (Pss. 89:35-36; 110:4; Isa. 9:7). Other passages, however, showed that he would (Isa. 53:5-9). Jesus' words did not mesh with their concept of the Messiah. First he had to suffer and die—then he would one day set up his eternal Kingdom. What kind of Messiah, or Savior, are you seeking? Beware of trying to force Jesus into your own mold—he won't fit.

AUGUST

Jesus and His Message
JOHN 12:37-50

But despite all the miraculous signs he had done, most of the people did not believe in him. ³⁸This is exactly what Isaiah the prophet had predicted:

> "Lord, who has believed our message?
> To whom will the Lord reveal his saving power?"

³⁹But the people couldn't believe, for as Isaiah also said,

> ⁴⁰"The Lord has blinded their eyes
> and hardened their hearts—
> so their eyes cannot see,
> and their hearts cannot understand,
> and they cannot turn to me
> and let me heal them."

⁴¹Isaiah was referring to Jesus when he made this prediction, because he was given a vision of the Messiah's glory. ⁴²Many people, including some of the Jewish leaders, believed in him. But they wouldn't admit it to anyone because of their fear that the Pharisees would expel them from the synagogue. ⁴³For they loved human praise more than the praise of God.

⁴⁴Jesus shouted to the crowds, "If you trust me, you are really trusting God who sent me. ⁴⁵For when you see me, you are seeing the one who sent me. ⁴⁶I have come as a light to shine in this dark world, so that all who put their trust in me will no longer remain in the darkness. ⁴⁷If anyone hears me and doesn't obey me, I am not his judge—for I have come to save the world and not to judge it. ⁴⁸But all who reject me and my message will be judged at the day of judgment by the truth I have spoken. ⁴⁹I don't speak on my own authority. The Father who sent me gave me his own instructions as to what I should say. ⁵⁰And I know his instructions lead to eternal life; so I say whatever the Father tells me to say!"

〜〰〜 **What kinds of pressures make you hesitant to tell others about your belief in Christ?** Jesus had performed many miracles, but most people still didn't believe in him. Likewise, many today won't believe despite all God does. Don't be discouraged if your witness for Christ doesn't turn as many to him as you'd like. Your job is to continue as a faithful witness. You are responsible, not for the decisions of others, but simply to reach out to them.

Permission to Pray for Anything

MARK 11:20-33

The next morning as they passed by the fig tree [Jesus] had cursed, the disciples noticed it was withered from the roots. ²¹Peter remembered what Jesus had said to the tree on the previous day and exclaimed, "Look, Teacher! The fig tree you cursed has withered!"

²²Then Jesus said to the disciples, "Have faith in God. ²³I assure you that you can say to this mountain, 'May God lift you up and throw you into the sea,' and your command will be obeyed. All that's required is that you really believe and do not doubt in your heart. ²⁴Listen to me! You can pray for anything, and if you believe, you will have it. ²⁵But when you are praying, first forgive anyone you are holding a grudge against, so that your Father in heaven will forgive your sins, too."

²⁷By this time they had arrived in Jerusalem again. As Jesus was walking through the Temple area, the leading priests, the teachers of religious law, and the other leaders came up to him. They demanded, ²⁸"By whose authority did you drive out the merchants from the Temple? Who gave you such authority?"

²⁹"I'll tell who gave me authority to do these things if you answer one question," Jesus replied. ³⁰"Did John's baptism come from heaven or was it merely human? Answer me!"

³¹They talked it over among themselves. "If we say it was from heaven, he will ask why we didn't believe him. ³²But do we dare say it was merely human?" For they were afraid that the people would start a riot, since everyone thought that John was a prophet. ³³So they finally replied, "We don't know."

And Jesus responded, "Then I won't answer your question either."

〰️〰️ **How bold is your prayer life?** Jesus, our example for prayer, once prayed, "Everything is possible. . . . Yet I want your will, not mine" (Mark 14:36). Often when we pray, we are motivated by our own interests and desires. We like to hear that we can have anything. But Jesus prayed with God's interests in mind. When we pray, we are to express our desires, but we should want his will above ours. Check yourself to see if your prayers are focusing on your interests or on God's.

2

Two Parables
MATTHEW 21:28-46

[The religious leaders asked Jesus,] "But what do you think about this? A man with two sons told the older boy, 'Son, go out and work in the vineyard today.' ²⁹The son answered, 'No, I won't go,' but later he changed his mind and went anyway. ³⁰Then the father told the other son, 'You go,' and he said, 'Yes, sir, I will.' But he didn't go. ³¹Which of the two was obeying his father?"

They replied, "The first, of course."

Then Jesus explained his meaning: "I assure you, corrupt tax collectors and prostitutes will get into the Kingdom of God before you do. ³²For John the Baptist came and showed you the way to life, and you didn't believe him, while tax collectors and prostitutes did. And even when you saw this happening, you refused to turn from your sins and believe him.

³³"Now listen to this story. A certain landowner planted a vineyard, built a wall around it, dug a pit for pressing out the grape juice, and built a lookout tower. Then he leased the vineyard to tenant farmers and moved to another country. ³⁴At the time of the grape harvest he sent his servants to collect his share of the crop. ³⁵But the farmers grabbed his servants, beat one, killed one, and stoned another. ³⁶So the landowner sent a larger group of his servants to collect for him, but the results were the same.

³⁷"Finally, the owner sent his son, thinking, 'Surely they will respect my son.'

³⁸"But when the farmers saw his son coming, they said to one another, 'Here comes the heir to this estate. Come on, let's kill him and get the estate for ourselves!' ³⁹So they grabbed him, took him out of the vineyard, and murdered him.

⁴⁰"When the owner of the vineyard returns," Jesus asked, "what do you think he will do to those farmers?"

⁴¹The religious leaders replied, "He will put the wicked men to a horrible death and lease the vineyard to others who will give him his share of the crop after each harvest."

⁴²Then Jesus asked them, "Didn't you ever read this in the Scriptures?

'The stone rejected by the builders
    has now become the cornerstone.
This is the Lord's doing,
    and it is marvelous to see.'

⁴³What I mean is that the Kingdom of God will be taken away from you and given to a nation that will produce the proper fruit. ⁴⁴Anyone who stumbles over that stone will be broken to pieces, and it will crush anyone on whom it falls."

⁴⁵When the leading priests and Pharisees heard Jesus, they realized he was pointing at them—that they were the farmers in his story. ⁴⁶They wanted to

arrest him, but they were afraid to try because the crowds considered Jesus to be a prophet.

~*\/*~ **Which son do you resemble most?** The son who said he would obey and then didn't represented the nation of Israel in Jesus' day. They said they wanted to do God's will, but they constantly disobeyed. It is dangerous to pretend to obey God when our heart is far from him because God knows the intentions of our heart. Our actions must match our words.

Jesus Tells about the Wedding Feasts

SEPTEMBER

3

MATTHEW 22:1-14

Jesus told them several other stories to illustrate the Kingdom. He said, ²"The Kingdom of Heaven can be illustrated by the story of a king who prepared a great wedding feast for his son. ³Many guests were invited, and when the banquet was ready, he sent his servants to notify everyone that it was time to come. But they all refused! ⁴So he sent other servants to tell them, 'The feast has been prepared, and choice meats have been cooked. Everything is ready. Hurry!'" ⁵But the guests he had invited ignored them and went about their business, one to his farm, another to his store. ⁶Others seized his messengers and treated them shamefully, even killing some of them.

⁷"Then the king became furious. He sent out his army to destroy the murderers and burn their city. ⁸And he said to his servants, 'The wedding feast is ready, and the guests I invited aren't worthy of the honor. ⁹Now go out to the street corners and invite everyone you see.'

¹⁰"So the servants brought in everyone they could find, good and bad alike, and the banquet hall was filled with guests. ¹¹But when the king came in to meet the guests, he noticed a man who wasn't wearing the proper clothes for a wedding. ¹²'Friend,' he asked, 'how is it that you are here without wedding clothes?' And the man had no reply. ¹³Then the king said to his aides, 'Bind him hand and foot and throw him out into the outer darkness, where there is weeping and gnashing of teeth.' ¹⁴For many are called, but few are chosen.'"

~*\/*~ **At what point in your life did you realize that you were invited? How did you respond?** In this culture, two invitations were expected when banquets were given. The first invitation asked the guests to attend; the second announced that all was ready. Here the king (God) invited his guests three times—and each time they refused to come. God wants us to join him at his banquet that will last for eternity. That's why he sends us invitations again and again. Have you accepted his invitation?

339

4

Jesus Answers Questions
LUKE 20:20-40

Watching for their opportunity, the leaders sent secret agents pretending to be honest men. They tried to get Jesus to say something that could be reported to the Roman governor so he would arrest Jesus. [21]They said, "Teacher, we know that you speak and teach what is right and are not influenced by what others think. You sincerely teach the ways of God. [22]Now tell us—is it right to pay taxes to the Roman government or not?"

[23]He saw through their trickery and said, [24]"Show me a Roman coin. Whose picture and title are stamped on it?"

"Caesar's," they replied.

[25]"Well then," he said, "give to Caesar what belongs to him. But everything that belongs to God must be given to God." [26]So they failed to trap him in the presence of the people. Instead, they were amazed by his answer, and they were silenced.

[27]Then some Sadducees stepped forward—a group of Jews who say there is no resurrection after death. [28]They posed this question: "Teacher, Moses gave us a law that if a man dies, leaving a wife but no children, his brother should marry the widow and have a child who will be the brother's heir. [29]Well, there were seven brothers. The oldest married and then died without children. [30]His brother married the widow, but he also died. Still no children. [31]And so it went, one after the other, until each of the seven had married her and died, leaving no children. [32]Finally, the woman died, too. [33]So tell us, whose wife will she be in the resurrection? For all seven were married to her!"

[34]Jesus replied, "Marriage is for people here on earth. [35]But that is not the way it will be in the age to come. For those worthy of being raised from the dead won't be married then. [36]And they will never die again. In these respects they are like angels. They are children of God raised up to new life. [37]But now, as to whether the dead will be raised—even Moses proved this when he wrote about the burning bush. Long after Abraham, Isaac, and Jacob had died, he referred to the Lord as 'the God of Abraham, the God of Isaac, and the God of Jacob.' [38]So he is the God of the living, not the dead. They are all alive to him."

[39]"Well said, Teacher!" remarked some of the teachers of religious law who were standing there. [40]And that ended their questions; no one dared to ask any more.

〜�办〆 **How do you really feel about living forever?** The Sadducees came to Jesus with a trick question. Not believing in the Resurrection, they wanted Jesus to say something they could refute. Even so, Jesus did not ignore or belittle their question. He answered it and then went beyond it to the real issue. When people ask you tough religious questions, such as "How can a loving God allow people to starve?" or, "If God knows what I'm going to do, do I have any free choice?" follow Jesus' example. First answer the question to the best of your ability; then look for the real issue—hurt over a personal tragedy, for example, or difficulty in making a decision. Often the spoken question is only a test, not of your ability to answer hard questions, but of your willingness to listen and care.

Questions Given and Taken

MARK 12:28-37

One of the teachers of religious law was standing there listening to the discussion. He realized that Jesus had answered well, so he asked, "Of all the commandments, which is the most important?"

²⁹Jesus replied, "The most important commandment is this: 'Hear, O Israel! The Lord our God is the one and only Lord. ³⁰And you must love the Lord your God with all your heart, all your soul, all your mind, and all your strength.' ³¹The second is equally important: 'Love your neighbor as yourself.' No other commandment is greater than these."

³²The teacher of religious law replied, "Well said, Teacher. You have spoken the truth by saying that there is only one God and no other. ³³And I know it is important to love him with all my heart and all my understanding and all my strength, and to love my neighbors as myself. This is more important than to offer all of the burnt offerings and sacrifices required in the law."

³⁴Realizing this man's understanding, Jesus said to him, "You are not far from the Kingdom of God." And after that, no one dared to ask him any more questions.

³⁵Later, as Jesus was teaching the people in the Temple, he asked, "Why do the teachers of religious law claim that the Messiah will be the son of David? ³⁶For David himself, speaking under the inspiration of the Holy Spirit, said,

'The LORD said to my Lord,
Sit in honor at my right hand
until I humble your enemies beneath your feet.'

³⁷Since David himself called him Lord, how can he be his son at the same time?" And the crowd listened to him with great interest.

〰〰 Whom do you know who is not far from the Kingdom of God?
God's laws are not burdensome in number or detail. They can be reduced to two simple rules for life: love God, and love others. These commands are from the Old Testament (Lev. 19:18; Deut. 6:5). When you love God completely and

care for others as you care for yourself, then you have fulfilled the intent of the Ten Commandments and the other Old Testament laws. According to Jesus, these two rules summarize all of God's laws. Let them rule your thoughts, decisions, and actions. When you are uncertain about what to do, ask yourself which course of action best demonstrates love for God and love for others.

6

Jesus: Warnings and Grieving

MATTHEW 23:1-39

Then Jesus said to the crowds and to his disciples, [2]"The teachers of religious law and the Pharisees are the official interpreters of the Scriptures. [3]So practice and obey whatever they say to you, but don't follow their example. For they don't practice what they teach. [4]They crush you with impossible religious demands and never lift a finger to help ease the burden.

[5]"Everything they do is for show. On their arms they wear extra wide prayer boxes with Scripture verses inside, and they wear extra long tassels on their robes. [6]And how they love to sit at the head table at banquets and in the most prominent seats in the synagogue! [7]They enjoy the attention they get on the streets, and they enjoy being called 'Rabbi.' [8]Don't ever let anyone call you 'Rabbi,' for you have only one teacher, and all of you are on the same level as brothers and sisters. [9]And don't address anyone here on earth as 'Father,' for only God in heaven is your spiritual Father. [10]And don't let anyone call you 'Master,' for there is only one master, the Messiah. [11]The greatest among you must be a servant. [12]But those who exalt themselves will be humbled, and those who humble themselves will be exalted.

[13]"How terrible it will be for you teachers of religious law and you Pharisees. Hypocrites! For you won't let others enter the Kingdom of Heaven, and you won't go in yourselves. [15]Yes, how terrible it will be for you teachers of religious law and you Pharisees. For you cross land and sea to make one convert, and then you turn him into twice the son of hell as you yourselves are.

[16]"Blind guides! How terrible it will be for you! For you say that it means nothing to swear 'by God's Temple'—you can break that oath. But then you say that it is binding to swear 'by the gold in the Temple.' [17]Blind fools! Which is greater, the gold, or the Temple that makes the gold sacred? [18]And you say that to take an oath 'by the altar' can be broken, but to swear 'by the gifts on the altar' is binding! [19]How blind! For which is greater, the gift on the altar, or the altar that makes the gift sacred? [20]When you swear 'by the altar,' you are swearing by it and by everything on it. [21]And when you swear 'by the Temple,' you are swearing by it and by God, who lives in it. [22]And when you swear 'by heaven,' you are swearing by the throne of God and by God, who sits on the throne.

[23]"How terrible it will be for you teachers of religious law and you Phari-

sees. Hypocrites! For you are careful to tithe even the tiniest part of your income, but you ignore the important things of the law—justice, mercy, and faith. You should tithe, yes, but you should not leave undone the more important things. ²⁴Blind guides! You strain your water so you won't accidentally swallow a gnat; then you swallow a camel!

²⁵"How terrible it will be for you teachers of religious law and you Pharisees. Hypocrites! You are so careful to clean the outside of the cup and the dish, but inside you are filthy—full of greed and self-indulgence! ²⁶Blind Pharisees! First wash the inside of the cup, and then the outside will become clean, too.

²⁷"How terrible it will be for you teachers of religious law and you Pharisees. Hypocrites! You are like whitewashed tombs—beautiful on the outside but filled on the inside with dead people's bones and all sorts of impurity. ²⁸You try to look like upright people outwardly, but inside your hearts are filled with hypocrisy and lawlessness.

²⁹"How terrible it will be for you teachers of religious law and you Pharisees. Hypocrites! For you build tombs for the prophets your ancestors killed and decorate the graves of the godly people your ancestors destroyed. ³⁰Then you say, 'We never would have joined them in killing the prophets.'

³¹"In saying that, you are accusing yourselves of being the descendants of those who murdered the prophets. ³²Go ahead. Finish what they started. ³³Snakes! Sons of vipers! How will you escape the judgment of hell? ³⁴I will send you prophets and wise men and teachers of religious law. You will kill some by crucifixion and whip others in your synagogues, chasing them from city to city. ³⁵As a result, you will become guilty of murdering all the godly people from righteous Abel to Zechariah son of Barachiah, whom you murdered in the Temple between the altar and the sanctuary. ³⁶I assure you, all the accumulated judgment of the centuries will break upon the heads of this very generation.

³⁷"O Jerusalem, Jerusalem, the city that kills the prophets and stones God's messengers! How often I have wanted to gather your children together as a hen protects her chicks beneath her wings, but you wouldn't let me. ³⁸And now look, your house is left to you, empty and desolate. ³⁹For I tell you this, you will never see me again until you say, 'Bless the one who comes in the name of the Lord!' "

〰〰 **Which of these seven warnings most directly relate to your life?** Jesus condemned the Pharisees and religious leaders for appearing saintly and holy but remaining full of corruption and greed on the inside. Living our Christianity merely as a show for others is like washing a cup on the outside only. When we are clean on the inside, our cleanliness on the outside won't be phony.

7

Jesus Talks about
the Future
LUKE 21:1-24

While Jesus was in the Temple, he watched the rich people putting their gifts into the collection box. [2]Then a poor widow came by and dropped in two pennies. [3]"I assure you," he said, "this poor widow has given more than all the rest of them. [4]For they have given a tiny part of their surplus, but she, poor as she is, has given everything she has."

[5]Some of his disciples began talking about the beautiful stonework of the Temple and the memorial decorations on the walls. But Jesus said, [6]"The time is coming when all these things will be so completely demolished that not one stone will be left on top of another."

[7]"Teacher," they asked, "when will all this take place? And will there be any sign ahead of time?"

[8]He replied, "Don't let anyone mislead you. For many will come in my name, claiming to be the Messiah and saying, 'The time has come!' But don't believe them. [9]And when you hear of wars and insurrections, don't panic. Yes, these things must come, but the end won't follow immediately." [10]Then he added, "Nations and kingdoms will proclaim war against each other. [11]There will be great earthquakes, and there will be famines and epidemics in many lands, and there will be terrifying things and great miraculous signs in the heavens.

[12]"But before all this occurs, there will be a time of great persecution. You will be dragged into synagogues and prisons, and you will be accused before kings and governors of being my followers. [13]This will be your opportunity to tell them about me. [14]So don't worry about how to answer the charges against you, [15]for I will give you the right words and such wisdom that none of your opponents will be able to reply! [16]Even those closest to you—your parents, brothers, relatives, and friends—will betray you. And some of you will be killed. [17]And everyone will hate you because of your allegiance to me. [18]But not a hair of your head will perish! [19]By standing firm, you will win your souls.

[20]"And when you see Jerusalem surrounded by armies, then you will know that the time of its destruction has arrived. [21]Then those in Judea must flee to the hills. Let those in Jerusalem escape, and those outside the city should not enter it for shelter. [22]For those will be days of God's vengeance, and the prophetic words of the Scriptures will be fulfilled. [23]How terrible it will be for pregnant women and for mothers nursing their babies. For there will be great distress in the land and wrath upon this people. [24]They will be brutally killed by the sword or sent away as captives to all the nations of the world. And Jerusalem will be conquered and trampled down by the Gentiles until the age of the Gentiles comes to an end."

〜〜 **What do your giving habits say about your level of trust in God?**
This widow gave all she had to live on, in contrast to the way most of us handle
our money. When we consider giving a certain percentage of our income as a
great accomplishment, we resemble those who gave out of their abundance.
Here, Jesus was admiring generous and sacrificial giving. As believers, we
should consider increasing our giving—whether money, time, or talents—to a
point beyond convenience or safety.

Jesus on Being Prepared

LUKE 21:25-38

[Jesus said,] "And there will be strange events in the skies—signs in the sun,
moon, and stars. And down here on earth the nations will be in turmoil,
perplexed by the roaring seas and strange tides. ^{26}The courage of many
people will falter because of the fearful fate they see coming upon the earth,
because the stability of the very heavens will be broken up. ^{27}Then everyone
will see the Son of Man arrive on the clouds with power and great glory.
^{28}So when all these things begin to happen, stand straight and look up, for
your salvation is near!"

^{29}Then he gave them this illustration: "Notice the fig tree, or any other
tree. ^{30}When the leaves come out, you know without being told that summer is near. ^{31}Just so, when you see the events I've described taking place,
you can be sure that the Kingdom of God is near. ^{32}I assure you, this generation will not pass from the scene until all these events have taken place.
^{33}Heaven and earth will disappear, but my words will remain forever.

^{34}"Watch out! Don't let me find you living in careless ease and drunkenness, and filled with the worries of this life. Don't let that day catch you
unaware, ^{35}as in a trap. For that day will come upon everyone living on the
earth. ^{36}Keep a constant watch. And pray that, if possible, you may escape
these horrors and stand before the Son of Man."

^{37}Every day Jesus went to the Temple to teach, and each evening he
returned to spend the night on the Mount of Olives. ^{38}The crowds gathered
early each morning to hear him.

〜〜 **What does your schedule today say about your watchfulness?**
Jesus told the disciples to keep a constant watch for his return. Although nearly
two thousand years have passed since he spoke these words, their truth
remains: Christ is coming again, and we need to watch and be spiritually fit.
This means working faithfully at the tasks God has given us. Don't let your mind
and spirit be dulled by careless living, drinking, or the foolish pursuit of pleasure. Don't let life's anxieties overburden you. Instead, be ready to move at
God's command.

Parables about Being Prepared

MATTHEW 25:1-30

[Jesus said,] "The Kingdom of Heaven can be illustrated by the story of ten bridesmaids who took their lamps and went to meet the bridegroom. ²Five of them were foolish, and five were wise. ³The five who were foolish took no oil for their lamps, ⁴but the other five were wise enough to take along extra oil. ⁵When the bridegroom was delayed, they all lay down and slept. ⁶At midnight they were roused by the shout, 'Look, the bridegroom is coming! Come out and welcome him!'

⁷"All the bridesmaids got up and prepared their lamps. ⁸Then the five foolish ones asked the others, 'Please give us some of your oil because our lamps are going out.' ⁹But the others replied, 'We don't have enough for all of us. Go to a shop and buy some for yourselves.'

¹⁰"But while they were gone to buy oil, the bridegroom came, and those who were ready went in with him to the marriage feast, and the door was locked. ¹¹Later, when the other five bridesmaids returned, they stood outside, calling, 'Sir, open the door for us!' ¹²But he called back, 'I don't know you!'

¹³"So stay awake and be prepared, because you do not know the day or hour of my return.

¹⁴"Again, the Kingdom of Heaven can be illustrated by the story of a man going on a trip. He called together his servants and gave them money to invest for him while he was gone. ¹⁵He gave five bags of gold to one, two bags of gold to another, and one bag of gold to the last—dividing it in proportion to their abilities—and then left on his trip. ¹⁶The servant who received the five bags of gold began immediately to invest the money and soon doubled it. ¹⁷The servant with two bags of gold also went right to work and doubled the money. ¹⁸But the servant who received the one bag of gold dug a hole in the ground and hid the master's money for safekeeping.

¹⁹"After a long time their master returned from his trip and called them to give an account of how they had used his money. ²⁰The servant to whom he had entrusted the five bags of gold said, 'Sir, you gave me five bags of gold to invest, and I have doubled the amount.' ²¹The master was full of praise. 'Well done, my good and faithful servant. You have been faithful in handling this small amount, so now I will give you many more responsibilities. Let's celebrate together!'

²²"Next came the servant who had received the two bags of gold, with the report, 'Sir, you gave me two bags of gold to invest, and I have doubled the amount.' ²³The master said, 'Well done, my good and faithful servant. You have been faithful in handling this small amount, so now I will give you many more responsibilities. Let's celebrate together!'

²⁴"Then the servant with the one bag of gold came and said, 'Sir, I know you are a hard man, harvesting crops you didn't plant and gathering crops

you didn't cultivate. ²⁵I was afraid I would lose your money, so I hid it in the earth and here it is.'

²⁶"But the master replied, 'You wicked and lazy servant! You think I'm a hard man, do you, harvesting crops I didn't plant and gathering crops I didn't cultivate? ²⁷Well, you should at least have put my money into the bank so I could have some interest. ²⁸Take the money from this servant and give it to the one with the ten bags of gold. ²⁹To those who use well what they are given, even more will be given, and they will have an abundance. But from those who are unfaithful, even what little they have will be taken away. ³⁰Now throw this useless servant into outer darkness, where there will be weeping and gnashing of teeth.' "

⁓⋏⋎⊱ **With which of the people in these two stories do you identify most?** These parables describe the consequences of two attitudes to Christ's return. The person who diligently prepares for it by investing his or her time and talent to serve God will be rewarded. The person who has no heart for the work of the Kingdom will be punished. God rewards faithfulness. Those who bear no fruit for God's Kingdom cannot expect to be treated the same as those who are faithful.

Jesus on the Final Judgment

MATTHEW 25:31-46

[Jesus said,] "But when the Son of Man comes in his glory, and all the angels with him, then he will sit upon his glorious throne. ³²All the nations will be gathered in his presence, and he will separate them as a shepherd separates the sheep from the goats. ³³He will place the sheep at his right hand and the goats at his left. ³⁴Then the King will say to those on the right, 'Come, you who are blessed by my Father, inherit the Kingdom prepared for you from the foundation of the world. ³⁵For I was hungry, and you fed me. I was thirsty, and you gave me a drink. I was a stranger, and you invited me into your home. ³⁶I was naked, and you gave me clothing. I was sick, and you cared for me. I was in prison, and you visited me.'

³⁷"Then these righteous ones will reply, 'Lord, when did we ever see you hungry and feed you? Or thirsty and give you something to drink? ³⁸Or a stranger and show you hospitality? Or naked and give you clothing? ³⁹When did we ever see you sick or in prison, and visit you?' ⁴⁰And the King will tell them, 'I assure you, when you did it to one of the least of these my brothers and sisters, you were doing it to me!'

⁴¹"Then the King will turn to those on the left and say, 'Away with you, you cursed ones, into the eternal fire prepared for the Devil and his demons! ⁴²For I was hungry, and you didn't feed me. I was thirsty, and you

didn't give me anything to drink. ⁴³I was a stranger, and you didn't invite me into your home. I was naked, and you gave me no clothing. I was sick and in prison, and you didn't visit me.'

⁴⁴"Then they will reply, 'Lord, when did we ever see you hungry or thirsty or a stranger or naked or sick or in prison, and not help you?' ⁴⁵And he will answer, 'I assure you, when you refused to help the least of these my brothers and sisters, you were refusing to help me.' ⁴⁶And they will go away into eternal punishment, but the righteous will go into eternal life."

 Are you treating the people in your life in ways you would treat Christ? God will separate his obedient followers from pretenders and unbelievers. The real evidence of our belief is the way we act. To treat all persons we encounter as if they were Jesus is no easy task. What we do for others demonstrates what we really think about Jesus' words to us—feed the hungry, give the homeless a place to stay, visit the sick. How well do your actions separate you from pretenders and unbelievers?

11

SEPTEMBER

Preparing the Last Supper
LUKE 22:1-13

The Festival of Unleavened Bread, which begins with the Passover celebration, was drawing near. ²The leading priests and teachers of religious law were actively plotting Jesus' murder. But they wanted to kill him without starting a riot, a possibility they greatly feared.

³Then Satan entered into Judas Iscariot, who was one of the twelve disciples, ⁴and he went over to the leading priests and captains of the Temple guard to discuss the best way to betray Jesus to them. ⁵They were delighted that he was ready to help them, and they promised him a reward. ⁶So he began looking for an opportunity to betray Jesus so they could arrest him quietly when the crowds weren't around.

⁷Now the Festival of Unleavened Bread arrived, when the Passover lambs were sacrificed. ⁸Jesus sent Peter and John ahead and said, "Go and prepare the Passover meal, so we can eat it together."

⁹"Where do you want us to go?" they asked him.

¹⁰He replied, "As soon as you enter Jerusalem, a man carrying a pitcher of water will meet you. Follow him. At the house he enters, ¹¹say to the owner, 'The Teacher asks, Where is the guest room where I can eat the Passover meal with my disciples?' ¹²He will take you upstairs to a large room that is already set up. That is the place. Go ahead and prepare our supper there."

¹³They went off to the city and found everything just as Jesus had said, and they prepared the Passover supper there.

Satan's part in
the betrayal of Jesus does not remove any of the responsibility from Judas.
Disillusioned because Jesus was talking about dying rather than about setting
up his Kingdom, Judas may have been trying to force Jesus' hand and make
him use his power to prove he was the Messiah. Or perhaps Judas, not understanding Jesus' mission, no longer believed that Jesus was God's chosen one.
Whatever Judas thought, Satan assumed that Jesus' death would end Jesus'
mission and thwart God's plan. Like Judas, he did not know that Jesus' death
and resurrection were the most important parts of God's plan all along. Jesus
gave the ultimate sacrifice for you. The next time you take Communion at
church, remember what Jesus did on the cross for you.

Jesus Washes His Disciples' Feet

SEPTEMBER

12

JOHN 13:1-20

Before the Passover celebration, Jesus knew that his hour had come to leave
this world and return to his Father. He now showed the disciples the full
extent of his love. [2]It was time for supper, and the Devil had already enticed
Judas, son of Simon Iscariot, to carry out his plan to betray Jesus. [3]Jesus
knew that the Father had given him authority over everything and that he
had come from God and would return to God. [4]So he got up from the table,
took off his robe, wrapped a towel around his waist, [5]and poured water into
a basin. Then he began to wash the disciples' feet and to wipe them with the
towel he had around him.

[6]When he came to Simon Peter, Peter said to him, "Lord, why are you
going to wash my feet?"

[7]Jesus replied, "You don't understand now why I am doing it; someday
you will."

[8]"No," Peter protested, "you will never wash my feet!"

Jesus replied, "But if I don't wash you, you won't belong to me."

[9]Simon Peter exclaimed, "Then wash my hands and head as well, Lord,
not just my feet!"

[10]Jesus replied, "A person who has bathed all over does not need to wash,
except for the feet, to be entirely clean. And you are clean, but that isn't true
of everyone here." [11]For Jesus knew who would betray him. That is what he
meant when he said, "Not all of you are clean."

[12]After washing their feet, he put on his robe again and sat down and
asked, "Do you understand what I was doing? [13]You call me 'Teacher' and
'Lord,' and you are right, because it is true. [14]And since I, the Lord and
Teacher, have washed your feet, you ought to wash each other's feet. [15]I have
given you an example to follow. Do as I have done to you. [16]How true it is
that a servant is not greater than the master. Nor are messengers more

important than the one who sends them. [17]You know these things—now do them! That is the path of blessing.

[18]"I am not saying these things to all of you; I know so well each one of you I chose. The Scriptures declare, 'The one who shares my food has turned against me,' and this will soon come true. [19]I tell you this now, so that when it happens you will believe I am the Messiah. [20]Truly, anyone who welcomes my messenger is welcoming me, and anyone who welcomes me is welcoming the Father who sent me."

〰〰 **What is the greatest service someone has done for you? How do you serve others?** Jesus was the model servant, and he showed this attitude to his disciples. Washing guests' feet was a job for a household servant when guests arrived. But Jesus wrapped a towel around him, as the lowliest slave would do, and washed his disciples' feet. If even he, God in the flesh, was willing to serve, we, his followers, must also be servants, willing to serve in any way in order to glorify God. Are you willing to follow Christ's example of serving? Whom can you serve today?

13 SEPTEMBER

A Sad Prediction
JOHN 13:21-38

Now Jesus was in great anguish of spirit, and he exclaimed, "The truth is, one of you will betray me!"

[22]The disciples looked at each other, wondering whom he could mean. [23]One of Jesus' disciples, the one Jesus loved, was sitting next to Jesus at the table. [24]Simon Peter motioned to him to ask who would do this terrible thing. [25]Leaning toward Jesus, he asked, "Lord, who is it?"

[26]Jesus said, "It is the one to whom I give the bread dipped in the sauce." And when he had dipped it, he gave it to Judas, son of Simon Iscariot. [27]As soon as Judas had eaten the bread, Satan entered into him. Then Jesus told him, "Hurry. Do it now." [28]None of the others at the table knew what Jesus meant. [29]Since Judas was their treasurer, some thought Jesus was telling him to go and pay for the food or to give some money to the poor. [30]So Judas left at once, going out into the night.

[31]As soon as Judas left the room, Jesus said, "The time has come for me, the Son of Man, to enter into my glory, and God will receive glory because of all that happens to me. [32]And God will bring me into my glory very soon. [33]Dear children, how brief are these moments before I must go away and leave you! Then, though you search for me, you cannot come to me—just as I told the Jewish leaders. [34]So now I am giving you a new commandment: Love each other. Just as I have loved you, you should love each other. [35]Your love for one another will prove to the world that you are my disciples."

[36]Simon Peter said, "Lord, where are you going?"

And Jesus replied, "You can't go with me now, but you will follow me later."

[37]"But why can't I come now, Lord?" he asked. "I am ready to die for you."

[38]Jesus answered, "Die for me? No, before the rooster crows tomorrow morning, you will deny three times that you even know me."

〰〰 **How well do you feel Christ knows you?** John describes these few moments in clear detail. We can see that Jesus knew exactly what was going to happen. He knew about Judas and about Peter, but he did not change the situation, nor did he stop loving them. In the same way, Jesus knows exactly what you will do to hurt him. Yet he still loves you unconditionally and will forgive you whenever you ask. Judas couldn't understand this, and his life ended tragically. Peter understood, and, despite his shortcomings, his life ended triumphantly because he never let go of his faith in the one who loved him.

SEPTEMBER **14**

Jesus Is the Way
JOHN 14:1-14

[Jesus said,] "Don't be troubled. You trust God, now trust in me. [2]There are many rooms in my Father's home, and I am going to prepare a place for you. If this were not so, I would tell you plainly. [3]When everything is ready, I will come and get you, so that you will always be with me where I am. [4]And you know where I am going and how to get there."

[5]"No, we don't know, Lord," Thomas said. "We haven't any idea where you are going, so how can we know the way?"

[6]Jesus told him, "I am the way, the truth, and the life. No one can come to the Father except through me. [7]If you had known who I am, then you would have known who my Father is. From now on you know him and have seen him!"

[8]Philip said, "Lord, show us the Father and we will be satisfied."

[9]Jesus replied, "Philip, don't you even yet know who I am, even after all the time I have been with you? Anyone who has seen me has seen the Father! So why are you asking to see him? [10]Don't you believe that I am in the Father and the Father is in me? The words I say are not my own, but my Father who lives in me does his work through me. [11]Just believe that I am in the Father and the Father is in me. Or at least believe because of what you have seen me do.

[12]"The truth is, anyone who believes in me will do the same works I have done, and even greater works, because I am going to be with the Father. [13]You can ask for anything in my name, and I will do it, because the work of the Son brings glory to the Father. [14]Yes, ask anything in my name, and I will do it!"

How would you rate your present level of understanding of Christ and his teachings? Jesus says he is the *only* way to God the Father. Some people may argue that this is too narrow. In reality, it is wide enough for the whole world if the world chooses to accept it. Instead of worrying about how limited it sounds to have only one way, we should be saying, "Thank you, God, for providing a sure way to get to you!"

15

SEPTEMBER

Jesus Promises the Comforter

JOHN 14:15-31

[Jesus said,] "If you love me, obey my commandments. [16]And I will ask the Father, and he will give you another Counselor, who will never leave you. [17]He is the Holy Spirit, who leads into all truth. The world at large cannot receive him, because it isn't looking for him and doesn't recognize him. But you do, because he lives with you now and later will be in you. [18]No, I will not abandon you as orphans—I will come to you. [19]In just a little while the world will not see me again, but you will. For I will live again, and you will, too. [20]When I am raised to life again, you will know that I am in my Father, and you are in me, and I am in you. [21]Those who obey my commandments are the ones who love me. And because they love me, my Father will love them, and I will love them. And I will reveal myself to each one of them."

[22]Judas (not Judas Iscariot, but the other disciple with that name) said to him, "Lord, why are you going to reveal yourself only to us and not to the world at large?"

[23]Jesus replied, "All those who love me will do what I say. My Father will love them, and we will come to them and live with them. [24]Anyone who doesn't love me will not do what I say. And remember, my words are not my own. This message is from the Father who sent me. [25]I am telling you these things now while I am still with you. [26]But when the Father sends the Counselor as my representative—and by the Counselor I mean the Holy Spirit—he will teach you everything and will remind you of everything I myself have told you.

[27]"I am leaving you with a gift—peace of mind and heart. And the peace I give isn't like the peace the world gives. So don't be troubled or afraid. [28]Remember what I told you: I am going away, but I will come back to you again. If you really love me, you will be very happy for me, because now I can go to the Father, who is greater than I am. [29]I have told you these things before they happen so that you will believe when they do happen.

[30]"I don't have much more time to talk to you, because the prince of this world approaches. He has no power over me, [31]but I will do what the Father requires of me, so that the world will know that I love the Father. Come, let's be going."

_≈ᶰ/∿_ **How have you experienced the Comforter?** The end result of the Holy Spirit's work in our life is deep and lasting peace. Unlike worldly peace, which is usually defined as the absence of conflict, this peace is confident assurance in any circumstance; with Christ's peace, we have no need to fear the present or the future. If your life is full of stress, allow the Holy Spirit to fill you with Christ's peace.

Jesus on the Vine and the Branches

SEPTEMBER

16

JOHN 15:1-16

[Jesus said,] "I am the true vine, and my Father is the gardener. ²He cuts off every branch that doesn't produce fruit, and he prunes the branches that do bear fruit so they will produce even more. ³You have already been pruned for greater fruitfulness by the message I have given you. ⁴Remain in me, and I will remain in you. For a branch cannot produce fruit if it is severed from the vine, and you cannot be fruitful apart from me.

⁵"Yes, I am the vine, you are the branches. Those who remain in me, and I in them, will produce much fruit. For apart from me you can do nothing. ⁶Anyone who parts from me is thrown away like a useless branch and withers. Such branches are gathered into a pile to be burned. ⁷But if you stay joined to me and my words remain in you, you may ask any request you like, and it will be granted! ⁸My true disciples produce much fruit. This brings great glory to my Father.

⁹"I have loved you even as the Father has loved me. Remain in my love. ¹⁰When you obey me, you remain in my love, just as I obey my Father and remain in his love. ¹¹I have told you this so that you will be filled with my joy. Yes, your joy will overflow! ¹²I command you to love each other in the same way that I love you. ¹³And here is how to measure it—the greatest love is shown when people lay down their lives for their friends. ¹⁴You are my friends if you obey me. ¹⁵I no longer call you servants, because a master doesn't confide in his servants. Now you are my friends, since I have told you everything the Father told me. ¹⁶You didn't choose me. I chose you. I appointed you to go and produce fruit that will last, so that the Father will give you whatever you ask for, using my name."

_≈ᶰ/∿_ **What kind of fruit has the Gardener produced in you?** Many people try to be good, honest people who do what is right. But Jesus says that the only way to live a truly good life is to stay close to him, like a branch attached to the vine. Apart from Christ our efforts are unfruitful. Are you receiving the nourishment and life offered by Christ, the Vine? If not, you are missing a special gift he has for you.

17

SEPTEMBER

Jesus Warns about
Troubles
JOHN 15:17–16:4

[Jesus said,] "I command you to love each other.
¹⁸"When the world hates you, remember it hated me before it hated you.
¹⁹The world would love you if you belonged to it, but you don't. I chose you
to come out of the world, and so it hates you. ²⁰Do you remember what I
told you? 'A servant is not greater than the master.' Since they persecuted
me, naturally they will persecute you. And if they had listened to me, they
would listen to you! ²¹The people of the world will hate you because you
belong to me, for they don't know God who sent me. ²²They would not be
guilty if I had not come and spoken to them. But now they have no excuse
for their sin. ²³Anyone who hates me hates my Father, too. ²⁴If I hadn't done
such miraculous signs among them that no one else could do, they would
not be counted guilty. But as it is, they saw all that I did and yet hated both
of us—me and my Father. ²⁵This has fulfilled what the Scriptures said:
'They hated me without cause.'

²⁶"But I will send you the Counselor—the Spirit of truth. He will come to
you from the Father and will tell you all about me. ²⁷And you must also tell
others about me because you have been with me from the beginning.

¹⁶:¹"I have told you these things so that you won't fall away. ²For you will
be expelled from the synagogues, and the time is coming when those who
kill you will think they are doing God a service. ³This is because they have
never known the Father or me. ⁴Yes, I'm telling you these things now, so
that when they happen, you will remember I warned you. I didn't tell you
earlier because I was going to be with you for a while longer."

� **What have you learned recently about loving others?** Christians
will get plenty of hatred from the world; from each other we need love and support. Do you allow small problems to get in the way of loving other believers?
Jesus commands that you love them, and he will give you the strength to do it.

18

SEPTEMBER

Jesus on the Holy Spirit
and Prayers
JOHN 16:5-33

[Jesus said,] "But now I am going away to the one who sent me, and none
of you has asked me where I am going. ⁶Instead, you are very sad. ⁷But it is
actually best for you that I go away, because if I don't, the Counselor won't
come. If I do go away, he will come because I will send him to you. ⁸And
when he comes, he will convince the world of its sin, and of God's righteousness, and of the coming judgment. ⁹The world's sin is unbelief in me.

¹⁰Righteousness is available because I go to the Father, and you will see me no more. ¹¹Judgment will come because the prince of this world has already been judged.

¹²"Oh, there is so much more I want to tell you, but you can't bear it now. ¹³When the Spirit of truth comes, he will guide you into all truth. He will not be presenting his own ideas; he will be telling you what he has heard. He will tell you about the future. ¹⁴He will bring me glory by revealing to you whatever he receives from me. ¹⁵All that the Father has is mine; this is what I mean when I say that the Spirit will reveal to you whatever he receives from me.

¹⁶"In just a little while I will be gone, and you won't see me anymore. Then, just a little while after that, you will see me again."

¹⁷The disciples asked each other, "What does he mean when he says, 'You won't see me, and then you will see me'? And what does he mean when he says, 'I am going to the Father'? ¹⁸And what does he mean by 'a little while'? We don't understand."

¹⁹Jesus realized they wanted to ask him, so he said, "Are you asking yourselves what I meant? I said in just a little while I will be gone, and you won't see me anymore. Then, just a little while after that, you will see me again. ²⁰Truly, you will weep and mourn over what is going to happen to me, but the world will rejoice. You will grieve, but your grief will suddenly turn to wonderful joy when you see me again. ²¹It will be like a woman experiencing the pains of labor. When her child is born, her anguish gives place to joy because she has brought a new person into the world. ²²You have sorrow now, but I will see you again; then you will rejoice, and no one can rob you of that joy. ²³At that time you won't need to ask me for anything. The truth is, you can go directly to the Father and ask him, and he will grant your request because you use my name. ²⁴You haven't done this before. Ask, using my name, and you will receive, and you will have abundant joy.

²⁵"I have spoken of these matters in parables, but the time will come when this will not be necessary, and I will tell you plainly all about the Father. ²⁶Then you will ask in my name. I'm not saying I will ask the Father on your behalf, ²⁷for the Father himself loves you dearly because you love me and believe that I came from God. ²⁸Yes, I came from the Father into the world, and I will leave the world and return to the Father."

²⁹Then his disciples said, "At last you are speaking plainly and not in parables. ³⁰Now we understand that you know everything and don't need anyone to tell you anything. From this we believe that you came from God."

³¹Jesus asked, "Do you finally believe? ³²But the time is coming—in fact, it is already here—when you will be scattered, each one going his own way, leaving me alone. Yet I am not alone because the Father is with me. ³³I have told you all this so that you may have peace in me. Here on earth you will have many trials and sorrows. But take heart, because I have overcome the world."

〰️〰️ **Which of these verses give you peace of heart and mind?**
What a contrast between the disciples and the world! The world rejoiced as the disciples wept, but the disciples would see Jesus again (in three days) and rejoice. The world's values are often the opposite of God's values. This can cause Christians to feel like misfits. But even if life is difficult now, one day we will rejoice. Keep your eye on the future and on God's promises!

SEPTEMBER

Jesus Prays
JOHN 17:1-26

When Jesus had finished saying all these things, he looked up to heaven and said, "Father, the time has come. Glorify your Son so he can give glory back to you. ²For you have given him authority over everyone in all the earth. He gives eternal life to each one you have given him. ³And this is the way to have eternal life—to know you, the only true God, and Jesus Christ, the one you sent to earth. ⁴I brought glory to you here on earth by doing everything you told me to do. ⁵And now, Father, bring me into the glory we shared before the world began.

⁶"I have told these men about you. They were in the world, but then you gave them to me. Actually, they were always yours, and you gave them to me; and they have kept your word. ⁷Now they know that everything I have is a gift from you, ⁸for I have passed on to them the words you gave me; and they accepted them and know that I came from you, and they believe you sent me.

⁹"My prayer is not for the world, but for those you have given me, because they belong to you. ¹⁰And all of them, since they are mine, belong to you; and you have given them back to me, so they are my glory! ¹¹Now I am departing the world; I am leaving them behind and coming to you. Holy Father, keep them and care for them—all those you have given me— so that they will be united just as we are. ¹²During my time here, I have kept them safe. I guarded them so that not one was lost, except the one headed for destruction, as the Scriptures foretold.

¹³"And now I am coming to you. I have told them many things while I was with them so they would be filled with my joy. ¹⁴I have given them your word. And the world hates them because they do not belong to the world, just as I do not. ¹⁵I'm not asking you to take them out of the world, but to keep them safe from the evil one. ¹⁶They are not part of this world any more than I am. ¹⁷Make them pure and holy by teaching them your words of truth. ¹⁸As you sent me into the world, I am sending them into the world. ¹⁹And I give myself entirely to you so they also might be entirely yours.

²⁰"I am praying not only for these disciples but also for all who will ever believe in me because of their testimony. ²¹My prayer for all of them is that they will be one, just as you and I are one, Father—that just as you are in

me and I am in you, so they will be in us, and the world will believe you sent me. ²²"I have given them the glory you gave me, so that they may be one, as we are—²³I in them and you in me, all being perfected into one. Then the world will know that you sent me and will understand that you love them as much as you love me. ²⁴Father, I want these whom you've given me to be with me, so they can see my glory. You gave me the glory because you loved me even before the world began!

²⁵"O righteous Father, the world doesn't know you, but I do; and these disciples know you sent me. ²⁶And I have revealed you to them and will keep on revealing you. I will do this so that your love for me may be in them and I in them."

〰️ **Where do you find yourself in this prayer?** Jesus didn't ask God to take believers *out* of the world but instead to use them *in* the world. Because Jesus sends us into the world, we should not try to escape from the world or avoid all relationships with non-Christians. We are called to be salt and light (Matt. 5:13-16), and we are to do the work God sent us to do.

SEPTEMBER **20**

A Repeated Prediction
MARK 14:26-52

Then [Jesus and the disciples] sang a hymn and went out to the Mount of Olives. ²⁷"All of you will desert me," Jesus told them. "For the Scriptures say,

> 'God will strike the Shepherd,
>   and the sheep will be scattered.'

²⁸But after I am raised from the dead, I will go ahead of you to Galilee and meet you there."

²⁹Peter said to him, "Even if everyone else deserts you, I never will."

³⁰"Peter," Jesus replied, "the truth is, this very night, before the rooster crows twice, you will deny me three times."

³¹"No!" Peter insisted. "Not even if I have to die with you! I will never deny you!" And all the others vowed the same.

³²And they came to an olive grove called Gethsemane, and Jesus said, "Sit here while I go and pray." ³³He took Peter, James, and John with him, and he began to be filled with horror and deep distress. ³⁴He told them, "My soul is crushed with grief to the point of death. Stay here and watch with me."

³⁵He went on a little farther and fell face down on the ground. He prayed that, if it were possible, the awful hour awaiting him might pass him by. ³⁶"Abba, Father," he said, "everything is possible for you. Please take this cup of suffering away from me. Yet I want your will, not mine."

37Then he returned and found the disciples asleep. "Simon!" he said to Peter. "Are you asleep? Couldn't you stay awake and watch with me even one hour? 38Keep alert and pray. Otherwise temptation will overpower you. For though the spirit is willing enough, the body is weak."

39Then Jesus left them again and prayed, repeating his pleadings. 40Again he returned to them and found them sleeping, for they just couldn't keep their eyes open. And they didn't know what to say.

41When he returned to them the third time, he said, "Still sleeping? Still resting? Enough! The time has come. I, the Son of Man, am betrayed into the hands of sinners. 42Up, let's be going. See, my betrayer is here!"

43And immediately, as he said this, Judas, one of the twelve disciples, arrived with a mob that was armed with swords and clubs. They had been sent out by the leading priests, the teachers of religious law, and the other leaders. 44Judas had given them a prearranged signal: "You will know which one to arrest when I go over and give him the kiss of greeting. Then you can take him away under guard."

45As soon as they arrived, Judas walked up to Jesus. "Teacher!" he exclaimed, and gave him the kiss. 46Then the others grabbed Jesus and arrested him. 47But someone pulled out a sword and slashed off an ear of the high priest's servant.

48Jesus asked them, "Am I some dangerous criminal, that you come armed with swords and clubs to arrest me? 49Why didn't you arrest me in the Temple? I was there teaching every day. But these things are happening to fulfill what the Scriptures say about me."

50Meanwhile, all his disciples deserted him and ran away. 51There was a young man following along behind, clothed only in a linen nightshirt. When the mob tried to grab him, 52they tore off his clothes, but he escaped and ran away naked.

〰〰 **What practical prayer problems do you need to work on?** While praying, Jesus was aware of what doing the Father's will would cost him. He understood the suffering he was about to encounter, and he did not want to have to endure the horrible experience. But Jesus prayed, "I want your will, not mine." Anything worth having costs something. What does your commitment to God cost you? Be willing to pay the price to gain something worthwhile in the end.

21

SEPTEMBER

Jesus Betrayed and Abandoned
JOHN 18:1-24

After saying these things, Jesus crossed the Kidron Valley with his disciples and entered a grove of olive trees. 2Judas, the betrayer, knew this place, because Jesus had gone there many times with his disciples. 3The leading priests and Pharisees had given Judas a battalion of Roman soldiers and Temple guards to accompany him. Now with blazing torches, lanterns, and weapons, they arrived at the olive grove.

⁴Jesus fully realized all that was going to happen to him. Stepping forward to meet them, he asked, "Whom are you looking for?"

⁵"Jesus of Nazareth," they replied.

"I am he," Jesus said. Judas was standing there with them when Jesus identified himself. ⁶And as he said, "I am he," they all fell backward to the ground! ⁷Once more he asked them, "Whom are you searching for?"

And again they replied, "Jesus of Nazareth."

⁸"I told you that I am he," Jesus said. "And since I am the one you want, let these others go." ⁹He did this to fulfill his own statement: "I have not lost a single one of those you gave me."

¹⁰Then Simon Peter drew a sword and slashed off the right ear of Malchus, the high priest's servant. ¹¹But Jesus said to Peter, "Put your sword back into its sheath. Shall I not drink from the cup the Father has given me?"

¹²So the soldiers, their commanding officer, and the Temple guards arrested Jesus and tied him up. ¹³First they took him to Annas, the father-in-law of Caiaphas, the high priest that year. ¹⁴Caiaphas was the one who had told the other Jewish leaders, "Better that one should die for all."

¹⁵Simon Peter followed along behind, as did another of the disciples. That other disciple was acquainted with the high priest, so he was allowed to enter the courtyard with Jesus. ¹⁶Peter stood outside the gate. Then the other disciple spoke to the woman watching at the gate, and she let Peter in. ¹⁷The woman asked Peter, "Aren't you one of Jesus' disciples?"

"No," he said, "I am not."

¹⁸The guards and the household servants were standing around a charcoal fire they had made because it was cold. And Peter stood there with them, warming himself.

¹⁹Inside, the high priest began asking Jesus about his followers and what he had been teaching them. ²⁰Jesus replied, "What I teach is widely known, because I have preached regularly in the synagogues and the Temple. I have been heard by people everywhere, and I teach nothing in private that I have not said in public. ²¹Why are you asking me this question? Ask those who heard me. They know what I said."

²²One of the Temple guards standing there struck Jesus on the face. "Is that the way to answer the high priest?" he demanded.

²³Jesus replied, "If I said anything wrong, you must give evidence for it. Should you hit a man for telling the truth?"

²⁴Then Annas bound Jesus and sent him to Caiaphas, the high priest.

〰〰 **How close have you come to denying Christ?** We can easily get angry at the Jewish Supreme Court for their injustice in condemning Jesus, but Peter and the rest of the disciples also contributed to Jesus' pain by deserting and denying him. While most of us are not like the religious leaders, we are all like the disciples, for all of us have been guilty of denying Christ as Lord in vital areas of our life. Don't excuse yourself by pointing at others whose sins seem worse than yours. Instead, come to Jesus for forgiveness and healing, and be committed to stand up for him.

22 SEPTEMBER

Trial and Denial
MATTHEW 26:57-75

Then the people who had arrested Jesus led him to the home of Caiaphas, the high priest, where the teachers of religious law and other leaders had gathered. 58Meanwhile, Peter was following far behind and eventually came to the courtyard of the high priest's house. He went in, sat with the guards, and waited to see what was going to happen to Jesus.

59Inside, the leading priests and the entire high council were trying to find witnesses who would lie about Jesus, so they could put him to death. 60But even though they found many who agreed to give false witness, there was no testimony they could use. Finally, two men were found 61who declared, "This man said, 'I am able to destroy the Temple of God and rebuild it in three days.' "

62Then the high priest stood up and said to Jesus, "Well, aren't you going to answer these charges? What do you have to say for yourself?" 63But Jesus remained silent. Then the high priest said to him, "I demand in the name of the living God that you tell us whether you are the Messiah, the Son of God."

64Jesus replied, "Yes, it is as you say. And in the future you will see me, the Son of Man, sitting at God's right hand in the place of power and coming back on the clouds of heaven."

65Then the high priest tore his clothing to show his horror, shouting, "Blasphemy! Why do we need other witnesses? You have all heard his blasphemy. 66What is your verdict?"

"Guilty!" they shouted. "He must die!"

67Then they spit in Jesus' face and hit him with their fists. And some slapped him, 68saying, "Prophesy to us, you Messiah! Who hit you that time?"

69Meanwhile, as Peter was sitting outside in the courtyard, a servant girl came over and said to him, "You were one of those with Jesus the Galilean."

70But Peter denied it in front of everyone. "I don't know what you are talking about," he said.

71Later, out by the gate, another servant girl noticed him and said to those standing around, "This man was with Jesus of Nazareth."

72Again Peter denied it, this time with an oath. "I don't even know the man," he said.

^{73}A little later some other bystanders came over to him and said, "You must be one of them; we can tell by your Galilean accent."
^{74}Peter said, "I swear by God, I don't know the man." And immediately the rooster crowed. ^{75}Suddenly, Jesus' words flashed through Peter's mind: "Before the rooster crows, you will deny me three times." And he went away, crying bitterly.

〰〰 **In what ways has being a follower of Jesus complicated your life?** There were three stages to Peter's denial. First, he acted confused and tried to divert attention from himself by changing the subject. Second, he vehemently denied Jesus. Third, he denied Jesus with an oath. Believers who deny Christ often begin doing so by subtly pretending not to know him. When opportunities to discuss religious issues come up, they walk away or pretend they don't know the answers. With only a little more pressure, they can be induced to flatly deny their relationship with Christ. If you find yourself subtly avoiding occasions to talk about Christ, watch out. You may be on the road to denying him.

The Religious Trial and Judas's Death

SEPTEMBER

MATTHEW 27:1-10

23

Very early in the morning, the leading priests and other leaders met again to discuss how to persuade the Roman government to sentence Jesus to death. ^{2}Then they bound him and took him to Pilate, the Roman governor.
^{3}When Judas, who had betrayed him, realized that Jesus had been condemned to die, he was filled with remorse. So he took the thirty pieces of silver back to the leading priests and other leaders. ^{4}"I have sinned," he declared, "for I have betrayed an innocent man."

"What do we care?" they retorted. "That's your problem." ^{5}Then Judas threw the money onto the floor of the Temple and went out and hanged himself. ^{6}The leading priests picked up the money. "We can't put it in the Temple treasury," they said, "since it's against the law to accept money paid for murder." ^{7}After some discussion they finally decided to buy the potter's field, and they made it into a cemetery for foreigners. ^{8}That is why the field is still called the Field of Blood. ^{9}This fulfilled the prophecy of Jeremiah that says,

> "They took the thirty pieces of silver—
> the price at which he was valued by the people of Israel—
> ^{10}and purchased the potter's field,
> as the Lord directed."

~v\z **When you think of sin's consequences, what personal examples come to mind?** Jesus' formal accuser wanted to drop his charges, but the religious leaders refused to halt the trial. When Judas first betrayed Jesus, perhaps he was trying to force Jesus' hand to get him to lead a revolt against Rome. This did not work, of course. Whatever his reason, Judas changed his mind, but it was too late. Many of the plans we set into motion cannot be reversed. It is best to think of the potential consequences before we launch into an action we may later regret.

SEPTEMBER

Two Political Trials
LUKE 23:1-12

Then the entire council took Jesus over to Pilate, the Roman governor. ²They began at once to state their case: "This man has been leading our people to ruin by telling them not to pay their taxes to the Roman government and by claiming he is the Messiah, a king."

³So Pilate asked him, "Are you the King of the Jews?"

Jesus replied, "Yes, it is as you say."

⁴Pilate turned to the leading priests and to the crowd and said, "I find nothing wrong with this man!"

⁵Then they became desperate. "But he is causing riots everywhere he goes, all over Judea, from Galilee to Jerusalem!"

⁶"Oh, is he a Galilean?" Pilate asked. ⁷When they answered that he was, Pilate sent him to Herod Antipas, because Galilee was under Herod's jurisdiction, and Herod happened to be in Jerusalem at the time.

⁸Herod was delighted at the opportunity to see Jesus, because he had heard about him and had been hoping for a long time to see him perform a miracle. ⁹He asked Jesus question after question, but Jesus refused to answer. ¹⁰Meanwhile, the leading priests and the teachers of religious law stood there shouting their accusations. ¹¹Now Herod and his soldiers began mocking and ridiculing Jesus. Then they put a royal robe on him and sent him back to Pilate. ¹²Herod and Pilate, who had been enemies before, became friends that day.

~v\z **In what ways did your childhood and background prepare you to respond to Jesus?** Pilate was the Roman governor of Judea, where Jerusalem was located. He seemed to take special pleasure in harassing the Jews. For example, Pilate had taken money from the Temple treasury and had used it to build an aqueduct. And he had insulted the Jewish religion by bringing imperial images into the city. As Pilate well knew, such acts could backfire. If the people were to lodge a formal complaint against his administration, Rome might remove him from his post. Pilate was already beginning to feel insecure in his position when the Jewish leaders brought Jesus to trial. Would he continue to badger the Jews and risk his political future, or would he give in to their demands and condemn a man who, he was quite sure, was innocent? That was the question facing Pilate that springtime Friday morning nearly two thousand years ago. Under the circumstances, how would you have responded?

SEPTEMBER

Sentencing and Torture

MARK 15:6-24

Now it was the governor's custom to release one prisoner each year at Passover time—anyone the people requested. [7]One of the prisoners at that time was Barabbas, convicted along with others for murder during an insurrection. [8]The mob began to crowd in toward Pilate, asking him to release a prisoner as usual. [9]"Should I give you the King of the Jews?" Pilate asked. [10](For he realized by now that the leading priests had arrested Jesus out of envy.) [11]But at this point the leading priests stirred up the mob to demand the release of Barabbas instead of Jesus. [12]"But if I release Barabbas," Pilate asked them, "what should I do with this man you call the King of the Jews?"

[13]They shouted back, "Crucify him!"

[14]"Why?" Pilate demanded. "What crime has he committed?"

But the crowd only roared the louder, "Crucify him!"

[15]So Pilate, anxious to please the crowd, released Barabbas to them. He ordered Jesus flogged with a lead-tipped whip, then turned him over to the Roman soldiers to crucify him.

[16]The soldiers took him into their headquarters and called out the entire battalion. [17]They dressed him in a purple robe and made a crown of long, sharp thorns and put it on his head. [18]Then they saluted, yelling, "Hail! King of the Jews!" [19]And they beat him on the head with a stick, spit on him, and dropped to their knees in mock worship. [20]When they were finally tired of mocking him, they took off the purple robe and put his own clothes on him again. Then they led him away to be crucified.

[21]A man named Simon, who was from Cyrene, was coming in from the country just then, and they forced him to carry Jesus' cross. (Simon is the father of Alexander and Rufus.) [22]And they brought Jesus to a place called Golgotha (which means Skull Hill). [23]They offered him wine drugged with myrrh, but he refused it. [24]Then they nailed him to the cross. They gambled for his clothes, throwing dice to decide who would get them.

〜〜 **Was there a time you chose to do the wrong thing on purpose? Why? What happened?** Although Jesus was innocent according to Roman law, Pilate caved in under political pressure. He abandoned what he knew was right. He tried to second-guess the Jewish leaders and give a decision that would please everyone while keeping himself safe. When we ignore God's clear statements of right and wrong and make decisions based on our audience, we fall into compromise and lawlessness. God promises to honor those who do right, not those who make everyone happy.

26

Jesus Crucified

LUKE 23:32-49

Two others, both criminals, were led out to be executed with him. ³³Finally, they came to a place called The Skull. All three were crucified there—Jesus on the center cross, and the two criminals on either side.

³⁴Jesus said, "Father, forgive these people, because they don't know what they are doing." And the soldiers gambled for his clothes by throwing dice.

³⁵The crowd watched, and the leaders laughed and scoffed. "He saved others," they said, "let him save himself if he is really God's Chosen One, the Messiah." ³⁶The soldiers mocked him, too, by offering him a drink of sour wine. ³⁷They called out to him, "If you are the King of the Jews, save yourself!" ³⁸A signboard was nailed to the cross above him with these words: "This is the King of the Jews."

³⁹One of the criminals hanging beside him scoffed, "So you're the Messiah, are you? Prove it by saving yourself—and us, too, while you're at it!"

⁴⁰But the other criminal protested, "Don't you fear God even when you are dying? ⁴¹We deserve to die for our evil deeds, but this man hasn't done anything wrong." ⁴²Then he said, "Jesus, remember me when you come into your Kingdom."

⁴³And Jesus replied, "I assure you, today you will be with me in paradise."

⁴⁴By this time it was noon, and darkness fell across the whole land until three o'clock. ⁴⁵The light from the sun was gone. And suddenly, the thick veil hanging in the Temple was torn apart. ⁴⁶Then Jesus shouted, "Father, I entrust my spirit into your hands!" And with those words he breathed his last.

⁴⁷When the captain of the Roman soldiers handling the executions saw what had happened, he praised God and said, "Surely this man was innocent." ⁴⁸And when the crowd that came to see the crucifixion saw all that had happened, they went home in deep sorrow. ⁴⁹But Jesus' friends, including the women who had followed him from Galilee, stood at a distance watching.

〜〜 **What do you feel as you read the description of the Crucifixion?** Jesus asked God to forgive the people who were putting him to death— the Jewish leaders, Roman politicians and soldiers, bystanders—and God answered that prayer by opening up the way of salvation even to Jesus' murderers. The Roman officer and soldiers who witnessed the Crucifixion said, "Truly, this was the Son of God!" (Matt. 27:54). Soon many priests were converted to the Christian faith (Acts 6:7). Since we are all sinners, we all played a part in putting Jesus to death. The good news is that God is gracious. He will forgive us and give us new life through his Son.

Jesus' Body Placed in a Guarded Tomb

MATTHEW 27:57-66

As evening approached, Joseph, a rich man from Arimathea who was one of Jesus' followers, [58]went to Pilate and asked for Jesus' body. And Pilate issued an order to release it to him. [59]Joseph took the body and wrapped it in a long linen cloth. [60]He placed it in his own new tomb, which had been carved out of the rock. Then he rolled a great stone across the entrance as he left. [61]Both Mary Magdalene and the other Mary were sitting nearby watching.

[62]The next day—on the first day of the Passover ceremonies—the leading priests and Pharisees went to see Pilate. [63]They told him, "Sir, we remember what that deceiver once said while he was still alive: 'After three days I will be raised from the dead.' [64]So we request that you seal the tomb until the third day. This will prevent his disciples from coming and stealing his body and then telling everyone he came back to life! If that happens, we'll be worse off than we were at first."

[65]Pilate replied, "Take guards and secure it the best you can." [66]So they sealed the tomb and posted guards to protect it.

What have you seen people do in their resistance to Christ?
The religious leaders took Jesus' resurrection claims more seriously than the disciples did. The Pharisees were so afraid of Jesus' predictions about his resurrection that they made sure the tomb was thoroughly sealed and guarded. Because the tomb was hewn out of rock in the side of a hill, there was only one entrance. The tomb was sealed by stringing a cord over the stone that was rolled across the entrance and sealing it at each end with clay. But the religious leaders took a further precaution, asking that guards be placed at the tomb's entrance. The disciples didn't remember Jesus' teaching about his resurrection, but the religious leaders did. Because of his claims, they were almost as afraid of Jesus after his death as when he was alive. They tried to take every precaution to see that his body would remain in the tomb. If you had been one of the disciples, what would you have been thinking? How would you have felt knowing that Jesus' body was in a sealed and guarded tomb? How would you have explained Jesus' words about rising again?

28

Jesus Is Alive!

JOHN 20:1-18

Early Sunday morning, while it was still dark, Mary Magdalene came to the tomb and found that the stone had been rolled away from the entrance. ²She ran and found Simon Peter and the other disciple, the one whom Jesus loved. She said, "They have taken the Lord's body out of the tomb, and I don't know where they have put him!"

³Peter and the other disciple ran to the tomb to see. ⁴The other disciple outran Peter and got there first. ⁵He stooped and looked in and saw the linen cloth lying there, but he didn't go in. ⁶Then Simon Peter arrived and went inside. He also noticed the linen wrappings lying there, ⁷while the cloth that had covered Jesus' head was folded up and lying to the side. ⁸Then the other disciple also went in, and he saw and believed—⁹for until then they hadn't realized that the Scriptures said he would rise from the dead. ¹⁰Then they went home.

¹¹Mary was standing outside the tomb crying, and as she wept, she stooped and looked in. ¹²She saw two white-robed angels sitting at the head and foot of the place where the body of Jesus had been lying. ¹³"Why are you crying?" the angels asked her.

"Because they have taken away my Lord," she replied, "and I don't know where they have put him."

¹⁴She glanced over her shoulder and saw someone standing behind her. It was Jesus, but she didn't recognize him. ¹⁵"Why are you crying?" Jesus asked her. "Who are you looking for?"

She thought he was the gardener. "Sir," she said, "if you have taken him away, tell me where you have put him, and I will go and get him."

¹⁶"Mary!" Jesus said.

She turned toward him and exclaimed, "Teacher!"

¹⁷"Don't cling to me," Jesus said, "for I haven't yet ascended to the Father. But go find my brothers and tell them that I am ascending to my Father and your Father, my God and your God."

¹⁸Mary Magdalene found the disciples and told them, "I have seen the Lord!" Then she gave them his message.

What makes Easter an important celebration in your life?

Jesus' resurrection is the key to the Christian faith. Why? (1) Just as he said, Jesus rose from the dead. We can be confident, therefore, that he will accomplish all he has promised. (2) Jesus' bodily resurrection shows us that the living Christ, not a false prophet or imposter, is ruler of God's eternal Kingdom. (3) We can be certain of our own resurrection because Jesus was resurrected. Death is not the end—there is a future life. (4) The divine power that brought Jesus back to life is now available to bring spiritually dead people back to life. (5) The Resurrection is the basis for the church's witness to the world. When you go to church on Easter Sunday, rejoice in what the Resurrection means for you.

Reactions to the Resurrection

SEPTEMBER 29

MATTHEW 28:8-15

The women ran quickly from the tomb. They were very frightened but also filled with great joy, and they rushed to find the disciples to give them the angel's message. ⁹And as they went, Jesus met them. "Greetings!" he said. And they ran to him, held his feet, and worshiped him. ¹⁰Then Jesus said to them, "Don't be afraid! Go tell my brothers to leave for Galilee, and they will see me there."

¹¹As the women were on their way into the city, some of the men who had been guarding the tomb went to the leading priests and told them what had happened. ¹²A meeting of all the religious leaders was called, and they decided to bribe the soldiers. ¹³They told the soldiers, "You must say, 'Jesus' disciples came during the night while we were sleeping, and they stole his body.' ¹⁴If the governor hears about it, we'll stand up for you and everything will be all right." ¹⁵So the guards accepted the bribe and said what they were told to say. Their story spread widely among the Jews, and they still tell it today.

~√⁄~ **What would be your first words to Jesus if he appeared to you?** Jesus' resurrection was already causing a great stir in Jerusalem. A group of women was moving quickly through the streets, looking for the disciples to tell them the amazing news that Jesus was alive. At the same time, a group of religious leaders was plotting how to cover up the Resurrection. Today there is still a great stir over the Resurrection, and there are still only two choices—to believe that Jesus rose from the dead or to be closed to the truth, denying it, ignoring it, or rationalizing it away. What has been your choice? Why?

Appearances of Jesus

SEPTEMBER 30

LUKE 24:13-43

That same day two of Jesus' followers were walking to the village of Emmaus, seven miles out of Jerusalem. ¹⁴As they walked along they were talking about everything that had happened. ¹⁵Suddenly, Jesus himself came along and joined them and began walking beside them. ¹⁶But they didn't know who he was, because God kept them from recognizing him.

[17]"You seem to be in a deep discussion about something," he said. "What are you so concerned about?"

They stopped short, sadness written across their faces. [18]Then one of them, Cleopas, replied, "You must be the only person in Jerusalem who hasn't heard about all the things that have happened there the last few days."

[19]"What things?" Jesus asked.

"The things that happened to Jesus, the man from Nazareth," they said. "He was a prophet who did wonderful miracles. He was a mighty teacher, highly regarded by both God and all the people. [20]But our leading priests and other religious leaders arrested him and handed him over to be condemned to death, and they crucified him. [21]We had thought he was the Messiah who had come to rescue Israel. That all happened three days ago. [22]Then some women from our group of his followers were at his tomb early this morning, and they came back with an amazing report. [23]They said his body was missing, and they had seen angels who told them Jesus is alive! [24]Some of our men ran out to see, and sure enough, Jesus' body was gone, just as the women had said."

[25]Then Jesus said to them, "You are such foolish people! You find it so hard to believe all that the prophets wrote in the Scriptures. [26]Wasn't it clearly predicted by the prophets that the Messiah would have to suffer all these things before entering his time of glory?" [27]Then Jesus quoted passages from the writings of Moses and all the prophets, explaining what all the Scriptures said about himself.

[28]By this time they were nearing Emmaus and the end of their journey. Jesus would have gone on, [29]but they begged him to stay the night with them, since it was getting late. So he went home with them. [30]As they sat down to eat, he took a small loaf of bread, asked God's blessing on it, broke it, then gave it to them. [31]Suddenly, their eyes were opened, and they recognized him. And at that moment he disappeared!

[32]They said to each other, "Didn't our hearts feel strangely warm as he talked with us on the road and explained the Scriptures to us?" [33]And within the hour they were on their way back to Jerusalem, where the eleven disciples and the other followers of Jesus were gathered. When they arrived, they were greeted with the report, [34]"The Lord has really risen! He appeared to Peter!"

[35]Then the two from Emmaus told their story of how Jesus had appeared to them as they were walking along the road and how they had recognized him as he was breaking the bread. [36]And just as they were telling about it, Jesus himself was suddenly standing there among them. He said, "Peace be with you." [37]But the whole group was terribly frightened, thinking they were seeing a ghost! [38]"Why are you frightened?" he asked. "Why do you doubt who I am? [39]Look at my hands. Look at my feet. You can see that it's really me. Touch me and make sure that I am not a ghost, because ghosts don't have bodies, as you see that I do!" [40]As he spoke, he held out his hands for them to see, and he showed them his feet.

[11]Still they stood there doubting, filled with joy and wonder. Then he asked them, "Do you have anything here to eat?" [12]They gave him a piece of broiled fish, [43]and he ate it as they watched.

~✝︎~ **Would you recognize Jesus if you saw him today? How?** The two disciples returning to Emmaus at first missed the significance of history's greatest event because they were too focused on their disappointments and problems. In fact, they didn't recognize Jesus when he was walking beside them. To compound the problem, they were walking in the wrong direction— away from the fellowship of believers in Jerusalem. We are likely to miss Jesus and withdraw from the strength found in other believers when we become pre-occupied with our dashed hopes and frustrated plans. Only when we are looking for Jesus in our midst will we experience the power and help he can bring.

More Appearances of Jesus

JOHN 20:24–21:14

One of the disciples, Thomas (nicknamed the Twin), was not with the others when Jesus came. [25]They told him, "We have seen the Lord!" But he replied, "I won't believe it unless I see the nail wounds in his hands, put my fingers into them, and place my hand into the wound in his side."

[26]Eight days later the disciples were together again, and this time Thomas was with them. The doors were locked; but suddenly, as before, Jesus was standing among them. He said, "Peace be with you." [27]Then he said to Thomas, "Put your finger here and see my hands. Put your hand into the wound in my side. Don't be faithless any longer. Believe!"

[28]"My Lord and my God!" Thomas exclaimed.

[29]Then Jesus told him, "You believe because you have seen me. Blessed are those who haven't seen me and believe anyway."

[30]Jesus' disciples saw him do many other miraculous signs besides the ones recorded in this book. [31]But these are written so that you may believe that Jesus is the Messiah, the Son of God, and that by believing in him you will have life.

[21:1]Later Jesus appeared again to the disciples beside the Sea of Galilee. This is how it happened. [2]Several of the disciples were there—Simon Peter, Thomas (nicknamed the Twin), Nathanael from Cana in Galilee, the sons of Zebedee, and two other disciples.

[3]Simon Peter said, "I'm going fishing."

"We'll come, too," they all said. So they went out in the boat, but they caught nothing all night.

[4]At dawn the disciples saw Jesus standing on the beach, but they couldn't see who he was. [5]He called out, "Friends, have you caught any fish?"

"No," they replied.

[6]Then he said, "Throw out your net on the right-hand side of the boat, and you'll get plenty of fish!" So they did, and they couldn't draw in the net because there were so many fish in it.

[7]Then the disciple whom Jesus loved said to Peter, "It is the Lord!" When

Simon Peter heard that it was the Lord, he put on his tunic (for he had stripped for work), jumped into the water, and swam ashore. ⁸The others stayed with the boat and pulled the loaded net to the shore, for they were only out about three hundred feet. ⁹When they got there, they saw that a charcoal fire was burning and fish were frying over it, and there was bread.

¹⁰"Bring some of the fish you've just caught," Jesus said. ¹¹So Simon Peter went aboard and dragged the net to the shore. There were 153 large fish, and yet the net hadn't torn.

¹²"Now come and have some breakfast!" Jesus said. And no one dared ask him if he really was the Lord because they were sure of it. ¹³Then Jesus served them the bread and the fish. ¹⁴This was the third time Jesus had appeared to his disciples since he had been raised from the dead.

 How has Christ answered your doubts? Jesus wasn't hard on Thomas for his doubts. Despite his skepticism, Thomas was still loyal to the believers and to Jesus himself. Some people need to doubt before they believe. If doubt leads to questions and questions lead to answers and the answers are accepted, then doubt has done good work. It is when doubt becomes stubborn-ness, and stubbornness becomes a lifestyle that doubt harms faith. When you doubt, don't stop there, but let your doubt deepen your faith as you continue to search for the answer.

OCTOBER

Jesus Talks with Peter
JOHN 21:15-25

After breakfast Jesus said to Simon Peter, "Simon son of John, do you love me more than these?"

"Yes, Lord," Peter replied, "you know I love you."

"Then feed my lambs," Jesus told him.

¹⁶Jesus repeated the question: "Simon son of John, do you love me?"

"Yes, Lord," Peter said, "you know I love you."

"Then take care of my sheep," Jesus said.

¹⁷Once more he asked him, "Simon son of John, do you love me?"

Peter was grieved that Jesus asked the question a third time. He said, "Lord, you know everything. You know I love you."

Jesus said, "Then feed my sheep. ¹⁸The truth is, when you were young, you were able to do as you liked and go wherever you wanted to. But when you are old, you will stretch out your hands, and others will direct you and take you where you don't want to go." ¹⁹Jesus said this to let him know what kind of death he would die to glorify God. Then Jesus told him, "Follow me."

²⁰Peter turned around and saw the disciple Jesus loved following them— the one who had leaned over to Jesus during supper and asked, "Lord, who among us will betray you?" ²¹Peter asked Jesus, "What about him, Lord?"

²²Jesus replied, "If I want him to remain alive until I return, what is that to you? You follow me." ²³So the rumor spread among the community of believers that that disciple wouldn't die. But that isn't what Jesus said at all. He only said, "If I want him to remain alive until I return, what is that to you?"

²⁴This is that disciple who saw these events and recorded them here. And we all know that his account of these things is accurate.

²⁵And I suppose that if all the other things Jesus did were written down, the whole world could not contain the books.

〜⋏〳⋎〱 **What difference would it make to you to read these verses with your name in the place of Simon Peter's?** Peter asked Jesus how John would die. Jesus replied that Peter should not concern himself with that. We tend to compare our life to others, whether to rationalize our own level of devotion to Christ or to question God's justice. Jesus responds to us as he did to Peter: "What is that to you? *You* follow me!"

Jesus Gives the Great Commission

OCTOBER

3

MATTHEW 28:16-20

Then the eleven disciples left for Galilee, going to the mountain where Jesus had told them to go. ¹⁷When they saw him, they worshiped him—but some of them still doubted!

¹⁸Jesus came and told his disciples, "I have been given complete authority in heaven and on earth. ¹⁹Therefore, go and make disciples of all the nations, baptizing them in the name of the Father and the Son and the Holy Spirit. ²⁰Teach these new disciples to obey all the commands I have given you. And be sure of this: I am with you always, even to the end of the age."

〜⋏〳⋎〱 **What are you doing specifically to obey Christ's words?** When someone is dying or leaving us, his last words are very important. Jesus left the disciples with these last words of instruction: They were under his authority, they were to make more disciples, they were to baptize and teach them to obey him, and he would be with them always. Whereas in previous missions Jesus had sent his disciples only to the Jews, their mission from now on would be worldwide. Jesus is Lord of the earth, and he died for the sins of all those who trust him, everywhere. We are to go—whether it is next door or to another country—and make disciples. It is not an option but a command to all who call Jesus Lord. All of us are not evangelists, but we have all received gifts that we can use in helping to fulfill the great commission. As we obey, we have comfort in the knowledge that Jesus is always with us.

4

Jesus Says Farewell
LUKE 24:44-53

Then [Jesus] said, "When I was with you before, I told you that everything written about me by Moses and the prophets and in the Psalms must all come true." ⁴⁵Then he opened their minds to understand these many Scriptures. ⁴⁶And he said, "Yes, it was written long ago that the Messiah must suffer and die and rise again from the dead on the third day. ⁴⁷With my authority, take this message of repentance to all the nations, beginning in Jerusalem: 'There is forgiveness of sins for all who turn to me.' ⁴⁸You are witnesses of all these things.

⁴⁹"And now I will send the Holy Spirit, just as my Father promised. But stay here in the city until the Holy Spirit comes and fills you with power from heaven."

⁵⁰Then Jesus led them to Bethany, and lifting his hands to heaven, he blessed them. ⁵¹While he was blessing them, he left them and was taken up to heaven. ⁵²They worshiped him and then returned to Jerusalem filled with great joy. ⁵³And they spent all of their time in the Temple, praising God.

How do you find Christ opening your mind as you read the Bible? Jesus opened these people's minds to understand the Scriptures. The Holy Spirit does this in our life today when we study the Bible. Have you ever wondered what a difficult Bible passage meant? Besides reading surrounding passages, asking other people, and consulting reference works, pray that the Holy Spirit will open your mind to understand, giving you the needed insight to put God's Word into action in your life.

5

The Departure of Jesus
ACTS 1:1-11

Dear Theophilus:

In my first book I told you about everything Jesus began to do and teach ²until the day he ascended to heaven after giving his chosen apostles further instructions from the Holy Spirit. ³During the forty days after his crucifixion, he appeared to the apostles from time to time and proved to them in many ways that he was actually alive. On these occasions he talked to them about the Kingdom of God.

⁴In one of these meetings as he was eating a meal with them, he told them, "Do not leave Jerusalem until the Father sends you what he prom-

ised. Remember, I have told you about this before. [5]John baptized with water, but in just a few days you will be baptized with the Holy Spirit."

[6]When the apostles were with Jesus, they kept asking him, "Lord, are you going to free Israel now and restore our kingdom?"

[7]"The Father sets those dates," he replied, "and they are not for you to know. [8]But when the Holy Spirit has come upon you, you will receive power and will tell people about me everywhere—in Jerusalem, throughout Judea, in Samaria, and to the ends of the earth."

[9]It was not long after he said this that he was taken up into the sky while they were watching, and he disappeared into a cloud. [10]As they were straining their eyes to see him, two white-robed men suddenly stood there among them. [11]They said, "Men of Galilee, why are you standing here staring at the sky? Jesus has been taken away from you into heaven. And someday, just as you saw him go, he will return!"

⌇⌇⌇ **What one thing would you be sure to do if you knew Jesus was coming back today?** Today there are still people who doubt Jesus' resurrection. But Jesus appeared to the apostles on many occasions after his resurrection, proving that he was alive. Look at the change the Resurrection made in the disciples' lives. At Jesus' death, they scattered. They were disillusioned and feared for their lives. After seeing the resurrected Christ, they were fearless and risked everything to spread the Good News about him around the world. They faced imprisonment, beatings, rejection, and martyrdom, yet they never compromised their mission. These men would not have risked their lives for something they knew was a fraud. They knew Jesus was raised from the dead, and the early church was fired with enthusiasm to tell others.

OCTOBER 6

First Things First

ACTS 1:12-26

The apostles were at the Mount of Olives when this happened, so they walked the half mile back to Jerusalem. [13]Then they went to the upstairs room of the house where they were staying. Here is the list of those who were present:

> Peter,
> John,
> James,
> Andrew,
> Philip,
> Thomas,
> Bartholomew,

Matthew,
James (son of Alphaeus),
Simon (the Zealot),
and Judas (son of James).

¹⁴They all met together continually for prayer, along with Mary the mother of Jesus, several other women, and the brothers of Jesus.

¹⁵During this time, on a day when about 120 believers were present, Peter stood up and addressed them as follows:

¹⁶"Brothers, it was necessary for the Scriptures to be fulfilled concerning Judas, who guided the Temple police to arrest Jesus. This was predicted long ago by the Holy Spirit, speaking through King David. ¹⁷Judas was one of us, chosen to share in the ministry with us."

¹⁸(Judas bought a field with the money he received for his treachery, and falling there, he burst open, spilling out his intestines. ¹⁹The news of his death spread rapidly among all the people of Jerusalem, and they gave the place the Aramaic name *Akeldama*, which means "Field of Blood.")

²⁰Peter continued, "This was predicted in the book of Psalms, where it says, 'Let his home become desolate, with no one living in it.' And again, 'Let his position be given to someone else.'

²¹"So now we must choose someone else to take Judas's place. It must be someone who has been with us all the time that we were with the Lord Jesus—²²from the time he was baptized by John until the day he was taken from us into heaven. Whoever is chosen will join us as a witness of Jesus' resurrection."

²³So they nominated two men: Joseph called Barsabbas (also known as Justus) and Matthias. ²⁴Then they all prayed for the right man to be chosen. "O Lord," they said, "you know every heart. Show us which of these men you have chosen ²⁵as an apostle to replace Judas the traitor in this ministry, for he has deserted us and gone where he belongs." ²⁶Then they cast lots, and in this way Matthias was chosen and became an apostle with the other eleven.

〰〰 **What is your idea of the right amount of time for prayer?** After Christ was taken up into heaven, the disciples immediately returned to Jerusalem and had a prayer meeting. Jesus had said they would be baptized with the Holy Spirit in a few days, so they waited and prayed. When you face a difficult task, an important decision, or a baffling dilemma, don't rush, hoping it will come out right. Instead, your first step should be to pray for the Holy Spirit's power and guidance.

An Amazing Gift

ACTS 2:1-13

On the day of Pentecost, seven weeks after Jesus' resurrection, the believers were meeting together in one place. ²Suddenly, there was a sound from heaven like the roaring of a mighty windstorm in the skies above them, and it filled the house where they were meeting. ³Then, what looked like flames or tongues of fire appeared and settled on each of them. ⁴And everyone present was filled with the Holy Spirit and began speaking in other languages, as the Holy Spirit gave them this ability.

⁵Godly Jews from many nations were living in Jerusalem at that time. ⁶When they heard this sound, they came running to see what it was all about, and they were bewildered to hear their own languages being spoken by the believers.

⁷They were beside themselves with wonder. "How can this be?" they exclaimed. "These people are all from Galilee, ⁸and yet we hear them speaking the languages of the lands where we were born! ⁹Here we are—Parthians, Medes, Elamites, people from Mesopotamia, Judea, Cappadocia, Pontus, the province of Asia, ¹⁰Phrygia, Pamphylia, Egypt, and the areas of Libya toward Cyrene, visitors from Rome (both Jews and converts to Judaism), ¹¹Cretans, and Arabians. And we all hear these people speaking in our own languages about the wonderful things God has done!" ¹²They stood there amazed and perplexed. "What can this mean?" they asked each other. ¹³But others in the crowd were mocking. "They're drunk, that's all!" they said.

〰〰〰 **What is the main purpose of any gift God might have given you?** God made his presence known to this group of believers in a spectacular way—a mighty wind, fire, and his Holy Spirit. Would you like God to reveal himself to you in such recognizable ways? He may do so, but be wary of forcing your expectations on God. In 1 Kings 19:10-13, Elijah also needed a message from God. There was a great wind, then an earthquake, and finally a fire. But God's message came in a "gentle whisper." God may use dramatic methods to work in your life—or he may speak in a still small voice. Wait patiently and listen.

Peter's First Sermon

ACTS 2:14-40

Then Peter stepped forward with the eleven other apostles and shouted to the crowd, "Listen carefully, all of you, fellow Jews and residents of Jerusalem! Make no mistake about this. ¹⁵Some of you are saying these people are drunk. It isn't true! It's much too early for that. People don't get drunk by nine o'clock in the morning. [16]No, what you see this morning was predicted centuries ago by the prophet Joel:

[17] 'In the last days, God said,
  I will pour out my Spirit upon all people.
  Your sons and daughters will prophesy,
    your young men will see visions,
    and your old men will dream dreams.
[18] In those days I will pour out my Spirit
    upon all my servants, men and women alike,
    and they will prophesy.
[19] And I will cause wonders in the heavens above
    and signs on the earth below—
    blood and fire and clouds of smoke.
[20] The sun will be turned into darkness,
    and the moon will turn bloodred,
    before that great and glorious day of the Lord arrives.
[21] And anyone who calls on the name of the Lord
    will be saved.'

[22]"People of Israel, listen! God publicly endorsed Jesus of Nazareth by doing wonderful miracles, wonders, and signs through him, as you well know. [23]But you followed God's prearranged plan. With the help of lawless Gentiles, you nailed him to the cross and murdered him. [24]However, God released him from the horrors of death and raised him back to life again, for death could not keep him in its grip. [25]King David said this about him:

'I know the Lord is always with me.
  I will not be shaken, for he is right beside me.
[26] No wonder my heart is filled with joy,
    and my mouth shouts his praises!
  My body rests in hope.
[27] For you will not leave my soul among the dead
    or allow your Holy One to rot in the grave.
[28] You have shown me the way of life,
    and you will give me wonderful joy in your presence.'

[29]"Dear brothers, think about this! David wasn't referring to himself when he spoke these words I have quoted, for he died and was buried, and his tomb is still here among us. [30]But he was a prophet, and he knew God had promised with an oath that one of David's own descendants would sit on David's throne as the Messiah. [31]David was looking into the future and predicting the Messiah's resurrection. He was saying that the Messiah would not be left among the dead and that his body would not rot in the grave.

[32]"This prophecy was speaking of Jesus, whom God raised from the dead, and we all are witnesses of this. [33]Now he sits on the throne of highest

honor in heaven, at God's right hand. And the Father, as he had promised, gave him the Holy Spirit to pour out upon us, just as you see and hear today. [34]For David himself never ascended into heaven, yet he said,

> 'The LORD said to my Lord,
> Sit in honor at my right hand
> [35] until I humble your enemies,
> making them a footstool under your feet.'

[36]So let it be clearly known by everyone in Israel that God has made this Jesus whom you crucified to be both Lord and Messiah!"

[37]Peter's words convicted them deeply, and they said to him and to the other apostles, "Brothers, what should we do?"

[38]Peter replied, "Each of you must turn from your sins and turn to God, and be baptized in the name of Jesus Christ for the forgiveness of your sins. Then you will receive the gift of the Holy Spirit. [39]This promise is to you and to your children, and even to the Gentiles—all who have been called by the Lord our God." [40]Then Peter continued preaching for a long time, strongly urging all his listeners, "Save yourselves from this generation that has gone astray!"

〜〰〜 **How would you put this sermon into your own words?** Peter had been an unstable leader during Jesus' ministry, letting his bravado be his downfall, even denying that he knew Jesus. But Christ forgave and restored Peter after his denial. This was a new Peter, humble but bold. His confidence came from the Holy Spirit, who made him a powerful and dynamic speaker. Have you ever felt as though you've made such bad mistakes that God could never forgive and use you? No matter what sins you have committed, God says he will forgive you and make you useful for his Kingdom. Confess your sins and allow God to use you effectively to serve him.

Daily Life in the Early Church

OCTOBER

9

ACTS 2:41–3:11

Those who believed what Peter said were baptized and added to the church—about three thousand in all. [42]They joined with the other believers and devoted themselves to the apostles' teaching and fellowship, sharing in the Lord's Supper and in prayer.

[43]A deep sense of awe came over them all, and the apostles performed many miraculous signs and wonders. [44]And all the believers met together constantly and shared everything they had. [45]They sold their possessions and shared the proceeds with those in need. [46]They worshiped together at the Temple each day, met in homes for the Lord's Supper, and shared their

meals with great joy and generosity—⁴⁷all the while praising God and enjoying the goodwill of all the people. And each day the Lord added to their group those who were being saved.

³:¹Peter and John went to the Temple one afternoon to take part in the three o'clock prayer service. ²As they approached the Temple, a man lame from birth was being carried in. Each day he was put beside the Temple gate, the one called the Beautiful Gate, so he could beg from the people going into the Temple. ³When he saw Peter and John about to enter, he asked them for some money.

⁴Peter and John looked at him intently, and Peter said, "Look at us!" ⁵The lame man looked at them eagerly, expecting a gift. ⁶But Peter said, "I don't have any money for you. But I'll give you what I have. In the name of Jesus Christ of Nazareth, get up and walk!"

⁷Then Peter took the lame man by the right hand and helped him up. And as he did, the man's feet and anklebones were healed and strengthened. ⁸He jumped up, stood on his feet, and began to walk! Then, walking, leaping, and praising God, he went into the Temple with them.

⁹All the people saw him walking and heard him praising God. ¹⁰When they realized he was the lame beggar they had seen so often at the Beautiful Gate, they were absolutely astounded! ¹¹They all rushed out to Solomon's Colonnade, where he was holding tightly to Peter and John. Everyone stood there in awe of the wonderful thing that had happened.

〰️ **What part of these early days of the church would you have enjoyed the most?** The lame beggar asked for money, but Peter gave him something much better—the use of his legs. We often ask God to solve a small problem, but he wants to give us a new life and help for *all* our problems. When we ask God for help, he may say, "I've got something even better for you." Ask God for what you want, but don't be surprised when he gives you what you really *need*.

OCTOBER

Peter's Second Sermon
ACTS 3:12–4:4

Peter saw his opportunity and addressed the crowd. "People of Israel," he said, "what is so astounding about this? And why look at us as though we had made this man walk by our own power and godliness? ¹³For it is the God of Abraham, the God of Isaac, the God of Jacob, the God of all our ancestors who has brought glory to his servant Jesus by doing this. This is the same Jesus whom you handed over and rejected before Pilate, despite Pilate's decision to release him. ¹⁴You rejected this holy, righteous one and instead demanded the release of a murderer. ¹⁵You killed the author of life, but God raised him to life. And we are witnesses of this fact!

[16]"The name of Jesus has healed this man—and you know how lame he was before. Faith in Jesus' name has caused this healing before your very eyes. [17]"Friends, I realize that what you did to Jesus was done in ignorance; and the same can be said of your leaders. [18]But God was fulfilling what all the prophets had declared about the Messiah beforehand—that he must suffer all these things. [19]Now turn from your sins and turn to God, so you can be cleansed of your sins. [20]Then wonderful times of refreshment will come from the presence of the Lord, and he will send Jesus your Messiah to you again. [21]For he must remain in heaven until the time for the final restoration of all things, as God promised long ago through his prophets. [22]Moses said, 'The Lord your God will raise up a Prophet like me from among your own people. Listen carefully to everything he tells you.' [23]Then Moses said, 'Anyone who will not listen to that Prophet will be cut off from God's people and utterly destroyed.'

[24]"Starting with Samuel, every prophet spoke about what is happening today. [25]You are the children of those prophets, and you are included in the covenant God promised to your ancestors. For God said to Abraham, 'Through your descendants all the families on earth will be blessed.' [26]When God raised up his servant, he sent him first to you people of Israel, to bless you by turning each of you back from your sinful ways."

[4:1]While Peter and John were speaking to the people, the leading priests, the captain of the Temple guard, and some of the Sadducees came over to them. [2]They were very disturbed that Peter and John were claiming, on the authority of Jesus, that there is a resurrection of the dead. [3]They arrested them and, since it was already evening, jailed them until morning. [4]But many of the people who heard their message believed it, so that the number of believers totaled about five thousand men, not counting women and children.

✒ **If you were given three minutes to tell the story of your spiritual life, what would you say?** Not often will sharing the gospel send us to jail as it did Peter and John. Still, we run risks in trying to win others to Christ. We might be willing to face a night in jail if it would bring five thousand people to Christ, but shouldn't we also be willing to suffer for the sake of even one? What do you risk in witnessing—rejection, persecution? Whatever the risks, realize that nothing done for God is ever wasted.

OCTOBER **11**

Hostile Reactions

ACTS 4:5-22

The next day the council of all the rulers and elders and teachers of religious law met in Jerusalem. [6]Annas the high priest was there, along with Caiaphas, John, Alexander, and other relatives of the high priest. [7]They brought in the two disciples and demanded, "By what power, or in whose name, have you done this?"

[8]Then Peter, filled with the Holy Spirit, said to them, "Leaders and elders of our nation, [9]are we being questioned because we've done a good deed for a crippled man? Do you want to know how he was healed? [10]Let me clearly state to you and to all the people of Israel that he was healed in the name and power of Jesus Christ from Nazareth, the man you crucified, but whom God raised from the dead. [11]For Jesus is the one referred to in the Scriptures, where it says,

'The stone that you builders rejected
has now become the cornerstone.'

[12]There is salvation in no one else! There is no other name in all of heaven for people to call on to save them."

[13]The members of the council were amazed when they saw the boldness of Peter and John, for they could see that they were ordinary men who had had no special training. They also recognized them as men who had been with Jesus. [14]But since the man who had been healed was standing right there among them, the council had nothing to say. [15]So they sent Peter and John out of the council chamber and conferred among themselves.

[16]"What should we do with these men?" they asked each other. "We can't deny they have done a miraculous sign, and everybody in Jerusalem knows about it. [17]But perhaps we can stop them from spreading their propaganda. We'll warn them not to speak to anyone in Jesus' name again." [18]So they called the apostles back in and told them never again to speak or teach about Jesus.

[19]But Peter and John replied, "Do you think God wants us to obey you rather than him? [20]We cannot stop telling about the wonderful things we have seen and heard."

[21]The council then threatened them further, but they finally let them go because they didn't know how to punish them without starting a riot. For everyone was praising God [22]for this miraculous sign—the healing of a man who had been lame for more than forty years.

〰️ **What excuses are you most likely to use to keep from sharing your faith?** Although the evidence was overwhelming and irrefutable (changed lives and a healed man), the religious leaders refused to believe in Christ and continued to try to suppress the truth. Don't be surprised if some people reject you and your positive witness for Christ. When minds are closed, even the clearest presentation of the facts can't open them. But don't give up. Pray for those people and continue to spread the gospel. Peter and John's zeal for the Lord was so strong that they could not keep quiet. If your courage to witness for God has weakened, pray that your boldness may increase.

Praying and Sharing

ACTS 4:23-37

As soon as they were freed, Peter and John found the other believers and told them what the leading priests and elders had said. [24]Then all the believers were united as they lifted their voices in prayer: "O Sovereign Lord, Creator of heaven and earth, the sea, and everything in them—[25]you spoke long ago by the Holy Spirit through our ancestor King David, your servant, saying,

'Why did the nations rage?
Why did the people waste their time with futile plans?
[26]The kings of the earth prepared for battle;
the rulers gathered together
against the Lord
and against his Messiah.'

[27]"That is what has happened here in this city! For Herod Antipas, Pontius Pilate the governor, the Gentiles, and the people of Israel were all united against Jesus, your holy servant, whom you anointed. [28]In fact, everything they did occurred according to your eternal will and plan. [29]And now, O Lord, hear their threats, and give your servants great boldness in their preaching. [30]Send your healing power; may miraculous signs and wonders be done through the name of your holy servant Jesus."

[31]After this prayer, the building where they were meeting shook, and they were all filled with the Holy Spirit. And they preached God's message with boldness.

[32]All the believers were of one heart and mind, and they felt that what they owned was not their own; they shared everything they had. [33]And the apostles gave powerful witness to the resurrection of the Lord Jesus, and God's great favor was upon them all. [34]There was no poverty among them, because people who owned land or houses sold them [35]and brought the money to the apostles to give to others in need.

[36]For instance, there was Joseph, the one the apostles nicknamed Barnabas (which means "Son of Encouragement"). He was from the tribe of Levi and came from the island of Cyprus. [37]He sold a field he owned and brought the money to the apostles for those in need.

〜〜 **When was the last time you shared something with someone else?** None of these Christians felt that what they had was their own, and so they were able to give and share, eliminating poverty among them. They would not let a brother or sister suffer when others had plenty. How do you feel about your possessions? We should adopt the attitude that everything we have comes from God, and we are only sharing what is already his.

13

Strange Events
ACTS 5:1-16

There was also a man named Ananias who, with his wife, Sapphira, sold some property. [2]He brought part of the money to the apostles, but he claimed it was the full amount. His wife had agreed to this deception.

[3]Then Peter said, "Ananias, why has Satan filled your heart? You lied to the Holy Spirit, and you kept some of the money for yourself. [4]The property was yours to sell or not sell, as you wished. And after selling it, the money was yours to give away. How could you do a thing like this? You weren't lying to us but to God."

[5]As soon as Ananias heard these words, he fell to the floor and died. Everyone who heard about it was terrified. [6]Then some young men wrapped him in a sheet and took him out and buried him.

[7]About three hours later his wife came in, not knowing what had happened. [8]Peter asked her, "Was this the price you and your husband received for your land?"

"Yes," she replied, "that was the price."

[9]And Peter said, "How could the two of you even think of doing a thing like this—conspiring together to test the Spirit of the Lord? Just outside that door are the young men who buried your husband, and they will carry you out, too."

[10]Instantly, she fell to the floor and died. When the young men came in and saw that she was dead, they carried her out and buried her beside her husband. [11]Great fear gripped the entire church and all others who heard what had happened.

[12]Meanwhile, the apostles were performing many miraculous signs and wonders among the people. And the believers were meeting regularly at the Temple in the area known as Solomon's Colonnade. [13]No one else dared to join them, though everyone had high regard for them. [14]And more and more people believed and were brought to the Lord—crowds of both men and women. [15]As a result of the apostles' work, sick people were brought out into the streets on beds and mats so that Peter's shadow might fall across some of them as he went by. [16]Crowds came in from the villages around Jerusalem, bringing their sick and those possessed by evil spirits, and they were all healed.

〰️ **How often are you tempted to take God lightly?** The sin that Ananias and Sapphira committed was not stinginess or holding back part of the money. It was their choice whether or not to sell the land and how much to give. Their sin was lying to God and God's people—saying they gave the whole amount but holding back some for themselves and trying to make themselves appear more generous than they really were. This act was judged harshly because dishonesty, greed, and covetousness are destructive in a church, preventing the Holy Spirit from working effectively. All lying is bad, but when we lie to try to deceive God and his people about our relationship with him, we destroy our testimony about Christ.

Arrested!

ACTS 5:17-42

14

The high priest and his friends, who were Sadducees, reacted with violent jealousy. [18]They arrested the apostles and put them in the jail. [19]But an angel of the Lord came at night, opened the gates of the jail, and brought them out. Then he told them, [20]"Go to the Temple and give the people this message of life!" [21]So the apostles entered the Temple about daybreak and immediately began teaching.

When the high priest and his officials arrived, they convened the high council, along with all the elders of Israel. Then they sent for the apostles to be brought for trial. [22]But when the Temple guards went to the jail, the men were gone. So they returned to the council and reported, [23]"The jail was locked, with the guards standing outside, but when we opened the gates, no one was there!"

[24]When the captain of the Temple guard and the leading priests heard this, they were perplexed, wondering where it would all end. [25]Then someone arrived with the news that the men they had jailed were out in the Temple, teaching the people.

[26]The captain went with his Temple guards and arrested them, but without violence, for they were afraid the people would kill them if they treated the apostles roughly. [27]Then they brought the apostles in before the council. [28]"Didn't we tell you never again to teach in this man's name?" the high priest demanded. "Instead, you have filled all Jerusalem with your teaching about Jesus, and you intend to blame us for his death!"

[29]But Peter and the apostles replied, "We must obey God rather than human authority. [30]The God of our ancestors raised Jesus from the dead after you killed him by crucifying him. [31]Then God put him in the place of honor at his right hand as Prince and Savior. He did this to give the people of Israel an opportunity to turn from their sins and turn to God so their sins would be forgiven. [32]We are witnesses of these things and so is the Holy Spirit, who is given by God to those who obey him."

[33]At this, the high council was furious and decided to kill them. [34]But one member had a different perspective. He was a Pharisee named Gamaliel, who was an expert on religious law and was very popular with the people. He stood up and ordered that the apostles be sent outside the council chamber for a while. [35]Then he addressed his colleagues as follows: "Men of

Israel, take care what you are planning to do to these men! ³⁶Some time ago there was that fellow Theudas, who pretended to be someone great. About four hundred others joined him, but he was killed, and his followers went their various ways. The whole movement came to nothing. ³⁷After him, at the time of the census, there was Judas of Galilee. He got some people to follow him, but he was killed, too, and all his followers were scattered.

³⁸"So my advice is, leave these men alone. If they are teaching and doing these things merely on their own, it will soon be overthrown. ³⁹But if it is of God, you will not be able to stop them. You may even find yourselves fighting against God."

⁴⁰The council accepted his advice. They called in the apostles and had them flogged. Then they ordered them never again to speak in the name of Jesus, and they let them go. ⁴¹The apostles left the high council rejoicing that God had counted them worthy to suffer dishonor for the name of Jesus. ⁴²And every day, in the Temple and in their homes, they continued to teach and preach this message: "The Messiah you are looking for is Jesus."

〰〰 **How do you react when you are treated unfairly?** Have you ever thought of persecution as a blessing? This beating suffered by Peter and John was the first time any of the apostles had been physically abused for their faith. These men knew how Jesus had suffered, and they praised God that he allowed them to be persecuted like their Lord. If you are mocked or persecuted for your faith, it isn't because you are doing something wrong but because God has counted you "worthy to suffer dishonor for the name of Jesus."

15

OCTOBER

Stephen: Special Servant
ACTS 6:1-15

But as the believers rapidly multiplied, there were rumblings of discontent. Those who spoke Greek complained against those who spoke Hebrew, saying that their widows were being discriminated against in the daily distribution of food. ²So the Twelve called a meeting of all the believers.

"We apostles should spend our time preaching and teaching the word of God, not administering a food program," they said. ³"Now look around among yourselves, friends, and select seven men who are well respected and are full of the Holy Spirit and wisdom. We will put them in charge of this business. ⁴Then we can spend our time in prayer and preaching and teaching the word."

⁵This idea pleased the whole group, and they chose the following: Stephen (a man full of faith and the Holy Spirit), Philip, Procorus, Nicanor, Timon, Parmenas, and Nicolas of Antioch (a Gentile convert to the Jewish faith, who had now become a Christian). ⁶These seven were presented to the apostles, who prayed for them as they laid their hands on them.

⁷God's message was preached in ever-widening circles. The number of believers greatly increased in Jerusalem, and many of the Jewish priests were converted, too.

⁸Stephen, a man full of God's grace and power, performed amazing miracles and signs among the people. ⁹But one day some men from the Synagogue of Freed Slaves, as it was called, started to debate with him. They were Jews from Cyrene, Alexandria, Cilicia, and the province of Asia. ¹⁰None of them was able to stand against the wisdom and Spirit by which Stephen spoke.

¹¹So they persuaded some men to lie about Stephen, saying, "We heard him blaspheme Moses, and even God." ¹²Naturally, this roused the crowds, the elders, and the teachers of religious law. So they arrested Stephen and brought him before the high council. ¹³The lying witnesses said, "This man is always speaking against the Temple and against the law of Moses. ¹⁴We have heard him say that this Jesus of Nazareth will destroy the Temple and change the customs Moses handed down to us." ¹⁵At this point everyone in the council stared at Stephen because his face became as bright as an angel's.

〰〰 **What specific responsibilities do you have in your local church?** As the early church increased in size, so did its needs. One great need was to organize the distribution of food to the poor. The apostles needed to focus on preaching, so they chose others to administer the food program. Each person has a vital part to play in the life of the church. If you are in a position of leadership and find yourself overwhelmed by responsibilities, determine *your* God-given abilities and priorities and then find others to help. If you are not in leadership, offer the gifts that you have to God for service in various areas of the church's ministry.

OCTOBER **16**

History Review 1
ACTS 7:1-29

Then the high priest asked Stephen, "Are these accusations true?"

²This was Stephen's reply: "Brothers and honorable fathers, listen to me. Our glorious God appeared to our ancestor Abraham in Mesopotamia before he moved to Haran. ³God told him, 'Leave your native land and your relatives, and come to the land that I will show you.' ⁴So Abraham left the land of the Chaldeans and lived in Haran until his father died. Then God brought him here to the land where you now live. ⁵But God gave him no inheritance here, not even one square foot of land. God did promise, however, that eventually the whole country would belong to Abraham and his descendants—though he had no children yet. ⁶But God also told him that his descendants would live in a foreign country where they would be mistreated as slaves for four hundred years. ⁷But I will punish the nation that

enslaves them,' God told him, 'and in the end they will come out and worship me in this place.' ⁸God also gave Abraham the covenant of circumcision at that time. And so Isaac, Abraham's son, was circumcised when he was eight days old. Isaac became the father of Jacob, and Jacob was the father of the twelve patriarchs of the Jewish nation.

⁹"These sons of Jacob were very jealous of their brother Joseph, and they sold him to be a slave in Egypt. But God was with him ¹⁰and delivered him from his anguish. And God gave him favor before Pharaoh, king of Egypt. God also gave Joseph unusual wisdom, so that Pharaoh appointed him governor over all of Egypt and put him in charge of all the affairs of the palace.

¹¹"But a famine came upon Egypt and Canaan. There was great misery for our ancestors, as they ran out of food. ¹²Jacob heard that there was still grain in Egypt, so he sent his sons to buy some. ¹³The second time they went, Joseph revealed his identity to his brothers, and they were introduced to Pharaoh. ¹⁴Then Joseph sent for his father, Jacob, and all his relatives to come to Egypt, seventy-five persons in all. ¹⁵So Jacob went to Egypt. He died there, as did all his sons. ¹⁶All of them were taken to Shechem and buried in the tomb Abraham had bought from the sons of Hamor in Shechem.

¹⁷"As the time drew near when God would fulfill his promise to Abraham, the number of our people in Egypt greatly increased. ¹⁸But then a new king came to the throne of Egypt who knew nothing about Joseph. ¹⁹This king plotted against our people and forced parents to abandon their newborn babies so they would die.

²⁰"At that time Moses was born—a beautiful child in God's eyes. His parents cared for him at home for three months. ²¹When at last they had to abandon him, Pharaoh's daughter found him and raised him as her own son. ²²Moses was taught all the wisdom of the Egyptians, and he became mighty in both speech and action.

²³"One day when he was forty years old, he decided to visit his relatives, the people of Israel. ²⁴During this visit, he saw an Egyptian mistreating a man of Israel. So Moses came to his defense and avenged him, killing the Egyptian. ²⁵Moses assumed his brothers would realize that God had sent him to rescue them, but they didn't.

²⁶"The next day he visited them again and saw two men of Israel fighting. He tried to be a peacemaker. 'Men,' he said, 'you are brothers. Why are you hurting each other?'

²⁷"But the man in the wrong pushed Moses aside and told him to mind his own business. 'Who made you a ruler and judge over us?' he asked. ²⁸'Are you going to kill me as you killed that Egyptian yesterday?' ²⁹When Moses heard that, he fled the country and lived as a foreigner in the land of Midian, where his two sons were born."

〰✍ **How familiar are you becoming with "his story" in history?**
Stephen's review of Jewish history gives a clear testimony of God's faithfulness and sovereignty. Despite the continued failures of his chosen people and the

swirling world events, God was working out his plan. When faced by a confusing array of circumstances, remember: (1) God is in control—nothing surprises him. (2) This world is not all there is—it will pass away, but God is eternal. (3) God is just, and he will make things right—punishing the wicked and rewarding the faithful. (4) God wants to use you (like Joseph, Moses, and Stephen) to make a difference in the world.

History Review 2

ACTS 7:30-60

[Stephen testified,] "Forty years later, in the desert near Mount Sinai, an angel appeared to Moses in the flame of a burning bush. ³¹Moses saw it and wondered what it was. As he went to see, the voice of the Lord called out to him, ³²'I am the God of your ancestors—the God of Abraham, Isaac, and Jacob.' Moses shook with terror and dared not look.

³³"And the Lord said to him, 'Take off your sandals, for you are standing on holy ground. ³⁴You can be sure that I have seen the misery of my people in Egypt. I have heard their cries. So I have come to rescue them. Now go, for I will send you to Egypt.' ³⁵And so God sent back the same man his people had previously rejected by demanding, 'Who made you a ruler and judge over us?' Through the angel who appeared to him in the burning bush, Moses was sent to be their ruler and savior. ³⁶And by means of many miraculous signs and wonders, he led them out of Egypt, through the Red Sea, and back and forth through the wilderness for forty years.

³⁷"Moses himself told the people of Israel, 'God will raise up a Prophet like me from among your own people.' ³⁸Moses was with the assembly of God's people in the wilderness. He was the mediator between the people of Israel and the angel who gave him life-giving words on Mount Sinai to pass on to us.

³⁹"But our ancestors rejected Moses and wanted to return to Egypt. ⁴⁰They told Aaron, 'Make us some gods who can lead us, for we don't know what has become of this Moses, who brought us out of Egypt.' ⁴¹So they made an idol shaped like a calf, and they sacrificed to it and rejoiced in this thing they had made. ⁴²Then God turned away from them and gave them up to serve the sun, moon, and stars as their gods! In the book of the prophets it is written,

'Was it to me you were bringing sacrifices
    during those forty years in the wilderness, Israel?
⁴³ No, your real interest was in your pagan gods—
    the shrine of Molech,
    the star god Rephan,
    and the images you made to worship them.

So I will send you into captivity
    far away in Babylon.'

⁴⁴"Our ancestors carried the Tabernacle with them through the wilderness. It was constructed in exact accordance with the plan shown to Moses by God. ⁴⁵Years later, when Joshua led the battles against the Gentile nations that God drove out of this land, the Tabernacle was taken with them into their new territory. And it was used there until the time of King David.

⁴⁶"David found favor with God and asked for the privilege of building a permanent Temple for the God of Jacob. ⁴⁷But it was Solomon who actually built it. ⁴⁸However, the Most High doesn't live in temples made by human hands. As the prophet says,

⁴⁹ 'Heaven is my throne,
    and the earth is my footstool.
    Could you ever build me a temple as good as that?'
        asks the Lord.
    'Could you build a dwelling place for me?
⁵⁰   Didn't I make everything in heaven and earth?'

⁵¹"You stubborn people! You are heathen at heart and deaf to the truth. Must you forever resist the Holy Spirit? But your ancestors did, and so do you! ⁵²Name one prophet your ancestors didn't persecute! They even killed the ones who predicted the coming of the Righteous One—the Messiah whom you betrayed and murdered. ⁵³You deliberately disobeyed God's law, though you received it from the hands of angels."

⁵⁴The Jewish leaders were infuriated by Stephen's accusation, and they shook their fists in rage. ⁵⁵But Stephen, full of the Holy Spirit, gazed steadily upward into heaven and saw the glory of God, and he saw Jesus standing in the place of honor at God's right hand. ⁵⁶And he told them, "Look, I see the heavens opened and the Son of Man standing in the place of honor at God's right hand!"

⁵⁷Then they put their hands over their ears, and drowning out his voice with their shouts, they rushed at him. ⁵⁸They dragged him out of the city and began to stone him. The official witnesses took off their coats and laid them at the feet of a young man named Saul.

⁵⁹And as they stoned him, Stephen prayed, "Lord Jesus, receive my spirit." ⁶⁰And he fell to his knees, shouting, "Lord, don't charge them with this sin!" And with that, he died.

〰〰 **In what ways would you want to be more like Stephen?**
Stephen saw the glory of God and Jesus the Messiah standing at God's right hand. Stephen's vision supported Jesus' claim of being the Messiah and angered the Jewish leaders who had condemned Jesus to death for blasphemy. They would not tolerate Stephen's words, so they dragged him out of the city

and killed him. People may not kill us for witnessing about Christ, but they will let us know they don't want to hear the truth and often try to silence us. Keep honoring God in your conduct and words; though many may turn against you and your message, some will follow Christ. Remember, Stephen's death made a profound impact on Paul, who later became the world's greatest missionary. Even those who oppose you now may later turn to Christ.

Benefits of Persecution

ACTS 8:1-25

Saul was one of the official witnesses at the killing of Stephen.

A great wave of persecution began that day, sweeping over the church in Jerusalem, and all the believers except the apostles fled into Judea and Samaria. ²(Some godly people came and buried Stephen with loud weeping.) ³Saul was going everywhere to devastate the church. He went from house to house, dragging out both men and women to throw them into jail.

⁴But the believers who had fled Jerusalem went everywhere preaching the Good News about Jesus. ⁵Philip, for example, went to the city of Samaria and told the people there about the Messiah. ⁶Crowds listened intently to what he had to say because of the miracles he did. ⁷Many evil spirits were cast out, screaming as they left their victims. And many who had been paralyzed or lame were healed. ⁸So there was great joy in that city.

⁹A man named Simon had been a sorcerer there for many years, claiming to be someone great. ¹⁰The Samaritan people, from the least to the greatest, often spoke of him as "the Great One—the Power of God." ¹¹He was very influential because of the magic he performed. ¹²But now the people believed Philip's message of Good News concerning the Kingdom of God and the name of Jesus Christ. As a result, many men and women were baptized. ¹³Then Simon himself believed and was baptized. He began following Philip wherever he went, and he was amazed by the great miracles and signs Philip performed.

¹⁴When the apostles back in Jerusalem heard that the people of Samaria had accepted God's message, they sent Peter and John there. ¹⁵As soon as they arrived, they prayed for these new Christians to receive the Holy Spirit. ¹⁶The Holy Spirit had not yet come upon any of them, for they had only been baptized in the name of the Lord Jesus. ¹⁷Then Peter and John laid their hands upon these believers, and they received the Holy Spirit.

¹⁸When Simon saw that the Holy Spirit was given when the apostles placed their hands upon people's heads, he offered money to buy this power. ¹⁹"Let me have this power, too," he exclaimed, "so that when I lay my hands on people, they will receive the Holy Spirit!"

²⁰But Peter replied, "May your money perish with you for thinking God's

gift can be bought! [21]You can have no part in this, for your heart is not right before God. [22]Turn from your wickedness and pray to the Lord. Perhaps he will forgive your evil thoughts, [23]for I can see that you are full of bitterness and held captive by sin."

[24]"Pray to the Lord for me," Simon exclaimed, "that these terrible things won't happen to me!"

[25]After testifying and preaching the word of the Lord in Samaria, Peter and John returned to Jerusalem. And they stopped in many Samaritan villages along the way to preach the Good News to them, too.

〜〜〜 **Which difficulties in your life has God used to help you grow spiritually?** Persecution forced the believers out of their homes in Jerusalem, but with them went the gospel. Often we have to become uncomfortable before we'll move. Discomfort may be unwanted, but it is not undesirable, for out of our hurting God works his purposes. The next time you are tempted to complain about uncomfortable or painful circumstances, stop and consider that God may be preparing you for a special task.

OCTOBER

Unexpected Appointment

ACTS 8:26-40

As for Philip, an angel of the Lord said to him, "Go south down the desert road that runs from Jerusalem to Gaza." [27]So he did, and he met the treasurer of Ethiopia, a eunuch of great authority under the queen of Ethiopia. The eunuch had gone to Jerusalem to worship, [28]and he was now returning. Seated in his carriage, he was reading aloud from the book of the prophet Isaiah.

[29]The Holy Spirit said to Philip, "Go over and walk along beside the carriage."

[30]Philip ran over and heard the man reading from the prophet Isaiah; so he asked, "Do you understand what you are reading?"

[31]The man replied, "How can I, when there is no one to instruct me?" And he begged Philip to come up into the carriage and sit with him. [32]The passage of Scripture he had been reading was this:

> "He was led as a sheep to the slaughter.
>   And as a lamb is silent before the shearers,
>   he did not open his mouth.
> [33]He was humiliated and received no justice.
>   Who can speak of his descendants?
>   For his life was taken from the earth."

[34]The eunuch asked Philip, "Was Isaiah talking about himself or someone else?" [35]So Philip began with this same Scripture and then used many others to tell him the Good News about Jesus.

[36]As they rode along, they came to some water, and the eunuch said, "Look! There's some water! Why can't I be baptized?" [38]He ordered the carriage to stop, and they went down into the water, and Philip baptized him.

[39]When they came up out of the water, the Spirit of the Lord caught Philip away. The eunuch never saw him again but went on his way rejoicing. [40]Meanwhile, Philip found himself farther north at the city of Azotus! He preached the Good News there and in every city along the way until he came to Caesarea.

~∿∠ **How can you find an opening in sharing your faith with others?**
Philip found the Ethiopian man reading Scripture. Taking advantage of this opportunity to explain the gospel, Philip asked the man if he understood what he was reading. Philip followed the Spirit's leading and, beginning the discussion where the man was (immersed in the prophecies of Isaiah), explained how Jesus Christ fulfilled Isaiah's prophecies. When we share the gospel, we should start where the other person's concerns are focused. Then we can bring the gospel to bear on those concerns.

OCTOBER

Paul Meets Jesus
ACTS 9:1-19a

Meanwhile, Saul was uttering threats with every breath. He was eager to destroy the Lord's followers, so he went to the high priest. [2]He requested letters addressed to the synagogues in Damascus, asking their cooperation in the arrest of any followers of the Way he found there. He wanted to bring them—both men and women—back to Jerusalem in chains.

[3]As he was nearing Damascus on this mission, a brilliant light from heaven suddenly beamed down upon him! [4]He fell to the ground and heard a voice saying to him, "Saul! Saul! Why are you persecuting me?"

[5]"Who are you, sir?" Saul asked.

And the voice replied, "I am Jesus, the one you are persecuting! [6]Now get up and go into the city, and you will be told what you are to do."

[7]The men with Saul stood speechless with surprise, for they heard the sound of someone's voice, but they saw no one! [8]As Saul picked himself up off the ground, he found that he was blind. [9]So his companions led him by the hand to Damascus. He remained there blind for three days. And all that time he went without food and water.

[10]Now there was a believer in Damascus named Ananias. The Lord spoke to him in a vision, calling, "Ananias!"

"Yes, Lord!" he replied.

¹¹The Lord said, "Go over to Straight Street, to the house of Judas. When you arrive, ask for Saul of Tarsus. He is praying to me right now. ¹²I have shown him a vision of a man named Ananias coming in and laying his hands on him so that he can see again."

¹³"But Lord," exclaimed Ananias, "I've heard about the terrible things this man has done to the believers in Jerusalem! ¹⁴And we hear that he is authorized by the leading priests to arrest every believer in Damascus."

¹⁵But the Lord said, "Go and do what I say. For Saul is my chosen instrument to take my message to the Gentiles and to kings, as well as to the people of Israel. ¹⁶And I will show him how much he must suffer for me."

¹⁷So Ananias went and found Saul. He laid his hands on him and said, "Brother Saul, the Lord Jesus, who appeared to you on the road, has sent me so that you may get your sight back and be filled with the Holy Spirit." ¹⁸Instantly something like scales fell from Saul's eyes, and he regained his sight. Then he got up and was baptized. ¹⁹Afterward he ate some food and was strengthened.

〰〰 **What unusual events has God used to catch your attention?**
As Paul traveled to Damascus, pursuing Christians, he was confronted by the risen Christ and brought face-to-face with the truth of the gospel. Sometimes God breaks into a life in a spectacular manner, and sometimes conversion is a quiet experience. Beware of people who insist that you must have a particular type of conversion experience. The right way to come to faith in Jesus is whatever way God brings *you*.

21 OCTOBER

Paul's New Life
ACTS 9:19b-31

Saul stayed with the believers in Damascus for a few days. ²⁰And immediately he began preaching about Jesus in the synagogues, saying, "He is indeed the Son of God!"

²¹All who heard him were amazed. "Isn't this the same man who persecuted Jesus' followers with such devastation in Jerusalem?" they asked. "And we understand that he came here to arrest them and take them in chains to the leading priests."

²²Saul's preaching became more and more powerful, and the Jews in Damascus couldn't refute his proofs that Jesus was indeed the Messiah. ²³After a while the Jewish leaders decided to kill him. ²⁴But Saul was told about their plot, and that they were watching for him day and night at the city gate so they could murder him. ²⁵So during the night, some of the other believers let him down in a large basket through an opening in the city wall.

²⁶When Saul arrived in Jerusalem, he tried to meet with the believers, but

they were all afraid of him. They thought he was only pretending to be a believer! ²⁷Then Barnabas brought him to the apostles and told them how Saul had seen the Lord on the way to Damascus. Barnabas also told them what the Lord had said to Saul and how he boldly preached in the name of Jesus in Damascus. ²⁸Then the apostles accepted Saul, and after that he was constantly with them in Jerusalem, preaching boldly in the name of the Lord. ²⁹He debated with some Greek-speaking Jews, but they plotted to murder him. ³⁰When the believers heard about it, however, they took him to Caesarea and sent him on to his hometown of Tarsus.

³¹The church then had peace throughout Judea, Galilee, and Samaria, and it grew in strength and numbers. The believers were walking in the fear of the Lord and in the comfort of the Holy Spirit.

〜〰〜 **What are three ways that Christ has changed your life?** It is difficult to change your reputation, and Saul had a terrible reputation with the Christians. But Barnabas, a Jewish convert, became the bridge between Saul and the apostles. New Christians (especially those with tarnished reputations) need sponsors, people who will come alongside, encourage, teach, and introduce them to other believers. Find ways that you can become a Barnabas to new believers.

OCTOBER
22

God Uses Peter
ACTS 9:32-42

Peter traveled from place to place to visit the believers, and in his travels he came to the Lord's people in the town of Lydda. ³³There he met a man named Aeneas, who had been paralyzed and bedridden for eight years. ³⁴Peter said to him, "Aeneas, Jesus Christ heals you! Get up and make your bed!" And he was healed instantly. ³⁵Then the whole population of Lydda and Sharon turned to the Lord when they saw Aeneas walking around.

³⁶There was a believer in Joppa named Tabitha (which in Greek is Dorcas). She was always doing kind things for others and helping the poor. ³⁷About this time she became ill and died. Her friends prepared her for burial and laid her in an upstairs room. ³⁸But they had heard that Peter was nearby at Lydda, so they sent two men to beg him, "Please come as soon as possible!"

³⁹So Peter returned with them; and as soon as he arrived, they took him to the upstairs room. The room was filled with widows who were weeping and showing him the coats and other garments Dorcas had made for them. ⁴⁰But Peter asked them all to leave the room; then he knelt and prayed. Turning to the body he said, "Get up, Tabitha." And she opened her eyes! When she saw Peter, she sat up! ⁴¹He gave her his hand and helped her up.

Then he called in the widows and all the believers, and he showed them that she was alive. ⁴²The news raced through the whole town, and many believed in the Lord.

〰〰 **This past week, what special ability did you use to meet someone's need?** Dorcas made an enormous impact on her community by "always doing kind things for others and helping the poor." When she died, the room was filled with mourners, people she had helped. And when she was brought back to life, the news raced through the town. God uses great preachers like Peter and Paul, but he also uses those who have gifts of kindness like Dorcas. Rather than wishing you had other gifts, make good use of the gifts God has given you.

 OCTOBER

Peter Sees a Lesson
ACTS 10:1-23

In Caesarea there lived a Roman army officer named Cornelius, who was a captain of the Italian Regiment. ²He was a devout man who feared the God of Israel, as did his entire household. He gave generously to charity and was a man who regularly prayed to God. ³One afternoon about three o'clock, he had a vision in which he saw an angel of God coming toward him. "Cornelius!" the angel said.

⁴Cornelius stared at him in terror. "What is it, sir?" he asked the angel.

And the angel replied, "Your prayers and gifts to the poor have not gone unnoticed by God! ⁵Now send some men down to Joppa to find a man named Simon Peter. ⁶He is staying with Simon, a leatherworker who lives near the shore. Ask him to come and visit you."

⁷As soon as the angel was gone, Cornelius called two of his household servants and a devout soldier, one of his personal attendants. ⁸He told them what had happened and sent them off to Joppa.

⁹The next day as Cornelius's messengers were nearing the city, Peter went up to the flat roof to pray. It was about noon, ¹⁰and he was hungry. But while lunch was being prepared, he fell into a trance. ¹¹He saw the sky open, and something like a large sheet was let down by its four corners. ¹²In the sheet were all sorts of animals, reptiles, and birds. ¹³Then a voice said to him, "Get up, Peter; kill and eat them."

¹⁴"Never, Lord," Peter declared. "I have never in all my life eaten anything forbidden by our Jewish laws."

¹⁵The voice spoke again, "If God says something is acceptable, don't say it isn't." ¹⁶The same vision was repeated three times. Then the sheet was pulled up again to heaven.

¹⁷Peter was very perplexed. What could the vision mean? Just then the

men sent by Cornelius found the house and stood outside at the gate. [18]They asked if this was the place where Simon Peter was staying. [19]Meanwhile, as Peter was puzzling over the vision, the Holy Spirit said to him, "Three men have come looking for you. [20]Go down and go with them without hesitation. All is well, for I have sent them." [21]So Peter went down and said, "I'm the man you are looking for. Why have you come?"

[22]They said, "We were sent by Cornelius, a Roman officer. He is a devout man who fears the God of Israel and is well respected by all the Jews. A holy angel instructed him to send for you so you can go to his house and give him a message." [23]So Peter invited the men to be his guests for the night. The next day he went with them, accompanied by some other believers from Joppa.

〜〜〜 **What lessons has God had to repeat in your life?** "What about the heathen who have never heard about Christ?" This is a common question asked about God's justice. Cornelius wasn't a Christian, but he was seeking God, and he was a reverent and generous man. Therefore, God sent Peter to tell Cornelius about Jesus. This shows us that God "rewards those who sincerely seek him" (Heb. 11:6). Those who sincerely seek God will find him! God made Cornelius's knowledge complete.

OCTOBER

Peter Learns a Lesson

ACTS 10:24-48

[Peter] arrived in Caesarea the following day. Cornelius was waiting for him and had called together his relatives and close friends to meet Peter. [25]As Peter entered his home, Cornelius fell to the floor before him in worship. [26]But Peter pulled him up and said, "Stand up! I'm a human being like you!" [27]So Cornelius got up, and they talked together and went inside where the others were assembled.

[28]Peter told them, "You know it is against the Jewish laws for me to come into a Gentile home like this. But God has shown me that I should never think of anyone as impure. [29]So I came as soon as I was sent for. Now tell me why you sent for me."

[30]Cornelius replied, "Four days ago I was praying in my house at three o'clock in the afternoon. Suddenly, a man in dazzling clothes was standing in front of me. [31]He told me, 'Cornelius, your prayers have been heard, and your gifts to the poor have been noticed by God! [32]Now send some men to Joppa and summon Simon Peter. He is staying in the home of Simon, a leatherworker who lives near the shore.' [33]So I sent for you at once, and it was good of you to come. Now here we are, waiting before God to hear the message the Lord has given you."

³⁴Then Peter replied, "I see very clearly that God doesn't show partiality. ³⁵In every nation he accepts those who fear him and do what is right. ³⁶I'm sure you have heard about the Good News for the people of Israel—that there is peace with God through Jesus Christ, who is Lord of all. ³⁷You know what happened all through Judea, beginning in Galilee after John the Baptist began preaching. ³⁸And no doubt you know that God anointed Jesus of Nazareth with the Holy Spirit and with power. Then Jesus went around doing good and healing all who were oppressed by the Devil, for God was with him.

³⁹"And we apostles are witnesses of all he did throughout Israel and in Jerusalem. They put him to death by crucifying him, ⁴⁰but God raised him to life three days later. Then God allowed him to appear, ⁴¹not to the general public, but to us whom God had chosen beforehand to be his witnesses. We were those who ate and drank with him after he rose from the dead. ⁴²And he ordered us to preach everywhere and to testify that Jesus is ordained of God to be the judge of all—the living and the dead. ⁴³He is the one all the prophets testified about, saying that everyone who believes in him will have their sins forgiven through his name."

⁴⁴Even as Peter was saying these things, the Holy Spirit fell upon all who had heard the message. ⁴⁵The Jewish believers who came with Peter were amazed that the gift of the Holy Spirit had been poured out upon the Gentiles, too. ⁴⁶And there could be no doubt about it, for they heard them speaking in tongues and praising God.

Then Peter asked, ⁴⁷"Can anyone object to their being baptized, now that they have received the Holy Spirit just as we did?" ⁴⁸So he gave orders for them to be baptized in the name of Jesus Christ. Afterward Cornelius asked him to stay with them for several days.

✦ **How has God helped you change some attitudes?** Perhaps the greatest barrier to the spread of the gospel in the first century was the Jewish-Gentile conflict. Most of the early believers were Jewish, and to them it was scandalous even to think of associating with Gentiles. But God told Peter to take the gospel to a Roman, and Peter obeyed despite his background and personal feelings. God was making it clear that the Good News of Christ is for everyone! We should not allow any barrier—language, culture, prejudice, geography, economic level, or educational level—to keep us from telling others about Christ.

OCTOBER

Gentiles Get a Chance

ACTS 11:1-18

Soon the news reached the apostles and other believers in Judea that the Gentiles had received the word of God. ²But when Peter arrived back in Jerusalem, some of the Jewish believers criticized him. ³"You entered the home of Gentiles and even ate with them!" they said.

⁴Then Peter told them exactly what had happened. ⁵"One day in Joppa," he said, "while I was praying, I went into a trance and saw a vision. Something like a large sheet was let down by its four corners from the sky. And it came right down to me. ⁶When I looked inside the sheet, I saw all sorts of small animals, wild animals, reptiles, and birds that we are not allowed to eat. ⁷And I heard a voice say, 'Get up, Peter; kill and eat them.'

⁸" 'Never, Lord,' I replied. 'I have never eaten anything forbidden by our Jewish laws.'

⁹"But the voice from heaven came again, 'If God says something is acceptable, don't say it isn't.'

¹⁰"This happened three times before the sheet and all it contained was pulled back up to heaven. ¹¹Just then three men who had been sent from Caesarea arrived at the house where I was staying. ¹²The Holy Spirit told me to go with them and not to worry about their being Gentiles. These six brothers here accompanied me, and we soon arrived at the home of the man who had sent for us. ¹³He told us how an angel had appeared to him in his home and had told him, 'Send messengers to Joppa to find Simon Peter. ¹⁴He will tell you how you and all your household will be saved!'

¹⁵"Well, I began telling them the Good News, but just as I was getting started, the Holy Spirit fell on them, just as he fell on us at the beginning. ¹⁶Then I thought of the Lord's words when he said, 'John baptized with water, but you will be baptized with the Holy Spirit.' ¹⁷And since God gave these Gentiles the same gift he gave us when we believed in the Lord Jesus Christ, who was I to argue?"

¹⁸When the others heard this, all their objections were answered and they began praising God. They said, "God has also given the Gentiles the privilege of turning from sin and receiving eternal life."

~⌁⌁ **On which of your prejudices is God still working?** When Peter brought the news of Cornelius's conversion back to Jerusalem, the believers were shocked that he had eaten with Gentiles. After they heard the whole story, however, they began praising God. Their reactions teach us how to handle disagreements with other Christians. Before judging the behavior of fellow believers, it is important to hear them out. The Holy Spirit may have something important to teach us through them.

Christians Helping One Another

OCTOBER

26

ACTS 11:19-29

Meanwhile, the believers who had fled from Jerusalem during the persecution after Stephen's death traveled as far as Phoenicia, Cyprus, and Antioch of Syria. They preached the Good News, but only to Jews. ²⁰However, some of the believers who went to Antioch from Cyprus and Cyrene began preaching to Gentiles about the Lord Jesus. ²¹The power of the Lord was upon them, and large numbers of these Gentiles believed and turned to the Lord.

²²When the church at Jerusalem heard what had happened, they sent Barnabas to Antioch. ²³When he arrived and saw this proof of God's favor, he was filled with joy, and he encouraged the believers to stay true to the Lord. ²⁴Barnabas was a good man, full of the Holy Spirit and strong in faith. And large numbers of people were brought to the Lord.

²⁵Then Barnabas went on to Tarsus to find Saul. ²⁶When he found him, he brought him back to Antioch. Both of them stayed there with the church for a full year, teaching great numbers of people. (It was there at Antioch that the believers were first called Christians.)

²⁷During this time, some prophets traveled from Jerusalem to Antioch. ²⁸One of them named Agabus stood up in one of the meetings to predict by the Spirit that a great famine was coming upon the entire Roman world. (This was fulfilled during the reign of Claudius.) ²⁹So the believers in Antioch decided to send relief to the believers in Judea, everyone giving as much as they could.

〰〰 **What do you do when you hear stories of extreme poverty or hardship among Christians in other parts of the world?** There were serious food shortages during the reign of the Roman emperor Claudius (A.D. 41–54) because of a drought that had extended across much of the Roman Empire for many years. It is significant that the church in Antioch assisted the church in Jerusalem. The daughter church had grown enough to be able to help the established church. The people of Antioch were motivated to give generously because they cared about the needs of others. This is the cheerful giving that the Bible commends (2 Cor. 9:7). Reluctant giving reflects a lack of concern for people. Focus your concern on the needy, and you will be motivated to give.

27 OCTOBER

A Great Escape and Capital Punishment
ACTS 12:1-25

About that time King Herod Agrippa began to persecute some believers in the church. ²He had the apostle James (John's brother) killed with a sword. ³When Herod saw how much this pleased the Jewish leaders, he arrested Peter during the Passover celebration ⁴and imprisoned him, placing him under the guard of four squads of four soldiers each. Herod's intention was to bring Peter out for public trial after the Passover. ⁵But while Peter was in prison, the church prayed very earnestly for him.

⁶The night before Peter was to be placed on trial, he was asleep, chained between two soldiers, with others standing guard at the prison gate. ⁷Suddenly, there was a bright light in the cell, and an angel of the Lord stood before Peter. The angel tapped him on the side to awaken him and said, "Quick! Get up!" And the chains fell off his wrists. ⁸Then the angel told him, "Get dressed and put on your sandals." And he did. "Now put on your coat and follow me," the angel ordered.

⁹So Peter left the cell, following the angel. But all the time he thought it was a vision. He didn't realize it was really happening. ¹⁰They passed the first and second guard posts and came to the iron gate to the street, and this opened to them all by itself. So they passed through and started walking down the street, and then the angel suddenly left him.

¹¹Peter finally realized what had happened. "It's really true!" he said to himself. "The Lord has sent his angel and saved me from Herod and from what the Jews were hoping to do to me!"

¹²After a little thought, he went to the home of Mary, the mother of John Mark, where many were gathered for prayer. ¹³He knocked at the door in the gate, and a servant girl named Rhoda came to open it. ¹⁴When she recognized Peter's voice, she was so overjoyed that, instead of opening the door, she ran back inside and told everyone, "Peter is standing at the door!"

¹⁵"You're out of your mind," they said. When she insisted, they decided, "It must be his angel."

¹⁶Meanwhile, Peter continued knocking. When they finally went out and opened the door, they were amazed. ¹⁷He motioned for them to quiet down and told them what had happened and how the Lord had led him out of jail. "Tell James and the other brothers what happened," he said. And then he went to another place.

¹⁸At dawn, there was a great commotion among the soldiers about what had happened to Peter. ¹⁹Herod Agrippa ordered a thorough search for him. When he couldn't be found, Herod interrogated the guards and sentenced them to death. Afterward Herod left Judea to stay in Caesarea for a while.

²⁰Now Herod was very angry with the people of Tyre and Sidon. So they sent a delegation to make peace with him because their cities were dependent upon Herod's country for their food. They made friends with Blastus, Herod's personal assistant, ²¹and an appointment with Herod was granted. When the day arrived, Herod put on his royal robes, sat on his throne, and made a speech to them. ²²The people gave him a great ovation, shouting, "It is the voice of a god, not of a man!"

²³Instantly, an angel of the Lord struck Herod with a sickness, because he accepted the people's worship instead of giving the glory to God. So he was consumed with worms and died.

²⁴But God's Good News was spreading rapidly, and there were many new believers.

²⁵When Barnabas and Saul had finished their mission in Jerusalem, they returned to Antioch, taking John Mark with them.

~~How do you react when God answers your prayers?~~ Why did God allow James to die and yet miraculously save Peter? Life is full of difficult questions like this. Why is one child physically handicapped and another child athletically gifted? Why do people die before realizing their potential? These are questions we cannot possibly answer in this life because we do not see all that God sees. God has chosen to allow evil in this world for a time, but we can trust his leading because he has promised to destroy all evil one day. In the meantime, we know that God will help us use our suffering in a way that strengthens us and glorifies him.

28

OCTOBER

Paul and Barnabas: Travel Preaching
ACTS 13:1-12

Among the prophets and teachers of the church at Antioch of Syria were Barnabas, Simeon (called "the black man"), Lucius (from Cyrene), Manaen (the childhood companion of King Herod Antipas), and Saul. ²One day as these men were worshiping the Lord and fasting, the Holy Spirit said, "Dedicate Barnabas and Saul for the special work I have for them." ³So after more fasting and prayer, the men laid their hands on them and sent them on their way.

⁴Sent out by the Holy Spirit, Saul and Barnabas went down to the seaport of Seleucia and then sailed for the island of Cyprus. ⁵There, in the town of Salamis, they went to the Jewish synagogues and preached the word of God. (John Mark went with them as their assistant.)

⁶Afterward they preached from town to town across the entire island until finally they reached Paphos, where they met a Jewish sorcerer, a false prophet named Bar-Jesus. ⁷He had attached himself to the governor, Sergius Paulus, a man of considerable insight and understanding. The governor invited Barnabas and Saul to visit him, for he wanted to hear the word of God. ⁸But Elymas, the sorcerer (as his name means in Greek), interfered and urged the governor to pay no attention to what Saul and Barnabas said. He was trying to turn the governor away from the Christian faith.

⁹Then Saul, also known as Paul, filled with the Holy Spirit, looked the sorcerer in the eye and said, ¹⁰"You son of the Devil, full of every sort of trickery and villainy, enemy of all that is good, will you never stop perverting the true ways of the Lord? ¹¹And now the Lord has laid his hand of punishment upon you, and you will be stricken awhile with blindness." Instantly mist and darkness fell upon him, and he began wandering around begging for someone to take his hand and lead him. ¹²When the governor saw what had happened, he believed and was astonished at what he learned about the Lord.

~~√\√⁄~~ **What Christians do you know who might help you discover more clearly how God wants you to invest your time and abilities?** The church set apart Barnabas and Saul to the work God had for them. They were dedicated for a special purpose. We, too, should dedicate our pastors, missionaries, and Christian workers for their tasks. We can also dedicate ourselves to use our time, money, and talents for God's work. Ask God what he wants you to set apart for him.

OCTOBER

29

Response and Reaction
ACTS 14:1-28

In Iconium, Paul and Barnabas went together to the synagogue and preached with such power that a great number of both Jews and Gentiles believed. ²But the Jews who spurned God's message stirred up distrust among the Gentiles against Paul and Barnabas, saying all sorts of evil things about them. ³The apostles stayed there a long time, preaching boldly about the grace of the Lord. The Lord proved their message was true by giving them power to do miraculous signs and wonders. ⁴But the people of the city were divided in their opinion about them. Some sided with the Jews, and some with the apostles.

⁵A mob of Gentiles and Jews, along with their leaders, decided to attack and stone them. ⁶When the apostles learned of it, they fled for their lives. They went to the region of Lycaonia, to the cities of Lystra and Derbe and the surrounding area, ⁷and they preached the Good News there.

⁸While they were at Lystra, Paul and Barnabas came upon a man with crippled feet. He had been that way from birth, so he had never walked. ⁹He was listening as Paul preached, and Paul noticed him and realized he had faith to be healed. ¹⁰So Paul called to him in a loud voice, "Stand up!" And the man jumped to his feet and started walking.

¹¹When the listening crowd saw what Paul had done, they shouted in their local dialect, "These men are gods in human bodies!" ¹²They decided that Barnabas was the Greek god Zeus and that Paul, because he was the chief speaker, was Hermes. ¹³The temple of Zeus was located on the outskirts of the city. The priest of the temple and the crowd brought oxen and wreaths of flowers, and they prepared to sacrifice to the apostles at the city gates.

¹⁴But when Barnabas and Paul heard what was happening, they tore their clothing in dismay and ran out among the people, shouting, ¹⁵"Friends, why are you doing this? We are merely human beings like yourselves! We have come to bring you the Good News that you should turn from these worthless things to the living God, who made heaven and earth, the sea, and everything in them. ¹⁶In earlier days he permitted all the nations to go their own ways, ¹⁷but he never left himself without a witness. There were always

his reminders, such as sending you rain and good crops and giving you food and joyful hearts." [18]But even so, Paul and Barnabas could scarcely restrain the people from sacrificing to them.

[19]Now some Jews arrived from Antioch and Iconium and turned the crowds into a murderous mob. They stoned Paul and dragged him out of the city, apparently dead. [20]But as the believers stood around him, he got up and went back into the city. The next day he left with Barnabas for Derbe.

[21]After preaching the Good News in Derbe and making many disciples, Paul and Barnabas returned again to Lystra, Iconium, and Antioch of Pisidia, [22]where they strengthened the believers. They encouraged them to continue in the faith, reminding them that they must enter into the Kingdom of God through many tribulations. [23]Paul and Barnabas also appointed elders in every church and prayed for them with fasting, turning them over to the care of the Lord, in whom they had come to trust. [24]Then they traveled back through Pisidia to Pamphylia. [25]They preached again in Perga, then went on to Attalia.

[26]Finally, they returned by ship to Antioch of Syria, where their journey had begun and where they had been committed to the grace of God for the work they had now completed. [27]Upon arriving in Antioch, they called the church together and reported about their trip, telling all that God had done and how he had opened the door of faith to the Gentiles, too. [28]And they stayed there with the believers in Antioch for a long time.

〜〰〜 **How does the gospel act like good news in your life?** We may wish we could perform a miraculous act that would convince everyone once and for all that Jesus is the Lord. But we see here that even if we could perform a miracle, it wouldn't convince everyone. God gave these men power to do great wonders as confirmation of the message of grace, but people were still divided. Don't spend your time and energy wishing for miracles. Sow your seeds of the Good News on the best ground you can find in the best way you can, and leave the convincing to the Holy Spirit.

30 OCTOBER

A Church Conference
ACTS 15:1-21

While Paul and Barnabas were at Antioch of Syria, some men from Judea arrived and began to teach the Christians: "Unless you keep the ancient Jewish custom of circumcision taught by Moses, you cannot be saved." [2]Paul and Barnabas, disagreeing with them, argued forcefully and at length. Finally, Paul and Barnabas were sent to Jerusalem, accompanied by some local believers, to talk to the apostles and elders about this question. [3]The church sent the delegates to Jerusalem, and they stopped along the way in

Phoenicia and Samaria to visit the believers. They told them—much to everyone's joy—that the Gentiles, too, were being converted.

⁴When they arrived in Jerusalem, Paul and Barnabas were welcomed by the whole church, including the apostles and elders. They reported on what God had been doing through their ministry. ⁵But then some of the men who had been Pharisees before their conversion stood up and declared that all Gentile converts must be circumcised and be required to follow the law of Moses.

⁶So the apostles and church elders got together to decide this question. ⁷At the meeting, after a long discussion, Peter stood and addressed them as follows: "Brothers, you all know that God chose me from among you some time ago to preach to the Gentiles so that they could hear the Good News and believe. ⁸God, who knows people's hearts, confirmed that he accepts Gentiles by giving them the Holy Spirit, just as he gave him to us. ⁹He made no distinction between us and them, for he also cleansed their hearts through faith. ¹⁰Why are you now questioning God's way by burdening the Gentile believers with a yoke that neither we nor our ancestors were able to bear? ¹¹We believe that we are all saved the same way, by the special favor of the Lord Jesus."

¹²There was no further discussion, and everyone listened as Barnabas and Paul told about the miraculous signs and wonders God had done through them among the Gentiles.

¹³When they had finished, James stood and said, "Brothers, listen to me. ¹⁴Peter has told you about the time God first visited the Gentiles to take from them a people for himself. ¹⁵And this conversion of Gentiles agrees with what the prophets predicted. For instance, it is written:

> ¹⁶ 'Afterward I will return,
>   and I will restore the fallen kingdom of David.
>   From the ruins I will rebuild it,
>   and I will restore it,
> ¹⁷ so that the rest of humanity might find the Lord,
>   including the Gentiles—
>   all those I have called to be mine.
>   This is what the Lord says,
> ¹⁸   he who made these things known long ago.'

¹⁹And so my judgment is that we should stop troubling the Gentiles who turn to God, ²⁰except that we should write to them and tell them to abstain from eating meat sacrificed to idols, from sexual immorality, and from consuming blood or eating the meat of strangled animals. ²¹For these laws of Moses have been preached in Jewish synagogues in every city on every Sabbath for many generations."

〰️〰️ **How important is it for you to talk over your problems with other Christians?** James's judgment was that Gentile believers did not have to be circumcised, but they should stay away from food offered to idols, from

sexual immorality (a common part of idol worship), from eating meat of strangled animals, and from consuming blood (reflecting the biblical teaching that
the life is in the blood—Lev. 17:14). If Gentile Christians would abstain from
these practices, they would please God and get along better with their Jewish
brothers and sisters in Christ. Of course, there were other actions inappropriate
for believers, but the Jews were especially concerned about these four. This
compromise helped the church grow unhindered by the cultural differences of
Jews and Gentiles. When we share our message across cultural and economic
boundaries, we must be sure that the requirements for faith we set up are
God's, not people's.

31 OCTOBER

The Gentiles Are Accepted

ACTS 15:22-41

Then the apostles and elders and the whole church in Jerusalem chose delegates, and they sent them to Antioch of Syria with Paul and Barnabas to
report on this decision. The men chosen were two of the church leaders—
Judas (also called Barsabbas) and Silas. ²³This is the letter they took along
with them:

> "This letter is from the apostles and elders, your brothers in
> Jerusalem. It is written to the Gentile believers in Antioch, Syria,
> and Cilicia. Greetings!
> ²⁴"We understand that some men from here have troubled you
> and upset you with their teaching, but they had no such instruc-
> tions from us. ²⁵So it seemed good to us, having unanimously
> agreed on our decision, to send you these official representatives,
> along with our beloved Barnabas and Paul, ²⁶who have risked their
> lives for the sake of our Lord Jesus Christ. ²⁷So we are sending
> Judas and Silas to tell you what we have decided concerning your
> question.
> ²⁸"For it seemed good to the Holy Spirit and to us to lay no
> greater burden on you than these requirements: ²⁹You must abstain
> from eating food offered to idols, from consuming blood or eating
> the meat of strangled animals, and from sexual immorality. If you
> do this, you will do well. Farewell."

³⁰The four messengers went at once to Antioch, where they called a
general meeting of the Christians and delivered the letter. ³¹And there was
great joy throughout the church that day as they read this encouraging
message.
³²Then Judas and Silas, both being prophets, spoke extensively to the
Christians, encouraging and strengthening their faith. ³³They stayed for a

while, and then Judas and Silas were sent back to Jerusalem, with the blessings of the Christians, to those who had sent them. ³⁵Paul and Barnabas stayed in Antioch to assist many others who were teaching and preaching the word of the Lord there.

³⁶After some time Paul said to Barnabas, "Let's return to each city where we previously preached the word of the Lord, to see how the new believers are getting along." ³⁷Barnabas agreed and wanted to take along John Mark. ³⁸But Paul disagreed strongly, since John Mark had deserted them in Pamphylia and had not shared in their work. ³⁹Their disagreement over this was so sharp that they separated. Barnabas took John Mark with him and sailed for Cyprus. ⁴⁰Paul chose Silas, and the believers sent them off, entrusting them to the Lord's grace. ⁴¹So they traveled throughout Syria and Cilicia to strengthen the churches there.

〰〰 **In what ways is God affecting the way you live and plan?** Paul and Barnabas disagreed sharply over Mark. Paul didn't want to take him along because he had left them earlier (Acts 13:13). This disagreement caused the two great preachers to form two teams, opening up two missionary endeavors instead of one. God works even through conflict and disagreements. Later, Mark became vital to Paul's ministry (Col. 4:10). Christians do not always agree, but problems can be solved by agreeing to disagree and letting God work his will.

Paul, Silas, and Timothy
Acts 16:1-15

Paul and Silas went first to Derbe and then on to Lystra. There they met Timothy, a young disciple whose mother was a Jewish believer, but whose father was a Greek. [2]Timothy was well thought of by the believers in Lystra and Iconium, [3]so Paul wanted him to join them on their journey. In deference to the Jews of the area, he arranged for Timothy to be circumcised before they left, for everyone knew that his father was a Greek. [4]Then they went from town to town, explaining the decision regarding the commandments that were to be obeyed, as decided by the apostles and elders in Jerusalem. [5]So the churches were strengthened in their faith and grew daily in numbers.

[6]Next Paul and Silas traveled through the area of Phrygia and Galatia, because the Holy Spirit had told them not to go into the province of Asia at that time. [7]Then coming to the borders of Mysia, they headed for the province of Bithynia, but again the Spirit of Jesus did not let them go. [8]So instead, they went on through Mysia to the city of Troas.

[9]That night Paul had a vision. He saw a man from Macedonia in northern Greece, pleading with him, "Come over here and help us." [10]So we decided to leave for Macedonia at once, for we could only conclude that God was calling us to preach the Good News there.

[11]We boarded a boat at Troas and sailed straight across to the island of Samothrace, and the next day we landed at Neapolis. [12]From there we reached Philippi, a major city of the district of Macedonia and a Roman colony; we stayed there several days.

[13]On the Sabbath we went a little way outside the city to a riverbank, where we supposed that some people met for prayer, and we sat down to speak with some women who had come together. [14]One of them was Lydia from Thyatira, a merchant of expensive purple cloth. She was a worshiper of God. As she listened to us, the Lord opened her heart, and she accepted what Paul was saying. [15]She was baptized along with other members of her household, and she asked us to be her guests. "If you agree that I am faith-

ful to the Lord," she said, "come and stay at my home." And she urged us until we did.

〰〰 **How would you describe the spiritual team of which you are part?** We don't know how the Holy Spirit told Paul that he and his men were not to go into Asia. It may have been through a prophet, a vision, an inner conviction, or some circumstance. To know God's will does not mean we must hear his voice. He leads in different ways. When seeking God's will: (1) Make sure your plan is in harmony with God's Word. (2) Ask mature Christians for their advice. (3) Check your motives—are you trying to do what you want or what you think God wants? (4) Pray for God to open and close the doors of circumstances.

NOVEMBER

Adventures in Jail
ACTS 16:16-40

One day as we were going down to the place of prayer, we met a demon-possessed slave girl. She was a fortune-teller who earned a lot of money for her masters. [17]She followed along behind us shouting, "These men are servants of the Most High God, and they have come to tell you how to be saved."

[18]This went on day after day until Paul got so exasperated that he turned and spoke to the demon within her. "I command you in the name of Jesus Christ to come out of her," he said. And instantly it left her.

[19]Her masters' hopes of wealth were now shattered, so they grabbed Paul and Silas and dragged them before the authorities at the marketplace. [20]"The whole city is in an uproar because of these Jews!" they shouted. [21]"They are teaching the people to do things that are against Roman customs."

[22]A mob quickly formed against Paul and Silas, and the city officials ordered them stripped and beaten with wooden rods. [23]They were severely beaten, and then they were thrown into prison. The jailer was ordered to make sure they didn't escape. [24]So he took no chances but put them into the inner dungeon and clamped their feet in the stocks.

[25]Around midnight, Paul and Silas were praying and singing hymns to God, and the other prisoners were listening. [26]Suddenly, there was a great earthquake, and the prison was shaken to its foundations. All the doors flew open, and the chains of every prisoner fell off! [27]The jailer woke up to see the prison doors wide open. He assumed the prisoners had escaped, so he drew his sword to kill himself. [28]But Paul shouted to him, "Don't do it! We are all here!"

[29]Trembling with fear, the jailer called for lights and ran to the dungeon and fell down before Paul and Silas. [30]He brought them out and asked, "Sirs, what must I do to be saved?"

³¹They replied, "Believe on the Lord Jesus and you will be saved, along with your entire household." ³²Then they shared the word of the Lord with him and all who lived in his household. ³³That same hour the jailer washed their wounds, and he and everyone in his household were immediately baptized. ³⁴Then he brought them into his house and set a meal before them. He and his entire household rejoiced because they all believed in God.

³⁵The next morning the city officials sent the police to tell the jailer, "Let those men go!" ³⁶So the jailer told Paul, "You and Silas are free to leave. Go in peace."

³⁷But Paul replied, "They have publicly beaten us without trial and jailed us—and we are Roman citizens. So now they want us to leave secretly? Certainly not! Let them come themselves to release us!"

³⁸When the police made their report, the city officials were alarmed to learn that Paul and Silas were Roman citizens. ³⁹They came to the jail and apologized to them. Then they brought them out and begged them to leave the city. ⁴⁰Paul and Silas then returned to the home of Lydia, where they met with the believers and encouraged them once more before leaving town.

〜〜〜 **How would you react to God using a difficult situation of yours to help another person discover him?** Paul and Silas's reputation in Philippi was well known. When the jailer realized his own true condition and need, he risked everything to find the answer. The Good News of salvation is simply expressed: Believe on the Lord Jesus, and you will be saved. When we recognize Jesus as Lord and trust in him, salvation is assured to us. If you have never trusted in Jesus to save you, do so quickly. Your life can be filled with joy, just as the jailer's was.

Different Responses from Two Cities

NOVEMBER

ACTS 17:1-15

Now Paul and Silas traveled through the towns of Amphipolis and Apollonia and came to Thessalonica, where there was a Jewish synagogue. ²As was Paul's custom, he went to the synagogue service, and for three Sabbaths in a row he interpreted the Scriptures to the people. ³He was explaining and proving the prophecies about the sufferings of the Messiah and his rising from the dead. He said, "This Jesus I'm telling you about is the Messiah." ⁴Some who listened were persuaded and became converts, including a large number of godly Greek men and also many important women of the city.

⁵But the Jewish leaders were jealous, so they gathered some worthless fellows from the streets to form a mob and start a riot. They attacked the home of Jason, searching for Paul and Silas so they could drag them out to the crowd. ⁶Not finding them there, they dragged out Jason and some of the

other believers instead and took them before the city council. "Paul and Silas have turned the rest of the world upside down, and now they are here disturbing our city," they shouted. [7]"And Jason has let them into his home. They are all guilty of treason against Caesar, for they profess allegiance to another king, Jesus."

[8]The people of the city, as well as the city officials, were thrown into turmoil by these reports. [9]But the officials released Jason and the other believers after they had posted bail.

[10]That very night the believers sent Paul and Silas to Berea. When they arrived there, they went to the synagogue. [11]And the people of Berea were more open-minded than those in Thessalonica, and they listened eagerly to Paul's message. They searched the Scriptures day after day to check up on Paul and Silas, to see if they were really teaching the truth. [12]As a result, many Jews believed, as did some of the prominent Greek women and many men.

[13]But when some Jews in Thessalonica learned that Paul was preaching the word of God in Berea, they went there and stirred up trouble. [14]The believers acted at once, sending Paul on to the coast, while Silas and Timothy remained behind. [15]Those escorting Paul went with him to Athens; then they returned to Berea with a message for Silas and Timothy to hurry and join him.

〰️〰️ **What part does the Bible play in your evaluation of what you hear and read?** How do you evaluate sermons and teachings? The people in Berea opened the Scriptures for themselves and searched to verify or disprove the message they heard. Always compare what you hear with what the Bible says. A preacher or teacher who gives God's true message will never contradict or explain away anything in God's Word.

4

Paul in Athens
Acts 17:16-34

While Paul was waiting for them in Athens, he was deeply troubled by all the idols he saw everywhere in the city. [17]He went to the synagogue to debate with the Jews and the God-fearing Gentiles, and he spoke daily in the public square to all who happened to be there.

[18]He also had a debate with some of the Epicurean and Stoic philosophers. When he told them about Jesus and his resurrection, they said, "This babbler has picked up some strange ideas." Others said, "He's pushing some foreign religion."

[19]Then they took him to the Council of Philosophers. "Come and tell us more about this new religion," they said. [20]"You are saying some rather startling things, and we want to know what it's all about." [21](It should be

explained that all the Athenians as well as the foreigners in Athens seemed to spend all their time discussing the latest ideas.)

²²So Paul, standing before the Council, addressed them as follows: "Men of Athens, I notice that you are very religious, ²³for as I was walking along I saw your many altars. And one of them had this inscription on it—'To an Unknown God.' You have been worshiping him without knowing who he is, and now I wish to tell you about him.

²⁴"He is the God who made the world and everything in it. Since he is Lord of heaven and earth, he doesn't live in man-made temples, ²⁵and human hands can't serve his needs—for he has no needs. He himself gives life and breath to everything, and he satisfies every need there is. ²⁶From one man he created all the nations throughout the whole earth. He decided beforehand which should rise and fall, and he determined their boundaries.

²⁷"His purpose in all of this was that the nations should seek after God and perhaps feel their way toward him and find him—though he is not far from any one of us. ²⁸For in him we live and move and exist. As one of your own poets says, 'We are his offspring.' ²⁹And since this is true, we shouldn't think of God as an idol designed by craftsmen from gold or silver or stone. ³⁰God overlooked people's former ignorance about these things, but now he commands everyone everywhere to turn away from idols and turn to him. ³¹For he has set a day for judging the world with justice by the man he has appointed, and he proved to everyone who this is by raising him from the dead."

³²When they heard Paul speak of the resurrection of a person who had been dead, some laughed, but others said, "We want to hear more about this later." ³³That ended Paul's discussion with them, ³⁴but some joined him and became believers. Among them were Dionysius, a member of the Council, a woman named Damaris, and others.

〰〰 **What symbols of God's presence do you see around you in society?** Paul was well prepared to speak to these philosophers. He came from Tarsus, an educational center, and had the training and knowledge to present his beliefs clearly and persuasively. Paul was a rabbi, taught by the finest scholar of his day, Gamaliel, and he had spent much of his life thinking and reasoning through the Scriptures. While it is important to share our faith with conviction, we, like Paul, must also be prepared. The more we know about the Bible—what it means and how to apply it to our life—the more convincing our words will be. This does not mean that we should avoid presenting the gospel until we feel adequately prepared. We should work with what we know but always seek to know more in order to reach more people and answer their questions and arguments more effectively.

5

Paul in Ephesus
ACTS 19:1-20

While Apollos was in Corinth, Paul traveled through the interior provinces. Finally, he came to Ephesus, where he found several believers. ²"Did you receive the Holy Spirit when you believed?" he asked them.

"No," they replied, "we don't know what you mean. We haven't even heard that there is a Holy Spirit."

³"Then what baptism did you experience?" he asked.

And they replied, "The baptism of John."

⁴Paul said, "John's baptism was to demonstrate a desire to turn from sin and turn to God. John himself told the people to believe in Jesus, the one John said would come later."

⁵As soon as they heard this, they were baptized in the name of the Lord Jesus. ⁶Then when Paul laid his hands on them, the Holy Spirit came on them, and they spoke in other tongues and prophesied. ⁷There were about twelve men in all.

⁸Then Paul went to the synagogue and preached boldly for the next three months, arguing persuasively about the Kingdom of God. ⁹But some rejected his message and publicly spoke against the Way, so Paul left the synagogue and took the believers with him. Then he began preaching daily at the lecture hall of Tyrannus. ¹⁰This went on for the next two years, so that people throughout the province of Asia—both Jews and Greeks—heard the Lord's message.

¹¹God gave Paul the power to do unusual miracles, ¹²so that even when handkerchiefs or cloths that had touched his skin were placed on sick people, they were healed of their diseases, and any evil spirits within them came out.

¹³A team of Jews who were traveling from town to town casting out evil spirits tried to use the name of the Lord Jesus. The incantation they used was this: "I command you by Jesus, whom Paul preaches, to come out!" ¹⁴Seven sons of Sceva, a leading priest, were doing this. ¹⁵But when they tried it on a man possessed by an evil spirit, the spirit replied, "I know Jesus, and I know Paul. But who are you?" ¹⁶And he leaped on them and attacked them with such violence that they fled from the house, naked and badly injured.

¹⁷The story of what happened spread quickly all through Ephesus, to Jews and Greeks alike. A solemn fear descended on the city, and the name of the Lord Jesus was greatly honored. ¹⁸Many who became believers confessed their sinful practices. ¹⁹A number of them who had been practicing magic brought their incantation books and burned them at a public bonfire. The value of the books was several million dollars. ²⁰So the message about the Lord spread widely and had a powerful effect.

In what situations are you most likely to become discouraged?
Ephesus was considered a center for black magic and other occult practices. The people sought spells to give them wealth, happiness, and success in marriage. Superstition and sorcery were commonplace. God clearly forbids such practices (Deut. 18:9-13). You cannot be a believer and hold onto the occult, black magic, or sorcery. Once you begin to dabble in these areas, it is extremely easy to become obsessed by them because Satan is very powerful. But God's power is even greater. If you are mixed up or even interested in the occult, learn a lesson from the Ephesians and get rid of anything that lures you into such practices.

NOVEMBER

The Riot

ACTS 19:21-41

Afterward Paul felt impelled by the Holy Spirit to go over to Macedonia and Achaia before returning to Jerusalem. "And after that," he said, "I must go on to Rome!" [22]He sent his two assistants, Timothy and Erastus, on ahead to Macedonia while he stayed awhile longer in the province of Asia.

[23]But about that time, serious trouble developed in Ephesus concerning the Way. [24]It began with Demetrius, a silversmith who had a large business manufacturing silver shrines of the Greek goddess Artemis. He kept many craftsmen busy. [25]He called the craftsmen together, along with others employed in related trades, and addressed them as follows:

"Gentlemen, you know that our wealth comes from this business. [26]As you have seen and heard, this man Paul has persuaded many people that handmade gods aren't gods at all. And this is happening not only here in Ephesus but throughout the entire province! [27]Of course, I'm not just talking about the loss of public respect for our business. I'm also concerned that the temple of the great goddess Artemis will lose its influence and that Artemis—this magnificent goddess worshiped throughout the province of Asia and all around the world—will be robbed of her prestige!"

[28]At this their anger boiled, and they began shouting, "Great is Artemis of the Ephesians!" [29]A crowd began to gather, and soon the city was filled with confusion. Everyone rushed to the amphitheater, dragging along Gaius and Aristarchus, who were Paul's traveling companions from Macedonia. [30]Paul wanted to go in, but the believers wouldn't let him. [31]Some of the officials of the province, friends of Paul, also sent a message to him, begging him not to risk his life by entering the amphitheater.

[32]Inside, the people were all shouting, some one thing and some another. Everything was in confusion. In fact, most of them didn't even know why they were there. [33]Alexander was thrust forward by some of the Jews, who encouraged him to explain the situation. He motioned for silence and tried

to speak in defense. ³⁴But when the crowd realized he was a Jew, they started shouting again and kept it up for two hours: "Great is Artemis of the Ephesians! Great is Artemis of the Ephesians!"

³⁵At last the mayor was able to quiet them down enough to speak. "Citizens of Ephesus," he said. "Everyone knows that Ephesus is the official guardian of the temple of the great Artemis, whose image fell down to us from heaven. ³⁶Since this is an indisputable fact, you shouldn't be disturbed, no matter what is said. Don't do anything rash. ³⁷You have brought these men here, but they have stolen nothing from the temple and have not spoken against our goddess. ³⁸If Demetrius and the craftsmen have a case against them, the courts are in session and the judges can take the case at once. Let them go through legal channels. ³⁹And if there are complaints about other matters, they can be settled in a legal assembly. ⁴⁰I am afraid we are in danger of being charged with rioting by the Roman government, since there is no cause for all this commotion. And if Rome demands an explanation, we won't know what to say." ⁴¹Then he dismissed them, and they dispersed.

∿⌇ When are you most likely to forget that God is in control?

When Paul preached in Ephesus, Demetrius and his fellow craftsmen did not quarrel with his doctrine. Their anger boiled because his preaching threatened their profits. They made silver statues of the Ephesian goddess Diana. The craftsmen knew that if people started believing in God and discarding the idols, their livelihood would suffer. Demetrius's strategy for stirring up a riot was to appeal to his fellow workmen's love of money and then to encourage them to hide their greed behind the mask of patriotism and religious loyalty. The rioters couldn't see the selfish motives for their rioting—instead they saw themselves as heroes for the sake of their land and beliefs. It is amazing the lengths to which people will go even today to silence Christians. We must be always ready to defend our faith, no matter what the consequences.

7

NOVEMBER

Sleeping in Church
ACTS 20:1-12

When it was all over, Paul sent for the believers and encouraged them. Then he said good-bye and left for Macedonia. ²Along the way, he encouraged the believers in all the towns he passed through. Then he traveled down to Greece, ³where he stayed for three months. He was preparing to sail back to Syria when he discovered a plot by some Jews against his life, so he decided to return through Macedonia.

⁴Several men were traveling with him. They were Sopater of Berea, the son of Pyrrhus; Aristarchus and Secundus, from Thessalonica; Gaius, from Derbe; Timothy; and Tychicus and Trophimus, who were from the province

of Asia. [5]They went ahead and waited for us at Troas. [6]As soon as the Passover season ended, we boarded a ship at Philippi in Macedonia and five days later arrived in Troas, where we stayed a week.

[7]On the first day of the week, we gathered to observe the Lord's Supper. Paul was preaching; and since he was leaving the next day, he talked until midnight. [8]The upstairs room where we met was lighted with many flickering lamps. [9]As Paul spoke on and on, a young man named Eutychus, sitting on the windowsill, became very drowsy. Finally, he sank into a deep sleep and fell three stories to his death below. [10]Paul went down, bent over him, and took him into his arms. "Don't worry," he said, "he's alive!" [11]Then they all went back upstairs and ate the Lord's Supper together. And Paul continued talking to them until dawn; then he left. [12]Meanwhile, the young man was taken home unhurt, and everyone was greatly relieved.

〜〜〜 **How does God respond to your human weaknesses?** The combination of the heat from the candles and the number of people in the upstairs room making the room very warm, and the late hour, no doubt, helped Eutychus fall asleep and then tumble out the window. Notice that Paul showed concern for the young man, not anger at the interruption. How do you deal with others' weaknesses? Are you able to show compassion?

Saying Good-Bye to Ephesus

NOVEMBER

8

ACTS 20:13-38

Paul went by land to Assos, where he had arranged for us to join him, and we went on ahead by ship. [14]He joined us there and we sailed together to Mitylene. [15]The next day we passed the island of Kios. The following day, we crossed to the island of Samos. And a day later we arrived at Miletus.

[16]Paul had decided against stopping at Ephesus this time because he didn't want to spend further time in the province of Asia. He was hurrying to get to Jerusalem, if possible, for the Festival of Pentecost. [17]But when we landed at Miletus, he sent a message to the elders of the church at Ephesus, asking them to come down to meet him.

[18]When they arrived he declared, "You know that from the day I set foot in the province of Asia until now [19]I have done the Lord's work humbly— yes, and with tears. I have endured the trials that came to me from the plots of the Jews. [20]Yet I never shrank from telling you the truth, either publicly or in your homes. [21]I have had one message for Jews and Gentiles alike— the necessity of turning from sin and turning to God, and of faith in our Lord Jesus.

[22]"And now I am going to Jerusalem, drawn there irresistibly by the Holy Spirit, not knowing what awaits me, [23]except that the Holy Spirit has told me in

city after city that jail and suffering lie ahead. [24]But my life is worth nothing unless I use it for doing the work assigned me by the Lord Jesus—the work of telling others the Good News about God's wonderful kindness and love.

[25]"And now I know that none of you to whom I have preached the Kingdom will ever see me again. [26]Let me say plainly that I have been faithful. No one's damnation can be blamed on me, [27]for I didn't shrink from declaring all that God wants for you.

[28]"And now beware! Be sure that you feed and shepherd God's flock— his church, purchased with his blood—over whom the Holy Spirit has appointed you as elders. [29]I know full well that false teachers, like vicious wolves, will come in among you after I leave, not sparing the flock. [30]Even some of you will distort the truth in order to draw a following. [31]Watch out! Remember the three years I was with you—my constant watch and care over you night and day, and my many tears for you.

[32]"And now I entrust you to God and the word of his grace—his message that is able to build you up and give you an inheritance with all those he has set apart for himself.

[33]"I have never coveted anyone's money or fine clothing. [34]You know that these hands of mine have worked to pay my own way, and I have even supplied the needs of those who were with me. [35]And I have been a constant example of how you can help the poor by working hard. You should remember the words of the Lord Jesus: 'It is more blessed to give than to receive.' "

[36]When he had finished speaking, he knelt and prayed with them. [37]They wept aloud as they embraced him in farewell, [38]sad most of all because he had said that they would never see him again. Then they accompanied him down to the ship.

~∿⁄_ **When have painful good-byes worked for the best in your life?**
Paul's relationship with these believers is a beautiful example of Christian fellowship. He had cared for them and loved them, even cried over their needs. They responded with love and care for him and sorrow over his leaving. They had prayed together and comforted one another. Like Paul, you can build strong relationships with other Christians by sharing, caring, sorrowing, rejoicing, and praying with them. You will gather others around you only by giving yourself away to them.

9

Difficult Decision
ACTS 21:1-17

After saying farewell to the Ephesian elders, we sailed straight to the island of Cos. The next day we reached Rhodes and then went to Patara. [2]There we boarded a ship sailing for the Syrian province of Phoenicia. [3]We sighted the island of Cyprus, passed it on our left, and landed at the harbor of Tyre, in Syria, where the ship was to unload. [4]We went ashore, found the local believers, and stayed with them a week. These disciples prophesied through the Holy Spirit that Paul should not go on to Jerusalem. ⁵When we returned to the ship at the end of the week, the entire congregation, including wives and children, came down to the shore with us. There we knelt, prayed, ⁶and said our farewells. Then we went aboard, and they returned home.

⁷The next stop after leaving Tyre was Ptolemais, where we greeted the believers but stayed only one day. ⁸Then we went on to Caesarea and stayed at the home of Philip the Evangelist, one of the seven men who had been chosen to distribute food. ⁹He had four unmarried daughters who had the gift of prophecy.

¹⁰During our stay of several days, a man named Agabus, who also had the gift of prophecy, arrived from Judea. ¹¹When he visited us, he took Paul's belt and bound his own feet and hands with it. Then he said, "The Holy Spirit declares, 'So shall the owner of this belt be bound by the Jewish leaders in Jerusalem and turned over to the Romans.' " ¹²When we heard this, we who were traveling with him, as well as the local believers, begged Paul not to go on to Jerusalem.

¹³But he said, "Why all this weeping? You are breaking my heart! For I am ready not only to be jailed at Jerusalem but also to die for the sake of the Lord Jesus." ¹⁴When it was clear that we couldn't persuade him, we gave up and said, "The will of the Lord be done."

¹⁵Shortly afterward we packed our things and left for Jerusalem. ¹⁶Some believers from Caesarea accompanied us, and they took us to the home of Mnason, a man originally from Cyprus and one of the early disciples. ¹⁷All the believers in Jerusalem welcomed us cordially.

~~⁓⁓~~ **What hard decisions do you have to make?** Paul knew that he would be imprisoned in Jerusalem. His friends pleaded with him to not go there because of the suffering he would endure, but Paul knew he had to because God wanted him to. No one wants to face hardship or suffering, but a faithful disciple wants above all else to please God. Our desire to please God should overshadow our desire to avoid hardship and suffering. When we really want to do God's will, we must accept all that comes with it—even the pain. Then we can say with Paul, "The will of the Lord be done."

NOVEMBER

Paul in Jerusalem
ACTS 21:18-36

10

The next day Paul went in with us to meet with James, and all the elders of the Jerusalem church were present. ¹⁹After greetings were exchanged, Paul gave a detailed account of the things God had accomplished among the Gentiles through his ministry.

²⁰After hearing this, they praised God. But then they said, "You know,

dear brother, how many thousands of Jews have also believed, and they all take the law of Moses very seriously. ²¹Our Jewish Christians here at Jerusalem have been told that you are teaching all the Jews living in the Gentile world to turn their backs on the laws of Moses. They say that you teach people not to circumcise their children or follow other Jewish customs. ²²Now what can be done? For they will certainly hear that you have come.

²³"Here's our suggestion. We have four men here who have taken a vow and are preparing to shave their heads. ²⁴Go with them to the Temple and join them in the purification ceremony, and pay for them to have their heads shaved. Then everyone will know that the rumors are all false and that you yourself observe the Jewish laws.

²⁵"As for the Gentile Christians, all we ask of them is what we already told them in a letter: They should not eat food offered to idols, nor consume blood, nor eat meat from strangled animals, and they should stay away from all sexual immorality."

²⁶So Paul agreed to their request, and the next day he went through the purification ritual with the men and went to the Temple. Then he publicly announced the date when their vows would end and sacrifices would be offered for each of them.

²⁷The seven days were almost ended when some Jews from the province of Asia saw Paul in the Temple and roused a mob against him. They grabbed him, ²⁸yelling, "Men of Israel! Help! This is the man who teaches against our people and tells everybody to disobey the Jewish laws. He speaks against the Temple—and he even defiles it by bringing Gentiles in!" ²⁹(For earlier that day they had seen him in the city with Trophimus, a Gentile from Ephesus, and they assumed Paul had taken him into the Temple.)

³⁰The whole population of the city was rocked by these accusations, and a great riot followed. Paul was dragged out of the Temple, and immediately the gates were closed behind him. ³¹As they were trying to kill him, word reached the commander of the Roman regiment that all Jerusalem was in an uproar. ³²He immediately called out his soldiers and officers and ran down among the crowd. When the mob saw the commander and the troops coming, they stopped beating Paul. ³³The commander arrested him and ordered him bound with two chains. Then he asked the crowd who he was and what he had done. ³⁴Some shouted one thing and some another. He couldn't find out the truth in all the uproar and confusion, so he ordered Paul to be taken to the fortress. ³⁵As they reached the stairs, the mob grew so violent the soldiers had to lift Paul to their shoulders to protect him. ³⁶And the crowd followed behind shouting, "Kill him, kill him!"

~\/\~ **How important is it to respect the consciences of others?** The Jerusalem Council (Acts 15) had settled the issue of circumcision of Gentile believers. Evidently there was a rumor that Paul had gone far beyond their decision, even forbidding Jews to circumcise their children. This, of course, was not true, and so Paul willingly submitted to Jewish custom to show that he was not working against the council's decision and that he was still Jewish in his life-style. Sometimes we must go the second mile to avoid offending others, especially when not doing so would hinder God's work.

Paul Speaks

ACTS 21:37–22:29

11

As Paul was about to be taken inside, he said to the commander, "May I have a word with you?"

"Do you know Greek?" the commander asked, surprised. ³⁸"Aren't you the Egyptian who led a rebellion some time ago and took four thousand members of the Assassins out into the desert?"

³⁹"No," Paul replied, "I am a Jew from Tarsus in Cilicia, which is an important city. Please, let me talk to these people." ⁴⁰The commander agreed, so Paul stood on the stairs and motioned to the people to be quiet. Soon a deep silence enveloped the crowd, and he addressed them in their own language, Aramaic.

22:1"Brothers and esteemed fathers," Paul said, "listen to me as I offer my defense." ²When they heard him speaking in their own language, the silence was even greater. ³"I am a Jew, born in Tarsus, a city in Cilicia, and I was brought up and educated here in Jerusalem under Gamaliel. At his feet I learned to follow our Jewish laws and customs very carefully. I became very zealous to honor God in everything I did, just as all of you are today. ⁴And I persecuted the followers of the Way, hounding some to death, binding and delivering both men and women to prison. ⁵The high priest and the whole council of leaders can testify that this is so. For I received letters from them to our Jewish brothers in Damascus, authorizing me to bring the Christians from there to Jerusalem, in chains, to be punished.

⁶"As I was on the road, nearing Damascus, about noon a very bright light from heaven suddenly shone around me. ⁷I fell to the ground and heard a voice saying to me, 'Saul, Saul, why are you persecuting me?'

⁸" 'Who are you, sir?' I asked. And he replied, 'I am Jesus of Nazareth, the one you are persecuting.' ⁹The people with me saw the light but didn't hear the voice.

¹⁰"I said, 'What shall I do, Lord?' And the Lord told me, 'Get up and go into Damascus, and there you will be told all that you are to do.'

¹¹"I was blinded by the intense light and had to be led into Damascus by my companions. ¹²A man named Ananias lived there. He was a godly man in his devotion to the law, and he was well thought of by all the Jews of Damascus. ¹³He came to me and stood beside me and said, 'Brother Saul, receive your sight.' And that very hour I could see him!

¹⁴"Then he told me, 'The God of our ancestors has chosen you to know

421

his will and to see the Righteous One and hear him speak. [15]You are to take his message everywhere, telling the whole world what you have seen and heard. [16]And now, why delay? Get up and be baptized, and have your sins washed away, calling on the name of the Lord.'

[17]"One day after I returned to Jerusalem, I was praying in the Temple, and I fell into a trance. [18]I saw a vision of Jesus saying to me, 'Hurry! Leave Jerusalem, for the people here won't believe you when you give them your testimony about me.'

[19]" 'But Lord,' I argued, 'they certainly know that I imprisoned and beat those in every synagogue who believed on you. [20]And when your witness Stephen was killed, I was standing there agreeing. I kept the coats they laid aside as they stoned him.'

[21]"But the Lord said to me, 'Leave Jerusalem, for I will send you far away to the Gentiles!' "

[22]The crowd listened until Paul came to that word; then with one voice they shouted, "Away with such a fellow! Kill him! He isn't fit to live!" [23]They yelled, threw off their coats, and tossed handfuls of dust into the air.

[24]The commander brought Paul inside and ordered him lashed with whips to make him confess his crime. He wanted to find out why the crowd had become so furious. [25]As they tied Paul down to lash him, Paul said to the officer standing there, "Is it legal for you to whip a Roman citizen who hasn't even been tried?"

[26]The officer went to the commander and asked, "What are you doing? This man is a Roman citizen!"

[27]So the commander went over and asked Paul, "Tell me, are you a Roman citizen?"

"Yes, I certainly am," Paul replied.

[28]"I am, too," the commander muttered, "and it cost me plenty!"

"But I am a citizen by birth!"

[29]The soldiers who were about to interrogate Paul quickly withdrew when they heard he was a Roman citizen, and the commander was frightened because he had ordered him bound and whipped.

〰〰 **How can you relate what Paul is saying to what God has done in your life?** After gaining a hearing and establishing common ground with his audience, Paul gave his testimony. He shared how he had come to faith in Christ. Sound reasoning is good, but it is also important to simply share what Christ has done in our life. But no matter how we present the message, not everyone will accept it, as Paul knew. We must faithfully and responsibly present the gospel and leave the results to God.

A Plan to Kill Paul

ACTS 22:30–23:22

12

The next day the commander freed Paul from his chains and ordered the leading priests into session with the Jewish high council. He had Paul brought in before them to try to find out what the trouble was all about.

²³:¹Gazing intently at the high council, Paul began: "Brothers, I have always lived before God in all good conscience!"

²Instantly Ananias the high priest commanded those close to Paul to slap him on the mouth. ³But Paul said to him, "God will slap you, you white-washed wall! What kind of judge are you to break the law yourself by ordering me struck like that?"

⁴Those standing near Paul said to him, "Is that the way to talk to God's high priest?"

⁵"I'm sorry, brothers. I didn't realize he was the high priest," Paul replied, "for the Scriptures say, 'Do not speak evil of anyone who rules over you.' "

⁶Paul realized that some members of the high council were Sadducees and some were Pharisees, so he shouted, "Brothers, I am a Pharisee, as were all my ancestors! And I am on trial because my hope is in the resurrection of the dead!"

⁷This divided the council—the Pharisees against the Sadducees—⁸for the Sadducees say there is no resurrection or angels or spirits, but the Pharisees believe in all of these. ⁹So a great clamor arose. Some of the teachers of religious law who were Pharisees jumped up to argue that Paul was all right. "We see nothing wrong with him," they shouted. "Perhaps a spirit or an angel spoke to him." ¹⁰The shouting grew louder and louder, and the men were tugging at Paul from both sides, pulling him this way and that. Finally, the commander, fearing they would tear him apart, ordered his soldiers to take him away from them and bring him back to the fortress.

¹¹That night the Lord appeared to Paul and said, "Be encouraged, Paul. Just as you have told the people about me here in Jerusalem, you must preach the Good News in Rome."

¹²The next morning a group of Jews got together and bound themselves with an oath to neither eat nor drink until they had killed Paul. ¹³There were more than forty of them. ¹⁴They went to the leading priests and other leaders and told them what they had done. "We have bound ourselves under oath to neither eat nor drink until we have killed Paul. ¹⁵You and the high council should tell the commander to bring Paul back to the council again," they requested. "Pretend you want to examine his case more fully. We will kill him on the way."

¹⁶But Paul's nephew heard of their plan and went to the fortress and told Paul. ¹⁷Paul called one of the officers and said, "Take this young man to the commander. He has something important to tell him."

¹⁸So the officer did, explaining, "Paul, the prisoner, called me over and asked me to bring this young man to you because he has something to tell you."

¹⁹The commander took him by the arm, led him aside, and asked, "What is it you want to tell me?"

²⁰Paul's nephew told him, "Some Jews are going to ask you to bring Paul before the Jewish high council tomorrow, pretending they want to get some more information. ²¹But don't do it! There are more than forty men hiding along the way ready to jump him and kill him. They have vowed not to eat or drink until they kill him. They are ready, expecting you to agree to their request."

²²"Don't let a soul know you told me this," the commander warned the young man as he sent him away.

〜〰〰 **How well do you know your rights and fulfill your responsibilities as a citizen of your country?** Paul's outburst came as a result of the illegal command that Ananias had given. Ananias had violated Jewish law by assuming that Paul was guilty without a trial and ordering his punishment (see Deut. 19:15). Paul didn't recognize Ananias as the High Priest, probably because Ananias's command broke the law he was pledged to represent. As Christians, we are to represent Christ. When those around you say, "We didn't know you were a Christian," you have failed to represent Jesus as you should. You are not merely Christ's follower; you are his representative to others.

NOVEMBER

Paul in Prison
ACTS 23:23–24:27

Then the commander called two of his officers and ordered, "Get two hundred soldiers ready to leave for Caesarea at nine o'clock tonight. Also take two hundred spearmen and seventy horsemen. ²⁴Provide horses for Paul to ride, and get him safely to Governor Felix." ²⁵Then he wrote this letter to the governor:

²⁶"From Claudius Lysias, to his Excellency, Governor Felix. Greetings! ²⁷This man was seized by some Jews, and they were about to kill him when I arrived with the troops. When I learned that he was a Roman citizen, I removed him to safety. ²⁸Then I took him to their high council to try to find out what he had done. ²⁹I soon discovered it was something regarding their religious law—certainly nothing worthy of imprisonment or death. ³⁰But when I was informed of a plot to kill him, I immediately sent him on to you. I have told his accusers to bring their charges before you."

³¹So that night, as ordered, the soldiers took Paul as far as Antipatris. ³²They returned to the fortress the next morning, while the horsemen took him on to Caesarea. ³³When they arrived in Caesarea, they presented Paul and the letter to Governor Felix. ³⁴He read it and then asked Paul what province he was from. "Cilicia," Paul answered.

³⁵"I will hear your case myself when your accusers arrive," the governor told him. Then the governor ordered him kept in the prison at Herod's headquarters.

²⁴:¹Five days later Ananias, the high priest, arrived with some of the Jewish leaders and the lawyer Tertullus, to press charges against Paul. ²When Paul was called in, Tertullus laid charges against Paul in the following address to the governor:

"Your Excellency, you have given peace to us Jews and have enacted reforms for us. ³And for all of this we are very grateful to you. ⁴But lest I bore you, kindly give me your attention for only a moment as I briefly outline our case against this man. ⁵For we have found him to be a troublemaker, a man who is constantly inciting the Jews throughout the world to riots and rebellions against the Roman government. He is a ringleader of the sect known as the Nazarenes. ⁶Moreover he was trying to defile the Temple when we arrested him. ⁸You can find out the truth of our accusations by examining him yourself." ⁹Then the other Jews chimed in, declaring that everything Tertullus said was true.

¹⁰Now it was Paul's turn. The governor motioned for him to rise and speak. Paul said, "I know, sir, that you have been a judge of Jewish affairs for many years, and this gives me confidence as I make my defense. ¹¹You can quickly discover that it was no more than twelve days ago that I arrived in Jerusalem to worship at the Temple. ¹²I didn't argue with anyone in the Temple, nor did I incite a riot in any synagogue or on the streets of the city. ¹³These men certainly cannot prove the things they accuse me of doing.

¹⁴"But I admit that I follow the Way, which they call a sect. I worship the God of our ancestors, and I firmly believe the Jewish law and everything written in the books of prophecy. ¹⁵I have hope in God, just as these men do, that he will raise both the righteous and the ungodly. ¹⁶Because of this, I always try to maintain a clear conscience before God and everyone else.

¹⁷"After several years away, I returned to Jerusalem with money to aid my people and to offer sacrifices to God. ¹⁸My accusers saw me in the Temple as I was completing a purification ritual. There was no crowd around me and no rioting. ¹⁹But some Jews from the province of Asia were there—and they ought to be here to bring charges if they have anything against me! ²⁰Ask these men here what wrongdoing the Jewish high council found in me, ²¹except for one thing I said when I shouted out, 'I am on trial before you today because I believe in the resurrection of the dead!' "

²²Felix, who was quite familiar with the Way, adjourned the hearing and said, "Wait until Lysias, the garrison commander, arrives. Then I will decide

the case." [23]He ordered an officer to keep Paul in custody but to give him some freedom and allow his friends to visit him and take care of his needs. [24]A few days later Felix came with his wife, Drusilla, who was Jewish. Sending for Paul, they listened as he told them about faith in Christ Jesus. [25]As he reasoned with them about righteousness and self-control and the judgment to come, Felix was terrified. "Go away for now," he replied. "When it is more convenient, I'll call for you again." [26]He also hoped that Paul would bribe him, so he sent for him quite often and talked with him.

[27]Two years went by in this way; then Felix was succeeded by Porcius Festus. And because Felix wanted to gain favor with the Jewish leaders, he left Paul in prison.

~ᐱᐯᑣ **What would be harder for you, the pressure or the prison?** The Roman commander ordered Paul sent to Caesarea. Jerusalem was the seat of Jewish government, but Caesarea was the Roman headquarters for the area. God works in amazing and amusing ways. There were many ways that God could have used to get Paul to Caesarea, but he chose to use the Roman army to deliver Paul from his enemies. God's ways are not ours—we are limited, he is not. Don't limit God by asking him to respond your way. When God intervenes, anything can happen, much more and much better than you could ever anticipate.

14
NOVEMBER

Paul Speaks to Festus
ACTS 25:1-27

Three days after Festus arrived in Caesarea to take over his new responsibilities, he left for Jerusalem, [2]where the leading priests and other Jewish leaders met with him and made their accusations against Paul. [3]They asked Festus as a favor to transfer Paul to Jerusalem. (Their plan was to waylay and kill him.) [4]But Festus replied that Paul was at Caesarea and he himself would be returning there soon. [5]So he said, "Those of you in authority can return with me. If Paul has done anything wrong, you can make your accusations."

[6]Eight or ten days later he returned to Caesarea, and on the following day Paul's trial began. [7]On Paul's arrival in court, the Jewish leaders from Jerusalem gathered around and made many serious accusations they couldn't prove. [8]Paul denied the charges. "I am not guilty," he said. "I have committed no crime against the Jewish laws or the Temple or the Roman government."

[9]Then Festus, wanting to please the Jews, asked him, "Are you willing to go to Jerusalem and stand trial before me there?"

[10]But Paul replied, "No! This is the official Roman court, so I ought to be tried right here. You know very well I am not guilty. [11]If I have done something worthy of death, I don't refuse to die. But if I am innocent, neither

you nor anyone else has a right to turn me over to these men to kill me. I appeal to Caesar!"

[12]Festus conferred with his advisers and then replied, "Very well! You have appealed to Caesar, and to Caesar you shall go!"

[13]A few days later King Agrippa arrived with his sister, Bernice, to pay their respects to Festus. [14]During their stay of several days, Festus discussed Paul's case with the king. "There is a prisoner here," he told him, "whose case was left for me by Felix. [15]When I was in Jerusalem, the leading priests and other Jewish leaders pressed charges against him and asked me to sentence him. [16]Of course, I quickly pointed out to them that Roman law does not convict people without a trial. They are given an opportunity to defend themselves face to face with their accusers.

[17]"When they came here for the trial, I called the case the very next day and ordered Paul brought in. [18]But the accusations made against him weren't at all what I expected. [19]It was something about their religion and about someone called Jesus who died, but whom Paul insists is alive. [20]I was perplexed as to how to conduct an investigation of this kind, and I asked him whether he would be willing to stand trial on these charges in Jerusalem. [21]But Paul appealed to the emperor. So I ordered him back to jail until I could arrange to send him to Caesar."

[22]"I'd like to hear the man myself," Agrippa said.

And Festus replied, "You shall—tomorrow!"

[23]So the next day Agrippa and Bernice arrived at the auditorium with great pomp, accompanied by military officers and prominent men of the city. Festus ordered that Paul be brought in. [24]Then Festus said, "King Agrippa and all present, this is the man whose death is demanded both by the local Jews and by those in Jerusalem. [25]But in my opinion he has done nothing worthy of death. However, he appealed his case to the emperor, and I decided to send him. [26]But what shall I write the emperor? For there is no real charge against him. So I have brought him before all of you, and especially you, King Agrippa, so that after we examine him, I might have something to write. [27]For it doesn't seem reasonable to send a prisoner to the emperor without specifying the charges against him!"

〜〰〜 **If Christianity were outlawed, what evidence could be brought against you to prove you are a Christian?** Paul was in prison, but that didn't stop him from making the most of his situation. Military officers and prominent city leaders met in the palace room with Agrippa to hear this case. Paul saw this new audience as yet another opportunity to present the gospel. Rather than complain about your present situation, look for ways to use every opportunity to serve God and share him with others. Your problems may be opportunities in disguise.

15

Paul Speaks to Agrippa
ACTS 26:1-32

Then Agrippa said to Paul, "You may speak in your defense."

So Paul, with a gesture of his hand, started his defense: ²"I am fortunate, King Agrippa, that you are the one hearing my defense against all these accusations made by the Jewish leaders, ³for I know you are an expert on Jewish customs and controversies. Now please listen to me patiently!

⁴"As the Jewish leaders are well aware, I was given a thorough Jewish training from my earliest childhood among my own people and in Jerusalem. ⁵If they would admit it, they know that I have been a member of the Pharisees, the strictest sect of our religion. ⁶Now I am on trial because I am looking forward to the fulfillment of God's promise made to our ancestors. ⁷In fact, that is why the twelve tribes of Israel worship God night and day, and they share the same hope I have. Yet, O king, they say it is wrong for me to have this hope! ⁸Why does it seem incredible to any of you that God can raise the dead?

⁹"I used to believe that I ought to do everything I could to oppose the followers of Jesus of Nazareth. ¹⁰Authorized by the leading priests, I caused many of the believers in Jerusalem to be sent to prison. And I cast my vote against them when they were condemned to death. ¹¹Many times I had them whipped in the synagogues to try to get them to curse Christ. I was so violently opposed to them that I even hounded them in distant cities of foreign lands.

¹²"One day I was on such a mission to Damascus, armed with the authority and commission of the leading priests. ¹³About noon, Your Majesty, a light from heaven brighter than the sun shone down on me and my companions. ¹⁴We all fell down, and I heard a voice saying to me in Aramaic, 'Saul, Saul, why are you persecuting me? It is hard for you to fight against my will.'

¹⁵" 'Who are you, sir?' I asked.

"And the Lord replied, 'I am Jesus, the one you are persecuting. ¹⁶Now stand up! For I have appeared to you to appoint you as my servant and my witness. You are to tell the world about this experience and about other times I will appear to you. ¹⁷And I will protect you from both your own people and the Gentiles. Yes, I am going to send you to the Gentiles, ¹⁸to open their eyes so they may turn from darkness to light, and from the power of Satan to God. Then they will receive forgiveness for their sins and be given a place among God's people, who are set apart by faith in me.'

¹⁹"And so, O King Agrippa, I was not disobedient to that vision from heaven. ²⁰I preached first to those in Damascus, then in Jerusalem and throughout all Judea, and also to the Gentiles, that all must turn from their sins and turn to God—and prove they have changed by the good things

they do. [21]Some Jews arrested me in the Temple for preaching this, and they tried to kill me. [22]But God protected me so that I am still alive today to tell these facts to everyone, from the least to the greatest. I teach nothing except what the prophets and Moses said would happen—[23]that the Messiah would suffer and be the first to rise from the dead as a light to Jews and Gentiles alike."

[24]Suddenly, Festus shouted, "Paul, you are insane. Too much study has made you crazy!"

[25]But Paul replied, "I am not insane, Most Excellent Festus. I am speaking the sober truth. [26]And King Agrippa knows about these things. I speak frankly, for I am sure these events are all familiar to him, for they were not done in a corner! [27]King Agrippa, do you believe the prophets? I know you do—"

[28]Agrippa interrupted him. "Do you think you can make me a Christian so quickly?"

[29]Paul replied, "Whether quickly or not, I pray to God that both you and everyone here in this audience might become the same as I am, except for these chains."

[30]Then the king, the governor, Bernice, and all the others stood and left. [31]As they talked it over they agreed, "This man hasn't done anything worthy of death or imprisonment." [32]And Agrippa said to Festus, "He could be set free if he hadn't appealed to Caesar!"

〜〜 **How comfortable are you in explaining your faith?** Paul was setting forth the *facts*: People were still alive who had heard Jesus and seen his miracles, the empty tomb could still be seen, and the Christian message was turning the world upside down. The history of Jesus' life and the early church are facts that are still there for us to examine. We still have eyewitness accounts of Jesus' life in the Bible as well as historical and archaeological records of the early church to study. Examine the events and facts as verified by many witnesses. Reconfirm your faith with the truth of these accounts.

NOVEMBER 16

The Storm at Sea
ACTS 27:1-26

When the time came, we set sail for Italy. Paul and several other prisoners were placed in the custody of an army officer named Julius, a captain of the Imperial Regiment. [2]And Aristarchus, a Macedonian from Thessalonica, was also with us. We left on a boat whose home port was Adramyttium; it was scheduled to make several stops at ports along the coast of the province of Asia.

[3]The next day when we docked at Sidon, Julius was very kind to Paul and let him go ashore to visit with friends so they could provide for his needs. [4]Putting out to sea from there, we encountered headwinds that made it

difficult to keep the ship on course, so we sailed north of Cyprus between the island and the mainland. [5]We passed along the coast of the provinces of Cilicia and Pamphylia, landing at Myra, in the province of Lycia. [6]There the officer found an Egyptian ship from Alexandria that was bound for Italy, and he put us on board.

[7]We had several days of rough sailing, and after great difficulty we finally neared Cnidus. But the wind was against us, so we sailed down to the leeward side of Crete, past the cape of Salmone. [8]We struggled along the coast with great difficulty and finally arrived at Fair Havens, near the city of Lasea. [9]We had lost a lot of time. The weather was becoming dangerous for long voyages by then because it was so late in the fall, and Paul spoke to the ship's officers about it.

[10]"Sirs," he said, "I believe there is trouble ahead if we go on—shipwreck, loss of cargo, injuries, and danger to our lives." [11]But the officer in charge of the prisoners listened more to the ship's captain and the owner than to Paul. [12]And since Fair Havens was an exposed harbor—a poor place to spend the winter—most of the crew wanted to go to Phoenix, farther up the coast of Crete, and spend the winter there. Phoenix was a good harbor with only a southwest and northwest exposure.

[13]When a light wind began blowing from the south, the sailors thought they could make it. So they pulled up anchor and sailed along close to shore. [14]But the weather changed abruptly, and a wind of typhoon strength (a "northeaster," they called it) caught the ship and blew it out to sea. [15]They couldn't turn the ship into the wind, so they gave up and let it run before the gale.

[16]We sailed behind a small island named Cauda, where with great difficulty we hoisted aboard the lifeboat that was being towed behind us. [17]Then we banded the ship with ropes to strengthen the hull. The sailors were afraid of being driven across to the sandbars of Syrtis off the African coast, so they lowered the sea anchor and were thus driven before the wind.

[18]The next day, as gale-force winds continued to batter the ship, the crew began throwing the cargo overboard. [19]The following day they even threw out the ship's equipment and anything else they could lay their hands on. [20]The terrible storm raged unabated for many days, blotting out the sun and the stars, until at last all hope was gone.

[21]No one had eaten for a long time. Finally, Paul called the crew together and said, "Men, you should have listened to me in the first place and not left Fair Havens. You would have avoided all this injury and loss. [22]But take courage! None of you will lose your lives, even though the ship will go down. [23]For last night an angel of the God to whom I belong and whom I serve stood beside me, [24]and he said, 'Don't be afraid, Paul, for you will surely stand trial before Caesar! What's more, God in his goodness has granted safety to everyone sailing with you.' [25]So take courage! For I believe God. It will be just as he said. [26]But we will be shipwrecked on an island."

~~~W~~ **What is your attitude when you are part of a group and are going through difficulties?** Julius, a hardened Roman centurion, was assigned to guard Paul. Obviously, he had to remain close to Paul at all times. Through this contact, Julius developed a respect for Paul. He gave Paul a certain amount of freedom and later spared his life. How would your character look, up close and personal?

NOVEMBER 17

The Shipwreck

ACTS 27:27-44

About midnight on the fourteenth night of the storm, as we were being driven across the Sea of Adria, the sailors sensed land was near. [28]They took soundings and found the water was only 120 feet deep. A little later they sounded again and found only 90 feet. [29]At this rate they were afraid we would soon be driven against the rocks along the shore, so they threw out four anchors from the stern and prayed for daylight. [30]Then the sailors tried to abandon the ship; they lowered the lifeboat as though they were going to put out anchors from the prow. [31]But Paul said to the commanding officer and the soldiers, "You will all die unless the sailors stay aboard." [32]So the soldiers cut the ropes and let the boat fall off.

[33]As the darkness gave way to the early morning light, Paul begged everyone to eat. "You haven't touched food for two weeks," he said. [34]"Please eat something now for your own good. For not a hair of your heads will perish." [35]Then he took some bread, gave thanks to God before them all, and broke off a piece and ate it. [36]Then everyone was encouraged, [37]and all 276 of us began eating—for that is the number we had aboard. [38]After eating, the crew lightened the ship further by throwing the cargo of wheat overboard.

[39]When morning dawned, they didn't recognize the coastline, but they saw a bay with a beach and wondered if they could get between the rocks and get the ship safely to shore. [40]So they cut off the anchors and left them in the sea. Then they lowered the rudders, raised the foresail, and headed toward shore. [41]But the ship hit a shoal and ran aground. The bow of the ship stuck fast, while the stern was repeatedly smashed by the force of the waves and began to break apart.

[42]The soldiers wanted to kill the prisoners to make sure they didn't swim ashore and escape. [43]But the commanding officer wanted to spare Paul, so he didn't let them carry out their plan. Then he ordered all who could swim to jump overboard first and make for land, [44]and he told the others to try for it on planks and debris from the broken ship. So everyone escaped safely ashore!

⌇⋋⋌⌇ **What disasters in your life has God used to teach you?** The soldiers would pay with their own lives if any of their prisoners escaped. Their instinctive reaction was to kill the prisoners so they wouldn't get away. Julius, the centurion, was impressed with Paul and wanted to save his life. Julius was the highest ranking official and therefore could make this decision. This act preserved Paul for his later ministry in Rome and fulfilled Paul's prediction that all the people on the ship would be saved.

18

NOVEMBER

The Winter on Malta

ACTS 28:1-14

Once we were safe on shore, we learned that we were on the island of Malta. ²The people of the island were very kind to us. It was cold and rainy, so they built a fire on the shore to welcome us and warm us.

³As Paul gathered an armful of sticks and was laying them on the fire, a poisonous snake, driven out by the heat, fastened itself onto his hand. ⁴The people of the island saw it hanging there and said to each other, "A murderer, no doubt! Though he escaped the sea, justice will not permit him to live." ⁵But Paul shook off the snake into the fire and was unharmed. ⁶The people waited for him to swell up or suddenly drop dead. But when they had waited a long time and saw no harm come to him, they changed their minds and decided he was a god.

⁷Near the shore where we landed was an estate belonging to Publius, the chief official of the island. He welcomed us courteously and fed us for three days. ⁸As it happened, Publius's father was ill with fever and dysentery. Paul went in and prayed for him, and laying his hands on him, he healed him. ⁹Then all the other sick people on the island came and were cured. ¹⁰As a result we were showered with honors, and when the time came to sail, people put on board all sorts of things we would need for the trip.

¹¹It was three months after the shipwreck that we set sail on another ship that had wintered at the island—an Alexandrian ship with the twin gods as its figurehead. ¹²Our first stop was Syracuse, where we stayed three days. ¹³From there we sailed across to Rhegium. A day later a south wind began blowing, so the following day we sailed up the coast to Puteoli. ¹⁴There we found some believers, who invited us to stay with them seven days. And so we came to Rome.

⌇⋋⋌⌇ **How often are you aware of God in everyday occurrences?** God had promised safe passage to Paul (27:23-25), and he would let nothing stop his servant. The poisonous viper that bit Paul was unable to harm him. Our life is in God's hands, to continue on or to come to an end in his good timing. God still had work for Paul to do.

Paul in Rome

ACTS 28:15–31

19

The believers in Rome had heard we were coming, and they came to meet us at the Forum on the Appian Way. Others joined us at The Three Taverns. When Paul saw them, he thanked God and took courage.

¹⁶When we arrived in Rome, Paul was permitted to have his own private lodging, though he was guarded by a soldier.

¹⁷Three days after Paul's arrival, he called together the local Jewish leaders. He said to them, "Brothers, I was arrested in Jerusalem and handed over to the Roman government, even though I had done nothing against our people or the customs of our ancestors. ¹⁸The Romans tried me and wanted to release me, for they found no cause for the death sentence. ¹⁹But when the Jewish leaders protested the decision, I felt it necessary to appeal to Caesar, even though I had no desire to press charges against my own people. ²⁰I asked you to come here today so we could get acquainted and so I could tell you that I am bound with this chain because I believe that the hope of Israel—the Messiah—has already come."

²¹They replied, "We have heard nothing against you. We have had no letters from Judea or reports from anyone who has arrived here. ²²But we want to hear what you believe, for the only thing we know about these Christians is that they are denounced everywhere."

²³So a time was set, and on that day a large number of people came to Paul's house. He told them about the Kingdom of God and taught them about Jesus from the Scriptures—from the five books of Moses and the books of the prophets. He began lecturing in the morning and went on into the evening. ²⁴Some believed and some didn't. ²⁵But after they had argued back and forth among themselves, they left with this final word from Paul: "The Holy Spirit was right when he said to our ancestors through Isaiah the prophet,

²⁶ 'Go and say to my people,
You will hear my words,
   but you will not understand;
you will see what I do,
   but you will not perceive its meaning.
²⁷For the hearts of these people are hardened,
   and their ears cannot hear,
   and they have closed their eyes—
so their eyes cannot see,
   and their ears cannot hear,
   and their hearts cannot understand,
and they cannot turn to me
   and let me heal them.'

[28]So I want you to realize that this salvation from God is also available to the Gentiles, and they will accept it."

[30]For the next two years, Paul lived in his own rented house. He welcomed all who visited him, [31]proclaiming the Kingdom of God with all boldness and teaching about the Lord Jesus Christ. And no one tried to stop him.

〰〰 **What would you most like to be doing when your time on this earth is over?** Paul wanted to preach the gospel in Rome, and he eventually got there—in chains, through shipwreck, and after many trials. Although Paul may have wished for an easier passage, he knew that God had blessed him greatly in allowing him to meet the believers in Rome and preach the message to both Jews and Gentiles in that great city. God worked all things for good for Paul, and you can trust him to do the same for you. God does not promise you comfort or security, but he will provide the opportunity and means to do his work.

20

NOVEMBER

Faith Brings Joy
ROMANS 5:1-11

Therefore, since we have been made right in God's sight by faith, we have peace with God because of what Jesus Christ our Lord has done for us. [2]Because of our faith, Christ has brought us into this place of highest privilege where we now stand, and we confidently and joyfully look forward to sharing God's glory.

[3]We can rejoice, too, when we run into problems and trials, for we know that they are good for us—they help us learn to endure. [4]And endurance develops strength of character in us, and character strengthens our confident expectation of salvation. [5]And this expectation will not disappoint us. For we know how dearly God loves us, because he has given us the Holy Spirit to fill our hearts with his love.

[6]When we were utterly helpless, Christ came at just the right time and died for us sinners. [7]Now, no one is likely to die for a good person, though someone might be willing to die for a person who is especially good. [8]But God showed his great love for us by sending Christ to die for us while we were still sinners. [9]And since we have been made right in God's sight by the blood of Christ, he will certainly save us from God's judgment. [10]For since we were restored to friendship with God by the death of his Son while we were still his enemies, we will certainly be delivered from eternal punishment by his life. [11]So now we can rejoice in our wonderful new relationship with God—all because of what our Lord Jesus Christ has done for us in making us friends of God.

~∿⌒ **When was the last time you thanked God for all he's done for you?** Paul tells us that in the future we will *become*, but until then we must *overcome*. This means we will experience difficulties that help us grow. Problems we run into will develop our patience, which in turn will strengthen our character, deepen our trust in God, and give us greater confidence about the future. You probably find your patience tested in some way every day. Thank God for these opportunities to grow, and deal with them in his strength.

Truly Free from Sin

ROMANS 8:1-18

So now there is no condemnation for those who belong to Christ Jesus. ²For the power of the life-giving Spirit has freed you through Christ Jesus from the power of sin that leads to death. ³The law of Moses could not save us, because of our sinful nature. But God put into effect a different plan to save us. He sent his own Son in a human body like ours, except that ours are sinful. God destroyed sin's control over us by giving his Son as a sacrifice for our sins. ⁴He did this so that the requirement of the law would be fully accomplished for us who no longer follow our sinful nature but instead follow the Spirit.

⁵Those who are dominated by the sinful nature think about sinful things, but those who are controlled by the Holy Spirit think about things that please the Spirit. ⁶If your sinful nature controls your mind, there is death. But if the Holy Spirit controls your mind, there is life and peace. ⁷For the sinful nature is always hostile to God. It never did obey God's laws, and it never will. ⁸That's why those who are still under the control of their sinful nature can never please God.

⁹But you are not controlled by your sinful nature. You are controlled by the Spirit if you have the Spirit of God living in you. (And remember that those who do not have the Spirit of Christ living in them are not Christians at all.) ¹⁰Since Christ lives within you, even though your body will die because of sin, your spirit is alive because you have been made right with God. ¹¹The Spirit of God, who raised Jesus from the dead, lives in you. And just as he raised Christ from the dead, he will give life to your mortal body by this same Spirit living within you.

¹²So, dear Christian friends, you have no obligation whatsoever to do what your sinful nature urges you to do. ¹³For if you keep on following it, you will perish. But if through the power of the Holy Spirit you turn from it and its evil deeds, you will live. ¹⁴For all who are led by the Spirit of God are children of God.

¹⁵So you should not be like cowering, fearful slaves. You should behave instead like God's very own children, adopted into his family—calling him

"Father, dear Father." [16]For his Holy Spirit speaks to us deep in our hearts and tells us that we are God's children. [17]And since we are his children, we will share his treasures—for everything God gives to his Son, Christ, is ours, too. But if we are to share his glory, we must also share his suffering. [18]Yet what we suffer now is nothing compared to the glory he will give us later.

〰️ **In what areas are you still struggling with your sinful nature?** Paul divides people into two categories—those who let themselves be controlled by their lower natures and those who follow after the Holy Spirit. All of us would be in the first category if Jesus hadn't offered us a way out. Once we have said yes to Jesus, we will want to continue following him because his way brings life and peace. Daily we must consciously choose to center our life on God. Use the Bible to discover God's guidelines, and then follow them. Ask yourself in every perplexing situation, What would Jesus want me to do? When the Holy Spirit points out what is right, do it eagerly.

22
NOVEMBER

How God Loves
ROMANS 8:19-39

For all creation is waiting eagerly for that future day when God will reveal who his children really are. [20]Against its will, everything on earth was subjected to God's curse. [21]All creation anticipates the day when it will join God's children in glorious freedom from death and decay. [22]For we know that all creation has been groaning as in the pains of childbirth right up to the present time. [23]And even we Christians, although we have the Holy Spirit within us as a foretaste of future glory, also groan to be released from pain and suffering. We, too, wait anxiously for that day when God will give us our full rights as his children, including the new bodies he has promised us. [24]Now that we are saved, we eagerly look forward to this freedom. For if you already have something, you don't need to hope for it. [25]But if we look forward to something we don't have yet, we must wait patiently and confidently.

[26]And the Holy Spirit helps us in our distress. For we don't even know what we should pray for, nor how we should pray. But the Holy Spirit prays for us with groanings that cannot be expressed in words. [27]And the Father who knows all hearts knows what the Spirit is saying, for the Spirit pleads for us believers in harmony with God's own will. [28]And we know that God causes everything to work together for the good of those who love God and are called according to his purpose for them. [29]For God knew his people in advance, and he chose them to become like his Son, so that his Son would be the firstborn, with many brothers and sisters. [30]And having chosen them, he called them to come to him. And he gave them right standing with himself, and he promised them his glory.

³¹What can we say about such wonderful things as these? If God is for us, who can ever be against us? ³²Since God did not spare even his own Son but gave him up for us all, won't God, who gave us Christ, also give us everything else?

³³Who dares accuse us whom God has chosen for his own? Will God? No! He is the one who has given us right standing with himself. ³⁴Who then will condemn us? Will Christ Jesus? No, for he is the one who died for us and was raised to life for us and is sitting at the place of highest honor next to God, pleading for us.

³⁵Can anything ever separate us from Christ's love? Does it mean he no longer loves us if we have trouble or calamity, or are persecuted, or are hungry or cold or in danger or threatened with death? ³⁶(Even the Scriptures say, "For your sake we are killed every day; we are being slaughtered like sheep.") ³⁷No, despite all these things, overwhelming victory is ours through Christ, who loved us.

³⁸And I am convinced that nothing can ever separate us from his love. Death can't, and life can't. The angels can't, and the demons can't. Our fears for today, our worries about tomorrow, and even the powers of hell can't keep God's love away. ³⁹Whether we are high above the sky or in the deepest ocean, nothing in all creation will ever be able to separate us from the love of God that is revealed in Christ Jesus our Lord.

What things do you feel might be able to separate you from the love of Christ? These verses contain one of the most comforting promises in all Scripture. Believers have always had to face hardships in many forms: persecution, illness, imprisonment, even death. These hardships can cause us to fear that we have been abandoned by Christ. But Paul exclaims that it is *impossible* to be separated from Christ. His death for us is proof of his unconquerable love. Nothing can stop his constant presence with us. God tells us how great his love is so that we will feel totally secure in him. If we believe these wonderful promises, we will not be afraid.

NOVEMBER

23

Living Sacrifice

ROMANS 12:1-21

And so, dear Christian friends, I plead with you to give your bodies to God. Let them be a living and holy sacrifice—the kind he will accept. When you think of what he has done for you, is this too much to ask? ²Don't copy the behavior and customs of this world, but let God transform you into a new person by changing the way you think. Then you will know what God wants you to do, and you will know how good and pleasing and perfect his will really is.

³As God's messenger, I give each of you this warning: Be honest in your estimate of yourselves, measuring your value by how much faith God has given you. ⁴Just as our bodies have many parts and each part has a special function, ⁵so it is with Christ's body. We are all parts of his one body, and each of us has different work to do. And since we are all one body in Christ, we belong to each other, and each of us needs all the others.

⁶God has given each of us the ability to do certain things well. So if God has given you the ability to prophesy, speak out when you have faith that God is speaking through you. ⁷If your gift is that of serving others, serve them well. If you are a teacher, do a good job of teaching. ⁸If your gift is to encourage others, do it! If you have money, share it generously. If God has given you leadership ability, take the responsibility seriously. And if you have a gift for showing kindness to others, do it gladly.

⁹Don't just pretend that you love others. Really love them. Hate what is wrong. Stand on the side of the good. ¹⁰Love each other with genuine affection, and take delight in honoring each other. ¹¹Never be lazy in your work, but serve the Lord enthusiastically.

¹²Be glad for all God is planning for you. Be patient in trouble, and always be prayerful. ¹³When God's children are in need, be the one to help them out. And get into the habit of inviting guests home for dinner or, if they need lodging, for the night.

¹⁴If people persecute you because you are a Christian, don't curse them; pray that God will bless them. ¹⁵When others are happy, be happy with them. If they are sad, share their sorrow. ¹⁶Live in harmony with each other. Don't try to act important, but enjoy the company of ordinary people. And don't think you know it all!

¹⁷Never pay back evil for evil to anyone. Do things in such a way that everyone can see you are honorable. ¹⁸Do your part to live in peace with everyone, as much as possible.

¹⁹Dear friends, never avenge yourselves. Leave that to God. For it is written,

> "I will take vengeance;
> I will repay those who deserve it,"
> says the Lord.

²⁰Instead, do what the Scriptures say:

> "If your enemies are hungry, feed them.
> If they are thirsty, give them something to drink,
>   and they will be ashamed of what they have done to you."

²¹Don't let evil get the best of you, but conquer evil by doing good.

〰️〰️ **What act of a living sacrifice might God allow you to do today?**
In this day of constant lawsuits and incessant demands for legal rights, Paul's command sounds almost impossible. When someone hurts you deeply, instead of giving him what he deserves, Paul says to befriend him. Why does Paul tell

us to forgive our enemies? (1) Forgiveness may break a cycle of retaliation and lead to mutual reconciliation. (2) It may make the enemy feel ashamed and change his ways. (3) Returning evil for evil hurts you just as much as it hurts your enemy. Even if your enemy never repents, forgiving him will free you of a heavy load of bitterness.

NOVEMBER

Real Love

1 CORINTHIANS 13:1-13

24

If I could speak in any language in heaven or on earth but didn't love others, I would only be making meaningless noise like a loud gong or a clanging cymbal. [2]If I had the gift of prophecy, and if I knew all the mysteries of the future and knew everything about everything, but didn't love others, what good would I be? And if I had the gift of faith so that I could speak to a mountain and make it move, without love I would be no good to anybody. [3]If I gave everything I have to the poor and even sacrificed my body, I could boast about it; but if I didn't love others, I would be of no value whatsoever.

[4]Love is patient and kind. Love is not jealous or boastful or proud [5]or rude. Love does not demand its own way. Love is not irritable, and it keeps no record of when it has been wronged. [6]It is never glad about injustice but rejoices whenever the truth wins out. [7]Love never gives up, never loses faith, is always hopeful, and endures through every circumstance.

[8]Love will last forever, but prophecy and speaking in unknown languages and special knowledge will all disappear. [9]Now we know only a little, and even the gift of prophecy reveals little! [10]But when the end comes, these special gifts will all disappear.

[11]It's like this: When I was a child, I spoke and thought and reasoned as a child does. But when I grew up, I put away childish things. [12]Now we see things imperfectly as in a poor mirror, but then we will see everything with perfect clarity. All that I know now is partial and incomplete, but then I will know everything completely, just as God knows me now.

[13]There are three things that will endure—faith, hope, and love—and the greatest of these is love.

〰️ **Which quality of real love do you most need to ask God to increase in your life?** Our society confuses love and lust. Unlike lust, God's kind of love is directed outward toward others, not inward toward ourselves. It is utterly unselfish. This kind of love goes against our natural inclinations. It involves unselfish service to others and gives evidence that we care. *Faith* is the foundation and content of God's message; *hope* is the attitude and focus; *love* is the action. When faith and hope are in line, we are free to love completely because we understand how God loves. It is only as God helps us set aside our own desires and instincts that we can give this love while expecting nothing in return. Thus, the more we become like Christ, the more love we will show to others.

25

The Basic Gospel
1 CORINTHIANS 15:1-20

Now let me remind you, dear brothers and sisters, of the Good News I preached to you before. You welcomed it then and still do now, for your faith is built on this wonderful message. [2]And it is this Good News that saves you if you firmly believe it—unless, of course, you believed something that was never true in the first place.

[3]I passed on to you what was most important and what had also been passed on to me—that Christ died for our sins, just as the Scriptures said. [4]He was buried, and he was raised from the dead on the third day, as the Scriptures said. [5]He was seen by Peter and then by the twelve apostles. [6]After that, he was seen by more than five hundred of his followers at one time, most of whom are still alive, though some have died by now. [7]Then he was seen by James and later by all the apostles. [8]Last of all, I saw him, too, long after the others, as though I had been born at the wrong time. [9]For I am the least of all the apostles, and I am not worthy to be called an apostle after the way I persecuted the church of God.

[10]But whatever I am now, it is all because God poured out his special favor on me—and not without results. For I have worked harder than all the other apostles, yet it was not I but God who was working through me by his grace. [11]So it makes no difference whether I preach or they preach. The important thing is that you believed what we preached to you.

[12]But tell me this—since we preach that Christ rose from the dead, why are some of you saying there will be no resurrection of the dead? [13]For if there is no resurrection of the dead, then Christ has not been raised either. [14]And if Christ was not raised, then all our preaching is useless, and your trust in God is useless. [15]And we apostles would all be lying about God, for we have said that God raised Christ from the grave, but that can't be true if there is no resurrection of the dead. [16]If there is no resurrection of the dead, then Christ has not been raised. [17]And if Christ has not been raised, then your faith is useless, and you are still under condemnation for your sins. [18]In that case, all who have died believing in Christ have perished! [19]And if we have hope in Christ only for this life, we are the most miserable people in the world.

[20]But the fact is that Christ has been raised from the dead. He has become the first of a great harvest of those who will be raised to life again.

~~√\/↙~~ **What parts of the gospel are especially helpful to you in times of doubt or stress?** There will always be people who will say that Jesus didn't rise from the dead. Paul assures us that many people saw Jesus after his resurrection, including more than five hundred believers. The Resurrection is a historical fact. Don't be discouraged by doubters who deny it. The resurrection of Christ is the focus of our Christian faith. Because Christ rose from the dead as he promised, we know that what he said is true—he is God. Because he rose, we have certainty that our sins are forgiven. Because he rose, he lives and represents us to God. Because he rose and defeated death, we know we will also be raised.

NOVEMBER

26

Destiny!
1 CORINTHIANS 15:42-58

It is the same way for the resurrection of the dead. Our earthly bodies, which die and decay, will be different when they are resurrected, for they will never die. [43]Our bodies now disappoint us, but when they are raised, they will be full of glory. They are weak now, but when they are raised, they will be full of power. [44]They are natural human bodies now, but when they are raised, they will be spiritual bodies. For just as there are natural bodies, so also there are spiritual bodies.

[45]The Scriptures tell us, "The first man, Adam, became a living person." But the last Adam—that is, Christ—is a life-giving Spirit. [46]What came first was the natural body, then the spiritual body comes later. [47]Adam, the first man, was made from the dust of the earth, while Christ, the second man, came from heaven. [48]Every human being has an earthly body just like Adam's, but our heavenly bodies will be just like Christ's. [49]Just as we are now like Adam, the man of the earth, so we will someday be like Christ, the man from heaven.

[50]What I am saying, dear brothers and sisters, is that flesh and blood cannot inherit the Kingdom of God. These perishable bodies of ours are not able to live forever.

[51]But let me tell you a wonderful secret God has revealed to us. Not all of us will die, but we will all be transformed. [52]It will happen in a moment, in the blinking of an eye, when the last trumpet is blown. For when the trumpet sounds, the Christians who have died will be raised with transformed bodies. And then we who are living will be transformed so that we will never die. [53]For our perishable earthly bodies must be transformed into heavenly bodies that will never die.

[54]When this happens—when our perishable earthly bodies have been transformed into heavenly bodies that will never die—then at last the Scriptures will come true:

"Death is swallowed up in victory.
⁵⁵O death, where is your victory?
O death, where is your sting?"

⁵⁶For sin is the sting that results in death, and the law gives sin its power. ⁵⁷How we thank God, who gives us victory over sin and death through Jesus Christ our Lord!
⁵⁸So, my dear brothers and sisters, be strong and steady, always enthusiastic about the Lord's work, for you know that nothing you do for the Lord is ever useless.

〰〰 **How much are you looking forward to all Christ has planned for you?** Paul said that because of the Resurrection, nothing we do is wasted. Sometimes we hesitate to do good because we don't see any results. In order to see the good resulting from our efforts, we need to maintain a heavenly perspective. Truly believing that Christ has won the ultimate victory will affect the way we live right now. Don't let discouragement over an apparent lack of results keep you from working. Do the good that you have opportunity to do, knowing that your work will have eternal results.

27
NOVEMBER

Weak Containers, Strong Contents
2 CORINTHIANS 4:1-18

And so, since God in his mercy has given us this wonderful ministry, we never give up. ²We reject all shameful and underhanded methods. We do not try to trick anyone, and we do not distort the word of God. We tell the truth before God, and all who are honest know that.
³If the Good News we preach is veiled from anyone, it is a sign that they are perishing. ⁴Satan, the god of this evil world, has blinded the minds of those who don't believe, so they are unable to see the glorious light of the Good News that is shining upon them. They don't understand the message we preach about the glory of Christ, who is the exact likeness of God.
⁵We don't go around preaching about ourselves; we preach Christ Jesus, the Lord. All we say about ourselves is that we are your servants because of what Jesus has done for us. ⁶For God, who said, "Let there be light in the darkness," has made us understand that this light is the brightness of the glory of God that is seen in the face of Jesus Christ.
⁷But this precious treasure—this light and power that now shine within us—is held in perishable containers, that is, in our weak bodies. So everyone can see that our glorious power is from God and is not our own.
⁸We are pressed on every side by troubles, but we are not crushed and broken. We are perplexed, but we don't give up and quit. ⁹We are hunted down, but God never abandons us. We get knocked down, but we get up

again and keep going. [10]Through suffering, these bodies of ours constantly share in the death of Jesus so that the life of Jesus may also be seen in our bodies. [11]Yes, we live under constant danger of death because we serve Jesus, so that the life of Jesus will be obvious in our dying bodies. [12]So we live in the face of death, but it has resulted in eternal life for you.

[13]But we continue to preach because we have the same kind of faith the psalmist had when he said, "I believed in God, and so I speak." [14]We know that the same God who raised our Lord Jesus will also raise us with Jesus and present us to himself along with you. [15]All of these things are for your benefit. And as God's grace brings more and more people to Christ, there will be great thanksgiving, and God will receive more and more glory.

[16]That is why we never give up. Though our bodies are dying, our spirits are being renewed every day. [17]For our present troubles are quite small and won't last very long. Yet they produce for us an immeasurably great glory that will last forever! [18]So we don't look at the troubles we can see right now; rather, we look forward to what we have not yet seen. For the troubles we see will soon be over, but the joys to come will last forever.

〰〰 **With which of the difficult situations Paul mentions do you identify most clearly?** Our troubles should not diminish our faith or disillusion us. Instead, we should realize that there is a purpose in our suffering. Problems and human limitations have several benefits: (1) They help us remember Christ's suffering for us. (2) They help keep us from pride. (3) They help us look beyond this brief life. (4) They prove our faith to others. (5) They give God the opportunity to demonstrate his great power. Don't resent your troubles—see them as opportunities!

Two Radically Different Lives

NOVEMBER **28**

GALATIANS 5:13-26

For you, dear friends, have been called to live in freedom—not freedom to satisfy your sinful nature, but freedom to serve one another in love. [14]For the whole law can be summed up in this one command: "Love your neighbor as yourself." [15]But if instead of showing love among yourselves you are always biting and devouring one another, watch out! Beware of destroying one another.

[16]So I advise you to live according to your new life in the Holy Spirit. Then you won't be doing what your sinful nature craves. [17]The old sinful nature loves to do evil, which is just opposite from what the Holy Spirit wants. And the Spirit gives us desires that are opposite from what the sinful nature desires. These two forces are constantly fighting each other, and your

choices are never free from this conflict. [18]But when you are directed by the Holy Spirit, you are no longer subject to the law.

[19]When you follow the desires of your sinful nature, your lives will produce these evil results: sexual immorality, impure thoughts, eagerness for lustful pleasure, [20]idolatry, participation in demonic activities, hostility, quarreling, jealousy, outbursts of anger, selfish ambition, divisions, the feeling that everyone is wrong except those in your own little group, [21]envy, drunkenness, wild parties, and other kinds of sin. Let me tell you again, as I have before, that anyone living that sort of life will not inherit the Kingdom of God.

[22]But when the Holy Spirit controls our lives, he will produce this kind of fruit in us: love, joy, peace, patience, kindness, goodness, faithfulness, [23]gentleness, and self-control. Here there is no conflict with the law.

[24]Those who belong to Christ Jesus have nailed the passions and desires of their sinful nature to his cross and crucified them there. [25]If we are living now by the Holy Spirit, let us follow the Holy Spirit's leading in every part of our lives. [26]Let us not become conceited, or irritate one another, or be jealous of one another.

⌇⌇⌇ **Who comes to mind as someone you need to love as you love yourself?** When we are not motivated by love, we become critical of others. We stop looking for good in them and see only their faults. Soon the unity of believers becomes broken. Have you talked behind someone's back? Have you focused on others' shortcomings instead of their strengths? Remind yourself of Jesus' command to love others as we love ourself. When you begin to feel critical of someone, make a list of that person's positive qualities. And don't say anything behind his back that you wouldn't say to his face.

29 NOVEMBER

God's Action
EPHESIANS 1:3-23

How we praise God, the Father of our Lord Jesus Christ, who has blessed us with every spiritual blessing in the heavenly realms because we belong to Christ. [4]Long ago, even before he made the world, God loved us and chose us in Christ to be holy and without fault in his eyes. [5]His unchanging plan has always been to adopt us into his own family by bringing us to himself through Jesus Christ. And this gave him great pleasure.

[6]So we praise God for the wonderful kindness he has poured out on us because we belong to his dearly loved Son. [7]He is so rich in kindness that he purchased our freedom through the blood of his Son, and our sins are forgiven. [8]He has showered his kindness on us, along with all wisdom and understanding.

[9]God's secret plan has now been revealed to us; it is a plan centered on

Christ, designed long ago according to his good pleasure. [10]And this is his plan: At the right time he will bring everything together under the authority of Christ—everything in heaven and on earth. [11]Furthermore, because of Christ, we have received an inheritance from God, for he chose us from the beginning, and all things happen just as he decided long ago. [12]God's purpose was that we who were the first to trust in Christ should praise our glorious God. [13]And now you also have heard the truth, the Good News that God saves you. And when you believed in Christ, he identified you as his own by giving you the Holy Spirit, whom he promised long ago. [14]The Spirit is God's guarantee that he will give us everything he promised and that he has purchased us to be his own people. This is just one more reason for us to praise our glorious God.

[15]Ever since I first heard of your strong faith in the Lord Jesus and your love for Christians everywhere, [16]I have never stopped thanking God for you. I pray for you constantly, [17]asking God, the glorious Father of our Lord Jesus Christ, to give you spiritual wisdom and understanding, so that you might grow in your knowledge of God. [18]I pray that your hearts will be flooded with light so that you can understand the wonderful future he has promised to those he called. I want you to realize what a rich and glorious inheritance he has given to his people.

[19]I pray that you will begin to understand the incredible greatness of his power for us who believe him. This is the same mighty power [20]that raised Christ from the dead and seated him in the place of honor at God's right hand in the heavenly realms. [21]Now he is far above any ruler or authority or power or leader or anything else in this world or in the world to come. [22]And God has put all things under the authority of Christ, and he gave him this authority for the benefit of the church. [23]And the church is his body; it is filled by Christ, who fills everything everywhere with his presence.

〰〰 **In what ways has God marked your life?** Paul said, "God chose us," to emphasize that salvation depends totally on God. We are not saved because we deserve salvation but because God is gracious and freely gives it. We did not influence God's decision to save us; he did it according to his plan. Thus, there is no way to take credit for our salvation or to find room for pride. The mystery of salvation originated in the timeless mind of God long before we existed. It is hard to understand how God could accept us, but because of Christ, we are holy and blameless in his eyes. God chose you, and when you belong to him through Jesus Christ, he looks at you as if you had never sinned.

30

God's Plan
EPHESIANS 2:1-22

Once you were dead, doomed forever because of your many sins. ²You used to live just like the rest of the world, full of sin, obeying Satan, the mighty prince of the power of the air. He is the spirit at work in the hearts of those who refuse to obey God. ³All of us used to live that way, following the passions and desires of our evil nature. We were born with an evil nature, and we were under God's anger just like everyone else.

⁴But God is so rich in mercy, and he loved us so very much, ⁵that even while we were dead because of our sins, he gave us life when he raised Christ from the dead. (It is only by God's special favor that you have been saved!) ⁶For he raised us from the dead along with Christ, and we are seated with him in the heavenly realms—all because we are one with Christ Jesus. ⁷And so God can always point to us as examples of the incredible wealth of his favor and kindness toward us, as shown in all he has done for us through Christ Jesus.

⁸God saved you by his special favor when you believed. And you can't take credit for this; it is a gift from God. ⁹Salvation is not a reward for the good things we have done, so none of us can boast about it. ¹⁰For we are God's masterpiece. He has created us anew in Christ Jesus, so that we can do the good things he planned for us long ago.

¹¹Don't forget that you Gentiles used to be outsiders by birth. You were called "the uncircumcised ones" by the Jews, who were proud of their circumcision, even though it affected only their bodies and not their hearts. ¹²In those days you were living apart from Christ. You were excluded from God's people, Israel, and you did not know the promises God had made to them. You lived in this world without God and without hope. ¹³But now you belong to Christ Jesus. Though you once were far away from God, now you have been brought near to him because of the blood of Christ.

¹⁴For Christ himself has made peace between us Jews and you Gentiles by making us all one people. He has broken down the wall of hostility that used to separate us. ¹⁵By his death he ended the whole system of Jewish law that excluded the Gentiles. His purpose was to make peace between Jews and Gentiles by creating in himself one new person from the two groups. ¹⁶Together as one body, Christ reconciled both groups to God by means of his death, and our hostility toward each other was put to death. ¹⁷He has brought this Good News of peace to you Gentiles who were far away from him, and to us Jews who were near. ¹⁸Now all of us, both Jews and Gentiles, may come to the Father through the same Holy Spirit because of what Christ has done for us.

¹⁹So now you Gentiles are no longer strangers and foreigners. You are citizens along with all of God's holy people. You are members of God's family.

^{20}We are his house, built on the foundation of the apostles and the prophets. And the cornerstone is Christ Jesus himself. ^{21}We who believe are carefully joined together, becoming a holy temple for the Lord. ^{22}Through him you Gentiles are also joined together as part of this dwelling where God lives by his Spirit.

~~∿∼~~ **When have you recently reminded yourself and God that you want your life to be used for his purposes?** We become Christians through God's unmerited grace, not as the result of any effort, ability, intelligent choice, or act of service on our part. However, out of gratitude for this free gift, we will seek to help and serve others with kindness, love, and gentleness, and not merely to please ourselves. While no action or work we do can help us obtain salvation, God's intention is that our salvation will result in acts of service. We are saved not merely for our own benefit but to serve Christ and build up the church.

Picture of the Church

EPHESIANS 4:1-16

Therefore I, a prisoner for serving the Lord, beg you to lead a life worthy of your calling, for you have been called by God. ²Be humble and gentle. Be patient with each other, making allowance for each other's faults because of your love. ³Always keep yourselves united in the Holy Spirit, and bind yourselves together with peace.

⁴We are all one body, we have the same Spirit, and we have all been called to the same glorious future. ⁵There is only one Lord, one faith, one baptism, ⁶and there is only one God and Father, who is over us all and in us all and living through us all. ⁷However, he has given each one of us a special gift according to the generosity of Christ. ⁸That is why the Scriptures say,

> "When he ascended to the heights,
>   he led a crowd of captives
>   and gave gifts to his people."

⁹Notice that it says "he ascended." This means that Christ first came down to the lowly world in which we live. ¹⁰The same one who came down is the one who ascended higher than all the heavens, so that his rule might fill the entire universe.

¹¹He is the one who gave these gifts to the church: the apostles, the prophets, the evangelists, and the pastors and teachers. ¹²Their responsibility is to equip God's people to do his work and build up the church, the body of Christ, ¹³until we come to such unity in our faith and knowledge of God's Son that we will be mature and full grown in the Lord, measuring up to the full stature of Christ.

¹⁴Then we will no longer be like children, forever changing our minds about what we believe because someone has told us something different or because someone has cleverly lied to us and made the lie sound like the truth. ¹⁵Instead, we will hold to the truth in love, becoming more and more in every way like Christ, who is the head of his body, the church. ¹⁶Under his direction, the whole body is fitted together perfectly. As each part does

its own special work, it helps the other parts grow, so that the whole body is healthy and growing and full of love.

〰〰 **What is your role in Christ's body?** Our oneness in Christ does not destroy our individuality. The Holy Spirit has given each Christian special abilities for building up the church. Now that we have these gifts, it is crucial to use them. Are you spiritually mature, exercising the gifts God has given you? If you know what your gifts are, look for opportunities to serve. If you don't know, ask God to show you, or ask the help of your minister or Christian friends. Then, as you begin to recognize your special abilities, use them to strengthen and encourage the church.

2

DECEMBER

Armor of God
EPHESIANS 6:10-20

A final word: Be strong with the Lord's mighty power. ¹¹Put on all of God's armor so that you will be able to stand firm against all strategies and tricks of the Devil. ¹²For we are not fighting against people made of flesh and blood, but against the evil rulers and authorities of the unseen world, against those mighty powers of darkness who rule this world, and against wicked spirits in the heavenly realms.

¹³Use every piece of God's armor to resist the enemy in the time of evil, so that after the battle you will still be standing firm. ¹⁴Stand your ground, putting on the sturdy belt of truth and the body armor of God's righteousness. ¹⁵For shoes, put on the peace that comes from the Good News, so that you will be fully prepared. ¹⁶In every battle you will need faith as your shield to stop the fiery arrows aimed at you by Satan. ¹⁷Put on salvation as your helmet, and take the sword of the Spirit, which is the Word of God. ¹⁸Pray at all times and on every occasion in the power of the Holy Spirit. Stay alert and be persistent in your prayers for all Christians everywhere.

¹⁹And pray for me, too. Ask God to give me the right words as I boldly explain God's secret plan that the Good News is for the Gentiles, too. ²⁰I am in chains now for preaching this message as God's ambassador. But pray that I will keep on speaking boldly for him, as I should.

〰〰 **Which of these weapons do you need to learn to use better?** These who are not "flesh and blood" are demons over whom Satan has control. They are not mere fantasies—they are very real. We face a powerful army whose goal is to defeat Christ's church. When we believe in Christ, these beings become our enemies, and they try every device to turn us away from him and back to sin. Although we are assured of victory, we must engage in the struggle until Christ returns. Because Satan is constantly battling against all who are on the Lord's side, we need supernatural power to defeat him. God provides this by giving us his Holy Spirit within us and his armor surrounding us. If you feel discouraged, remember that Jesus promises to fight the battle for you as you trust in him.

The Mind of Jesus

PHILIPPIANS 2:1-18

Is there any encouragement from belonging to Christ? Any comfort from his love? Any fellowship together in the Spirit? Are your hearts tender and sympathetic? ²Then make me truly happy by agreeing wholeheartedly with each other, loving one another, and working together with one heart and purpose.

³Don't be selfish; don't live to make a good impression on others. Be humble, thinking of others as better than yourself. ⁴Don't think only about your own affairs, but be interested in others, too, and what they are doing.

⁵Your attitude should be the same that Christ Jesus had. ⁶Though he was God, he did not demand and cling to his rights as God. ⁷He made himself nothing; he took the humble position of a slave and appeared in human form. ⁸And in human form he obediently humbled himself even further by dying a criminal's death on a cross. ⁹Because of this, God raised him up to the heights of heaven and gave him a name that is above every other name, ¹⁰so that at the name of Jesus every knee will bow, in heaven and on earth and under the earth, ¹¹and every tongue will confess that Jesus Christ is Lord, to the glory of God the Father.

¹²Dearest friends, you were always so careful to follow my instructions when I was with you. And now that I am away you must be even more careful to put into action God's saving work in your lives, obeying God with deep reverence and fear. ¹³For God is working in you, giving you the desire to obey him and the power to do what pleases him.

¹⁴In everything you do, stay away from complaining and arguing, ¹⁵so that no one can speak a word of blame against you. You are to live clean, innocent lives as children of God in a dark world full of crooked and perverse people. Let your lives shine brightly before them. ¹⁶Hold tightly to the word of life, so that when Christ returns, I will be proud that I did not lose the race and that my work was not useless. ¹⁷But even if my life is to be poured out like a drink offering to complete the sacrifice of your faithful service (that is, if I am to die for you), I will rejoice, and I want to share my joy with all of you. ¹⁸And you should be happy about this and rejoice with me.

〰️〰️ **In what ways would having Christ's mind or attitude help you face this day differently?** Often people excuse selfishness, pride, or evil by claiming their "rights." They think, *I can cheat on this test; after all, I deserve to pass this class,* or *I can spend all this money on myself—I worked for it,* or *I* can get an abortion—*I have a right to control my own body.* But as believers, we should have a different attitude, an attitude that enables us to give up our rights for the good of others—in order to serve others. If we say we follow Christ, we must also want to live as he lived. We should develop his attitude of humble service, even when we are not likely to get recognition for our efforts. Are you selfishly clinging to your rights, or are you willing to serve?

4 DECEMBER

Learning Joy

PHILIPPIANS 3:1-21

Whatever happens, dear friends, may the Lord give you joy. I never get tired of telling you this. I am doing this for your own good. ²Watch out for those dogs, those wicked men and their evil deeds, those mutilators who say you must be circumcised to be saved. ³For we who worship God in the Spirit are the only ones who are truly circumcised. We put no confidence in human effort. Instead, we boast about what Christ Jesus has done for us.

⁴Yet I could have confidence in myself if anyone could. If others have reason for confidence in their own efforts, I have even more! ⁵For I was circumcised when I was eight days old, having been born into a pure-blooded Jewish family that is a branch of the tribe of Benjamin. So I am a real Jew if there ever was one! What's more, I was a member of the Pharisees, who demand the strictest obedience to the Jewish law. ⁶And zealous? Yes, in fact, I harshly persecuted the church. And I obeyed the Jewish law so carefully that I was never accused of any fault.

⁷I once thought all these things were so very important, but now I consider them worthless because of what Christ has done. ⁸Yes, everything else is worthless when compared with the priceless gain of knowing Christ Jesus my Lord. I have discarded everything else, counting it all as garbage, so that I may have Christ ⁹and become one with him. I no longer count on my own goodness or my ability to obey God's law, but I trust Christ to save me. For God's way of making us right with himself depends on faith. ¹⁰As a result, I can really know Christ and experience the mighty power that raised him from the dead. I can learn what it means to suffer with him, sharing in his death, ¹¹so that, somehow, I can experience the resurrection from the dead!

¹²I don't mean to say that I have already achieved these things or that I have already reached perfection! But I keep working toward that day when I will finally be all that Christ Jesus saved me for and wants me to be. ¹³No, dear friends, I am still not all I should be, but I am focusing all my energies on this one thing: Forgetting the past and looking forward to what lies ahead, ¹⁴I strain to reach the end of the race and receive the prize for which God, through Christ Jesus, is calling us up to heaven.

[15]I hope all of you who are mature Christians will agree on these things. If you disagree on some point, I believe God will make it plain to you. [16]But we must be sure to obey the truth we have learned already.

[17]Dear friends, pattern your lives after mine, and learn from those who follow our example. [18]For I have told you often before, and I say it again with tears in my eyes, that there are many whose conduct shows they are really enemies of the cross of Christ. [19]Their future is eternal destruction. Their god is their appetite, they brag about shameful things, and all they think about is this life here on earth. [20]But we are citizens of heaven, where the Lord Jesus Christ lives. And we are eagerly waiting for him to return as our Savior. [21]He will take these weak mortal bodies of ours and change them into glorious bodies like his own, using the same mighty power that he will use to conquer everything, everywhere.

〰〰〰 **What areas of your life could God be using to teach you joy?**
Paul challenged the Philippians to pursue Christlikeness by following Paul's own example. This did not mean, of course, that they should copy everything he did, for he stated that he was not perfect. But as he focused his life on being like Christ, so should they. The Gospels may not yet have been in circulation, so Paul could not tell them to read the Bible to see what Christ was like. Therefore he urged them to imitate him. That Paul could tell people to follow his example is a testimony to his character. Can you do the same? What kind of follower would a new Christian become if he or she imitated you?

DECEMBER **5**

What We Have in Christ
COLOSSIANS 2:1-15

I want you to know how much I have agonized for you and for the church at Laodicea, and for many other friends who have never known me personally. [2]My goal is that they will be encouraged and knit together by strong ties of love. I want them to have full confidence because they have complete understanding of God's secret plan, which is Christ himself. [3]In him lie hidden all the treasures of wisdom and knowledge.

[4]I am telling you this so that no one will be able to deceive you with persuasive arguments. [5]For though I am far away from you, my heart is with you. And I am very happy because you are living as you should and because of your strong faith in Christ.

[6]And now, just as you accepted Christ Jesus as your Lord, you must continue to live in obedience to him. [7]Let your roots grow down into him and draw up nourishment from him, so you will grow in faith, strong and vigorous in the truth you were taught. Let your lives overflow with thanksgiving for all he has done.

[8]Don't let anyone lead you astray with empty philosophy and high-

sounding nonsense that come from human thinking and from the evil powers of this world, and not from Christ. [9]For in Christ the fullness of God lives in a human body, [10]and you are complete through your union with Christ. He is the Lord over every ruler and authority in the universe. [11]When you came to Christ, you were "circumcised," but not by a physical procedure. It was a spiritual procedure—the cutting away of your sinful nature. [12]For you were buried with Christ when you were baptized. And with him you were raised to a new life because you trusted the mighty power of God, who raised Christ from the dead.

[13]You were dead because of your sins and because your sinful nature was not yet cut away. Then God made you alive with Christ. He forgave all our sins. [14]He canceled the record that contained the charges against us. He took it and destroyed it by nailing it to Christ's cross. [15]In this way, God disarmed the evil rulers and authorities. He shamed them publicly by his victory over them on the cross of Christ.

〜〰〜 **What dangerous philosophy is present in your environment that could affect your relationship with Christ?** Paul writes against any philosophy of life based only on human ideas and experiences. Paul himself was a gifted philosopher, so he is not condemning philosophy. He is condemning teaching that credits humanity, not Christ, with being the answer to life's problems. That approach becomes a false religion. There are many man-made approaches to life's problems that totally disregard God. To resist heresy you must use your mind, keep your eyes on Christ, and study God's Word. When we know Jesus Christ, we don't need to seek God by means of other religions, cults, or worldly philosophies as the Colossians were doing. Christ alone holds the answers to the true meaning of life because he *is* life. Christ is the unique source of knowledge and power for the Christian life. No Christian needs anything in addition to what Christ has provided to be saved. We are complete in him.

6

DECEMBER

Christian Relationships

COLOSSIANS 3:1-17

Since you have been raised to new life with Christ, set your sights on the realities of heaven, where Christ sits at God's right hand in the place of honor and power. [2]Let heaven fill your thoughts. Do not think only about things down here on earth. [3]For you died when Christ died, and your real life is hidden with Christ in God. [4]And when Christ, who is your real life, is revealed to the whole world, you will share in all his glory.

[5]So put to death the sinful, earthly things lurking within you. Have nothing to do with sexual sin, impurity, lust, and shameful desires. Don't be greedy for the good things of this life, for that is idolatry. [6]God's terrible anger will come upon those who do such things. [7]You used to do them

when your life was still part of this world. [8]But now is the time to get rid of anger, rage, malicious behavior, slander, and dirty language. [9]Don't lie to each other, for you have stripped off your old evil nature and all its wicked deeds. [10]In its place you have clothed yourselves with a brand-new nature that is continually being renewed as you learn more and more about Christ, who created this new nature within you. [11]In this new life, it doesn't matter if you are a Jew or a Gentile, circumcised or uncircumcised, barbaric, uncivilized, slave, or free. Christ is all that matters, and he lives in all of us.

[12]Since God chose you to be the holy people whom he loves, you must clothe yourselves with tenderhearted mercy, kindness, humility, gentleness, and patience. [13]You must make allowance for each other's faults and forgive the person who offends you. Remember, the Lord forgave you, so you must forgive others. [14]And the most important piece of clothing you must wear is love. Love is what binds us all together in perfect harmony. [15]And let the peace that comes from Christ rule in your hearts. For as members of one body you are all called to live in peace. And always be thankful.

[16]Let the words of Christ, in all their richness, live in your hearts and make you wise. Use his words to teach and counsel each other. Sing psalms and hymns and spiritual songs to God with thankful hearts. [17]And whatever you do or say, let it be as a representative of the Lord Jesus, all the while giving thanks through him to God the Father.

〜〰〜 **What do you envision when you think about heaven?** Paul writes that we should have as little desire for this world as a dead person would have. The Christian's real home is where Christ lives. This truth gives us a different perspective on our lives here on earth. To "set your sights on the realities of heaven" means to look at life from God's perspective and seek what he desires. This is the antidote to materialism; we gain the proper perspective on material goods when we take God's view of them. The more we regard the world around us as God does, the more we will live in harmony with him. We must not become too attached to what is only temporary.

DECEMBER

7

Spiritual Reputation

1 THESSALONIANS 1:1-10

This letter is from Paul, Silas, and Timothy.

It is written to the church in Thessalonica, you who belong to God the Father and the Lord Jesus Christ.

May his grace and peace be yours.

[2]We always thank God for all of you and pray for you constantly. [3]As we talk to our God and Father about you, we think of your faithful work, your loving deeds, and your continual anticipation of the return of our Lord Jesus Christ.

455

⁴We know that God loves you, dear brothers and sisters, and that he chose you to be his own people. ⁵For when we brought you the Good News, it was not only with words but also with power, for the Holy Spirit gave you full assurance that what we said was true. And you know that the way we lived among you was further proof of the truth of our message. ⁶So you received the message with joy from the Holy Spirit in spite of the severe suffering it brought you. In this way, you imitated both us and the Lord. ⁷As a result, you yourselves became an example to all the Christians in Greece. ⁸And now the word of the Lord is ringing out from you to people everywhere, even beyond Greece, for wherever we go we find people telling us about your faith in God. We don't need to tell them about it, ⁹for they themselves keep talking about the wonderful welcome you gave us and how you turned away from idols to serve the true and living God. ¹⁰And they speak of how you are looking forward to the coming of God's Son from heaven— Jesus, whom God raised from the dead. He is the one who has rescued us from the terrors of the coming judgment.

⌇⌇ **How do you think others would evaluate your spiritual life?** All of us should respond to the Good News as the Thessalonians did: Turn to God, serve God, and wait for his Son, Jesus Christ, to return from heaven. We should turn from sin to God because Christ is coming to judge the earth. We should be fervent in our service because we have little time before Christ returns. We should be prepared for Christ to return because we don't know when he will come.

8

DECEMBER

Living for God

1 THESSALONIANS 4:1-18

Finally, dear brothers and sisters, we urge you in the name of the Lord Jesus to live in a way that pleases God, as we have taught you. You are doing this already, and we encourage you to do so more and more. ²For you remember what we taught you in the name of the Lord Jesus. ³God wants you to be holy, so you should keep clear of all sexual sin. ⁴Then each of you will control your body and live in holiness and honor—⁵not in lustful passion as the pagans do, in their ignorance of God and his ways.

⁶Never cheat another Christian in this matter by taking his wife, for the Lord avenges all such sins, as we have solemnly warned you before. ⁷God has called us to be holy, not to live impure lives. ⁸Anyone who refuses to live by these rules is not disobeying human rules but is rejecting God, who gives his Holy Spirit to you.

⁹But I don't need to write to you about the Christian love that should be shown among God's people. For God himself has taught you to love one another. ¹⁰Indeed, your love is already strong toward all the Christians in all

of Macedonia. Even so, dear friends, we beg you to love them more and more. [11] This should be your ambition: to live a quiet life, minding your own business and working with your hands, just as we commanded you before. [12] As a result, people who are not Christians will respect the way you live, and you will not need to depend on others to meet your financial needs.

[13] And now, brothers and sisters, I want you to know what will happen to the Christians who have died so you will not be full of sorrow like people who have no hope. [14] For since we believe that Jesus died and was raised to life again, we also believe that when Jesus comes, God will bring back with Jesus all the Christians who have died.

[15] I can tell you this directly from the Lord: We who are still living when the Lord returns will not rise to meet him ahead of those who are in their graves. [16] For the Lord himself will come down from heaven with a commanding shout, with the call of the archangel, and with the trumpet call of God. First, all the Christians who have died will rise from their graves. [17] Then, together with them, we who are still alive and remain on the earth will be caught up in the clouds to meet the Lord in the air and remain with him forever. [18] So comfort and encourage each other with these words.

What specific action could you take today simply out of obedience to God? Because Jesus Christ came back to life, so will all believers. All Christians, including those living when Christ returns, will live with Christ forever. Therefore, we need not despair when loved ones die or world events take a tragic turn. God will turn our tragedies to triumphs, our poverty to riches, our pain to glory, and our defeat to victory. All believers throughout history will stand in God's very presence, safe and secure. As Paul comforted the Thessalonians with the promise of the resurrection, so we should comfort and reassure each other with this great hope.

DECEMBER

Encouragement
2 THESSALONIANS 1:1-12

This letter is from Paul, Silas, and Timothy.

It is written to the church in Thessalonica, you who belong to God our Father and the Lord Jesus Christ.

[2] May God our Father and the Lord Jesus Christ give you grace and peace.

[3] Dear brothers and sisters, we always thank God for you, as is right, for we are thankful that your faith is flourishing and you are all growing in love for each other. [4] We proudly tell God's other churches about your endurance and faithfulness in all the persecutions and hardships you are suffering. [5] But God will use this persecution to show his justice. For he will make you worthy of his Kingdom, for which you are suffering, [6] and in his justice he

will punish those who persecute you. [7]And God will provide rest for you who are being persecuted and also for us when the Lord Jesus appears from heaven. He will come with his mighty angels, [8]in flaming fire, bringing judgment on those who don't know God and on those who refuse to obey the Good News of our Lord Jesus. [9]They will be punished with everlasting destruction, forever separated from the Lord and from his glorious power [10]when he comes to receive glory and praise from his holy people. And you will be among those praising him on that day, for you believed what we testified about him.

[11]And so we keep on praying for you, that our God will make you worthy of the life to which he called you. And we pray that God, by his power, will fulfill all your good intentions and faithful deeds. [12]Then everyone will give honor to the name of our Lord Jesus because of you, and you will be honored along with him. This is all made possible because of the undeserved favor of our God and Lord, Jesus Christ.

~~\/~~ **What Christians could you encourage today?** As we live for Christ, we will experience troubles and hardships. Some say that troubles are a result of sin or lack of faith, but Paul teaches that they may be a part of God's plan for believers. Our problems help us to look upward and forward, not inward; they help build strong character; and they help us to be sensitive to others who also must struggle. In addition, problems are unavoidable because we are trying to be godly people in an ungodly world. Our troubles may well be a sign of effective Christian living.

10 DECEMBER

Final Requests

2 THESSALONIANS 3:1-18

Finally, dear brothers and sisters, I ask you to pray for us. Pray first that the Lord's message will spread rapidly and be honored wherever it goes, just as when it came to you. [2]Pray, too, that we will be saved from wicked and evil people, for not everyone believes in the Lord. [3]But the Lord is faithful; he will make you strong and guard you from the evil one. [4]And we are confident in the Lord that you are practicing the things we commanded you, and that you always will. [5]May the Lord bring you into an ever deeper understanding of the love of God and the endurance that comes from Christ.

[6]And now, dear brothers and sisters, we give you this command with the authority of our Lord Jesus Christ: Stay away from any Christian who lives in idleness and doesn't follow the tradition of hard work we gave you. [7]For you know that you ought to follow our example. We were never lazy when we were with you. [8]We never accepted food from anyone without paying for it. We worked hard day and night so that we would not be a burden to any of you. [9]It wasn't that we didn't have the right to ask you to feed us, but we

wanted to give you an example to follow. [10]Even while we were with you, we gave you this rule: "Whoever does not work should not eat."

[11]Yet we hear that some of you are living idle lives, refusing to work and wasting time meddling in other people's business. [12]In the name of the Lord Jesus Christ, we appeal to such people—no, we command them: Settle down and get to work. Earn your own living. [13]And I say to the rest of you, dear brothers and sisters, never get tired of doing good.

[14]Take note of those who refuse to obey what we say in this letter. Stay away from them so they will be ashamed. [15]Don't think of them as enemies, but speak to them as you would to a Christian who needs to be warned.

[16]May the Lord of peace himself always give you his peace no matter what happens. The Lord be with you all.

[17]Now here is my greeting, which I write with my own hand—PAUL. I do this at the end of all my letters to prove that they really are from me.

[18]May the grace of our Lord Jesus Christ be with you all.

How aware and involved are you in the worldwide spread of the gospel? Some people in the Thessalonian church were falsely teaching that because Christ would return any day, people should set aside their responsibilities, quit work, do no future planning, and just wait for the Lord. But their lack of activity only led them into sin. They became a burden to the church, which was supporting them, and they wasted time that could have been used for helping others. These church members may have thought that they were being more spiritual by not working, but Paul tells them to be responsible and get back to work. Being ready for Christ means obeying him in every area of life. Because we know that Christ is coming, we must live in such a way that our faith and our daily life will please him when he arrives.

DECEMBER

Always Going Forward
1 TIMOTHY 4:1-16

Now the Holy Spirit tells us clearly that in the last times some will turn away from what we believe; they will follow lying spirits and teachings that come from demons. [2]These teachers are hypocrites and liars. They pretend to be religious, but their consciences are dead.

[3]They will say it is wrong to be married and wrong to eat certain foods. But God created those foods to be eaten with thanksgiving by people who know and believe the truth. [4]Since everything God created is good, we should not reject any of it. We may receive it gladly, with thankful hearts. [5]For we know it is made holy by the word of God and prayer.

[6]If you explain this to the others, you will be doing your duty as a worthy servant of Christ Jesus, one who is fed by the message of faith and the true teaching you have followed. [7]Do not waste time arguing over godless ideas

and old wives' tales. Spend your time and energy in training yourself for spiritual fitness. [8]Physical exercise has some value, but spiritual exercise is much more important, for it promises a reward in both this life and the next. [9]This is true, and everyone should accept it. [10]We work hard and suffer much in order that people will believe the truth, for our hope is in the living God, who is the Savior of all people, and particularly of those who believe.

[11]Teach these things and insist that everyone learn them. [12]Don't let anyone think less of you because you are young. Be an example to all believers in what you teach, in the way you live, in your love, your faith, and your purity. [13]Until I get there, focus on reading the Scriptures to the church, encouraging the believers, and teaching them.

[14]Do not neglect the spiritual gift you received through the prophecies spoken to you when the elders of the church laid their hands on you. [15]Give your complete attention to these matters. Throw yourself into your tasks so that everyone will see your progress. [16]Keep a close watch on yourself and on your teaching. Stay true to what is right, and God will save you and those who hear you.

Which of these instructions need to be given a higher priority in your life? Are you in shape both physically and spiritually? In our society much emphasis is placed on physical fitness, but spiritual health (godliness) is even more important. Our physical health is susceptible to disease and injury, but faith can sustain us through these tragedies. To train ourselves to be godly, we must develop our faith by using our God-given abilities in the service of the church. Are you developing your spiritual muscles?

DECEMBER

A Friend's Final Words
1 TIMOTHY 6:3-21

Some false teachers may deny these things, but these are the sound, wholesome teachings of the Lord Jesus Christ, and they are the foundation for a godly life. [4]Anyone who teaches anything different is both conceited and ignorant. Such a person has an unhealthy desire to quibble over the meaning of words. This stirs up arguments ending in jealousy, fighting, slander, and evil suspicions. [5]These people always cause trouble. Their minds are corrupt, and they don't tell the truth. To them religion is just a way to get rich.

[6]Yet true religion with contentment is great wealth. [7]After all, we didn't bring anything with us when we came into the world, and we certainly cannot carry anything with us when we die. [8]So if we have enough food and clothing, let us be content. [9]But people who long to be rich fall into temptation and are trapped by many foolish and harmful desires that plunge them into ruin and destruction. [10]For the love of money is at the root of all kinds

of evil. And some people, craving money, have wandered from the faith and pierced themselves with many sorrows.

[11]But you, Timothy, belong to God; so run from all these evil things, and follow what is right and good. Pursue a godly life, along with faith, love, perseverance, and gentleness. [12]Fight the good fight for what we believe. Hold tightly to the eternal life that God has given you, which you have confessed so well before many witnesses. [13]And I command you before God, who gives life to all, and before Christ Jesus, who gave a good testimony before Pontius Pilate, [14]that you obey his commands with all purity. Then no one can find fault with you from now until our Lord Jesus Christ returns. [15]For at the right time Christ will be revealed from heaven by the blessed and only almighty God, the King of kings and Lord of lords. [16]He alone can never die, and he lives in light so brilliant that no human can approach him. No one has ever seen him, nor ever will. To him be honor and power forever. Amen.

[17]Tell those who are rich in this world not to be proud and not to trust in their money, which will soon be gone. But their trust should be in the living God, who richly gives us all we need for our enjoyment. [18]Tell them to use their money to do good. They should be rich in good works and should give generously to those in need, always being ready to share with others whatever God has given them. [19]By doing this they will be storing up their treasure as a good foundation for the future so that they may take hold of real life.

[20]Timothy, guard what God has entrusted to you. Avoid godless, foolish discussions with those who oppose you with their so-called knowledge. [21]Some people have wandered from the faith by following such foolishness.

May God's grace be with you all.

〰〰 **How does your attitude toward money match Paul's advice?**
Despite overwhelming evidence to the contrary, most people still believe that money brings happiness. Rich people craving greater riches can be caught in an endless cycle that only ends in ruin and destruction. How can you keep away from the love of money? Paul gives us some guidelines: (1) Realize that one day riches will all be gone (vv. 7, 17). (2) Be content with what you have (v. 8). (3) Monitor what you are willing to do to get more money (vv. 9-10). (4) Love people more than money (v. 10-11). (5) Love God's work more than money (v. 10-11). (6) Freely share what you have with others (v. 18).

The Importance of Examples
2 TIMOTHY 1:1-18

DECEMBER **13**

This letter is from Paul, an apostle of Christ Jesus by God's will, sent out to tell others about the life he has promised through faith in Christ Jesus. [2]It is written to Timothy, my dear son.

May God our Father and Christ Jesus our Lord give you grace, mercy, and peace.

³Timothy, I thank God for you. He is the God I serve with a clear conscience, just as my ancestors did. Night and day I constantly remember you in my prayers. ⁴I long to see you again, for I remember your tears as we parted. And I will be filled with joy when we are together again.

⁵I know that you sincerely trust the Lord, for you have the faith of your mother, Eunice, and your grandmother, Lois. ⁶This is why I remind you to fan into flames the spiritual gift God gave you when I laid my hands on you. ⁷For God has not given us a spirit of fear and timidity, but of power, love, and self-discipline. ⁸So you must never be ashamed to tell others about our Lord. And don't be ashamed of me, either, even though I'm in prison for Christ. With the strength God gives you, be ready to suffer with me for the proclamation of the Good News.

⁹It is God who saved us and chose us to live a holy life. He did this not because we deserved it, but because that was his plan long before the world began—to show his love and kindness to us through Christ Jesus. ¹⁰And now he has made all of this plain to us by the coming of Christ Jesus, our Savior, who broke the power of death and showed us the way to everlasting life through the Good News. ¹¹And God chose me to be a preacher, an apostle, and a teacher of this Good News.

¹²And that is why I am suffering here in prison. But I am not ashamed of it, for I know the one in whom I trust, and I am sure that he is able to guard what I have entrusted to him until the day of his return.

¹³Hold on to the pattern of right teaching you learned from me. And remember to live in the faith and love that you have in Christ Jesus. ¹⁴With the help of the Holy Spirit who lives within us, carefully guard what has been entrusted to you.

¹⁵As you know, all the Christians who came here from the province of Asia have deserted me; even Phygelus and Hermogenes are gone. ¹⁶May the Lord show special kindness to Onesiphorus and all his family because he often visited and encouraged me. He was never ashamed of me because I was in prison. ¹⁷When he came to Rome, he searched everywhere until he found me. ¹⁸May the Lord show him special kindness on the day of Christ's return. And you know how much he helped me at Ephesus.

〜〜〜 **Who has been a good spiritual example for you? How can you thank him or her?** Timothy's mother and grandmother, Eunice and Lois, were early Christian converts, possibly through Paul's ministry in their home city of Lystra. They had communicated their strong Christian faith to Timothy, even though his father was probably not a believer. Don't hide your light at home: your family is a fertile field for planting gospel seeds. Let your parents, brothers, and sisters know of your faith in Jesus, and be sure they see Christ's love, helpfulness, and joy in you.

Last Days

2 TIMOTHY 3:1-17

You should also know this, Timothy, that in the last days there will be very difficult times. ²For people will love only themselves and their money. They will be boastful and proud, scoffing at God, disobedient to their parents, and ungrateful. They will consider nothing sacred. ³They will be unloving and unforgiving; they will slander others and have no self-control; they will be cruel and have no interest in what is good. ⁴They will betray their friends, be reckless, be puffed up with pride, and love pleasure rather than God. ⁵They will act as if they are religious, but they will reject the power that could make them godly. You must stay away from people like that.

⁶They are the kind who work their way into people's homes and win the confidence of vulnerable women who are burdened with the guilt of sin and controlled by many desires. ⁷Such women are forever following new teachings, but they never understand the truth. ⁸And these teachers fight the truth just as Jannes and Jambres fought against Moses. Their minds are depraved, and their faith is counterfeit. ⁹But they won't get away with this for long. Someday everyone will recognize what fools they are, just as happened with Jannes and Jambres.

¹⁰But you know what I teach, Timothy, and how I live, and what my purpose in life is. You know my faith and how long I have suffered. You know my love and my patient endurance. ¹¹You know how much persecution and suffering I have endured. You know all about how I was persecuted in Antioch, Iconium, and Lystra—but the Lord delivered me from all of it. ¹²Yes, and everyone who wants to live a godly life in Christ Jesus will suffer persecution. ¹³But evil people and impostors will flourish. They will go on deceiving others, and they themselves will be deceived.

¹⁴But you must remain faithful to the things you have been taught. You know they are true, for you know you can trust those who taught you. ¹⁵You have been taught the holy Scriptures from childhood, and they have given you the wisdom to receive the salvation that comes by trusting in Christ Jesus. ¹⁶All Scripture is inspired by God and is useful to teach us what is true and to make us realize what is wrong in our lives. It straightens us out and teaches us to do what is right. ¹⁷It is God's way of preparing us in every way, fully equipped for every good thing God wants us to do.

〰️〰️ **How can you tell true teachers from false?** The whole Bible is God's inspired Word. Because it is inspired and trustworthy, we should *read* it and *apply* it to our life. The Bible is our standard for testing everything else that claims to be true. It is our safeguard against false teaching and our source of guidance for how we should live. The Bible is our only source of knowledge about how we can be saved. God wants to show you what is true and equip you to live for him. How much time do you spend in God's Word? Read it regularly to discover God's truth and to become confident in your life and faith. Develop a plan for reading the whole Bible and don't read just the same familiar passages.

15 DECEMBER

Good Counsel

TITUS 3:1-11; PHILEMON 1:4-7

Remind your people to submit to the government and its officers. They should be obedient, always ready to do what is good. ²They must not speak evil of anyone, and they must avoid quarreling. Instead, they should be gentle and show true humility to everyone.

³Once we, too, were foolish and disobedient. We were misled by others and became slaves to many wicked desires and evil pleasures. Our lives were full of evil and envy. We hated others, and they hated us.

⁴But then God our Savior showed us his kindness and love. ⁵He saved us, not because of the good things we did, but because of his mercy. He washed away our sins and gave us a new life through the Holy Spirit. ⁶He generously poured out the Spirit upon us because of what Jesus Christ our Savior did. ⁷He declared us not guilty because of his great kindness. And now we know that we will inherit eternal life. ⁸These things I have told you are all true. I want you to insist on them so that everyone who trusts in God will be careful to do good deeds all the time. These things are good and beneficial for everyone.

⁹Do not get involved in foolish discussions about spiritual pedigrees or in quarrels and fights about obedience to Jewish laws. These kinds of things are useless and a waste of time. ¹⁰If anyone is causing divisions among you, give a first and second warning. After that, have nothing more to do with that person. ¹¹For people like that have turned away from the truth. They are sinning, and they condemn themselves.

Philemon 1:4I always thank God when I pray for you, Philemon, ⁵because I keep hearing of your trust in the Lord Jesus and your love for all of God's people. ⁶You are generous because of your faith. And I am praying that you will really put your generosity to work, for in so doing you will come to an understanding of all the good things we can do for Christ. ⁷I myself have gained much joy and comfort from your love, my brother, because your kindness has so often refreshed the hearts of God's people.

〜〜 **Which of these commands apply directly to your life?** Paul summarized what Christ does for us when he saves us. We move from a life full of sin to one where we are led by God's Holy Spirit. *All* our sins, not merely some, are washed away. In becoming a Christian, the believer acknowledges Christ as Lord and recognizes Christ's saving work. We gain eternal life with *all* its treasures. We have the *renewing* of our heart by the Holy Spirit. None of this occurs because we earned or deserved it; it is all God's gift.

The New Life

HEBREWS 10:19-39

And so, dear friends, we can boldly enter heaven's Most Holy Place because of the blood of Jesus. ²⁰This is the new, life-giving way that Christ has opened up for us through the sacred curtain, by means of his death for us.
²¹And since we have a great High Priest who rules over God's people, ²²let us go right into the presence of God, with true hearts fully trusting him. For our evil consciences have been sprinkled with Christ's blood to make us clean, and our bodies have been washed with pure water.
²³Without wavering, let us hold tightly to the hope we say we have, for God can be trusted to keep his promise. ²⁴Think of ways to encourage one another to outbursts of love and good deeds. ²⁵And let us not neglect our meeting together, as some people do, but encourage and warn each other, especially now that the day of his coming back again is drawing near.
²⁶Dear friends, if we deliberately continue sinning after we have received a full knowledge of the truth, there is no other sacrifice that will cover these sins. ²⁷There will be nothing to look forward to but the terrible expectation of God's judgment and the raging fire that will consume his enemies. ²⁸Anyone who refused to obey the law of Moses was put to death without mercy on the testimony of two or three witnesses. ²⁹Think how much more terrible the punishment will be for those who have trampled on the Son of God and have treated the blood of the covenant as if it were common and unholy. Such people have insulted and enraged the Holy Spirit who brings God's mercy to his people.
³⁰For we know the one who said,

"I will take vengeance.
I will repay those who deserve it."

He also said,

"The Lord will judge his own people."

³¹It is a terrible thing to fall into the hands of the living God.
³²Don't ever forget those early days when you first learned about Christ. Remember how you remained faithful even though it meant terrible suffering. ³³Sometimes you were exposed to public ridicule and were beaten, and sometimes you helped others who were suffering the same things. ³⁴You suffered along with those who were thrown into jail. When all you owned was taken from you, you accepted it with joy. You knew you had better things waiting for you in eternity.
³⁵Do not throw away this confident trust in the Lord, no matter what happens. Remember the great reward it brings you! ³⁶Patient endurance is what

you need now, so you will continue to do God's will. Then you will receive all that he has promised.

> ³⁷ "For in just a little while,
> the Coming One will come and not delay.
> ³⁸ And a righteous person will live by faith.
> But I will have no pleasure in anyone who turns away."

³⁹But we are not like those who turn their backs on God and seal their fate. We have faith that assures our salvation.

〰〽〰 **What do your prayer habits and church habits say about the real importance of faith in your life?** To neglect church meetings is to give up the encouragement and help of other Christians. We gather together to share our faith and strengthen each other in the Lord. As we get closer to the time of Christ's return, we may face many spiritual struggles, tribulations, and even persecution. Anti-Christian forces will grow in strength. Difficulties should never be excuses for missing church services. Rather, as difficulties arise, we should make an even greater effort to be faithful in church attendance.

17 DECEMBER

A Review of Faith
HEBREWS 11:1-40

What is faith? It is the confident assurance that what we hope for is going to happen. It is the evidence of things we cannot yet see. ²God gave his approval to people in days of old because of their faith.

³By faith we understand that the entire universe was formed at God's command, that what we now see did not come from anything that can be seen.

⁴It was by faith that Abel brought a more acceptable offering to God than Cain did. God accepted Abel's offering to show that he was a righteous man. And although Abel is long dead, he still speaks to us because of his faith.

⁵It was by faith that Enoch was taken up to heaven without dying— "suddenly he disappeared because God took him." But before he was taken up, he was approved as pleasing to God. ⁶So, you see, it is impossible to please God without faith. Anyone who wants to come to him must believe that there is a God and that he rewards those who sincerely seek him.

⁷It was by faith that Noah built an ark to save his family from the flood. He obeyed God, who warned him about something that had never happened before. By his faith he condemned the rest of the world and was made right in God's sight.

⁸It was by faith that Abraham obeyed when God called him to leave home and go to another land that God would give him as his inheritance. He went without knowing where he was going. ⁹And even when he reached

the land God promised him, he lived there by faith—for he was like a foreigner, living in a tent. And so did Isaac and Jacob, to whom God gave the same promise. [10]Abraham did this because he was confidently looking forward to a city with eternal foundations, a city designed and built by God.

[11]It was by faith that Sarah together with Abraham was able to have a child, even though they were too old and Sarah was barren. Abraham believed that God would keep his promise. [12]And so a whole nation came from this one man, Abraham, who was too old to have any children—a nation with so many people that, like the stars of the sky and the sand on the seashore, there is no way to count them.

[13]All these faithful ones died without receiving what God had promised them, but they saw it all from a distance and welcomed the promises of God. They agreed that they were no more than foreigners and nomads here on earth. [14]And obviously people who talk like that are looking forward to a country they can call their own. [15]If they had meant the country they came from, they would have found a way to go back. [16]But they were looking for a better place, a heavenly homeland. That is why God is not ashamed to be called their God, for he has prepared a heavenly city for them.

[17]It was by faith that Abraham offered Isaac as a sacrifice when God was testing him. Abraham, who had received God's promises, was ready to sacrifice his only son, Isaac, [18]though God had promised him, "Isaac is the son through whom your descendants will be counted." [19]Abraham assumed that if Isaac died, God was able to bring him back to life again. And in a sense, Abraham did receive his son back from the dead.

[20]It was by faith that Isaac blessed his two sons, Jacob and Esau. He had confidence in what God was going to do in the future.

[21]It was by faith that Jacob, when he was old and dying, blessed each of Joseph's sons and bowed in worship as he leaned on his staff.

[22]And it was by faith that Joseph, when he was about to die, confidently spoke of God's bringing the people of Israel out of Egypt. He was so sure of it that he commanded them to carry his bones with them when they left!

[23]It was by faith that Moses' parents hid him for three months. They saw that God had given them an unusual child, and they were not afraid of what the king might do.

[24]It was by faith that Moses, when he grew up, refused to be treated as the son of Pharaoh's daughter. [25]He chose to share the oppression of God's people instead of enjoying the fleeting pleasures of sin. [26]He thought it was better to suffer for the sake of the Messiah than to own the treasures of Egypt, for he was looking ahead to the great reward that God would give him. [27]It was by faith that Moses left the land of Egypt. He was not afraid of the king. Moses kept right on going because he kept his eyes on the one who is invisible. [28]It was by faith that Moses commanded the people of Israel to keep the Passover and to sprinkle blood on the doorposts so that the angel of death would not kill their firstborn sons.

[29]It was by faith that the people of Israel went right through the Red Sea

as though they were on dry ground. But when the Egyptians followed, they were all drowned.

³⁰It was by faith that the people of Israel marched around Jericho seven days, and the walls came crashing down.

³¹It was by faith that Rahab the prostitute did not die with all the others in her city who refused to obey God. For she had given a friendly welcome to the spies.

³²Well, how much more do I need to say? It would take too long to recount the stories of the faith of Gideon, Barak, Samson, Jephthah, David, Samuel, and all the prophets. ³³By faith these people overthrew kingdoms, ruled with justice, and received what God had promised them. They shut the mouths of lions, ³⁴quenched the flames of fire, and escaped death by the edge of the sword. Their weakness was turned to strength. They became strong in battle and put whole armies to flight. ³⁵Women received their loved ones back again from death.

But others trusted God and were tortured, preferring to die rather than turn from God and be free. They placed their hope in the resurrection to a better life. ³⁶Some were mocked, and their backs were cut open with whips. Others were chained in dungeons. ³⁷Some died by stoning, and some were sawed in half; others were killed with the sword. Some went about in skins of sheep and goats, hungry and oppressed and mistreated. ³⁸They were too good for this world. They wandered over deserts and mountains, hiding in caves and holes in the ground.

³⁹All of these people we have mentioned received God's approval because of their faith, yet none of them received all that God had promised. ⁴⁰For God had far better things in mind for us that would also benefit them, for they can't receive the prize at the end of the race until we finish the race.

〰〰 **How deep is your commitment to Christ?** Do you remember how you felt when you were little and your birthday approached? You were excited and anxious. You knew you would certainly receive gifts and other special treats. But some things would be a surprise. Birthdays combined assurance and anticipation, and so does faith! Faith is the conviction based on past experience that God's new and fresh surprises will surely be ours. Two words describe our faith: confidence and certainty. These two qualities need a secure beginning and ending point. The beginning point of faith is believing in God's character—he *is* who he says. The end point is believing in God's promises—he will *do* what he says. We believe that God will fulfill his promises even though we don't see those promises materializing *now*—this is true faith.

Our Turn

HEBREWS 12:1-13

Therefore, since we are surrounded by such a huge crowd of witnesses to the life of faith, let us strip off every weight that slows us down, especially the sin that so easily hinders our progress. And let us run with endurance the race that God has set before us. ²We do this by keeping our eyes on Jesus, on whom our faith depends from start to finish. He was willing to die a shameful death on the cross because of the joy he knew would be his afterward. Now he is seated in the place of highest honor beside God's throne in heaven. ³Think about all he endured when sinful people did such terrible things to him, so that you don't become weary and give up. ⁴After all, you have not yet given your lives in your struggle against sin.

⁵And have you entirely forgotten the encouraging words God spoke to you, his children? He said,

> "My child, don't ignore it when the Lord disciplines you,
>   and don't be discouraged when he corrects you.
> ⁶ For the Lord disciplines those he loves,
>   and he punishes those he accepts as his children."

⁷As you endure this divine discipline, remember that God is treating you as his own children. Whoever heard of a child who was never disciplined? ⁸If God doesn't discipline you as he does all of his children, it means that you are illegitimate and are not really his children after all. ⁹Since we respect our earthly fathers who disciplined us, should we not all the more cheerfully submit to the discipline of our heavenly Father and live forever?

¹⁰For our earthly fathers disciplined us for a few years, doing the best they knew how. But God's discipline is always right and good for us because it means we will share in his holiness. ¹¹No discipline is enjoyable while it is happening—it is painful! But afterward there will be a quiet harvest of right living for those who are trained in this way.

¹²So take a new grip with your tired hands and stand firm on your shaky legs. ¹³Mark out a straight path for your feet. Then those who follow you, though they are weak and lame, will not stumble and fall but will become strong.

〰️ **Which of these directions would have a significant impact on your faith?** Who loves his child more—the father who allows the child to do as he pleases or the one who corrects, trains, and even punishes the child to help him learn what is right? It is never pleasant to be corrected and disciplined by God, but his discipline is a sign of his deep love for us. We may respond to discipline in several ways: (1) We can accept it with resignation. (2) We can accept it with self-pity, thinking we really don't deserve it. (3) We can be angry and resentful toward God. Or (4) we can accept it gratefully, as the appropriate response we owe a loving Father.

19

Tough Times, Happy People
JAMES 1:2-27

Dear brothers and sisters, whenever trouble comes your way, let it be an opportunity for joy. ³For when your faith is tested, your endurance has a chance to grow. ⁴So let it grow, for when your endurance is fully developed, you will be strong in character and ready for anything.

⁵If you need wisdom—if you want to know what God wants you to do— ask him, and he will gladly tell you. He will not resent your asking. ⁶But when you ask him, be sure that you really expect him to answer, for a doubtful mind is as unsettled as a wave of the sea that is driven and tossed by the wind. ⁷People like that should not expect to receive anything from the Lord. ⁸They can't make up their minds. They waver back and forth in everything they do.

⁹Christians who are poor should be glad, for God has honored them. ¹⁰And those who are rich should be glad, for God has humbled them. They will fade away like a flower in the field. ¹¹The hot sun rises and dries up the grass; the flower withers, and its beauty fades away. So also, wealthy people will fade away with all of their achievements.

¹²God blesses the people who patiently endure testing. Afterward they will receive the crown of life that God has promised to those who love him. ¹³And remember, no one who wants to do wrong should ever say, "God is tempting me." God is never tempted to do wrong, and he never tempts any- one else either. ¹⁴Temptation comes from the lure of our own evil desires. ¹⁵These evil desires lead to evil actions, and evil actions lead to death. ¹⁶So don't be misled, my dear brothers and sisters.

¹⁷Whatever is good and perfect comes to us from God above, who created all heaven's lights. Unlike them, he never changes or casts shifting shadows. ¹⁸In his goodness he chose to make us his own children by giving us his true word. And we, out of all creation, became his choice possession.

¹⁹Dear friends, be quick to listen, slow to speak, and slow to get angry. ²⁰Your anger can never make things right in God's sight.

²¹So get rid of all the filth and evil in your lives, and humbly accept the mes- sage God has planted in your hearts, for it is strong enough to save your souls.

²²And remember, it is a message to obey, not just to listen to. If you don't obey, you are only fooling yourself. ²³For if you just listen and don't obey, it is like looking at your face in a mirror but doing nothing to improve your appearance. ²⁴You see yourself, walk away, and forget what you look like. ²⁵But if you keep looking steadily into God's perfect law—the law that sets

you free—and if you do what it says and don't forget what you heard, then God will bless you for doing it. [26]If you claim to be religious but don't control your tongue, you are just fooling yourself, and your religion is worthless. [27]Pure and lasting religion in the sight of God our Father means that we must care for orphans and widows in their troubles, and refuse to let the world corrupt us.

〜〴〵 **In what difficulty could you use the "James plan" right now?**
We can't really know the depth of our character until we see how we react under pressure. It is easy to be kind to others when everything is going well, but can we still be kind when others are treating us unfairly? God wants to make us perfect and complete, not keep us from all pain. Instead of complaining about our struggles, we should see them as opportunities for growth. Thank God for promising to be with you in rough times. Ask him to help you solve your problems or to give you the strength to endure them. Then be patient. God will not leave you alone with your problems; he will stay close and help you grow.

DECEMBER **20**

Valuing Other People

JAMES 2:1-13

My dear brothers and sisters, how can you claim that you have faith in our glorious Lord Jesus Christ if you favor some people more than others? [2]For instance, suppose someone comes into your meeting dressed in fancy clothes and expensive jewelry, and another comes in who is poor and dressed in shabby clothes. [3]If you give special attention and a good seat to the rich person, but you say to the poor one, "You can stand over there, or else sit on the floor"—well, [4]doesn't this discrimination show that you are guided by wrong motives?

[5]Listen to me, dear brothers and sisters. Hasn't God chosen the poor in this world to be rich in faith? Aren't they the ones who will inherit the kingdom God promised to those who love him? [6]And yet, you insult the poor man! Isn't it the rich who oppress you and drag you into court? [7]Aren't they the ones who slander Jesus Christ, whose noble name you bear?

[8]Yes indeed, it is good when you truly obey our Lord's royal command found in the Scriptures: "Love your neighbor as yourself." [9]But if you pay special attention to the rich, you are committing a sin, for you are guilty of breaking that law.

[10]And the person who keeps all of the laws except one is as guilty as the person who has broken all of God's laws. [11]For the same God who said, "Do not commit adultery," also said, "Do not murder." So if you murder someone, you have broken the entire law, even if you do not commit adultery.

[12]So whenever you speak, or whatever you do, remember that you will be judged by the law of love, the law that set you free. [13]For there will be no

mercy for you if you have not been merciful to others. But if you have been merciful, then God's mercy toward you will win out over his judgment against you.

〰〰 **Which tendencies do you have to watch out for in how you treat others?** Often we treat a well-dressed, impressive-looking person better than someone who looks poor. We do this because we would rather identify with successful people than with apparent failures. We feel better about ourselves when we associate with people we admire. The irony, as James reminds us, is that the supposed winners may have gained their impressive lifestyle at our expense. In addition, the rich find it hard to identify with the Lord Jesus who came as a humble servant. Are you easily impressed by status, wealth, or fame? Are you partial to the "haves" while ignoring the "have nots"? This prejudice is sin. God views all people as equals, and if he favors anyone, it is the poor and the powerless who cannot help themselves. We should follow his example.

21 DECEMBER

Words as Weapons
JAMES 3:1-12

Dear brothers and sisters, not many of you should become teachers in the church, for we who teach will be judged by God with greater strictness.
²We all make many mistakes, but those who control their tongues can also control themselves in every other way. ³We can make a large horse turn around and go wherever we want by means of a small bit in its mouth. ⁴And a tiny rudder makes a huge ship turn wherever the pilot wants it to go, even though the winds are strong. ⁵So also, the tongue is a small thing, but what enormous damage it can do. A tiny spark can set a great forest on fire. ⁶And the tongue is a flame of fire. It is full of wickedness that can ruin your whole life. It can turn the entire course of your life into a blazing flame of destruction, for it is set on fire by hell itself.
⁷People can tame all kinds of animals and birds and reptiles and fish, ⁸but no one can tame the tongue. It is an uncontrollable evil, full of deadly poison. ⁹Sometimes it praises our Lord and Father, and sometimes it breaks out into curses against those who have been made in the image of God. ¹⁰And so blessing and cursing come pouring out of the same mouth. Surely, my brothers and sisters, this is not right! ¹¹Does a spring of water bubble out with both fresh water and bitter water? ¹²Can you pick olives from a fig tree or figs from a grapevine? No, and you can't draw fresh water from a salty pool.

~~✓~~ **How sharp would others consider your tongue?** What you say and what you *don't* say are both important. Proper speech is not only saying the right words at the right time but controlling your desire to say what you shouldn't. Examples of wrongly using the tongue include gossiping, putting others down, bragging, manipulating, false teaching, exaggerating, complaining, flattering, and lying. Before you speak, ask, Is it true, is it necessary, and is it kind?

Living Stones

1 PETER 2:1-25

So get rid of all malicious behavior and deceit. Don't just pretend to be good! Be done with hypocrisy and jealousy and backstabbing. [2]You must crave pure spiritual milk so that you can grow into the fullness of your salvation. Cry out for this nourishment as a baby cries for milk, [3]now that you have had a taste of the Lord's kindness.
[4]Come to Christ, who is the living cornerstone of God's temple. He was rejected by the people, but he is precious to God who chose him.
[5]And now God is building you, as living stones, into his spiritual temple. What's more, you are God's holy priests, who offer the spiritual sacrifices that please him because of Jesus Christ. [6]As the Scriptures express it,

> "I am placing a stone in Jerusalem,
> a chosen cornerstone,
> and anyone who believes in him
> will never be disappointed."

[7]Yes, he is very precious to you who believe. But for those who reject him,

> "The stone that was rejected by the builders
> has now become the cornerstone."

[8]And the Scriptures also say,

> "He is the stone that makes people stumble,
> the rock that will make them fall."

They stumble because they do not listen to God's word or obey it, and so they meet the fate that has been planned for them.
[9]But you are not like that, for you are a chosen people. You are a kingdom of priests, God's holy nation, his very own possession. This is so you can show others the goodness of God, for he called you out of the darkness into his wonderful light.

¹⁰ "Once you were not a people;
now you are the people of God.
Once you received none of God's mercy;
now you have received his mercy."

¹¹Dear brothers and sisters, you are foreigners and aliens here. So I warn you to keep away from evil desires because they fight against your very souls. ¹²Be careful how you live among your unbelieving neighbors. Even if they accuse you of doing wrong, they will see your honorable behavior, and they will believe and give honor to God when he comes to judge the world.

¹³For the Lord's sake, accept all authority—the king as head of state, ¹⁴and the officials he has appointed. For the king has sent them to punish all who do wrong and to honor those who do right.

¹⁵It is God's will that your good lives should silence those who make foolish accusations against you. ¹⁶You are not slaves; you are free. But your freedom is not an excuse to do evil. You are free to live as God's slaves. ¹⁷Show respect for everyone. Love your Christian brothers and sisters. Fear God. Show respect for the king.

¹⁸You who are slaves must accept the authority of your masters. Do whatever they tell you—not only if they are kind and reasonable, but even if they are harsh. ¹⁹For God is pleased with you when, for the sake of your conscience, you patiently endure unfair treatment. ²⁰Of course, you get no credit for being patient if you are beaten for doing wrong. But if you suffer for doing right and are patient beneath the blows, God is pleased with you.

²¹This suffering is all part of what God has called you to. Christ, who suffered for you, is your example. Follow in his steps. ²²He never sinned, and he never deceived anyone. ²³He did not retaliate when he was insulted. When he suffered, he did not threaten to get even. He left his case in the hands of God, who always judges fairly. ²⁴He personally carried away our sins in his own body on the cross so we can be dead to sin and live for what is right. You have been healed by his wounds! ²⁵Once you were wandering like lost sheep. But now you have turned to your Shepherd, the Guardian of your souls.

〰〰 **Which would you choose as the biggest personal challenge in these verses?** One characteristic all children share is that they want to grow up, to be like the big kids or like their parents. When we are born again, we are spiritual babies. If we are healthy, we will want to grow. It's sad when we are satisfied to stay where we are as the months and years roll by. Crying for milk is a natural instinct for a baby, but an adult may have to learn to want spiritual nourishment. Once we see our need and begin to find comfort and fulfillment in Christ, however, our spiritual appetite will increase, and we will start to mature. How strong is your desire to grow spiritually? What spiritual food can you take today?

Relationships and Pain

1 PETER 3:1-22

In the same way, you wives must accept the authority of your husbands, even those who refuse to accept the Good News. Your godly lives will speak to them better than any words. They will be won over ²by watching your pure, godly behavior.

³Don't be concerned about the outward beauty that depends on fancy hairstyles, expensive jewelry, or beautiful clothes. ⁴You should be known for the beauty that comes from within, the unfading beauty of a gentle and quiet spirit, which is so precious to God. ⁵That is the way the holy women of old made themselves beautiful. They trusted God and accepted the authority of their husbands. ⁶For instance, Sarah obeyed her husband, Abraham, when she called him her master. You are her daughters when you do what is right without fear of what your husbands might do.

⁷In the same way, you husbands must give honor to your wives. Treat her with understanding as you live together. She may be weaker than you are, but she is your equal partner in God's gift of new life. If you don't treat her as you should, your prayers will not be heard.

⁸Finally, all of you should be of one mind, full of sympathy toward each other, loving one another with tender hearts and humble minds. ⁹Don't repay evil for evil. Don't retaliate when people say unkind things about you. Instead, pay them back with a blessing. That is what God wants you to do, and he will bless you for it. ¹⁰For the Scriptures say,

> "If you want a happy life and good days,
>   keep your tongue from speaking evil,
>   and keep your lips from telling lies.
> ¹¹Turn away from evil and do good.
>   Work hard at living in peace with others.
> ¹²The eyes of the Lord watch over those who do right,
>   and his ears are open to their prayers.
> But the Lord turns his face
>   against those who do evil."

¹³Now, who will want to harm you if you are eager to do good? ¹⁴But even if you suffer for doing what is right, God will reward you for it. So don't be afraid and don't worry. ¹⁵Instead, you must worship Christ as Lord of your life. And if you are asked about your Christian hope, always be ready to explain it. ¹⁶But you must do this in a gentle and respectful way. Keep your conscience clear. Then if people speak evil against you, they will be ashamed when they see what a good life you live because you belong to Christ. ¹⁷Remember, it is better to suffer for doing good, if that is what God wants, than to suffer for doing wrong!

[18]Christ also suffered when he died for our sins once for all time. He never sinned, but he died for sinners that he might bring us safely home to God. He suffered physical death, but he was raised to life in the Spirit. [19]So he went and preached to the spirits in prison—[20]those who disobeyed God long ago when God waited patiently while Noah was building his boat. Only eight people were saved from drowning in that terrible flood. [21]And this is a picture of baptism, which now saves you by the power of Jesus Christ's resurrection. Baptism is not a removal of dirt from your body; it is an appeal to God from a clean conscience.

[22]Now Christ has gone to heaven. He is seated in the place of honor next to God, and all the angels and authorities and powers are bowing before him.

〰〰 **How willing are you to conduct your relationships God's way, even when there are difficulties?** In our sinful world, it is often acceptable to tear people down verbally or get back at them if we feel hurt. Remembering Jesus' teaching to turn the other cheek, Peter encourages his readers to pay back wrongs by praying for the offenders. In God's Kingdom, revenge is unacceptable behavior. So is insulting a person, no matter how indirectly it is done. Rise above getting back at those who hurt you. Instead of reacting angrily to those people, pray for them.

24 DECEMBER

Knowing God
2 PETER 1:2-21

May God bless you with his special favor and wonderful peace as you come to know Jesus, our God and Lord, better and better.

[3]As we know Jesus better, his divine power gives us everything we need for living a godly life. He has called us to receive his own glory and goodness! [4]And by that same mighty power, he has given us all of his rich and wonderful promises. He has promised that you will escape the decadence all around you caused by evil desires and that you will share in his divine nature.

[5]So make every effort to apply the benefits of these promises to your life. Then your faith will produce a life of moral excellence. A life of moral excellence leads to knowing God better. [6]Knowing God leads to self-control. Self-control leads to patient endurance, and patient endurance leads to godliness. [7]Godliness leads to love for other Christians, and finally you will grow to have genuine love for everyone. [8]The more you grow like this, the more you will become productive and useful in your knowledge of our Lord Jesus Christ. [9]But those who fail to develop these virtues are blind or, at least, very shortsighted. They have already forgotten that God has cleansed them from their old life of sin.

[10]So, dear friends, work hard to prove that you really are among those God has called and chosen. Doing this, you will never stumble or fall away.

¹¹And God will open wide the gates of heaven for you to enter into the eternal Kingdom of our Lord and Savior Jesus Christ.
¹²I plan to keep on reminding you of these things—even though you already know them and are standing firm in the truth. ¹³Yes, I believe I should keep on reminding you of these things as long as I live. ¹⁴But the Lord Jesus Christ has shown me that my days here on earth are numbered and I am soon to die. ¹⁵So I will work hard to make these things clear to you. I want you to remember them long after I am gone.

¹⁶For we were not making up clever stories when we told you about the power of our Lord Jesus Christ and his coming again. We have seen his majestic splendor with our own eyes. ¹⁷And he received honor and glory from God the Father when God's glorious, majestic voice called down from heaven, "This is my beloved Son; I am fully pleased with him." ¹⁸We ourselves heard the voice when we were there with him on the holy mountain.

¹⁹Because of that, we have even greater confidence in the message proclaimed by the prophets. Pay close attention to what they wrote, for their words are like a light shining in a dark place—until the day Christ appears and his brilliant light shines in your hearts. ²⁰Above all, you must understand that no prophecy in Scripture ever came from the prophets themselves ²¹or because they wanted to prophesy. It was the Holy Spirit who moved the prophets to speak from God.

How would you answer someone who asked you what it means to know God? Outstanding coaches constantly review the basics of a sport with their teams, and good athletes can execute the fundamentals consistently well. We must not neglect the basics of our faith as we go on to study deeper truths. Just as an athlete needs constant practice, we need constant reminders of the fundamentals of our faith and of how we came to believe in the first place. Don't allow yourself to be bored or impatient with messages on the basics of the Christian life. Instead, take the attitude of an athlete who continues to practice and refine the basics even as he or she learns more advanced skills. Our faith must go beyond what we believe, it must become a dynamic part of all we do, resulting in good fruit and spiritual maturity. Salvation does not depend on good works, but it results in good works. If you claim to be saved while remaining unchanged, you have not understood faith or what God has done for you.

DECEMBER

The Way of Forgiveness

1 John 1:1-10

The one who existed from the beginning is the one we have heard and seen. We saw him with our own eyes and touched him with our own hands. He is Jesus Christ, the Word of life. ²This one who is life from God was shown to us, and we have seen him. And now we testify and announce to you that he is the one who is eternal life. He was with the Father, and then he was shown to us. ³We are telling you about what we ourselves have actually seen and heard, so that you may have fellowship with us. And our fellowship is with the Father and with his Son, Jesus Christ.

⁴We are writing these things so that our joy will be complete.

⁵This is the message he has given us to announce to you: God is light and there is no darkness in him at all. ⁶So we are lying if we say we have fellowship with God but go on living in spiritual darkness. We are not living in the truth. ⁷But if we are living in the light of God's presence, just as Christ is, then we have fellowship with each other, and the blood of Jesus, his Son, cleanses us from every sin.

⁸If we say we have no sin, we are only fooling ourselves and refusing to accept the truth. ⁹But if we confess our sins to him, he is faithful and just to forgive us and to cleanse us from every wrong. ¹⁰If we claim we have not sinned, we are calling God a liar and showing that his word has no place in our hearts.

〰〰 **What part does confession have in your life?** True confession will free us to enjoy fellowship with Christ. It will ease our conscience and lighten our cares. But some Christians do not understand how confession works. They feel so guilty that they confess the same sins over and over, and then they wonder if they have forgotten something. Other Christians believe that God forgives them for only the sins they confess, but if they died with unconfessed sins, they would be lost forever. These Christians do not understand that *God wants to forgive us.* He allowed his beloved Son to die just so he could pardon us. When we come to Christ, he forgives all the sins we have committed or will ever commit. We don't need to confess the same sins all over again, and we don't need to be afraid that God will reject us if we don't keep our slate perfectly clear at all times. Of course we want to continue to confess our sins but not because we think failure to do so will make us lose our salvation. Our hope in Christ is secure. Instead, we should confess so that we can enjoy maximum fellowship and joy with Christ. True confession also involves a commitment not to continue in sin. We are not genuinely confessing our sins before God if we are planning to commit the sin again and just want temporary forgiveness. We must pray for strength to resist the temptation the next time.

26 DECEMBER

God Is Love
1 JOHN 3:1-24

See how very much our heavenly Father loves us, for he allows us to be called his children, and we really are! But the people who belong to this world don't know God, so they don't understand that we are his children. ²Yes, dear friends, we are already God's children, and we can't even imagine what we will be like when Christ returns. But we do know that when he comes we will be like him, for we will see him as he really is. [3]And all who believe this will keep themselves pure, just as Christ is pure.

[4]Those who sin are opposed to the law of God, for all sin opposes the law of God. [5]And you know that Jesus came to take away our sins, for there is no sin in him. [6]So if we continue to live in him, we won't sin either. But those who keep on sinning have never known him or understood who he is.

[7]Dear children, don't let anyone deceive you about this: When people do what is right, it is because they are righteous, even as Christ is righteous. [8]But when people keep on sinning, it shows they belong to the Devil, who has been sinning since the beginning. But the Son of God came to destroy these works of the Devil. [9]Those who have been born into God's family do not sin, because God's life is in them. So they can't keep on sinning, because they have been born of God. [10]So now we can tell who are children of God and who are children of the Devil. Anyone who does not obey God's commands and does not love other Christians does not belong to God.

[11]This is the message we have heard from the beginning: We should love one another. [12]We must not be like Cain, who belonged to the evil one and killed his brother. And why did he kill him? Because Cain had been doing what was evil, and his brother had been doing what was right. [13]So don't be surprised, dear brothers and sisters, if the world hates you.

[14]If we love other Christians, it proves that we have passed from death to eternal life. But a person who doesn't love them is still dead. [15]Anyone who hates another Christian is really a murderer at heart. And you know that murderers don't have eternal life within them. [16]We know what real love is because Christ gave up his life for us. And so we also ought to give up our lives for our Christian friends. [17]But if one of you has enough money to live well, and sees a brother or sister in need and refuses to help—how can God's love be in that person?

[18]Dear children, let us stop just saying we love each other; let us really show it by our actions. [19]It is by our actions that we know we are living in the truth, so we will be confident when we stand before the Lord, [20]even if our hearts condemn us. For God is greater than our hearts, and he knows everything.

[21]Dear friends, if our conscience is clear, we can come to God with bold confidence. [22]And we will receive whatever we request because we obey him and do the things that please him. [23]And this is his commandment: We must believe in the name of his Son, Jesus Christ, and love one another, just as he commanded us. [24]Those who obey God's commandments live in fellowship with him, and he with them. And we know he lives in us because the Holy Spirit lives in us.

~∿∕⁄∼ **How can you tell if your love is growing?** Real love is an action, not a feeling. It produces selfless, sacrificial giving. The greatest act of love anyone can do is to give himself or herself for others. How can we lay down our lives? Sometimes it is easier to say we will die for others than to truly live for them. That involves putting others' desires before ours.

27

DECEMBER

The Life God Gives

1 JOHN 5:1-21

Everyone who believes that Jesus is the Christ is a child of God. And everyone who loves the Father loves his children, too. [2]We know we love God's children if we love God and obey his commandments. [3]Loving God means keeping his commandments, and really, that isn't difficult. [4]For every child of God defeats this evil world by trusting Christ to give the victory. [5]And the ones who win this battle against the world are the ones who believe that Jesus is the Son of God.

[6]And Jesus Christ was revealed as God's Son by his baptism in water and by shedding his blood on the cross—not by water only, but by water and blood. And the Spirit also gives us the testimony that this is true. [7]So we have these three witnesses—[8]the Spirit, the water, and the blood—and all three agree. [9]Since we believe human testimony, surely we can believe the testimony that comes from God. And God has testified about his Son. [10]All who believe in the Son of God know that this is true. Those who don't believe this are actually calling God a liar because they don't believe what God has testified about his Son.

[11]And this is what God has testified: He has given us eternal life, and this life is in his Son. [12]So whoever has God's Son has life; whoever does not have his Son does not have life.

[13]I write this to you who believe in the Son of God, so that you may know you have eternal life. [14]And we can be confident that he will listen to us whenever we ask him for anything in line with his will. [15]And if we know he is listening when we make our requests, we can be sure that he will give us what we ask for.

[16]If you see any Christian sinning in a way that does not lead to death, you should pray, and God will give that person life. But there is a sin that leads to death, and I am not saying you should pray for those who commit it. [17]Every wrong is sin, but not all sin leads to death.

[18]We know that those who have become part of God's family do not make a practice of sinning, for God's Son holds them securely, and the evil one cannot get his hands on them. [19]We know that we are children of God and that the world around us is under the power and control of the evil one. [20]And we know that the Son of God has come, and he has given us understanding so that we can know the true God. And now we are in God because we are in his Son, Jesus Christ. He is the only true God, and he is eternal life.

480

²¹Dear children, keep away from anything that might take God's place in your hearts.

〰〰 **How do you know that you have eternal life?** Some people *hope* they will be given eternal life. John says that we can *know* we have it. Our certainty is based on God's promise that he has given us eternal life through his Son. This is true whether you feel close to God or distant from him. Eternal life is not based on feelings but on facts. You can know you have eternal life if you believe God's truth. If you lack assurance as to whether you are a Christian, ask yourself if you have honestly committed your life to Christ as your Savior and Lord. If so, you know by faith that you are indeed a child of God.

Family Matters

2 JOHN 1:4-6; 3 JOHN 1:5-8; JUDE 1:17-25

How happy I was to meet some of your children and find them living in the truth, just as we have been commanded by the Father. ⁵And now I want to urge you, dear lady, that we should love one another. This is not a new commandment, but one we had from the beginning. ⁶Love means doing what God has commanded us, and he has commanded us to love one another, just as you heard from the beginning.

3 John 1:5 Dear friend, you are doing a good work for God when you take care of the traveling teachers who are passing through, even though they are strangers to you. ⁶They have told the church here of your friendship and your loving deeds. You do well to send them on their way in a manner that pleases God. ⁷For they are traveling for the Lord and accept nothing from those who are not Christians. ⁸So we ourselves should support them so that we may become partners with them for the truth.

Jude 1:17 But you, my dear friends, must remember what the apostles of our Lord Jesus Christ told you, ¹⁸that in the last times there would be scoffers whose purpose in life is to enjoy themselves in every evil way imaginable. ¹⁹Now they are here, and they are the ones who are creating divisions among you. They live by natural instinct because they do not have God's Spirit living in them.

²⁰But you, dear friends, must continue to build your lives on the foundation of your holy faith. And continue to pray as you are directed by the Holy Spirit. ²¹Live in such a way that God's love can bless you as you wait for the eternal life that our Lord Jesus Christ in his mercy is going to give you. ²²Show mercy to those whose faith is wavering. ²³Rescue others by snatching them from the flames of judgment. There are still others to whom you need to show mercy, but be careful that you aren't contaminated by their sins.

²⁴And now, all glory to God, who is able to keep you from stumbling, and

who will bring you into his glorious presence innocent of sin and with great joy. [25]All glory to him, who alone is God our Savior, through Jesus Christ our Lord. Yes, glory, majesty, power, and authority belong to him, in the beginning, now, and forevermore. Amen.

〰️✍️ **How often do you go out of your way to meet the needs of other Christians?** In the church's early days, traveling prophets, evangelists, and teachers were helped on their way by people who housed and fed them. Hospitality is a lost art for many Christians today. We would do well to invite more people for meals—fellow church members, young people, traveling missionaries, those in need, visitors. This is an active and much-appreciated way to show your love. In fact, it is probably more important today. Because of our individualistic, self-centered society, there are many lonely people who wonder if anyone cares whether they live or die. If you find such a lonely person, show him or her that *you* care!

29
DECEMBER

Jesus the King
REVELATION 1:1-20

This is a revelation from Jesus Christ, which God gave him concerning the events that will happen soon. An angel was sent to God's servant John so that John could share the revelation with God's other servants. [2]John faithfully reported the word of God and the testimony of Jesus Christ—everything he saw.

[3]God blesses the one who reads this prophecy to the church, and he blesses all who listen to it and obey what it says. For the time is near when these things will happen.

[4]This letter is from John to the seven churches in the province of Asia. Grace and peace from the one who is, who always was, and who is still to come; from the sevenfold Spirit before his throne; [5]and from Jesus Christ, who is the faithful witness to these things, the first to rise from the dead, and the commander of all the rulers of the world.

All praise to him who loves us and has freed us from our sins by shedding his blood for us. [6]He has made us his kingdom and his priests who serve before God his Father. Give to him everlasting glory! He rules forever and ever! Amen!

[7]Look! He comes with the clouds of heaven. And everyone will see him—even those who pierced him. And all the nations of the earth will weep because of him. Yes! Amen!

[8]"I am the Alpha and the Omega—the beginning and the end," says the Lord God. "I am the one who is, who always was, and who is still to come, the Almighty One."

[9]I am John, your brother. In Jesus we are partners in suffering and in the

Kingdom and in patient endurance. I was exiled to the island of Patmos for preaching the word of God and speaking about Jesus. [10]It was the Lord's Day, and I was worshiping in the Spirit. Suddenly, I heard a loud voice behind me, a voice that sounded like a trumpet blast. [11]It said, "Write down what you see, and send it to the seven churches: Ephesus, Smyrna, Pergamum, Thyatira, Sardis, Philadelphia, and Laodicea."

[12]When I turned to see who was speaking to me, I saw seven gold lampstands. [13]And standing in the middle of the lampstands was the Son of Man. He was wearing a long robe with a gold sash across his chest. [14]His head and his hair were white like wool, as white as snow. And his eyes were bright like flames of fire. [15]His feet were as bright as bronze refined in a furnace, and his voice thundered like mighty ocean waves. [16]He held seven stars in his right hand, and a sharp two-edged sword came from his mouth. And his face was as bright as the sun in all its brilliance.

[17]When I saw him, I fell at his feet as dead. But he laid his right hand on me and said, "Don't be afraid! I am the First and the Last. [18]I am the living one who died. Look, I am alive forever and ever! And I hold the keys of death and the grave. [19]Write down what you have seen—both the things that are now happening and the things that will happen later. [20]This is the meaning of the seven stars you saw in my right hand and the seven gold lampstands: The seven stars are the angels of the seven churches, and the seven lampstands are the seven churches.

What do you think Jesus looks like? John recognized Jesus because he lived with him for three years and had seen him both as the Galilean Preacher and as the glorified Son of God at the Transfiguration. Here Jesus appears as the mighty Son of Man. His white hair indicates his wisdom and divine nature; his blazing eyes symbolize judgment of all evil; the golden band around his chest reveals him as the High Priest who goes into God's presence to obtain forgiveness of sin for those who have believed in him. Jesus is portrayed as an all-powerful King, victorious in battle, glorious in peace. He is not just a humble earthly teacher; he is the glorious God. When you read John's description of the vision, keep in mind that his words are not just good advice; they are truth from the King of kings. Don't just read his words for their interesting and amazing portrayal of the future. Let the truth about Christ penetrate your life, deepen your faith in him, and strengthen your commitment to follow him no matter what the cost.

30

Everything Made New

Then I saw a new heaven and a new earth, for the old heaven and the old earth had disappeared. And the sea was also gone. ²And I saw the holy city, the new Jerusalem, coming down from God out of heaven like a beautiful bride prepared for her husband. ³I heard a loud shout from the throne, saying, "Look, the home of God is now among his people! He will live with them, and they will be his people. God himself will be with them. ⁴He will remove all of their sorrows, and there will be no more death or sorrow or crying or pain. For the old world and its evils are gone forever."

⁵And the one sitting on the throne said, "Look, I am making all things new!" And then he said to me, "Write this down, for what I tell you is trustworthy and true." ⁶And he also said, "It is finished! I am the Alpha and the Omega—the Beginning and the End. To all who are thirsty I will give the springs of the water of life without charge! ⁷All who are victorious will inherit all these blessings, and I will be their God, and they will be my children. ⁸But cowards who turn away from me, and unbelievers, and the corrupt, and murderers, and the immoral, and those who practice witchcraft, and idol worshipers, and all liars—their doom is in the lake that burns with fire and sulfur. This is the second death."

⁹Then one of the seven angels who held the seven bowls containing the seven last plagues came and said to me, "Come with me! I will show you the bride, the wife of the Lamb."

¹⁰So he took me in spirit to a great, high mountain, and he showed me the holy city, Jerusalem, descending out of heaven from God. ¹¹It was filled with the glory of God and sparkled like a precious gem, crystal clear like jasper. ¹²Its walls were broad and high, with twelve gates guarded by twelve angels. And the names of the twelve tribes of Israel were written on the gates. ¹³There were three gates on each side—east, north, south, and west. ¹⁴The wall of the city had twelve foundation stones, and on them were written the names of the twelve apostles of the Lamb.

¹⁵The angel who talked to me held in his hand a gold measuring stick to measure the city, its gates, and its wall. ¹⁶When he measured it, he found it was a square, as wide as it was long. In fact, it was in the form of a cube, for its length and width and height were each 1,400 miles. ¹⁷Then he measured the walls and found them to be 216 feet thick (the angel used a standard human measure).

¹⁸The wall was made of jasper, and the city was pure gold, as clear as glass. ¹⁹The wall of the city was built on foundation stones inlaid with twelve gems: the first was jasper, the second sapphire, the third agate, the fourth emerald, ²⁰the fifth onyx, the sixth carnelian, the seventh chrysolite,

the eighth beryl, the ninth topaz, the tenth chrysoprase, the eleventh jacinth, the twelfth amethyst. ^{21}The twelve gates were made of pearls—each gate from a single pearl! And the main street was pure gold, as clear as glass. ^{22}No temple could be seen in the city, for the Lord God Almighty and the Lamb are its temple. ^{23}And the city has no need of sun or moon, for the glory of God illuminates the city, and the Lamb is its light. ^{24}The nations of the earth will walk in its light, and the rulers of the world will come and bring their glory to it. ^{25}Its gates never close at the end of day because there is no night. ^{26}And all the nations will bring their glory and honor into the city. ^{27}Nothing evil will be allowed to enter—no one who practices shameful idolatry and dishonesty—but only those whose names are written in the Lamb's Book of Life.

〜〜〜 **What difference do you think will be most noticeable between the new world and the old?** Have you ever wondered what eternity will be like? The "holy city, the new Jerusalem" is described as the place where God "will wipe away all tears." Forevermore, there will be no death, pain, sorrow, or crying. What a wonderful truth! No matter what you are going through, it's not the last word. God has written the final chapter, and it includes eternal joy for those who love him. We do not know as much as we would like, but it is enough to know that eternity with God will be more wonderful than we can imagine.

DECEMBER **31**

Life in the New City

REVELATION 22:1-21

And the angel showed me a pure river with the water of life, clear as crystal, flowing from the throne of God and of the Lamb, ^{2}coursing down the center of the main street. On each side of the river grew a tree of life, bearing twelve crops of fruit, with a fresh crop each month. The leaves were used for medicine to heal the nations.

^{3}No longer will anything be cursed. For the throne of God and of the Lamb will be there, and his servants will worship him. ^{4}And they will see his face, and his name will be written on their foreheads. ^{5}And there will be no night there—no need for lamps or sun—for the Lord God will shine on them. And they will reign forever and ever.

^{6}Then the angel said to me, "These words are trustworthy and true: 'The Lord God, who tells his prophets what the future holds, has sent his angel to tell you what will happen soon.'"

^{7}"Look, I am coming soon! Blessed are those who obey the prophecy written in this scroll."

⁸I, John, am the one who saw and heard all these things. And when I saw and heard these things, I fell down to worship the angel who showed them to me. ⁹But again he said, "No, don't worship me. I am a servant of God, just like you and your brothers the prophets, as well as all who obey what is written in this scroll. Worship God!"

¹⁰Then he instructed me, "Do not seal up the prophetic words you have written, for the time is near. ¹¹Let the one who is doing wrong continue to do wrong; the one who is vile, continue to be vile; the one who is good, continue to do good; and the one who is holy, continue in holiness."

¹²"See, I am coming soon, and my reward is with me, to repay all according to their deeds. ¹³I am the Alpha and the Omega, the First and the Last, the Beginning and the End."

¹⁴Blessed are those who wash their robes so they can enter through the gates of the city and eat the fruit from the tree of life. ¹⁵Outside the city are the dogs—the sorcerers, the sexually immoral, the murderers, the idol worshipers, and all who love to live a lie.

¹⁶"I, Jesus, have sent my angel to give you this message for the churches. I am both the source of David and the heir to his throne. I am the bright morning star."

¹⁷The Spirit and the bride say, "Come." Let each one who hears them say, "Come." Let the thirsty ones come—anyone who wants to. Let them come and drink the water of life without charge. ¹⁸And I solemnly declare to everyone who hears the prophetic words of this book: If anyone adds anything to what is written here, God will add to that person the plagues described in this book. ¹⁹And if anyone removes any of the words of this prophetic book, God will remove that person's share in the tree of life and in the holy city that are described in this book.

²⁰He who is the faithful witness to all these things says, "Yes, I am coming soon!"

Amen! Come, Lord Jesus!

²¹The grace of the Lord Jesus be with you all.

⌇⌇⌇ **When was the last time you were excited about heaven?**
Revelation closes human history as Genesis opened it—in paradise. But there is one distinct difference in Revelation—evil is gone forever. Genesis describes Adam and Eve walking and talking with God; Revelation describes people worshiping him face-to-face. Genesis describes a garden with an evil serpent; Revelation describes a perfect city with no evil. The Garden of Eden was destroyed by sin; but paradise is recreated in the new Jerusalem. The book of Revelation ends with an urgent request: "Come, Lord Jesus!" In a world of problems, persecution, evil, and immorality, Christ calls us to endure in our faith. Our efforts to better our world are important, but their results cannot compare with the transformation that Jesus will bring about when he returns. He alone

controls human history and forgives sin, and he will recreate the earth and bring lasting peace. No matter what happens on earth, God is in control. Evil will not last forever, and there will be a wonderful reward waiting for all those who believe in Jesus Christ as Savior and Lord.